D1498851

Childhood Information Resources

Marda Woodbury

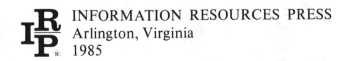

INFORMATION RESOURCES PRESS
Arlington, Virginia
1985

Z7164
C5
W58
1985

Available from
Information Resources Press
1700 North Moore Street
Suite 700
Arlington, Virginia 22209

Library of Congress Catalog Card Number 84-080534
ISBN 0-87815-051-X

The right to *affection, love, and understanding.*
The right to *adequate nutrition and medical care.*
The right to *free education.*
The right to *full opportunity for play and recreation.*
The right to *a name and nationality.*
The right to *special care, if handicapped.*
The right to *be among the first to receive relief in
    times of disaster.*
The right to *be a useful member of society and to develop
    individual abilities.*
The right to *be brought up in a spirit of peace and
    universal brotherhood.*
The right to *enjoy these rights, regardless of race,
    color, sex, religion, national or social origin.*

— *U.N. Declaration of the Rights of the Child*

The Author

MARDA WOODBURY, a reference librarian, library consultant, and free-lance researcher, has worked in public and research libraries in the sciences, social sciences, medicine, and education.

Ms. Woodbury's previous work, *A Guide to Sources of Educational Information* (2nd Edition, 1982), is the recognized standard work in its field. Another of her works, the three-volume *Selecting Materials for Instruction,* received the following accolade: "If awards are given for quality presentations of handbook information, this series. . .should receive the blue ribbon." (Alice Naylor, in *Voice of Youth Advocates.*)

Originally trained at Bard College in chemistry and political science, Ms. Woodbury holds an M.S. in Library Science from Columbia University. She has more than thirty years' experience in a broad range of library and library-related positions and has done graduate work in education and journalism at the University of California at Berkeley. At present, she is an information consultant and part-time librarian. Ms. Woodbury is a member of the Medical Library Association and the National Association for the Education of Young Children. She is on the board of the Educational Products Information Exchange and on the editorial board of *Reference Librarian.*

Contents

Preface

And [Solomon] said, Divide the living child in two,
and give half to the one, and half to the other.

The theme of this book is childhood, but it is neither a book for children nor a book about them. Rather, it is a compilation of scattered information sources on children for an audience of parents, researchers, concerned citizens, and professionals. Ever since the International Year of the Child (1979), I have wanted to put together a global guide to major information sources on all aspects of childhood. In 1982, I began the task of cumulating and annotating significant sources of information from the many disciplines that intersect in some way with childhood. Of course, the problems of children cannot be solved simply by accumulating information; still, this volume is the best contribution that I can make to the well-being of children. As a librarian and generalist—not a specialist in any child-related discipline—I hope that this book will help in establishing a common body of knowledge on childhood and that it will facilitate the collaboration and exchange of knowledge among all professionals and lay persons concerned with children.

In the early 1900s, when the Children's Bureau was founded to provide a single overview bureau on the child, "child study" as a discipline tended to view children more holistically than they are viewed today. We now have women's studies, black studies, and gerontology, but no discipline of child study as such. Those who work with children commit themselves to one discipline or another that treats the child and childhood only as subsets of its major content, such as law, police work, or psychology. Furthermore, we no longer have a single federal institution serving all children. Children fall through the cracks in these separate disciplines, as they fall through the cracks in the real world. Both constitute serious gaps in research and information.

Whatever their individual perceptions, adults who work with children tend, as professionals, to focus on single aspects of the child. Social workers focus on the family setting, teachers on learning capacity, health workers on presenting symptoms, and advertisers on the child as consumer. The education of professionals who work with children is equally fragmented, concentrating again on the part that is teachable, legally dependent, or badly parented, without studying the child as a whole. Fragmentation is perpetuated because individual professionals, although well intentioned, have become accustomed to their particular disciplines and technologies. Many professionals recognize the deficiency in this approach. For example, in 1978, the Task Force on Pediatric Education reported that more than half the pediatricians surveyed felt that their educations and residencies were inadequate for understanding developmental and behavioral aspects of childhood.

Too often the libraries that support these disparate disciplines similarly scatter the information. With very few exceptions, interdisciplinary research involves an undue amount of time, travel, and expertise in using the tools spread among a variety of libraries. Since there are so many sources to search and so many approaches, the pursuit of even simple questions can become quite complicated. While researching sources of information on childhood in the libraries of the University of California at Berkeley during one of California's wetter winters, I sloshed through the rain day after day, eventually visiting 12 different campus libraries and spending more time and money than I care to remember at the Interlibrary Loan Office. Not one department or library at this prestigious university offered an overview of childhood or a selection policy that covered childhood as a whole.

This book is an attempt to bridge agencies and disciplines to make accessible to all who work with children the extensive sources and statistics that have been laboriously compiled by the many groups that collect information on children. Six years ago,

Marion Edelman, of the Children's Defense Fund, strongly recommended that we develop a national agenda for children. *Childhood Information Resources* provides a place to start for those who wish to partake in this task.

Children today are documented victims of cutbacks in government programs that lack an overview of the child's basic needs and of a philosophical value system that blames the victim. Practitioners who work with children (and other dependent groups) are under siege. Often harried and with insufficient staff, they find it difficult to take a long-range view; indeed, it is all they can do to keep things running day to day.

We badly need all the wisdom and knowledge we can assemble on children. As part of this world, children share its problems and bear a disproportionately large part of the burden. The institutions set up to protect and nurture children—schools, day care, foster homes and child care institutions, juvenile courts, and even the family—seem to be crumpling under a thousand assaults. Childhood itself is vanishing, according to David Elkind and Marie Winn, who document its decline in *The Hurried Child* and *Children Without Childhood.* Even groups as mainstream as the 4-H Council are now issuing discussion kits on stress to be used with children aged 9–12, and the Federal Emergency Management Administration has developed coloring sheets for children entitled "Color What You Need in a Shelter." The specter of nuclear war looms large in the dreams of our children.

Children under age 15 constitute 36 percent of the total world population; 80 percent of these are in less-developed regions. In some countries, children comprise almost half the populations, but few of these countries can provide for them at even minimally adequate levels. Up to 40 percent of the children in underdeveloped countries receive almost no education. Particularly since the massive air attacks on civilians in World War II, children have been bombed and strafed, rendered homeless through war, and doomed to accompany their families as refugees. According to the Direct Relief Association, most refugees in the world today are women and children. Amnesty International searches for children who have disappeared.

No longer shielded by childhood, children are victims of parental unemployment, poverty, and environments they cannot understand or control. As the American Academy of Pediatrics noted in its "Lengthening Shadows" report in 1970, many child health problems are related to social change and socioeconomic factors, including adolescent pregnancies; increased use of drugs; lead poisoning in cities; and exposure to pollution in food, water, and air. Even mother's milk contains pesticides. Although nearly all social policies have implications for children, policies that affect children typically are inadvertent outcomes of policies directed toward adults or society in general.

Issues concerning children are inevitably multidimensional. Child abuse, for example, has legal, medical, emotional, economic, and educational ramifications, and, of course, it reflects our society and social structures. Yet, when we as a society try to solve such problems, our solutions and our research are often simplistic and one-dimensional. As a society, we lean toward policies and research that will yield a simple solution to a complex problem, preferably with only a modest, short-term expenditure of public funds. For example, we establish screening programs without considering the intricate relations between health and welfare or nutrition and learning and without considering the difficulties that various agencies in different disciplines and different branches of government with different constraints may have in working together.

National coordinated information networks on all topics and at all levels are needed to provide quick access to integrated statistics, information on hazards and poisons, registers of missing children, and a single source of information on organ donors. Unfortunately, during a period of government retrenchments in information gathering and publishing, national projects like these are unlikely. The moratorium that President Reagan issued on government periodicals, pamphlets, and audiovisuals has slowly been lifted from all departments except the U.S. Department of Health and Human Services. Under this information cutback, valuable titles like *Status of Children, Youth, and Families; The Poison Control Center Bulletin;* and *The National Immunization Survey* have been canceled. Other publishing has been shifted to the private sector, with a notable jump in price

and (sometimes) a decline in quality. Some agencies can no longer provide free copies of child-related publications; others have
fewer copies to give away. Agencies such as the Child Welfare
Resource Information Exchange, set up to identify good child
welfare programs, have vanished without trace; others have
short life expectancies. Despite numerous letters, phone calls,
and personal visits, I have found it exceedingly difficult to ascer-
tain just what most government agencies are doing for children.
Unfortunately, information and advocacy services of those child
advocacy organizations that receive federal grants or contract
funds are threatened by proposed regulations that would virtually eliminate the rights of these organizations to participate in
government decisions or to offer their substantial expertise to
government officials.

Other positive trends are under way, however. The House Select Committee on Children, Youth, and Families, chaired by
Rep. George Miller (D-Calif.), with 25 members, was authorized
by the 98th Congress during the spring of 1983 as an overview
committee. It considers children and families its constituency
and is attempting to assess the status of children and families on
a long-range basis and to recommend cost-effective methods to
meet their needs. The committee is currently gathering information on the changing needs of children and families. Although
select committees cannot approve legislation, they can call attention to problems ignored by less-focused committees. (Programs and policies that affect children now come before more
than 13 full House committees and numerous subcommittees.)
The Senate, too, has an informal Caucus for Children, cochaired
by Senators Christopher J. Dodd (D-Conn.) and Arlen Specter
(R-Pa.). Similarly, the National Governors' Association (NGA),
at its 1982–1983 winter meeting, voted to create a special task
force on children's issues and has prepared policy recommendations supporting specific children's policies. State legislatures,
city mayors, and county associations are similarly expressing
concern.

This cross-disciplinary book is an attempt to bring together in
one volume childhood information resources from different dis-

ciplines and lay sources. It concerns childhood as a whole, primarily emphasizing current information sources on American children from conception through age 12—some 47.5 million children. (Even this figure was difficult to obtain from the available printed sources.) Of these children, one in five is poor, two million are not getting the schooling they need, one million are abused, and nearly half a million are growing up in foster care or institutions. Since children are more than one-third of the total world population, I also have included a few information sources on children worldwide, as well as several historical sources.

In attempting to provide access to information sources, I have tried to help the readers of this book reach a fuller, more rounded awareness of possible approaches, as well as a knowledge of what is available. This material is based on what I could find, and, of course, is not an ideal, well-rounded exposition of children. Some professions (psychology, for one) are more articulate and better organized than others. I have found less information than I would like on other fields, such as religion and economics.

I have used a reference librarian's approach to tie together major accessible sources, checking my judgments against those of many child workers and information professionals. Most of the tools here are print and nonprint sources that consolidate information, keep information current, or lead to other sources of information. (My bias is toward lesser known, but very useful, tools.) Other sources are organizations and agencies that collect and dispense information on various aspects of childhood. The rest are special search and bibliographic services (mostly commercial) that provide rapid access to information. In my annotations, I have tried to convey the scope, uses, strengths, and weaknesses of the selections for a varied audience of child workers.

In keeping with my cross-disciplinary approach, most chapters are organized by types of materials (bibliographies, periodicals, audiovisuals, data bases, and so on) rather than by subject or discipline, so that users will be aware of sources they do not typically use. Four separate multidisciplinary chapters, however, deal with the special topics of statistics, tests and assessments, books and children, and parent education. The first section of Chapter 1 more fully explains the book's organization.

My research for this book was based largely on visits to many libraries and organizations during 1982 and 1983, heavy use of the reference tools cited in this book, personal inspection of works cited, extensive correspondence with organizations and publishers during that period, and reliance on newsletters to alert me of new publications and services. Because of my work at different times as an education librarian and author, medical librarian, and reference librarian in the social sciences, I started with a knowledge of or acquaintance with many basic tools. Furthermore, because this book has been in the back of my mind since 1979, I have been storing up awareness of suitable works.

As always, I am indebted to a multitude of colleagues and strangers. I am grateful to all those who took the time to fill out my organization questionnaire thoughtfully and thoroughly and to those who sent me review copies. (I am grateful also to those who didn't, since I had fewer items to annotate.) I appreciate the moral support and the critiques of Stevanne Auerbach, Stephen Menchini, Rephah Berg, Alice Wittig, Liz Flynn, Marilyn Halpern, Donna Richardson, and Sonya Kaufman. During the course of research, I spent many hours in local libraries and made lightning visits to libraries, clearinghouses, and research organizations in New York, Washington, D.C., and Los Angeles and to the Boys Town Search Center near Omaha, Nebraska. I would especially like to thank the library/clearinghouse staffs of the Bank Street College of Education, Child Welfare League, American Foundation for Maternal and Child Health, Columbia University School of Social Work, Teachers College, Early Childhood Resource and Information Center, Sex Information and Education Council of the United States (SIECUS), Information Center on Children's Cultures, Catalyst, Business and Professional Women's League, U.S. Department of Education, U.S. Department of Health and Human Services, National Clearinghouse on Health, National Clearinghouse on Child Abuse and Neglect, National Clearinghouse on Bilingual Education, Child Protection Report (CPR) Directory Service, the reference department of the University of California at Los Angeles, the Reiss-Davis Child Study Center, and the Center for Early Education. In the San Francisco Bay Area, I would like to thank the staffs of the Institute for Childhood Resources; the Berkeley Public Library; and the branch libraries of Public Health, Education-

Psychology, Law, Documents, and Library Science at the University of California at Berkeley. My correspondents have been invaluable, and the National Referral Center has been almost embarrassingly prolific.

I appreciate the exemplary assistance of Laurie Bagley. I also appreciate the patience of Steve McMahon, Dan Drasin, Karen Trocki, and other members of my computer users' group, whose advice and support were significant factors in the completion of this work. My editor at Information Resources Press, Nancy Winchester, has been—as always—most patient and competent.

I would like to thank all the individuals and organizations that helped me collect information sources on children. I hope that as a result of our cooperation, those who work with children will be a little better informed and the future of the world's children a little brighter.

PART I

Overview

1 / Research Approaches

This chapter covers some basic means for locating information in the interdisciplinary field of childhood, concentrating on overall approaches and major tools. Subsequent chapters provide detailed information on particular sources. Since my background is that of a reference librarian turned researcher, the approach I take in Chapter 1 is to explain the values and limitations of different categories of research tools (e.g., government documents, periodicals, indexes, data bases, audiovisual catalogs, and current sources). Because I strongly believe in an interdisciplinary approach to childhood information and wish to emphasize interrelationships, sources are generally divided by format rather than subject. The annotations are intended to explain the scope, coverage, and applications of each tool; in addition, the index to this book contains ample subject guidance.

Chapters 2 through 11 deal with major research tools, both print and nonprint. Chapters 12 and 13 annotate institutions that provide information, such as clearinghouses, libraries, government agencies, associations, and advocacy organizations. They include only those organizations whose responses indicated that they were willing and able to supply information. Chapters 14 through 17 provide interdisciplinary treatments of special subjects: tests and assessments, statistics, children and books, and parent education. The appendix contains a preliminary interdisciplinary library collection, composed mainly of handbooks and basic texts, divided by broad subjects.

Included herein are both the tools found in large academic libraries and inexpensive paperbacks that organize information intelligently and concisely. In many cases, sources do not deal directly with children but encompass peripheral fields that contain information on children. I have tried to choose works that are still in print or widely available, and, except for a very few sources that I was unable to locate outside libraries, I have given the source for every work. (The availability of government documents is discussed at the end of this chapter.)

Essentially, those searching for information must be able to identify what they already know and what they need to know and to link pieces of information into a coherent whole. The following CHECKLIST FOR RESEARCH QUESTIONS, adapted from the *Guide to Sources of Educational Information* (2nd Edition, by Marda Woodbury, Arlington, Va., Information Resources Press, 1982), helps one prepare for a search. The checklist is followed by a discussion of certain tools and search methods as they relate to childhood information resources.

CHECKLIST FOR RESEARCH QUESTIONS

I. BASIC QUESTIONS

   A. *What do I want to know? For what purpose?*

   Subjects, synonyms, related concepts, approaches
   Vocabulary: dictionaries, encyclopedias, thesauri

   B. *What do I already know?*

   C. *Who might have performed similar research and why? Where is it apt to be?*

   Source guides, bibliographies

   Individuals, groups or organizations, structures, hearings, records, other

   Choice of directories, organizations, periodicals, newsletters, current news, data bases

   D. *What summarizing or descriptive literature is available?*

   Statistics, directories, reviews, annuals, monographs, bibliographies, encyclopedias

II. ASPECT QUESTIONS

    A. *What aspects am I interested in?*

        Parental, psychological, legal, welfare, developmental, health or medical, financial, interpersonal, familial, group, intergroup, social, cultural, anthropological, historical, religious, moral, administrative, economic, environmental, theoretical, overview

        Choice of indexes, data bases, annuals, reviews, periodicals, newsletters

III. LIMITATION AND RESTRICTION QUESTIONS

    A. *Do I have restrictions or limitations?*

        Age, ethnic group, sex, geography, education, level of ability, income, educational level of parents, other

        Choice of vocabulary, indexes, data bases, other reference tools, search approaches

IV. TIME QUESTIONS

    A. *For which time spans do I need information? What kinds of information for each?*

        What is? What was? What will be? What can be?

        Choice of indexes, data bases, reference tools, search approaches, time parameters

    B. *Would my collection of information be affected by recurrent or other temporal events?*

        Elections, administrative changes, budget hearings, conventions or conferences, training programs, legislative sessions, paperwork deadlines, policy decisions

        Choice of reference tools, search approaches, time parameters

V. SUBJECTIVE ASPECT QUESTIONS

    A. *What are my values, prejudices, biases, and points of ignorance in these areas?*

    B. *Will I let these prejudice or limit my research in any manner?*

        Choice of vocabulary and indexing terms, choice of research tools, selection of data, evaluation of work of individuals, inclusion of conflicting theories, note taking, reporting or annotating data, arrangement of data, conclusions

In searching, as in journalism, the basic questions are *who, what, when,* and *where.* A knowledge of any of these can lead to the accumulation of more knowledge. Perhaps searches most frequently start with *what* (the subject). To be successful, the searcher must use the correct vocabulary and apply it to the appropriate sources.

VOCABULARY (Subject Searching)

Before the advent of the computer and keyword indexing, the traditional first step in research was to convert personal terminology into words and phrases that were used in subject catalogs, bibliographies, encyclopedias, and periodical indexes. This is still a useful approach, particularly because the study of children and childhood draws from many disciplines and areas. The keyword indexing approach (based on language in documents) will uncover materials bypassed by the subject indexing approach, but, in a field such as this, keyword searching can produce extraneous materials. Even in computer searching, the targeted logical subject approach is a useful supplement to searching based exclusively on the language found in particular documents.

The dictionaries, encyclopedias, and thesauri included in Chapter 2 provide information in context and often relate it to other sources that might provide additional information.

Library of Congress Subject Headings (9th Edition, Washington, D.C., Library of Congress, 1980), a two-volume guide to the subject headings used by the Library of Congress, is the standard source for subject headings. It has been applied or adapted in many bibliographic tools, including *Books in Print* and *Associations' Publications in Print;* it is also used in some data bases, such as LEGAL RESOURCE INDEX. These headings were established by the Library of Congress in 1897 and were derived from a book collection of millions of volumes. They are sometimes a bit ponderous or out-of-date and are not always suitable for articles or brief documents. Furthermore, they tend not to be revised (because of the enormous effort involved in recataloging) until revision is long overdue. Still, these headings (Figure 1), and variations thereof, are likely to be used and adapted in book catalogs and indexes, including computer indexes.

Lists of subject headings, or thesauri, indicate by library codes which subject terms are used and refer users from terms that are not used to terms that are used. They indicate how terms are divided so that users can locate specific headings. Some thesauri include scope notes that define uses of terms; others refer users to related headings. The library codes for *Subject Headings* are "sa" (related or subordinate topics), "xx" (additional related topics), and "x" (the term is not used).

In traditional card catalogs and indexes, form subdivisions are often added to indicate types of materials. In general, these correspond to types of reference books and can be useful for locating specific formats (such as bibliographies or directories) in subject searches. They are also helpful in most computer searches, either as indexing terms or vocabulary. I found, for example, that the word *annotated* in computer searches helped me locate appropriate bibliographies and directories. Following is a list of typical subdivisions used in subject searches:

–Abstracts
–Bibliographies
–Biographies
–Case studies
–Collections
–Dictionaries
–Directories
–Exhibitions
–Film catalogs
–Handbooks, manuals, and so on
–Indexes
–Outlines
–Statistics
–Study and teaching guides
–Yearbooks

x Deaf children
  Deafness in children
  Hard-of-hearing children
  Hearing-impaired children
  Hypoacoustic children
xx Deaf
  Hearing disorders in children
  Physically handicapped children
— Education
  See Deaf—Education
— Language
  xx Language and languages
    Speech
Children, Exceptional
  See Exceptional children
Children, First-born *(HQ754.F5)*
  sa Primogeniture
    Redemption of the first-born
  x Eldest child
    First-born children
  xx Birth order
    Infants
    Primogeniture
Children, Folk-lore of
  See Folk-lore of children
Children, Hindu
  See Hindu children
Children, Hospitalized
  See Children—Hospital care
Children, Islamic
  See Muslim children
Children, Italian American
  See Italian American children
Children, Jewish
  See Jewish children
Children, Mexican American
  See Mexican American children
Children, Muslim
  See Muslim children
Children, Oriental
  See Oriental children
Children, Photography of

Children and adults
  sa Children—Management
    Children and strangers
    Children and the aged
    Conflict of generations
    Parent and child
    Teacher-student relationships
  x Adult and child
    Adult-child relationships
    Adults and children
    Child-adult relationships
    Child and adult
    Children—Relationship with adults
  xx Authority
    Child psychology
    Interpersonal relations
Children and alcohol
  See Alcohol and children
Children and animals *(BF723.A45)*
  sa Pets—Social aspects
  x Animals and children
  xx Pets—Social aspects
Children and cartoons
  See Cartoons and children
Children and comic books
  See Comic books and children
Children and dancing
  See Dancing and children
Children and death
  sa Terminally ill children
    Youth and death
  x Death and children
  xx Death
    Death—Psychological aspects
Children and erotica
  x Erotica and children
  xx Erotic literature
    Literature, Immoral
Children and folk-lore
  See Folk-lore and children
Children and mass media
  See Mass media and children

  xx Children in art
    Children's art
    Folk art
    Gifted children
Children as authors *(Child study. BF723.A8; Literature, PN171.C5)*
  sa Children in literature
  x Child authors
    Children as poets
  xx Authors
    Authorship
    Children in literature
    Gifted children
  Notes under Children's literature; Children's writings
Children as collectors
  xx Collectors and collecting
Children as consumers
  See Youth as consumers
Children as musicians *(ML83)*
  sa Rhythm bands and orchestras
  xx Gifted children
    Musicians
Children as poets
  See Children as authors
Children as printers *(Indirect)*
  xx Printers
Children as soldiers
  See United States—History—Civil War,
    1861-1865—Juvenile participants
    World War, 1939-1945—Juvenile
      participants
Children as witnesses *(Indirect)*
  xx Evidence (Law)
    Psychology, Forensic
    Witnesses
Children in art *(Indirect)* *(N7640-7649)*
  sa Boys—Portraits
    Children—Portraits
    Children as artists
    Gainsborough, Thomas, 1727-1788.
      Painter's daughters chasing a

Children, Preaching to
  See Preaching to children
Children, Puerto Rican
  See Puerto Rican children
Children, Retarded
  See Mentally handicapped children
    Slow learning children
Children, Runaway
  See Runaway children
Children, Sick
  See Sick children
Children, Vagrant *(Indirect)*
  sa Runaway children
  x Child vagrants
    Vagrant children
  xx Child welfare
    Homelessness
    Juvenile delinquency
    Tramps
    Vagrancy
Children (Christian theology) *(BT705)*
  xx Man (Christian theology)
    Theology, Doctrinal
Children (Hindu law)
  xx Children—Law
Children (in religion, folklore, etc.)
  See Folk-lore of children
Children (International law)
  xx Children—Law
    International law
Children (Islamic law)
Children (Jewish law)
  xx Children—Law
Children (Roman-Dutch law)
  xx Children—Law
Children (Roman law)
  xx Children—Law

  See Moving-pictures and children
Children and newspapers
  See Newspapers and children
Children and poetry
  See Poetry and children
Children and politics *(HQ784.P5)*
  x Politics and children
Children and pyschical research
  See Pyschical research and children
Children and radio
  See Radio and children
Children and strangers
  x Strangers and children
  xx Children—Management
    Children and adults
Children and television
  See Television and children
Children and the aged *(Indirect)*
    (HQ784.A34)
  xx Aged
    Children and adults
Children and the performing arts
  See Performing arts and children
Children and traffic safety
  See Traffic safety and children
Children as actors *(Indirect)* *(PN3157)*
  sa Children's plays
    Drama in education
  x Child actors
  xx Actors
    Children's plays
    Drama in education
    Gifted children
Children as artists *(N352)*
  sa Children in art
    Children's art
    Finger painting
    Folk art

Girls—Portraits
    Photography of children
  xx Art
    Children as artists
    Figure drawing
    Humans in art
Children in cities
  See City children
Children in literature
  sa Boys in literature
    Child labor in literature
    Children as authors
    Girls in literature
    Youth in literature
  x Children in poetry
  xx Characters and characteristics in
    literature
    Children as authors
    Literature
    Youth in literature
Children in motion pictures
  xx Moving-pictures
    Moving-pictures and children
  Note under Moving-pictures—Plots, themes,
    etc.
Children in poetry
  See Children in literature
Children in the Bible *(BS576-8: New
    Testament, BS2446)*
  sa Children—Biblical teaching
  x Bible—Children
    Boys in the Bible
    Girls in the Bible
  xx Bible—Biography
    Biography—Juvenile literature
    Boys—Biography
    Children—Biblical teaching
    Children—Biography

Figure 1 Sample page from the 9th Edition of the *Library of Congress Subject Headings.*

Library of Congress subject headings are used in most large libraries and book catalogs. In smaller libraries, *Sears Subject Headings,* a simplified, although similar, system is often used. Neither is universal, however. In a multidisciplinary field such as childhood, which is searchable in many indexes, libraries, and subject disciplines, users need to be aware of variations in terminology in and across disciplines and to keep in mind that terminology usually changes over time.

Important thesauri discussed in Chapter 2 include *Medical Subject Headings,* for searches in health fields; *Thesaurus of ERIC Descriptors,* for education; and *Thesaurus of Psychological Index Terms,* for psychology.

The dictionaries and encyclopedias covered in Chapter 2 add depth and meaning to the terms found in the thesauri and can indicate how terms are used and how meanings are altered in different fields. Terms from these thesauri and subject heading lists, as well as terms gleaned from the indexes themselves, should serve as entry terms for most searches.

Most periodical indexes include self-contained cross-references within each yearly volume. Although traditional indexes frequently use logical terms that are often variations of the terms here, it is generally a good idea to start searches in such indexes with the latest bound volume to get a good overview of terms and synonyms. *Social Sciences Citation Index* has its own *Permuterm Subject Index,* which can be used to garner search terms. For computer searches, it is advisable to use thesauri and vocabularies before beginning searches or to check the appropriate terms in a print counterpart, if one is available.

ASPECTS

The aspect and limitation questions in the CHECKLIST FOR RESEARCH QUESTIONS deal with *what* and *where.* Some aspects correspond roughly to certain disciplines and professions that study parts of the child (e.g., law, medicine, sociology, and social work) and can be used to narrow or widen searches and to determine what indexes or data bases to use and/or what groups might be worth consulting. For example, although materials on such topics as child abuse, child custody, child suicide, or hyperactive children can be found in many indexes and data bases, a searcher—say, a lawyer for a school district—might be interested primarily in legal and educational implications and legal liability aspects of childhood problem areas. For this individual, comprehensive bibliographies updated by legal indexes and education indexes would be suitable tools. He could keep informed of current developments in the field through appropriate newsletters or periodicals on school health, school administration, school law, and family law and might consider joining a legal association concerned with children. A legislator or other policymaker interested in the same topics might be looking for a total overview and be particularly interested in statistics, model laws, and evaluations of current programs. His search would take him through public affairs indexes, a comprehensive search of public documents, and statistical sources. He could ask the National Council of State Legislators to put him in touch with other legislators and staffs interested in the same areas and to keep him informed of new legislation.

LIMITATIONS AND TIME SPANS

Geographic and other target audience limitations affect both search strategies and tools. If the lawyer in the preceding example was Canadian, he would do well to search the *Canadian Education Index* in addition to or instead of American reference works. If he was interested only in elementary or secondary students, he could skip items on children of other ages when browsing a print index or set up a limitation strategy in a computer search. If he was concerned with the problems of non-English-speaking children, *Bilingual Education Bibliographic Abstracts* would be a logical place to search. *Exceptional Child Education Resources* would be his best bet if his concern was handicapped children.

A person preparing a master's thesis or a doctoral dissertation might be interested in searching over a long time span and would probably include dissertations in his search. He would need to choose indexes or data bases accordingly, so that the tools would correspond in content and time to his research plan. An individual seeking a few recent practical references would likely omit dissertations but would check a frequently updated print or computer index. Other searches might require only a few well-targeted reference books, say, an appropriate directory or a subject bibliography.

THE RESEARCH PROCESS COMPOSITE OUTLINE that follows is useful for researching child-related topics. I have included some representative childhood information sources for purposes of illustration.

THE RESEARCH PROCESS
COMPOSITE OUTLINE

   I. Define the question
  II. Locate appropriate library, clearinghouse, or other source
 III. Search background and refine question through reference works

    A. For general background and vocabulary

       DICTIONARIES, ENCYCLOPEDIAS, AND THESAURI

       Encyclopedia of Bioethics
       Encyclopedia of Social Work
       NICSEM Special Education Thesaurus

       HISTORIES AND HANDBOOKS

       Basic Handbook of Child Psychiatry
       Children and Youth in America: A Documentary History

       SOURCE BOOKS AND LIBRARY GUIDES

       A Guide to Sources of Educational Information
       Resource Guide for Psychology
       Sources of Information in the Social Sciences
       Catalog of the Jean Piaget Archives

    B. For information on people and institutions

       DIRECTORIES

       Children's Media Market Place
       National Directory of Children & Youth Services
       Who's Who Biographical Record—Child Development

ON-LINE DIRECTORIES

AMERICAN MEN AND WOMEN OF SCIENCE
FAMILY RESOURCES DATABASE
FEDERAL ASSISTANCE PROGRAMS RETRIEVAL SYSTEM
NATIONAL CLEARINGHOUSE ON CHILD ABUSE AND NEGLECT
NATIONAL FOUNDATIONS

REFERRAL AGENCIES AND CLEARINGHOUSES

National Health Information Clearinghouse
National Referral Center
Resource and Referral Service

C. For updating or statistical information

ANNUALS

Associations' Publications in Print
Bibliography of Developmental Medicine and Child Neurology
Inventory of Marriage and Family Literature
Review of Child Development Research
Yearbook of Pediatrics

STATISTICS

America's Children and Their Families
Characteristics of American Children and Youth

STATISTICAL DATA BASES

AMERICAN STATISTICS INDEX
POPLINE

D. For summaries of knowledge

SUBJECT BIBLIOGRAPHIES

Child Abuse: An Annotated Bibliography
Child Health Assessment: A Literature Search
The Education of Poor and Minority Children
The Young Child: Reviews of Research

HANDBOOKS AND ENCYCLOPEDIAS

The Educator and Child Abuse
Encyclopedia of Pediatric Psychology
Legal Issues in Pediatrics and Adolescent Medicine
Young People with Cancer: A Handbook

IV. If more information is needed, use information from Steps A through D
for relevant names and search terms.

A. For monographs

   LIBRARY CARD CATALOG OR IN-HOUSE COMPUTER

   CUMULATIVE BOOK CATALOG or BIBLIOGRAPHY
   or BIBLIOGRAPHIC DATA BASE

   Books in Print

B. For periodical articles and documents

   PRINT INDEXES AND ABSTRACT JOURNALS

   Child Development Abstracts and Bibliography
   Exceptional Child Education Resources
   Kindex
   PsycSCAN: Developmental Psychology

   REVIEW JOURNALS

   Courrier
   International Child Welfare Review Supplement

   COMPUTERIZED DATA BASES

   BILINGUAL EDUCATION BIBLIOGRAPHIC ABSTRACTS
   CHILD ABUSE AND NEGLECT
   ERIC
   FAMILY RESOURCES DATABASE

   DOCUMENT INDEXES

   Monthly Catalog of U.S. Government Publications
   P.A.I.S. Bulletin
   Resources in Education

C. For the most current information

   Personal contacts

   NEWSLETTERS AND PERIODICALS

   CDF Reports
   Child Care Information Exchange
   Childhood Education
   Child Protection Report
   Children in the Tropics
   Children's Legal Rights Journal
   Children Today
   Gifted Child Newsletter

ADVOCACY AND PROFESSIONAL ORGANIZATIONS

Association for Children and Adults with Learning Disabilities
Black Child Development Institute
Child Welfare League
Clearinghouse on the Handicapped
La Leche League International

CURRENT EVENTS DATA BASES

CONGRESSIONAL RECORD ABSTRACTS
INFOBANK (The New York Times)
NEWSSEARCH

D. For unpublished data

People and institutions located through Step C.

As THE RESEARCH PROCESS COMPOSITE OUTLINE indicates, certain types of reference books are best suited for answering certain types of questions, and, because of the multidisciplinary aspects of childhood, certain types of materials are more important in this field than they are in narrower fields that are easier to research.

Following are some comments on the value and accessibility of certain types of childhood information sources.

Dictionaries, Encyclopedias, Thesauri (Chapter 2): Basically discussed under VOCABULARY (pp. 6–9). In child studies, these tools are valuable for locating background and for learning lesser known meanings of common words. Useful for suggesting search terms and other references.

Literature Guides and Library Catalogs (Chapter 3): Both suggest relevant titles; literature guides provide strategies and/or tools for further research. Since few guides in child studies deal mainly with sources of information on childhood, these are useful for learning the basic sources in related disciplines.

Histories (Chapter 4): Histories provide a common framework and a common core of knowledge. Historical indexes and data bases (Chapters 8 and 11) can be used to amplify these sources, whereas some bibliographies (Chapter 6) and directories (Chapter 10) indicate historical materials. At least two periodicals in Chapter 9 deal with the history of childhood.

Ongoing Bibliographies (Chapter 5): These include annual reviews, book reviews, and the like, and enable one to keep abreast of the literature. Combinations of these allow users to keep up with certain categories of materials, such as published monographs, reference works, book reviews, bibliographies, or government documents.

Bibliographies (Chapter 6): In any field, bibliographies keep one from reinventing the wheel. They are particularly important in childhood research, since few other reference works deal directly with childhood or are as well targeted or multidisciplinary. Chapter 6 brings together a significant cross-section of laboriously compiled cross-disciplinary research and research on important child-related topics. The bibliographies included in the chapter summarize the knowledge in a particular area and provide a foundation from which to survey current literature. Bibliographies for parents and on parent-education materials are annotated in Chapter 17. The indexes of Chapter 8 and the data bases of Chapter 11 are frequently used to compile bibliographies. In addition, bibliographies can be followed or located through some of the tools given in Chapter 5.

Audiovisual Catalogs and Mediaographies (Chapter 7): Audiovisuals are particularly valuable for presentations to large groups and for documenting sights or sounds not conveyed well through print or verbal means. Although bibliographic controls for audiovisuals are not as comprehensive as they are for books, the organizations, mediaographies, and catalogs in Chapter 7 provide access to a variety of audiovisuals for adults concerned with children. They are also listed in general bibliographies for adults and children (Chapters 6 and 16), parent-education materials (Chapter 17), and some of the periodical indexes and on-line data bases of Chapters 8 and 11. They are reviewed or noted in a number of the periodicals cited in Chapter 9. Many of the organizations in Chapters 12 and 13 produce, collect, or disseminate audiovisuals.

Periodical Indexes and Abstract Journals (Chapter 8): The tools in this chapter provide access to current and retrospective research and publications. In addition, they allow users time to browse, to refine their search vocabularies, and to note relevant and irrelevant sources. They provide subject and author access (and sometimes abstracts) to the contents of periodicals, fugitive documents, government documents, dissertations, brief monographs, multi-author publications, and pamphlets. Most periodical indexes locate articles on a topic within a certain time frame, whereas citation indexes find articles related through citations to those one has already discovered. (Since many authors copy each other's bibliographies, this is not always valuable.) Many indexes and abstract journals provide some sort of access to the materials they list, ranging from interlibrary loans, fee photocopying, and tear sheet services to provision of addresses and prices of the publications they include. Unfortunately, most indexes and abstract journals cover specific disciplines, of which childhood is only a subset.

Periodicals and Newsletters (Chapter 9): Newsletters on childhood are produced by associations, special-interest groups, interested individuals, and government agencies at all levels. Individually and collectively, they are an inexpensive, yet extremely helpful, means of keeping up with current developments. Periodicals, although less current than newsletters, are issued continuously and supply more depth and context. They are more apt to be multidisciplinary than the periodical indexes and abstract journals that index, abstract, or announce them.

Directories (Chapter 10): Directories lead to people, funds, and institutions (the *who, what, where*) concerned with children and serve as references to other sources, including libraries with collections on childhood. Directories are often compiled by those who need to locate, contact, promote, or award individuals or groups in a particular field (e.g., pediatricians, authors of books on children, foster homes, research organizations, or funding groups). Others are issued by publishers specializing in directories. Typically, they respond to a felt need. Chapter 10 includes both directories targeted at childhood and youth and directories of fields that are important for children (such as health and welfare).

Directory information is also available in source guides (Chapter 3), encyclopedias (Chapter 2), statistical works (Chapter 15), on-line data bases (Chapter 11), and periodical indexes (Chapter 8) and through institutions (Chapters 12 and 13) that compile information on other groups working toward the same goal or in the same area.

Data Bases (Chapter 11): Many on-line data bases are nonprint counterparts or comparable in function to the periodical indexes and abstract journals discussed in Chapter 8. Others provide directory information on persons, institutions, and funding or direct access to statistics, congressional activities, and publications. Many list very recent sources and are used increasingly by libraries to verify references. Computers allow speedy searches and facilitate searches that combine several topics or that require multiple access points through both document terminology and standard terms. Computer searches are particularly worthwhile for uncovering recent material. Documents can sometimes be ordered on-line for a price.

Organizations (Chapters 12 and 13): These chapters provide directory and bibliographic information on advocacy and volunteer organizations concerned with children and youth, professional associations, government agencies, and groups that collect relevant information. Such sources (and those in Chapters 7 and 14–16) can answer specific questions or provide print and nonprint materials in many areas related to children. Collectively, they produce bibliographies, directories, and data bases; collect or produce films and statistics; and interact with groups and individuals who share their concerns.

Tests (Chapter 14): Bibliographies, descriptions, and sources for a wide variety of tests and measurements applicable to children are annotated here. Collectively, they portray certain aspects of children subject to measurement and quantification.

Statistics (Chapter 15): The statistics in this chapter are garnered from a wide variety of agencies that provide demographic, economic, or health information on children, nationally and worldwide. The data might actually describe the functions of the agencies more than the children they study. Some of these statistical collections influence the flow of dollars, since data on census, demography, and income are used in allocating certain state, federal, and international funds.

Children's Books (Chapter 16): Books for children, like books for adults, cover the whole range of human knowledge and are updated as that knowledge changes. Their uses for factual information and emotional catharsis have been studied thoroughly by bibliotherapists, children's librarians, parents, early childhood educators, and experts in children's literature. Reading and language aspects have been studied by linguists, reading professionals, and elementary school teachers. This chapter is a multidisciplinary approach to sources that aid in selecting and using books with children.

Parent Education Materials (Chapter 17): The bibliographies, directories, and encyclopedic sources annotated in Chapter 17 are directed toward parents and parent educators and are included in this book for the reader's convenience. Although they consider many of the same issues as works in other chapters, they tend to be popular rather than scholarly, but, of course, this need not diminish their value. Chapter 13 covers some organizations concerned with parental or family values.

Handbooks (Appendix): Handbooks are similar to single-subject encyclopedias. They tend to contain concise, authoritative, and current knowledge logically arranged. Since there are few comprehensive encyclopedias on children, handbooks are particularly important for areas related to childhood.

Government Documents: Federal documents, an important source of information on government statistics, activities, agencies, and research on children, are announced and compiled in 300 subject bibliographies, ERIC (Chapter 12), and the *Monthly*

Catalog (Chapter 5), among other sources. They include bibliographies (Chapter 6), directories (Chapter 10), statistics (Chapter 15), and parent-education materials (Chapter 17). Federal documents are indexed in some periodical indexes (Chapter 8) such as the *P.A.I.S. Bulletin* and certain data bases (Chapter 11). Federal documents are sold through the U.S. Government Printing Office, Washington, DC 20402 and its bookstores throughout the country. (Addresses appear inside the cover of the *Monthly Catalog*.)

Single copies of many publications are available free from the issuing agencies. The National Center for Education in Maternal and Child Health (L25) provides single copies of professional and public education materials related to child and maternal health and well-being. Federal publications are not copyrighted and are available for inspection at 1,300 depository public and university libraries throughout the United States. Many libraries are partial depository libraries, and most have some government publications. The U.S. Government Printing Office also publishes materials in microform.

State documents are found in state libraries and are sometimes distributed free by issuing agencies or sold by the state printer or designated distributing agency. (Copies are often free to libraries and professionals.) Legal and public affairs indexes cover many of these publications, which are also collected by organizations (Chapters 12 and 13) interested in particular functions, such as juvenile justice, child support enforcement, or state legislatures.

Local documents are collected in municipal, school, and law libraries. Single copies can sometimes be obtained free. If not, sales agencies are listed in local telephone directories.

International and foreign documents are directly available through the issuing agencies (such as the organizations annotated in the last section of Chapter 12). Unipub, 1180 Avenue of the Americas, New York, NY 10036, distributes and announces documents of the United Nations and other international organizations. Contact the headquarters office to get announcement services or to get on mailing lists; prepaid orders should be sent to Unipub, Box 433, Murray Hill Sta., New York, NY 10157. Publications of the United Nations and nearly 100 other intergovernmental organizations are recorded in *International Bibliog-*

raphy: Publications of Intergovernmental Organizations, a Unipub quarterly. The International Bureau of Education's *Educational Documentation and Information* provides good coverage of education and education-related topics.

Microforms: Micropublishing, although not necessarily popular with users, has been around since the 1920s. It has been used to reproduce rare books, back files of newspapers, tax returns, test collections, indexes, conference reports, and substitutes for library card catalogs. Major microfiche collections discussed in this guide include those of the Human Relations Area Files (HRAF), the Educational Resources Information Center (ERIC), and the National Technical Information Service (NTIS) (Chapters 11 and 12).

The *Guide to Microforms in Print* is an annual cumulative listing of books, journals, and other available materials and is comparable to *Books in Print.* A companion, the *Subject Guide to Microforms in Print,* is divided into broad subject areas. *Microform Marketplace* provides information on the organizations that produce microformats. Current publications are annotated in the *Microform Review.* These current bibliographic tools are supplemented by four printed catalogs of the Library of Congress: the *National Register of Microform Masters,* a catalog of master microforms reported by institutional and commercial publishers; *Newspapers in Microform: United States* and *Newspapers in Microform: Foreign Countries,* which report microform masters of newspapers; and the *National Union Catalog,* which reports library locations of microforms.

Currently, many journal files are available in microformats from University Microfilms International (UMI). Statistical publications are available on microfiche from the Congressional Information Service, which publishes the *American Statistics Index* and the *Statistical Reference Index,* and from the U.S. Bureau of the Census. The Test Collection Division of the Educational Testing Service offers *Tests in Microfiche.* The Foundation Center has tax returns and reports of searches in microfiche format. Research collections, such as the William S. Gray Research Collection in Reading, are also available in microformats, as are theses and dissertations.

University Microfilms International (300 N. Zeeb Rd., Ann
Arbor, MI 48106, (313) 761-4700) specializes in providing access to hard-to-locate dissertations, books, periodical articles,
and monographs in microform. The UMI collection of periodicals
now contains more than 12,000 titles in *Serials in Microform;* it
also can supply copies of articles. The *Researcher's Guide to Dissertation Information Services,* free on request from UMI, describes
UMI's products and services on theses and dissertations.

PART II

Printed Reference Works

2 / *Dictionaries, Encyclopedias, Thesauri*

Dictionaries and encyclopedias are the first tools to consult for vocabulary and authoritative introductory articles when conducting literature searches. Dictionaries, like glossaries, attempt to create a common vocabulary or language, whereas encyclopedias compile a common body of knowledge. Thesauri are generally produced by groups that organize or disseminate information. By elucidating the interrelationships of terms, they provide valuable clues for locating or organizing information.

Encyclopedias and dictionaries usually attempt to embrace either the total world of knowledge, a group of academic disciplines (such as the life sciences), or a single discipline. Since the study of children is part of many academic disciplines rather than an independent academic study, there are few dictionaries or encyclopedias devoted exclusively to children (Chapter 17, on parent education, also includes helpful dictionaries and encyclopedias on child care.) The vocabulary tools selected here can be supplemented by general unabridged dictionaries. Contemporary handbooks in disciplines like child psychology, family law, and pediatrics lack the convenient alphabetic order of encyclopedias but are good substitutes for providing competent introductory articles and surveys of current trends. Appendix I lists some such handbooks.

Professional vocabularies dealing with childhood stem from many disciplines, so the same terms may be used differently in various contexts. For this reason, among others, I have tried to include, whenever possible, multidisciplinary dictionaries and encyclopedias that are clear and understandable, as well as authoritative and precise.

Some reference books cited in this guide include glossaries of terms; these are noted in the annotations. Items containing glossaries can be found under the term "Glossaries" in the index.

DICTIONARIES

A1   **A COMPREHENSIVE DICTIONARY OF AUDIOLOGY** By James H. Delk. Sioux City, Iowa, Hearing Aid Journal, 1974. 175 pp. (Out of print)

Contains more than 5,500 entries on vocabulary, acronyms, tests, and eponyms, with pronunciations and definitions; appendixes of abbreviations; and word lists in English, Spanish, French, and German. Includes color diagrams and black-and-white photographs of hearing equipment.

A2   **A COMPREHENSIVE DICTIONARY OF PSYCHOLOGICAL AND PSYCHOANALYTICAL TERMS: A Guide to Usage** By H. B. English and A. C. English. New York, Longmans, Green, 1958. 594 pp. (Out of print)

Old, but still considered a classic dictionary for terms used in special or technical senses by psychologists. Explains more than 13,000 terms (including related terms from fields like medicine and mathematics), sometimes with separate definitions for laypersons and for psychologists. Includes extensive cross-references.

A3   **THE CONCISE DICTIONARY OF EDUCATION** By Gene R. Hawes and Lynne S. Hawes. New York, Van Nostrand Reinhold, 1982. 249 pp. $18.95.

A concise dictionary for the nonspecialist, most useful for defining terms that have come into use since the publication of Carter Good's *Dictionary of Education* (A5).

A4   **DICTIONARY OF BEHAVIORAL SCIENCE** Compiled and edited by Benjamin B. Wolman. New York, Van Nostrand Reinhold, 1973. 478 pp. $24.50; paperback, $12.95.

Ninety collaborators in the fields of psychiatry, psychopharmacology, and clinical practice provide concise definitions for more than 12,000 terms, entered under the noun whenever possible. This dictionary covers prominent persons and all behavioral sciences. Graphs, tables, and illustrations are used to define terms. Appendixes include the American Psychiatric Association's classification of behavioral disorders and ethical standards.

A5   **DICTIONARY OF EDUCATION** 3rd Edition. Edited by Carter V. Good. New York, McGraw-Hill, 1973. 681 pp. $30. (Foundations in Education Series)

This basic education dictionary contains clear definitions of the educational meanings of 33,000 terms (including cross-references) selected through a word analysis of education indexes, handbooks, thesauri, and subject literature. This edition omits foreign terms but includes relevant terms from allied fields such as philosophy, psychology, sociology, and statistics.

A6   **DICTIONARY OF PERSONNEL AND GUIDANCE TERMS** Including Professional Agencies and Associations. Edited by William E. Hopke. Chicago, Ill., Ferguson, 1968. 421 pp. (Out of print)

A superior dictionary of 3,000 personnel and guidance terms that provides clear, complete definitions with source references of terms taken from the fields of psychology, social work, and education.

A7   **A DICTIONARY OF READING AND RELATED TERMS** Edited by Theodore L. Harris and Richard E. Hodges. Newark, Del., International Reading Assn., 1981. 382 pp. Members, $12; nonmembers, $18.

A multifaceted dictionary of 5,400 terms from 54 disciplines that somehow deal with reading, including speech and hearing, literary analysis, cognition, grammar, tests and measurements, neurology, and Piaget. Definitions include pronunciation and part of speech, technical and nontechnical definitions, citations to illustrate selected terms, corresponding words in principal foreign languages, and variant usages and spellings in the United Kingdom. Some multiple-definition terms (such as "dyslexia" and "word") are introduced by brief essays.

A8   **DICTIONARY OF SOCIAL BEHAVIOR AND SOCIAL RESEARCH METHODS** By David J. Stang and Lawrence S. Wrightsman. Monterey, Calif., Brooks/Cole, 1981. 105 pp. $8.95 (paperback).

A dictionary for college students enrolled in social behavior courses, including communication, developmental or experimental psychology, human relations, environmental psychology, personality, research methods, linguistics, urban studies, and, especially, social psychology. Terms chosen were based on thorough research of the glossaries of texts, the index of the *Handbook of Social Psychology,* and APA's *Thesaurus of Psychological Index Terms.* Definitions are brief and clear; many terms relate to children.

A9 **DICTIONARY OF SPECIAL EDUCATION AND REHA-BILITATION** By Leo J. Kelly. Denver, Colo., Love, 1978. 210 pp. $5.95 (paperback).

A dictionary of approximately 1,500 terms in special education and rehabilitation, chosen from texts and reference books, and intended primarily for college students. The book, with cross-references and pronunciations for difficult words, provides understandable explanations rather than authoritative, exhaustive definitions. This book could be useful for parents.

A10 **A DIVORCE DICTIONARY: A BOOK FOR YOU AND YOUR CHILDREN** By Stuart M. Glass. Boston, Mass., Little, Brown, 1979. 71 pp. $7.95 (paperback).

A small, illustrated dictionary on the terminology of divorce, prepared for children in grades 4 and higher; supposedly usable for parents.

A11 **A GLOSSARY OF CERTAIN CHILD-WELFARE TERMS IN SPANISH, PORTUGUESE, FRENCH, AND ENGLISH** By Anna Kalet Smith. Washington, D.C., U.S. Government Printing Office, 1942. 115 pp. Paper. (Out of print) (Bureau Publication No. 271)

An old but still useful publication intended to facilitate an interchange of literature and personal communication among child welfare professionals in the Americas; originally proposed at the 6th Pan American Child Congress in 1930. Sections are Spanish-English/English-Spanish, Portuguese-English/English-Portuguese, and French-English/English-French. Most of the vocabulary is still in use.

A12 **A GLOSSARY OF MEASUREMENT TERMS: A Basic Vocabulary for Evaluation and Testing** Revised Edition. Monterey, Calif., CTB/McGraw-Hill, 1973. 23 pp. $1.75 (paper). From: Del Monte Research Park, Monterey, CA 93940.

A pamphlet that provides clear, cross-referenced definitions of 120 of the most frequently encountered terms in mental measurement textbooks, test manuals, and journals. Valuable for those who use tests in teaching and counseling. *A Parent's Guide to Understanding Tests* (single copies free from the same source) is a simple explanation of types of tests, interpretation of test scores, and ways to help children prepare for tests.

A13   **GLOSSARY OF SELECTED LEGAL TERMS FOR JUVE-NILE JUSTICE PERSONNEL**   By the National College of Juvenile Justice. Denver, Colo., 1978. 10 pp. $3 (paper). From: National College of Juvenile and Family Court Judges, P.O. Box 8978, Reno, NV 89507.

Defines 98 of the most commonly used legal terms relating to juvenile justice for nonlawyers participating in juvenile justice training programs at the National College. Explanations are clear, helpful, and well cross-referenced.

A14   **INTERDISCIPLINARY GLOSSARY ON CHILD ABUSE AND NEGLECT: Legal, Medical, Social Work Terms** Revised Edition. By the National Center on Child Abuse and Neglect. Washington, D.C., U.S. Government Printing Office, 1980. 45 pp. $4.75 (paperback). (DHEW Publication No. [OHDS] 78-30137)

Originally compiled by the Midwest Parent-Child Welfare Resources Center, this tool provides clear, concise definitions of legal, medical, and social work terms relevant to child-abuse-and-neglect treatment and prevention programs. It was intended to help facilitate communication about child abuse across professional borders and, hence, is aimed at a wide audience of attorneys, day-care personnel, family-life educators, health-care administrators, homemaker personnel, judges, law enforcement personnel, legislators, nurses, parent aides, physicians, psychologists, social planners, social workers, school administrators, students, teachers, volunteer child and family advocates, and concerned citizens.

A15   **THE LANGUAGE OF MENTAL HEALTH**   2nd Edition. By William E. Fann and Charles E. Goshen. St. Louis, Mo., Mosby, 1977. 165 pp. $12 (paperback).

Another dictionary for those who need to know the language of mental health or the behavioral sciences for secretarial, administrative, legal, or historical functions. The author notes that the behavioral sciences have extensive vocabularies lacking authoritative statements of definition. This book presents terminology in logical disciplinary categories that are subdivided by function. Abnormal psychology, for example, is divided into diagnostic terminology, systems, and psychopathology.

Each section has its own glossary. Major categories are human behavior, treatment terminology, and administrative and legal terminology. Additional terms are taken from the related fields of medicine, science, statistics, and computer technology. Appendixes include abbreviations, slang, and historical biographies.

A16   **LAW DICTIONARY** Revised Edition. By Steven H. Gifis. Woodbury, N.Y., Barron's Educational Series, 1983. 240 pp. $3.95 (paperback).

An easy-to-understand legal dictionary of more than 1,500 legal terms, intended for lay persons and students. Good typography and boldface cross-references in straightforward definitions that sometimes explain the background of terms and concepts.

A17   **LEXIQUE FRANÇAIS-ANGLAIS-ALLEMAND DES TERMES USUELS EN PSYCHIATRIE, NEURO-PSYCHIATRIE INFANTILE ET PSYCHOLOGIE PATHOLOGIQUE** (English-French-German glossary for psychiatry, child psychiatry, and abnormal psychiatry.) 3rd Edition. By Lise Moor. Paris, L'Expansion Scientifique Française, 1980. 234 pp. $12 (paperback).

Lists words by language with corresponding words in adjacent columns. There are three sets of vocabularies: French-English-German (on white paper), German-English-French (on yellow paper), and English-French-German (again on white paper). It provides a quick means of translation or of finding word equivalents, but does not include definitions.

A18   **THE LIVING WORD VOCABULARY** By Edgar Dale and Joseph O'Rourke. Chicago, Ill., World Book/Childcraft, 1981. 704 pp. $49.95.

An interesting word list that includes 43,000 words or terms (each with a single meaning) followed by a percentage score, which indicates the proportion of students in a certain grade (4, 6, 8, 10, 12, 13, 16) familiar with a particular word or term. These scores were obtained from a three-choice test that has continued since 1954. The approach was originally used by *World Book Encyclopedia* as an objective scale for determining word recognition.

A19   **MANUAL ON TERMINOLOGY AND CLASSIFICATION IN MENTAL RETARDATION** 3rd Edition. Edited by Herbert J. Grossman. Washington, D.C., American Association on Mental Deficiency, 1977. 204 pp. $14.85.

The latest in a series of efforts by the American Association on Mental Deficiency to provide definitions and a classification system for mental retardation. The terminology and classification sections take up approximately half the book, with some good diagrams and interesting discussions of medical and behavioral classification and statistical reporting. The glossary, which occupies the other half of the book, uses good typography, with terms in boldface type and cross-references in italics. Its precise definitions cover nearly every aspect of the causes, prevention, and treatment of mental retardation.

A20 **OBSTETRIC-GYNECOLOGIC TERMINOLOGY, With Section on Neonatology and Glossary of Congenital Anomalies** Edited by Edward C. Hughes for the Committee on Terminology of the American College of Obstetricians and Gynecologists. Philadelphia, Pa., Davis, 1972. 731 pp. (Out of print)
This work is a major effort to standardize terms in obstetrics, gynecology, and neonatology, with a supporting grant from the Children's Bureau. Includes eponyms, abbreviations, synonyms, and mode of inheritance (in the section on genetics).

A21 **PIAGET: DICTIONARY OF TERMS** By Antonio M. Battro. Translated and edited by Elizabeth Rutschi-Hermann and Sarah F. Campbell. New York, Pergamon, 1973. 186 pp. $28.
Defines 1,200 terms used by Piaget and his collaborators in their works on genetic epistemology. Uses American spelling and an alphabetic arrangement but adheres closely to the definitions and translations of the original French. It includes bibliographies of books and articles.

A22 **PSYCHIATRIC DICTIONARY** 5th Edition. By Robert Jean Campbell. New York, Oxford University Press, 1981. 693 pp. $35.
A continuing version of the *Psychiatric Dictionary* by Leland E. Hinsie and Jacob Shatzky first published in 1940, updated to cover technological advances; current approaches; and attitudinal, economic, and legal changes.

A23 **TABER'S CYCLOPEDIC MEDICAL DICTIONARY** 14th Edition. Philadelphia, Pa., Davis, 1981. 1,818 pp. $15.95.
Somewhat easier to read and understand than the other two basic medical dictionaries (*Stedman's* and *Dorland's*), with definitions based on actual usage. Includes antidotes, warnings, and procedures and conveniently supplies abbreviations and synonyms for terms immediately

after their definitions. The 228 appendixes include lists of poison control centers, medical emergencies, and foreign phrase equivalents.

A24   **VOCABULAIRE DE PSYCHO-PEDAGOGIE ET DE PSY-
      CHIATRIE DE L'ENFANT**   3rd Edition. By R. Lafon. Paris,
      Presses Universitaires de France (New York, French & Euro-
      pean Publications, Inc.), 1973. 868 pp. $57.50.
Provides signed definitions of terms prepared by specialists. Includes
etymology; numerous cross-references; and German, English, Spanish, and Italian equivalents of entry words.

ENCYCLOPEDIAS

A25   **AMERICAN EDUCATOR'S ENCYCLOPEDIA**   By Edward
      L. Dejnozka and David E. Kapel. Westport, Conn., Greenwood,
      1982. 634 pp. $65.
A current, one-volume ready-reference work with approximately 2,000
brief but scholarly articles on almost all facets of elementary to higher
education, many with bibliographies. Articles are comprehensive and
include up-to-date information on federal programs and legislation,
special education, and minority and bilingual education, as well as administration and curriculum areas. The work provides a topical index
and good cross-references. Substantial appendixes cover significant
federal education legislation and addresses of state departments of
education, among other things.

A26   **BASIC HANDBOOK OF CHILD PSYCHIATRY**   Edited by
      Joseph D. Noshpitz, Justin D. Call, Richard L. Cohen, and
      Irving N. Berlin. New York, Basic Books, 1979–1980. 4 Vols.
      $148/set.
Although it is not arranged in encyclopedic format, this massive handbook, the work of almost 300 experts in child psychology, neurology,
developmental biochemistry, and social work, covers current theory,
research, and practice from conception through adolescence and is illustrated with tables, charts, sample tests, and black-and-white illustrations. The first volume, *Development,* explores in 57 chapters the
course of normal development, sociocultural factors, family structures,
various advantages, severe handicaps, assessment, diagnosis, and
examination. The bulk of the 40 chapters in the second volume, *Disturbances in Development, Etiology, Nosology,* deal with 31 syndromes; re-
maining chapters cover etiology and nosology. The third volume is en-

titled *Therapeutic Interventions,* and the fourth, *Prevention and Current Issues.* Each volume has its own author and title indexes, and Volume 4 includes a cumulative name index of 3,000 individuals whose works are discussed in the set.

A27 ENCYCLOPEDIA OF BIOETHICS Edited by Warren T. Reich. New York, Free Press, 1978. 4 Vols. $250/set.

This encyclopedia for the new field of bioethics was compiled by 285 contributors from 15 countries as a comprehensive source of information on ethical and social issues in the life sciences, medicine, and the health professions. Articles are intended to supply background information for students and researchers and to help professionals develop policy and make decisions. This encyclopedia covers problems imposed by new techniques, such as amniocentesis and prolongation of life, as well as age-old ethical dilemmas. Articles provide information on historical development, the basic concepts and principles that define a problem, the ethical theories and religious traditions involved, and the like. The comprehensive index reveals many articles on children, adolescents, and infants on such topics as health care, legitimacy, organ donation, proxy consent, rights, and sexual development. Other categories such as race differences in intelligence, racism and mental health, and sexual behavior have highly relevant entries. Nontechnical, signed articles, geared to the intelligent lay person, are followed by selective bibliographies.

A28 THE ENCYCLOPEDIA OF EDUCATION Edited by Lee C. Deighton et al. New York, Macmillan, 1971. 10 Vols. $199/set.

Provides reasonably current, well-rounded articles on approximately 1,000 topics in education, largely excluding individuals and institutions. The final index volume is very helpfully detailed.

A29 ENCYCLOPEDIA OF PEDIATRIC PSYCHOLOGY By Logan Wright, Arlene B. Schaefer, and Gerald Solomons. Baltimore, Md., University Park Press, 1979. 933 pp. $39.95.

A convenient encyclopedia on the medical psychology of children, covering, in alphabetic order, 114 topics in pediatric medicine. Articles from abortion to battered children and weaning deal with those common areas in childhood illness or disability in which emotional, behavioral, or psychological factors are important. The articles, accessible through the table of contents, range in length from one paragraph to 10 pages. In general, they are interesting and understandable. Some include charts and diagrams; all have citations to research. The book includes glossaries of tests and terms and nearly 300 pages of references.

A30 **ENCYCLOPEDIA OF SOCIAL WORK** 17th Edition. Edited by John B. Turner et al. Washington, D.C., National Association of Social Workers, 1977. 2 Vols. 1,702 pp. $40/set.

A well-written encyclopedia with a substantial amount of information on aspects of child welfare, child health, aid to dependent children, protective services for children, children's mental health, and mental illness. The approach is practical but scholarly; the articles contain bibliographies; and the index is detailed. The tendency is toward long articles on important topics (e.g., 76 pages on child welfare). The scope, however, goes beyond social work to relevant aspects of public affairs, urban and regional planning, anthropology, and sociology. The book also includes interesting biographies of prominent specialists in social work and social welfare, and the final section of 54 statistical tables contains significant data on children.

A31 **INTERNATIONAL ENCYCLOPEDIA OF PSYCHIATRY, PSYCHOLOGY, PSYCHOANALYSIS, AND NEUROLOGY** Edited by Benjamin B. Wolman. New York, Van Nostrand Reinhold for Aesculapius, 1977. 12 Vols. $675/set. *Progress Volume I,* Aesculapius, 1983, $69.

This monumental 12-volume work, which took seven years to complete, is the effort of 1,500 contributors and 300 editors and consultants and contains 2,000 signed, original articles with bibliographies. Articles provide readable, comprehensive reviews of research, theory, and practice in the study of the human mind and its ills. The set contains numerous articles on various aspects of children and childhood, many of which can be located through cross-references under the subject term "Child, childhood, children" in the main text. Other topics can be located through the index volume, which contains name and subject indexes. The American Library Association applauded the *International Encyclopedia* for its "outstanding quality and significance." Starting in 1983, the work uses *Progress Volumes* to update the areas that require fresh approaches and new appraisals.

A32 **INTERNATIONAL ENCYCLOPEDIA OF THE SOCIAL SCIENCES** Edited by David L. Sills. New York, Free Press, 1977. 8 Vols. $275/set. *Biographical Supplement,* 1979. $80.

Contains 1,900 authoritative articles by some 1,500 contributors on all aspects of social science, emphasizing sociology, psychology, theory, and methodology, with bibliographies and cross-references. The detailed index includes 40,000 analytical terms. The *Biographical Supplement* may be useful in locating relevant biographies.

THESAURI

The Library of Congress's *Subject Headings,* discussed in Chapter 1, is used or adapted in many research tools. The thesauri that follow can help suggest vocabulary and searching terms for more ambitious searches.

A33 **CHILD ABUSE AND NEGLECT THESAURUS** Washington, D.C., National Center on Child Abuse and Neglect (NCCAN), 1983. 149 pp. $7.

A compilation of standardized words and terms used to describe child abuse and neglect information, intended as a guide to terms and synonyms and a dictionary of contemporary terminology. It is used as the terminology source for describing and indexing the documents, research summaries, and program descriptors in the NCCAN data base. Based on an earlier (1975) thesaurus, it includes terms from medicine, law, social work, psychology, management, planning, program administration, research, facilities, and therapy. This thesaurus includes an alphabetic display, a permuted display, and descriptions of groups.

A34 **MEDICAL SUBJECT HEADINGS: Annotated, Alphabetical List, 1984** Bethesda, Md., National Library of Medicine, 1983. 760 pp. $17.

An alphabetic listing of subject descriptors used for periodical indexes and on-line searches, with notes and cross-references. Helpful for searches in nursing, medicine, and hospital literature.

A35 **NICSEM SPECIAL EDUCATION THESAURUS** The Controlled Indexing Vocabulary for the NICSEM Special Education Data Base. 2nd Edition. Albuquerque, N. Mex., National Information Center for Educational Media, 1980. 74 pp. $16 (paperback).

A three-part comprehensive searching vocabulary on special education; useful for areas like learner characteristics and skills, placement, evaluation, curriculum, and instruction. Includes a hierarchical display with definitions of terms, an alphabetic display, and a permuted term display.

A36 **TERMINOLOGY, UNESCO: IBE Education Thesaurus** A Faceted List of Terms for Indexing and Retrieving Documents and Data in the Field of Education with French and Spanish

Equivalents. By the International Bureau of Education. Paris, Unesco, 1978. 348 pp. $15.75 (paperback). From: Unipub, Box 433, Murray Hill Sta., New York, NY 10157.

Prepared by documentation experts to provide a culture-free set of terms, *Terminology, UNESCO* is similar to the *Thesaurus of ERIC Descriptors* (A37), with equivalents in English, French, and Spanish. Since the work is arranged by English-language terms, with informative scope notes, it could be useful in searching international topics and materials.

Three similar international tools are *Terminology: Special Education* (Paris, Unesco, 1976, $15.75 [paperback]), *International Standard Classification of Education (ISCED)* (Paris, Unesco, 1976), and *EUDISED Multilingual Thesaurus for Information Processing in the Field of Education* (Hawthorne, N.Y., Mouton, 1974, $19.50 [paperback]).

A37 **THESAURUS OF ERIC DESCRIPTORS** 10th Edition. Phoenix, Ariz., Oryx, 1984. 614 pp. $45.

The basic tool for indexing and researching documents and articles in *Resources in Education* and *Current Index to Journals in Education,* the *Thesaurus of ERIC Descriptors* contains more than 5,000 terms, many of which go well beyond education to a wide range of topics related to children. A supplementary *Identifier Authority List* is an added aid for searching ERIC.

A38 **A THESAURUS OF INDEX TERMS FOR DEVELOPMEN-TAL PSYCHOLOGY** A System of Classification for the Florence L. Goodenough Collection. Compiled by Wendy Pradt Lougee. Minneapolis, Minn., Institute of Child Development, University of Minnesota, 1977. 20 pp. Free (paper). From: 51 E. River Rd., Minneapolis, MN 55455.

A convenient pamphlet that arranges developmental terms alphabetically, with cross-references and scope notes. Can be used in book indexing and arranging reprint files.

A39 **THESAURUS OF PSYCHOLOGICAL INDEX TERMS** 3rd Edition. Washington, D.C., American Psychological Assn., 1982. 336 pp. $40.

A well-designed searching vocabulary of 4,000 terms to use in the PsycINFO data base or any of the allied print services. An alphabetic listing of all index terms includes terms that are broader, narrower, and related to specific terms being indexed. The relationship section includes scope notes for about one-third of the terms, and a rotated alphabetic section lists terms under all keywords.

3 / Guides to the Literature and Library Catalogs

The ideal way to begin research is to locate a recent comprehensive "guide to the literature" that provides an overview and/or summary of significant print, human, and institutional sources of information. Typically, such guides are issued by scholars or librarians experienced in a particular discipline. Since the study of children per se, however, is not an academic discipline, there is, to my knowledge, no English-language guide other than this book that attempts a systematic exposition of print and nonprint resources. Bibliographies and guides exist that are intended primarily for parents, and many do a creditable job of providing access to a well-rounded assortment of literature on the child, since parents' awareness in this area tends to encompass more facets than the awareness of subject specialists. These guides are annotated and discussed in Chapter 17. Directories of information resources on children's books and literature (extensively compiled by librarians and professors of English) are covered in Chapter 16.

This chapter treats guides to related, often broader, fields that concern children, such as child welfare, education, or child psychology. The focus is largely American and current, but I am including an exemplary (although almost unobtainable) 1979 guide to French sources on the child.

The most useful guides are generally paperbacks issued by organizations that collect information for their own use and then

37

publish it as a service to their colleagues. Unfortunately, some of these sources are out of print, but I am including several that were distributed to libraries. As funds and time permit, others may be reissued.

Similar directory/bibliographic information can be found elsewhere in this book. Some of the bibliographies annotated in Chapter 6 include related organizations, data bases, and periodical indexes, in addition to specific titles. Benjamin Schlesinger's bibliographies, for example, usually provide such sources. So do some handbooks. Often, collections of statistics indicate original data sources; *Child and Family Indicators: A Report with Recommendations* is one example. Review articles, too, may provide lists of sources along with summaries of literature and findings. For example, Jane S. Port's "The Effects of Maternal Alcohol and Substance Abuse on the Newborn" (*Advances in Alcohol and Substance Abuse, 1*[3/4], 1982) contains a helpful, selective guide to current reference sources. I have tried to indicate in the annotations when such information is included.

Readers interested in particular aspects of childhood not covered here, such as biology, medicine, physical anthropology, art, or theater, can look for an appropriate guide to the broad field. Such works typically are reviewed in *American Reference Books Annual* or annotated in guides to reference books, such as Eugene P. Sheehy's *Guide to Reference Books* (9th Edition, plus *Supplements,* Chicago, Ill., American Library Assn., 1976) or Alfred J. Walford's British *Guide to Reference Materials,* which contains many European titles.

GUIDES TO RESEARCH SOURCES

B1   **L'ENFANCE: GUIDE DES SOURCES DOCUMEN-TAIRES**   Coordinated by Luce Kellerman for La Documentation Française. Paris, Association des Documentalistes et Bibliothecairés Specialisés (ADBS), 1979. Approximately 140 pp. Price not available (paper). From: 29–31 quai Voltaire 75 340, Paris, Cedex 7, France.

A valuable, but extremely difficult to obtain, guide to French documentary sources on the child. It provides hundreds of references in 10 chapters, including addresses and annotations for 103 periodicals, 55 information and documentation centers, and 9 university centers. The first eight chapters deal with the child in contemporary French society, the rights of children, medical and social problems, the child and the family, children and school, the child and his/her environment, needs of the child, and children and mass media. The last two chapters are a directory of centers and a catalog of periodicals. Each of the first eight chapters has its own literature list of approximately 70 items. An appendix includes a French text of the Universal Declaration of the Rights of the Child. There is a subject index to the entire book.

B2   **FAMILY RESEARCH: A Source Book, Analysis, and Guide to Federal Funding** By Wakefield Washington Associates. Westport, Conn., Greenwood, 1979. 2 Vols., continuously paged. $95.

Wakefield Washington Associates is a management firm that specializes in planning research policy, designing information systems, forecasting national policy, and monitoring national research. *Family Research* provides informative profiles of relevant agencies and their programs. The first chapter describes 50 research programs in 24 agencies, with abstracts of 703 research projects. The appendix contains 1,100 abstracts, mostly research projects ongoing in fiscal year 1976. Volume 2 contains the current status and priorities of family research in these agencies.

B3   **FEDfind** By Richard D'Aleo. Springfield, Va., ICUC Press, 1982. 278 pp. $8.95, plus $1.00 postage (paperback). From: P.O. Box 1447, Springfield, VA 22151.

A convenient, current overview of and guide to the labyrinth of sources and services that disseminate information from or about the Federal Government; includes both government sources and specialized publishers. FEDfind is arranged in 16 chapters that cover federal personnel, legislative, presidential, judicial, budget, statistical, and map operations, as well as major sources of publications like the U.S. Government Printing Office (GPO), the National Technical Information Service (NTIS), specific agencies, and private publishers. It includes lengthy descriptions of publications and services (with sources and stock numbers as needed), a detailed table of contents, and a title index. Since so many programs for children are related to the Federal Government, this reference can be helpful.

B4   **A GUIDE TO INFORMATION SOURCES AND SERVICES FOR VOLUNTARY HUMAN SERVICE AGENCIES** Compiled and edited by Harold Schutzman. New York, National As-

sembly of National Voluntary Health and Social Welfare
Organizations, 1979. 112 pp. $4, plus $1 postage and handling
(paper). Limited supply. From: 1346 Connecticut Ave., NW,
Suite 424A, Washington, DC 20036.

The National Assembly, which recently moved to Washington, D.C.,
has compiled a most helpful and cogent guide to information services
for voluntary service agencies. It annotates approximately 160 information sources, including updating and loose-leaf services (such as those
of Commerce Clearinghouse), data bases, federally sponsored and private information services, and reference books. "Overwhelmed by the
multiplicity of sources," the assembly categorized, compiled, listed,
and described selected sources for decision makers in human service
agencies. Includes a detailed table of contents but no index.

B5   **GUIDE TO POPULATION/FAMILY PLANNING INFOR-
       MATION SOURCES**   2nd Edition. Edited by Judith M. Wil-
       kinson. Clarion, Pa., Association for Population/Family Plan-
       ning Libraries and Information Centers—International (APLIC),
       1979. 50 pp. $8 (paper). (APLIC Special Publication No. 2)

This project of the New York regional chapter of APLIC annotates
bibliographies, directories, dictionaries, indexes, and other reference
works concerned with population and family planning and also covers
periodicals and newsletters, publishers, and organizations. Treats these
particular sources more comprehensively than do other guides.

B6   **GUIDE TO SOCIAL SCIENCE RESOURCES IN WO-
       MEN'S STUDIES**   By Elizabeth H. Oakes and Kathleen E.
       Sheldon. Santa Barbara, Calif., ABC-Clio, 1978. 162 pp. $24.75.

Prepared under the auspices of the Women's Studies Program at the
University of California, Los Angeles, this well-assembled guide
annotates, classifies, and indexes 654 bibliographies in the fields of
anthropology, economics, history, psychology, sociology, and contemporary feminist thought. Good subject and author indexes; the
former lists 34 citations concerned specifically with child care and 18
dealing with childhood. Many others are on peripherally related topics.

B7   **A GUIDE TO SOURCES OF EDUCATIONAL INFORMA-
       TION**   2nd Edition. By Marda Woodbury. Arlington, Va., In-
       formation Resources Press, 1982. 430 pp. $39.50, plus $2.30
       postage and handling.

A comprehensive, selective guide to the massive field of education;
considered the current standard guide to educational information
sources. Annotates more than 500 printed sources (mostly reference

works), 26 data banks, and 152 organizations. A five-section work in 20 chapters, it covers the research process, print and organizational research tools, and resources for subjects such as finance and government, special education, instructional materials, and tests and assessment instruments. Chapters are included on state library services for educators and guides for educational writers. Useful for educators and child experts who want a one-volume perspective on educational sources. Includes a detailed index.

B8   **INFORMATION SOURCES OF POLITICAL SCIENCE** 3rd Edition. By Frederick L. Holler. Santa Barbara, Calif., ABC-Clio, 1981. 278 pp. $65.

Useful for locating materials related to law and governance, this guide includes 1,750 numbered citations divided into six parts (each with its own introduction and table of contents): general reference sources; social sciences; American government, politics, and public law; international relations and organizations; comparative and area studies; and political theory and public administration. The literature for each field is covered thoroughly and usually includes guidebooks, bibliographies, dictionaries and encyclopedias, handbooks, and biographical sources. The annotations for each work are full and descriptive. Author, title, and subject indexes, with entries for particular formats (e.g., bibliography, dictionary, handbook) in the subject index.

B9   **NEW FEMINIST SCHOLARSHIP: A GUIDE TO BIBLIOGRAPHIES** By Jane Williamson. Old Westbury, N.Y., Feminist Press, 1979. 144 pp. $15.

A directory of feminist bibliographies divided into many topic areas. Several helpful sections cover child care, life cycles, marriage and the family, and work. The book includes introductions for each section and author and title indexes.

B10   **REFERENCE RESOURCES: A SYSTEMATIC APPROACH** Edited by James M. Doyle and George H. Grimes. Metuchen, N.J., Scarecrow, 1976. 292 pp. $13.

Combines a systematic searcher's manual with discipline resource packages in the fields of general social sciences, psychology, business and economics, education, law, philosophy and religion, language and literature, fine arts, physical and life sciences, and general reference works. The first two sections cover the structure and identification of reference resources and demonstrate the search process. The third section provides annotated lists of reference materials and periodicals by subject experts.

42 PRINTED REFERENCE WORKS

B11 **REFERENCE SOURCES IN SOCIAL WORK: AN ANNO-
TATED BIBLIOGRAPHY** By James H. Conrad. Metuchen,
N.J., Scarecrow, 1982. 201 pp. $15.

Brings together in six sections 656 major reference sources in social
work and allied disciplines (basically the social and behavioral sciences)
for librarians, practitioners, and educators. The first (general) section
covers broad-scope abstracts, bibliographies, manuals, encyclopedias,
and handbooks. The second section presents the history of social work.
The third covers major reference works in the allied fields of psychiatry
and psychology, sociology and anthropology, economics, political affairs, and urban affairs. The fourth section covers reference works in
particular fields, such as adoption, aging, alcoholism, child abuse, child
welfare, and so on. The fifth and sixth deal with service methods and
the social work profession. Appendixes treat social work journals,
organizations, and libraries. Even though the author concentrates on
works published from 1970 through 1981 and uses a cutoff date of 1974
for directories, some of the entries, as is almost inevitable, are out-
of-date. The book does not include data bases and clearinghouses, but
these are covered in other guides. Author and subject indexes.

B12 **RESEARCH GUIDE FOR PSYCHOLOGY** By Raymond
G. McInnes. Westport, Conn., Greenwood, 1982. 604 pp.
$45. (Reference Sources for the Social Sciences and Humani-
ties, No. 1)

A 1,200-entry research guide compiled by a social sciences librarian
who attempts to "include the principal information sources in a logically
integrated and critically analytical format." Of the 17 sections of reference works, those on child psychology and development psychology
are perhaps the most significant for professionals concerned with children. For each category, McInnes discusses specific tools and classes of
reference books, such as recurrent and retrospective bibliographies.
Particular works are identified by a letter code and cited by the same
code in a separate section. Since McInnes has an encyclopedic knowledge of sources, the discussions are helpful and precise, although one
has to flip through the pages to tie citations to discussions. This book
should be consulted by anyone who wants to research beyond the child
psychology and psychiatry resources contained in this guide.

B13 **THE RESOURCE DIRECTORY FOR FUNDING AND
MANAGING NONPROFIT ORGANIZATIONS** Compiled
by Ann M. Heywood. New York, Edna McConnell Clark Foun-

dation, 1982. 83 pp. $4, with quantity discount (paperback).
From: 250 Park Ave., New York, NY 10017.
Funded by Exxon and the Edna McConnell Clark Foundation, *The Resource Directory* is an excellent guide to the organizations and printed reference sources that can help nonprofit organizations deal effectively with raising money and managing programs. Provides specific and thorough discussions of key service organizations for grant seekers; directories and search methods for foundation, corporate, and governmental funding; periodicals and data bases; classified lists of sources (e.g., on arts, justice, youth, and religion); a geographic (state and regional) guide to sources; references on fund raising and proposal writing; and, finally, a most useful classified guide to organizations and publications that provide assistance in general management, accounting and budgeting, program planning and evaluation, public relations, and other technical areas.

B14   **SOCIAL SCIENCE REFERENCE SOURCES: A PRACTI-CAL GUIDE** By Tze-chung Li. Westport, Conn., Greenwood, 1980. 315 pp. $29.95. (Contributions in Librarianship and Information Science, No. 30)
Apparently intended for reference librarians in the social sciences, this book covers guides, bibliographies, indexes and abstract journals, compilations, digests, encyclopedias, dictionaries, directories, and biographical sources for all the social sciences—800 items in all. More current than *Sources of Information in the Social Sciences* (B15).

B15   **SOURCES OF INFORMATION IN THE SOCIAL SCI-ENCES: A Guide to the Literature** 2nd Edition, revised. By Carl M. White et al. Chicago, Ill., American Library Assn., 1973. 1,500 pp. $25.
The basic scholarly guide to reference books and other printed sources in the social sciences, well cross-referenced and indexed, with annotations and short bibliographic essays. Areas covered include the social sciences in general, history, geography, economics and business, sociology, anthropology, psychology, education, and political science.

B16   **STARTING POINTS: RESOURCES FOR THE RESIDEN-TIAL/CHILD WELFARE FIELD** Edited by Linda Simpson Potter et al. Chapel Hill, University of North Carolina School of Social Work, Group Child Care Consultant Services, 1981. 34 pp. Paper. (Out of print)

A convenient directory and guide to clearinghouses, national and regional organizations, federal agencies, funding sources, and directories, indexed by title and category of service. Includes an "alphabet soup" of acronyms. Might be revised and reprinted if funds and time permit.

B17   **THE TROUBLED FAMILY: SOURCES OF INFORMA-TION** By Theodore P. Peck. Jefferson, N.C., McFarland & Co., 1982. 258 pp. $19.95 (paper).

A guide for counselors and researchers concerned with troubled families, listing 2,639 organizations or bibliographic references on related topics. The first three parts list organizations—government, private, and others. The fourth part is a series of bibliographies or reading lists on topics like child abuse and neglect, divorce, finances, military personnel, families of prisoners, parent/child relations, and the like. These include journal articles, books, and reports. The fifth part contains brief listings of other sources like data bases, directories, handbooks, reference guides, periodical indexes, and periodicals. The volume is an ambitious undertaking, but not too well realized. Most of the reference works cited are several years old, but the bibliographies are representations of some current approaches. The bibliographies on finances and the families of prisoners and military personnel, however, include citations of works not usually noted elsewhere. Although other directories and bibliographies cover most of the areas more thoroughly, this guide has something for everyone. Subject index.

B18   **URBAN NEEDS: A BIBLIOGRAPHY AND DIRECTORY FOR COMMUNITY RESOURCE CENTERS** By Paula Kline. Metuchen, N.J., Scarecrow, 1978. 257 pp. $14.50.

Not a library guide, but a guide to information sources for community agencies and resource centers. Lists local, state, federal, private, and nonprivate agencies and organizations; directories of their programs and services; and manuals, handbooks, and guides useful in starting programs. It excludes bibliographies and materials directed toward professionals but covers areas of education, consumer protection, legal services, community development, health care, recreation, information services, and social services. Materials on child advocacy, juvenile delinquency, child health services and programs, child care, child abuse, and other areas related to children and youth are included. Author/title/subject index.

B19   **WHERE DO YOU LOOK? WHOM DO YOU ASK? HOW DO YOU KNOW?** An Information Resource for Child

Advocates. By Janet Shur and Paul V. Smith. Washington, D.C., Children's Defense Fund, 1980. 129 pp. $5.50 (paper).
A workbook and outline of federal documents, surveys, and statistics, with an emphasis on census documents. Indicates sources and explains how to locate materials on federal and state programs for children in the areas of health, employment, income assistance, social services, and juvenile justice. Appendixes include a guide to sources in the text, lists of selected directories, selected federal depository libraries, and state directors of cooperative health statistics systems.

LIBRARY CATALOGS

The catalogs listed in this section provide subject, author, and title access to a wide variety of holdings of major libraries specializing in some aspect of childhood or child thought processes. The first two are produced by G. K. Hall, which also publishes the *Dictionary Catalog of the Teacher's College Library* (Columbia University, New York City), updated annually with the *Bibliographic Guide to Education.* Another, similar publication of Hall is the *Bibliographic Guide to Psychology.* Usually, such guides can be located in large academic libraries.

B20   **CATALOG OF THE JEAN PIAGET ARCHIVES, UNIVERSITY OF GENEVA, SWITZERLAND** Boston, Mass., G. K. Hall, 1975. (Out of print)
A three-part catalog comprising a bibliography of the writings of child psychologist Jean Piaget, a bibliography of the works of his collaborators, and a list of secondary literature relating to Piagetian psychology. Subject headings, taken from the original, are in French. Materials are arranged chronologically, then by publication form (monograph, periodical, report, and so on). Translations of Piaget's works follow the original French edition and other languages chronologically, with English translations first. A new edition is planned.

B21   **CATALOG OF THE RESEARCH LIBRARY OF THE REISS-DAVIS CHILD STUDY CENTER.** Boston, Mass., G. K. Hall, 1978. 2 Vols. (Out of print)
Reproduces the dictionary catalog (i.e., author, title, subject) of a library collection of approximately 12,000 volumes reflecting an interdisciplinary approach to emotional problems of children.

B22   **MARRIAGE AND THE FAMILY: PRELIMINARY CHECK LIST OF NATIONAL LIBRARY HOLDINGS**
Compiled by Maryna Nowosielski. Ottawa, National Library of Canada, 1980. 130 pp. Spiral bound. (Apparently out of print)
A checklist of a research collection on marriage, children, the family, and related topics, developed by the National Library of Canada with a grant from the Vanier Institute of the Family. Includes approximately 2,000 monographs, theses, pamphlets, and government publications and 100 periodical titles, primarily in English but also in French and other European languages. The materials are arranged by author or title in three sections: reference sources, serials, and monographs.

4 / Histories and Concepts

As a substitute for the somewhat elusive encyclopedias on childhood, the sources in this chapter provide several histories and surveys that deal extensively with certain aspects of childhood. They are comprehensive and well documented and should provide a helpful overview of the condition of children in the past, including how children were perceived by adults. These sources contain extensive references or bibliographies.

Many of the bibliographies in Chapter 6 have historical implications, such as *Childhood and History in America* (E35), *History of the Family and Kinship* (E85), and *Play and Playthings: A Reference Guide* (E111); all lead to additional works. *Social Service Organizations and Agencies Directory* (I63) and the directory of adoption agencies in *Adoption Agencies, Orphanages and Maternity Homes: An Historical Directory* (I12) contain much historical information on social service organizations concerned with children. AMERICAN HISTORY AND LIFE (J14), available in print and on-line, and FAMILY RESOURCES DATABASE (J24) are two good sources for the history of childhood in the United States. HISTORICAL ABSTRACTS (J25) provides international coverage. The *Journal of Psychohistory* (H106) and the *Journal of Family History* (H97) access current research. Other historical works can be located through the index.

C1 **CENTURIES OF CHILDHOOD: A Social History of Family Life** By Philippe Aries. New York, Vintage Books (a division of Random House), 1965. 447 pp. $5.95 (paperback).

Uses a survey of medieval literature and a wealth of anecdotes as the basis for interpreting the place, role, and concept of childhood in civilization from the Middle Ages to the early twentieth century. The author describes the discovery of childhood and covers changes in certain aspects of child life (such as games, clothes, and schooling) as they mirror society's increasing awareness of child development. Published originally in France in 1960.

C2   **THE CHILD AND THE STATE**   Select Documents, with Introductory Notes. Edited by Grace Abbott. Chicago, Ill., University of Chicago Press, 1938. 2 Vols. (Out of print)

A collection of original documents and source materials from the late eighteenth century to the 1930s, this book provides a realistic history of family relationships, the roles of children in industrial development, and the effects of changing societies on children. It includes firsthand accounts by concerned officials, judges, and even factory inspectors. The first volume (679 pages) explores the legal status of the child in the family and apprenticeship and child labor legislation in the United States, Great Britain, and internationally. The second volume (701 pages) covers various relations between the state and the dependent child, including child offenders, children of unmarried parents, and organizations that serve children. Includes volume bibliographies and indexes.

C3   **CHILDREN AND YOUTH IN AMERICA: A DOCUMENTARY HISTORY**   Edited by Robert H. Bremner et al. Cambridge, Mass., Harvard University Press, 1971-1974. Vol. I: 1600-1865, $35. Vol. II: 1866-1932, 2 books, $55/set. Vol. III: 1933-1973, 2 books, $50/set; paperback, $30/set.

An exhaustive history of childhood and youth (and related public policies) in the United States, which uses documents chosen and organized by an outstanding team of editors aided by consultants from such fields as health, education, family law, delinquency, dependency, and child labor. The book's purpose is "to be useful to students of history and to those who are now considering how to strengthen and improve existing services and create new programs in accord with advances in knowledge of child health and development." The authors have included significant sections of documents, adding explanations only when necessary. The histories of events are organized chronologically by broad topics such as child labor, youth employment, child welfare services, adoption, custody, illegitimacy, juvenile delinquency, health care, and education. There is more hard demographic data in Volume

3, which moves forward from Franklin Roosevelt's New Deal. Each volume contains a selected bibliography and excellent author and subject indexes.

C4   **CHILDREN OF CRISIS** By Robert Coles. Boston, Mass., Atlantic Monthly Press, 1967–1976. Vol. 1: *A Study of Courage and Fear,* 1967, $16.95; paper, $10.95. Vol. 2: *Migrants, Sharecroppers, Mountaineers,* 1972, $15.00; paper, $10.95. Vol. 3: *The South Goes North,* 1972, $10.95 (paper). Vol. 4: *Eskimos, Chicanos, Indians,* 1977 (out of print). Vol. 5: *Privileged Ones: The Well-Off and Rich in America,* 1977, $12.95 (paper).

The first four volumes of this social history are based on personal contact and interviews. The author, a child psychiatrist, interviewed, taped, and collected drawings from poor children (ages 5–14) — black, white, Chicano, Indian, Eskimoan — moving from the country to city ghettos and finding poverty and rootlessness in both. For the last volume, Coles interviewed well-off children and found that they, too, were suffering.

C5   **CHILDREN OF SIX CULTURES: A Psycho-Cultural Analysis** By Bernice B. Whiting and John W. M. Whiting. Cambridge, Mass., Harvard University Press, 1975. 128 pp. $14; paperback, $6.95.

Part of a Six Cultures Project, this publication presents initial results of extensive research on child-parent relations in six distinct cultures: the United States, North India, the Philippines, Okinawa, Mexico, and Kenya. Includes maps, descriptions, and photographs.

C6   **THE CHILDREN'S BUREAU: Its History, Activities and Organization** By James A. Tobey. New York, AMS Press, 1974. 83 pp. $21.50. (The Brookings Institution, Institute for Government Research, Service Monographs, U.S. Government Reprint A25)

A reprint of a 1925 official publication that provides a history of the origin and concepts of the Children's Bureau.

C7   **CRUSADE FOR THE CHILDREN** A History of the National Child Labor Committee and Child Labor Reform in America. By Walter I. Trattner. Chicago, Ill., Quadrangle Books, 1970. 319 pp. (Out of print)

Although the author modestly denies that this is an exhaustive treatment of child labor reform in America, it makes extensive use of manuscripts and committee records to cover 100 years of important develop-ments and trends at the state and federal levels up to World War II. There are many analogies to today's reform movements on the well-being of children. The notes are essentially an annotated, 85-page bibliography.

C8 **DECLARATION OF THE RIGHTS OF THE CHILD** By Eliska Chanlett and G. M. Mourrier. In: *International Child Welfare Review, 1*:4–8, 1968.

An excellent article that traces the evolution of the declaration from the 1924 version after World War I, through the amended draft version of 1948, to the declaration in its 1959 form.

C9 **EDUCATION IN THE UNITED STATES: A Documentary History** Edited by Sol Cohen. Westport, Conn., Greenwood, 1974. 5 Vols. $200/set.

A competent documentary history of American education from 1607 through 1973, *Education in the United States* uses more than 1,300 documents arranged topically and chronologically. These include let-ters, laws, essays, and reports that convey a feeling of time and place. The book covers broad areas such as reform movements, education of minorities and social classes, the history of the teaching profession, and political issues in education. Introductions span American education from 1607 to 1789, 1789 to 1895, and 1895 to 1973. A useful coverage of a major section of child life in America.

C10 **THE HISTORY OF CHILDHOOD** Edited by Lloyd De-Mause. New York, Harper & Row, 1974. 460 pp. $9.50 (paper-back). (New York, Psychohistory Press, 1974, $28 [hardcover].)

DeMause, an expert on psychohistory and editor of the *Journal of Psy-chohistory,* believes that Western civilization has waged a continuous war against children.

C11 **200 YEARS OF CHILDREN** Edited by Edith H. Grotberg. Washington, D.C., U.S. Office of Child Development, 1976. 486 pp. Paperback. (Out of print)

A thematically arranged compilation of some of the major events, pat-terns, and ideas of the last 200 years that prompted changes in the lives of children and of the social institutions that have affected them— related in the perspective of the 1970s. Covers immigration and migra-tion of families and federal and state structures concerned with the well-being of children. Also deals with health, education, recreation and play, child development, children's literature, and children and the law.

5 / Ongoing Annuals, Bibliographies, and Book Reviews

The materials in Chapters 2–4 provide overviews of history, vocabulary, subject fields, and research methods to aid research on children. This chapter provides several alternative means of keeping up with professional research and ongoing print materials, including annual reviews and yearbooks, recurring bibliographies, sources of bibliographic information, and book reviews. (Of course, the encyclopedias, histories, and sourcebooks cited in Chapters 2–4 usually contain supportive and extensive bibliographies.)

ANNUAL REVIEWS

Annual reviews and yearbooks provide a convenient means of keeping up with research and professional developments in particular areas so that practitioners and interested individuals can share a common knowledge. There are quite a few annual reviews of different types in fields related to children, perhaps because other means of keeping up (such as well-targeted abstract journals or periodical indexes) are deficient. These review publications are particularly prolific in different aspects of child psychology and psychopathology.

The common purpose of all annual reviews and yearbooks is to keep their readers apprised of changes and developments in particular fields, but these publications use different means to attain this goal. Some editors of annual reviews assiduously collect significant articles published within the year; others provide yearly listings or annotations (possibly classified or indexed) of publications that meet certain criteria; still others solicit review or topical articles from prominent individuals in the field. All these approaches have their advantages and disadvantages, and all are used in professions concerned with childhood.

In general, yearly review publications tend to reflect the concerns of an editorial board surveying and assessing major trends, whereas individual review articles and appraisals may stem from independent or particular viewpoints. The latter are more apt to pull together disparate literature or to investigate controversial areas; the former might be more bland or objective. Similar review issues or articles in many other disciplines might cover facets that relate to childhood. For example, annual reviews in law and sociology and the *Annals of the American Academy of Political and Social Science* carry substantial articles on public policies affecting families. Review articles containing more than 50 references can often be located through the *Bibliographic Index* (D40).

Some annual reviews or yearbooks also provide statistical data. Yearbooks primarily devoted to this purpose are dealt with in Chapter 15. I have not included all annuals here. Some that may be occasionally useful are the International Reading Association's *Summary of Investigations Relating to Reading* and the *Annual Review of Child Abuse and Neglect Research* (no longer published).

D1   **ADVANCES IN BEHAVIORAL PEDIATRICS** Edited by Mark Wolraich and Donald K. Routh. Greenwich, Conn., JAI Press, 1980– . Annual. Individuals, $20; institutions, $40.
Contains around 10 chapters in each issue, covering infancy and early development, neuropsychology, and general psychological problems. Articles deal with psychosocial aspects of child and adolescent medicine, including addictions, interventions, prevention of behavioral and medical problems, and learning disabilities. Not indexed internally but indexed in *Psychological Abstracts* and *Social Sciences Citation Index*.

D2   **ADVANCES IN CHILD DEVELOPMENT AND BEHAV-
IOR** Edited by Hayne W. Reese and Lewis P. Lipsitt. New
York, Academic, 1963– . Annual. $34; microfiche, $24.
Usually includes six or seven high-quality reviews of important and/or
controversial issues, representing a useful selection of viewpoints. The
studies discussed are noted at the ends of the articles, and the entire
issue has author and subject indexes. The topics covered vary over
time; each issue lists contents of previous issues.

D3   **ADVANCES IN CLINICAL CHILD PSYCHOLOGY** Edited by Benjamin P. Lahey. New York, Plenum, 1977– . Annual.
$35.
"Designed to provide researchers and clinicians with a medium for dis-
cussing new and innovative approaches to the problems of children."
Includes approximately 10 well-written and (usually) well-referenced
articles on different themes. Volume index.

D4   **ADVANCES IN EARLY EDUCATION AND DAY CARE:
An Annual Compilation of Research and Therapy** Edited by
Sally Kilmer. Greenwich, Conn., JAI Press, 1980– . Annual. Individuals, $20; institutions, $40.
Intended to stimulate research and enhance communication among
scholars in early childhood education, child development, and related
fields, with original research, critical reviews, and conceptual analyses—the only academic reference work in this area. Contains approximately eight articles per issue. Indexed in *Social Sciences Citation Index*.

D5   **ADVANCES IN INFANCY RESEARCH** Edited by Lewis
P. Lipsitt and Carolyn E. Rovee-Collier. Norwood, N.J., Ablex,
1981– . Annual. 1983 edition, $32.50.
Intended as a forum for invitational mid-size (between the length of
journal articles and monographs) technical and scholarly articles that
combine overviews of critical topics with substantive contributions.
Articles serve as primary references for studies on infancy research,
critical collections of diverse data on common themes, and constructive
attacks on old issues (with new inputs). The first issue had seven
articles, authored by leaders in the field, with a detailed table of contents and subject and author indexes.

D6   **ADVANCES IN INTERNATIONAL MATERNAL AND
CHILD HEALTH** Edited by D. B. Jelliffe and E. F. P. Jelliffe.
New York, Oxford, 1981– . Annual. $45.

A publication with an international editorial board that includes around a dozen articles containing interesting comparative data on such things as national nutrition surveys, epidemic hysteria in schoolchildren, the interactions of culture and child health care, and the health implications of promoting infant formulas. Includes an index.

D7 ADVANCES IN LAW AND CHILD DEVELOPMENT Edited by Robert L. Sprague. Greenwich, Conn., JAI Press, 1982– . Annual. Individuals, $20; institutions, $40.

Examines the broad area of law and governmental activities pertaining to child development. Includes legislation, litigation, regulations, and guidelines by schools and government agencies at all levels. Indexed in *Current Index to Journals in Education* and *Social Sciences Citation Index.* Author/subject index.

D8 ADVANCES IN PEDIATRICS Edited by Lewis A. Barness. Chicago, Ill., Year Book Medical Publishers, 1942– . Annual. $49.50.

By reputation, this publication provides well-considered scholarly reviews of pediatric subjects covering the understanding, management, and diagnosis of common and/or refractory pediatric disorders. Commissioned articles provide current updates on a variety of topics; some issues cover particular areas in depth (e.g., Volume 29 deals with ambulatory pediatrics and contains articles on child advocacy and data needs for health services).

D9 ADVANCES IN PERINATAL MEDICINE Edited by Aubrey Milunsky et al. New York, Plenum, 1981– . Annual. $9.50.

Includes around six articles and a journal index per issue.

D10 ADVANCES IN THE BEHAVIORAL MEASUREMENT OF CHILDREN Edited by Roslyn A. Glow. Greenwich, Conn., JAI Press, 1983– . Annual. Individuals, $20; institutions, $40.

Concentrates on studies concerning the measurement of behavior from infancy through adolescence; directed toward researchers and practitioners.

D11 ANNUAL PROGRESS IN CHILD PSYCHIATRY AND CHILD DEVELOPMENT Edited by Stella Chess and Alexander Thomas. New York, Brunner-Mazel, 1968– . Annual. 1983 edition, $35.

A convenient series recommended for immediate information and long-term reference in child development. Includes both original and review articles. Original pieces are intended to contribute to an understanding of the child; review articles are supposed to present a clear and systematic assessment of scientific knowledge. Approximately 30 articles are included in each issue and are divided into around 10 subject areas. Typically, these include learning and cognition, risk factors in childhood, temperament, family therapy, childhood psychosis, hyperactivity, learning disabilities, adolescence, racial issues, and parent/child interaction, but articles are selected for intrinsic merit rather than to fit a predetermined series of topics. Good introduction to each section; no index.

D12 **ANNUAL PROGRESS IN CHILD PSYCHOLOGY AND CHILD DEVELOPMENT** London, Butterworth, 1968– . Annual. Price not available.

Selections from the year's leading contributions in child psychology and child development, usually with some 30 articles in around a dozen areas.

D13 **BIRTH DEFECTS: ORIGINAL ARTICLE SERIES** New York, Alan R. Liss, 1965– . Irregular. Price varies. From: 150 Fifth Ave., New York, NY 10011.

A series of original commissioned articles on birth defects, with subjects ranging from intrauterine infections to inherited eye diseases; includes an *Annual Review of Birth Defects*.

Volume 18, Number 5 is the *Cumulative Index: Birth Defects: Original Article Series, Volumes 1 (1965) to 16 (1980)* (by Natalie W. Paul, 570 pp., $96). It includes an author index, an exhaustive subject index, the full tables of contents of the journals, and a guide to using the index. Almost all individual issues are indexed.

D14 **CHILD PERSONALITY AND PSYCHOPATHOLOGY: CURRENT TOPICS** New York, Wiley, 1974– . Annual. $21.95.

Articles concern theoretical, applied, and, mainly, empirical research, noting findings. Each issue includes a few review articles and an index.

D15 **CURRENT TOPICS IN EARLY CHILDHOOD EDUCATION** Edited by Lilian G. Katz et al. Norwood, N.J., Ablex, 1977– . Annual. 1982 edition, $27.50; paperback, $16.95.

Aims at providing reviews of research and development in early childhood education to an interdisciplinary audience, including those working with young children or training others to do so. Includes approximately 10 integrative articles per issue on topics from assessment of
motor skills to peer relationships, symbolic play, and staff burnout in
child care; provides references on each article. Contains a guide to the
ERIC system and information on obtaining ERIC documents.

D16 **FAMILY STUDIES REVIEW YEARBOOK** Edited by
     David H. Olson and Brent C. Miller. Beverly Hills, Calif., Sage,
     1983– . Annual. $37.50.
A representative interdisciplinary selection of contemporary published
and unpublished works in family studies. The 1983 edition includes 53
articles in 10 sections covering family policy; family stress and coping;
divorce and child custody; marital and family violence; alcoholism,
drug abuse, and the family; work and the family; family economics;
and family therapy.

D17 **LIFE-SPAN DEVELOPMENT AND BEHAVIOR** Edited
     by Paul Baltes. New York, Academic, 1978– . Annual. 1984 edi-
     tion, Vol. 6, $56.
Covers literature on behavioral changes and developmental processes
throughout life. Volumes include 8–10 articles covering 50–200 research reports on topics such as cognitive development, life-span development theory, and feminine role orientations from childhood to adulthood. Has bibliographies at ends of articles, with subject and author
indexes to the whole volume.

D18 **MENTAL RETARDATION AND DEVELOPMENTAL
     DISABILITIES: An Annual Review** Edited by Joseph
     Wartis. New York, Brunner-Mazel, 1970– . Annual. $25.
Covers the entire field of service and research on mental retardation in
15–20 articles, each of which typically includes 50 or more references,
with a subject index to the whole volume. Different topics are reviewed
each year. Issues include calendars of significant occurrences in the
preceding year and of events scheduled for the current year.

D19 **MINNESOTA SYMPOSIA ON CHILD PSYCHOLOGY**
     Hillsdale, N.J., Erlbaum, 1968– . Annual. 1983 edition, $24.95.
     From: 365 Broadway, Hillsdale, NJ 07642. (Earlier volumes
     published by University of Minnesota Press.)

Reports of the yearly conference sponsored by the Institute of Child Development of the University of Minnesota. These papers are similar to commissioned articles and report significant issues to the profession. Each report includes six presentations by eminent researchers (often on a theme), with comments and reactions included in each volume. The most recent volume is *Development and Policy Concerning Children with Special Needs.*

D20 **PROGRESS IN LEARNING DISABILITIES** Edited by Helmer R. Myklebust. New York, Grune & Stratton, 1968- . Irregular. 1983 edition, $29.50.

Intended as periodic updates in the field of learning disabilities. Each volume contains approximately 10 articles. Emphases vary, although all issues attempt interdisciplinary coverage. Discussed works are cited at the ends of the chapters. Subject indexes for each volume.

D21 **THE PSYCHOANALYTIC STUDY OF THE CHILD** New Haven, Conn., Yale University Press, 1945- . Annual. 1983 edition, $45.

This collection of original theoretical and clinical papers, launched by Anna Freud and peers, has served for years as a repository of concerned, articulate thought on all aspects of the development of children within a psychoanalytic framework. In earlier years, papers were targeted toward clinicians directly involved with children; they have since become increasingly relevant for a broader audience. Most issues include articles on development, cognition and intellect, child psychopathology, child and family, and mental health services. The first 25 volumes of this publication are indexed and abstracted in *Abstracts: The Psychoanalytic Study of the Child, Vols. 1-25* (Rockville, Md., National Institute of Mental Health, 1972). This comprehensive compilation and indexing of 516 abstracts was performed by the National Institute of Mental Health in collaboration with the Committee on Indexing of the American Psychoanalytic Association. Abstracts are arranged by broad areas that reflect major investigations and clinical experience. The work includes author and keyword/subject indexes.

D22 **PSYCHOLOGY OF LEARNING AND MOTIVATION: ADVANCES IN RESEARCH** Edited by Gordon Bower. New York, Academic, 1967- . Annual. 1981 edition, $32.

Includes six to eight technical reviews of recent published studies, with chapter references and author and subject volume indexes. Volume 15 has articles on conditioning and short-term information processing, as well as on children's knowledge of events.

D23 **REVIEW OF CHILD DEVELOPMENT RESEARCH** Prepared under the auspices of the Society for Research in Child Development. Chicago, Ill., University of Chicago Press, 1964–. 1982 edition, $40.

Provides interesting, informative, comprehensive reviews for practitioners and researchers, making a conscientious effort to minimize professional jargon and methodological details. Includes around 10–20 articles that may be on a theme or solicited from foreign scholars. Includes separate author and subject indexes.

D24 **REVIEW OF RESEARCH IN EDUCATION** Edited by Dave C. Berliner. Washington, D.C., American Educational Research Assn., 1973–. Annual. 1984 edition, $18.

Sponsored by the American Educational Research Association as a "disciplined inquiry. . .through critical and synthesizing essays," not necessarily limited to the past few years. Most issues deal with several themes, which have included the relations between human development and research in teaching and instruction, guidance counseling, exceptional children, and bilingual/bicultural education. Articles include long bibliographies.

D25 **SOURCEBOOK OF EQUAL EDUCATIONAL OPPORTUNITY** 3rd Edition. Chicago, Ill., Marquis Academic Media, 1979. Irregular. 601 pp. $39.50.

Something between a yearbook and a guide to sources, this continues Marquis's *Yearbook of Equal Educational Opportunity* at irregular intervals, with an interesting smorgasbord of recent articles and excerpts from books, covering general issues, blacks, native Americans, Asian Americans, disadvantaged/white ethnics, Hispanics, and women. Different issues contain different directory information. This issue has statistical data, a bibliography of legislation, addresses of network centers, fellowship programs, and materials development centers. Includes an inadequate index. The *Yearbook of Special Education,* also issued by Marquis, is another irregularly issued "yearbook."

D26 **YEAR BOOK OF PEDIATRICS** Edited by Frank A. Oski and James A. Stockman III. Chicago, Ill., Year Book Medical Publishers, 1933–. Annual. $39.95; $25.00 for physicians serving residencies.

A clinically oriented reference work that attempts to evaluate and summarize the most important pediatric publications of the year. The 1983 edition, for example, provides clear and concise reviews of 288 articles chosen from 74 journals (450 publications were perused). Includes an index and editorial comments.

RECURRING BIBLIOGRAPHIES

Recurring or cumulative bibliographies are another way of keeping up with printed materials in some field. In areas such as education and law, an institution or commercial publisher takes responsibility for periodically compiling a comprehensive listing. Although few recurring bibliographies of this scope that deal specifically with children are published in the United States, two European magazines described in Chapter 9, *Courrier* and the *International Child Welfare Review's Library Supplement,* provide ongoing multilingual annotations of many of the books and journal articles added to the libraries of their parent organizations. *American Family* is now issuing a similar supplement, which is annotated in item D27.

Essentially, the abstracting and indexing services discussed in Chapter 8 also serve as ongoing bibliographies for the formats and topics they index and abstract. Some of them provide supplementary tools to facilitate locating other references. *Index Medicus,* for example, offers a subject bibliography of review articles at the beginning of each issue. This is particularly convenient to research in the annual *Cumulated Index Medicus.* (The National Library of Medicine also issues a separate *Bibliography of Medical Reviews* that can be searched for articles on children.) Because of their structure, citation indexes like the *Social Sciences Citation Index* (*SSCI*) indicate references (or quasi-bibliographies) with the symbol "R" in the entry of a cited work, which points to the location of a bibliography or a review of research in which that work is cited. The *Source Index of SSCI* lists (in extremely brief format) all works cited in all volumes indexed. In most periodical indexes and abstract journals, the heading or subheading "bibliography(ies)" can generally be used to locate bibliographies. This is almost always true in computer searches.

Two types of recurring bibliographies are described in the annotations that follow. These are recurring subject bibliographies (or inventories) and guides that provide ongoing information on particular types of publications such as books, reference books, government documents, or publications of associations. Bibliographic guides to books and U.S. government documents are now available via computer.

G. K. Hall issues two annuals that some users might find relevant: *Bibliographic Guide to Education* and *Bibliographic Guide to Psychology*. These should be available in large academic libraries specializing in psychology and education. R. R. Bowker provides an annual bibliography of law and related areas entitled *Law Information: Current Books, Pamphlets, Serials,* which can be found in large law libraries.

D27 **AMERICAN FAMILY [Supplement]: BIBLIOGRAPHY OF FAMILY PUBLICATIONS** Edited by Rowan A. Wakefield and Joan Mooney. Washington, D.C., American Family, 1982– . Monthly. $15/year.

A new service offered by *American Family* newsletter, consisting of lengthy annotations or brief reviews of books, magazines, films, and other media and some particularly relevant articles from journals and magazines focusing on family policy and programs, with selected books on family history and family therapy when they relate to public policy. Includes a section on the family and computers. The bibliography is current but may go back one year or more for especially useful materials; usually notes around 18 items per issue.

D28 **AMERICAN REFERENCE BOOKS ANNUAL (ARBA)** Edited by Bohdan S. Wynar. Littleton, Colo., Libraries Unlimited, 1970– . Annual. 1983 edition, Vol. 14, $47.50.

A well-annotated record of reference books published in the United States during the previous year, with some international titles and U.S. government publications. Arranged by subject into approximately 40 chapters, ARBA presents some 1,600–1,800 signed reviews by knowledgeable librarians and subject specialists on new dictionaries, encyclopedias, indexes, directories, guides, and other types of reference materials. No section is devoted to children, but the volumes are well-indexed so that reference books on children can be located either through the index or by browsing in the chapters on education, psychology, sociology, and the like.

D29 **ASSOCIATIONS' PUBLICATIONS IN PRINT** 2nd Edition. New York, R. R. Bowker, 1981- . Annual. 1982 edition, $120.

This welcome guide is most helpful in locating publications issued by associations concerned in some way with children, as well as occasional publications on children issued by other associations. Materials can be searched either by subject or association. The guide covers 100,000 pamphlets, journals, newsletters, bulletins, books, audiovisuals, and other items from approximately 4,000 organizations, arranged and cross-referenced by subject. Many, if not most, of these items are omitted from standard bibliographies. Each entry includes the full title, author and editor, publisher, distributor, publication date, frequency of publication, price, binding, and catalog and order numbers to facilitate purchase. The set includes a subject index to publications and audiovisual materials, separate title indexes for publications and audiovisuals, an association name index, an acronym index, and a key to abbreviations. Topics are arranged by Library of Congress subject heading terms. Subjects are well cross-referenced.

D30 **BIBLIOGRAPHY OF DEVELOPMENTAL MEDICINE AND CHILD NEUROLOGY: SELECTED BOOKS AND ARTICLES** Edited by Martin C. O. Bax for Spastics International Medical Publications. London, Spastics International with William Heinemann Medical Books, 1963- . Annual. Free to subscribers of *Developmental Medicine and Child Neurology;* $12 to nonsubscribers. From: J. B. Lippincott, E. Washington Sq., Philadelphia, PA 19105.

An annual bibliography of selected international periodical and monograph literature in developmental medicine and child neurology; supplements the publications abstracted and cited in *Developmental Medicine and Child Neurology* (H43). The 1982 issue (Supplement 46) cited 225 books and nearly 1,000 journal articles. The articles are arranged by author under broad topics and indexed by subject and author. Topics for 1982 included genetics, cytogenetics, embryology and teratology, developmental abnormalities, neonatal studies, cerebral palsy, epilepsy, Down's syndrome, other neurological disorders, disorders of communication, neurophysiology and neuroanatomy, developmental studies, orthopedics of malformations, metabolic disorders, muscular disorders, mental handicaps, psychology and psychiatry, and general. This list sounds formidable, but not all the books and articles are technical. The books, in particular, are interesting, with good representation of titles by international organizations and British publishers.

Topics include breast-feeding, verbal processes in children, ecology of preschool behavior, family patterns, and health. Each issue includes a list of journals cited (around 200).

D31   **BOOKS IN PRINT 1984–85** New York, R. R. Bowker, 1948– . Annual. 1984 Edition: 2 Parts, 6 Vols. (Vols. 1–3, *Authors;* Vols. 4–6, *Titles.*) $185.

One of a series of comprehensive guides issued by Bowker that indexes by author and title approximately 500,000 books issued by standard American publishers. Includes price, publication, and order data for each title, and pagination for more recent titles, with a complete directory of publishers in the titles set.

Subject Guide to Books in Print, revised each fall, provides subject access to these titles by Library of Congress subject headings. *Forthcoming Books in Print,* issued during the year, lists and cumulates books published subsequent to the latest *Books in Print* and books scheduled to be published within the next five months. *Subject Guide to Forthcoming Books* indexes these titles. The Bowker series also includes *Children's Books in Print, Medical Books in Print, Paperbound Books in Print,* and many others. The complete data file can now be searched on-line via DIALOG.

D32   **CHILDREN AND YOUTH: SUBJECT BIBLIOGRAPHY** Washington, D.C., U.S. Government Printing Office, 1983. Irregular. 29 pp. Free (paper). From: U.S. Government Printing Office, Washington, DC 20402 or local government bookstores.

The nearly 300 *Subject Bibliographies* issued by the U. S. Government Printing Office are listings of in-print materials available for purchase from GPO. The listing on children and youth is arranged under broad categories by title and includes price, pagination, and document number. Topics in the 1982 issue include alcohol and drugs, early development, employment and unemployment, family life, the handicapped and learning-disabled, health and nutrition, literature, prenatal and neonatal care, safety, and sexuality. Other relevant free *Subject Bibliographies* include No. 196, *Elementary Education;* No. 164, *Reading;* No. 150, *Library Science;* No. 163, *Drug Education;* No. 167, *Mental Health;* No. 122, *Public Health;* No. 273, *Statistical Publications;* and No. 30, *Social Welfare and Services.*

D33   **EDUCATIONAL DOCUMENTATION AND INFORMATION** Geneva, International Bureau of Education, 1927– .

Quarterly. 52 French francs/year. From: Unipub, Box 433, Murray Hill Sta., New York, NY 10157.

A quarterly annotated thematic bibliography on subjects or themes related to the education program of Unesco. Often these bibliographies include institutions and organizations, as well as publications. Each issue appears in English, French, and Spanish and includes around 300 references to materials chosen by subject specialists on the criteria of recency and geographic distribution, as well as cogency. Reviews are analytic rather than critical; topics often deal with the whole child or the whole context of childhood. Valuable issues are *Early Childhood Education* (No. 224, 1982), *Family, Community and Media in the Education of the Disadvantaged Child* (No. 214, 1980), and *Education of the Disadvantaged: Non-School Factors* (No. 212, 1979).

D34   INTERNATIONAL BIBLIOGRAPHY: PUBLICATIONS OF INTERGOVERNMENTAL ORGANIZATIONS (Formerly *International Bibliography, Information, Documentation.*) New York, Unipub, 1972– . Quarterly. United States and Canada, $48/year; $55/year foreign.

Provides a bibliographic record of books, periodicals, microforms, and audiovisual materials issued by the United Nations and nearly 100 other international organizations. Useful for international aspects of children and childhood. The bibliographic record section arranges publications other than periodicals alphabetically by title in broad subject categories. The periodicals record section arranges periodicals by title with tables of contents. Includes annotations of sales publications and some publications omitted from agency catalogs. Provides subject and title indexes and names and addresses of organizations.

Another announcement service of the United Nations is the *United Nations Documentation News,* issued by the Dag Hammarskjöld Library (United Nations, New York, NY 10071) free to some depository libraries and United Nations information centers. Lists new sales publications and prices.

D35   INVENTORY OF MARRIAGE AND FAMILY LITERATURE (IMFL) Edited by David H. Olson and Roxanne Markoff. Beverly Hills, Calif., Sage, 1975– . Annual. 510 pp. Vol. 9 (1983), $75 (hardcover only).

The continuation of an earlier bibliographic series that covered published literature on marriage and the family back to 1900 under the title *International Bibliography of Research in Marriage and the Family.* The current series now provides an annual inventory of all relevant articles and all articles published in leading marriage and family journals. Volume VIII (1982) contains abstracts of 3,000 English-language articles by 4,500 authors, published in 990 journals, and indexed by authors, subjects, and keywords in titles.

Inventory of Marriage and Family Literature is the print output of some current English-language accessions incorporated into the National Council on Family Relations' FAMILY RESOURCES DATABASE (J24) and is discussed more fully in Chapter 11.

Volumes in this set were published from 1967 to 1974 by the University of Minnesota Press; biennially from 1975 to 1977 by Family Social Science; and annually from 1979 on by Sage. Titles are as follows:

–*International Bibliography of Research in Marriage and the Family, 1900–1964* (Vol. I), edited by Joan Aldous and Reuben Hill, Minneapolis, University of Minnesota Press, 1967. Includes 12,850 references, of which 11,294 are English-language works; has keyword-in-context (KWIC) index, subject index, author list, periodicals list, and complete reference lists.

–*International Bibliography of Research in Marriage and the Family, 1965–1972* (Vol. II), edited by Joan Aldous and Nancy Dahl, Minneapolis, University of Minnesota Press, 1974.

–*Inventory of Marriage and Family Literature, 1973–1974* (Vol. III), edited by David H. Olson and Nancy Dahl, St. Paul, Minn., Family Social Science, 1975.

–*Inventory of Marriage and Family Literature, 1975–1976* (Vol. IV), edited by David H. Olson and Nancy Dahl, St. Paul, Minn., Family Social Science, 1977.

–*Inventory of Marriage and Family Literature, 1977–1978* (Vol. V), edited by David H. Olson, Beverly Hills, Calif., Sage, 1979.

Subsequent issues have been published by Sage.

D36   **MONTHLY CATALOG OF UNITED STATES GOVERN-
      MENT PUBLICATIONS** Washington, D.C., U.S. Government Printing Office, 1895– . Monthly, including *Serials Supplement,* $95/year; semiannual cumulative indexes, $17/year; annual cumulative index, $30/year.

This monthly catalog is a standard tool for keeping up with recent (supposedly the previous month's) publications by the Federal Government—except for certain categories like ERIC microfiche and NTIS publications. It has a very broad range, encompassing books, pamphlets, maps, and periodicals of all types. Includes departmental, congressional, and bureau publications, arranged alphabetically by department or bureau; fully cataloged, with title, author, date, pagination, price, availability, and various classification numbers to simplify ordering and organization. Addresses of retail government bookstores are listed inside the back cover, and tear-out order forms are now provided. Each issue has a monthly index; indexes are cumulated semiannually and annually. The corresponding data base, GPO MONTHLY CATALOG (J11), is now available on-line through DIALOG and BRS. *Monthly Catalog* updates *Children and Youth: Subject Bibliography* (D32) and the DHHS *Publications Catalog* (D37).

D37   **PUBLICATIONS CATALOG OF THE U.S. DEPARTMENT OF HEALTH AND HUMAN SERVICES**   Edited by Mary Kent Prowitt for the Office of the Secretary, Assistant Secretary for Public Affairs. Washington, D.C., 1982- . Annual. Free while supply lasts. From: 200 Independence Ave., SW, Washington, DC 20201.

An excellent catalog of publications (the 1982 edition covers everything published during 1981) that also provides an organization chart of the Department of Health and Human Services with addresses of divisions that produce and distribute publications. Most major agencies concerned with children are part of DHHS. Similar in format to the *Monthly Catalog* (D36), the *Publications Catalog* arranges fully cataloged publications (638 in 1982) by agency, with assigned subjects. It is indexed by author, title, subject, series, stock number, classification number, and keyword title. Prices and sources are included.

D38   **SOCIAL SERVICE RESEARCH: REVIEWS OF STUDIES**   Edited by Henry S. Maas. Silver Spring, Md., National Association of Social Workers, 1978. 232 pp. $12.95.

The Research Series of the National Association of Social Workers reviews research approximately every six years. This current volume reviews social service research studies done between 1970 and 1977. Populations examined include children in adoptive homes, children in foster homes and institutions, and troubled people. *Research Included in Social Services: A Five-Year Review* (1971, 232 pp., $8) comprises 1964–1969 studies in child welfare, family services, and casework. *Five Fields of Social Service: Reviews of Research* (1966, 208 pp., $8) reviews the literature prior to 1964, covering child welfare and family services, among other areas.

BIBLIOGRAPHIES OF BIBLIOGRAPHIES

Another traditional way to locate subject bibliographies is to use a bibliography of bibliographies. These are somewhat similar to the source guides in Chapter 3 but are limited to bibliographies. The standard guide is Theodore Besterman's *World Bibliography of Bibliographies* (4th Edition, Totowa, N.J., Rowman & Little-field, 1963). This is a fine multivolumed bibliography of 117,000 monographic bibliographies up to 1963 and can be found in many large academic libraries. Another compilation with the same title, by Alice F. Toomey (Totowa, N.J., Rowman & Little-field, 1977), updates Besterman from 1964 to 1974 with 18,000 titles represented by Library of Congress catalog cards. These massive bibliographic works can be supplemented by recurring bibliographies such as those listed in the previous section. The following titles may be more valuable for locating current bibliographies on children.

D39 **AN ANNOTATED BIBLIOGRAPHY OF ERIC BIBLI-OGRAPHIES, 1966–1980** Compiled by Joseph Gerald Drazan. Westport, Conn., Greenwood, 1982. 519 pp. $45.
The 3,200 bibliographies in this publication were garnered through the subject indexes of ERIC's *Resources in Education* (G46) from 1966 through 1980 and then rearranged (in 600 subject categories), reanno-tated, cross-referenced, and indexed. This bibliography provides convenient one-stop searching for inexpensive, relatively accessible bibliographies on a variety of topics related to education and to children.

D40 **BIBLIOGRAPHIC INDEX: A Cumulative Bibliography of Bibliographies** New York, H. W. Wilson, 1938– . 3 issues/year, including annual cumulation. Sold on a service basis.
An alphabetic subject listing of bibliographies published separately or appearing as parts of books, pamphlets, and periodicals. Selection is made from bibliographies that have 50 citations or more. Surveys 1,500 periodicals regularly, concentrating on titles in the Romance and Germanic languages. Uses typical subject headings (similar to those in the *Readers' Guide to Periodical Literature*). The August 1982 issue contained citations of bibliographies on adoption, birth order, child abuse, child molesting, child analysis, child development, child psychiatry, child psychology, child psychotherapy, child language, autistic chil-

dren, blind children, children of divorced parents, suicidal behavior of children, hospital care of children, government policies toward children in Latin America, and many other topics.

D41 **BIBLIOGRAPHY OF UNITED STATES GOVERNMENT BIBLIOGRAPHIES** By Roberta A. Scull. Ann Arbor, Mich., Pierian, 1974 (covers 1968-1973), 1979 (covers 1974-1976). 2 Vols. $50/set.

These two volumes provide an annotated listing of approximately 2,000 bibliographies published by the U.S. government from 1968 to 1976, arranged by broad disciplines like psychology, anthropology, and ethnology. Includes many bibliographies relating to children and many on peripheral topics. Since the Federal Government is a massive producer of needed, but short-lived, bibliographies that are neither advertised nor widely reviewed — many from agencies concerned with children — this bibliography makes it easy to verify and locate these tools. The documents cited within are in the public domain and can be copied. Another tool for locating some government bibliographies is the biennial *Government Reference Books,* issued since 1977 by Libraries Unlimited.

BOOK REVIEWS

Bibliographic tools facilitate the identification of relevant materials but may not indicate the quality of the materials they include (although in some cases selection implies merit or at least relevance). The tools in this section, however, either review books or lead to book reviews through summaries and/or indexing. Many of the periodicals discussed in Chapter 9 review books on children, and most of the periodical indexes and abstract journals discussed in Chapter 8 note reviews in some structured way, but reviews of particular titles are not always easy to locate. The best sources for this follow.

D42 **BOOK REVIEW DIGEST** Edited by Martha T. Mooney. New York, H. W. Wilson, 1905- . Monthly, with annual cumulation. Sold on a service basis (based on annual book budget).

Provides a synopsis of selected English-language books and excerpts from and citations to reviews in 85 selected periodicals and journals in all fields. Popular (but thoughtful) rather than scholarly, it covers around 6,000 books per year and is an excellent reviewing tool. Digests of reviews are arranged alphabetically by author with price, publisher, descriptive notes, and complete citations. Title and subject indexes in every volume are cumulated every five years for efficient reference. *Book Review Digest* covers most best-sellers and extensively reviewed books, including books for and about children.

D43 **BOOK REVIEW INDEX (BRI)** Edited by Gary C. Harbert. Detroit, Mich., Gale Research, 1965– . Bimonthly, with annual cumulation. Bimonthly indexes, $84/year; annual cumulation, $84; 11-year cumulation (1969–1979), $510.

A computer-produced index to reviews in 400 professional and general periodicals and newspapers that cites around 16,000 reviews of 8,100 titles per issue. Each entry includes author, title of book, reviewing publication, and date on which reviews appeared, with a code denoting whether the material is a children's book, youth's book, periodical, or reference book. Each issue has a title index and source list. Issued six times per year, with every alternate issue cumulating the preceding issue. Valuable for its comprehensiveness and currency; can be searched via computer back to 1969.

D44 **CHICOREL INDEX TO MENTAL HEALTH BOOK RE-VIEWS** An Annotated Guide to Books and Book Reviews in the Behavioral Sciences. Edited by Marietta Chicorel. New York, Chicorel, 1974– . Annual cumulation. $70. From: 275 Central Park, W., New York, NY 10024.

Provides very brief reviews of some 1,900 books per year in the behavioral sciences, with citations to 2,500 reviews in 140 journals and a subject index so that one can locate books under the headings of child abuse and child psychology and development. It fails, however, to cover many of the journals on children. It can be supplemented with another publication from the same source, *Chicorel Index to Reading and Learning Disabilities.* An earlier index to mental health literature, the *Mental Health Book Review Index,* was published by the Council on Research in Bibliography at New York University from 1956 through 1972 and provided lengthier abstract reviews of significant works taken from approximately 200 publications in the behavioral sciences.

D45 **INDEX TO BOOK REVIEWS IN THE HUMANITIES** Edited by Philip Thomson. Williamston, Mich., Thomson,

1960– . Annual. $30/year. From: 836 Georgia Ave., Williamston, MI 48895.

Annual index to reviews appearing in 405 humanities journals, arranged by author, with a source list. Entries include author, title, reviewer, abbreviated periodical title, date, and pagination.

6 / Bibliographies

This chapter contains nearly 150 retrospective subject bibliographies selected from the thousands available. They have been laboriously compiled because it is so difficult to obtain satisfactory information on children from traditional tools like periodicals and recurring bibliographies. In selecting bibliographies for this chapter, I looked for interdisciplinary and multidisciplinary bibliographies, well-done bibliographies on important topics, and bibliographies compiled since 1970. Bibliographies compiled before 1970 were included only if they provide retrospective information on a massive amount of research. I also have included only bibliographies that are still available through purchase or through ERIC or that are likely to be found in large academic libraries or libraries that contain depositories of government documents. I searched for those that covered certain facets of childhood not covered elsewhere, such as religious development or medical environments. On some topics, such as child abuse and child psychology, many bibliographies exist. I have tried to select the most useful of these and to indicate which refer to other bibliographies. Individually and collectively, these bibliographies can save a great deal of time for those researching children and childhood.

Other subject and retrospective bibliographies can be located through the periodical indexes and abstracts discussed in Chapter 8, especially *Psychological Abstracts,* and the bibliographies of bibliographies annotated in Chapter 5, particularly the guides to

ERIC bibliographies and government documents. Since ERIC bibliographies can be located through *Resources in Education* (*RIE*) and a computerized search, only a few are included in this chapter.

E1   **ABSTRACTS ON CHILD PLAY AREAS AND CHILD SUPPORT FACILITIES**   By Ann B. Hill and Carol G. Lane. Milwaukee, Wis., Center for Architecture and Urban Planning Research, 1978. 102 pp. $5 (paperback). From: P.O. Box 413, Milwaukee, WI 53201.

Detailed abstracts of 40 significant works on children and the built environment, organized into sections on theories of child care and play, child-environment research, descriptions of facilities, design guides, and bibliographies, with sample drawings from each source. These were abstracted from the *Bibliography on Children and the Physical Environment* (E20), a comprehensive bibliography of more than 1,500 items.

E2   **ADOPTION BIBLIOGRAPHY AND MULTIETHNIC SOURCEBOOK**   By Elizabeth Wharton Van Why. Hartford, Conn., Open Door Society of Connecticut, 1977. 320 pp. $7.50 (paperback).

Designed both for parents who contemplate adoption and for professionals concerned in some way with adoption (lawyers, doctors, teachers, social workers, and the like), this book includes 1,250 entries in its first section, the adoption bibliography, which arranges materials by format, that is, as articles, nonfiction (general, personal narratives, dissertations), fiction, children's books, audiovisuals, periodicals, and bibliographies. Includes an addenda. The bibliography covers all aspects of adoption, with citations on blacks, native Americans, handicapped, older people, and sibling adoptees; intercultural, international, and single-parent adoptions; and organizations. Citations give author, title, price, date, and availability; some are annotated.

   The second part of the book—the multiethnic sourcebook—is an annotated directory of 130 tools that provide materials (dolls, toys, calendars, games, children's books, audiovisuals, programs, and services) to help parents rear adopted children of different races.

E3   **ADOPTION FACTS AND FALLACIES**   A Review of Research in the United States, Canada and Great Britain between 1948 and 1965. By M. L. Kellmer Pringle. London, Longmans, 1967. 251 pp. (Out of print) (Studies in Child Development)

An annotated bibliography, with abstracts of completed research and annotated lists of ongoing research projects at date of publication. Prepared cooperatively with the National Bureau for Co-operation in Child Care.

E4 **ANNOTATED BIBLIOGRAPHY OF BOOKS AND SHORT STORIES ON CHILDHOOD AND YOUTH** Compiled by the Council on Social Work Education. New York, 1968. 52 pp. Price not available (paperback).

A selection of literature (mostly fiction, short stories, and biographies) intended to develop teaching materials on child welfare to enhance the sensitivity, knowledge, and competence of social work students and all those who work with children in human service professions and occupations. The list is divided into two sections arranged by author: books (approximately 150) and short stories (around 80). Each citation is annotated and coded for such things as child's age, handicap, and family structure. The brief annotations succeed very well in conveying how or why a particular book or story could contribute to the understanding of some aspect of childhood.

E5 **ANNOTATED BIBLIOGRAPHY OF THE REMARRIED, THE LIVING TOGETHER, AND THEIR CHILDREN** By Libby Walker et al. New York, Jewish Board of Family and Children's Services, 1979. 20 pp. In: *Family Process, 18*(2):193–212, June 1979.

Approximately 80 annotated entries on remarried persons and individuals living together in committed relationships and the effects on their children. Citations through 1978 are grouped in six sections: demography of remarriage, remarried couples, stepparents and stepchildren, divorce as a precursor to remarriage, children of divorce (in relation to remarriage), and therapeutic agents in remarriage.

E6 **ANNOTATED BIBLIOGRAPHY ON CHILDHOOD SCHIZOPHRENIA, 1955–1964** By James R. Tilton, Marian K. DeMyer, and Lois Hendrickson Loew. New York, Grune & Stratton, 1966. 136 pp. (Out of print)

Compiled for the Clinical Research Center on Early Childhood Schizophrenia, this annotated bibliography covers nearly all English-language works published from 1954 through 1964 dealing with children from birth through age 12. It considers autistic children, childhood psychoses, symbiotic psychoses, and atypical children. The 346 papers it cites are grouped into seven sections dealing with historical and general reviews; description and diagnosis; etiology; biochemical, neurological, and physiological studies; family characteristics; treatment and care; and follow-up studies. Papers with secondary themes are cross-referenced appropriately. A few papers that could not be obtained through interlibrary loan are listed separately. There is an author index to the entire work.

This book complements the *Annotated Bibliography of Childhood Schizophrenia Reported in the English Language through 1954* (by William Goldfarb and Marilyn M. Dorsen, New York, Basic Books, 1955, 170 pp., no index; out of print, but available in some libraries). Together, the two books provide access to virtually all papers and books on childhood schizophrenia from the mid-nineteenth century through 1964.

E7   AN ANNOTATED BIBLIOGRAPHY ON MOVEMENT
      EDUCATION   By Theresa G. Rizzitiello. Reston, Va., American Alliance for Health, Physical Education, Recreation, and Dance, 1977. 49 pp. $4.25 (paper).

A selective bibliography of major publications on the theory and practice of movement education (i.e., the provision of learning experiences to help children fulfill their potential). The bibliography, which is well cross-referenced, covers theories and perspectives, foundation of movement and motor development, practice, basic movement, dance and drama, gymnastics, and sports.

E8   ANNOTATED BIBLIOGRAPHY ON PERCEPTUAL-
      MOTOR DEVELOPMENT   By Margaret Clifton et al. Reston, Va., American Alliance for Health, Physical Education, Recreation, and Dance, 1973. 115 pp. $5.25 (paper).

A thorough three-section guide to perceptual motor development. The first section covers the works of specialists A. Jean Ayres and Newell Kephart. The second section provides movement-related bibliographies on auditory perception, body image, depth and distance perception, feedback and regulation, figure-ground perception, reduced and supplementary perceptual cues, and visual and size perception. The third section is a well-annotated compilation of tests, programs, material sources, assessment instruments, and films. The bulk of the items are relevant for impaired children.

E9   ARTS EDUCATION AND BRAIN RESEARCH   By
      Thomas A. Regelski. Reston, Va., Music Educators National Conference, and Washington, D.C., Alliance for Arts Education, 1978. 32 pp. $2 (paper).

A literature review of new research on functions of the brain; covers the learning process, aesthetic education, and future research directions.

E10 **ART THERAPY IN MENTAL HEALTH** Rockville, Md., National Institute of Mental Health, 1981. 125 pp. Single copies free (paper). (NIMH Literature Survey Series, No. 3)
An annotated bibliography of English-language books, dissertations, and journal articles published between June 1973 and June 1980 on the use of art therapy in treating mental disorders. Items are arranged by author, and authors' addresses are provided for some items. Several hundred items deal with children. Keyword and author indexes.

This updates a previous bibliography, entitled *Art Therapy: A Bibliography,* by Linda Gantt and Marilyn Strauss Schmal (Rockville, Md., NIMH, 1974, 174 pp.), which had around 150 references from 1940 to 1973 on art therapy for children and adolescents and additional references on families.

E11 **AUTISM: A RESOURCE GUIDE FOR EDUCATORS** By the Garden City Public Schools. Garden City, Mich., 1982. Paged in sections. Price not available (paper).
This guide, funded by the Michigan Department of Education, provides extensive information about programs, services, assessment instruments, and instructional materials appropriate for autistic students. Although it concentrates on Michigan, it has extensive national information selected for special education teachers and other school personnel concerned with autistic children. *Autism* includes bibliographies for books, journals, and MEDLARS.

E12 **BACKGROUND AND TREATMENT OF THE EMOTIONAL BEHAVIOR DISORDERS OF CHILDREN: A Bibliography of Research, 1925–1970** By Zanvel E. Klein. Chicago, Ill., University of Chicago, Department of Psychiatry, 1970. 89 pp. Paper. (Out of print)
A topical listing of 1,037 references primarily dealing with outpatient treatment of emotional-behavior disorders. Includes books, articles, dissertations, and papers covering the fields of psychiatry, psychology, education, social work, and public health. Author index.

E13 **BEHAVIOR MODIFICATION AND THE CHILD: An Annotated Bibliography** By Hazel B. Benson. Westport, Conn., Greenwood, 1979. 398 pp. $27.50. (Contemporary Problems of Childhood Series, No. 3)

An impressively thorough bibliography by a speech therapist/librarian who heads the health sciences library at Ohio State University. It includes 2,309 entries (2,164 of which are annotated), mostly literature from 1956 to 1977, with a few citations from earlier years and a few new unannotated selections from 1977 and 1978. Materials were chosen through a search of 38 indexes and include books, book chapters, journal articles, reports, dissertations, and 20 previous bibliographies, all arranged in 11 complexly subdivided sections. The main classifications are bibliographies, books of reprinted articles, introductory materials, behavioral techniques for specific behaviors, behavioral techniques for the handicapped, educational applications, behavior modifications by specific professions, training in behavior modification, and research. The eleventh section consists of three appendixes: a list of the research tools used in compiling the bibliography; an annotated listing of 50 films and audiovisuals, with information on intended audiences and distributors; and a glossary of common terms in behavioral modification. The book also features an author index, a selective keyword index to words taken from titles (supplements the classified arrangement), and an alphabetic list of all journals cited in the text. This is part of the interdisciplinary *Contemporary Problems of Childhood Series,* which attempts to locate and organize scattered information for researchers.

E14   THE BEREAVED CHILD: ANALYSIS, EDUCATION AND
        TREATMENT: An Abstracted Bibliography   By Gillian S.
        Mace, Faren R. Akins, and Dianna L. Akins. New York, IFI/Plenum, 1981. 284 pp. $75.

Contains 558 annotated entries, most from material published after 1960, on materials that deal with the reactions and coping mechanisms of children and adolescents when faced with the death of parents, siblings, friends, teachers, pets, and presidents, as well as annotated descriptions of four journals that deal exclusively with death and dying. Abstracts of books and periodicals were obtained from *Psychological Abstracts* or from the original article or were written by the authors. The book includes an author index and an unspecific subject index that lists up to 70 numerical references on topics like the concept of death and death education; it includes "assassination" and "pet death," but omits terms like "adolescence," "twins," and "parental death," even though entries deal with these topics. The book also includes 33 late additions that are neither annotated nor indexed.

E15   BIBLIOGRAPHY OF AGGRESSIVE BEHAVIOR   A Reader's Guide to the Research Literature. Edited by J. Michael

Crabtree and Kenneth E. Moyer. New York, Alan R. Liss. Vol.
I: 1977, 416 pp., $49; Vol. II: 1981, 476 pp., $46.
Volume I is an extensive (3,856 items) classified bibliography of research materials on aggression. Approximately 250 items are specifically on childhood aggression, and many other areas (e.g., mass media,
psychoanalytic concepts, and learning and imitation) include relevant
entries. Volume I is updated and supplemented by Volume II.

E16 **BIBLIOGRAPHY OF CHILD PSYCHIATRY AND CHILD
MENTAL HEALTH WITH A SELECTED LIST OF
FILMS** Edited by Irving N. Berlin. New York, Human Sciences Press, 1976. 508 pp. $34.95. (Child Psychiatry and Child
Psychology Series)
A well-organized comprehensive compilation of 4,257 references on all
aspects of child psychiatry, prepared for child mental health professionals. Materials cover the historical, developmental, cultural, and psychoanalytic bases of child psychiatry. It has a wide scope, arranged developmentally (so that citations on earlier years are listed first), and
covers such topics as learning and school disturbances, hyperactivity,
mental retardation, creativity, problems of adolescence, child abuse,
preventive measures, and therapeutics. The main bibliography is followed by a select list of films. All items are annotated; the most important items are asterisked. Subject and author indexes.

E17 **BIBLIOGRAPHY OF CHILD STUDY: 1898–1912** By
Louis N. Wilson. New York, Arno, 1975. 350 pp. $20. (Classics
in Child Development)
A reprint of a 1907–1912 summary (originally compiled by the librarian
of Clark University, Worcester, Mass. and published by Clark University Press and the U.S. Government Printing Office) of articles on childhood and adolescence that first appeared in G. Stanley Hall's *Pedagogi-
cal Seminary* and *The American Journal of Psychology.* Many seminal
works and important genres in this early period of child development
research are included. Contains nearly 4,000 items. This new edition is
nicely bound and convenient to use.

E18 **BIBLIOGRAPHY OF INFANT FOODS AND NUTRI-
TION, 1938 TO 1977** By Jane O. Henderson. Victoria,
Australia, Commonwealth Scientific and Industrial Research
Organization, 1978. 322 pp. $16.
An easy-to-use classified compilation of 2,259 references published be-
tween 1938 and 1977, located through *Dairy Science Abstracts, Nutrition
Abstracts and Reviews, Food Science and Technology Abstracts,* and *Ag-*

ricola SDI Service. Certain items concentrate on nutritional aspects of infant foods. Although there are no annotations, items are so intelligently classified and indexed that it is easy to locate appropriate materials. Milk, for instance, is subdivided into 16 subcategories ranging from mother's milk to the milk of cows, buffaloes, ewes, and mares; homogenized milk; whey; and comparative data. Nearly all nutritional aspects of infant foods are included, with a truly international perspective. Citations indicate where an abstract is located. Separate author and subject (keyword) indexes.

E19   **BIBLIOGRAPHY OF WORLD LITERATURE ON MENTAL RETARDATION, JANUARY 1940–MARCH 1963** The President's Panel on Mental Retardation, 1963. 564 pp. *Supplement: Mar. 1963–Dec. 31, 1964.* Washington, D.C., National Institute of Child Health and Human Development, 1965. 99 pp. (Out of print)
An integrated, systematic, and comprehensive bibliography of the major world literature search carried out through major abstracting services such as *Index Medicus, Education Index,* and *Psychological Abstracts* and through searching of individual journal titles. The bibliography is restricted to professional and scientific literature that directly discusses mental retardation and/or conditions and diseases associated with it. Within that scope, the compilers estimate that errors of omission are only 1–3 percent. The book includes 16,096 references, arranged by author. There is a massive author/subject index with functional categories representing processes, programs, treatments, diseases, and conditions. The *Supplement* includes 2,372 additional items.

E20   **BIBLIOGRAPHY ON CHILDREN AND THE PHYSICAL ENVIRONMENT: Child Care Centers, Outdoor Play Environments, and Other Children's Environments** By Gary T. Moore, Carol G. Lane, and Lisa A. Lindberg. Milwaukee, Wis., Center for Architecture and Urban Planning Research, 1979. 130 pp. $7.50 (paper). From: P.O. Box 413, Milwaukee, WI 53201.
A comprehensive, nonevaluative bibliography of all kinds of materials relating to the planning and design of indoor and outdoor facilities for children aged 6 weeks through 12 years. More than 1,500 items were collected as part of the center's Children's Environments Project, garnered through searches of bibliographies and indexes on studies of the effect of the environment on behavior, architecture, early childhood education, and developmental psychology. Covers the role of the physi-

cal environment in child development and in overcoming developmental disabilities and the role of overall housing and neighborhood environment in children's play and development. Environments studied include children's hospitals, recreation centers, elementary and secondary schools, libraries, housing, zoos, museums, and designing for handicapped children. Materials cited range from reports and articles; to journals, periodicals, and newspapers; to informative pamphlets; to major empirical works. This project also resulted in the production of guidelines for children's centers and detailed recommendations for play areas and child care centers. *Abstracts on Child Play Areas and Child Support Facilities* (E1) abstracts some of the more significant items here.

E21 **BIBLIOGRAPHY ON HUMAN INTELLIGENCE** By Logan Wright for the National Clearinghouse for Mental Health Information. Washington, D.C., U.S. Government Printing Office, 1970. 222 pp. (Out of print) (Public Health Publication No. 1839)

A thorough summary, up-to-date to 1970, with 6,736 numbered entries on the psychology of human intelligence, including books, articles, and dissertations. Materials are arranged alphabetically by author, and a topical outline and index provide a subject approach. Some relevant categories include historical antecedents, related concepts, theoretical works, nature of intelligence, factors influencing intelligence, and group intelligence tests.

E22 **BIBLIOGRAPHY ON SPEECH, HEARING AND LANGUAGE IN RELATION TO MENTAL RETARDATION, 1900–1968** By Maryann Peins. Washington, D.C., U.S. Public Health Service, 1969. 156 pp. (Out of print, but available from ERIC as ED 044 858.)

"This bibliography was prepared to serve as a specialized, yet comprehensive, reference guide for those scientists, teachers, researchers, students and professional persons who are concerned with the communicative processes of the mentally retarded." Materials are classified in six main sections: speech and language behavior; assessment of speech and language of the mentally retarded; hearing; habilitation procedures for speech, language, and oral communication; research monographs and chapters; and dissertations. A total of 1,969 references were garnered mainly from major abstract journals.

E23   BIBLIOGRAPHY ON THE TREATMENT OF PSYCHO-
      LOGICAL DISORDERS IN CHILDREN   By Donald K.
      Routh. Washington, D.C., American Psychological Assn.,
      1979. 148 pp. $14 (paper); $4 (microfiche).

An "informal bibliography" of approximately 2,000 citations—articles,
books, and book chapters—related to the treatment of psychological
disorders in children. Materials, arranged under 57 headings, reflect
the author's collection and his bias toward treatment approaches subject
to controlled evaluative research. Topics include research, prevention,
treatment modalities, impairment and problem areas, liaison with
other professionals, school problems, delinquency, treatment of adolescents, and child abuse and neglect.

E24   BLACK CHILD DEVELOPMENT IN AMERICA, 1927–
      1977: An Annotated Bibliography   By Hector F. Myers and
      Phyllis G. Rana. Westport, Conn., Greenwood, 1979. 470 pp.
      $35.

A timesaving compilation and guide to 1,275 abstracts of social science
studies on the black child that appeared from 1927 to 1977. The entries, taken from eight major abstract journals, usually contain the original abstracts and are arranged alphabetically by author under broad
categories that relate to the language, physical, cognitive, personality,
and social development of the black child. An interpretive introduction
reviews some of the salient issues and theories on black child development. The book includes a well-arranged, intelligently hierarchical subject index and an author index.

E25   BLACK CHILDREN AND THEIR FAMILIES   A Bibli-
      ography. By Charlotte J. Dunmore. San Francisco, R&E
      Associates, 1976. 103 pp. $11 (paperback). From: 4843 Mission
      St., San Francisco, CA 94112.

Less scholarly and research-oriented than *Black Child Development in
America* (E24) but useful for practitioners, this unannotated bibliography covers approximately 1,200 citations under eight subject headings:
adoption; education; health; family life; life in the ghetto; mental
health; sex, contraception, and family planning; and miscellaneous.
Except for a few "classics," most items were published after 1960. Encompasses a variety of sources including fiction and popular weekly
magazines but lacks an index.

E26   THE BLACK FAMILY IN THE UNITED STATES: A Se-
      lected Bibliography of Annotated Books, Articles, and Disser-

tations on Black Families in America   By Lenwood G. Davis.
Westport, Conn., Greenwood, 1978. 132 pp. $15.
A selected, evaluative bibliography of 386 items covering the period
from 1908 to 1976. In this bibliography, the black family is seen as a
unit of individuals: children, workers, slaves, free men, husbands, and
wives. Each item is described, categorized (e.g., factual, descriptive,
sociological), and evaluated (good, fair, excellent). It considers three
types of literature: literature that emphasizes the evils of the black
family (such as black family disorganization after slavery), literature
that records such pathological conditions as low academic achievement
and delinquency, and literature that reviews the inadequate methodology of works in the first two categories. Author and selective keyword
subject indexes.

E27   **CHILD ABUSE: AN ANNOTATED BIBLIOGRAPHY**
      Compiled by Dorothy P. Wells. Metuchen, N.J., Scarecrow,
      1980. 450 pp. $22.
An impressive, comprehensive annotated bibliography that covers
2,484 items in 21 chapters ranging alphabetically from bibliographies
and case studies through etiology, history, hospital's role, incidence,
laws, management, medical aspects, psychological and sociological aspects, school's role, and unclassified foreign-language publications.
There are more than 200 case studies, 230 items on detection and diagnosis, 400 on legal aspects, and 250 on protective cooperation and
services. The focus is on physical and psychological abuse and intentional neglect of children and largely omits materials dealing solely with
neglect or sexual molestation. The author used *Abstracts for Social
Workers, Criminal Justice Abstracts,* and *Psychiatry Excerpta Medica,*
among other sources, including French and German articles. Many of
her annotations draw on these abstracts. Although some tools (including historical sources) predate 1962, most items were published between 1962 and 1976, with multidisciplinary selections from many
formats: newspapers, pamphlets, journal articles, reference books,
books and parts of books, government publications, dissertations,
films, and videocassettes. The chapter on education includes many curricula and audiovisual materials for a variety of audiences including
medical workers, social workers, and parents. This bibliography is most
thorough and competent up to 1976, but needs to be supplemented for
more recent materials.

E28   **CHILD ABUSE AND NEGLECT**   A Literature Review and
      Selected Bibliography. By Marian Eskin and Marjorie Kravitz.

Washington, D.C., National Criminal Justice Reference Service
and Aspen Systems Corp., 1980. 118 pp. Paper. (Out of print)
(National Criminal Justice Reference Service NCJ 62013)
This overview of the current status of the literature on child abuse and
neglect reviews the major historical, legal, social, and medical issues;
describes the prevention and treatment programs funded at time of
compilation; indicates the legislation that has been enacted; and suggests future research and programs. Appendixes cover sources, resource agencies, and child abuse legislation.

E29   **CHILD ABUSE AND NEGLECT: An Annotated Bibliogra-
       phy** By Beatrice J. Kalisch. Westport, Conn., Greenwood,
       1978. 535 pp. $35. (Contemporary Problems of Childhood
       Series, No. 2)
An interdisciplinary bibliography of more than 2,000 English-language
items published between 1800 and 1976, with most materials from the
1960s and 1970s. The bibliography, compiled by computer and manual
literature searches, includes all sorts of materials—books, book
chapters, articles, government documents, dissertations, conference
proceedings, pamphlets, and committee reports—arranged alphabetically by author within broad subject divisions. Fairly lengthy annotations cover the scope and content of the entries, sometimes the findings
and results of research, and the number of entries in other bibliographies. The book includes popular and scholarly articles from a wide
variety of disciplines. Medical aspects receive excellent coverage, but
the criminal justice field is not as well represented as other disciplines,
and the coverage of state and federal documents is spotty. Appendix A
is a list of the bibliographic tools used in compiling this work. Author
and keyword subject indexes.

E30   **CHILD ABUSE: A Selected Bibliography of an Alarming
       Social Problem** By Phyllis Cohen. Monticello, Ill., Vance
       Bibliographies, 1981. 30 pp. $4.50 (paper). (Public Administra-
       tion Series P771)
Fairly accessible materials from the 1950s to present drawn from the
fields of social work, medicine, and psychiatry. The intended audience
is community planners, social workers, and other interested individuals.

E31   **CHILD ABUSE: COMMISSION AND OMISSION**
       Edited by Joanne Valiant Cook and Roy Tyler Bowes. Toronto,
       Butterworth, 1980. 509 pp. Price not available.

Contains brief but thoughtful literature review and bibliography of "readily accessible, current scholarly knowledge," mostly from the late 1970s, that delineates the contributions and limitations of research. Includes papers reflecting the range of abuse from physical and sexual assault (commission) to neglect or failure to protect (omission), as well as papers that critically address the controversial issues of causation and social policy. Materials are divided into four main parts: the forms of abuse, the sources of abuse, social policy issues, and the victims and consequences of abuse, with abstracts of articles in the introductions, followed by papers. An appendix includes a 55-item select abstract bibliography on treatment and prevention programs.

E32 **CHILD CARE AND WORKING PARENTS: An Introductory Bibliography** By Phyllis Cohen. Monticello, Ill., Vance Bibliographies, 1981. 19 pp. $3 (paper). (Public Administration Series P770)

This brief bibliography from Vance's Public Administration Series has no annotations or index and is arranged by author only. Books, articles, and research reports were selected for an audience of community planners, social workers, and others who plan child care centers and facilities for working families. References chosen were assumed to be accessible in major research libraries or attainable through interlibrary loan; most are from the 1970s, although a few go back to the 1960s. Many Federal Government hearings and reports are listed under "U.S."

E33 **CHILD CARE SERVICES—DAY CARE** By Project SHARE. Rockville, Md., 1981, 31 pp. $2 (paperback; quantity discount). (Human Services Bibliography Series)

A selected annotated bibliography with 45 references covering training for child care, program evaluation for child care services, and personnel management policy issues.

E34 **CHILD HEALTH ASSESSMENT: Part I - A Literature Review** Edited By Kathryn E. Barnard and Helen Bee Douglas. Bethesda, Md., U.S. Public Health Service, Health Resources Administration, Division of Nursing, 1974. 211 pp. $6 (paper).

Part of a two-volume set on child health assessment, this literature review was undertaken by the Division of Nursing in cooperation with the University of Washington at Seattle as a preliminary aid in the planning of an assessment format and methodology incorporating relevant characteristics of health, development, behavior, and environment for young children. Its ultimate purpose is to enable nurses to identify and care for health and development problems in children and to help nurses identify groups that are "high risk" due to physical, emotional, educational, or psychological dysfunctions so that appropriate preventive services can be offered.

Consultants from a variety of disciplines offered advice on the direction of the literature search and the subsequent design for testing assessment procedures. Each of the 13 chapters is a narrative literature review by one or two authors, followed by references. The book devotes six chapters to "predictor variables" like prenatal and perinatal influences, congenital abnormalities, nutrition, parents' perception of their children, the animate environment, and the inanimate environment. Six other chapters cover "outcome variables" such as physical growth and development, sleep patterns, childhood accidents, language, mental development, and social development. An overview chapter on the Seattle Study emphasizes the interaction of variables and points out that measures of a child's functioning are really measures of predictors, as well as outcomes. The individual chapters are interesting, clearly written, and sometimes illustrated; the references are intelligently selective rather than comprehensive.

E35 **CHILDHOOD AND HISTORY IN AMERICA** By Glenn Davis. New York, Psychohistory Press (Division of Atcom), 1976. 281 pp. $16.95; paperback, $8.95.

An extensive literature review of the evolution from 1840 to 1965 of the concept of childhood in America, arranged by chronological period. Includes an index, an overview of the psychogenic theory of history, and an appendix from Lloyd DeMause's *Overgrams for a Unified Psychohistory.*

E36 **CHILD NEGLECT: An Annotated Bibliography** By N. A. Polansky et al. Washington, D.C., U.S. Department of Health, Education, and Welfare, Community Services Administration, 1975. 90 pp. Paper.

A companion piece to Polansky's "Profile of Neglect," this extremely well-annotated bibliography includes approximately 150 abstracts on the prevention, identification, causation, treatment, and consequences of child neglect. Intended as a ready reference for disciplines such as medicine, law, education, and social work and for public and voluntary agencies that serve neglecting families and their children. The annotations include helpful evaluations, comments, and cross-references.

E37 **CHILDREN AND ADVERTISING: An Annotated Bibliography** Edited by Laurene Meringoff. New York, Council of Better Business Bureaus, Inc., Children's Advertising Review Unit, 1980. 87 pp. $15 (paperback). From: 845 Third Ave., New York, NY 10022.

A well-done, comprehensive bibliography of 750 references that includes a directory of relevant organizations and groups. References in the main section, "Core References," deals with children under age 12 and with advertising; "Related References" provides additional sources on children, advertising, television and other media, and particular content areas. The "overriding objective guiding selection" was to provide readers with "the full picture" and to select entries representing the diversity and eclecticism of available evidence and opinion. Meringoff has done an outstanding job of locating references from government, business, academia, consumer groups, and educators in various formats (speeches, petitions, films and rules, and books and articles). Subjects covered include the ability of children to understand the persuasive intent of commercials, the efficacy of these commercials, their influence on the development of consumer skills in children, and the self-regulation of the industry.

Materials are briefly annotated (with more depth for significant references) and are indexed under broad areas such as cognitive development, consumer socialization, and parent-child relations. The work is well produced and well organized, with good typography. One time-saving feature is a comprehensive directory of relevant groups including academia, private research companies concerned with children, firms that survey the public or television audiences, broadcasters, nonprofit trade organizations, consumer groups and educational organizations, and federal agencies.

E38 **CHILDREN AND ARCHITECTURE: Play Needs—A Checklist of Sources** By M. Lynne Struthers Swanick. Monticello, Ill., Vance Bibliographies, 1980. 11 pp. $2 (paper). (Architecture Series A278)

Although brief and unannotated, this bibliography contains more than 100 entries from all kinds of sources, including the Consumer Product Safety Commission, *Sunset Magazine, Good Housekeeping, Journal of Creative Behavior,* and *American City.* Most entries are accessible journal articles from the late 1970s.

E39 **CHILDREN AND THE BUILT ENVIRONMENT** An Annotated Bibliography of Representative Research of Children

and Housing, School Design and Environmental Stress. By
Sherry Ahrentzen. Monticello, Ill., Vance Bibliographies, 1982.
62 pp. $9 (paper). (Architecture Series A764)
A thoughtful, substantially annotated bibliography focusing and com-
menting on empirical research into the child's major environments:
home and school. Deals with such factors and stressors as density,
noise, physical design, size, and access and includes laboratory research
on environmental stressors. After a solid introduction that provides an
overview of research, the bibliography devotes approximately one page
per item to author, citation, hypothesis, subjects, setting, limitations,
variables, measures, summaries, and other possible interpretations.
Items cited are monographs and journal articles from the 1970s.

E40   **CHILDREN AND THEIR ENVIRONMENTS** By Willem
      van Vliet. Monticello, Ill., Vance Bibliographies, 1980. 34 pp. $4
      (paper). (Architecture Series A333)
A well-arranged, classified bibliography of journals and monographs
covering foreign-language materials over a long time span (although
most items are from the 1970s). Items deal with children aged 6–16 and
are grouped into 10 broad categories: urban and suburban environments; housing environments; play environments; leisure; transportation and traffic; development and health; perception and cognition; environmental change; environmental education and awareness; and
methods for research, design, and planning. The last category includes
five recent references on child participation in planning and design.

E41   **CHILDREN AS A FACTOR IN MARITAL SATISFAC-
      TION: A Selected Bibliography** Compiled by Carole Baker
      Goldman. Washington, D.C., National Alliance for Optional
      Parenthood, 1979. 14 pp. Paper. (Out of print)
In this bibliography, "marital satisfaction," not a conceptually precise
term, is sometimes used as a synonym for such terms as marital success, happiness, or adjustment or may imply feelings of love, perma-
nence, consensus, or such goals sought in marriage as companionship,
sexual adjustment, and social relations. This selected annotated bibliography includes research dealing with the many different goals and
values in marriage and how children affect the attainment of these
goals.

E42   **CHILDREN, DEATH, AND DYING: An Annotated Bibli-
      ography** By John C. Patterson. Washington, D.C., American
      Psychological Assn., 1979. 17 pp. $4 (paper); $2 (microfiche).

This bibliography—designed primarily for clinicians and researchers—
is a thorough (but not exhaustive) treatment of the area, drawing from
psychology, psychiatry, social work, nursing, and education. It includes
both classic and recent studies, divided into five topic areas: general,
developmental research, effects of early parental loss, treatment of the
bereaved or dying child, and death education. The first section (general) includes literature reviews and issues unique to children, family process, and research ethics. The developmental section includes Piagetian
and psychoanalytic explanations of children's experiences with death.

E43   **CHILDREN IN THE BUILT ENVIRONMENT: A Bibli-
      ography** By U.S. Department of Housing and Urban Develop-
      ment (HUD), Office of International Affairs. Washington, D.C.,
      1979. 21 pp. Price not available (paper).
A bibliography prepared during the International Year of the Child by
the library and the Office of International Affairs of HUD. Includes 130
unannotated references reflecting foreign experience and the United
States and covers children at home, at play, at school, and in the
community. Lists nine bibliographies and provides the names and addresses of 30 relevant American and foreign periodicals.

E44   **CHILDREN WHO NEED PROTECTION: An Annotated
      Bibliography** Compiled by Dorothy M. Jones. Washington,
      D.C., U.S. Children's Bureau, 1966. 75 pp. (Out of print)
An early effort that selected and annotated approximately 400 of the
most significant English-language books and articles of the previous 25
years, covering all aspects of child neglect except cultural deprivation.
Topics covered include abuse and neglect, foster care, homemaker services, maternal deprivation, and social casework. Materials are arranged
by author under topics; citations include full information and a brief
annotation. Author index.

E45   **CHILD SEXUAL ABUSE: INCEST, ASSAULT, AND SEX-
      UAL EXPLOITATION** Washington, D.C., Children's Bu-
      reau, 1981. 18 pp. Single copy free while supply lasts.
A brief overview of recent research findings on the nature, extent,
dynamics, and effects of child sexual abuse, as well as promising treatment techniques.

E46   **CHILD SEXUAL ASSAULT AND INCEST: A Bibliography**
      By Elizabeth Midlarsky. Washington, D.C., American Psy-
      chological Assn., 1978. 12 pp. $4 (paper); $2 (microfiche).

Includes 157 references (from 1881 to 1978) from the literature of psychology, sociology, medicine, social work, nursing, and education; intended to focus attention on an area the author perceives as neglected.

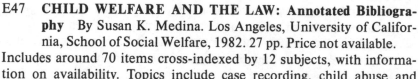

E47 **CHILD WELFARE AND THE LAW: Annotated Bibliography** By Susan K. Medina. Los Angeles, University of California, School of Social Welfare, 1982. 27 pp. Price not available.

Includes around 70 items cross-indexed by 12 subjects, with information on availability. Topics include case recording, child abuse and neglect, children's rights, expert testimony/evidence, foster care and permanency planning, juvenile justice, guardianship, and Indian child welfare.

E48 **CHILD WELFARE TRAINING AND PRACTICE: An Annotated Bibliography** Compiled by John T. Pardeck et al. Westport, Conn., Greenwood, 1982. 131 pp. $27.50.

Intended to draw together materials for and on training practices in the broad field of child welfare for an audience of trainers, educators, practitioners, and students. Criteria for inclusion were recency (1964 or later), availability, and appropriateness for training purposes. Chosen materials—453 entries altogether—include books, articles, training manuals, and audiovisuals grouped into seven sections that correspond to child welfare specializations or interests: abuse and neglect, law, substitute care, in-home services and parent education, institutions and special-needs children, minority clients, and training and interviewing methods. Items are fully cited and annotated. Author and subject indexes and an index to audiovisuals.

E49 **THE CHILD WITH A CHRONIC MEDICAL PROBLEM:** Cardiac Disorders, Diabetes, Hemophilia; Social, Emotional and Educational Adjustment: An Annotated Bibliography. By Doria Pilling. Windsor, England, National Foundation for Educational Research in England and Wales, 1973. 71 pp. $7 (paper). From: Humanities Press, 171 First Ave., Atlantic Highlands, NJ 07716.

Includes lengthy abstracts of 107 references to journal articles, books, dissertations, British government reports, and World Health Organization materials published between 1958 and 1972. Abstracts are arranged chronologically in three sections: emotional and social adjustment, family adjustment, and educational attainment. Emphasizes leading as normal a life-style as possible, given medical supervision and greater-than-average parental care. Author index.

E50 **THE CHILD WITH SPINA BIFIDA. SOCIAL, EMOTIONAL AND EDUCATIONAL ADJUSTMENT: An Annotated Bibliography** By Doria Pilling. Windsor, England, National Foundation for Educational Research in England and Wales, 1973. 46 pp. $7 (paper). From: Humanities Press, 171 First Ave., Atlantic Highlands, NJ 07716. (A National Children's Bureau Report)

Covers research and general literature on the adjustments and attainments of children with spina bifida; intended for teachers, parents, and social workers. Detailed annotations and author index.

A similar work by Pilling is *The Orthopaedically Handicapped Child. Social, Emotional and Educational Adjustment: An Annotated Bibliography,* which includes more than 120 abstracts covering attitudes to disability, emotional and social adjustment, educational attainments, and parental attitudes.

E51 **COGNITIVE AND MENTAL DEVELOPMENT IN THE FIRST FIVE YEARS OF LIFE: A Review of Recent Research** By Philip Lichtenberg and Dolores G. Norton. Rockville, Md., National Institute of Mental Health, 1970. 111 pp. (Out of print)

Primarily a survey of authors who have received NIMH grants to investigate the first five years of children's lives. (It does include, however, other writers but does not include all grantees or all the works of any grantee.) It is an attempt to identify the themes, ideas, perspectives, and issues emerging from these studies to eventually formulate and evaluate social policies related to infant and child development. Consequently, ideas and authors are reviewed and correlated by theme and cited in a final bibliography. A summary of general themes sets forth some of the major concepts in broad terms.

E52 **COGNITIVE STYLES: An Annotated Bibliography** By James A. Vasquez and Tobias M. Gonzales. Arlington, Va., National Clearinghouse for Bilingual Education, 1980. 24 pp. $3.25 (paper).

This annotated bibliography includes approximately 100 research and general items referring to individual intellectual behavior in information processing—for example, reflective versus impulsive, analytical versus global, and field dependent versus field independent strategies. Many items deal with cognitive flexibility and with the cognitive styles of such ethnic minorities as blacks, Chicanos, and native Americans. In general, they explore the implications of cognitive style and learning patterns for academic achievement.

E53   CONCEPT DEVELOPMENT AND THE DEVELOPMENT
       OF THE GOD CONCEPT IN THE CHILD: A Bibliography
       By V. Peter Pitts. Schenectady, N.Y., Character Research Press,
       1977. 62 pp. $2.75.
This unusual multifaceted study of the development of a God concept
stemmed from Pitts' research and classification of children's drawings
of God, which suggested to him that children's conceptions of God
change in a Piagetian fashion across age levels. He is concerned with
the *what* and *when* of religious education of various sorts and in different cultures. The bibliography itself contains around 600 references
(some reaching as far back as 1888) from a variety of disciplines. Forty-
one references deal with the evolution of the God concept from childhood to adulthood; 51 deal with concept development; 77 cover child
development and developmental psychology; 51 are concerned with
the problems of religious education, especially the methods and forms
appropriate for various age groups; 78 specifically treat religious conceptual development; 22 cover symbols, signs, and religious imagery;
92 are historical and contemporary references on children's art; 15 are
on the related topic of artistic development and the psychology of art;
18 deal with the belief systems of particular religious denominations;
35 are on aesthetics and creativity; 43 relate to the sociology,
psychology, and philosophy of religion; and 65 include reference books
and general works relating to God concepts or conceptual development. Citations include both books and periodical articles (mostly in
English but also in French, German, and Italian) covering a long time
span. The author index includes both individual authors and periodical
titles. Unfortunately, the work is not annotated, although it ties together research from many disciplines (e.g., anthropology, child development, and religious education) in a pathfinding way.

E54   THE CONSUMER BEHAVIOR OF CHILDREN AND
       TEENAGERS: An Annotated Bibliography Compiled by
       Robert O. Herrmann. Chicago, Ill., American Marketing Assn.,
       1969. 160 pp. (Out of print)
Contains 300 abstracts of easily accessible research studies published
since 1955, as well as a few selected speculative and interpretive
articles. Although the author is concerned mainly with youth, the age
range covers infancy through college age (unmarried only). Topics include the influence of children on family spending; the youth market;
problems, needs, and interests; social influences on youth; business influences on youth; the young consumer; and preferences and consumption in a variety of fields. Author index.

E55 **CONSUMER SOCIALIZATION OF YOUNG PEOPLE: A Bibliography** By Ronald Faber and Scott Ward. Cambridge, Mass., Marketing Science Institute, 1976. 38 pp. Paper. (Out of print)

A bibliography of 380 citations focusing on phenomena having to do with young people's developing patterns of interaction with the marketplace. Approximately 22 percent of the citations are theoretical overviews, 8 percent are empirical overviews, 42 percent deal with the effects of television advertising on children and youth, and 28 percent deal with consumer socialization skills and knowledge. Although there is no index, items are easily located through a detailed table of contents.

E56 **CREATIVITY IN HUMAN DEVELOPMENT: An Interpretive and Annotated Bibliography** By A. Reza Arasteh and Josephine D. Arasteh. New York, Schrenkman, 1976. 154 pp. $11.95.

An engrossing and creative bibliography that provides excellent summaries of research and substantial introductory articles on creativity, both in general and in young children (138 references), adolescents (36 references), and adults. Contains significant references from the late 1920s to 1973. These books and periodical articles are from a wide variety of sources and could easily have been bypassed in less-thorough searches. The book is not indexed, but it is well-arranged and provides easy access to such topics as socioeconomic, cultural, and sex factors in creativity; the effects of parental behavior; and the relationships between creativity and conformity.

E57 **DAY CARE: AN ANNOTATED BIBLIOGRAPHY** By Alberta Wills. Minneapolis, Minn., Day Care Policy Studies Group, Institute for Interdisciplinary Studies, 1971. 353 pp. (Out of print)

A well-done annotated bibliography of 1,500 items examined by the Day Care Policy Studies Group. Materials are arranged by general issues, child development, specific programs, personnel, economic issues, licensing standards, legislation and regulation, special issues, evaluation, facilities and supplies, general resources, and public schools. It provides a good overview of the state of the art as of 1971.

E58 **THE DESIGN OF MEDICAL ENVIRONMENTS FOR CHILDREN AND ADOLESCENTS: An Annotated Bibliography** By Wendy Sarkissian with Cheryl Donaldson Spagnoletti and Kathy Isam. Monticello, Ill., Vance Bibliographies, 1980. 65 pp. $7 (paper). (Architecture Series A261)

A thoroughly researched bibliography first produced in Australia, this is a discursive three-part work. The first section provides general references on the design of medical facilities from the patient's viewpoint, the second section annotates books and monographs on medical environments for children and adolescents, and the third covers journal articles on the same topic. There is an emphasis on adolescents, since the authors found their medical needs most neglected. Materials were gathered through a MEDLARS search and through extensive correspondence and personal inquiry. Materials are cited on topics like stimuli, perception, and territoriality, and substantial annotations and discussions are included on otherwise obscure (although relevant) documents from countries such as Sweden and Canada. The third appendix is a helpful international directory of suggested resources, including the names of contact persons.

E59   **DETERMINANTS AND CONSEQUENCES OF MATERNAL EMPLOYMENT: An Annotated Bibliography, 1968–80** By Marsha Hurst and Ruth E. Zambrana. Washington, D.C., Business and Professional Women's Foundation, 1981. 85 pp. $3.75, plus $1.00 postage (paperback). From: 2012 Massachusetts Ave., NW, Washington, DC 20036.

A systematic and comprehensive review of the diverse literature on maternal employment and its effects on women, their children, and their families, topically arranged within genres. It includes technical and governmental reports and papers, books about working mothers, articles in professional journals, "working mother" sections in popular books on child rearing, children's books about working mothers, professional articles, clinical studies, and related bibliographies. The fine introductions and annotations succeed in organizing and clarifying what is known about why mothers work and how it affects their families. The bibliography contains 213 annotated items and a short unnumbered, unannotated listing of technical and government reports. Approximately 50 of these are professional articles on the effects of maternal employment on children, around 30 review the "working mother" chapters of popular child-rearing books, and 15 are children's books about working mothers.

E60   **DISCIPLINE AND CLASSROOM CONTROL** Compiled by Sara Lake. Phoenix, Ariz., Oryx, 1980. 63 pp. $15 (paper). (A Special Interest Resource Guide in Education)

A convenient synthesis of journal articles, documents, and books on student control—generally more practical than theoretical—that might be of interest to parents, as well as teachers, administrators, counselors, and other educators. Items were mainly culled from searches in ERIC, PSYCHOLOGICAL ABSTRACTS, MAGAZINE INDEX, COMPREHENSIVE DISSERTATIONS INTERNATIONAL, and other relevant data bases for the years 1975–1979. Items are arranged by number in four broad sections: historical overview, programs and practices, practical guidelines, and administrator concerns. Subject index.

E61 **DIVORCE: A SELECTED ANNOTATED BIBLIOGRAPHY** By Mary McKenney. Metuchen, N.J., Scarecrow, 1975. 157 pp. $11.
Like other comprehensive bibliographies on divorce, this includes materials on the effects of divorce on children. It covers the legal and psychological effects of divorce and has appendixes that list resource people and American divorce laws by state. Author and subject indexes.

E62 **DIVORCE IN THE 70s: A SUBJECT BIBLIOGRAPHY** Compiled by Kenneth D. Sell. Phoenix, Ariz., Oryx, 1981. 191 pp. $45.
A multidisciplinary search by a sociologist and librarian that groups its extensive citations under the headings of social and behavioral science, legal literature, Judeo-Christian literature, popular literature, and nonprint materials. Under these broad categories, subheadings such as alimony, child custody, and desertion are arranged alphabetically. The materials were garnered through searching 73 relevant indexes and abstract journals, of which only 20 were searchable on-line. The result is a comprehensive—nearly complete—compilation of books, articles, and nonprint items. Author, subject, and geographic indexes provide good access to a wide array of materials.

E63 **DYSLEXIA: AN ANNOTATED BIBLIOGRAPHY** By Martha M. Evans. Westport, Conn., Greenwood, 1982. 644 pp. $49.95. (Contemporary Problems of Childhood, No. 5)
A comprehensive compilation of materials on dyslexia, defined in this bibliography as a severe reading disability in children who are normally intelligent and motivated, have adequate cultural backgrounds and educational opportunities, and are without obvious emotional problems. This bibliography provides 2,400 contemporary and retrospective English-language citations on dyslexia, covering indexing and abstracting services, books, book chapters, journal articles, dissertations, government documents, conference reports and proceedings, and pamphlets, drawn primarily from the fields of medicine, education, and

psychology. Materials are organized by type: comprehensive works, collected works, surveys, broadly based research, diagnosis, case studies, historical works, bibliographies, directories, dictionaries, and glossaries, among others. The appendix lists some basic bibliographic tools and some definitions of dyslexia. The work includes a glossary, an author index, a keyword subject index, and a list of journal abbreviations.

E64   **EARLY CHILDHOOD MUSICAL DEVELOPMENT: A Bibliography of Research Abstracts, 1960-1975, with Implications and Recommendations of Teaching and Research** By Gene M. Simons. Reston, Va., Music Educators National Conference, 1978. 136 pp. $3 (paperback).

This particular work brings together most of the published research from 1960 through 1975 (a period when increasing attention was paid to early childhood music learning) on musical behaviors, development, and responses of infants and young children—from prenatal conditioning to children up to seven years of age (with a few related studies dealing with older or exceptional children). The work is in two parts. The first synthesizes the research findings and suggests their importance for teaching and research. The second presents detailed abstracts of 99 research projects, providing the purpose, procedures, and results of each, as well as complete citations. Most relate musical and teaching concerns; others involve such topics as the cry of the newborn or prenatal rhythmic stimulation, conservation of melody, and children's galvanic skin responses to music. The bibliography includes a list of journal sources (mostly psychology and education), an author index, and a good subject index.

E65   **EDUCATION LITERATURE, 1907-1932** Edited by Malcolm Hamilton. New York, Garland, 1979. 12 Vols. $363.

This comprehensive set of indexes to 44,000 citations originally collected and indexed by the U.S. Office of Education between 1907 and 1932, is an extensive survey of the American and foreign educational literature of 50-75 years ago, including books, journals, pamphlets, reports, and periodicals). Overall, it indicates that the concerns of educators of that day had much in common with educators today. The references indexed include many on topics like child development (both physical and mental), behavior problems, intelligence, special educational concerns (namely, deaf, blind, crippled, and gifted children), speech defects, religious development, and statistics. The compilation provides good access to this period by simplifying and systematizing the indexing. It also includes an informative introduction, as well as a comprehensive list of names and subjects. Volume 1 also contains a list of 705 journals indexed in *Educational Literature* from 1907 to 1932, from *Adult Bible Class Monthly* through *Child Health Bulletin, Child Labor Bulletin, Mother and Child,* and *Zuid en Noord.*

E66   **THE EDUCATION OF POOR AND MINORITY CHIL-
      DREN: A World Bibliography**   Compiled by Meyer Wein-
      berg. Westport, Conn., Greenwood, 1981. 2 Vols. $95/set.
A worldwide major definitive bibliography that encompasses 40,000 bibliographical references in five accessible languages (English, Spanish, French, German, and Italian), arranged under 22 broad categories. A massive work of scholarship that took 12 years to compile (single-handedly), it is impressive in unearthing and retrieving significant and usually overlooked works by minority authors and minority groups. It draws from both popular and scholarly publications in law, history, education, and the social sciences, from the early twentieth century through the 1970s, and includes newspapers, dissertations, books, periodical articles, legal proceedings, government documents at all levels, and relevant excerpts from the biographies of doers and shakers.

Materials are arranged under topics (such as "history" and "the American scene"); particular groups (e.g., "children" and "Spanish-speaking peoples"); structures (such as "school organization" and "community"); movements and approaches; and geographic locations. Some sections are intricately subdivided; for instance, "American Indians" is subdivided by tribe. Most major sections end with citations of earlier bibliographies.

Approximately 30,000 items deal with conditions in the United States; 10,000 cover the rest of the world, with major emphasis on Canada and Great Britain. Since there is no subject index, the table of contents and author index provide access to the book. The table of contents should be studied in detail to locate relevant sections, which are not always where one would expect. For example, excellent sections on tests and measurement and on intelligence quotients are found under the heading "Children."

E67   **EFFECTIVENESS OF PREVENTIVE CHILD HEALTH
      CARE**   By William Shadish, for Health Care Financing Admin-
      istration. Baltimore, Md., U.S. Public Health Service, Health
      Care Financing Administration, 1981. 51 pp. Price not available

(paper). (Health Care Financing Grants and Contracts Report Series)

The author of this narrative review (with citations) perused 150 books and articles to identify 38 controlled studies on the effectiveness of preventive health care in children, in such areas as comprehensive care, dental care, health education, iron deficiency anemia, lead poisoning, and screening tests. The report discusses evidence for each of these and explores the credibility of the studies, with conclusions and references following. The author concludes that the bulk of the evidence suggests that preventive health care is beneficial.

E68   **THE EFFECT OF THE INFANT ON ITS CAREGIVER**
       Edited by Michael Lewis and Leonard A. Rosenblum. New York, Wiley, 1974. 265 pp. $32.95. (The Origins of Behavior Series)

A multiauthor literature review with extensive references in all 10 chapters. Areas covered include contributions of human infants to care giving and social interactions, the origins of reciprocity, the effect of the infant on the care giver, development variations and changes, and interactions between blind infants and their mothers; two chapters deal with mother monkeys and their offspring.

E69   **EFFECTS AND FUNCTIONS OF TELEVISION: CHILDREN AND ADOLESCENTS: A Bibliography of Selected Research Literature, 1970–1978** By Manfred Meyer and Ursula Nissen. Hamden, Conn., Linnet Books, 1981. 172 pp. $16. (Communication Research and Broadcasting Series)

The 914 items cited in this well-done bibliography include materials taken from government publications, communications journals, market research sources, and publications on child psychology. Most of them refer to empirical studies published from 1970 through 1978 and are grouped into subject categories like "cognitive and emotional effects" or "aspects of socialization." The work includes many ERIC documents and some European (mostly German) studies. It has an extensive author index and a subject index.

E70   **THE EMOTIONAL AND SOCIAL ADJUSTMENT OF BLIND CHILDREN: Abstracts with a Critical View of the Literature Published Between 1928 and 1962** By M. L. Kellmer Pringle. London, National Foundation for Educational Research in England and Wales, 1964. 72 pp. (Out of print) (Occasional Publication No. 10)

Includes 123 entries, of which 56 have abstracts.

E71 **ENVIRONMENTS FOR PHYSICALLY AND MENTALLY HANDICAPPED CHILDREN** By Robert P. Bartholomew. Monticello, Ill., Vance Bibliographies, 1980. 11 pp. $2 (paper). (Architecture Series A261)

An unannotated and unindexed bibliography, arranged by author, that includes mostly books and monographs from the 1970s (with a few from the 1960s), drawn largely from sources on special education, government, and architecture. Includes some standards and architectural publications not mentioned in other bibliographies.

E72 **THE ESSENTIAL MONTESSORI: An Introduction to the Woman, the Writings, the Method, and the Movement** By Elizabeth G. Hainstock. New York, New American Library, 1978. $1.95 (paperback).

A brief but well-organized overview and introduction that includes sufficient detail for individuals to locate particular sources and concepts. The overview uses cited quotes and summaries tied to the original, so that ideas can be traced to their sources. Appendixes deal with terminology, classroom materials, information sources, and research, among other topics.

E73 **FAILURE TO THRIVE: August 1977 through July 1982** By Charlotte Kenton. Bethesda, Md., National Library of Medicine, 1982. 14 pp. Free (paper). (National Library of Medicine Literature Search 82-16.) From: 8600 Rockville Pike, Bethesda, MD 20209. (Enclose your address on gummed label.)

Contains 184 medical citations dealing with the concepts or symptoms of growth failure in infants and children; updates Literature Search No. 77-10.

E74 **THE FAMILY** Compiled by Project SHARE. Rockville, Md., 1980. 58 pp. $2 (paperback; quantity discount). (Human Services Bibliography Series)

Provides excellent summaries of nearly 100 well-selected, but not widely known, studies on the family.

E75 **FAMILY COUNSELING: An Annotated Bibliography** Edited by Kristi Brown. Cambridge, Mass., Oelgeschlager, Gunn & Hain, 1981. 204 pp. $22.50.

Largely a tool for counselors and others who want to keep abreast of changes in family counseling from 1975 on, *Family Counseling* provides well-annotated listings and abstracts of important works from this period. Sections on research, prevention of problems and worsening situations, supervision, and programs should be valuable for an even wider audience.

E76   **THE FAMILY LAW DECISION-MAKING PROCESS: Annotated Law, Psychiatry, and Policy Science Bibliography** By John Batt and William James. Buffalo, N.Y., William S. Hein, 1979. 262 pp. $25 (paper).

This book, by a law professor and law librarian, includes approximately 700 50- to 60-word somewhat abstract abstracts on topics related to family law in a legalistic context. The materials, however, are of interest to individuals other than lawyers. Section IV, "Protection of the Child" (which covers foster care, child abuse, neglect, and termination of parental rights), and section VII, "Adoption," are most relevant to childhood. The section on the financial dimensions of divorce and dissolution includes citations on child support, and a section on child custody conflicts includes references to materials on child snatching. The paternity and illegitimacy section has materials on unwed mothers and teenage fathers. The articles generally are well chosen by authors who made a sincere effort to "mine the literature of law, psychiatry, psychoanalysis, psychology, sociology, and medicine" to expand the thinking of those "forced to work within narrow and incomplete monoprofessional models." Author and topical indexes.

E77   **FAMILY SUPPORT COUNSELING FOR PARENTS OF EXCEPTIONAL CHILDREN: An Annotated and Categorical Bibliography** By Robert L. Marion and Terri L. McCaslin. Austin, Tex., National Educational Laboratory Publishers, 1977. 85 pp. $7 (paperback).

A comprehensive resource guide for all professionals (psychologists, counselors, social workers, teachers, health workers, rehabilitation workers, and so on) involved in counseling parents of exceptional children. It contains some 450 citations, arranged in brief chapters relating to specific disabilities or areas of interest, such as cerebral palsy, child abuse, deafness and blindness, death and dying, early childhood, emotional disturbance, genetic counseling, health impairment, hearing impairment, learning disabilities, mental retardation, physical handicaps, resources for parents, sex education and counseling, speech impairment, the teacher as counselor, and visual impairment. The selections are chosen from a wide variety of sources (mostly medical, psychological, and educational) over a time span covering the 1950s to 1975; most seem truly valuable for their intended audiences. The annotations, which tend to be brief, are similarly discriminating.

E78   **FAMILY THERAPY AND RESEARCH: An Annotated Bibliography of Articles and Books Published 1950–1970**   By Ira D. Glick and Jay Haley. New York, Grune & Stratton, 1971. 280 pp. $39.50.

A survey of books and articles published from 1950 to 1970 that attempts to include everything written on family therapy, as well as published family research studies that relate to psychiatry, psychology, and social work (excluding popular works, anthropology, and sociology). References are arranged by broad subjects such as family descriptions, types of families, and literature surveys (with articles listed in one or more categories as needed) and are supplemented by an author index. This work supplements Brown's *Family Counseling* (E75).

E79   **FATHERING: A BIBLIOGRAPHY**   By Alice Sterling Honig. Urbana, Ill., ERIC Clearinghouse on Early Childhood Education, 1977. 73 pp. Paper. (Out of print) (ED 142 293)

An interesting, partially annotated bibliography whose 700 references are divided into 10 chapters reflecting the major areas to which "theorists, researchers and clinicians. . .have addressed their inquiries and thoughts in the past few decades." The entries—books, articles, and dissertations—stem mostly from the fields of child development, psychology, and family relations. Topics include general references on the role of the. father; the father and socialization; the contribution of fathering to sex role development; fathers' relations to their children's cognitive competence; fathers and infants; fathers and behavior problems; children's views of fathering; nontraditional fathering; correlations between fathers' status and children; and the effects of father absence, loss, or neglect on child behavior. Although there is no index, a detailed table of contents makes it relatively easy to locate references on a particular topic.

E80   **FATHER'S ROLE IN FAMILY SYSTEMS: An Annotated Bibliography**   Compiled by the School of Family Resources and Consumer Services under the supervision of Pauline G. Boss. Madison, University of Wisconsin, 1979. 239 pp. $6. From: 1430 Linden Dr., Madison, WI 53706.

A comprehensive annotated bibliography of approximately 700 items produced by students in a graduate seminar on the father's role in the family. It includes a very wide range of materials in health and social science fields grouped into four main categories: father and child development/father-child interaction; the fathering experience/the father role; father absence; and general father theory. The first section includes materials on sex role socialization and on gifted children. The father experience section includes interesting references on the biological and physiological aspects of fatherhood, expectant fathers, teenage fathers, single fathers, unwed fathers, and changing father roles. The section on father's absence considers the physical and psychological effects of absence, neglect, and the like, on the family and on the mother. Because of the broadness of the categories and the inadequacy of the index (which codes 700 references into 30 areas), materials are not as accessible as they should be.

E81 **FOLK LITERATURE AND CHILDREN: An Annotated Bibliography** Compiled by George W. B. Shannon. Westport, Conn., Greenwood, 1981. 124 pp. $22.50.
An unusual bibliography that surveys printed materials from 1693 to 1979 concerned somehow with interactions between folklore and children. Entries (English-language materials only; no esoteric studies) are arranged alphabetically by author in three main categories: literature, education, and psychology. Most items cited are twentieth-century journal articles from these three disciplines, as well as general magazines and books. The annotations are descriptive rather than evaluative, usually 50 words or less. Subject, author, and title indexes provide easy access to specific references. The materials cited here and their implications could prove interesting to many adults who work with children.

E82 **FOSTER FAMILY SERVICES SELECTED READING LIST** Compiled by Bea Garrett and Vardrine S. Carter for the Children's Bureau. Washington, D.C., U.S. Children's Bureau, 1967. 78 pp. Paperback. (Out of print)
An annotated reading list on foster family services intended mostly for social workers, but also useful for foster parents and potential foster parents. Materials, on topics like "emergency services," "licensing of foster families," "current general research," and the like, can be located through the table of contents, which is well organized and thorough. Items included were published from 1965 through March 1976.

E83 **FOSTER PARENTING: An Updated Review of the Literature** By Rosemarie Carbino. New York, Child Welfare League of America, Inc., 1980. 43 pp. $4.95 (paperback).
An update of a 1967 literature review that analyzes new issues and trends in practice, policy, and research. Areas covered are characteristics of foster families, definitions of foster parent roles (including new roles), monetary aspects, recruitment and attrition, foster parent edu-

cation and training, and special issues. Includes 102 items with substantial commentary; no index.

E84 **THE GIFTED STUDENT: An Annotated Bibliography** By Jean Laubenfels. Westport, Conn., Greenwood, 1977. 220 pp. $17.50. (Contemporary Problems of Childhood, No. 1)
A bibliography that lists and annotates more than 1,300 items—books, articles, documents, and dissertations—published since 1961 on gifted students. Although the word *student* appears in the title, not all of the items deal exclusively with the gifted child as student. For example, the categories "Characteristics," "Identification," and "Longitudinal Studies" (3 of the 10 overlapping categories used to organize these references) include broader materials. The citations are thorough and indicate such things as the number of references in an article and whether an entry is a bibliography. The book includes an author index and a selective keyword subject index. Appendixes list individuals and organizations concerned with the gifted, assessment instruments commonly used with the gifted, and audiovisual materials for this group.

E85 **HISTORY OF THE FAMILY AND KINSHIP: A Select International Bibliography** Edited by Gerald L. Soliday et al. Millwood, N.Y., Kraus International Publications, 1980. 410 pp. $50.
This project of the *Journal of Family History* was initiated in 1976 under a grant from the National Endowment for the Humanities, with the intent of studying the internal structure and characteristics of family and kinship and their interaction with the larger society and community and educational institutions.

Intended as a reference tool for demographers, anthropologists, and social scientists, and for students of economic, cultural, and legal history, this intensive, selective bibliography contains more than 6,000 entries of secondary works in the area of family history from all around the world, transliterated into the Roman alphabet and translated into English. Materials are arranged geographically and by time period, cross-referenced by subject, and indexed by author.

E86 **THE HOSPITALIZED CHILD: PSYCHOSOCIAL ISSUES—An Abstracted Bibliography** By Dianna Lyell Akins, Gillian S. Mace, and Faren R. Akins. New York, IFI/Plenum, 1981. 294 pp. $75. (IFI Data Base Library)
A comprehensive, abstract bibliography of 514 numbered items, emphasizing the psychosocial issues related to the hospital experience itself (whether long term, short term, or recurrent) rather than to

illness. It covers such areas as anxiety over medical procedures or separation from the family, restrictions on physical activity, absence from school, forced dependency, and so on. It also reviews the programs and therapies created to solve these problems, ranging from foster grandparent programs, to surgical orientations, to such therapies as play therapy, bibliotherapy, or puppet therapy. Also covers changes in hospital policy and design. All items in the main section were published after 1970; abstracts are from *Psychological Abstracts* or were written by one of the authors. Authors and categorical indexes are supplied for these citations; 255 additional citations, from 1960 to 1969, are included, but not annotated, in a separate section. A "stop press" section at the end of the book includes 41 post-1970 articles discovered too late to annotate.

E87   **HUMAN INTERACTION WITH THE PHYSICAL ENVI-RONMENT**   Patterns of Living, Socialization, Behavior, and Environmental Cognition in Various Cultures—Selected Annotated Bibliography. By Nathan Jerry Maltz. Monticello, Ill., Vance Bibliographies, 1979. 29 pp. $3 (paper). (Public Administration Series P173)

An annotated bibliography of approximately 200 well-chosen entries from the 1940s to date dealing with various interactions between humans and their environments, such as life-styles, cross-cultural interactions, cognition, and social behaviors in various settings, neighborhoods, and urban structures. Two sections deal specifically with children: "Processes of Socialization and Education" and "Individual Development and Behavior in Childhood and Adolescence."

E88   **THE HYPERKINETIC CHILD: An Annotated Bibliography, 1974–1979**   Compiled by Carol Ann Winchell. Westport, Conn., Greenwood, 1981. 488 pp. $35.

An exemplary compilation of more than 2,000 annotated entries from a wide variety of disciplines, ranging from medicine to education, child development, psychology, social work, nursing, sociology, rehabilitation, and law, on all aspects of hyperkinesis. It begins with a thoughtful introduction and is arranged complexly but intelligently, with access through a detailed table of contents and excellent author, keyword, and subject indexes. Appendixes include a glossary of terms; a table of drugs; and guides to audiovisual materials, science organizations, and basic bibliographic tools. *The Hyperkinetic Child* updates Winchell's earlier work, *The Hyperkinetic Child: A Bibliography of Medical, Education, and Behavioral Studies* (Westport, Conn., Greenwood, 1975), which covered 1,874 works from the 1950s to mid-1974.

E89 **INDEX OF SCIENTIFIC WRITINGS ON CREATIVITY: General, 1566–1964** By Albert Rothenberg and Bette Greenberg. Hamden, Conn., Shoe String, 1976. 274 pp. $17.50.

A structured classification of 6,823 world references on creativity, with many works in foreign languages. It covers general creativity, creativity and psychopathology, developmental studies, creativity in the fine arts, science, industry, engineering, and business, and the creativity of women. Approximately 800 items in the developmental section, and others elsewhere, deal with children, although they are not always easy to locate through the subject index. Includes an author index.

E90 **INFANT CARE: ABSTRACTS OF THE LITERATURE** By Tannis M. Williams. Washington, D.C., U.S. Children's Bureau, Consortium on Early Childbearing and Childrearing, 1972. 218 pp. (Out of print)

Provides lengthy summaries of approximately 200 papers selected as the best and/or most relevant from a comprehensive survey of research and demonstration work on infant development, infant care, mother-infant interaction, intervention projects, child-rearing practices, and adolescent parenting. This research basically was oriented toward the ramifications for young parents and their infants, but materials cited deal with parents and infants in general. Major areas covered are infant development; infant-adult relationships; child-rearing patterns; infant education, intervention, and day care; and theoretical and methodological issues. Includes an index.

E91 **INFANT FEEDING: AN ANNOTATED BIBLIOGRAPHY** Compiled by Christine Marie Crowhurst and Bonnie Lee Kumer. Toronto, Ryerson Polytechnical Institute, Nutrition Information Service, 1982. 154 pp. $8.95 (paper). From: 350 Victoria St., Room 1955, Toronto, Ontario M5B 1E8, Canada.

A comprehensive review of approximately 700 books, pamphlets, journal articles, and audiovisuals of interest to professionals and parents concerned with the feeding of normal infants during their first year. Covers breast-feeding, infant formulas, comparisons of breast- and bottle-feeding methods, solid foods, infant formula use in developing countries, preterm and low-birth-weight infants, clinical concerns, recipes, and audiovisuals.

E92   **THE INFLUENCE OF THE CINEMA ON CHILDREN AND ADOLESCENTS: An Annotated International Bibliography** Compiled and published by Unesco. Paris, 1961. Westport, Conn., Greenwood, 1975. 106 pp. (Out of print)
This bibliography annotates the works of 400 writers in 13 countries from 1930 to 1959 (with a few earlier entries). It is one of the very few serious compilations on how movies (i.e., cinema rather than educational films) affect children. For each study, it includes the purpose, the research methods, and the main conclusions.

E93   **THE JEWISH FAMILY: A Survey and Annotated Bibliography** By Benjamin Schlesinger. Toronto, University of Toronto Press, 1971. 175 pp. Price not available.
The first part of this volume consists of four articles surveying the Jewish family in retrospect, family life in the kibbutz of Israel, American Jewish families, and Jewish intermarriage in the United States. The second part is a topical annotated bibliography that covers in detail the areas of home, marriage, intermarriage, sexuality, health and welfare, divorce, and death and mourning among Jews. Also included are chapters on family life arranged by time period and geographic area. The book covers a substantial amount of materials on children, youth, and family life in the United States. Appendixes cover Jewish family life in fiction and world Jewish population statistics, as well as the demographics of Israel. Contains only an author index, but the materials are clearly arranged within chapters.

E94   **LATINO MENTAL HEALTH, BIBLIOGRAPHY AND ABSTRACTS** By Amado M. Padilla and Raul Aranda. Rockville, Md., Department of Health, Education, and Welfare, 1976. 288 pp. (Out of print)
An exhaustive bibliography that summarizes and indexes articles from a wide variety of sources that relate somehow to the mental health of those who are Spanish surnamed, Spanish speaking, or of Spanish origin. Well-written, informative abstracts summarize articles from the literature of anthropology, psychology, psychiatry, sociology, and social work. Items are arranged by author, with a subject index at the end. A list of related dissertations is also included.

E95   **LEOPOLD'S BIBLIOGRAPHY OF CHILD LANGUAGE** Revised and augmented by Dan Isaac Slobin. Bloomington, Ind., Indiana University Press, 1972. 202 pp. (Out of print)

A massive revision of Werner F. Leopold's *Bibliography of Child Language,* published in 1952. It includes 746 entries from this work, plus thousands of additional entries—not annotated, but each entry is completely coded according to a contents code devised by Slobin and his associates. This work is intended to be "as exhaustive a compendium as possible of writings on the child's acquisition of language, covering research in America, Western and Eastern Europe, and, to a lesser extent, Japan; and embracing a time span from 1250 to June 1976." There are three indexes that thoroughly cover language and content, and appendixes on recent research on the acquisition of languages other than English and on Hungarian child language development.

This work and Leopold's original opus (reprinted by AMS Press) take care of past research. *Language and Language Behavior Abstracts,* which began in 1967, can be used to update this bibliography.

E96 **LONGITUDINAL STUDIES OF CHILD PERSONALITY: ABSTRACTS WITH INDEX** By Alan A. Stone and Gloria Cochrane Onque. Cambridge, Mass., Harvard University Press for the Commonwealth Fund, 1959. 314 pp. (Out of print)

The aim of this painstaking annotated bibliography was to provide a perspective on the contributions of longitudinal research; it is limited to studies concerned with psychological (emotional and social) behavior in infants and children. Includes well-done summaries of the essential findings of 297 studies, complete up to 1955. Summaries are arranged by author and indexed by subject.

E97 **MAINSTREAMING THE EXCEPTIONAL CHILD: A BIBLIOGRAPHY** Compiled by Mary Cervantes Clarkson. San Antonio, Tex., Trinity University Press, 1982. 240 pp. $25. (Checklists in the Humanities and Education, No. 6)

A comprehensive checklist of 3,122 references on mainstreaming, with one-half classified as general and the other half assigned to areas of exceptionality: the gifted, hearing impaired, learning disabled and emotionally disturbed, mentally handicapped, physically handicapped, speech handicapped, and visually handicapped. Includes 400 late discoveries in a supplement, which is also arranged by general and disability categories. This is the most extensive bibliography on mainstreaming to date, with a subject index that enables users to search from a variety of viewpoints. It includes books, journal articles, ERIC documents, theses and dissertations, government documents, proceedings, and pamphlets going back to 1964.

E98   THE MALE SEX ROLE: A Selected and Annotated Bibliog-
      raphy   By Kathleen E. Grady, Robert Brennan, and Joseph H.
      Pleck. Rockville, Md., National Institute on Mental Health,
      1979. 196 pp. (Out of print)
An annotated bibliography of more than 250 items of representative research and theoretical perspectives selected as valuable for researchers.
Evaluative annotations of research items cover the methods, the population studied, and the findings. For theoretical reports, the authors include premises, conclusions, and comments. It is divided into 14 topics
and subtopics, including socialization, marriage, fatherhood, and mas-
culinity in other countries.

E99   THE MULTI-PROBLEM FAMILY: A Review and Anno-
      tated Bibliography   3rd Edition. By Benjamin Schlesinger. To-
      ronto, University of Toronto Press, 1970. 191 pp. Price not
      available.
Includes introductory articles on the multiproblem family (in general
and in Canada) and on community treatment programs, as well as abbreviations and lists of addresses. The bibliography section, arranged
by geographic area, covers Australia, Britain, Canada, France, Holland,
the United States, and miscellaneous. A bibliography from 1962 to
1965 is given in an appendix. Author index.

E100 MUSICAL   CHARACTERISTICS   OF   CHILDREN   By
      Marilyn P. Zimmerman. Reston, Va., Music Educators National
      Conference, 1971. 32 pp. $2 (paper).
Provides a literature review and references of research studies on the
perceptual, conceptual, affective, vocal, and manipulative development
of and individual differences among children as related to music. Each
topic is given a separate chapter.

E101 NEEDS AND CHARACTERISTICS OF STUDENTS IN THE
      INTERMEDIATE YEARS, AGES 12-16: A Comprehensive
      Review of the Literature 1930-1974   With Recommendations
      for Educational Practice. By Lionel Desjardins et al. Ontario, On-
      tario Ministry of Education, 1975. 393 pp. Price not available
      (paper).
A comprehensive literature review and synthesis of information (taken
from approximately 600 "quality" research studies) on the physical,
intellectual, emotional, and social characteristics of adolescents aged
12-16. The first section is an overview on the theories, meaning, and

goals of adolescence; the psychological consequences of biological change; the effect of such changes; the changes in cognitive functioning; and the educational implications. The second section is a detailed literature review of growth and other physiological levels and events in adolescence. The third deals with early adolescent cognitive functioning and intellectual growth, and the last section provides an empirical base for the emotional and social development of normal adolescents.

E102 **NONORGANIC FAILURE TO THRIVE—CHILD ABUSE: An Abstract Bibliography** By Sara M. Derrick. Bowling Green, Ohio, Bowling Green State University Popular Press, 1981. 48 pp. $5 (paperback).

This two-part abstract bibliography expands the literature on child abuse and neglect to include the syndrome of nonorganic failure to thrive, that is, retardation of growth of infants and children reared in their own homes by their own families. The first part covers the characteristics of these children and their families; the second covers articles on laws, treatments, and programs relating to physical child abuse. Although there are fewer than 70 citations, these were intelligently chosen from writings by physicians, social workers, psychologists, educators, and legal workers. Author index.

E103 **NORMAL CHILD DEVELOPMENT: An Annotated Bibliography of Books and Articles Published 1950-1969** By Janice B. Schulman and Robert C. Prall. New York, Grune & Stratton, 1971. 326 pp. $33.

A well-arranged, useful compilation of child development research up to 1969, with 733 citations and summaries arranged by author in 18 topical chapters. The book deals with such broad areas as adjustment, self-perception, family relationships, sexual knowledge and behavior, religious and moral values, and physical health. Each chapter starts with definitions and scope notes. Cross-references are provided for age, socioeconomic status, and family composition. The references were culled from a comprehensive survey of research literature of the United States, Canada, and England pertaining to studies involving 30 or more children. The authors excluded experimental studies and overly technical materials that were not comprehensible and readable, unless they approximated the normal range of children's experiences. Although the literature survey goes back only to 1950, the bibliography includes some books and articles of particular value from the 1940s. There is an author index to the whole volume.

E104 **THE ONE-PARENT FAMILY: PERSPECTIVES AND ANNOTATED BIBLIOGRAPHY** 4th Edition. By Benjamin Schlesinger. Toronto, University of Toronto Press, 1978. 224 pp. $17.50.
This edition starts with six review essays that reflect current trends and deal with motherless families, fatherless families, divorce and children, the crisis of widowhood, the unmarried mother who keeps her child, and single-parent adoptions. The annotated bibliography is arranged in three chronological sections, 1930–1969, 1970–1974, and 1975–1978. These sections are in turn subdivided into topics that differ slightly for each time period. The topics in the last group are basically similar to the initial essays, with the addition of remarriage and bibliographies. One appendix is an annotated list of books for children who are experiencing family changes because of divorce, separation, or adjustment to a re-constituted family. The book also provides an author index and a directory of publishers. The emphasis of the book is slightly Canadian.

E105 **PARENTAL ACCEPTANCE AND REJECTION: A Review and Annotated Bibliography of Research and Theory** By Ronald P. Rohner and Caroline C. Neilsen. New Haven, Conn., Human Relations Area Files, 1978. 2 Vols. (continuous paging). 357 pp. $30. (HRAFlex Books, Cross-Cultural Research Series, ws-006)
This two-volume work contains a critical review of the research literature from 1940 through 1977 on the antecedents and effects of parental acceptance and rejection, a complex index of topics, and an annotated bibliography of some 600 items arranged by author and categorized according to 27 major topics. The categories, which are fully explained in the index, include maternal deprivation, maternal overprotection, attachment, separation, behavior disorders, achievement, intelligence quotient, handicapped children, personality characteristics, sex differences, working mothers, father's influence, longitudinal studies, and cross-cultural comparisons, among many others. Each annotation provides information on the sample, method, and results of the study, as well as a brief discussion.

E106 **PARENT-CHILD SEPARATION: Psychosocial Effects on Development—An Abstracted Bibliography** By Faren R. Akins, Dianna L. Akins, and Gillian S. Mace. New York, IFI/Plenum, 1981. 356 pp. $85. (IFI Data Base Library)
A substantial abstract bibliography on the ways that parent separation (for reasons other than parental death) affects the developing child and

adolescent. Includes books, articles, and dissertations on maternal or paternal absence due to desertion, military duty, parental institutionalization, and divorce. It also contains restricted parenting articles that deal with the effects of maternal or paternal inattention rather than physical abuse. Essentially, *Parent-Child Separation* covers professional rather than popular literature and intentionally excludes laboratory studies. The main section contains 690 cited abstracts published after 1960 that were prepared by *Psychological Abstracts,* the original authors, or written specially for this book. Abstracts are numbered and arranged alphabetically by author and indexed by subject and author. The index is not always helpful; although some terms are specific, it has only 24 categories, some of which are overly general and some of which overlap. For example, there are more than 70 numbers following the term "psychopathology." An unindexed section provides 184 "historical references" of materials mostly from the 1940s and 1950s. A "stop press" section contains 37 additional, unindexed late additions.

E107 **PERSPECTIVES ON RESIDENTIAL CHILD CARE: An Annotated Bibliography** Research and Other Literature in the United States, Canada and Great Britain, 1966–74. By Hilary Prosser. Windsor, England, NFER Publishing Co., 1976. 109 pp. $9.75 (paperback). Distributed by Humanities Press, 171 First Ave., Atlantic Highlands, NJ 07716.

Originally published under the auspices of Great Britain's National Children's Bureau, this book updates R. Dinage and M. K. Pringle's *Residential Child Care Facts and Fallacies* (Longmans, 1967), which covered research through 1965. The specific field treated is residential care of normal children. It excludes both the care of children in community schools and handicapped children, except when they are compared in the literature to normal children. Most of the items are detailed summaries of research literature that specify the scope, purpose, samples, methodology, and findings of particular studies. The authors also include a small number of somewhat shorter accounts of "impressionistic" materials. Research materials are divided into four sections: the consequences of residential care for children; the characteristics of children in care; evaluations of the care and treatment of children; and aspects of the characteristics, training, and working conditions of the residential staff. The impressionistic material is divided into three categories: policy and practice, residential child care staff, and historic considerations.

E108 **PHILOSOPHY, POLICIES AND PROGRAMS FOR EAR-
LY ADOLESCENT EDUCATION: An Annotated Bibliogra-
phy** By Dale A. Blyth and Elizabeth Leuder Karnes. Westport,
Conn., Greenwood, 1981. 704 pp. $49.95.

Contains 12 chapters comprising 1,600 annotated entries of books,
journals, dissertations, and school district reports that deal with major
issues in early adolescent education. Most of the materials are slanted
toward the concerns of educators, but the materials on guidance programs, philosophy and theory, extracurricular materials, research, and
student behavior are more generally valuable. Annotations, which vary
in length, are, for the most part, thoughtful, although they sometimes
omit conclusions. Chapters contain thorough, helpful scope notes. The
book has a general subject index.

E109 **THE PHYSICALLY HANDICAPPED: An Annotated Bibliography of Empirical Research Studies, 1970–1979** By William A. Pearman and Philip Starr. New York, Garland, 1981.
132 pp. $30.

Directed at clinicians, with the aim of reducing the gap between social
research and the delivery of services, this book summarizes research
findings and provides annotated references to 330 important empirical
studies published in a broad grouping of medical, educational, and
social and behavioral science journals from 1970 to 1979. The annotations, which are lengthy and informative, are arranged by author; there
is an author index at the end. The extensive subject index reveals many
items relating to children. The book begins with an extensive chapter
on measurement and methodology problems in physical disability research and includes a list of the journals searched.

E110 **PIAGETIAN RESEARCH; COMPILATION AND COM-
MENTARY** Edited by Sohan Modgil and Celia Modgil. Windsor, England, NFER Publishing Co., 1976. 8 Vols. Vol. 1, $12.50
(paper); Vol. 2, $17.25; Vols. 3 and 4, $20.75 each; Vol. 5,
$28.25; Vol. 6, $17.25; Vol. 7, $16.00; Vol. 8, $16.00. Distributed by Humanities Press, 171 First Ave., Atlantic Highlands, NJ
07716.

This series, with a previous guide, is designed to make available Piaget-
oriented research of Piaget and his followers; it covers 3,700 references
on replications and extensions of Piaget's work, as well as reflections,
speculations, and analyses. Includes theses and published and unpublished research projects up to 1975. Each volume covers a particular
area and can be studied separately.

E111 **PLAY AND PLAYTHINGS: A REFERENCE GUIDE** By
Bernard Mergen. Westport, Conn., Greenwood, 1982. 288 pp.
$35. (American Popular Culture)
This reference guide begins with an in-depth historical essay, surveying
American children's games, toys, and playthings from colonial times to
the present, including games of Puritan children, slave children, and
children of the nineteenth century. Covers the "discovery" of children's play; the significance of games, toys, and play vis-à-vis theories
of child development; and the changes in play that emerged as a result
of movies and television. The second part of the book is a guide to
books and articles, histories of childhood and play, source materials,
anthropology and folklore, and guides to periodicals and research collections.

E112 **THE POLITICAL AND CIVIC SOCIALIZATION OF
CHILDREN** By Terry Lutes. Monticello, Ill., Vance Bibliographies, 1981. 11 pp. $2 (paper). (Public Administration
Series P859)
A research bibliography focusing on one aspect of political socialization
and cognitive development—namely, children's development of civic
and political attitudes during the last five years of elementary school
(between the ages of 9 and 13). Values and attitudes covered include
perception of roles of citizenship and attitudes toward authority. Most
of the books and articles cited were written in the 1960s and the 1970s,
with many taken from the fields of political science and the social
sciences.

E113 **POLITICS AND CHILDREN** By Robert Goehlert. Monticello, Ill., Vance Bibliographies, 1982. 39 pp. $6 (paper). (Public
Administration Series P1007)
Approximately 550 well-selected items on many dimensions of the interactions between politics and children and adolescents. Most are journal articles from sociology and political science journals (and some
behavioral science journals) dealing with areas such as socialization,
care taking, and party identification. There is a definite international
flavor to this melange. Unfortunately, this thoughtful selection is less
useful than it should be, since unannotated items are arranged by author and are not indexed.

E114 **POVERTY AND MALNUTRITION IN LATIN AMERICA:
EARLY CHILDHOOD INTERVENTION PROGRAMS**
By Ernesto Pollitt. New York, Praeger, 1980. 162 pp. $23.95.

An exposition and a literature review on the interrelationships among sociocultural settings, malnutrition, and mental and behavioral development in children in Latin America (mostly South America). The book manages a concise review of complex materials, where each chapter builds on the issues raised in the last. For example, Chapter 1 describes the significance and incidence of poverty in Latin America; Chapter 2 explores the complex relations between poverty, cognitive development, and school enrollment; and the third chapter covers the severe deficiency diseases that accompany extreme poverty and their effect on brain function. Subsequent chapters cover various interventions.

E115 **THE PROGRESSIVE EDUCATION MOVEMENT: An Annotated Bibliography** By Mariann Pezzella Winick. New York, Garland, 1978. 130 pp. $19. (Reference Library of Social Science, No. 29)

Almost a history of the progressive education movement over the last 80 years, using 590 cross-referenced annotated citations arranged in topical chapters. Since this cooperative movement of social scientists and educators grew out of and fostered the child study movement, the chapters on history, theory, philosophy, curriculum, and parent involvement are relevant. The last chapter incorporates descriptions of state journals that might be useful for other research on children. Author index.

E116 **PROJECT HEAD START: A Legacy of the War on Poverty** Edited by Edward Zigler and Jeanette Valentine. New York, Free Press, 1979. 610 pp. $29.95.

A comprehensive view of Head Start. Chapters and bibliographic references cover its history, the preschool component, and the comprehensive development component. Four chapters are devoted to evolving concepts of evaluation. Discussions and references also cover day care, education, nutrition, parental involvement, career development, health care and health needs of children, and short- and long-term evaluation models. The bibliography contains 1,070 items.

E117 **REGIONALIZED SYSTEMS AS AN APPROACH TO PERINATAL HEALTH CARE: An Annotated Bibliography** By Barbara Pearce. Chicago, Ill., Council of Planning Librarians, 1981. 81 pp. $13 (paperback). (CPL Bibliography No. 54)

A detailed bibliography intended to help planners, administrators, and medical practitioners review and select therapies, management techniques, architectural designs, and/or programs associated with a reduction in maternal, fetal, and neonatal mortality rates, within the context of regionalization of perinatal care. (This is a system that coordinates and consolidates perinatal care among many institutions.) The bibliography includes brief abstracts and fairly detailed (sometimes extensive) summaries for approximately 70 articles selected from the literature of clinical applications, operative regionalized systems, and planning. Priority was given to locating descriptions of regionalized perinatal care in Illinois. Citations are arranged by author, following a preliminary categorization according to type of literature. Includes a good subject index.

E118 **THE RELATIONSHIP BETWEEN CHILD CARE AND FAMILY FUNCTIONING: AN ANNOTATED BIBLIOGRAPHY** By Karen Hill-Scott. Monticello, Ill., Vance Bibliographies, 1979. 33 pp. $4.50 (paper). (Public Administration Series P343)

A two-part review of the published literature of child care effects on the family. The first part is a collection of detailed annotations of around 20 works organized into six areas: family structure and function, maternal employment and its effects, the parent as a child care consumer, the effects of child care on the mother-child dyad, parent involvement in child care, and child care and public policy issues. The annotations vary in length, since the author discusses some particularly salient ideas in great detail. The second part is an exhaustive list of citations, from 1972 to 1977, pertaining to child care and family functioning. The introduction is most thoughtful and helpful.

E119 **THE RELATIONSHIP BETWEEN NUTRITION AND STUDENT ACHIEVEMENT, BEHAVIOR, AND HEALTH: A Review of the Literature** Compiled by Rose Y. L. Tseng, Joyce Mellon, and Karen Bammer. Sacramento, California State Department of Education, 1980. 150 pp. $4 (paperback).

A literature review, rather than a bibliography, of existing research—in California and elsewhere—on the relationships between nutrition and achievement, behavior, and health. Most items were located through searching the previous 10 years of the computerized data banks of ERIC and AGRICOLA, as well as the 1976 and 1977 editions of *Index Medicus* and the library of the Nutrition Clearinghouse. The cutoff date for research appears to be 1977, with most of the citations from the late 1970s.

The research is organized into separate, autonomous chapters that cover children's nutritional status, evidence of nutritional deficiency, evidence of improved nutritional status, general contributing factors in nutritional status, malnutrition and obesity, malnutrition and dental problems, hyperactivity, synergistic interaction between malnutrition and infection, growth and malnutrition, and the relations between behavior and malnutrition in animals and in humans. Each chapter contains its own conclusions and bibliographies. The authors conclude that nutrition is the most important and influential of all early environmental factors.

E120 **RESEARCH IN BLACK CHILD DEVELOPMENT: DOC-TORAL DISSERTATION ABSTRACTS, 1927–1979** Compiled by Hector F. Myers et al. Westport, Conn., Greenwood, 1982. 737 pp. $49.95.

A companion volume to *Black Child Development in America, 1927–1977,* covering the dissertation literature with lengthy annotations of 627 entries based on *Dissertation Abstracts International* and arranged alphabetically by author in five areas: language, physical, cognitive, personality, and social development. Author and subject indexes.

E121 **RESEARCH IN INFANT BEHAVIOR: A CROSS-IN-DEXED BIBLIOGRAPHY** Edited by Yvonne Brackbill. Baltimore, Md., Williams & Wilkins, 1964. 281 pp. (Out of print)

A careful, thorough attempt to bring together scattered research on infant behavior. This comprehensive bibliography "of maximal use to students, practitioners, and to research scientists," with thoughtful, explicit criteria for selection, includes 1,733 entries, mostly journal articles (going back to 1876) from some 290 serials and approximately 150 books. All entries are primary sources in empirical research, dealing with normal behavior in infants between birth and three years (or birth and four years for language studies). The book includes an author index and a form of coordinate subject indexing to locate articles within broad areas like sensation and perception, motor behavior, learning and conditioning, language, vocalization and communication, cognitive development, social behavior and social variables, and emotional and personality development.

E122 **RESEARCH IN THE CHILD PSYCHIATRIC AND GUID-ANCE CLINICS (1923–1970)** By Zanvel E. Klein. Chicago, Ill., University of Chicago, Department of Psychiatry, 1971. (ED 073 849). *Supplements,* 1973 and 1974. (ED 089 876, ED 089 877)

These reports, available from ERIC, are a bibliography of more than 1,000 investigations published between 1923 and 1972 of neurologically handicapped children under age 12 with problems that can be treated in guidance or in outpatient clinics. Reports are classified in 12 sections and indexed by author.

E123 **RESEARCH ON THE EFFECTS OF TELEVISION AD-VERTISING ON CHILDREN: A Review of the Literature and Recommendations for Future Research** Prepared for the National Science Foundation. Washington, D.C., 1977. 229 pp. $7.50.

A thoughtful, classified literature review that provides overviews of particular areas, arranged to facilitate the location of particular information. The first section provides an introduction and a background on children's viewing patterns. The second section is divided into 11 chapters on such things as children's ability to distinguish commercials from programs, the influence of format or volume and repetitions, the effects of premiums or food advertising, self-concept appeals, violence and unsafe acts on television, and the relation of advertising to consumer socialization or parent-child relations.

E124 **RESEARCH RELATING TO EMOTIONALLY DIS-TURBED CHILDREN** Compiled by the Children's Bureau. Washington, D.C., 1968. 182 pp. (Out of print)

A listing of all research projects on emotional disturbance reported to the Children's Bureau Clearinghouse for Research in Child Life from 1956 to 1967. Items are classified according to the main focus of the research, except that all studies involving schizophrenic children and all studies representing ongoing research (as of 1966–1967) are grouped together. Information on each study includes the title, expected duration dates, a citation to *Research Relating to Children,* subsequent publication references, and the names and addresses of principal investigators. Areas covered include general studies, incidence and prevalence, etiology, identification, diagnosis and classification, psychological testing, psychological characteristics, psychoses, associated manifestations, treatment methods and facilities, community programs, children with disturbed parents and siblings, and longitudinal studies. There is an investigator index at the end.

E125 **RESEARCH RELATING TO MENTALLY RETARDED CHILDREN** Compiled by the Clearinghouse for Research in

Child Life. Washington, D.C., U.S. Government Printing
Office, 1966. 126 pp. (Out of print)
A classified listing of all research projects on mental retardation reported by the Children's Bureau Clearinghouse between 1949 and 1966
(similar to E124). Categories include surveys, etiology, classification,
neurology and neurosurgery, endocrinology and biochemistry, phenylketonuria, mongolism, pharmacology, growth and development, family and community factors, therapy, special education, institutions,
community services, vocational training and employment, and current
(1965) projects.

E126 **RESOURCE GUIDE TO BILINGUAL EDUCATION: A
Selective Bibliography of Recent Publications** By Theodore
Andersson. Austin, Tex., National Educational Laboratory
Publishers, 1979. 105 pp. (Out of print) (Educational Bibliographies Series, No. 3)
An intelligently selective and well-designed bibliography of 769 items
divided into four sections based on types of materials: studies and
reports, government reports and hearings, bibliographies, and serials
and periodicals. These provide good documentation and background information on legal and political aspects of bilingual education, as well as
on the population of children involved. Government reports provide
sources of statistics; the bibliographies lead to retrospective data and
studies, and the titles and addresses of periodicals can help with ongoing research.

E127 **RESOURCES FOR EARLY CHILDHOOD: An Annotated
Bibliography and Guide for Educators, Librarians, Health
Care Professionals, and Parents** Compiled by Hannah Nuba
Scheffler. New York, Garland, 1983. 551 pp. $49.95.
In this timely work, almost 50 essays by well-known early-childhood
professionals introduce, follow, and surround the 16 subject bibliographies that collectively annotate around 1,200 recommended titles for
parents and professionals. The organizer is the librarian of the New
York Public Library's Early Childhood Resource and Information Center. The titles cited, the contributors, and the collection of this center
express contemporary thoughts and theories on child rearing and child
development. The work itself is a massive enterprise, involving essay-
ists, an editorial committee, 25 chapter coordinators, and approximately 160 contributors. Areas covered include pregnancy, birth, and the
first year; child development; the family; parenting; health; nutrition;
children's play; choices in child care and management of child care

settings; schooling; literature; expressive arts; multicultural education; special needs; nonsexist education; and film and television. There is a resource chapter that lists periodicals, newsletters, and organizations. The book also provides a subject index to the essays and author and title indexes to the cited works. As might be expected in a collective enterprise, the book is uneven and varies in focus. Some essays and annotations are concise and insightful; others are rambling and general. Overall, the quality is respectable, although the works cited appear to be more appropriate for parents than the declared professional audience. These chapters might best be considered a series of recommended reading lists by knowledgeable professionals. As such, the book serves an important function in providing thoughtful, contemporary background reading on a variety of topics, surrounded by essays that set each topic in perspective.

E128 **A REVIEW OF HEAD START RESEARCH SINCE 1969 AND AN ANNOTATED BIBLIOGRAPHY** By Ada Jo Mann, Adele Harrell, and Maure Hurt, Jr. Washington, D.C., Administration for Children, Youth, and Families, 1978. 158 pp. $7 (paper).
Includes a 44-page survey of Head Start research, followed by an annotated bibliography of 762 references to articles on Head Start children, services, and projects, arranged by author and indexed by author and subject. This selective bibliography was compiled to make significant books, articles, and papers on Head Start more accessible to researchers, evaluators, and policymakers. Priority for inclusion was given to works that presented qualitative or quantitative data on Head Start, reanalyzed this data, reviewed or synthesized the findings, criticized or defended Head Start studies, or described specific programs or processes. The introductory material covers the summaries of research on the impact of Head Start on the families, health, and social and cognitive development of participating children.

E129 **THE ROLE OF GOVERNMENT IN PROVIDING CHILD CARE FACILITIES: A Checklist of Sources** By Lynne Struthers Swanick. Monticello, Ill., Vance Bibliographies, 1978. 9 pp. Paper. (Out of print) (Public Administration Series P25)
Covers books, periodicals, and government publications from the 1970s focusing on the role of North American governments in providing child care facilities. Includes references to government regulations and guidelines for day care centers.

E130 **THE ROLE OF THE FATHER IN CHILD DEVELOP-
MENT** 2nd Edition. Edited by Michael E. Lamb. New York,
Wiley, 1981. 596 pp. $29.95.
A comprehensive multiauthored, multidisciplinary work on the many
dimensions of the father's role in child development. Lamb's introductory chapter reflects the growth of research in this field. Other chapters
deal with such things as historical perspectives, father influence in a
family context, and the father's role in infancy.

E131 **SECOND LANGUAGE LEARNING AMONG YOUNG
CHILDREN: A BIBLIOGRAPHY OF CURRENT RE-
SEARCH** Compiled by Emma González Stupp and Jennifer
Gage. Arlington, Va., National Clearinghouse for Bilingual Education (NCBE), 1982. 71 pp. $10.75 (paper).
Includes approximately 90 abstracts from NCBE's data base on various
aspects of the learning of a second language among young children.
Areas covered include acquisition and instruction, English as a second
language, foreign-language instruction in elementary schools, and im-
mersion programs. Provides information on the availability of items
cited. Author and title indexes.

E132 **A SELECTED ANNOTATED BIBLIOGRAPHY ON
BLACK FAMILIES** Compiled by Project THRIVE of the National Urban League. Washington, D.C., U.S. Government
Printing Office, 1978. 38 pp. Paper. (Out of print)
A bibliography on black families with a comprehensive perspective on
the totality of black families and family life (i.e., not focusing on problem families), designed to improve professional awareness and skills
and to foster minority participation and interdisciplinary cooperation in
the prevention and treatment of child abuse and neglect. Areas covered
include the family patterns and processes of black families, social welfare service delivery, and issues in conceptualizing services. The descriptions and perceptions of black creative writers are used, as well as
materials stemming from the fields of sociology, social planning, and
social work.

E133 **SELECTED BIBLIOGRAPHY: INTERNATIONAL MA-
TERNAL AND CHILD HEALTH** By Mary Kay Larson.
Monticello, Ill., Vance Bibliographies, 1980. 18 pp. $2.50
(paper). (Public Administration Series P438)
A bibliography, originally compiled for a class in public health, that con-
tains annotations of 75 English-language items on maternal and child

health in developing countries. The books, reports, and periodical articles cited are well chosen to cover all aspects of the field (cultural perspectives as well as medical realities); the annotations are detailed and helpful. Includes a source for additional materials.

E134 **THE SELECTIVE GUIDE TO PUBLICATIONS FOR MENTAL HEALTH AND FAMILY LIFE EDUCATION** 4th Edition. Edited by Hal Rifken. Chicago, Ill., Marquis Academic Media, 1979. $44.50 (paperback).
Provides complete order information and descriptive evaluations of recommended materials (books, pamphlets, leaflets, plays) in the areas of child growth and development, adult mental health, areas of special concern, and related reference works. Materials are fully described for their use in adult, community, and family life education by mental health professionals, community educators, parent educators, and others. The *Guide* has been updated by *Education-for-Health: The Selective Guide* (F12), annotated in Chapter 7.

E135 **SEPARATION AND SPECIAL-CARE BABY UNITS** Edited by F. S. W. Brimblecombe, M. P. M. Richards, and N. R. C. Roberton. London, Spastics International Medical Publications, 1978. 120 pp. $19.75. (Clinics in Developmental Medicine, No. 68) From: J. B. Lippincott, E. Washington Sq., Philadelphia, PA 19105.
A study of the current and future aspects of special baby care units that includes a review of possible effects of early separation from parents on later development of children.

E136 **SEX ROLES: A RESEARCH BIBLIOGRAPHY** By Helen S. Astin, Allison Parelman, and Anne Fisher. Washington, D.C., National Institute of Mental Health, 1975. 362 pp. (Out of print)
A multidisciplinary review of sex roles, incorporating research materials from anthropology, psychology, economics, biology, physiology, and other fields. Covers socialization and child-rearing practices; sex differences in cognitive and personality development; cross-cultural variations in behavior; anatomical, hormonal, and other biological characteristics; sex role expectations; sex role perceptions; sex stereotyping; and economic perspectives, among other things. Abstracts are indexed by keywords.

E137 **SEXUAL ABUSE OF CHILDREN: A RESOURCE GUIDE AND ANNOTATED BIBLIOGRAPHY** By Benjamin Schlesinger. Toronto, University of Toronto Press, 1982. 200 pp. $10 (paperback).

A handbook and bibliography focusing on the Canadian experience. Includes a 180-item bibliography (1937–1980) of materials from 55 journals (most since 1977), classified by subject. Appendixes include an inventory of findings, a basic library of information on sexual abuse, lists of films, guides to interviewing and examination, reviews of Canadian laws and Canadian studies, and addresses of information sources.

E138 **SPECIAL ADOPTIONS: An Annotated Bibliography on Transracial, Transcultural, and Nonconventional Adoption and Minority Children** By S. Peter Kim and the American Academy of Child Psychiatry. Rockville, Md., National Institute of Mental Health, 1983. 142 pp. Single copy free while supply lasts; phone (301) 443-4515 for information.

The references in this annotated bibliography were largely garnered through researching books, monographs, and journals published during the last 25 years in the fields of adoption, child development, pediatrics, psychiatry, psychology, social work, sociology, and other related areas. It includes an author index; a detailed subject index to 188 references on transracial, transcultural, and nonconventional adoption; and 271 references to adoption of minority children. The purpose was to help families and children involved in special adoptions by bringing together relevant materials to make mental health, health, and human service professionals aware of the changing patterns of adoption. The subject index is particularly helpful in locating materials on such topics as the sale of children.

E139 **STEPFATHER, WHAT THE LITERATURE REVEALS: A Literature Review and Annotated Bibliography** By Mona McCormick. La Jolla, Calif., Western Behavioral Sciences Institute, 1974. 75 pp. Paper. (Out of print)

Includes 39 pages of discussion based on materials of the 1950s, 1960s, and 1970s, with close analysis of such factors as jealousy, the presence of other children, and additional factors affecting the relationship. Covers legal aspects as well as social and psychological factors.

E140 **SUICIDE AMONG CHILDREN, ADOLESCENTS, AND STUDENTS: A Comprehensive Bibliography** By John L. McIntosh, with the assistance of John F. Santos. Monticello,

Ill., Vance Bibliographies, 1981. 106 pp. $5.25 (paperback). (Public Administration Series P685)
A multidisciplinary bibliography of around 1,000 items that concentrates on the 1970s but also includes some earlier material and some from as late as 1980. Materials stem from nearly every discipline involved, including anthropology, suicidology, psychology, and criminology, and include both English- and foreign-language articles, books, conferences, and dissertations. The bibliography was based on perusal of many individual journals, as well as use of 31 indexing and abstracting sources. It also refers to earlier bibliographies and indicates where abstracts can be located.

E141 **SUICIDE OR DEPRESSION IN CHILDHOOD AND ADOLESCENCE: January 1975 through February 1979** By Philip Wexler. Bethesda, Md., National Library of Medicine, 1979. 12 pp. Free. From: NLM, Literature Search Program, 8600 Rockville Pike, Bethesda, MD 20209. (Enclose a self-addressed gummed label.) (National Library of Medicine Literature Search 79-6)
Includes 179 citations of recent articles from the medical literature, in English and foreign languages, dealing with all aspects of depression, suicide, and suicidal tendencies in children and adolescents. An addendum includes monographs published from 1966 through 1977.

E142 **TELEVISION AND SOCIAL BEHAVIOR: An Annotated Bibliography of Research Focusing on Television's Impact on Children** Edited by Charles K. Atkin, John P. Murray, and Oguz B. Nayman for the National Institute of Mental Health. Rockville, Md., 1971. 150 pp. (Out of print) (Public Health Service Publication No. 2099)
The classic study on children and television, incorporating 496 references to monographs, journal articles, and dissertations on the ways children's behavior may be affected by television content, with some foreign literature included. The main section includes 285 annotated references arranged by author under broad topics; a supplementary 211 references are arranged alphabetically by author. The abstracts indicate the number of items cited in each work. There is a supplementary author index.

E143 **TELEVISION AND YOUTH: 25 Years of Research & Controversy** By John P. Murray. Omaha, Neb., Boys Town Center for the Study of Youth Development, 1980. 278 pp. $10 (paperback).

This comprehensive listing of research and commentary provides 2,886 categorized citations, 60 percent of which were published between 1975 and 1980. It reviews English-language publications, primarily from North America but also from Australia, Great Britain, Europe, and Scandinavia, with 400 "moderately accessible" non-English-language reports included.

Designed for researchers, broadcasters, legislators, and others (including parents) who affect policy, this book is published in three major sections. The first is a referenced review of research, commentary, and controversy; the second is the master bibliography from 1955 to 1980; the third consists of 13 specialized bibliographies covering violence, socialization, advertising, role portrayals, cognitive development and educational television, audience patterns, viewing policy, suggestions for policy, guidelines for action, bibliographies, and more.

E144 **TELEVISION'S IMPACT ON CHILDREN AND ADOLESCENTS** By Sara Lake. Phoenix, Ariz., Oryx, 1981. 107 pp. $15.

Provides 515 selections (from 1975 on) of research and opinion on television, arranged in five categories: viewing habits, perceptions of children and adolescents, impact of television on the young, television and teaching, and improvement of the situation. Materials include books, journals, articles, dissertations, proceedings, and papers located through searching nine data bases and consolidating and arranging the findings. Well arranged and well indexed, although the abstracts, like most data base abstracts, do not provide commentary or evaluations.

E145 **VIOLENCE AT HOME: An Annotated Bibliography** Compiled and edited by Mary Lystad. Rockville, Md., National Institute of Mental Health, 1974. 95 pp. (Out of print)

A very-well-done bibliography that annotates 190 books and scientific articles on violence in family life and arranges them by type of violence. The author points out that violence among adults is far more prevalent than child abuse, but, nevertheless, several categories (perhaps half the entries) in this bibliography concern children and violence: violence of parent to child, violence of child to parent, violence among siblings, socialization, and services to families with violent members. The abstracts are exceptionally well written and informative. The arrangement is easy to use and is supported by an author index.

E146 **THE YOUNG CHILD: Reviews of Research** Washington, D.C., National Association for the Education of Young Chil-

dren. 3 Vols. Vol. 1: Edited by Willard W. Hartup and Nancy L.
Smothergill, 1967, 312 pp. (Out of print); Vol. 2: Edited by Willard W. Hartup, 1972, 374 pp., $3.00; Vol. 3: Edited by Shirley
G. Moore and Catherine R. Cooper, 1982, 304 pp., $6.50.
Contains extensive literature reviews of research on the young child,
with subject indexes that allow good access to particular topics such as
attachment and sex-role learning. Topics in Volume 1 include role-
taking and communication skills, role of play in cognitive development, frustration and motivation, development of conscience, sex
roles, racial awareness, and peer acceptance. Topics in Volume 2 include language, punishment, memory, anxiety, and intelligence. Some
highlights of Volume 3 are socioeconomic development, language and
thinking, social relationships, biological factors, and special needs.

E147 **YOUNG PEOPLE'S ENVIRONMENTS: Selected References** By Willem van Vliet. Chicago, Ill., Council of Planning
Librarians, 1982. 42 pp. $8 (paperback). From: 1313 E. 60th
St., Chicago, IL 60637. (CPL Bibliography No. 78)
A rather inclusive bibliography concerned with the environments of
children aged 6–16 (except for research on children in schools and day
care centers). Sections deal with urban and suburban environments;
housing environments; play and leisure environments; vandalism and
delinquent behavior; transportation and traffic; development and
health; perception and cognition; environmental change; environmental education and awareness; methods for research, design, and planning; and special publications and bibliographies. Within each section,
items (mostly books and articles) are arranged by author. Important
items are asterisked; significant bibliographic sources are given two
asterisks. Because this work updates an earlier work by the same
author (*Children and Their Environments* [E40]), it provides supplementary references to topics covered in the previous work.

7 / Mediaographies: Catalogs and Bibliographies

Bibliographies and catalogs containing significant numbers of audiovisuals relating to children or useful in some way to adults who work with children are annotated in this chapter. A few relevant organizations are also included. The chapter does not contain mediaographies of films to use with children, but some of the guides, such as Mary Sive's *Selecting Instructional Media* (F26), contain such data, while *Children's Media Market Place* (I17) lists directories of producers and sources of children's media. Guides to children's books that are designed for school libraries, like the *Elementary School Library Collection,* identify recommended audiovisuals, as do some bibliotherapeutic guides, such as *Aging Adult in Children's Books* and *Single Parent in Children's Books.* See the annotations in Chapter 16 for more details.

The mediaographies in this chapter can be supplemented by those bibliographies in Chapter 6 that include media as well as print materials and by the data bases in Chapter 11 that identify media, such as FAMILY RESOURCES DATABASE, BILINGUAL EDUCATION BIBLIOGRAPHIC ABSTRACTS, and PsycINFO. Some periodical indexes cover audiovisuals—for example, the *Chicago Psychoanalytic Literature Index* and the *Cumulative Index to Nursing and Allied Health Literature* include films. Parent education materials in Chapter 17, such as the *Healthy Mothers Coalition Directory of Educational Materials,* can be good guides to media on parenting, prenatal health, and similar topics. Many organizations cited as nonprint sources in Chapters 12 and 13 produce, collect, or prepare their own bibliographies of films and other audiovisuals.

Audiovisuals for topics relating to health are fairly easy to locate. The *Cumulative Index to Nursing and Allied Health Literature* (G13) and its bimonthly issues have appendixes that list audiovisual reviews. The AVLINE on-line catalog of the National Library of Medicine also identifies audiovisuals in health-related fields, such as pediatrics, medicine, nursing, nutrition, psychology, and patient education, as does the HEALTH AUDIOVISUAL ON-LINE CATALOG (HAVC) of the Basic Medical Sciences Library, College of Medicine, Northeastern Ohio Universities, Rootstown, OH 44272. Some 12,000 items are accessible through AVLINE, and HAVC has approximately 5,000 records of allied health, psychology, medical, and nursing materials. Both of these use *Medical Subject Headings* (*MeSH*) as search terms. HAVC is available on-line, directly or through BRS, and has a microform version of its catalog available for $25/year. Access to AVLINE is described in the entry on MEDLARS (J30). Eutychia G. Londos has produced *AV Health: Current Publications of the United States Government* (Metuchen, N.J., Scarecrow, 1982, $17.50), essentially a catalog of audiovisual catalogs produced by federal agencies.

Some entries in this chapter identify specific appropriate materials, whereas others indicate sources. The latter tend to become out-of-date rapidly.

ORGANIZATIONS AND DATA BASES

Many of the organizations listed in Chapters 12 and 13 are sources of current information on audiovisuals on children or are active collectors, distributors, or organizers, as are the library organizations described in Chapter 16. Most advocacy organizations or organizations concerned with the well-being of children produce or distribute at least a few media items in their areas of concern. Some, like the March of Dimes, make many materials available at public and professional levels.

Although this chapter includes only a few media catalogs or film lists issued by organizations concerned with children, many groups produce or distribute films and other media. For example, the National Association for the Education of Young Children describes films previewed at its meetings in *A Festival of Films,* and the Information Center on Children's Cultures has slides, films, filmstrips, recordings, and other materials on children's cultures worldwide. I have tried to indicate such activities, collections, and productions through my citations and indexing.

This section includes two educational media data bases—essentially on-line catalogs—that produce print catalogs, and one organization for children that updates lists of films on children. The Child Development Film Archives of the University of Akron, Ohio is discussed in F13. Some other organizations that have significant collections or expertise are

1. The American Association for Counseling and Development (AACD), 5999 Stevenson Ave., Alexandria, VA 22304 distributes outstanding films and videotapes.
2. Boys Town's Communications and Public Services Division, Boys Town, NE 68010 has produced films suitable for teachers, parents, and counselors. Ask for its brochure.
3. Educational Film Library Association, 46 W. 61st St., New York, NY 10003—an exemplary reviewer of educational films with an outstanding *Manual on Film Evaluation;* expert in using films with children.
4. ERIC Clearinghouse on Information Resources, School of Education, Syracuse University, Syracuse, NY 13201 deals with information delivery through media, with helpful updating publications.
5. National Audio-Visual Association (NAVA), 3150 Spring St., Fairfax, VA 22031 is a good source for how-to information, as well as for information on funding for programs.
6. Unifilm, Inc., 419 Park Ave., S., New York, NY 10016 is a film library of Third World films, including children's films.

Selecting Materials for Instruction: Media and Curriculum (O66) discusses many more organizations with collections on childhood. Government agencies at many levels produce, collect, and distribute films, although films from federal agencies are no longer distributed as freely as they once were. Most of those appropriate for child workers in education are included in the NICEM (F2) and NICSEM/NIMIS (F3) data bases.

F1   **NATIONAL CHILDREN'S BUREAU** Information Service & Library, 8 Wakley St., London EC1V 7QE, England. (01) 378-9441

This organization, which last issued the *Index of Documentary Films About Children* in 1977, now distributes revised and updated entries through a series of inexpensive film lists (29 as of late 1983). The first list includes *Adolescence: General* (50 pence); *Education: General* (80 pence); *Ethnic Minorities and Race Relations* (50 pence); *Mental Handicap* (£1.00); *Physical Handicap* (£1.00); and *Child Development* (£1.00). Others will be issued.

F2   **NATIONAL INFORMATION CENTER FOR EDUCATIONAL MEDIA (NICEM)** P.O. Box 40130, Albuquerque, NM 87196. (800) 421-8711; in New Mexico, (505) 265-3591

A data base of some 350,000 items, from 1966 on, replaced biennially and covering nonprint educational media (broadly construed) in all subject areas and for all levels of education and instruction from preschool to postgraduate and professional. Includes training of teachers and other professionals. NICEM's data bank is used to issue and update a substantial series of indexes in paperback and microfiche formats. Most of these index materials by form (16mm film, 35mm filmstrips, educational slides, phonograph records, audiotapes, videotapes, 8mm motion picture cartridges, overhead transparencies, and so on); some, however, index by subject area. Indexes are comprehensive, but many users consider them oddly indexed and bibliographically sketchy. Mary Sive noted that the on-line files are not always current. Some 1984 titles and prices are *Index to 16mm Educational Films* (8th Edition: $240 [paper], $120 [microfiche]) and *Index to 35mm Educational Filmstrips* (8th Edition: $180 [paper], $90 [microfiche]).

The data base, like the indexes, can be searched by media type and grade level. Citations include producer and distributor, publication date, abstracts, subject heading code, and descriptors. Subject codes represent broad subject areas, such as social science, literature, and drama. Descriptors are single or multiword, such as urbanization or social processes. NICEM distributes the *NICEM Newsletter* and the *NICEM Subject Headings*.

NICEM is searchable as AVLINE through DIALOG, at approximately $70/hour on-line and $0.20 per record off-line.

F3   **NATIONAL INFORMATION CENTER FOR SPECIAL EDUCATION MATERIALS/NATIONAL INSTRUCTIONAL MATERIALS INFORMATION SYSTEM (NICSEM/ NIMIS)**   National Information Center for Educational Media, P.O. Box 40130, Albuquerque, NM 87196. (800) 421-8711; in New Mexico, (505) 265-3591

NICSEM/NIMIS contains approximately 40,000 records of instructional materials and objectives (including media and devices) developed from 1974 through 1980 for use with handicapped children and in special education. Although the bulk of the collection consists of instructional materials, it also includes assessment instruments, professional educational materials, materials for parents, media in all subject fields, and materials dealing with areas such as cognition, perceptual recognition, motor processes, guidance, and personal skills. Many of the materials are appropriate outside school situations.

NICSEM's printed access tools include *NICSEM Special Index Thesaurus, Special Education Index to Parent Materials, Special Education Index to In-Service Training Materials, Special Education Index to Assessment Materials, Family Life and Sex Education, Functional and Communication Skills,* and *Master Index of Special Education Materials.*

NICSEM as a data base is now a closed file.

CATALOGS AND BIBLIOGRAPHIES

F4   **AMERICAN FAMILY LIFE FILMS**   By Judith Trojan. Metuchen, N.J., Scarecrow, 1981. 425 pp. $25.

A major compendium of 2,096 short and feature-length documentaries and dramatic 16mm films covering the spectrum of family dynamics in America, compiled by a film reviewer who evaluates films for the Educational Film Library Association. The vast majority of the films annotated deal with American sensibilities and concerns up to 1978; a few specially selected Canadian films interpret Canada.

Basically two types of films are included: (1) short films and documentaries and (2) selected dramatic features (usually over 59 minutes). One entry, *The American Family,* included because of its outstanding value, is available only on videotape. Annotations are extensive but not evaluative—some are derived from the author's screening;

others are taken from producers' or distributors' catalogs. Films are
divided by type and then arranged alphabetically by title. There is an extensive subject index to topics that range from abortion to adolescence,
stepparenting, television, and values; most items are related to children. The whole collection should be highly valuable for social workers, family and guidance counselors, medical personnel, community
programmers, and librarians.

F5   **ANNOTATED LIST OF AUDIO-VISUAL LOAN MATERI-
ALS: C. Henry Kempe Center** Denver, Colo., C. Henry
Kempe National Center for the Prevention and Treatment of
Child Abuse and Neglect. Not dated, but updated occasionally.
18 pp. Free (paper). From: 1205 Oneida St., Denver, CO 80220.
A well-indexed listing of 99 well-chosen films, filmstrips, videocassettes, and slides, available for low-cost rental from the center. Indexes
are by audience (e.g., students, educators, community, lay therapists),
purpose (e.g., prevention, identification), and subject. Descriptions
cover format, length, and content.

F6   **AUDIOVISUAL RESOURCES IN FOOD AND NUTRI-
TION** 2nd Edition. Compiled by the National Agricultural
Library. Phoenix, Ariz., Oryx, 1984. 256 pp. $32.50 (paper-
back).
Replaces the *Audiovisual Guide to the Catalog of the Food and Nutrition
Information and Educational Materials Center,* formerly produced by the
U.S. Department of Agriculture. Contains annotated entries of audio-
visual materials received by the Food and Nutrition Information and
Educational Materials Center (FNIC), with subject, author, title, and
media indexes, as well as an introduction and an audiovisual glossary.
Relevant areas are child care, child development, child rearing, child
nutrition, and school food programs, in all kinds of media, for adults
and/or children. Since 1981, lending services for the materials listed
here have been limited to federal agencies and state health services.

F7   **CASSETTE TAPE CATALOGS** Hampton, Va., Child Care
Information Center, 1976– . Revised 1976 Edition. *1977 Adden-
dum. 1978/79 Unabridged Supplement. 1980/81 Unabridged Sup-
plement. 1982 Supplement.* Free. From: 532 Settlers Landing
Rd., P.O. Box 548, Hampton, VA 23669.
Staff of the Child Care Information Center, part of the American Child
Care Services, as a public service attend conferences and then record,

duplicate, and make available at cost tape recordings of conference speeches relating to work with children. These are compiled into free *Cassette Tape Catalogs,* arranged by conference, then described and cataloged. For most presentations, the catalog includes the name and credentials of the speaker, the title of the speech, a synopsis of its contents, the general subjects covered in the recording, and its length. Subjects range from administrative law to child care, foster parents, funding, group therapy, volunteers, and youth service—all major concerns of child care professionals.

As of June 1983, the center had recorded 2,565 presentations, available for only $3.50 per 90 minutes, plus $1.00 for each additional cassette (up to 90 minutes) in a presentation. The presentations are made more accessible through subject, speaker, title, and conference indexes.

F8   **CATALOG OF AUDIO-VISUAL MATERIALS** By Child Welfare League of America Informational Resource Services. New York, 1983 (updated occasionally). 14 pp. Free (paper). From: 67 Irving Pl., New York, NY 10003.

A catalog of the rental films, slide shows, and cassette tapes currently available from the Child Welfare League of America (CWL), perhaps 100 items altogether, selected by CWL's professional staff for content and suitability for educating child care staff, board members and community members, students, and special-interest groups. These cover all areas of child welfare, particularly adoption, foster care, work with unmarried parents, and residential treatment centers. Materials are arranged largely by subject and title. Annotations include media; length; content; possible uses; and, sometimes, source. All items can be rented from CWL, which occasionally sends additions to and alterations of its catalog.

F9   **CATALOG OF AUDIOVISUAL TEACHING PROGRAMS** 5th Edition. Compiled by Marcia Cox. Kansas City, Mo., University of Missouri–Kansas City (UMKC) School of Medicine, Office of Educational Resources, Audiovisual Library, 1980. $5. From: 2411 Holmes, Kansas City, MO 64108.

This edition lists more than 800 items available from the Audiovisual Library of the UMKC School of Medicine, arranged by topic. It includes videocassettes, slides, films, audiocassettes, overhead transparencies, and microfiche available free of charge to affiliated institutions and at a low cost to others.

F10　**CHILD ABUSE AND NEGLECT AUDIOVISUAL MATE-
RIALS**　Compiled by the National Center on Child Abuse and
Neglect (NCCAN). Washington, D.C., U.S. Government Printing Office, 1980. 93 pp. $5.50 (paperback). From: U.S. Govern-
ment Printing Office, Washington, DC 20402.

Includes information on 354 films, videotapes, slides, multimedia
packages, and other audiovisual materials on child abuse and neglect.
All materials included were reviewed by NCCAN and are described fully
and correlated well with other materials in the catalog. Items are arranged by media and, within a medium, by producer and accession
number. Items are indexed by subject, producer, and title. Unfortunately, the information given on availability is now incorrect, due to
changes in government policy. The catalog is still valuable for identifying and describing materials and can be updated through NCCAN's data
base of audiovisual materials.

F11　**EDUCATIONAL FILMS AND VIDEO: A RENTAL CATA-
LOG**　Ann Arbor, Mich., University of Michigan Media Re-
sources Center, 1983. Annual. Free. From: 400 Fourth St.,
Ann Arbor, MI 48109.

A comprehensive catalog of films available for rental by any individual
or institution in the United States. Contains many films on child
growth and development and on human behavior. Separate, smaller
catalogs, entitled *Child Growth and Development* and *Children's Stories,*
are available from the same source.

F12　**EDUCATION-FOR-HEALTH: THE SELECTIVE GUIDE**
(Audiovisuals and Publications for Health Promotion, Family
Life, and Mental Health) Edited by Alex Sareyan and Jack
Neher for the National Center for Health Education and the
Mental Health Materials Center. New York, National Center for
Health Education, 1983. 927 pp. $90. (Also distributed by Gale
Research Co., Book Tower, Detroit MI 48226.)

This two-section book is a collaborative effort of the National Center
for Health Education (the private-sector health education response to
the President's Committee on Health Education) and the Mental
Health Materials Center, which has 30 years' experience in evaluating
mental health materials. The first section reviews and evaluates 1,200
films and audiovisuals, and the second reviews and evaluates 1,000
publications. Materials included were selected from items previewed or
screened by more than 40 experts. Recommended items were then annotated for quality, content, and format, with suggestions for audience
and use. The reviews, which are excellent and particularly useful for

practitioners and professionals, were then rewritten and synthesized. Audiences, distributors, and costs are provided. Approximately one-fifth of the recommended materials are available at little or no cost.

Both parts are divided into nine sections: awareness for health, human growth and development, health and disabilities, care and treatment, emergencies and crisis intervention, community care and home care, environmental health, health careers, and program planning and design.

The section on human growth and development (which covers parenting, infancy, childhood, and adolescence) is probably the most pertinent, but all sections contain relevant items. For example, immunization is covered under awareness for health; family violence, incest, and first aid are covered under emergencies; and community care for the developmentally disabled is discussed under community care. The work includes alphabetic lists of titles, subject indexes, and practical articles that provide overviews and suggestions for creative, effective use of print and audiovisual materials.

F13   **FILM ARCHIVES ON CHILD DEVELOPMENT: THE IN-AUGURATION OF THE CHILD DEVELOPMENT ARCHIVES** By John A. Popplestone and Marion White McPherson. Washington, D.C., U.S. Department of Health, Education, and Welfare, Office of Human Development, 1978. $4.95. From: National Technical Information Service, 5285 Port Royal Rd., Springfield, VA 22161.

A report on some 4,000 films acquired by the Child Development Film Archives at the Bierce Library of the University of Akron (Akron, OH 44325; (216) 375-7285). Included are 2,048 films from Arnold Gesell of Yale University, 1,048 from the L. Joseph Store Collection, 264 from Margaret Mahler, and various others—all available for use on-site only.

The archives was established in 1976 as an adjunct to the Archives of the History of American Psychology to preserve these films and to make them available for research and teaching. Since many of the films were produced to deliver a strong visual image and many of the early behavioral studies provide data uncontaminated by experimenter bias, they are an invaluable resource for contemporary training and empirical research in child development. An inventory sheet for each film identifies the number, sex, age, ethnicity of the child or children, amount and nature of clothing, biopathology and psychopathology, milieu, purpose of the footage, whether sound is present, rating of visual and audio clarity, and many other details. The archives suggests that investigators telephone or write Bierce Library prior to visiting. A brochure and an inventory sheet are available on request. The archives is also described in ERIC's *Inauguration of the Child Development Archives: Final Report* (ED 188 577).

F14   **FILMOGRAPHY ON BEHAVIOR MODIFICATION, BEHAVIOR THERAPY, PROGRAMMED INSTRUCTION, LEARNING AND CONDITIONING** By Samuel Berkowitz. Columbia, Md., ABC's of Behavior Change, 1976. No pagination. Price not available.
Brief descriptions of films, videotapes, and slide programs, arranged by title. Omits dates and prices but includes length and sources. Most information comes from distributors' catalogs.

F15   **FILM REVIEWS IN PSYCHIATRY, PSYCHOLOGY AND MENTAL HEALTH** A Descriptive and Evaluative Listing of Educational and Instructional Films. Edited by Robert E. Froelich. Ann Arbor, Mich., Pierian, 1974. 142 pp. $16.95.
Includes detailed reviews, by a team from the American Psychological Association, of 123 films from 1962 on. Around half are related to children; for these, the work supplies helpful comments on contents and applications.

F16   **FILMS FOR EARLY CHILDHOOD: A Selected Annotated Bibliography** By Mariann Pezzella Winick. New York, Early Childhood Education Council of New York City, 1973. 124 pp. $3.50.
Items in this annotated mediaography of 400 films and film series for training early childhood education teachers are arranged by title under such categories as development, current trends, program planning, curriculum, parent education, teacher training, comparative education, children, and series and are rated from excellent to adequate on the basis of content; veracity; and aesthetic, sound, visual, and overall quality.

F17   **FILMS OF THE UNITED NATIONS FAMILY: 16MM FILM CATALOGUE, 1980–81** New York, United Nations, 1981. 119 pp. $5. From: United Nations Bookshop, United Nations, New York, NY 10017.
A catalog in French and English describing 600 films produced and distributed by United Nations organizations. Provides helpful film descriptions (including languages), a subject index, an index by agency, and

an agency directory. Many of the films are related to children, particularly those by UNICEF (United Nations Children's Fund), the Food and Agricultural Organization, and Unesco (United Nations Educational, Scientific and Cultural Organization). This is updated by the *United Nations Film and Video Catalogue: 1983,* available from United Nations, Department of Public Information, Radio and Visual Services Division, New York, NY 10017.

F18   **GUIDE TO AUDIOVISUAL RESOURCES FOR THE HEALTH CARE FIELD** Pittsburgh, Pa., Medical Media Publishers and American Hospital Publishing, 1981. $18. From: 4923 Centre Ave., Pittsburgh, PA 15213.
An ongoing guide to audiovisual resources for the health care field, prepared cooperatively with a subsidiary of the American Hospital Association. Audiovisuals, described by physical characteristics, contents, price, and audience level (on the basis of information supplied by producers and distributors), are arranged by subject. Some relevant areas are family and parent-child relations, mental health, pediatrics, pregnancy and childbirth, and safety. The *Guide* also includes information on new products, lending libraries and distributors, and other useful publications. A new edition (to be priced around $20 or $25) will be issued in 1985.

F19   **HUMAN SEXUALITY: METHODS AND MATERIALS FOR THE EDUCATION, FAMILY LIFE AND HEALTH PROFESSIONS** Vol. I: *An Annotated Guide to the Audiovisuals.* By Ronald S. Daniel. La Brea, Calif., Heuristicus, 1979. 507 pp. $35.00, plus $1.85 postage and handling.
Annotated listing of 3,100 audiovisuals arranged under 28 topics, with a subject index and charts that indicate target grade levels and audiences. Some relevant areas include gender-related materials (645 titles), medicine and health (616), pregnancy and birth (530), values and attitudes (401), adolescence and puberty (291), and sex education (95). The descriptions of the contents of the audiovisuals were gleaned from catalogs and brochures, newsletters, and reviews.

F20   **INDEX TO PSYCHOLOGY—Multimedia** 4th Edition. Albuquerque, N. Mex., National Information Center for Educational Media (NICEM), 1979. 862 pp. (Out of print, but widely available in libraries)
A comprehensive, although not current, directory of instructional materials at all levels from preschool to professional; includes 18,000

entries on psychology and related areas, such as counseling and guidance, sexual behavior, smoking, drugs and alcohol, and special education. A fairly high proportion of the items included are on the professional level; other titles may be useful with children. Typically, in these NICEM guides, unselected materials are arranged alphabetically by title and indexed (not too well) by subject. Items can also be searched in the NICEM data base. Descriptions include title, format, physical description, length, color, producer, distributor, year of release, grade level, and Library of Congress catalog number.

F21   **A LIST OF AUDIOVISUAL MATERIALS PRODUCED BY THE UNITED STATES GOVERNMENT FOR SOCIAL ISSUES** Washington, D.C., National Audiovisual Center, National Archives and Records Service, 1981. 24 pp. Free (paper). From: National Audiovisual Center, Washington, DC 20409.

One of a series of classified lists issued by the National Audiovisual Center. Topics include child abuse, family planning/sex education, human relations, mental health/psychology, and parenting. Other lists deal with alcohol and drug abuse and special education. Annotations include description, length, audience, and price for sales or rentals.

F22   **NICEM INDEX TO NONPRINT SPECIAL EDUCATION MATERIALS—Multimedia** (Professional Volume) Albuquerque, N. Mex., National Information Center for Educational Media, 1978. 244 pp. Books, $15; microfiche, $8.

Contains 5,192 titles relevant to the interests and needs of parents, teachers, and others working with handicapped children. Subject areas include guidance and counseling, health and safety, clinical psychology, developmental psychology, and social psychology. Similar in format to *Index to Psychology* (F20), this is one of a series of indexes to special education materials published by NICEM. Other volumes deal with materials for parents, materials for "learners," family life and sex education, and assessment materials.

F23   **PARENTING MATERIALS: An Evaluative Annotation of Audiovisuals for Effective Parenting** By Del Lawhon and Beth Dankert. Charleston, W.Va., Appalachia Education Laboratory, 1977. 195 pp. $5. From: P.O. Box 1348, Charleston, WV 25325.

Provides fairly detailed and clearly written summaries of 154 superior audiovisuals appropriate for parent education. The annotations provide format details, dates, sources, distributors, target audiences, and technical evaluations and are indexed by topic. The introduction indicates the criteria used for selection.

F24   **PCR: FILMS AND VIDEO IN THE BEHAVIORAL SCIENCES**   Edited by Lori A. Baldwin. University Park, Pennsylvania State University, Audiovisual Services, 1981. Biennial. 197 pp. Free. From: Pennsylvania State University, Audiovisual Services, University Park, PA 16802.

Contains brief but well-done annotations of 1,700 PCR (Psychological Cinema Register) films, arranged alphabetically by title. These are specialized films in the general areas of psychology, psychiatry, animal behavior, anthropology, and related behavioral sciences, selected primarily on the basis of scientific validity and their usefulness for research or university teaching. Includes many films concerned in some way with topics like child abuse, child development, behavior modification, communication, education, emotion, ethnography, family, learning, play, moral development, and single parents. Has a detailed subject index.

F25   **THE SCREEN IMAGE OF YOUTH: MOVIES ABOUT CHILDREN AND ADOLESCENTS**   By Ruth M. Goldstein and Edith Zornow. Metuchen, N.J., Scarecrow, 1980. 324 pp. $22.

A reference guide that provides insight to the ways youth has been presented on the screen in the last 50 years. The authors have identified 350 feature-length entertainment and documentary films dealing with children and have annotated these in terms of their treatment of the characters of children and adolescents. The annotations, ranging in length from 200–500 words, are readable and perceptive and succeed in capturing the essence of the films. Films are grouped in broad subject areas (such as growing pains, "finding" oneself, delinquency, and crime), supplemented by a title index, a bibliography, and a directory of film companies and distributors. The six-page preface is a thoughtful—if too short—introduction. This collection should be valuable not only to those interested in cultural mores and to students of film, but also to parents, teachers, librarians, guidance counselors, and other adults working with children.

F26   **SELECTING INSTRUCTIONAL MEDIA: A GUIDE TO AUDIOVISUAL AND OTHER MEDIA LISTS**   3rd Edition. By Mary Robinson Sive. Littleton, Colo., Libraries Unlimited, 1983. 330 pp. $22.50.

15-016   **They Need to Know: How to Teach Children About Death.** Audrey
                Gordon and Dennis Klass. Prentice-Hall. 1979. 274p. $10.95;
                $4.95pa.
Purpose: "Other Media" recommended for suggested objectives, pp. 142-209
Criteria: accuracy, relative absence of value statements
Grade level: all
Arrangement: by grade and objective (total 15)
Subjects: death education
Entries: appr. 50

     medium designation, running time, producer/distributor; contents note
        omitted: release date, physical description (FS), price
Indexes: none
Period covered: not known
Revision and updating:
Media represented: audio recordings, films, filmstrips, video recordings
Producers represented: various
Features: Arrangement by instructional objective is unique. Far more of the sug-
     gested resources are for reading, and teacher audiovisual resources are also
     noted.
Subject terms: death education

Figure 2   Mary R. Sive's *Selecting Instructional Media* contains detailed, structured annotations of print materials that lead to instructional media. This illustration is reprinted with the permission of the author.

A well-organized, descriptive annotated bibliography of nearly all extant catalogs and lists of instructional media. Arranged in three sections, it includes comprehensive lists, subject lists, and lists by types of
media, with an informative introduction to media selection. Although
it is intended primarily for teachers and media librarians in elementary
and secondary schools, it should be valuable for anyone selecting
media to use with children or child workers. Some of its relevant areas
are psychology and guidance, early childhood education, and health
and safety education, but it covers almost every area that is taught in
elementary or secondary schools. Entries provide bibliographic descriptions with address, purpose, grade level, subject, scope and numbers of
items in each list, general arrangement, special features, and means of
updating. Includes subject, media, instructional level, author, and title
indexes. A sample entry is shown in Figure 2.

8 / Indexing and Abstracting Publications

The indexing, abstracting, and announcement publications presented in this chapter have two major functions: They are means of keeping abreast of the mass of current literature (in that way, resembling the recurring bibliographies in Chapter 5) and are major tools for retrospective searches. Many of these are now accessible on-line. Whether they are used in printed or computer form, the initial problem is to select the right indexes and then to obtain appropriate materials located through these indexes. In general, for those who are able to browse, the printed format is superior for keeping current; the computer format, however, hastens subject searches considerably. The printed indexes and thesauri, such as those listed in Chapter 2, can be used to determine approaches and terminology appropriate for particular indexes.

In some subject areas or academic disciplines, individuals looking for current materials or searching the literature need to locate only one or two indexes. Unfortunately for those of us interested in children, only four—at most—of the hundreds of indexing, abstracting, and current-awareness tools available concentrate on children per se. Many more index or abstract some materials on children within the context of academic disciplines or broad subject/interest areas, although the materials they index or abstract might not be easy to locate or summarize. Furthermore, since children permeate our culture, it is hard to anticipate which abstracting or indexing journals might be used.

Those searching for current references on children and the media, for example, would probably do well to search *Communications Abstracts* or *Abstracts of Popular Culture.*

Because abstract journals and indexes are important tools, and since adults can locate significant childhood information sources through many indexes in many fields and libraries, I have annotated only those tools that seemed most cogent. Others are listed in *Ulrich's International Periodical Directory* under abstracting and indexing services or are described in *Periodical Indexes in the Social Sciences* (by Lois Harzfield, Metuchen, N.J., Scarecrow, 1978) and in *Abstracting and Indexing Services Directory* (edited by John Schmittroth, Jr., Detroit, Gale Research Co., 1982–1983, 3 vols.).

Beyond subject coverage, other criteria for choosing particular indexes are ease of use, presence of abstracts, types of materials covered, and time span covered. The section of this chapter on subject approaches includes some additional indexes and abstract journals that are not annotated here but that occasionally may be useful.

SUBJECT APPROACHES

Usually, the title of an abstracting or indexing publication indicates its subject. Subject searches involving children, however, tend to be multidisciplinary. Significant materials on topics like adoption or child abuse can be found in legal, medical, psychological, popular, public affairs, and education publications.

ANTHROPOLOGY: *Abstracts in Anthropology* is a good source for cross-cultural studies; general social sciences and popular publications also contain many titles.

CHILDREN: *Child Development Abstracts and Bibliography* and *PsycSCAN: Developmental Psychology* both deal with child development. *Kindex* covers children and the law, and *Exceptional Child Education Resources* deals with exceptional children. (*PsycSCAN: LD/MR* covers somewhat the same ground—learning disabilities and mental retardation—but includes adults as well.) *Research Relating to Children* reported on research from 1950 to 1979. The journals *Courrier* and *International Child Welfare Review Supplement,* annotated in Chapter 9, also serve as abstract journals; both have a very wide scope.

CURRENT EVENTS: Popular and alternate indexes cover current events, as do the newsletters discussed in Chapter 9. Newspaper indexes include *The New York Times Index,* which is included here. Others are *The* [London] *Times Index,* the *Newspaper Index,* and an interesting *NewsBank* service that combines a subject index to current events with microfiched clippings arranged by subject. The NEW YORK TIMES INFORMATION SERVICE, the NATIONAL NEWSPAPER INDEX, and other current events data bases are discussed in Chapter 11.

EDUCATION: Three indexes that cover the closely related field of education (broadly construed) are *Current Index to Journals in Education (CIJE), Education Index,* and *Resources in Education;* all contain many articles on children. *Bulletin Signalétique: Sciences de l'Éducation* is a European equivalent. The *British Education Index* and the *Canadian Education Index* cover the United Kingdom (with some continental reporting) and Canada, respectively, and deal with childhood as well as education. The *British Education Index,* for example, has headings for such topics as asthmatic children, babies, bereaved children, birth order, bullies, play groups, and welfare services for children. *A Guide to Sources of Educational Information* (B7) contains a chapter on education abstracts and indexes. Many materials on education can be located in indexes to public affairs and popular publications.

EXCEPTIONAL CHILDREN: Major sources for information on this topic are *Exceptional Child Education Resources, dsh Abstracts,* and *Rehabilitation Literature.* General education indexes include many materials, as do psychological indexes, especially *PsycSCAN: LD/MR.* (*Mental Retardation and Developmental Disability Abstracts* covered the field for many years; *PsycSCAN: LD/MR* offers coverage from 1982.)

FAMILY PLANNING/POPULATION: *Current Literature on Family Planning* and *Population Index* are two indexes annotated here. Public affairs, social science, and medical abstracts and indexes are also relevant.

FAMILY STUDIES: *Inventory of Marriage and Family Literature* and *Sage Family Studies Abstracts,* both issued by Sage, inventory and abstract family studies. Information on family studies can also be found in psychological, sociological, social science, and social welfare publications. The FAMILY RESOURCES DATABASE, which covers this field thoroughly, is discussed in Chapter 11.

HUMANITIES: Sources on the humanities include *American Humanities Index* and *Humanities Index.* There is also the *Arts and Humanities Citation Index,* which covers philosophy, psychology, psychohistory, religion, art, music, and language. From certain perspectives, the *Bibliography of Bioethics* is a humanistic publication.

LANGUAGE: Indexes listed here include *Language and Behavior Abstracts, Language Teaching,* and *Reading Abstracts.* The Modern Language Association's *MLA International Bibliography of Books and Articles on the Modern Languages and Literature* also includes materials on child language acquisition, memory, cognition, and neurology.

LAW AND JUSTICE: *Kindex* indexes only materials that deal with law and children. *Criminal Justice Abstracts* is concerned with law and justice. *CIS/Index* and *Federal Index* deal with laws as they are created. *Index to Foreign Legal Periodicals* and *Index to Legal Periodicals* are easier to locate than *Kindex.* LEGAL RESOURCE INDEX, which is very comprehensive, is treated as a data base in Chapter 11. Popular articles on law are apt to appear anywhere. Many articles can be located through medical, education, popular, and public affairs indexes.

MEDICINE, NURSING, AND HEALTH: A variety of indexes can be searched for materials that relate children and health, including *Cumulative Index to Nursing and Allied Health Literature, Exceptional Child Education Resources, FAMLI Medicine Literature Index, Bibliography of Bioethics, Index Medicus* (in various manifestations), and *International Nursing Index.* Other possibilities are *Excerpta Medica,* which has substantial coverage of pediatrics; a card index to pediatrics offered by the Medical Information Systems of Indianapolis; *Combined Cumulative Index to Pediatrics* (Buffalo, N.Y., Numarc Book Corp.), which indexes six major pediatric journals; and *Biological Abstracts* and its offshoots. *Physical Education Index,* for physical education and recreation instructors, covers growth and development, anthropometry, and perceptual and motor skills. *Rehabilitation Literature* deals with rehabilitation. School health can be followed through education indexes, and indexes to popular publications list medical reports written for parents and citizens.

MENTAL HEALTH: Popular, nursing, and psychological indexes cover mental health per se, whereas public affairs and social services indexes cover policy considerations. MENTAL HEALTH ABSTRACTS, a data base founded on the holdings of the National Institute of Mental Health, is discussed in Chapter 11. Education indexes also include some materials on child mental health.

NUTRITION AND NUTRITION EDUCATION: AGRICOLA (J13) and *Nutrition Abstracts and Reviews* deal specifically with nutrition. Other sources are education, medical and nursing, and popular indexes. Social science and public affairs indexes cover social aspects such as community programs and parental poverty.

POPULAR PUBLICATIONS: Nonscholarly materials can be located in *Abstracts of Popular Culture, Access, Alternative Press Index, The New York Times Index*, and the *Readers' Guide to Periodical Literature*. The *Magazine Index* is annotated in Chapter 11. *The Catholic Periodical and Literature Index* treats popular subjects from a Catholic perspective.

PSYCHOLOGY: A substantial portion of the *Chicago Psychoanalytic Literature Index* deals with articles on children; *Psychological Abstracts* is more comprehensive but has a smaller proportion of such articles. The *PsycSCAN* publications provide inexpensive coverage of developmental and learning disabilities. *Mental Retardation and Developmental Disability Abstracts* covered this area thoroughly for 40 years.

PUBLIC AFFAIRS: *CIS/Index* and the *P.A.I.S.* (Public Affairs Information Service) publications provide excellent coverage of Congress and public affairs. The *Monthly Catalog* (D36) announces government publications, and the *Federal Index* indexes some of them. *The New York Times Index* and other news indexes deal with public affairs, as do the indexes of popular or alternative publications. Three Sage abstract journals, not listed in this book, provide good abstracts on narrower topics: *Sage Public Administration Abstracts, Human Resources Abstracts,* and *Sage Urban Studies Abstracts.* All include a few abstracts on children. *Social Welfare, Planning/Policy, and Development (SOPODA)* applies sociology to public policy. *Refugee Abstracts* covers child refugees, and *Work Related Abstracts* covers child labor.

RELIGION AND ETHICS: *Bibliography of Bioethics* addresses ethical issues with biological overtones. *The Catholic Periodical and Literature Index* provides a Christian approach to significant topics in Catholic-authored or Catholic-interest books and periodicals. Ethical topics can appear anywhere and would most likely be covered by humanities or popular indexes.

SOCIAL SCIENCES: Two main indexes discussed in this chapter are the *Social Sciences Index* and the *Social Sciences Citation Index*. Specialized indexes not included here are *Abstracts in Anthropology* and Tavistock's *International Bibliography of the Social Sciences*. *Current Contents: Social and Behavioral Sciences* is the tool for keeping current. Some consider *P.A.I.S.* publications to be oriented to the social sciences.

SOCIAL SERVICES/SOCIAL WELFARE: Relevant indexes include *Journal of Human Services Abstracts; Refugee Abstracts; Rehabilitation Literature; Social Service Abstracts; Social Welfare, Planning/Policy, and Development (SOPODA),* and *Social Work Research & Abstracts.* Public affairs indexes, general indexes, and medical indexes also deal with this field.

SOCIOLOGY: *Sociological Abstracts* is the major abstracting journal. *The Combined Retrospective Index to Journals in Sociology* covers the years 1895–1974.

FORMATS

There are four common formats in these index and abstract publications. Presumably, most users are familiar with typical periodical indexes (e.g., the *Readers' Guide to Periodical Literature*), which reduce individual periodical articles, books, or pamphlets to bibliographic entries that can be located through detailed subject indexing.

Abstract journals supply bibliographic entries and summaries of the essential contents of selected or inclusive original documents, usually arrange these numerically, and provide access through supplementary author and subject and/or keyword indexes.

If abstract journals are extensive, they tend to be less easy to search manually than the aforementioned indexes, although the abstracts themselves can be very valuable. Some abstract journals (such as *Resources in Education*) abstract and announce affiliated microfiche publications of some or most items cited.

Citation indexes are probably the most difficult to use but are gaining importance in this era of computerized data retrieval. They allow users to search by author, cited authors, cited references, subject, and organization.

Announcement services, such as the *Current Contents* series, provide tables of contents and some minimal indexes for journals covered. The *Monthly Catalog* (D36) could also be considered an announcement publication.

ACCESS TO INDEXED PUBLICATIONS

Fortunately, most of the sources in this chapter provide some means for readers to acquire the items announced, indexed, or abstracted. Periodical indexes typically include publishers' addresses and price information at least once a year. Some abstract journals are coordinated with microfiche collections of documents. University Microfilms International (UMI), which produces *Dissertation Abstracts International,* provides microform or paper copies of dissertations and also supplies microform or paper copies of periodicals and periodical articles. It has recently launched a UMI Article Clearinghouse that provides articles from thousands of journals. *Current Contents* has a tear sheet service for the articles it announces and also supplies authors' addresses.

Libraries that issue or sponsor indexes may offer copy service or backup interlibrary loans for materials included in their indexes. *P.A.I.S.* offers this service through the New York Public Library. The *Chicago Psychoanalytic Literature Index, FAMLI,* and the *Cumulative Index to Nursing and Allied Health Literature* all offer such backup through their sponsoring libraries. Some vendors of computer data bases will order cited documents for their customers on a cost-plus basis.

Other indexing journals, like the *Readers' Guide to Periodical Literature* and *Education Index,* consider availability of publications as one criterion for deciding which publications to index.

TIME SPANS

For comparative or historical purposes, it is sometimes very worthwhile to locate an index with a long time span. The *Readers' Guide* goes back to 1900, the *P.A.I.S. Bulletin* to 1915, *Psychological Abstracts* to 1927, and the *Humanities Index* and the *Social Sciences Index* to 1907. *The Combined Retrospective Index to Journals in Sociology* covers 1895 to 1974. The starting dates of indexes—noted in the following citations—should be considered when choosing an index.

Popular indexes, *P.A.I.S.,* and Wilson indexes tend to be more current than abstract journals. Some (but not all) of the computer data bases in Chapter 11 are quite current; data base versions are more current than print versions.

G1   **ABC POL SCI, A BIBLIOGRAPHY OF CONTENTS: POLITICAL SCIENCE AND GOVERNMENT** Edited by Lloyd W. Garrison. Santa Barbara, Calif., ABC–Clio Press, 1969- . Five issues/year with annual index. Sold on a service basis. From: Riviera Campus, 2040 A.P.S., Box 4397, Santa Barbara, CA 93103.

Reproduces and indexes, by author and subject, the tables of contents of approximately 300 journals in political science, government, and the related disciplines of law, sociology, and economics. It covers some 10,000 articles per year, 5–10 percent of which are on children and youth. These articles can be found through the issue or annual indexes under subjects like children, child labor, family, aid to families with dependent children, UNICEF, and the like.

G2   **ALTERNATIVE PRESS INDEX: AN INDEX TO ALTERNATIVE AND RADICAL PUBLICATIONS** Edited by Peggy D'Adamo. Baltimore, Md., Alternative Press Center, 1969- . Quarterly. Individuals, high schools, and movement

groups, $25/year; libraries and institutions, $90/year. Paper. From: P.O. Box 7229, Baltimore, MD 21218.
A subject index of approximately 175 English-language left-of-center periodicals, newsletters, and scholarly journals from the United States, Canada, and the United Kingdom that cover such topics as alternative energy, radical education, the peace movement, feminism, gay rights, third world, the black movement, native Americans, and the like. The editor estimates that some 75 articles covered in each issue are on child-related topics like child abuse, child care centers, child custody, child health, child labor, child molesting, and child rearing. Around 25 articles are on related topics such as parent-child relations, juvenile delinquency, infant formulas, native American children, orphans, and third-world children. Perhaps a total of 400 articles per year are covered. Many of these—especially materials from lesbian, feminist, and third-world perspectives—are not apt to appear in any other index. Altogether, this index provides wide coverage, from scholarly articles on the theory of mothering to news-oriented articles on day care funding.

G3   **AMERICA: HISTORY AND LIFE (AHL)**   Edited by Gail
      A. Schlachter. Santa Barbara, Calif., ABC–Clio Press, 1964– .
      Four parts, issued at various intervals. Sold on a service basis.
      From: Riviera Campus, 2040 A.P.S., Box 4397, Santa Barbara,
      CA 93103.
Part A: *Article Abstracts and Citations,* which scans approximately 2,000 periodicals from 90 countries for articles on Canadian and American history and culture, is issued three times a year and cumulated in Part D.
    Part B: *Index to Book Reviews* scans 130 periodical titles and is issued twice a year. It covers around 1,750 titles per issue.
    Part C: *American History Bibliography* is the annual bibliography of periodical articles, books, and dissertations. It includes citations from Parts A and B, as well as relevant dissertations from *Dissertation Abstracts International.*
    Part D: *Annual Index* is a complex subject index to Parts A, B, and C, with additional author, book title, and book reviewer indexes.
    Parts A, B, and C are searchable on-line, as is a similar index, *Historical Abstracts,* which covers the history of the rest of the world.

G4   **AMERICAN HUMANITIES INDEX (AHI)**   Troy, N.Y.,
      Whitson Publishing Co., 1975– . Quarterly. $160/year. From:
      P.O. Box 958, Troy, NY 12181.

An author and subject index to approximately 300 creative, critical, and scholarly publications in the arts and humanities that are indexed in obscure indexing services or not at all. It includes occasional articles on children and the arts (literature, drama, poetry) that cannot be found elsewhere.

G5   **BIBLIOGRAPHY OF BIOETHICS**   Edited by LeRoy Walters. Washington, D.C., Georgetown University, Kennedy Institute of Ethics, Center for Bioethics, 1975- . Annual. $55/year. From: Free Press, 100B Brown St., Riverside, NJ 08370.

Annual bibliography of international literature dealing with value questions in the biomedical and behavioral fields—an interdisciplinary area of concern that has developed considerably since the 1970s, with literature appearing in widely scattered sources. This index is the product of a retrieval system designed to identify the central issues in bioethics, to develop an appropriate indexing language, and to provide comprehensive cross-disciplinary coverage of English-language materials stemming from such fields as medicine, law, religion, anthropology, and social sciences. Some issues related to children include abortion, informed consent, prolongation of life, research on children, care of the dying child, contraception, and child suicide, although these are only a small part of the whole. The 1981 edition included 65 articles on infants and newborns, 11 on adolescents, and 78 on children and minors (of approximately 2,000 items added during the year). The file can be searched on-line as BIOETHICSLINE, which is part of the MEDLARS system of the National Library of Medicine.

G6   **BULLETIN SIGNALÉTIQUE, 520: SCIENCES DE L'ÉDUCATION**   Paris, Centre National de la Recherche Scientifique, Centre de Documentation Sciences Humaines, 1947- . Quarterly. 340 French francs/year. From: 54 Boulevard Raspail, 72560 Paris, Cedex, France.

A classified index to educational materials (broadly viewed) that provides one point of access to European journals dealing with children and education. Around 6,000 items are included yearly. An English-language subject index makes these items more accessible to American users.

G7   **BUSINESS PERIODICALS INDEX (BPI)**   Edited by Betty Jane Third. Bronx, N.Y., H. W. Wilson, 1958- . Monthly, except August. Sold on a service basis.

Cumulative subject index to 278 English-language business periodicals dealing with such topics as communications, economics, marketing, finance, and labor, selected by subscriber vote from a list of suggested periodicals. As such, it provides coverage for interactions between children and the business world. The January 1983 issue, for instance, noted 12 articles on child care centers, 3 on child labor, 7 under children's literature, 2 under children's reading, and 1 each on child pornography, children of executives, and children's allowances. There were six subdivisions under "children," with five cross-references to topics like black children and runaways.

G8   **CHICAGO PSYCHOANALYTIC LITERATURE INDEX** Edited by Glenn Miller. Chicago, Ill., Institute for Psychoanalysis, 1970– . Quarterly, with annual cumulation. Students, $30/year; professionals, $75/year; libraries, $100/year. From: 180 N. Michigan Ave., Chicago, IL 60601.

A less-expensive alternative to *Psychological Abstracts,* based on the acquisitions of the library of the Institute for Psychoanalysis in the subject areas of psychiatry, psychoanalysis, psychosomatic medicine, psychology, and related areas in behavioral and social sciences. Covers approximately 150 journals (mostly English language) and some 1,000 reports, 200 proceedings, and 400 books each year. The main part of the index is arranged by subject, followed by a separate author index. Many of the indexed items relate to children. The index is maintained on magnetic tape and is being made available on-line. The library can supply copies of items cited.

G9   **CHILD DEVELOPMENT ABSTRACTS AND BIBLIOG- RAPHY**   Edited by Hoben Thomas for the Society for Research in Child Development. Chicago, Ill., University of Chicago Press, 1927– . 3 issues/year. $28/year. From: P.O. Box 37005, Chicago, IL 60637.

One of the very few abstract journals devoted exclusively to children, published since 1927 by the Society for Research in Child Development. Currently a two-part journal that includes abstracts of research literature selected from some 275 English- and foreign-language journals, as well as reviews of books and technical reports dealing in some way with the growth and development of children. Abstracts are classified into six major categories: biology-health-medicine; cognition-learning-perception; social-psychological-cultural-personality studies; educational processes; psychiatry-clinical psychology; and history-theory-methodology. The format is good, and citations are complete. Article summaries are clear and concise, although unevaluative, and include current addresses for some authors.

The book review section includes signed book reviews, some quite lengthy, and lists of books received but not reviewed—up to 100 titles in some issues. Every few issues, recent reference books are handily grouped together in "The Reference Shelf." All book notices provide the intent of the books as well as the reviewers' evaluations.

Each issue contains author and detailed subject indexes and lists of periodicals abstracted in that issue. All of these are cumulated annually in the October–December issue. There are approximately 1,300 selected entries in each volume.

G10 **CIS/INDEX** Edited by Bernard Hayden. Bethesda, Md., Congressional Information Service (CIS), 1970– . Monthly, with annual cumulation. Rates vary. From: 4520 East-West Highway, Bethesda, MD 20814.

Abstracts and indexes all of the publications (hearings, reports, prints, documents, and special publications) of the committees of Congress. Each year, CIS provides monthly abstracts and an annual cumulation for approximately 750,000 pages (or 4,400 titles) of new material; the percentage dealing with children and youth per se varies widely from administration to administration and from Congress to Congress and may increase or be easier to locate now that we have overview committees dealing with children. CIS estimates that, on the average, materials dealing with child welfare, preschool education, elementary and secondary education, adoption, juvenile delinquency, drugs and youth, toys, infant mortality, and related topics account for 10 percent of its coverage. For this 10 percent, CIS is a most valuable source. Informative abstracts (that may summarize testimony or note supplementary materials) are arranged by document type under issuing committee and are cited and indexed so fully that they can be located in many ways (through Library of Congress catalog numbers, document classification numbers, committee chairmen, and so on). Full-text microfiche reproductions of all publications covered by the *CIS/Index* are available in complete or selective files, as well as individually on demand. The CIS data base is fully searchable on-line.

G11 **COMBINED RETROSPECTIVE INDEX TO JOURNALS IN SOCIOLOGY, 1895–1974** With an Introduction and User's Guide. By Evan I. Farber. Washington, D.C., Carrollton Press, 1978. 6 Vols. $615. From: Research Publications, Inc.,

Reference Dept., 12 Lunar Dr., Drawer AB, Woodbridge, CT 06525.

This comprehensive index is part of a larger series of retrospective indexes in the social sciences intended to enable users to cover historical materials without searching volume after volume. This concept of indexing provides one-line keyword citations arranged chronologically under subject categories, with journal titles reduced to a code number. Volume 2, for example, covers the family (as an institution) with sections on childhood, adoption, and adolescence, among others, with keyword citations under these. The sociology set provides references to articles in 129 publications, with an author index in the final volume. Other sets in this series cover political science in 8 volumes and history in 11, with references to 928 journals overall.

G12 **CRIMINAL JUSTICE ABSTRACTS** National Council on Crime and Delinquency. Hackensack, N.J., 1970– . Quarterly. $50/year in the United States and Canada; $55/year foreign; single issues, $13.

Each issue of *Criminal Justice Abstracts* contains in-depth abstracts of current literature, worldwide in scope, as well as a comprehensive review article on a specific topic. Typically, detailed abstracts cover crime and the offender, law enforcement and the police, law and the courts, correction, and related social issues, with a cumulative subject index in the December issue. There are usually up to 10 articles per issue under the category "Juvenile Delinquency and the Delinquent," but the December 1981 issue had at least 100 entries under terms starting with "child," "children," and "juvenile." Abstracts are informative, comprehensive, and easy to understand.

G13 **CUMULATIVE INDEX TO NURSING AND ALLIED HEALTH LITERATURE (CINAHL)** Edited by DeLauna Lockwood. Glendale, Calif., Glendale Adventist Medical Center, 1961– . Bimonthly, with annual cumulation. $115/year. From: P.O. Box 871, Glendale, CA 91209.

A comprehensive and authoritative index designed originally for nurses and allied health practitioners, but also useful to those interested in following health care issues, consumer health, and patient education materials. It regularly indexes 300 allied health, nursing, and ancillary journals, as well as government publications of health agencies, and selectively covers such popular publications as *Psychology Today* and *Parents* and pertinent articles from some 2,600 biomedical journals indexed in *Index Medicus*. The bimonthly issues, entitled *Nursing and*

Allied Health Index, are cumulated each year into the *Cumulative Index.* Issues contain two sections, subject and author. The index is easy to use and highly legible, with a good format and many cross-references. It is a good source for articles on topics relating to childhood illness and hospitalization. An appendix indexes audiovisual materials, book reviews, and pamphlets. Copies of articles not available through local sources can be obtained through *CINAHL's* depository library, which issues an occasional newsletter for subscribers. *CINAHL* became available on-line in 1983.

G14 **CURRENT CONTENTS: SOCIAL AND BEHAVIORAL SCIENCES (CC/S&BS)** Philadelphia, Institute for Scientific Information, 1969– . Weekly. $210/year in the United States; $245/year, Mideast, Europe, and Americas; $280/year elsewhere. From: 3501 Market St., University City Science Center, Philadelphia, PA 19104.

A weekly current-awareness service that reproduces and indexes the tables of contents from more than 1,300 international journals and 800 multiauthored books in the social and behavioral sciences. Table of contents reproductions are arranged in broad sections, such as social issues and philosophy, law, psychology, sociology and anthropology, education, economics and business, linguistics, management, rehabilitation and special education, political science, and history. Each issue includes an alphabetic list of journals covered in that issue and an author index/directory (first author only) complete with addresses. A computer-produced index lists articles by significant words from journal titles; another section announces new technical books, proceedings, and symposia with full bibliographic information and order coupons. A journal index, cumulated every four months, indicates where particular title pages can be found. A directory of publishers is included with each issue, and a complete list of journals is issued twice a year.

Current Contents now provides occasional introductory essays with literature summaries by Eugene Garfield. Articles covered can be obtained through ISI's Original Article Tear Sheet Service (OATS). Similar *Current Contents* are issued for other fields.

G15 **CURRENT INDEX TO JOURNALS IN EDUCATION (CIJE)** Edited by Susan Slesinger. Phoenix, Ariz., Oryx, 1979– . (Published by Macmillan, 1969–February 1979). Monthly. $125/year; $136 foreign.

An index sponsored by the National Institute of Education that abstracts and indexes articles from approximately 760 social and behavioral education-related journals (around 1,400 articles per month), including approximately 100 foreign journals and some articles from journals not primarily concerned with education. The selection and indexing is performed at 16 ERIC clearinghouses. Items are assigned EJ (educational journal) numbers under 16 broad topics that represent the scope of these clearinghouses. Each citation has a one- or two-sentence resume and is indexed by terms chosen from the 5,100 index terms in the *Thesaurus of ERIC Descriptors,* as well as by author. This arrangement is more convenient for browsing and computer searches than for subject and author searches, since the user must go back and forth from subject terms or author entries to locate the EJ numbers in the main entry section. Since its cumulative indexes are published only twice a year and often arrive late, manual searching of *CIJE* late in the year can be a slow, time-consuming process.

Other features are an alphabetic journal/contents index and a source/journals index that lists the names, addresses, and prices of periodicals. To facilitate access to indexed journals that might be difficult to locate, ERIC has arranged with University Microfilms International to provide reprints of most articles indexed in *CIJE;* a three-day turnaround is typical.

Essentially, this is the journal component of the ERIC data base and is searchable on-line through many state and local school systems and commercial vendors.

G16   **CURRENT LITERATURE IN FAMILY PLANNING**
       Edited by Gloria A. Roberts. New York, Planned Parenthood Federation of America, 1966– . Monthly. $25/year. From: 810 Seventh Ave., New York, NY 10019.

A monthly classified publication that annotates books and articles in the field of family planning. It is based largely on the acquisitions of the Katherine Dexter McCormick Library of the Planned Parenthood Federation, although additional articles are located through *Current Contents* and other sources. The index, which contains approximately 50 items per issue, is divided into two parts: books and articles. It includes complete citations, excellent annotations, prices, publishers' addresses for books, and the library call number. An order form on the last page can be used for ordering copies or reprints of articles at $0.10 per page. The library accesses approximately 1,500 items per year, of which perhaps 15 percent are concerned with childhood and adolescence—mostly on reproductive health and freedom, human sexuality, sex education, and related statistics. For these specialized areas, this index offers high-quality annotations of materials not readily available from other sources. *Adolescent Sexuality: Special Subject Bibliography* (1982, $2) was compiled from *Current Literature* articles relating to adolescent sexuality, legal rights, and medical care.

G17 **DISSERTATION ABSTRACTS INTERNATIONAL (DAI)** (Formerly *Dissertation Abstracts.*) A–The Humanities and Social Sciences. Ann Arbor, Mich., University Microfilms International, 1938– . Monthly. $140/year.

Abstracts and indexes doctoral dissertations submitted to University Microfilms International by more than 380 institutions, mostly American, but some foreign. Arranged by broad academic disciplines rather than subject, with annual subject and author indexes. Each entry has a 600-word abstract, written by the doctoral candidate, and includes title, author, institution, adviser, number of pages, and ordering information for microform or photocopies. A variety of cumulated retrospective indexes can be used to search the data base as far back as 1861. DATRIX is a computerized search service to this data base; it is also available online through DIALOG and others.

G18 **dsh ABSTRACTS** Edited by Ernest J. Moncada. Washington, D.C., Deafness, Speech and Hearing Publications, 1960– . Quarterly. $24/year; $27/year foreign; students, $10/year. From: American Speech-Language-Hearing Association, 10801 Rockville Pike, Rockville, MD 20852.

An abstract quarterly produced as a joint venture of Gallaudet College and the American Speech-Language-Hearing Association that contains brief noncritical summaries of current scientific, technical, and educational literature on deafness, speech, and hearing from books, reports, proceedings, and approximately 500 international periodicals published in all major languages. Abstracts—around 500 per issue—are prepared by experts in speech and hearing and arranged by classified outline, with author and subject indexes. A list of periodical sources appears annually in the October issue. The emphasis is on research, although some practical articles are included. There are numerous citations on topics like speech and language development, speech therapy, stuttering, cleft palate, etiology of hearing disorders, and other subjects that contain frequent entries on children.

G19 **EDUCATION INDEX** Edited by Marylouise Hewitt. Bronx, N.Y., H. W. Wilson, 1929– . 10 issues/year, including cumulations and annual volume. Prices vary. Sold on a service basis.

The traditional subject and author index to educational periodical literature, issued monthly except in July and August, with frequent cumulations. Indexes around 320 of the better known English-language periodicals, selected by subscriber vote for subject balance and reference value. In addition to periodicals, *Education Index* also handles proceedings, yearbooks, monographs, and some U.S. government publications. Subjects include education and curricula in all subject areas (preschool to adult), school administration and finance, counseling and guidance, comparative and international education, special education, and rehabilitation. Entries are arranged in one alphabetic index that combines authors and subject terms, with fewer and more logical indexing terms than *CIJE* (G15). One convenient feature is the separate book review section, which indexes reviews by individual authors and titles. Each issue contains a list of periodical sources with publisher names and addresses and subscription information.

G20 **EXCEPTIONAL CHILD EDUCATION RESOURCES (ECER)** (Formerly *Exceptional Child Education Abstracts.*) Edited by June B. Jordan. Reston, Va., The Council for Exceptional Children (CEC), 1969– . Quarterly. Individuals, $35/year; institutions, $75/year. From: 1920 Association Dr., Reston, VA 22091.

An indispensable tool for persons involved with exceptional children that provides comprehensive abstract coverage of important publications in all aspects of special education—mental retardation; physical and learning disabilities; communication disorders; and homebound, hospitalized, and gifted children. Prepared by a long-standing membership organization that is now an ERIC clearinghouse. Scans around 300 periodical titles for articles and includes approximately 2,200 other items: dissertations, books and monographs, research reports, administrative surveys and guidelines, teachers' activity manuals, texts for professionals and beginning students, and nonprint media. Abstracts in the main section are arranged by accession number with computer-generated author, subject, and title indexes, as well as a source list of CEC periodicals. Cumulated annually. Each issue includes a source list of journals.

Approximately one-quarter of the publications abstracted in *ECER* are available in microfiche or paper copy from ERIC. Entries for such reports include ERIC accession numbers and the number of pages needed to compute the cost from the ERIC Documentation Reproduction Service. This data base can be searched by computer, usually through the same sources that search ERIC.

G21 **FAMILY MEDICINE LITERATURE INDEX (FAMLI)**
Edited by Dorothy Fitzgerald. London, Ontario, World Organization of National Colleges, Academies, and Academic Associations of General Practitioners/Family Physicians (WONCA),
1980- . Quarterly, with annual cumulation. $60 (Canadian)/
year. From: Canadian Library of Family Medicine, 4000 Leslie
St., Willowdale, Ontario M2K 2R9, Canada.

A concise and convenient two-part index to the world family medicine
literature. The first part, published in cooperation with the National Library of Medicine, includes articles on family medicine processed
through MEDLARS. The second section contains references to around
30 family medical journals not indexed in *Index Medicus;* some of these
are indexed selectively rather than completely in *FAMLI.* Although the
indexing is basically similar to that in *Index Medicus* (G24), *FAMLI*
contains a thesaurus of "key words in family medicine," that explains
and refers to appropriate terms. Includes numerous articles on family
health, family characteristics, family relations, family life cycle, and
similar topics that are not found in the larger medical indexes.

The annual issue also includes a comprehensive listing of new books
in family medicine, as well as a listing of publications by member organizations in WONCA and master's degree and medical degree theses
in family medicine.

G22 **FEDERAL INDEX** Edited by J. Kelley Summers. Washington, D.C., Capitol Services International, 1980- . Monthly.
$495/year. From: 415 Second St., NE, Washington, DC 20002.

An expensive monthly composite index to four major government publications: *Congressional Record, Federal Register, Weekly Compilation of
Presidential Documents,* and *United States Law Week.* It is organized by
government function, issuing agency, and groups affected. Like *CIS/
Index* (G10), it can be used to locate federal legislative, regulatory, and
judicial documents relating to children.

G23 **HUMANITIES INDEX** Edited by Elizabeth Pingree. Bronx,
N.Y., H. W. Wilson, 1974- . Quarterly, with annual bound cu-
mulative volume. Sold on a service basis. From: 950 University
Ave., Bronx, NY 10452.

A continuation of the *International Index* (1907-1965) and the *Social
Sciences and Humanities Index* (1965-1974) that indexes approximately
300 periodicals in archaeology, area studies, history, the classics,
folklore, criticism, philosophy, religion, performing arts, and related
topics. Each issue includes a list of periodical sources with publishers'

names, addresses, and subscription prices, as well as a book review index that arranges citations alphabetically under book author.

G24 **INDEX MEDICUS** Edited by Clifford A. Bachrach. Bethesda, Md., National Library of Medicine, 1960– . Monthly, with annual cumulation. $195.00/year; $243.75/year foreign. *Cumulated Index Medicus.* Annual. $260.00/year; $325.00/year foreign. From: U.S. Government Printing Office, Washington, DC 20402.

A subject and author index to current articles from around 2,600 worldwide biomedical journals, accessed and indexed by MEDLARS. Approximately 22,000 articles in medicine, the life sciences, and health-related fields are covered in each issue and indexed according to NLM's *Medical Subject Headings (MeSH).* An abridged version of this index, the *Abridged Index Medicus,* covers 117 of the more popular and accessible medical journals and would probably be adequate for many medical searches involving children and pediatrics. It is available for $43/year ($53.75 foreign) from the same source. The *Cumulated Abridged Index Medicus* costs $34/year in the United States and $42.50 elsewhere.

In these indexes, entries are arranged alphabetically by journal title under alphabetic subject headings and their subdivisions, except that English-language journal titles appear first.

One convenient aspect of this *Index Medicus* series is the "Bibliography of Medical Reviews," which has appeared in the front of each issue since 1967 and which cites survey articles and medical bibliographies under broad subjects. Citations include the number of references, as well as full bibliographic citations. This section provides a rapid means of locating bibliographies under topics related to children and/or pediatrics.

The *List of Journals Indexed in Index Medicus* is included in the January issue and is also issued as a separate publication. *Index Medicus* is available in microfiche or microfilm from Pergamon Press and is available on-line through the National Library of Medicine as well as through private vendors.

G25 **INDEX TO FOREIGN LEGAL PERIODICALS AND COLLECTIONS OF ESSAYS** Edited by W. A. Steiner. London, Institute of Advanced Legal Studies and American Association of Law Libraries, 1960– . Quarterly, with triannual cumulation. $250/year. From: 17 Russell Sq., London WC1B 5DR, England.

Similar to *Index to Legal Periodicals* (G26), with separate lists of periodicals and essay collections and subject, geographic, book review, and author indexes. Can be useful for a comparative study of family law and other laws involving children.

G26   **INDEX TO LEGAL PERIODICALS**   Edited by Stephen Rosen. Bronx, N.Y., H. W. Wilson, 1952– . Monthly, except September, with quarterly and annual cumulations. $100/year in the United States and Canada; $120/year elsewhere.

Provides subject and author indexing of legal periodicals from the United States, Canada, Great Britain, Ireland, Australia, and New Zealand that regularly publish "legal articles of high quality and permanent reference value"—some 400 periodicals altogether, as well as yearbooks and reviews. In the standard Wilson fashion, entries are arranged by article title under a combined alphabetic author/subject index. Each issue includes an alphabetic table of cases; a table of statutes, arranged by jurisdiction; a book review index arranged by book author; and a list of sources. Although it is a popular index and generally easy to use, it is not the best for searches involving children. There are relatively few articles found under topics like child abuse and child custody; "infants," a legal term, is preferred to "children."

G27   **INTERNATIONAL NURSING INDEX**   Edited by Frederick W. Pattison. New York, American Journal of Nursing, 1966– . Quarterly, with annual cumulation. $100/year. From: 555 W. 57th St., New York, NY 10019.

Quarterly index to 200 nursing publications and to articles related to nursing that appear in 2,600 nonnursing journals in the National Library of Medicine. Includes subject and name sections, lists of serials indexed, nursing books published, and nursing publications of organizations and agencies. The final issue of each year includes a list of nursing sources. Since this index is based in part on the NLM collection, it uses *MeSH* subject headings of *Index Medicus,* as well as terms taken from the *Nursing Thesaurus.* Its coverage of foreign nursing is somewhat more extensive than that of the *Cumulative Index* (G13).

G28   **JOURNAL OF HUMAN SERVICES ABSTRACTS**   Rockville, Md., Project SHARE, 1976– . Quarterly. $75/year; $20/issue. From: P.O. Box 2309, Rockville, MD 20852.

An announcement and abstracting service for Project SHARE, a clearinghouse that processes documents for those engaged in the planning, management, and delivery of human services. Each issue announces approximately 150 documents on topics like adoption, foster families, and self-help services. It is a well-done index in four parts, with abstracts arranged alphabetically by author and indexed by corporate author, title, and subject. Documents are available from NTIS in microfiche or paper.

G29 **KINDEX: AN INDEX TO LEGAL PERIODICAL LITERATURE CONCERNING CHILDREN** Edited by Thomas S. Vereb. Pittsburgh, Pa., National Center for Juvenile Justice, 1975– . Semiannual, with annual cumulation. $25/year. From: 701 Forbes Ave., Pittsburgh, PA 15219.

Another specific index devoted solely to children—in this case, international legal articles concerning children. *Kindex,* which began as an inhouse aid for the research efforts of the National Center for Juvenile Justice, now covers 400 English-language periodicals, with access by topical subject area, geographic location, and supreme court decisions. The main arrangement is alphabetic by subject, but *Kindex* also includes a list of journals (with abbreviations), a cross-index to subjects, a cumulative index to classifications by page number, and an author index. The format is not as easy to use as that of the *Index to Foreign Legal Periodicals and Collections of Essays* (G25) or the *Index to Legal Periodicals* (G26), but it focuses much better on children, with 270 subject terms on topics ranging from abortion to best interest, certification as an adult, child abuse, child custody, children in placement, status offenders, support, television, and youthful offenders, to name a few (see Figure 3). It provides good coverage of legislation and constitutional law. Each issue has around 600 citations.

Although *Kindex* has only been published since 1975, the first issue covers 10 years (1965–1974) of legal articles concerning children and is available from the center for $25. The center also provides automated searches for a fee; consult it for costs.

G30 **LANGUAGE AND LANGUAGE BEHAVIOR ABSTRACTS (LLBA)** Edited by Florian Andrade. San Diego, Calif., Sociological Abstracts, Inc., 1967– . Quarterly, with annual cumulated index. $130/year. From: P.O. Box 22206, San Diego, CA 92122-0206.

A scholarly reference work that screens almost 1,000 publications in 25 disciplines and more than 30 languages. Areas covered include anthropology, applied linguistics, communication sciences, education, pediatrics, psychiatry and psychology, psycholinguistics, and speech. It is easy to use, with well-written, current abstracts listed by accession number and classification order. Arranged by broad subject, relevant sections include child language acquisition, verbal learning, non-native

KENTUCKY

JOINT CUSTODY IN KENTUCKY.
BRATTON, R.M.
8 N. KY. L. REV. 553-576 (1981).

JUVENILE CODE.
PATTERSON, K.D.
70 KY. L.J. 343-393 (1982).

RESPONSE TO A CRISIS: REDUCING THE JUVENILE DETENTION RATE IN LOUISVILLE, KENTUCKY.
KIHM, R.C., BLOCK, J.A.
33 JUV. & FAM. CT. J. 37-44 (1982).

KIDNAPPING

ABDUCTION OF CHILD BY NONCUSTODIAL PARENT: DAMAGES FOR CUSTODIAL PARENT'S MENTAL DISTRESS.
46 MO. L. REV. 829-843 (1981).

AMERICA'S MISSING CHILDREN.
HOWELL, J.
16 PROSECUTOR 12-14 (1982).

CHILD CUSTODY JURISDICTION AND THE PARENTAL KIDNAPPING PREVENTION ACT: A DUE PROCESS DILEMMA?
SHERMAN, S.B.
17 TULSA L.J. 713-727 (1982).

CHILD SNATCHING.
HOFF, P.M.
5 FAM. ADVOCATE 38-43 (1982).

EFFECT OF THE PARENTAL KIDNAPPING PREVENTION ACT OF 1980 ON CHILD SNATCHING.
17 NEW ENG. L. REV. 499-526 (1982).

GRUBS V. ROSS: OREGON'S NEW APPROACH TO CHILD CUSTODY FORUM DETERMINATION.
HUTTERLI, C.G.
18 WILLAMETTE L. REV. 519-533 (1982).

HAGUE CONVENTION ON INTERNATIONAL CHILD ABDUCTION.
ANTON, A.E.
30 INT. & COMP. L.Q. 537-567 (1981).

LEGISLATIVE REFORMS TO REDUCE PARENTAL CHILD ABDUCTIONS.
AGOPIAN, M.W., ANDERSON, G.L.
6 J. JUV. L. 1-26 (1982).

1981 SURVEY OF NEW YORK LAW: FAMILY LAW.
FOSTER, H.H., JR., FREED, D.J.
33 SYRACUSE L. REV. 285-336 (1982).

PARENTAL CHILD-SNATCHING: OUT OF A NO-MAN'S LAND OF LAW.
13 ST. MARY'S L.J. 337-352 (1981).

PARENTAL KIDNAPPING: CAN THE UNIFORM CHILD CUSTODY JURISDICTION ACT AND THE FEDERAL PARENTAL KIDNAPPING PREVENTION ACT OF 1980 EFFECTIVELY DETER IT?
20 DUQUESNE L. REV. 43-70 (1981).

PROSECUTORS, POLICE AND PARENTAL KIDNAPPING.
FOLEY, C., HOFF, P.M.
16 PROSECUTOR 19-24 (1982).

LEGISLATION

UNIFORM CHILD CUSTODY JURISDICTION ACT AND THE PARENTAL KIDNAPPING PREVENTION ACT: DUAL RESPONSE TO INTERSTATE CHILD CUSTODY PROBLEMS.
39 WASH. & LEE L. REV. 149-163 (1982).

SEE ALSO CHILD CUSTODY

LABELING THEORY

RELATIVE REDEMPTION: LABELING IN JUVENILE RESTITUTION.
LEVI, K.
33 JUV. & FAM. CT. J. 3-13 (1982).

SEE ALSO CRIMINOLOGY, JUVENILE COURTS, PSYCHOLOGY, STATUS OFFENSES

LEARNING DISABILITIES

LEARNING DISABILITIES AND JUVENILE DELINQUENCY: A SUMMARY REPORT.
DUNIVANT, N.
6 ST. CT. J. 12-15 (1982).

LEARNING DISABILITIES AND JUVENILE DELINQUENTS.
CELLINI, H.R., SNOWMAN, J.
46 FED. PROB. 26-32 (1982).

SEE ALSO EDUCATION, JUVENILE DELINQUENCY

LEGISLATION

AVAILABILITY OF CHILD CARE FOR LOW-INCOME FAMILIES: STRATEGIES TO ADDRESS THE IMPACT OF THE ECONOMIC RECONCILIATION ACT OF 1981 AND THE OMNIBUS BUDGET RECONCILIATION ACT OF 1981.
ZEITLIN, J.H., CAMPBELL, N.D.
16 CLEARINGHOUSE REV. 285-313 (1982).

CHILD ABUSE REVISITED.
TINKHAM, T.
29 MED. TR. T.Q. 33-43 (1982).

CONFRONTING CHILD ABUSE.
DAVIDSON, H.A.
5 FAM. ADVOCATE 26-30, 41-42 (1982).

CUSTODY AND MAINTENANCE: THE ROLE OF PROVINCIAL LEGISLATION FOR DIVORCED FAMILIES.
3 CAN. J. FAM. L. 403-417 (1980).

EFFECT OF THE PARENTAL KIDNAPPING PREVENTION ACT OF 1980 ON CHILD SNATCHING.
17 NEW ENG. L. REV. 499-526 (1982).

IMPLEMENTING THE INDIAN CHILD WELFARE ACT.
DAVIES, B.
16 CLEARINGHOUSE REV. 179-196 (1982).

JUVENILE COURT PRACTICE AND PROCEDURE.
CLARK, G.W.
33 MERCER L. REV. 167-185 (1981).

JUVENILE JUSTICE: THE LEGISLATURE REVISITS CHAPTER 39.
EVANS, R.W.
55 FLA. B.J. 697-702 (1981).

Figure 3   *KINDEX* has 270 subject and geographic entries plus author entries for locating materials on children and the law. This page is reproduced with the permission of the National Center for Juvenile Justice.

language pedagogy, various topics on language testing and reading, writing, learning disabilities, and special education. The index reveals additional relevant topics, such as Piaget, bilingual education, and age differences in language. Includes author, subject, and source publication indexes and offers a reproduction service for articles. The LLBA data base from 1973 on is also available in a computer-searchable format.

G31 **LANGUAGE TEACHING, THE INTERNATIONAL AB-STRACTING JOURNAL FOR LANGUAGE TEACHERS AND APPLIED LINGUISTS** (Formerly *Language-Teaching Abstracts* and *Language Teaching and Linguistics: Abstracts.*) Edited by Valerie Kinsella. London, Cambridge University Press, 1968– . Quarterly. Individuals, $30/year; institutions, $55/year. From: 32 E. 57th St., New York, NY 10022.

A cross-disciplinary publication, edited jointly by the English-Teaching Information Centre and the Centre for Information on Language Teaching and Research, that aims to provide users with the latest research information in the areas of linguistics, psychology, and language behavior as they relate to language teaching, especially the teaching of modern foreign languages. To this end, it presents well-done objective English-language summaries of articles from 400 international journals, arranged alphabetically by topic, with a good assortment of articles on topics like language development of children and teaching English as a second language. Each issue includes a bibliographic supplement of brief book annotations (perhaps 10 books per issue) and a 7,000-word survey article with bibliographic citations on an important topic. Indexed by country, subject, and author. The January issue lists the periodicals reviewed.

G32 **MENTAL RETARDATION AND DEVELOPMENTAL DISABILITIES ABSTRACTS** (Formerly *Mental Retardation Abstracts.*) Office of Human Development, Developmental Disabilities Office. Washington, D.C., U.S. Government Printing Office, 1964–1979. Quarterly. (Out of print)

Although no longer printed, this is still a good source of information for a wide variety of materials related to childhood mental retardation and developmental handicaps. Numbered, classified abstracts cover books, book chapters, ERIC documents, and articles from medical journals (with a good representation of foreign publications). All facets are included: development, treatment, training, legislation, and planning. Excellent author and subject indexes.

G33   **THE NEW YORK TIMES INDEX** New York, The New York Times, 1913– . Bimonthly, with annual cumulations. $345/year.

A newspaper index to our national newspaper of record, widely dispersed across the United States, with detailed abstracts of each article. Backed by microfilm or paper copies of *The New York Times,* it provides extensive current access to significant national (and some international) events, names, and dates involving children.

G34   **NUTRITION ABSTRACTS AND REVIEWS: SERIES A, HUMAN AND EXPERIMENTAL** Edited by A. A. Woodham. Slough, England, Commonwealth Agricultural Bureaux (CAB), 1931– . Monthly, with indexes cumulated annually. £184/year; £120/year for new subscriptions. From: Farnham House, Farnham Royal, Slough SL2 3BN, England.

A British abstracting journal that provides worldwide coverage of periodicals, books, monographs, and reports on human nutrition and metabolism, foods, immunology, public health, and related topics taken largely from agricultural periodicals. Abstracts in the main section are arranged by number under broad subject headings and subheadings; each issue has author and subject indexes. A list of the 8,600 periodicals scanned is published annually. Photocopies of most articles published are available from CAB.

    The system also is available in microform and on magnetic tape, and on-line as part of the CAB ABSTRACTS data base.

G35   **POPULATION INDEX** Edited by Richard Hankinson. Princeton, N.J., Office of Population Research, 1935– . Quarterly, with annual cumulation of author and geographic indexes. $35/year. From: 21 Prospect Ave., Princeton, NJ 08544.

Abstracts and indexes the world literature on population studies, covering around 350 periodical titles and 1,000 books per year, plus reports, theses, proceedings, and working papers (approximately 1,000 abstracts per issue). Although much of the materials covered are not relevant, the index is a good source for locating statistics, bibliographies, directories, and other sources for demographic studies of the family. Abstracts are arranged by author under 20 broad subjects, with author and geographic indexes, news of the Population Association of America, and tables of population statistics. A list of periodical sources is included in the cumulated volume, which contains the yearly author and geographic indexes. *Population Index* is available in microfilm and microfiche from University Microfilms International; most citations from 1978 on are in the POPLINE data base accessible through NLM.

G36 **PSYCHOLOGICAL ABSTRACTS (PA)** Edited by Lois Granick. Washington, D.C., American Psychological Assn., (APA), 1927– . Monthly, with semiannual cumulations. $600/year.

A comprehensive international guide to the literature of psychology and related disciplines that compiles and indexes nonevaluative summaries and citations of selected reports and articles from 1,200 periodical titles (approximately 2,300 abstracts per issue). Traditionally, this has been the major indexing source for psychology. Up to January 1980, it also indexed books and dissertations; now these are included only in the PsycINFO computerized data base, therefore, the printed data bank is around 25 percent smaller than the computerized version.

Psychological Abstracts is arranged alphabetically by author under 16 broad (and subdivided) subject categories and is indexed by author and subject, using headings from APA's *Thesaurus of Psychological Index Terms.* Although materials on children can be found under all topics, the best areas to scan are "Developmental Psychology," "Educational Psychology," and "Psychometrics." A list of periodical sources is published annually, as are cumulated subject and author indexes. Three-year cumulative indexes are also available through 1983.

Microform editions of *PA* are available through University Microfilms International as well as Johnson Associates, P.O. Box 1017, Greenwich, CT 06830.

The PsycINFO data base, searchable directly from APA and through many vendors, contains all records since 1967 and some 9,000 dissertations per year.

The PsycSCAN publications (G37) and (G38) provide a considerably less-expensive means of keeping up with certain segments of psychology.

G37 **PsycSCAN: DEVELOPMENTAL PSYCHOLOGY** Edited by Lois Granick. Washington, D.C., American Psychological Assn. (APA), 1980– . Quarterly. Members, $10/year; nonmembers, $15/year; $18/year foreign.

One of a new APA series (based on *Psychological Abstracts*) intended for researchers, psychologists, and students as an inexpensive means of keeping up with the literature. Abstracts and indexes articles on developmental psychology (and related topics) taken from journals chosen by subscriber vote from APA's data base. Each issue contains around

400 abstracts, arranged alphabetically by publication title and then by pagination. Many of the 36 journals chosen and listed on the cover of *PsycSCAN: Developmental Psychology* are annotated in Chapter 9.

The convenient format is designed for ease and speed in reader scanning. Information elements associated with the concise informative abstracts include title, index terms (drawn from the *Thesaurus of Psychological Index Terms*), bibliographic citation, and the abstract number under which the items were originally published in *PA*. The abstracts provide clear overviews of the content of the original articles, and additional data elements suggest subjects to pursue further, with information for follow-up.

G38   **PsycSCAN: LD/MR**   Abstracts on Learning and Communication Disorders and Mental Retardation. Edited by Lois Granick. Washington, D.C., American Psychological Assn., 1982– . Quarterly. Members, $10/year; nonmembers, $15/year; $18/year foreign.

Intended for parents, therapists, psychologists, researchers, and educators, *PsycSCAN: LD/MR* provides selected classified abstracts to relevant articles from the entire PsycINFO data base of 1,200 journals. These are arranged by author under specific disabilities within broad subject categories. For example, the category "learning disorders" includes behavioral disorders, dyslexia, hyperkinesis, and psychoneurological disorders. "Communication disorders" includes disturbances in speech, hearing, and language. "Mental retardation" includes mild, moderate, and severe retardation, as well as autism. Each condition is subdivided by theory, research, and assessment; treatment and rehabilitation; and educational issues. Typical entries are similar to those in *PsycSCAN: Developmental Psychology.*

This index is backed by two valuable retrospective bibliographies, *PsycINFO Retrospective: Mental Retardation—An Abstracted Bibliography, 1971–1980* and *PsycINFO Retrospective: Learning and Communication Disorders—An Abstracted Bibliography, 1971–1980* (1982, $31.50 each). Each contains more than 4,000 abstracts.

G39   **PUBLIC AFFAIRS INFORMATION SERVICE (P.A.I.S.) BULLETIN**   Edited by Lawrence J. Woods. New York, Public Affairs Information Service, 1915– . Semimonthly, plus quarterly cumulations and annual bound volume. $200/year; cumulations and annual only, $150/year; annual only, $100. From: 11 W. 40th St., New York, NY 10018.

A subject index (and author index in the annual volume) to library materials in the fields of public affairs and public policy in the English language, based on the collection of the Economic and Public Affairs Division of the New York Public Library and selected by a nonprofit association of libraries. An excellent research tool, widely available in public libraries, *P.A.I.S.* tries to identify the public affairs information most interesting and useful to legislators, administrators, policy researchers, students, and the business and financial communities. It covers publications on all areas that bear on contemporary public issues—social, economic, and political—particularly, controversial issues in the public debate. It uses a wide variety of sources: the academic social sciences; professional publications in social work, law, education, business, and finance; and the general press, excluding technical materials or those of interest mainly to practitioners. It scans more than 800 English-language periodicals, as well as some 6,000 books, reports, pamphlets, proceedings, and government documents each year. It concentrates on factual and statistical materials to meet the needs of its member libraries and is an excellent source of information on bibliographies, directories, legislative handbooks, and statistics. *P.A.I.S.* is useful for locating relevant federal, state, municipal, and international documents; for example, one can check the term *directories* as a heading in the annual volume to locate new directories or new editions of old directories.

P.A.I.S. Bulletin is conveniently arranged with logical, concise index terms and adequate cross-references. As a current, cumulative index, it provides full bibliographic citations, sources, and prices. The last quarterly cumulation is a bound volume that supersedes the previous cumulations and contains an author index. With its currency, wide coverage, and frequent cumulations, it is a basic source for the social sciences, as well as for public policy issues.

In addition to the main subject indexes, the *P.A.I.S. Bulletin* also includes a variety of lists designed to make the entries accessible: a key to periodical references, an address directory of publishers and organizations, lists of publications analyzed, and lists of U.S. government agencies whose publications were included. Addresses of some small publishers are given in the entries, so that sources and prices are supplied for each item cited. For materials no longer in print, a backup service is provided by the New York Public Library's Photographic Services Department, which can generally supply copies at cost.

The P.A.I.S. data base, the machine-readable version of *P.A.I.S. Bulletin* and *P.A.I.S. Foreign Language Index* (G40) can be searched on-line.

The 60-year *Cumulative Subject Index to the P.A.I.S. Annual Bulletins, 1915-1974,* containing more than one million subject entries, was published by Carrollton Press (15 vols., Arlington, Va., 1978, $1,182).

G40   **PUBLIC AFFAIRS INFORMATION SERVICE (P.A.I.S.) FOREIGN LANGUAGE INDEX** Edited by Lawrence J. Woods. New York, Public Affairs Information Service, 1972- . Quarterly, plus bound annual volume. $195/year.

Supplements the *P.A.I.S. Bulletin* (G39) with foreign-language materials in French, German, Italian, Portuguese, and Spanish. Scans some 400 periodical titles, and indexes around 2,000 books, reports, pamphlets, proceedings, and government documents. As a foreign-language counterpart, it similarly includes materials on public policy, political science, court decisions, statistics, and international relations. Titles are entered in the original language and annotated as needed. Each issue includes a source list, an author index, and a directory of publishers and organizations. Like the *Bulletin,* it is part of the P.A.I.S. data base and can be searched on-line.

G41   **READERS' GUIDE TO PERIODICAL LITERATURE** Edited by Jean Marra. Bronx, N.Y., H. W. Wilson, 1900- . Semimonthly; monthly in July and August; quarterly and annual cumulations. $80/year. From: 950 University Ave., Bronx, NY 10452.

An author and subject index to general-interest periodical literature in the United States, particularly useful for locating accessible topical materials and for scanning the literature of the early twentieth century. Although "popular," it includes many articles that reflect, comment on, or investigate the social, cultural, and economic aspects of child life, including attitudes toward and treatment of children. Covers almost 200 magazines, ranging from weekly news to family reading and journals of opinion.

G42   **READING ABSTRACTS** Edited by Leo P. Chall. La Jolla, Calif., Essay Press, 1974- . Semiannual. Individuals, $25/year; institutions, $35/year. From: P.O. Box 2323, La Jolla, CA 92037.

Contains English-language abstracts of scholarly articles selected from the world's periodical literature on reading, arranged in classified order, with around 2,200 abstracts in each issue. The major topics— psycholinguistics, linguistics, orthography, interpersonal behavior and communication, sociolinguistics, hearing, language, learning disabilities, mental retardation, and speech education—are subdivided into smaller topics like child language acquisition, language testing, and reading readiness. Each issue provides subject, author, and source publication indexes.

G43 **REFUGEE ABSTRACTS** Edited by Mark Braham. Geneva, International Refugee Integration Resource Centre (IRIRC), 1982– . Quarterly. Individuals and organizations that aid refugees, $20/year; libraries, $30/year. From: 5-7, avenue de la Pais, CH-1202 Geneva, Switzerland.

Published by the computer-based documentation center of IRIRC, a center that gathers, stores, and disseminates information on all aspects of refugee reception, resettlement, and integration. The publication includes several sections: abstracts, news headlines, reviews, author index, subject index, and publishers' address lists. The abstracts are derived from the books, journals, and documents received in the center and are arranged in broad topics that represent current materials. In the March 1983 issue, for example, 102 numbered abstracts were divided among the following major topics: international, origins, exodus, asylum, resettlement, and repatriation. Other issues may differ slightly. The abstracts are in English (British), but the materials abstracted stem from French, English, German, and Spanish sources. Other languages may be developed over time, since this publication is evolving. The terms *child care* and *children* in the subject index of each volume reveal many abstracts whose main concern is children, whereas most other articles refer to populations that contain children. So long as children are pawns and refugees, this index is a necessity for locating information on refugee children. It is well done by knowledgeable people and provides compact access to a wide variety of source materials.

G44 **REHABILITATION LITERATURE** For Use by Professional Personnel and Students in All Disciplines Concerned with Rehabilitation of Persons with Disabilities. Chicago, Ill., National Easter Seal Society, 1939– . Bimonthly. $21/year. From: 2023 W. Ogden Ave., Chicago, IL 60612.

An interdisciplinary journal for students and professionals concerned with rehabilitation of persons with disabling conditions. Each issue contains original articles, excellent book reviews, brief abstracts of films and audiovisuals, notices of relevant publications, and approximately 50–70 well-done abstracts of current literature (monographs, periodical articles, and so on) arranged by topic.

G45   **RESEARCH RELATING TO CHILDREN**   By ERIC Clearinghouse on Early Childhood Education. Washington, D.C.,
U.S. Government Printing Office, 1950–1979. Occasional, at approximately one-year intervals. No longer published.
Unfortunately and ironically, this helpful abstract publication was discontinued with Volume 42 in 1979, the International Year of the Child.
First published by the U.S. Children's Bureau (nos. 1–26) and then assigned to the ERIC Clearinghouse on Early Childhood Education, this
intermittent publication reported research under way and research recently completed that involved children. Arranged by subject, it included a broad range of research covering long-term investigations, growth
and development, special groups of children, the child in the family,
socioeconomic and cultural factors, social services, health services, and
educational factors and services. For each project, it noted investigators, subjects, purpose, methods, findings, directions, cooperating
groups, and publications and was indexed by institution, investigator,
and subject. Although *Research Relating to Children* provided most
thorough coverage of individual projects, the scope was never complete, since a low budget forced it to rely on voluntary reporting. It is
still a valuable source for the years involved.

G46   **RESOURCES IN EDUCATION (RIE)**   (Formerly *Research
in Education.*)   Washington, D.C., National Institute of Education (NIE), Educational Resources Information Center (ERIC),
1966– . Monthly. $95.00/year; $118.75/year foreign. Semiannual
indexes, $29.00; $36.25 foreign. From: U.S. Government Printing Office, Washington, DC 20402.
Resources in Education, the monthly documents abstracting service of
ERIC, reports and indexes resumes of hard-to-find or limited distribution documents selected by 16 ERIC clearinghouses around the country.
Items include technical and research reports, conference papers, documents from school districts and state agencies, project descriptions,
bibliographies, books, guides, curriculum materials, and other reports
of interest to the education community—altogether around 1,200
items each month, a total of some 250,000 entries. Although a small
percentage of materials included are copyrighted, most documents abstracted are available in microfiche or paper copy from the ERIC Document Reproduction Service (EDRS), 3030 N. Fairfax Dr., Suite 200,
Arlington, VA 22201.
Resources in Education reports are arranged by clearinghouse and
then assigned ED numbers in the ERIC system so that the output of any

clearinghouse can be read each month. They are indexed by author and institution and by subject descriptors selected from the *Thesaurus of ERIC Descriptors*. Since 1979, a publication-type index and a cross-reference to clearinghouse numbers have been included. Each issue lists new *Thesaurus* terms and explains the format of the abstracts.

This is the companion volume to *Current Index to Journals in Education (CIJE)*, which treats educational periodical literature. Together they constitute the ERIC data base, which is widely available on-line. As the outline of ERIC on page 310 indicates, the clearinghouses collectively take a broad view of education and uncover many references on children.

G47 **SAGE FAMILY STUDIES ABSTRACTS** Edited by Eileen Peronneau. Beverly Hills, Calif., Sage, 1979- . Quarterly. Individuals, $50/year; institutions, $90/year; $4 additional foreign. From: 275 S. Beverly Dr., Beverly Hills, CA 90212.

An international information service designed to keep family scholars and practitioners apprised of the best of current literature in family studies and related fields. It selectively scans more than 2,000 scholarly journals and innumerable books, reports, dissertations, government documents, speeches, legislative research studies, unpublished manuscripts, and other fugitive materials in the field of family studies to select some 250 items per month to abstract. In each issue, materials are arranged in broad classes indicated in the table of contents (which changes slightly from issue to issue as research interests evolve). Broad topics in the May 1983 issue were historical and theoretical perspectives, developmental stages, family life-styles, cross-cultural perspectives, therapy and counseling, and social issues (all subdivided again). The editor estimates that at least 40 percent of the journal deals with development or problems of children and adolescents. The abstracts are well written, well selected, and highly interesting. Each issue includes a list of 60–75 related citations, an author index, and a good subject index. The August issue contains a source list of journals with addresses; cumulative indexes appear in the fall issue.

G48 **SOCIAL SCIENCES CITATION INDEX (SSCI)** Philadelphia, Pa., Institute for Scientific Information (ISI), 1973- . 3 issues/year, with annual cumulation. $2,100/year. Includes *Citation Index, Permuterm Subject Index, Source Index,* and *Corporate Index.* From: 3501 Market St., University City Science Center, Philadelphia, PA 19104.

A complete indexing system to 1,400 journals in the social sciences (in all languages) and to some 250 multiauthored books, with occasional articles from 3,100 selectively covered journals. The scope encompasses the social sciences, including anthropology, business and finance, community health, criminology, demography, ethnic studies, history, international relations, law, linguistics, philosophy, political science, psychology, sociology, statistics, and urban studies. A one-year subscription covers two triannual indexes and an annual cumulation incorporating the last four months of the year. These citation tools, which are completely machine produced, allow users to search for current authors, cited authors, references, organizations, and permuted keywords. Citation indexing uses keywords from titles and the subject orientation implied by authors' published citations to perform subject searches without having to use assigned subject heading terms or specialized nomenclature, a type of search easily performed by computer. SOCIAL SCISEARCH, the computer-readable version of *SSCI,* covers social, behavioral, and related sciences from 1972 on and is available on-line through DIALOG.

Copies of some of the articles indexed can be obtained through ISI's Original Article Tear Sheet Service (OATS). An ISI grant program provides *SSCI* at reduced rates to certain organizations.

G49 **SOCIAL SCIENCES INDEX** Edited by Joseph Bloomfield. Bronx, N.Y., H. W. Wilson, 1974- . Quarterly, with annual cumulation. Service basis. From: 950 University Ave., Bronx, NY 10452.

A quarterly author and subject index that evolved from the *International Index* (1907-1965) and the *Social Sciences and Humanities Index* (1965-1974). Essentially, this provides author and subject access to 308 periodicals in anthropology, economics, environmental sciences, geography, law and criminology, planning and public administration, political sciences, psychology, social aspects of medicine, sociology, and related subjects. The titles, addresses, and prices of these publications are supplied in each issue. As might be expected from its subject scope, this publication contains quite a few entries on various aspects of children. These are easy to locate with the journal's clear typography, consistent subject headings, and numerous cross-references (see Figure 4).

G50 **SOCIAL SERVICE ABSTRACTS** Edited by A. B. Cooper. London, Great Britain Department of Social Health and Social Security Library, 1974- . Monthly, with annual author and sub-

SOCIAL SCIENCES INDEX

Child welfare —*See also*—*cont.*
Foster home care
Maternal and infant welfare
Georgia
Child abuse in Georgia: a method to evaluate risk factors and reporting bias. J. Jason and others. Am J Pub Health 72:-1353-8 D '82
Great Britain
Wards of court. H. Sharron. New Statesm 105:12-13 F 25 '83
Sweden
Sweden's child support system: lessons for the United States. I. Garfinkel and A. Sørensen. Soc Work 27:509-15 N '82
United States
American urban riots revisited. M. Iris. bibl Am Behav Sci 26:333-52 Ja/F '83
Child support: new focus for social work practice. J. H. Cassetty. Soc Work 27:504-8 N '82
Econometric examination of the new federalism [with discussion]. E. M. Gramlich. Brookings Pa Econ Activ no2:327-70 '82
Follow-up study of foster children in permanent placements. J. Lahti. Soc Serv R 56:556-71 D '82
Investigation of prescribed and nonprescribed medicine use behavior within the household context. J. D. Jackson and others. Soc Sci & Med 16 no2:2009-15 '82
Services for minority children in out-of-home care. L. Olsen. Soc Serv R 56:572-85 D '82
Sweden's child support system: lessons for the United States. I. Garfinkel and A. Sørensen. Soc Work 27:509-15 N '82
Turnover in the AFDC population: an event history analysis. R. Plotnick. bibl J Hum Resources 18:65-81 Wint '83
See also
Adoption assistance and child welfare act, 1980
Childbearing age. See Maternal age
Childbirth
See also
Midwives
Study and teaching
Effect of childbirth preparation on women of different social classes. M. K. Nelson. J Health & Soc Behav 23:339-52 D '82
Childbirth education. See Childbirth—Study and teaching
Childhood. See Children
Children
See also
Adoption
Attitudes toward children
Child development
Deaf children
Elementary school students
Handicapped children
Infants
Man, Prehistoric—Children
Mentally handicapped children
Play
Preschool children
Social work with children
Television advertising and children
Television and children
Youth
Attitudes
See Children's attitudes
Care and hygiene
14 a minute. Economist 285:10 D 25 '82-Ja 7 '83
Medical care, living conditions, and children's well-being. C. E. Ross and R. S. Duff. bibl Soc Forces 61:456-74 D '82
See also
Child health services
Children—Medical examinations
Obesity in children
Pediatrics
Civil rights
Children's rights [symposium]. ed. by J. Knitzer. Am J Orthopsych 52:468-538 Jl '82
Crime
See Juvenile delinquency
Custody
See Custody of children
Dental care
Good toothbrushing game: a school-based dental hygiene program for increasing the toothbrushing effectiveness of children. J. J. Swain and others. bibl J App Behav Anal 15:171-6 Spr '82
Review and analysis of children's fearful behavior in dental settings. G. A. Winer. bibl Child Devel 53:1111-33 O '82
Diseases
See also
Measles

Growth
Body proportions of Warsaw children, 1959-79. A. Siniarska and N. Wolanski. Cur Anthrop 24:108-10 F '83
Clinical applications of physical anthropology. M. Robinow. bibl Am J Phys Anthrop supp3:169-79 '82
Effect of high altitude on the growth of children of high socioeconomic status in Bolivia. S. Stinson. bibl Am J Phys Anthrop 59:61-71 S '82
Ethnic and secular influences on the size and maturity of seven year old children living in Guatemala City. B. Bogin and R. B. MacVean. bibl Am J Phys Anthrop 59:393-8 D '82
Fatness and skeletal maturity of Belgian boys 12 through 17 years of age. G. Beunen and others. bibl Am J Phys Anthrop 59:387-92 D '82
Growth data as indicators of social inequalities: the case of Poland. T. Bielicki and Z. Welon. bibl Am J Phys Anthrop supp3:153-67 '82
Relation of growth to cognition in a well-nourished preschool population. E. Pollitt and others. bibl Child Devel 53:1157-63 O '82
Hospitals
See also
Sick children
Language
Acquisition of tag questions. M. Dennis and others. Child Devel 53:1254-7 O '82
Comprehension, production, and language acquisition. E. V. Clark and B. F. Hecht. bibl Ann R Psychol 34:325-49 '83
Control of animate and inanimate components in pretend play and language. R. Corrigan. bibl Child Devel 53:1343-53 O '82
Lady spaceman: children's perceptions of sex-stereotyped occupations. D. A. Rosenthal and D. C. Chapman. bibl Sex Roles 8:959-65 S '82
Prediction of IQ and language skill from perinatal status, child performance, family characteristics, and mother-infant interaction. H. L. Bee and others. bibl Child Devel 53:1135-56 O '82
Reproductive, perinatal, and environmental factors as predictors of the cognitive and language development of preterm and full-term infants. L. S. Siegel. bibl Child Devel 53:963-73 Ag '82
Role playing and the real thing: socialization and standard speech in Norway. K. A. Larson. bibl J Anthrop Res 38:-401-10 Wint '82
Sequence and principles in article system use: an examination of A, the, and null acquisition. A. M. Zehler and W. F. Brewer. bibl Child Devel 53:1268-74 O '82
Teaching comprehension and production. G. Holdgrafer. Percept & Motor Skills 55:306 Ag '82
Wh-questions: linguistic factors that contribute to the sequence of acquisition. L. Bloom and others. bibl Child Devel 53:1084-92 Ag '82
Legal status, laws, etc.
Aggregate beer and wine consumption; effects of changes in the minimum legal drinking age and a mandatory beverage container deposit law in Michigan. A. C. Wagenaar. J Stud Alcohol 43:469-87 My '82
Innocence for sale. G. Mitchell. il Police Mag 6:52-60 Ja '83
Is raising the legal drinking age warranted? T. L. Krieg. il Police Chief 49:32-4 D '82
Nonobscene child pornography and its categorical exclusion from constitutional protection. S. Z. Brown. J Crim Law & Criminol 73:1337-64 Wint '82
See also
Custody of children
Illegitimacy
Parent and child (law)
Management
See also
Classroom management
Parenting
Great Britain—History
No sufficient security: the reaction of the poor law authorities to boarding-out. M. Horsburgh. bibl J Soc Pol 12:51-73 Ja '83
Hawaii
Concordance between ethnographer and folk perspectives: observed performance and self-ascription of sibling caretaking roles. T. S. Weisner and others. bibl Hum Org 41:-237-44 Fall '82
Israel
Effects of father absence on young children in mother-headed families. R. Levy-Shiff. bibl Child Devel 53:1400-5 O '82
United States
Father absence and reproductive strategy: an evolutionary perspective. P. Draper and H. Harpending. bibl J Anthrop Res 38:255-73 Fall '82

Figure 4 This sample page from the quarterly index of *Social Sciences Index* indicates the scope of its coverage. Social Sciences Index Copyright © 1983 by The H. W. Wilson Company. Material reproduced by permission of the publisher.

ject indexes. £28.73/year. From: Stationery Office, P.O. Box 569, London SE1 9NH, England.
Provides approximately 150 abstracts per month on social services and social service issues, primarily in Great Britain. Areas covered include handicapped and homeless children, child abuse, social problems such as poverty, and the young offender. Abstracts are listed by entry number under broad subject categories. Each issue includes a subject index.

G51 **SOCIAL WELFARE, PLANNING/POLICY, AND DEVEL-OPMENT ABSTRACTS: An International Social Science Information Resource (SOPODA)** San Diego, Calif., Sociological Abstracts, Inc., 1979– . Semiannual. $130/year. Individual sections also available by subscription. From: P.O. Box 22206, San Diego, CA 92122.
A semiannual three-part index to worldwide periodical literature that emphasizes applied sociology: that is, social welfare, planning and policy, and development, with around 800 abstracts per issue from some 200 periodicals. Each issue is divided into subject sections and then subdivided, and each has its own subject, author, and source indexes. The social welfare section includes entries on child welfare as a problem in industrialized countries and in developing countries. There are also entries on childhood concerns in the planning and development sections, perhaps a total of 150 per year.
   SOPODA includes a supplement in each issue, *The International Review of Publications in Welfare, Policy and Development* (*IRPWPD*), which provides a bibliography of reviews from the periodicals abstracted in *SOPODA*. The *SOPODA* Reproduction Service can provide photocopies of many articles abstracted in *SOPODA*.

G52 **SOCIAL WORK RESEARCH & ABSTRACTS** Edited by Shirley L. Poole. New York, National Association of Social Workers, 1965– . Quarterly. Individuals, $45/year; institutions, $55/year; membership and student discounts. From: 257 Park Ave., S., 10th Floor, New York, NY 10010.
Originally published as *Abstracts for Social Workers,* this publication was expanded in 1977 to include original research articles in addition to abstracts. Articles generally relate to research methods, strategies, and theories in social work and analytic reviews of research. The abstracts (around 450 per issue) cover materials from 250 periodicals published worldwide in all languages (although priority is given to U.S. materials). These comprehensively cover social work, with selective coverage of related fields and disciplines. Approximately 1,700 signed abstracts

are published each year, of which a quarter relate to children and youth. Abstracts are arranged by author under subject category. Relevant areas include crime and delinquency, family and child welfare, and health and medical care. Some useful index terms are children, youths, adolescents, adoption, child abuse, child custody, child care, child neglect, child psychiatry, day care, and delinquents. Each issue includes author, title, and source indexes. Indexes are cumulated annually in the winter issue.

G53 **SOCIOLOGICAL ABSTRACTS (SA)**   Edited by Miriam Chall. San Diego, Calif., Sociological Abstracts, Inc., 1953- . 5 issues/year, with annual cumulative index. $270/year. From: Box 22206, San Diego, CA 92122.

Provides complete coverage of sociology in all languages, covering around 1,500 serials, 200 books, and some proceedings. Arranged intelligently under 32 classifications, the abstracts are well done and the selection is comprehensive. Includes as a supplement the *International Review of Publications in Sociology (IRPS)*, a bibliography of book reviews from abstracted journals. Each issue also includes complete source, author, and subject indexes (based on keywords and identifiers). Some issues contain supplements of abstracts of conference papers. Perhaps 200 items per issue deal in some way with children and youth; important areas are the sociology and socialization of children and families. The entire data base, going back to 1953, contains approximately 12,000 items on children and youth.

Photocopies of many abstracted articles are available from the SA Reproduction Service. The SOCIOLOGICAL ABSTRACTS data base, covering the world's literature on sociology since 1963, is searchable on-line through BRS, DIALOG, and other sources.

G54 **WOMEN STUDIES ABSTRACTS**   Edited by Sara Stauffer Whaley. Rush, N.Y., Rush Publishing Co., 1972- . Quarterly, with annual index. Individuals, $33/year; libraries, $66/year. From: P.O. Box 1, Rush, NY 14543.

Some relevant sections in this publication are education and socialization; sex roles and sex characteristics; family; pregnancy, family planning, childbirth, and abortion; and book reviews. Each issue comprises around 1,000 entries—articles, reports, and professional papers—from some 500 periodicals and other sources, including women's studies and women's liberation sources, as well as scholarly journals. Some items are abstracted; most are merely listed. Entries are arranged by subject; book reviews are referenced in a separate section.

The nicely detailed index reveals many entries on childhood and children under topics such as childhood needs, childhood responsibilities, and child—abuse, abusers, adjustment, advocates, care, care centers, care givers, custody, development, discipline, health, kidnapping, labor, molestation, mortality, neglect, nutrition, psychiatrics, rearing, sexual abuse, therapy, and welfare.

G55 **WORK RELATED ABSTRACTS** Edited by Florence Kretzschmar. Detroit, Information Coordinators, 1950- . Monthly, with quarterly and annual cumulated subject indexes. $360/year. From: 1435-37 Randolph St., Detroit, MI 48226.

Published as *Labor-Personnel Abstracts* from 1950-1958 and as *Employment Relations Abstracts* from 1959-1972, *Work Related Abstracts* is now published in loose-leaf format, with the monthly updates arranged in 20 broad categories and incorporated into a binder. Its Subject Heading List provides cross-references, geographic entries, and new terminology. On the whole, it succeeds in its intent to "extract the significant and the informative" from more than 250 management, professional, and university periodicals. Collectively, these provide thorough subject coverage and a variety of viewpoints and expertise. It is a prime source for locating materials on topics like child labor; child care; problems of working women with children; and the problems of youth, including age bias and high school dropouts.

9 / Periodicals and Newsletters

This chapter provides a multidisciplinary selection of periodicals and newsletters concerned in some way with the well-being of children. Although the periodicals, journals, and newsletters described and annotated herein are a varied group ranging widely in content, format, approaches, and length (from newsletters of a few pages to near monographs), collectively they are a most important segment of the literature on children. Most are ostensibly designed for particular practitioners (including the practice of parenting), although many aspire to be interdisciplinary. Typically, they are far more apt to transcend disciplinary boundaries than the reference sources discussed in previous chapters and are broader in scope than the textbooks and handbooks on children listed in the appendix. The periodicals and newsletters included in this chapter comprise articles and research, book reviews, news on children and publications, conferences and continuing education, and opportunities (through letters to the editors and other means) for two-way communication. Many are membership publications; some are old; some are responses to new conditions. I highly recommend extensive browsing.

Although only a few newsletters are described, I consider them a major (and usually inexpensive) source of information. Most are produced by associations, organizations, and clearinghouses (descriptions of some are subsumed under organizations in later chapters). Others are produced by interested individuals or some level of government, from local to international.

UNICEF and such international groups as the World Health Organization are the best sources for international newsletters. National reporting frequently comes from Washington, D.C. by associations and advocacy organizations that need to report the Washington scene to members. Other newsletters are issued by individuals or commercial organizations to speed up or amplify official sources. One good list of newsletters issued by organizations is contained in *The National Children's Directory.* General guides also exist, such as *The Oxbridge Directory of Newsletters* and the *National Directory of Newsletters and Reporting Services.* Check "Newsletters" in the index of this book to locate a few more titles.

I have not included all the periodicals on children, nor all those published in any particular discipline — that would call for a separate volume. I have tried, however, to describe the contents and special features of a representative cross-section of the more accessible and/or valuable journals and to indicate price, editorship, and where they are indexed. (The extensive indexing of many of these titles confirms that they do indeed cross disciplinary borders.) Other periodical titles can be gleaned through the journal lists in the periodical indexes cited in Chapter 8 (although some good titles are not indexed). I have checked prices with journal publishers and through the 1983 edition of *Ulrich's International Periodical Directory* (whose on-line version is described in J12). The current *Ulrich's* — in print and on-line — is a good source for locating additional titles and for checking to see if prices and addresses given here are still current. Back issues are usually available in libraries or through publishers or in microform from University Microfilms International.

The reference literature of most fields (other than child studies) generally includes a guide to periodicals. Haworth Press, for example, has issued the *Author's Guide to Journals in Psychology, Psychiatry and Social Work,* the *Author's Guide to Journals in the Health Field,* and similar titles. *Lippincott's Guide to Nursing Literature,* by Jane L. Binger and Lydia M. Jensen (Philadelphia, Pa., Lippincott, 1980), has an excellent discussion of journals in maternal and child nursing. There are four guides to education journals, including *Guide to Periodicals in Education and Its Academic Disciplines* (2nd Edition, by William L. Camp, Metuchen, N.J., Scarecrow, 1975). Bill Katz's *Magazines for Libraries* is, in effect, a consumer's guide to magazines, and the monthly *New Magazine Review*—also directed at librarians—provides illustrated reviews of new publications. Newsletters and periodicals (such as the *International Child Welfare Review*) frequently mention new periodicals.

In addition to these general guides, Haworth Press also issues a periodical entitled *Behavioral and Social Sciences Librarian,* which frequently contains annotated lists of periodicals in particular fields. For example, the fall 1983 issue included a core listing of journals on behaviorally disordered children (vol. 3, no. 1). *Children's Media Market Place* (I17) lists children's magazines and magazines that review children's media. *Ulrich's* includes sections on pediatrics periodicals and on periodicals for or about children.

H1   **ACADEMIC THERAPY**   Edited by Betty Lou Kratoville. Novato, Calif., Academic Therapy, 1965– . 5 issues/year. $15. From: 20 Commercial Blvd., Novato, CA 94947.

An interdisciplinary journal directed toward an international audience of classroom teachers, special teachers, parents, educational therapists, and specialists in all fields working with persons having reading, learning, and communication disorders. Basically focuses on "inefficient learners," that is, intellectually capable students unable to achieve academically with traditional educational methods; includes both scholarly articles and articles on materials and practices by psychologists, doctors, and educators. Lists approximately 10 professional books per issue. Indexed in *Bulletin Signalétique Sciences Humaine, Chicorel Abstracts to Reading and Learning Disabilities, Current Contents, dsh Abstracts, Exceptional Child Education Resources, Psychological Abstracts,* and *Rehabilitation Literature.*

H2   **ADOLESCENCE**   Edited by William Kroll. Roslyn Heights, N.Y., Libra, 1966– . Quarterly. Individuals, $30/year; institutions, $35/year. From: 391 Willets Rd., Roslyn Heights, NY 11577.

An international quarterly on the second decade of life, with articles for and by educators, psychologists, psychiatrists, sociologists, doctors, and other interested professionals. Editorial policy emphasizes interdisciplinary coordination. Good, brief book reviews. Indexed in *Biological Abstracts, Current Index to Journals in Education, Education Index, Excerpta Medica, Index Medicus, Psychological Abstracts, PsycSCAN: Developmental Psychology,* and *Social Sciences Citation Index.*

H3 **ADOPTION & FOSTERING** Edited by Sarah Curtis. London, British Agencies for Adoption & Fostering, 1976– . Quarterly. $10/year. From: 11 Southwark St., London SE1 1RQ, England.
A journal for professionals concerned with the welfare of children in foster care. Readers and contributors include social workers, lawyers, doctors, and academics. Contains "legal notes," books, and resources. Indexed in *Social Work Research and Abstracts.*

H4 **AMERICAN ANNALS OF THE DEAF** Edited by McCay Vernon. Silver Spring, Md., Convention of American Instructors of the Deaf, 1847– . Bimonthly. $33/year. From: 814 Thayer Ave., Silver Spring, MD 20910.
A national professional journal for teachers, specialists, and school administrators concerned with the education of deaf students. Includes articles on topics such as language or cognitive development in hearing-impaired children; also includes reviews, announcements, and letters to the editor. Indexed in *Biological Abstracts, Current Contents, Education Index, Excerpta Medica, P.A.I.S. Bulletin, Psychological Abstracts,* and *Social Sciences Citation Index.*

H5 **AMERICAN BABY: For Expectant and New Parents** Edited by Judith Nolte. New York, N.Y., American Baby, 1938– . Monthly. $9.95/year. Free six-month subscription. From: 575 Lexington Ave., New York, NY 10022.
Generally reliable, commonsense articles for new and expectant parents, with good pictorial features. The objective of this publication is to inform new and expectant parents about all aspects of pregnancy and baby care. Indexed in *Cumulative Index to Nursing and Allied Health Literature* and *Magazine Index.*

H6 **AMERICAN EDUCATION** Edited by William Horn. Washington, D.C., U.S. Department of Education, 1965– . Monthly (January/February, August/September, combined issues). $14/year. From: U.S. Government Printing Office, Washington, DC 20402.
A convenient overview that reports on federal legislation and education programs; includes statistics and a brief review section that covers most recent books on education issued by the U.S. Government Printing Office. Usually includes a guide to programs in the November issue. Indexed in *Education Index, P.A.I.S. Bulletin, Readers' Guide to Periodical Literature,* and elsewhere.

H7   **AMERICAN FAMILY: The National Newsletter on Family Policy and Programs** Edited by Rowan A. Wakefield. Washington, D.C., National Center for Family Studies, 1977- . Monthly, except August. $55/year; $70/year foreign. From: National Center for Family Studies, The Catholic University of America, Cardinal Sta., Washington, DC 20064.

American Family covers policy issues concerning the whole family life cycle, from early childhood to the elderly. Regularly featured in the monthly newsletter are sections on legislation, research, programs, organizations, trends, families and computers, publications, and meetings. The "Washington Focus" section covers the executive branch and national organizations in the nation's capital. Special issues, sold separately for $6 each, include one on military families and another on family mediation. The *Bibliographical Supplement* (D27) is cited in Chapter 5.

In 1984, American Family, Inc., merged its research, editing, and publishing operations with those of the Youth Policy Institute, Inc. of Washington, D.C., where the combined American Family and Youth Policy Institute staff maintains an extensive youth and family policy data base.

H8   **AMERICAN INDIAN CULTURE AND RESEARCH JOURNAL** Edited by William Oandasan. Los Angeles, University of California, American Indian Studies Center, 1971- . Quarterly. Individuals, $20/year; institutions, $30/year. From: University of California, 3220 Campbell Hall, 405 Hilgard Ave., Los Angeles, CA 90024.

Interdisciplinary forum for scholars concerned with the past, present, and future of American Indian life and knowledge. Often includes materials relevant to American Indian children; book reviews also are presented. Approximately 30 books on American Indian subjects are reviewed each year.

H9   **THE AMERICAN JOURNAL OF FAMILY THERAPY** Edited by S. Richard Sauber. New York, Brunner-Mazel, 1973- . Quarterly. Individuals, $28/year; institutions, $44/year. From: 19 Union Sq., W., New York, NY 10003.

Concentrates more on family therapy than on child therapy. Its book review section contains thoughtful reviews of many relevant titles, and the "Journal File" offers well-done abstracts of relevent articles from many journals. Indexed in *Current Contents*.

H10 **AMERICAN JOURNAL OF ORTHOPSYCHIATRY** Edited by Albert C. Cain. New York, American Orthopsychiatric Assn., 1930- . Quarterly. Individuals, $25/year; institutions, $35/year. From: 19 W. 44th St., New York, NY 10036.

A multidisciplinary, interpersonal journal with clinical, theoretical, research, and expository papers on topics related to mental health and human development. Includes reviews of current literature, perhaps seven or eight per issue. Some special issues tackle broad topics, such as the October 1982 edition on health and mental health problems associated with nuclear war.

Indexed in many abstract journals, including *Child Development Abstracts, Current Contents, Education Index, Excerpta Medica, Hospital Literature Index, Index Medicus, International Nursing Index, Language and Language Behavior Abstracts, Mental Retardation Abstracts, Psychological Abstracts, PsycSCAN: Developmental Psychology, Social Sciences Index,* and *Social Sciences Citation Index.*

The American Orthopsychiatric Association has published a 50-year cumulative index covering 1931–1980, with separate sections for authors, titles, subjects, and book reviews. It is available from JAI Press (Box 1678, 36 Sherwood Pl., Greenwich, CT 06830) at $65 for individuals and $95 for institutions.

H11 **THE ARTS IN PSYCHOTHERAPY: An International Journal** Edited by Myra F. Levick. Fayetteville, N.Y., Ankho Intl., 1973- . Quarterly. Members, $20/year; individuals, $40/year; institutions, $90/year; foreign institutions, $100/year. From: P.O. Box 426, Fayetteville, NY 13066.

Publishes original articles (including illustrations) by art, dance/movement, music, poetry, and drama psychotherapists; and by psychologists and psychiatrists for students and professionals in psychotherapy, mental health, and education. It attempts international, multidisciplinary coverage and contains news and book reviews for the field. Some issues have articles relating to children. For example, Volume 10, number 1 (1983) has relevant articles on improvisational drama with disturbed adolescents, children's drawings and storytelling resulting from psychiatric hospitalization, and art therapy with preschool children. Indexed in *Current Contents, Excerpta Medica, Psychological Abstracts,* and *Social Sciences Citation Index.*

H12 **ASSIGNMENT CHILDREN** (Appears in French under the title *Les Carnets de l'Enfance.*) Edited by P.-E. Mandel. Geneva, UNICEF, 1963- . 2 double issues/year. $16/year in the United

States, Canada, Australia, and New Zealand; $7.50/year for students and the third world; 46 French francs/year in Europe. From: Villa Le Bocage, Palais des Nations, 1211 Geneva 10, Switzerland.
An international multidisciplinary journal published by the United Nations Children's Fund, *Assignment Children* is concerned with major social development issues, especially those related to children, youth, and families. Most issues contain well-done book reviews and bibliographies. For example, the 59/60 double issue (1982) on community participation includes an annotated index of 92 articles on community participation published between 1976 and 1982, as well as another selective bibliography of 63 books and 52 journals on community participation.

H13 **BABY TALK MAGAZINE**   Edited by Patricia Irons. New York, Blessing Corp., 1935- . Monthly. $6.75/year. From: 185 Madison Ave., New York, NY 10016.
A parenting magazine with authoritative articles and many photographs. Often rewrites technical reports from scientific and pediatric journals for lay audiences.

H14 **BEHAVIORAL DISORDERS JOURNAL**   Edited by Robert B. Rutherford, Jr. Reston, Va., Council for Children with Behavior Disorders, 1976- . Quarterly. Individuals, $20/year; institutions, $40/year; $24/year foreign. From: Council for Exceptional Children, 1920 Association Dr., Reston, VA 22901.
A multidisciplinary journal concerned with all childhood behavioral disorders and children with special needs, including those of children committed to juvenile correctional facilities. Indexed in *Current Index to Journals in Education* and *Exceptional Child Education Resources.*

H15 **BIRTH**   Edited by Madeleine H. Shearer. Berkeley, Calif., Medical Consumer Communications (International Childbirth Education Association and American Society for Psychoprophylaxis in Obstetrics, cosponsors), 1973- . Quarterly. Individuals, $14/year; institutions, $20/year; $16/year foreign. From: 110 El Camino Real, Berkeley, CA 94705.
Original articles of research and commentary for perinatal care givers and educators; includes articles of general interest, research articles, letters to the editor, book reviews, reviews and summaries of slides and films, abstracts, an index to current literature, and a calendar. Indexed in *Current Contents, Excerpta Medica, Index Medicus, International Nursing Abstracts,* and *Psychological Abstracts.*

H16   **BLACK CHILD ADVOCATE** Washington, D.C., National Black Child Development Institute, 1971– . Quarterly. Free to members; nonmembers, $12.50. From: 1463 Rhode Island Ave., NW, Washington, DC 20005.
A quarterly newsletter that provides current and background national information on black children and their families in the areas of child development, child welfare, research, and public policy. Updates are sent through a supplementary *Black Flash*.

H17   **CDF REPORTS: The Monthly Newsletter of the Children's Defense Fund** Edited by Peggy Jarvis. Washington, D.C., Children's Defense Fund, 1979– . Monthly. $29.95/year. From: P.O. Box 7584, Washington, DC 20044.
A readable, competent source of current news on all aspects of federal, state, and local policies affecting children. Includes areas such as poverty, education, child care, child health and nutrition, child mental health, foster care and adoption, and child abuse. Offers excellent reporting that provides good background information on budget and legislative issues and court decisions. Also includes announcements of worthwhile books and programs and action alerts.

H18   **CHILD ABUSE AND NEGLECT: The International Journal** Edited by C. Henry Kempe. Denver, Colo., International Society for the Prevention of Child Abuse and Neglect, 1977– . Quarterly. Members, $50/year; institutions, $130/year. From: Pergamon Press, Maxwell House, Fairview Park, Elmsford, NY 10523.
A truly international journal, published in England and America, concerned with the prevention and treatment of child abuse and neglect, including sexual abuse; has an international editorial board. Indexed in *Child Development Abstracts, Current Contents, Psychological Abstracts,* and *Social Sciences Citation Index.*

H19   **CHILD AND FAMILY BEHAVIOR THERAPY** (Formerly *Child Behavior Therapy.*) Edited by Cyril M. Franks. New York, Haworth, 1978– . Quarterly. Individuals, $33/year; libraries, $85/year; other institutions, $48/year. From: 28 E. 22nd St., New York, NY 10010.
Includes general articles on behavior therapy, as well as research and clinical applications, in its "Clinical Corner." Some items deal with the enhancement of parenting. Most issues review 15–18 books (not too briefly) under "Briefly Noted" and include lengthy reviews of a few

additional titles. Indexed in *Behavioral Abstracts, Biological Abstracts, Bulletin Signalétique—Part 390 (Psychologie et Psychiatrie), Child Development Abstracts and Bibliography, Current Contents: Social and Behavioral Sciences, Current Index to Journals in Education, Education Index, Exceptional Child Education Resources, Pre-Psych Index, Psychological Abstracts, Rehabilitation Literature, Sage Family Studies Abstracts, Social Sciences Citation Index, Social Work Research and Abstracts, Sociological Abstracts, Sociology of Education Abstracts,* and the FAMILY RESOURCES DATABASE, among others.

H20 **CHILD & YOUTH SERVICES** Edited by Ranae Hanson. New York, Haworth, 1977- . Quarterly. Individuals, $35/year; libraries, $75/year; other institutions, $48/year. From: 28 E. 22nd St., New York, NY 10010.

Formerly provided reviews and abstracts of current literature; now primarily assembles original materials on emerging topics "that seem underrepresented in the established literature." Issues deal with broad themes or topics on the delivery of social and human services to youth and children, such as institutional abuse of children and youth. Since each issue is indexed, it can be used appropriately as text material for courses for which texts do not yet exist.

H21 **CHILD: CARE, HEALTH AND DEVELOPMENT** Edited by R. B. Jones. Oxford, England, Blackwell Scientific Publ., 1975- . Bimonthly. $75/year. From: 52 Beacon St., Boston, MA 02108.

"The journal aims to promote the study of the development of all children, but particularly those handicapped by physical, intellectual, emotional and social problems and to provide information on new methods to help overcome them. It is hoped the journal will contribute to the expansion of sound programmes of care and treatment and to a greater cooperation between the various disciplines concerned with child development." Includes book reviews. Indexed in *Current Contents, Excerpta Medica, Index Medicus,* and *PsycSCAN: Developmental Psychology.*

H22 **CHILD CARE INFORMATION EXCHANGE** Edited by Roger Neugebauer. Redmond, Wash., Child Care Information Exchange, 1978- . Bimonthly. $20/year. From: P.O. Box 2890, Redmond, WA 98052.

A helpful information exchange for directors of child care centers, with a management and administrative perspective. Includes materials on staff development; in-service education; child advocacy; and reviews of books, periodicals, and other resources—approximately six full reviews and 20–30 short listings per year. The exchange also publishes reprints and related books: *Caring for Infants and Toddlers: What Works and What Doesn't* (Vol. II, $10) covers issues, curriculum, health and safety, environments, parents, staff, administration, and resources.

H23 **CHILD CARE QUARTERLY** Edited by Dr. Jerome Beker. New York, Human Sciences Press, 1971– . Quarterly. Individuals, $28/year; institutions, $68/year. From: 72 Fifth Ave., New York, NY 10011.

An independent, yet scholarly, quarterly for professional child care workers; strongly concerned with upgrading the profession and child care standards in a variety of day and residential settings. Often includes information on topics like professional education. Around 10 book reviews per year. Indexed in *Social Work, Current Contents, Chicorel Abstracts to Reading and Learning Disabilities, Education Index, Exceptional Child Education Resources, Psychological Abstracts, PsycSCAN: Developmental Psychology, Sage Family Studies Abstracts,* and *Social Sciences Citation Index.*

H24 **CHILD DEVELOPMENT** Edited by E. Mavis Hetherington. Chicago, Ill., University of Chicago Press, 1930– . Bimonthly. $75/year; $81/year foreign. From: 5801 S. Ellis Ave., Chicago, IL 60637.

The basic research journal, issued by the Society for Research in Child Development, with original contributions in child development from the fetal period through adolescence, prepared by experts in such fields as psychology, sociology, and medicine. Each issue contains around 25 articles on current research and theory and a dozen brief reports, as well as occasional reviews or theoretical papers. Topics covered range from family relationships to cognition and learning, language and communication, social and personal development, and cross-cultural studies. Sometimes schedules special issues or special sections on significant current research areas such as infants at risk and developmental psychopathology. Indexed in *Biological Abstracts, Child Development Abstracts, Current Contents, dsh Abstracts, Education Index, Index Medicus, Language and Language Behavior Abstracts, Psychological Abstracts, PsycSCAN: Developmental Psychology, Social Sciences Citation Index,* and *Social Sciences Index.*

H25 **CHILDHOOD CITY QUARTERLY** (Formerly *Childhood City Newsletter.*) Edited by Roger Hart. New York, Graduate School of the City University of New York, Center for Human Environments, 1974– . Quarterly. Individuals, $12/year; libraries, $24/year; $16/year (individuals) foreign airmail. From: 33 W. 42nd St., New York, NY 10036.

Each thematic issue deals with some area of interaction between children and/or youths and the urban environment—issues such as toxics and children, city farms, children in transportation, environments for handicapped children, and urban wildlands. Each also includes announcements of conferences, workshops, special events, and exhibits; a resource section that covers new books, journals, films, and grant opportunities; and communications on the current research, design, educational, and planning projects of subscribers. The participation of children and youths in projects involving their environments is an important concern of the sponsoring group.

H26 **CHILDHOOD EDUCATION** Edited by Lucy Prete Martin. Washington, D.C., Association for Childhood Education International, 1924– . Bimonthly, from September to June. $32/year. From: 3615 Wisconsin Ave., NW, Washington, DC 20016.

A well-balanced childhood education publication for parents, teachers, and interested lay persons that covers education from infancy through early adolescence, with an international perspective. Includes good, brief reviews of books for children (approximately 200) and adults. Indexed in *Current Index to Journals in Education, Education Index,* and *Exceptional Child Education Resources.*

H27 **CHILD PROTECTION REPORT: The Independent Newsletter Covering Children/Youth Health and Welfare Services** Edited by William E. Howard. Washington, D.C., Child Protection Report (CPR), 1974– . Biweekly. $135/year, $250/2 years. From: 1301 20th St., NW, Washington, DC 20036.

Independent, knowledgeable, behind-the-scenes, no-holds-barred reporting of federal (mostly) and state actions that bear on the well-being of children, as well as what is happening in organizations that work for children or whose work affects children in some way. The editors are also the compilers of the *National Directory of Children & Youth Services* (I52) and know the scene. Subscribers have access to CPR's *Subscriber Inquiry Service* and may cancel at any time to receive a refund for unmailed issues.

H28 **CHILD PSYCHIATRY AND HUMAN DEVELOPMENT**
Edited by John C. Duffy. New York, Human Sciences Press,
1970– . Quarterly. Individuals, $32/year; institutions, $72/year.
From: 72 Fifth Ave., New York, NY 10011.
An interdisciplinary, international quarterly created to serve professionals in child psychology, psychiatry, pediatrics, social science, and
human development. Brings together the professional fields most concerned with the physical and psychological maturation of the child.
Well-documented, scholarly articles on children and adolescents provide a dialogue and exchange of ideas for a professionally diverse
audience. Indexed in *Chicorel Abstracts, Child Development Abstracts,
Current Contents, Current Index to Journals in Education, Education
Index, Exceptional Child Education Resources, Index Medicus, Psychological Abstracts, PsycSCAN: Developmental Psychology,* and *Social Sciences
Citation Index.*

H29 **CHILDREN AND YOUTH SERVICES REVIEW** Edited
by Duncan Lindsey. Elmsford, N.Y., Pergamon, 1979– .
Quarterly. Individuals, $30/year; institutions, $90/year. From:
Pergamon Press, Maxwell House, Fairview Park, Elmsford, NY
10523.
An international multidisciplinary quarterly review of the welfare of
young people. Indexed in *Current Contents, Exceptional Child Education
Resources, Psychological Abstracts, Social Sciences Citation Index,* and
Sociological Abstracts.

H30 **CHILDREN IN THE TROPICS** Edited by Dr. A. M. Masse-
Raimbault for the International Children's Center. Paris, Centre
International de l'Enfance, 1969– . Bimonthly. $17/year. From:
Chateau de Longchamp, Bois de Boulogne 75016, Paris, France.
Covers all childhood problems, as well as the training and education of
those who work with children. Many articles are concerned with children's health; others deal with social, psychological, educational, and
economic concerns. Some theme issues deal with children's health
habits, biological rhythms of children, children and their teeth, malnutrition, traditional medicine, and water quality. Indexed in *Biological
Abstracts.*

H31 **CHILDREN'S LEGAL RIGHTS JOURNAL** Edited by
Roberta Gottesman. New York, William S. Hein, 1979– .
Quarterly. Individuals, $23/year; agencies, $29/year. From:
1285 Main St., Buffalo, NY 14209.

Does a good job of covering children's rights as well as the rights and responsibilities of those concerned with children. In a typical issue, articles might range from a discussion of statutory rape to the rights of hyperactive children, to the role of religion in the classroom, to legal options for handicapped children. Other topics include children's rights vis-à-vis adoption or foster care and the public school system's responsibilities toward maltreated children. Each issue reviews legal issues and new cases in children's legal rights. Indexed in *Education Index, Book Review Index, Current Index to Journals in Education, Exceptional Child Education Resources,* and *Legal Resource Index.*

H32 **CHILDREN TODAY: An Interdisciplinary Journal for the Professions Serving Children** Edited by Judith Reed. Washington, D.C., U.S. Office of Child Development, 1954– . Bimonthly. $14/year. From: U.S. Government Printing Office, Washington, DC 20402.

Provides a comprehensive overview of current events, programs, and research from the stance of the Administration for Children, Youth, and Families. It includes an excellent book review section that covers up to 10 books per issue; some issues contain brief announcements of recent government publications. Each issue reports on current laws, grants, and studies. Topics reflect the full range of government concern and provide an overview of child health and welfare. Recent articles have covered child custody, foster care, family-based services, children of working parents, children with asthma, children of incarcerated parents, family life in the city, intellectually handicapped mothers, pediatric counseling, adolescent abuse, and discipline in the 1980s. Indexed in *Book Review Index, Cumulative Index to Nursing and Allied Health Literature, Current Index to Journals in Education, Education Index, Exceptional Child Education Resources, Hospital Literature Index, Magazine Index,* and *Readers' Guide to Periodical Literature.*

H33 **CHILD STUDY JOURNAL** (Formerly *Child Study Center Bulletin.*) Edited by Donald E. Carter. Buffalo, N.Y., State University of New York, 1970– . Quarterly. Individuals, $11; institutions, $22; students, $5. From: 1300 Elmwood Ave., Buffalo, NY 14222.

Still published by the Department of Behavioral and Humanistic Studies at the State University of New York at Buffalo, most articles deal with the interface of psychology and learning. Includes book reviews. Indexed in *Child Development Abstracts, Current Contents, Education Index, Exceptional Child Education Resources, Psychological Abstracts,*

PsycSCAN: Developmental Psychology, Social Sciences Citation Index, and *Sociological Abstracts.*

H34 **CHILD WELFARE: Journal of Policy, Practice and Program** Edited by Carl Schoenberg. New York, Child Welfare League of America, 1922– . Bimonthly. Individuals, $16/year; institutions, $25/year; students, $12/year. From: 67 Irving Pl., New York, NY 10003.

"Material submitted should extend knowledge in any child welfare or related service; on any aspect of administration supervision, casework, groupwork, community organization, teaching, research, interpretation; on any facet of interdisciplinary approaches to the field of child welfare; or on issues of social policy that bear on children's welfare." Most issues include general articles, practice forums, special reports, articles on programs, and reviews. Indexed in *Child Development Abstracts, Current Contents, Current Index to Journals in Education, Education Index, Exceptional Child Education Resources, Index Medicus, P.A.I.S. Bulletin, Human Resources Abstracts, Psychological Abstracts,* and *Social Sciences Citation Index.*

H35 **COGNITION** Edited by Jacques Mehler. Amsterdam, Associated Scientific Publishers and Elsevier Science Publishers, 1972– . 3 volumes of 3 issues/year. Individuals, $80.75/year; institutions, $162.75/year. From: Elsevier Science Publishers, 52 Vanderbilt Ave., New York, NY 10017.

An international journal publishing theoretical and experimental papers on the study of the mind; many articles deal with the minds and thinking of children (such as children's understanding of deception or the role of grammar in language use). Articles may arise from the fields of psychology, linguistics, neurophysiology, ethology, philosophy and epistemology; some deal with social policies involving behavioral science and the social and political aspects of cognitive studies. Includes book reviews only when they contribute to the field. Indexed in *Current Contents, Child Development Abstracts, Language and Language Behavior Abstracts, Psychological Abstracts, Social Sciences Citation Index,* and others.

H36 **COMPARATIVE EDUCATION REVIEW** Edited by Philip G. Altbach. Chicago, Ill., University of Chicago Press, 1957– . Triannual. Individuals, $22/year; institutions, $35/year. From: 5801 S. Ellis Ave., Chicago, IL 60637.

This periodical is valuable for its ongoing bibliography of comparative education, which has been included in various formats since 1969. It is currently a systematic subject index to 17 educational journals from Europe, Asia, and the Americas. Indexed in *Current Contents* and *Social Sciences Citation Index.*

H37 **CONTEMPORARY EDUCATION** Edited by Russell L. Hamm. Terre Haute, Indiana State University, School of Education, 1929– . Quarterly. $9/year. From: Statesman Towers West, Room 1005, Terre Haute, IN 47809.

Seeks to present competent discussions of contemporary problems in education, including controversial issues. For example, the Winter 1983 issue was a multifaceted presentation on ethnicity and multicultural education, including articles on learning disability classification, Asian-American culture, Indo-Chinese refugee children in Iowa, special needs of Mexican-American children, and so on. Indexed in *Current Contents, Current Index to Journals in Education, Chicorel Abstracts to Reading and Learning Disabilities, Language and Language Behavior Abstracts,* and *Social Sciences Citation Index.* Also available in microfilm from University Microfilms International.

H38 **CONTEMPORARY PSYCHOLOGY: A Journal of Reviews** Edited by Donald J. Foss. Arlington, Va., American Psychological Assn., 1956– . Monthly. Members, $20/year; nonmembers, $50/year; institutions, $100/year. Add $9 for foreign subscriptions. From: 1200 17th St., NW, Washington, DC 20036.

Contemporary Psychology contains critical reviews of books, films, tapes, and other media relevant to psychology; around 50 books per issue. Of these, perhaps 8–10 deal with children. This is a major source of reviews in psychology. Indexed in *Biological Abstracts, Book Review Index, Current Contents, Psychological Abstracts,* and *Social Sciences Citation Index.*

H39 **COURRIER: International Children's Center** Edited by Paul Resin. Paris, International Children's Center (Centre International de l'Enfance), 1950– . Bimonthly. 200 French francs in France; 250 French francs abroad. From: Chateau de Longchamp, Bois de Boulogne 75016, Paris, France.

This multidisciplinary, multilanguage journal contains original papers on health, nutrition, and social problems involving children, often with backup bibliographies. Its intended audience consists of pediatricians, obstetricians, health and social workers, educators, nutritionists, psychologists and psychiatrists, and magistrates of children's courts—with an emphasis on the needs of children and professionals in developing countries. It offers separate bibliographies on areas of concern, such as handicapped children.

Each issue also contains a "Medical, social and public health bibliography" that provides abstracts of some 800 papers from the world literature involving children. Typically, these deal with concerns, issues, and problems involving mothers, families, children, and adolescents. The abstracts, in French and English, are prepared by specialists and are followed by a book review section that provides French and English mini-reviews of 60–80 books per issue. This section is followed by citations of books received but not reviewed (usually 20–30 titles). Altogether, it mentions and/or reviews around 500 books yearly.

H40 **THE CREATIVE CHILD AND ADULT QUARTERLY**
     Edited by Wallace Draper. Cincinnati, Ohio, National Association for Creative Children and Adults (NACCA), 1976– .
     Members, $20/year; nonmembers, $25/year; institutions,
     $30/year. From: 8080 Spring Valley Dr., Cincinnati, OH 45236.
Published to help children and adults become the best they can be through understanding and applying research on creativity. Each issue includes approximately four research articles on topics like learning styles and ways to increase creativity in all spheres. Also included is a career guidance section with one or two articles and news and activities of NACCA. Some issues review books; others may contain lengthy classified lists of books received. Indexed in *Child Development Abstracts, Current Index to Journals in Education,* and *Psychological Abstracts.*

H41 **DAY CARE AND EARLY EDUCATION** Edited by Randa
     Roen. New York, Human Sciences Press, 1973– . Quarterly.
     Individuals, $19/year; institutions, $44/year. From: 72 Fifth
     Ave., New York, NY 10011.
This magazine is published "to provide the early childhood community with interesting, useful material," cognizant of the importance of the political process. Articles cover child development, families, facilities, day care administration, and preschool children. Its ongoing departments and columns include reviews of research in early childhood, reviews of books for young children, reviews of books for early childhood professionals, and activities for children. Around 6 professional books and 40 children's books are reviewed annually. Indexed in *Chico-*

rel Abstracts, Current Index to Journals in Education, Education Index, Exceptional Child Education Resources, and *Social Work Research and Abstracts.*

H42 **DAY CARE INFORMATION SERVICE** (Formerly the *Day Care & Child Development Reports.*) Edited by Jacqueline Zanca. Silver Spring, Md., United Communications Group, 1971– . Biweekly. $142/year. From: 8701 Georgia Ave., Suite 800, Silver Spring, MD 20910.

An information service for child care professionals that offers 26 issues of *Day Care USA Newsletter, Day Care Resources,* and *Day Care Special Reports* as part of its subscription service. *Day Care USA Newsletter* reports on day care issues and funding at local, state, and federal levels; *Day Care Resources* is an informative alerting service for publications and programs; and the *Special Reports* are full-scale analyses, such as highlights from unpublished government research reports or computerized information and referral. The subscription price includes a Day Care Hotline for legislation, regulations, programs, and developments and, currently, a bonus copy of the *Handbook for Day Care Professionals.*

H43 **DEVELOPMENTAL MEDICINE AND CHILD NEUROLOGY** Edited by Martin C. O. Bax for Spastics International Medical Publications. London, Spastics International Medical Publications (including American Academy for Cerebral Palsy and Developmental Medicine), 1958– . Bimonthly. $55/year. From: J. B. Lippincott, E. Washington Sq., Philadelphia, PA 19105.

Covers all problems concerned with child development and child neurology. Primarily medical and educational in scope, although articles range from a closer look at malnutrition in an African village to the study of the chromosomes of children with developmental language retardation, to teaching children with developmental language retardation, to teaching children with motor impairments, to postural care of the newborn. Each issue includes approximately 10 book reviews of well-selected significant books. Its annual bibliographic issue is noted in Chapter 5 (D30). Indexed in *Biological Abstracts, Current Contents, dsh Abstracts, Excerpta Medica, Index Medicus, Psychological Abstracts, Science Citation Index,* and others.

H44 **DEVELOPMENTAL PSYCHOLOGY** Edited by Sandra Scarr. Washington D.C., American Psychological Assn., 1969– . Bimonthly. Members, $20/year; nonmembers, $50/year; institutions, $100/year. Add $5 for foreign subscriptions. From: 1200 17th St., NW, Washington, DC 20036.

Contains articles and research reports on human development throughout a lifetime. Looks for research on socially important topics, including field research, cross-cultural studies, and longitudinal studies. Indexed in *Biological Abstracts, Current Contents, Psychological Abstracts,* and *PsycSCAN: Developmental Psychology.*

H45   **DIMENSIONS: A JOURNAL OF THE SOUTHERN AS-SOCIATION ON CHILDREN UNDER SIX**   Edited by Kay C. Powers. Little Rock, Ark., SACUS, 1972- . Quarterly. Free to members; nonmembers, $7/year. From: Box 5403, Brady Sta., Little Rock, AR 72215.

The editorial voice of a 13-state umbrella organization of many groups involved with the well-being and development of children under the age of six. Members range from university researchers and educators of teachers to school administrators and proprietors of day care centers and nursery schools, to parents and teachers of young children. It contains practical, interesting articles on topics such as improvement of self-concept through children's literature, helping children manage stress, and children's safety needs in play areas. Each issue includes reviews of research, a down-to-earth illustrated "ideas" section, excellent reviews of professional literature (usually three or four titles), and news involving children and/or the association. Reviews around 12–18 children's books, 10–12 professional books, and 10–15 new products per year.

H46   **THE DIRECTIVE TEACHER**   Edited by Larry A. Magliocca. Columbus, Ohio State University, National Center on Educational Media and Materials for the Handicapped (NCEMMH), 1978- . Semiannual. $5/year. From: Ohio State University, 356 Arps Hall, 1945 High St., Columbus, OH 43210.

Practical, yet often scholarly, general interest, and special theme articles on special education. Provides a good overview of the children who are being educated and their environments. Sometimes includes reviews or bibliographies of books and materials.

H47   **EARLY CHILD DEVELOPMENT AND CARE**   Edited by Roy Evans. London, Gordon and Breach, 1971- . Quarterly. Individuals, $81/year; institutions, $74/year. From: 1 Park Ave., New York, NY 10016.

A multidisciplinary publication, with an international editorial board, that covers all aspects of early child development and care for an audience of psychologists, educators, pediatricians, social workers, and other professionals concerned with research, planning, care, and education of infants and young children. Its articles include English-language translations and original articles in English; news and reports; and experimental and observational studies, critical reviews, and summary articles. Its book review section (around 10 pages of books reviewed and books received) includes foreign publications (generally European). Indexed in *Biological Abstracts* and *Excerpta Medica*.

H48   **EARLY   HUMAN   DEVELOPMENT: An   International Journal Concerned with the Continuity of Fetal and Postnatal Life**   Edited by John Dobbing. Amsterdam, Elsevier Biomedical Press, 1977– . 8 issues/year (2 Vols.). $176/year. From: Journal Division, P.O. Box 1527, 1000 BM Amsterdam, Netherlands.

A comprehensive interdisciplinary forum for papers concerned with early human growth and development, with an emphasis on the continuity among fetal life, the problems of the perinatal period, and those aspects of postnatal growth that are influenced by early events. The editors are concerned with safeguarding the quality of human survival. Papers are mostly original research with applications to the human species, appropriate for both clinicians and researchers, and are drawn mainly from the fields of reproduction and fertility, fetology, perinatology, pediatrics, growth and development, obstetrics, reproduction and fertility, behavioral sciences, nutrition and metabolism, and teratology, although other papers relating to early human development may be included from time to time. Book reviews are included as space permits (some issues have as many as 10 pages devoted to them). Indexed in *Current Contents: Life Sciences, Excerpta Medica,* and *Index Medicus.*

H49   **EARLY YEARS: A Magazine for Teachers of Preschool Through Grade Four**   Edited by Allen A. Raymond. Darien, Conn., Allen A. Raymond, Inc., 1971– . Monthly, from September to May. $13/year. From: Box 912, Farmingdale, NY 11735.

A magazine dedicated to the classroom teacher, preschool through fourth grade; deals with curriculum areas, classroom management techniques, and, occasionally, brings research down to the classroom level (as with a series of articles on learning styles). Rather busy but practical; covers a lot of information for this group.

H50   **EDUCATION**   Edited by Tudor David. London, Councils and
      Education Press, 1903– . Weekly. £37.50/year. From: Longman
      Journals, The Pinnacles, Fourth Ave., Harlow, Essex CM20
      1NE, England.
A weekly news journal that covers all aspects of education and education-related news in Britain, from child health and play groups to curriculum review and school meals. Notes or reviews around 250–300 new
books per year. Indexed in *British Education Index.*

H51   **EDUCATION LIBRARIES**   Edited by Susan Baughman.
      Cambridge, Mass., Special Libraries Assn., Education Div.,
      1976– . 3 issues/year. Individuals, $10/year; institutions, $15/
      year; $20/year foreign. From: Harvard University, Gutman
      Library, 6 Appian Way, Cambridge, MA 02138.
A magazine for and by education librarians that often helpfully consolidates information sources on topics like achievement or aptitude tests,
resources for teaching Indo-Chinese students, and on-line education
data bases. Also notes special issues of education journals and new
educational reference books and includes a column on ERIC.

H52   **EDUCATION OF THE VISUALLY HANDICAPPED**
      Edited by Mary Anna Bloch. Washington, D.C., Helen Dwight
      Reid Educational Foundation and Heldref Publications, 1951– .
      Quarterly. Members, $20/year. From: 4000 Albemarle St.,
      NW, Washington, DC 20016.
Takes a broad view of education, including such things as music therapy
and social skills. Indexed in *Current Contents, Current Index to Journals
in Education, Exceptional Child Education Resources, Psychological Abstracts,* and *Social Sciences Citation Index.*

H53   **ELEMENTARY SCHOOL GUIDANCE AND COUNSEL-
      ING**   Edited by Joseph C. Rotter. Alexandria, Va., American
      Association for Counseling and Development, 1967– .
      Quarterly. Members, $20/year. From: 5999 Stevenson Ave.,
      Alexandria, VA 22304.
Includes articles on research and practices in counseling children
during the elementary and middle school years, with discussions of
such issues as improving relations in stepfamilies, counseling transient
children or hearing-impaired children, and understanding social development during middle childhood. Indexed in *Education Index, Psychological Abstracts,* and *Social Work Research and Abstracts.*

H54 **ELT [ENGLISH LANGUAGE TEACHING] JOURNAL**
Edited by Richard Rossner. Oxford, England, Oxford University
Press, 1946- . Quarterly. $25. From: Walton St., Oxford OX2
6DP, England.
A publication for all professionals involved in teaching English as a
second or foreign language, whether in English-speaking countries or
elsewhere. *ELT Journal* seeks to bridge the gap between practice
(everyday concerns of teachers) and theory. Covers resources and
materials, case studies, and research from an international perspective.
Indexed in *British Education Index, Education Index,* and *Language and
Language Behavior Abstracts.*

H55 **ENVIRONMENT AND BEHAVIOR** Edited by Robert B.
Bechtel. Beverly Hills, Calif., Sage, 1969- . Bimonthly.
Individuals, $28/year; institutions, $62/year. From: 275 S.
Beverly Dr., Beverly Hills, CA 90212.
An interdisciplinary journal focusing on the influence of the physical
environment on human behavior at the individual, group, and institutional levels; includes articles on school and other childhood environments. Indexed in *Current Contents, Human Resources Abstracts, Psychological Abstracts, Social Sciences Citation Index, Social Sciences Index,*
and *Sociological Abstracts.*

H56 **EQUAL PLAY: A RESOURCE MAGAZINE FOR ADULTS
WHO ARE GUIDING YOUNG CHILDREN BEYOND STER-
EOTYPES** Edited by Jo Suchat Sanders. New York, Sex
Equity in Education Program of Women's Action Alliance,
1980- . Quarterly. Individuals, $12/year; institutions, $22/year.
From: 370 Lexington Ave., Room 603, New York, NY 10017.
For parents, teachers, and activists concerned with nonsexist and other
nonstereotyping education for children. Includes news and reviews of
curriculum and materials, television, and other media; programs, play,
and playthings; the toy industry, socialization, and children and
computers; and conferences and programs. In addition, it provides
many thoughtful reviews of books and media for children and adults.

H57 **ETHICS IN EDUCATION** Edited by Donald Craig.
Toronto, Ontario Institute for Studies in Education, 1981- . 10
issues/year during school year. $18/year; quantity discounts.
From: 252 Bloor St., W., Toronto, Ontario M5S 1V6, Canada.

A professional letter for parents, teachers, school principals, and school staff members at the elementary and high school levels. The objective of this publication is to make ethical education an integral part of classroom work, playground play, and school community life to develop consistent high standards of ethical thinking and behavior in school children. Reports cover basic ethics, applications of moral education theory, case reports from educators, and developments in ethical education. *Ethics in Education* also provides capsule reports on resources such as professional literature, relevant audiovisuals, texts, and supplementary classroom materials, as well as applicable television programs and films for the general public. It covers the United States well, but, as a Canadian publication, it draws heavily on Canadian and British experience. Reviews two to four books per year.

H58   **EXCEPTIONAL CHILDREN**   Edited by Dr. M. Angele Thomas. Reston, Va., Council for Exceptional Children, 1934– . 6 issues/year. $25/year; $29 foreign. From: 1920 Association Dr., Reston, VA 22901.

An official publication of the Council for Exceptional Children issued primarily for educators, *Exceptional Children* deals with many aspects of gifted and handicapped children. Provides capsule reports of research; overview articles (including debate articles on current issues); and articles on curriculum and classroom hints, programs, policies, and planning. It also reviews the media, including professional publications, tapes, and films, and contains a calendar of events, news notes, announcements of teaching aids and programs, and some book reviews. Indexed in *Education Index, Exceptional Child Education Resources, Excerpta Medica, Index Medicus, Psychological Abstracts, PsycSCAN: Developmental Psychology,* and *Social Sciences Citation Index.*

H59   **EXCEPTIONAL PARENT: Children with Disabilities/ Practical Information**   Edited by Stanley D. Klein and Maxwell J. Schleifer. Boston, Mass., Psy-Ed Corp., 1971– . 8 issues/year. Individuals, $16/year; institutions, $24/year. Add $3 for foreign subscriptions. From: 605 Commonwealth Ave., Boston, MA 02215.

A commonsense publication for parents of handicapped children and those who deal with these parents or children, with an emphasis on problem-solving at the parent-child and parent-professional levels. Typically, each issue contains articles on improving parent-professional relations, learning about family relationships, having fun with exceptional children, and managing finances (includes an annual income tax guide), as well as on travel, recreation, and religion for or with handicapped children (often backed up by directories); directories of parent and professional organizations that might be helpful to parents; and consumer guides to items like wheelchairs. Throughout, it has a consistent focus on communication and sharing of information. It provides occasional book reviews, announcements of publications, packets, and brochures and also operates The Exceptional Parent Bookstore to distribute relevant books to parents and teachers. Indexed in *Exceptional Child Education Resources, Index Medicus,* and *Psychological Abstracts.*

H60 **FAMILY ADVOCATE: A Practical Journal by the ABA Family Law Section**   Edited by Gary N. Skoloff. Chicago, Ill., American Bar Assn., Section on Family Law, 1978– . Quarterly. $25. From: 1155 E. 60th St., Chicago, IL 60637.

A lawyer's magazine on family practice that includes well-written, understandable articles on issues like divorce, child snatching, the rights of stepparents or unwed fathers, surrogate motherhood, and child custody. These articles may contain facts not easily located elsewhere, such as the estimated public costs of contested child custody cases or the impact of interviewing children in court. Sometimes entire issues are devoted to child-related topics such as adoption. *Family Advocate* announces laws and legal publications related to the well-being of children and reviews around 10 books per year. A section roster provides the names of officers, council, and chairpersons in the ABA's Section on Family Law. Indexed in *Legal Resource Index.*

H61 **FAMILY ECONOMICS REVIEW**   Edited by Kathleen K. Scholl. Hyattsville, Md., U.S. Department of Agriculture, Family Economics Research Group, 1983– . Quarterly. $8.50/year; $10.65/year foreign. From: U.S. Government Printing Office, Washington, DC 20402.

Reports on research done by its parent group and other research relating to economic aspects of family living, including up-to-date information on family finances, household production, and economic well-being of families (see Figure 5). From time to time, it includes information on its research project, the Cost of Raising a Child. It also abstracts relevant publications. Regular features include announcements of Department of Agriculture publications and reports on the cost of food at home. Writing is nontechnical and easy to understand.

Cost of raising a child born in 1966 [6]

Year	Age of child (years)	Total	Food at home[3]	Food away from home	Clothing	Housing[4]	Medical care	Education	Transportation	Other[5]
1966	Under 1	$1,316	$194	0	$66	$539	$70	0	$267	$180
1967	1	1,397	238	0	69	555	75	0	275	185
1968	2	1,372	245	0	118	508	79	0	247	175
1969	3	1,448	257	0	125	541	85	0	257	183
1970	4	1,620	310	$50	130	580	90	0	270	190
1971	5	1,688	317	53	134	606	96	0	284	198
1972	6	1,829	321	55	190	598	99	$43	287	236
1973	7	2,027	460	59	197	624	103	44	296	244
1974	8	2,254	528	66	211	697	112	47	330	263
1975	9	2,463	572	73	221	772	126	51	361	287
1976	10	2,713	695	78	229	820	138	53	397	303
1977	11	2,886	736	84	239	877	151	56	424	319
1978	12	3,366	831	109	357	971	164	70	478	386
1979	13	3,827	1,023	122	373	1,090	179	76	548	416
1980	14	4,282	1,105	135	397	1,262	199	83	645	456
1981	15	4,698	1,185	147	418	1,406	220	94	724	504
1982	16	5,469	1,371	155	592	1,562	244	107	832	606
1983	17	5,643	1,385	162	607	1,598	265	118	852	656
Total 1966–83..		50,298	11,773	1,348	4,673	15,606	2,495	842	7,774	5,787

Year	Age									
1984	Under 1	4,312	571	0	142	1,876	278	0	866	579
1985	1	4,664	736	0	149	1,970	292	0	910	607
1986	2	4,561	773	0	254	1,819	307	0	832	576
1987	3	4,789	812	0	266	1,910	322	0	874	605
1988	4	5,327	979	172	279	2,005	338	0	918	636
1989	5	5,593	1,028	181	293	2,105	355	0	964	667
1990	6	6,118	1,044	190	426	2,095	373	166	1,012	812
1991	7	6,678	1,352	199	448	2,200	391	174	1,062	852
1992	8	7,012	1,419	209	470	2,310	411	183	1,115	895
1993	9	7,364	1,490	220	494	2,425	432	192	1,171	940
1994	10	8,031	1,863	231	518	2,547	453	202	1,230	987
1995	11	8,431	1,956	242	544	2,674	476	212	1,291	1,036
1996	12	9,456	2,099	305	826	2,911	500	222	1,456	1,137
1997	13	10,175	2,449	321	867	3,057	525	234	1,528	1,194
1998	14	10,685	2,572	337	911	3,210	551	245	1,605	1,254
1999	15	11,217	2,700	354	956	3,370	578	258	1,685	1,316
2000	16	12,933	3,174	371	1,391	3,663	607	270	1,953	1,504
2001	17	13,581	3,333	390	1,461	3,846	638	284	2,050	1,579
Total 1984–2001		140,927	30,350	3,722	10,695	45,993	7,827	2,642	22,522	17,176

NOTE: Current dollar estimates[1] of the cost of raising a child[2] born in 1966 and in 1984 at the moderate cost level in the urban North Central region.

[1] Derived from table 8 of USDA Miscellaneous Publication No. 1411, USDA Estimates of the Cost of Raising a Child: A Guide to Their Use and Interpretation, October 1981, by Carolyn S. Edwards.

[2] Child in family of husband and wife and no more than 5 children.

[3] Includes home-produced foods and school lunches.

[4] Includes shelter, fuel, utilities, household operations, furnishings, and equipment.

[5] Includes personal care, recreation, reading, and other miscellaneous expenditures.

[6] Prices current in the years specified; calculated using indexes in table 2 rounded to nearest $1.

[7] Inflated from 1983 constant dollar estimates at annual rate of 5 percent and rounded to nearest $1.

Figure 5 The charts and articles in *Family Economics Review* provide a great deal of information on economic expenditures related to childhood. They also provide bibliographies of selected references on child cost estimates. (Shown is Table 3 from *Family Economics Review*, No. 3, 1984.)

H62   **FAMILY INVOLVEMENT JOURNAL** (Formerly *Involve-ment.*) Edited by John L. Brown. Toronto, Canadian Educational Programmes, 1968– . 5 issues/year. $15/year. From: 151 Placer Ct., Willowdale, Ontario M2H 3H9, Canada.
Jargon-free articles for teachers, nurses, social workers, child psychologists, and workers in allied fields on normal growth and development and on children and families. Some focus on providing normal life experiences for children with emotional problems or mental or physical handicaps. Contributors come from many countries and many disciplines.

H63   **FAMILY JOURNAL** Edited by Debra M. Gluck Gardner. Columbia, Mo., Family Journal Magazine, 1981– . Bimonthly. $15/year; $20/year in Canada; $25/year elsewhere. From: 1205 University Ave., Columbia, MO 65201.
An attractive, informative publication with news items, columns, and articles that provides coverage of nearly all issues of concern to parents of children up to eight years old, with emphasis on pregnancy and infancy. Many articles are written by professionals who also are parents. Ongoing columns include books for parents (around four per issue), books for children (perhaps seven per issue), a family news column, and a family health column (question and answer format). The magazine is pro-family and promotes causes that support effective parenting; its articles cover everything from storytelling to learning disabilities and the psychological problems children experience when they are very tall or very small.

H64   **FAMILY LAW REPORTER** Edited by Richard H. Cornfield. Washington, D.C., Bureau of National Affairs, 1974– . Weekly (50 weeks). $330/year. From: 1231 25th St., NW, Washington, DC 20037.
A legal reference compendium in loose-leaf format that provides continuous updating of pending legislation and recent decisions. Covers such topics as family violence, adoption, abortion, child custody, legitimacy, child support, foster care, and parental and children's rights. A survey of current developments, tables of current court cases, summaries and opinions of court decisions, legislative actions, Supreme Court decisions with full texts, news notes, and occasional monographs on family law subjects are included. The *Family Law Reporter* notes or reviews around a dozen books per year. Each issue provides a comprehensive cumulative index, culminating in a final index each year. Indexed in *Criminal Justice Periodical Index.*

H65   **FAMILY LIFE**   Los Angeles, American Institute of Family
Relations, 1945– . Bimonthly. $5/year. From: 4942 Vineland
Ave., North Hollywood, CA 91601.
Each bimonthly booklet provides a developmental overview and current counseling strategies for a particular family-related issue or group,
usually with references and recommended readings, pertinent book reviews, and institute news.

H66   **FAMILY PROCESS**   Edited by Carlos E. Sluzki. New York,
Family Process, 1962– . Quarterly. Individuals, $24/year;
institutions, $35/year. From: 149 E. 78th St., New York, NY
10021.
Emphasizes research, theory, and practice in the field of family health
and family psychotherapy, including family structure and parental communication. Includes around eight book reviews per issue and occasional reviews of audiovisual materials. Indexed in *Current Contents, Excerpta Medica, Psychological Abstracts,* and *Social Sciences Citation Index.*

H67   **FAMILY RELATIONS: JOURNAL OF APPLIED FAMI-
LY AND CHILD STUDIES**   Edited by Michael Sporakowski.
Minneapolis, Minn., National Council on Family Relations,
1952– . Quarterly. Individuals, $23.50/year; institutions,
$30.00/year. From: 1910 W. County Rd. B, Suite 147, St. Paul,
MN 55113.
Directed toward a somewhat diverse group of practitioners serving
families through education, counseling, and community services. This
journal reports practices (especially innovative work methods) in all
these fields, and includes articles on the applications of theory and research to practice. The articles are not of a "how-to" nature, but the authors are consistently concerned with the realities and consequences of
social work practices in the field of family relations. Recent issues include an array of short articles on varied topics, such as the impact of
family life events and family changes on the health of chronically ill
children, the obligations of stepparents, day care and single parents,
patterns of child care information seeking, and the education needs of
secondary students in learning how to become good parents. A helpful
book review section provides brief, but thoughtful, signed reviews of
perhaps 10 books and two media items in a typical issue. Indexed in
*Child Development Abstracts, Current Index to Journals in Education, Psy-
chological Abstracts, Sage Family Studies Abstracts,* and *Social Sciences Citation Index.*

H68   **FAMILY THERAPY: The Bulletin of Synergy** Edited by
      Martin G. Blinder. Roslyn Heights, N.Y., Libra Publishers,
      1972– . Triannual. Individuals, $25/year; institutions, $30/year.
      Add $1 for foreign subscriptions. From: 391 Willets Rd.,
      Roslyn Heights, NY 11577.
A clinical journal devoted to the practice of family, group, and other in-
teractional therapies that use the family unit as a base. Covers many
forms of treatment approaches and techniques. Indexed in *Psychological
Abstracts.*

H69   **FOCUS ON EXCEPTIONAL CHILDREN** Edited by Caro-
      lyn Acheson. Denver, Colo., Love Publishing, 1969– . Month-
      ly, from September to May. $18/year. From: 1777 S. Bellaire
      St., Denver, CO 80222.
Concerned with legal, educational, and psychological practical aid for
emotionally disturbed and mentally retarded children. Indexed in *Current Contents, Exceptional Child Education Resources,* and *Social Sciences
Citation Index.*

H70   **FUTURE** Edited by the UNICEF Regional Office for South
      Central Asia. New Delhi, India, UNICEF House, 1981– .
      Quarterly. $13/year in the United States; $11/year in Europe;
      $9/year in Asia and Africa. From: 73 Lodi Estate, New Delhi
      110003, India.
Future concerns the whole spectrum of child development and supportive facilities—that is, family, community, and society. It focuses on development issues related to children, especially in Asian countries such
as Afghanistan, Bhutan, India, Maldives, Mongolia, Nepal, and Sri
Lanka (although it also includes general articles). It is valuable in
providing information about the conditions of children, and, as an open
forum, does not exclusively advocate any development policy or model.

H71   **G/C/T [GIFTED/CREATIVE/TALENTED]** Edited by Mar-
      vin J. Gold. Mobile, Ala., G/C/T Publishing, 1978– .
      Bimonthly. $17.50/year; $20.00/year foreign. From: 350 Wei-
      nacker Ave., Mobile, AL 36604.
Self-proclaimed as the "world's most popular magazine for parents and
teachers of gifted, creative, and talented children," this attractive publication maintains a useful balance among discussions of contemporary
issues in gifted education, well-selected case studies, and practical
suggestions. It includes articles on creative parenting and mentors for
the gifted, ways to identify and counsel gifted students, and ways to

wedge critical thinking into school situations, as well as conceptual models and thoughtful articles with competent bibliographies on such topics as the relationship between cognitive abilities and moral development in gifted children. Also offers directories of summer programs for gifted youth and calendars of events for adults concerned with the gifted. Thirty reviews of books and articles were published in 1983. Indexed in *Exceptional Child Education Resources.*

H72 **GIFTED CHILD QUARTERLY** Edited by Donald J. Treffinger. St. Paul, Minn., National Association for Gifted Children, 1957– . Quarterly. $35/year. From: 5100 N. Edgewood Dr., St. Paul, MN 55112.

General, educational, and research articles on gifted children, from preschool through adolescence, aimed at furthering the education of the gifted and enhancing their personal activity. Includes articles on educational policies, research, theories, and curricula and reviews of four to six books per year. The association's newsletter, *Communique,* covers news events and reviews books of interest to parents and practitioners. Indexed in *Current Contents, Education Index,* and *Psychological Abstracts.*

H73 **GIFTED CHILDREN NEWSLETTER** Sewell, N.J., Gifted and Talented Publications, 1980– . Monthly. $24/year. From: P.O. Box 115, Sewell, NJ 08080.

A rather lengthy (around 20 pages) newsletter primarily for parents of the gifted but also useful for teachers and mentors. Contains short articles on topics like motivation, achievement, or mathematics education, often with suggested activities or additional readings. Each issue includes a calendar of events, as well as book, game, and toy reviews, and a "Spin-Off" pullout section of puzzles, games, and activities for gifted children. No index.

H74 **HUMAN DEVELOPMENT** Edited by J. A. Meacham. Basel, Switzerland, Karger, 1958– . Bimonthly. Individuals, $48.50/year; institutions, $97.00/year. From: 150 Fifth Ave., Suite 1103, New York, NY 10011.

Scholarly, multidisciplinary, and cross-cultural coverage of the spectrum of human development from infancy through aging, with frequent articles on aspects of childhood, child-rearing practices, language development, and the like, that affect cognitive and social development. Provides ongoing coverage through articles and integrative reviews of behavioral and social science research and work in education, anthropology, biology, history, and philosophy. A "Developmental Issues" section deals with significant issues and topics. Karger also publishes a monograph series, "Contributions to Human Development," that covers similar territory. Indexed in *Biological Abstracts, Current Contents, Education Index, Excerpta Medica, Psychological Abstracts, PsycSCAN: Developmental Psychology,* and *Social Sciences Citation Index.*

H75 **IMAGINATION, COGNITION AND PERSONALITY: Consciousness in Theory-Research-Clinical Practice** Edited by Kenneth S. Pope and Jerome L. Singer. Farmingdale, N.Y., Baywood Publishing, 1981– . Quarterly. Individuals, $30/year, plus postage; institutions, $55/year, plus postage. From: 120 Marine St., P.O. Box D, Farmingdale, NY 11735.

Provides a unique forum on studies of the imaginative processes, somewhat weighted toward psychology and psychotherapy. Each issue includes book reviews (around 15–18 per year) and news on conferences and research. No index.

H76 **INDEPENDENT SCHOOL** Edited by Blair McElroy. Boston, Mass., National Association of Independent Schools, 1941– . Quarterly. Members, $12.00/year; nonmembers, $14.50/year. From: 18 Tremont St., Boston, MA 02108.

An open forum for the exchange of ideas on quality education at elementary and secondary levels, especially in independent schools. Often contains thoughtful articles on topics like values, the "brain" behind the curriculum, and recruitment of minority students. Richard Barbieri's fine essay reviews and two or three other reviews in each issue search out books that can simultaneously enrich professional lives and stimulate readers. Indexed in *Current Index to Journals in Education* and *Education Index.*

H77 **INFANT MENTAL HEALTH JOURNAL** Edited by Jack M. Stack. New York, Human Sciences Press, 1980– . Quarterly. Individuals, $30/year; institutions, $72/year. From: 72 Fifth Ave., New York, NY 10011. Reprint service available through Institute for Scientific Information and University Microfilms International.

An interdisciplinary journal concerned with optimal development of infants; brings together ideas, programs, and approaches from many different care-giving specialties on topics like infant assessment and the social environment of infants. For example, a typical issue might have articles on the role of the adolescent father, day care, marital circumstances, community mental health, and private medical practice. The official publication of the Michigan Association for Infant Mental Health, it offers subscription discounts to its members and to members of affiliated associations. Includes book reviews mostly of interdisciplinary works. Abstracted in *Psychological Abstracts.* Indexed in *Child Development Abstracts, Excerpta Medica, Psychological Abstracts,* and *Sociological Abstracts.*

H78 **INTELLIGENCE: A Multidisciplinary Journal** Edited by Douglas K. Detterman. Norwood, N.J., Ablex, 1977– . Quarterly. Individuals, $20/year; institutions, $55/year. From: 355 Chestnut St., Norwood, NJ 07648.

Covers all aspects of intelligence in children and adults. A representative issue might contain articles on assessment; sex differences; cross-cultural aspects of intelligence; and the correlation of precocious reading with letter-naming time and digit span. Indexed in *Current Contents.*

H79 **INTERNATIONAL CHILDREN'S RIGHTS MONITOR** Geneva, Defense for Children International, 1983– . Quarterly. Individuals, $10/year; institutions, $20/year. From: P.O. Box 359, CH-1211 Geneva 4, Switzerland.

The first regular publication exclusively devoted to children's rights on a worldwide scale, it seeks to provide independent and objective information and analyses, not only to arouse awareness of problems, but to point out what has been, is being, and can be done at all levels to combat and resolve these problems. An advocate for children who may be imprisoned, tortured, separated from their families, forced into armies, or exploited or maltreated because of their helplessness, the *International Children's Rights Monitor* supplies international coverage of all kinds of child maltreatment and exploitation that occur beyond the family. The first issue, for example, included articles on the violation of children's rights in Iran, the female circumcision issue in Europe, international aspects of child kidnapping, curbing child marriages among immigrants in Sweden, and the circumstances of Amerasian children in Vietnam. The reporting is both timely and exemplary, with thorough background and documentation. Each issue includes a survey of developments, issues, and situations concerning children's rights during the preceding quarter.

H80 **INTERNATIONAL CHILD WELFARE REVIEW** Edited by Ceri Hammond. Geneva, International Union for Child Welfare (IUCW), 1926– . Quarterly, with supplemental *Biblio-*

theque/Library/Biblioteca. Switzerland, 37 Swiss francs; United States, Africa, Americas, Asia, 41 Swiss francs; Europe, 39 Swiss francs. From: P.O. Box 41, CH-1211 Geneva 20, Switzerland.

Intelligent reporting of international developments, available in English, Spanish, and French; sometimes includes interesting comparisons of treatment of children and legal rights or educational policies among nations and regions. Each issue provides news of meetings and reports of world organizations concerned with children and youth and a "Through the Grapevine" section that reports new organizations, new publications, and new services. Each issue also contains a separate multilingual *Library Supplement* on colored paper, which annotates around 25–30 books and 100 selected journal articles from the IUCW library in English, French, and Spanish. Books are arranged by Dewey decimal classification, whereas articles are grouped under the headings of psychology, sociology, statistics, law, economics, social welfare, education, and health. The supplement provides an excellent means of keeping current with significant materials related to children.

H81 **INTERNATIONAL JOURNAL OF BEHAVIORAL DE-VELOPMENT** Edited by Franz J. Moenks. Amsterdam, North-Holland, 1978– . Quarterly. Individuals, $65.50/year; institutions, $83.00/year. From: Box 211, 1000 AE Amsterdam, Netherlands.

The official journal of the International Society for the Study of Behavioral Development, it is concerned with the international and interdisciplinary study of behavior over a lifetime. Includes original research, review articles, comparative studies, applications of developmental theory and research, book reviews, and announcements of meetings. It also provides interesting cross-cultural reports (such as developmental psychology in China) and reprints of conference papers. Indexed in *Current Contents.*

H82 **INTERNATIONAL JOURNAL OF EARLY CHILDHOOD** Edited by Anne McKenna. Dublin, University College, Department of Psychology, 1969– . 2 issues/year. OMEP members, $7/year; nonmembers, $10/year. From: c/o Dr. Margaret Devine, 81 Irving Pl., New York, NY 10003.

Published for OMEP (World Organization for Early Childhood Education or Organisation Mondiale pour l'Education Prescolaire), the purpose of this journal is to disseminate information about the needs of children from birth to 7 or 8 years old, including child psychology, preschool education, child health and nutrition, good toys and play materials, playgrounds and play equipment, appropriate architecture, and parent education and information. It has an international editorial board, is published in three languages (English, French, and Spanish), and includes book reviews. Indexed in *Child Development Abstracts, Current Index to Journals in Education, ERIC Clearinghouse,* and *Social Sciences Index.*

H83 **INTERNATIONAL SOCIAL SCIENCE JOURNAL** Paris, Unesco, 1947– . Quarterly. $30/year. From: 7-9 Place de Fontenoy, 75700 Paris, France; or Unipub, Box 433, Murray Hill Sta., New York, NY 10016.

A good tool for keeping current with international and comparative developments in the social sciences. Occasionally, complete issues are devoted to topics such as patterns of child socialization. News on conferences, recent Unesco publications, and books received are also included. Indexed in *Current Contents, Excerpta Medica, P.A.I.S. Bulletin, Psychological Abstracts, Social Sciences Index,* and *Social Sciences Citation Index.*

H84 **JOURNAL OF ABNORMAL PSYCHOLOGY** Edited by Herbert C. Quay, New York, Plenum, 1973– . Bimonthly. $105/year. From: 233 Spring St., New York, NY 10013.

Devoted to research and theory concerned with psychopathology in childhood and adolescence. Priority is given to empirical investigations in etiology, assessment, treatment in the community and in correctional institutions, prognosis and follow-up, epidemiology, remediation in educational settings, pharmacological intervention, and the ecology of abnormal behavior. The target populations comprise subjects exhibiting a variety of neurotic and organic disorders, delinquency, psychosomatic conditions, and disorders of behavior in mental retardation. Emphasizes original experimental and correlational research but also publishes occasional significant case studies and brief reports on ongoing projects. Indexed in *Current Contents, Excerpta Medica, Index Medicus, PsycSCAN: Developmental Psychology,* and *Psychological Abstracts.*

H85 **JOURNAL OF ADOLESCENT HEALTH CARE** Edited by H. Verdain Barnes. New York, Elsevier/North-Holland, 1980– . Quarterly. Individuals, $30/year; institutions, $45/year; students, $15/year. From: 52 Vanderbilt Ave., New York, NY 10017.

A scientific publication of the Society for Adolescent Medicine, which is an interdisciplinary health care specialty that seeks to provide quality health care to adolescents, a medically neglected age group. This multidisciplinary magazine publishes significant works from disciplines involved in understanding the physiology, biochemistry, endocrinology, psychology, and sociology of adolescence and meeting the acute, chronic, and preventive health care needs of adolescents. Each issue includes research articles, subject reviews, case reports, and an annotated list of new publications in the field of adolescent medicine. Reviews or notes approximately 12–20 books per year.

H86 **JOURNAL OF AESTHETIC EDUCATION** Edited by Ralph A. Smith. Urbana, Ill., University of Illinois Press, 1966– . Quarterly. Individuals, $15.00/year; institutions, $25.00/year. Add $2.50 for foreign subscriptions. From: 54 E. Gregory, Box 5081, Sta. A, Champaign, IL 61820.

One of the few journals concerned with the interactions between children and the skills and concepts related to art and aesthetics. Includes book reviews, lists of books received, and occasional reviews of literature on topics like aesthetic responses of young children to visual arts. Reviews around 22–25 books per year and lists 125–150. Indexed in *Current Contents, Education Index, Psychological Abstracts,* and *Social Sciences Citation Index.*

H87 **JOURNAL OF AUTISM AND DEVELOPMENTAL DISORDERS** Edited by Eric Schopler. New York, Plenum, 1971– . Quarterly. Individuals, $33/year; institutions, $96/year. From: 233 Spring St., New York, NY 10013.

Devoted to all severe childhood psychopathologies, rather than limited to autism and childhood schizophrenia. Includes reports of experimental studies on biochemical, neurological, and genetic aspects; studies of social, group, and community factors and implications for normal development; and critical reviews of important research. Includes a book review section and a "Parents Speak" section. Abstracted or indexed in *Acta Paedopsychiatrica, Biological Abstracts, Chicorel Abstracts to Reading and Learning Disabilities, Child Development Abstracts and Bibliography, Current Contents, Current Index to Journals in Education, dsh Abstracts, Exceptional Child Education Resources, Excerpta Medica, Index Medicus, Psychological Abstracts, PsycSCAN: Developmental Psychology,* and others.

H88 **JOURNAL OF CHILD CARE** Edited by Gerry Fewster. Calgary, Canada, 1982– . 3 issues/year. Individuals, $30/year; institutions, $45/year; members of child care associations,

$20/year (Canadian funds). From: 117 Woodpark Blvd., SW, Calgary, Alberta T2W 2ZB, Canada. Intended primarily for the professional child care worker, but committed to disseminating information and knowledge to all individuals who assume responsibility for the well-being of children. This publication tackles interdisciplinary topics such as schooling and delinquency prevention; assessment in child care; and policies on reporting child abuse. Preference is given to articles by front-line practitioners. Chris Bagley heads the review section, which may exceed 20 pages.

H89 **JOURNAL OF CHILDHOOD COMMUNICATION DISORDERS: Bulletin of the Division for Children with Communication Disorders** Edited by Hiram L. McDade. Reston, Va., Council for Exceptional Children, 1978– . Semiannual. Free to members; individuals, $8/year; institutions, $16/year. From: 1920 Association Dr., Reston, VA 22091.
A peer review periodical issued under the auspices of the council's Division for Children with Communication Disorders, this journal attempts to address the needs of parents of communicatively handicapped children, as well as professionals in the area of speech-language pathology, audiology, deaf education, and learning disabilities. In addition, the journal publishes one theme issue each year; in 1982, it was entitled "Intervention with the Young Stutterer."

H90 **JOURNAL OF CHILD LANGUAGE** Edited by David Crystal. London, Cambridge University Press, 1974– . 3 issues/year. Individuals, $36/year; institutions, $85/year. From: 32 E. 57th St., New York, NY 10022.
Publishes material on all aspects of language behavior and development in children, including normal and pathological development and the study of monolingual and multilingual children. Reports on observation; therapy; education; and experiments involving sounds, grammar, semantics, dialects, and language use. Around seven book reviews and an index of books received are included in each issue. Indexed in *Biological Abstracts, Child Development Abstracts, Current Contents, Language and Language Behavior Abstracts, MLA Bibliography, PsycSCAN: Developmental Psychology,* and *Sociological Abstracts.*

H91 **JOURNAL OF CHILD PSYCHOLOGY AND PSYCHIATRY AND ALLIED DISCIPLINES** Edited by Eric Taylor. Oxford, England, Pergamon, 1960– . Students, $15/year; indi-

viduals whose institutions subscribe, $40/year; institutions, $130/year. From: Pergamon Press, Maxwell House, Fairview Park, Elmsford, NY 10523.
This official publication of Britain's Association for Child Pyschology and Psychiatry brings together contributions from different points of view to promote integration and a unified body of generally accepted facts. A typical issue might include articles on motor development of deaf children; a "stages-of-information" approach to hyperactivity; and a commentary on mother/infant interactions. Indexed in *Biological Abstracts, Education Index, Index Medicus, Psychological Abstracts,* and *PsycSCAN: Developmental Psychology.*

H92   **JOURNAL OF CHILD PSYCHOTHERAPY** Edited by Shirley Hoxter. London, Association of Child Psychotherapists, 1963- . £2/issue. From: Distribution Secretary, *Journal of Child Psychotherapy,* Burgh House, New End Sq., London NW3, England.
Largely case studies; includes some reviews.

H93   **JOURNAL OF CHILDREN IN CONTEMPORARY SOCIE-TY** (Formerly *Children in Contemporary Society.*) Edited by Mary Frank. New York, Haworth, 1967- . Quarterly. Individuals, $28/year; institutions, $48/year; libraries, $60/year. Quantity discount. From: 28 E. 22nd St., New York, NY 10010.
An interdisciplinary thematic quarterly that focuses on contemporary educational, social, medical, political, and economic issues influencing the growth and development of young children. Recent theme issues have dealt with such topics as childhood depression, young children in a computerized environment, and primary prevention of psychological and social problems for children and families. Arranged as texts of around 100 pages, these issues are sometimes edited by guest editors and may contain annotated bibliographies. Indexed in *Child Development Abstracts, Cumulative Index to Nursing and Allied Health Literature, Current Index to Journals in Education, Exceptional Child Education Resources, Resources in Education, Social Welfare/Planning Development Abstracts,* and *Sociological Abstracts.*

H94   **JOURNAL OF CLINICAL CHILD PSYCHOLOGY** Edited by June M. Tuma. Baton Rouge, La., American Psychological Assn., Clinical Child Psychology Section, 1972- . Triannual. Free to members; nonmembers, $25/year; institutions, $35/year. From: 318 Stanford Ave., Baton Rouge, LA 70808.

Oriented toward problems rather than disciplines, this journal is intended as a forum for reflective comment by those concerned with children and youth. It publishes the viewpoints of all child advocates, including nonpsychologist colleagues, students, and consumers of mental health services, and offers a wide range of articles on creative programs, models, service patterns, research, resources, and actions and ideas that promote the well-being of children and youth. Each issue has book reviews (around half a dozen, on varied topics like behavioral pediatrics, television, child custody, and learning disabilities) and lists books received. The "Announcements" section also notes books and periodicals, as well as organizations and symposia. Indexed in *Current Contents, Psychological Abstracts, PsycSCAN: Developmental Psychology,* and *Social Sciences Citation Index.*

H95 **JOURNAL OF DRUG EDUCATION** Edited by Seymour Eiseman. Farmingdale, N.Y., Baywood Publishing, 1971– . Quarterly. Individuals, $27/year, plus postage; institutions, $51/year, plus postage. From: 120 Marine St., P.O. Box D, Farmingdale, NY 11735.
Covers smoking, drinking, and prescription drugs, as well as drug use and prevention of abuse for an audience of health educators and researchers. Notes around 35 books per year. Indexed in *Abstracts of Criminology and Penology, Biosciences Information Service of Biological Abstracts, Counseling and Personnel Services Information Center, Current Contents, Current Index to Journals in Education, Drug Abuse and Alcoholism Review, Excerpta Medica, Psychological Abstracts,* and *Sociological Abstracts.*

H96 **JOURNAL OF EXPERIMENTAL CHILD PSYCHOLOGY** New York, Academic, 1964– . Bimonthly. Individuals, $80/year, $90/year foreign; institutions, $160/year, $192/year foreign. From: 111 Fifth Ave., New York, NY 10003.
Research and experimental reports cover the whole spectrum of child psychology, from cognition and development, to infant visual preferences, to the ways children evaluate consistency. Indexed in *Biological Abstracts, Current Contents, Education Index, Index Medicus, Psychological Abstracts, PsycSCAN: Developmental Psychology,* and *Social Sciences Citation Index.*

H97 **JOURNAL OF FAMILY HISTORY** Edited by Tamara K. Hareven. Minneapolis, Minn., National Council on Family Relations, 1975– . Quarterly. $25/year; $29/year foreign. From: 1910 W. County Rd. B, Suite 147, St. Paul, MN 55113.

Publishes essays on the history of the family and kinship in all periods and regions. Many essays involve the history of child rearing, attitudes toward children, and the like. Although the focus is primarily historical, current social changes also are discussed. Reviews approximately five books per year. Indexed in *Current Contents, Historical Abstracts, Human Resources Abstracts, Population Index, Sage Family Studies Abstracts, Social Sciences Citation Index, Social Sciences Index, Sociological Abstracts,* and others.

H98   **JOURNAL OF FAMILY ISSUES** Edited by Graham B. Spanier. Beverly Hills, Calif., Sage, 1980– . Quarterly. Individuals, $25/year; institutions, $52/year. Add $4 for foreign subscriptions. From: 275 S. Beverly Dr., Beverly Hills, CA 90212.

This journal, sponsored by the National Council on Family Relations, is devoted to contemporary social issues and social problems related to marriage and family life and to professional issues of concern to family workers and researchers. Two of the four issues are thematic, based on topics such as television and the family (June 1983); the other two include research and theoretical articles and occasional commentary and advocacy pieces on family issues. Indexed in *Current Contents, Social Sciences Citation Index, Sociological Abstracts,* and *Urban and Social Change Review.*

H99   **JOURNAL OF FAMILY LAW** Edited by Kevin Keeler. Louisville, Ky., University of Louisville, 1961– . Quarterly. $15/year. From: 2301 S. Third St., Louisville, KY 40292.

Includes articles on current and emerging issues related to family law and the historical and theoretical aspects of domestic law problems such as adoption and child custody. Includes notes, case notes, notes on current literature, legal essays, and book reviews, with a subject index to cases. Indexed in *Legal Resource Index.*

H100   **JOURNAL OF GENETIC PSYCHOLOGY: Developmental and Clinical Psychology** Edited by John E. Horrocks. Provincetown, Mass., The Journal Press, 1891– . Quarterly. $42/year. From: 2 Commercial St., Box 543, Provincetown, MA 02657.

Devoted to developmental and clinical psychology. Publishes occasional critical reviews of books of major importance and lists books received. The 15 or so articles per issue deal with topics like identity development, the relations between peer familiarity and play behavior, moral reasoning in childhood, and cross-cultural studies. A separate section on replications and refinements contains around five articles per issue. Indexed in *Biological Abstracts, Child Development Abstracts, Current Contents, Exceptional Child Education Resources, Excerpta Medica, Psychological Abstracts, Language and Language Behavior Abstracts, PsycSCAN: Developmental Psychology,* and *Sociology of Education Abstracts.*

H101 **JOURNAL OF JUVENILE LAW**   Edited by Carol Crow. La Verne, Calif., La Verne Law Review, Inc., 1977- . Semiannual. $8/year. From: 1950 Third St., La Verne, CA 91750.

Includes articles, notes and comments, and a digest of Supreme Court and state decisions affecting juveniles, as well as a digest of legislation affecting juveniles. Interesting articles deal with topics such as the death penalty for children, the surrogate child, privacy, child snatching, parental rights, owner restrictions on family occupancy, and the evolution of a successful delinquency diversion system. The Fall issue is simply a digest issue that surveys state and federal cases affecting juveniles. Indexed in *Index to Legal Periodicals* and *Legal Resource Index.*

H102 **JOURNAL OF LEARNING DISABILITIES**   Edited by Gerald M. Senf. Chicago, Ill., The Professional Press, 1968- . 10 issues/year. Individuals, $32/year; institutions, $45/year; $50/ year foreign. From: 11 E. Adams St., Chicago, IL 60603.

A multidisciplinary publication with articles on practice, research, and theory related to learning disabilities. Includes reports of research, opinion papers, case reports, and a discussion of issues related to the field. Provides a list of books received and has a "Books in Brief" section; together, these review around 30 books per year and note receipt of approximately 300. Indexed in *PsycSCAN: Developmental Psychology.*

H103 **JOURNAL OF NURSE-MIDWIFERY**   Edited by Mary Ann Shah. Washington, D.C., American College of Nurse-Midwives, 1954- . Bimonthly. Free to members; nonmembers, $25/year; institutions, $46/year. From: Elsevier Science Publishing Co., Inc., 52 Vanderbilt Ave., New York, NY 10017.

The official publication of the American College of Nurse-Midwives, the *Journal of Nurse-Midwifery* covers issues and research related to the practice and education of nurse-midwives in a manner that combines readability, humanism, and a solid professional approach. Each issue contains journal abstracts, research exchanges, media reviews, and book reviews of very high quality. Approximately 72 books are reviewed each year. Indexed in *Cumulative Index to Nursing and Allied Health Literature, Current Contents, International Nursing Index, Social Sciences Citation Index,* and others.

H104 JOURNAL OF PEDIATRIC PSYCHOLOGY Edited by Gerald P. Koocher. New York, Plenum, 1975- . Quarterly. $55/year. From: 233 Spring St., New York, NY 10013.

Includes articles that reflect the interests and concerns of psychologists working in interdisciplinary settings such as children's hospitals, developmental clinics, and group practices, except for materials on autism (or learning disabilities related to autism). Articles deal with theory, research, training, and practice, although they tend toward practice; family coping with childhood leukemia; management of common childhood bedtime problems; effect of mother's presence on children's reactions; follow-up on child surgery patients; and so on. Includes one or more book reviews each issue, perhaps 12-20 per year, as well as news and notes. Indexed in *Current Contents, Psychological Abstracts, PsycSCAN: Developmental Psychology,* and *Sociological Abstracts.*

H105 JOURNAL OF PEDIATRICS Edited by Joseph M. Garfunkel. St. Louis, Mo., C. V. Mosby, 1932- . Monthly. Individuals, $40.50/year; institutions, $68.50/year; students, $30.00/year. From: 11830 Westline Industrial Dr., St. Louis, MO 63146.

More clinical and technical than *Pediatrics* (H127) but nevertheless a basic journal with features and columns that cover the literature, the latest developments in the field, and reports on therapy. Contains original research articles and clinical and laboratory observations, information on medical care, pharmacology, and therapeutics. Reviews around 15-20 books per year and notes the receipt of some 200. Indexed in *Biological Abstracts, Chemical Abstracts, Excerpta Medica, Index Medicus,* and *Nutrition Abstracts.*

H106 JOURNAL OF PSYCHOHISTORY (Formerly *History of Childhood Quarterly.*) Edited by David Beisel. New York, Atcom, 1973- . Quarterly. $28/year. From: 2315 Broadway, New York, NY 10024.

Focuses on parent-child relationships in the context of history, literature, and the social sciences from the philosophical viewpoint of psychohistory. Studies personalities and historical and social movements. Indexed in *Child Development Abstracts, Psychological Abstracts,* and *Sociological Abstracts.*

H107 **JOURNAL OF SCHOOL HEALTH: Official Journal of the American School Health Association** Edited by Tom Reed. Kent, Ohio, American School Health Assn., 1930– . Monthly. Free to members (membership, $40/year); institutions, $35/year; $40/year foreign; single copies, $4. From: Box 708, Kent, OH 44240.

This interdisciplinary journal is a good source of information on health-care issues related to school-age children; typically covers health problems related to child development, disease control programs, current research in child health, administration of health programs, resources for health education, sex education, alcohol and drug abuse education, and the training of health providers. Includes competent reviews of books and films, announcements of brochures and publications, and occasional bibliographies on topics such as cross-cultural and international health. Some issues deal with broad topics; for example, the February 1983 issue was concerned with cross-cultural and international aspects of school health; the February 1984 issue is on consumer health. Index is cumulated once a year and once every 10 years. Indexed in *Biological Abstracts, Cumulative Index to Nursing and Allied Health Literature, Current Contents, Education Index, Index Medicus, International Nursing Index,* and *Social Sciences Citation Index.* Available in microform from University Microfilms International.

H108 **JOURNAL OF SOCIAL ISSUES** Edited by Joseph E. McGrath. Ann Arbor, Mich., Society for the Psychological Study of Social Issues, 1944– . Quarterly. Individuals, $25/year; institutions, $65/year. From: Plenum, 233 Spring St., New York, NY 10013.

Sponsored by the Society for the Psychological Study of Social Issues, a group of more than 3,000 psychologists and allied social scientists who share concern with research on the psychological aspects of important social issues. The journal's goal is to communicate scientific findings and interpretations in a nontechnical manner without sacrificing professional standards. Indexed in *Social Work Research and Abstracts, Abstracts in Anthropology, Abstracts on Criminology and Penology, Current Contents, Education Administration Abstracts, Human Resources Abstracts, Mental Health Index, Political Science Abstracts, Psychological Ab-*

stracts, Psychological Reader's Guide, Sage Family Studies Abstracts, Social Science and Humanities Index, Sociological Abstracts, and *Sociology of Educational Abstracts.*

H109 **JOURNAL OF THE AMERICAN ACADEMY OF CHILD PSYCHIATRY** Edited by Melvin Lewis. Baltimore, Md., Williams & Wilkins, 1962– . Bimonthly. Free to members; nonmembers, $50/year; institutions, $70/year. Add $10 for foreign subscriptions. From: 428 E. Preston St., Baltimore, MD 21202.

Includes special articles, scientific papers, brief communications, case reports, book reviews and lists of books received, and selected abstracts from *Pediatrics* (H127). Special articles may include contributions from other fields. Scientific papers cover all sorts of behaviors for all ages of children. Indexed in *Excerpta Medica, Index Medicus,* and *Psychological Abstracts.*

H110 **JOURNAL OF TROPICAL PEDIATRICS** Edited by D. B. Jeliffe and G. J. Ebrahim. Oxford, England, Oxford University Press, 1954– . Bimonthly. $69/year. From: Oxford University Press, Journals Subscriptions Dept., Walton St., Oxford OX2 6DP, England.

Devoted to all aspects of child health and nutrition, with an emphasis on the locality and quality of the environment. It enjoys a good reputation as one of very few journals concerned with the problems of children in the third world. Many papers report clinical and community research or program development. Also includes monographs or papers from conferences, review articles, and book reviews. Indexed in *Current Contents, Excerpta Medica,* and *Index Medicus.*

H111 **JOURNAL OF YOUTH AND ADOLESCENCE: A Multidisciplinary Research Publication** Edited by Daniel Offer. New York, Plenum, 1972– . Bimonthly. Individuals, $47.50/year; institutions, $140.00/year. From: 233 Spring St., New York, NY 10013.

Intended to provide single, high-level communication for psychiatrists, psychologists, biologists, sociologists, educators, and professionals in other disciplines concerned with children and youth. Articles deal with everything from grief reactions to diabetic control, gifted adolescents, and pregnancy. Indexed in *Abstracts on Criminology and Penology, Current Contents, Excerpta Medica, Psychological Abstracts, Sage Urban Studies Abstracts, Social Sciences Citation Index,* and *Sociological Abstracts.*

H112 **JUVENILE & FAMILY COURT JOURNAL** Edited by Toni Witt Hutcherson. Reno, Nev., National Council of Juvenile and Family Court Judges, 1949– . Quarterly. $24/year; $28/year foreign. From: University of Nevada, P.O. Box 8978, Reno, NV 89507.
Concerned with the U.S. juvenile justice system, juvenile delinquency, and juvenile and family courts. Contains approximately 10 thoughtful, well-documented articles in each issue, often with substantial tables and bibliographies. Indexed in *Current Contents* and *Social Sciences Citation Index.*

H113 **JUVENILE & FAMILY LAW DIGEST** Edited by Lindsay G. Arthur. Reno, Nev., National Council of Juvenile and Family Court Judges, 1968– . Monthly. $60/year. From: University of Nevada, Box 8978, Reno, NV 89507.
Recent significant court decisions on all topics of interest to judges, attorneys, paraprofessionals, probation officers, and others concerned with juvenile and family law, with an annual cumulative index of all rulings digested since 1974.

H114 **LANGUAGE ARTS: Official Journal of the National Council of Teachers of English** Edited by Julie M. Jensen. Urbana, Ill., National Council of Teachers of English, 1924– . Monthly. Individuals, $30/year; institutions, $35/year. Add $4 for foreign subscriptions. From: 1111 Kenyon Rd., Urbana, IL 61801.
This journal, which recently celebrated its 60th year, is primarily for teachers and teacher educators of children from preschool through middle school. It attempts to gather viewpoints from other academic areas, such as anthropology, linguistics, and psychology, that have implications for language teaching. It includes articles in a wide variety of formats from satires and photoessays to position papers and reviews. Each issue includes perspectives from outside the profession, research updates, reports from ERIC, reviews of professional resources and instructional materials, classified reviews of perhaps 30 children's books, and an in-depth profile of an author or illustrator. Indexed in *Current Index to Journals in Education* and *Education Index.*

H115 **LEARNING: The Magazine for Creative Teaching** Edited by Morton Malkofsky. Belmont, Calif., Pitman Learning, 1972– . Monthly, during the school year (nine issues). $12/year. From: 19 Davis Dr., Belmont, CA 94002.

A magazine for elementary teachers that publishes articles by important thinkers like Amitai Etzioni, not always taking a reverent view of educational givens. Includes reviews and updates on educational topics written in understandable English. Indexed in *Current Index to Journals in Education* and *Readers' Guide to Periodical Literature.*

H116 **MARRIAGE AND FAMILY REVIEW**   Edited by Marvin B. Sussman. New York, Haworth, 1977– . Quarterly. Individuals, $33/year; institutions, $72/year; libraries, $103/year. From: 28 E. 22nd St., New York, NY 10010.

Now a thematic journal, with each issue covering in-depth a single aspect of marriage and the family, ranging from government and the family to pets and the family. These issues are interdisciplinary syntheses that include solicited literature review articles. Many of the issues are concerned in some way with children in the family. Indexed in *Index Medicus, Psychological Abstracts, Social Sciences Citation Index,* and *Sociological Abstracts.*

H117 **MATERNAL-CHILD NURSING JOURNAL**   Edited by Corinne Barnes and Olive Rich. Pittsburgh, Pa., University of Pittsburgh, Nursing Care of Children and Maternity Nursing, 1972– . Quarterly. $15/year; 18/year in Canada; $20/year foreign. From: 437 Victoria Bldg., 3500 Victoria St., Pittsburgh, PA 15261.

Designed to serve the expert nurse practitioner in the care of mothers and children; also intended as a medium of exchange and stimulation in professional competence. Includes literature reviews, articles, and clinical contributions, as well as research reports. Recent topics include infant anxiety, how to help children deal with the stress of hospitalization, and a literature review of postpartum depression. Indexed in *Cumulative Index to Nursing and Allied Health Literature* and *International Nursing Review.*

H118 **MERRILL-PALMER QUARTERLY**   Edited by Carolyn U. Shantz. Detroit, Mich., Wayne State University Press, 1954– . Quarterly. Individuals, $20/year; institutions, $40/year; students, $12/year. From: 5959 Woodward Ave., Detroit, MI 48202.

A primary source of original research in the fields of human development and family life, with a special interest in integrative papers that are meaningful to professionals in diverse fields. Includes reviews, research reports, and commentary; provides selected book reviews; and lists books received (around 40 per year). Some issues are thematic; research reports may deal with topics such as cognitive content of parents' speech to preschoolers, evidence of effectiveness in early instruction in reading, and predictive validity of social-cognitive assessments. Indexed in *Child Development Abstracts, Current Contents, Current Index to Journals in Education, Language and Language Behavior Abstracts, Psychological Abstracts, PsycSCAN: Developmental Psychology, Social Sciences Citation Index, Social Work Research and Abstracts,* and *Sociology of Education Abstracts.*

H119 **MONTHLY LABOR REVIEW** Washington, D.C., U.S. Bureau of Labor Statistics, 1915– . Monthly. $26.00/year; $32.50/year foreign. From: U.S. Government Printing Office, Washington, DC 20402.

Good ongoing source of statistical and other information on family concerns related to work, such as child care arrangements by working parents, numbers of children with working mothers, and the like. Occasional articles on narrower topics. Announces Bureau of Labor Statistics reports in a timely way.

H120 **MOTHERS TODAY** (Formerly *Mothers' Manual.*) Edited by Janet Spencer King. New York, Mothers' Manual, 1966– . 8 issues/year. $6/year. From: Box 243, Franklin Lakes, NJ 07417.

A magazine for mothers and expectant mothers, with continuing departments on child health, women's bodies, expectant mothers, baby basics, parent perspectives, news notes, and discoveries.

H121 **NEW DIRECTIONS FOR CHILD DEVELOPMENT** Edited by William Damon. San Francisco, Jossey-Bass, 1978– . Quarterly. Individuals, $25.00/year; institutions, $35.00/year; $8.95 per issue. From: 433 California St., San Francisco, CA 94104.

A series of thematic sourcebooks on research topics in child development intended to present current, scholarly information at a manageable introductory level. Each issue has its own editors and index. Recent issues include *Child Development and International Development, Children and Divorce, Children's Planning Strategies, Children's Play,* and *Developmental Approaches to Giftedness and Creativity.* Indexed in *Child Development Abstracts and Bibliography, Education Index, Psychological Abstracts,* and others.

H122 **PARENTS' CHOICE: A REVIEW OF CHILDREN'S MEDIA** Edited by Diana Huss Green. Waban, Mass., Parents' Choice Foundation, 1978– . Quarterly. $10/year. From: Box 185, Waban, MA 02168.

A tabloid-size newsprint quarterly edited by a former teacher of children's literature. Its reviews of children's books, television, movies, music, story records, toys, computer software, and videodisks are aimed primarily at parents. Well written and well illustrated, with occasional essays or commentary by award-winning or big-name authors, *Parents' Choice* is valuable for anyone who deals with children. Reviews hundreds of items—including 75–100 books—each year from a nonprofessional, but intelligent and humanistic, perspective.

H123 **PARENTS: On Rearing Children from Crib to College** (Formerly Parents' Magazine.) Edited by Elizabeth Crow. New York, Parents' Magazine Enterprises, 1926– . Monthly. $14/year. From: 685 Third Ave., New York, NY 10017.

A popular magazine, with a host of previous titles; includes articles on child health, family fun, and successful child rearing from infancy to college. Indexed in *Readers' Guide to Periodical Literature.*

H124 **PARENTS VOICE** Edited by Alan Leighton. London, Journal of the National Society of Mentally Handicapped Children, 1950– . Quarterly. £3/year in England; £5/year elsewhere. From: Pembridge Sq., London EC1Y ORT, England.

A quarterly magazine with feature and news articles aimed at parents of mentally handicapped children and professionals working in the field, published by Britain's largest national parent organization. Reviews around 12–18 books per year.

H125 **PEDIATRIC ANNALS** Edited by Milton I. Levine. Thorofare, N.J., Slack, Inc., 1972– . Monthly. $38/year; $53/year foreign. From: 6900 Grove Rd., Thorofare, NJ 08086.

Dedicated to the continuing education of the practicing pediatrician, with review articles that serve as state-of-the-art benchmarks. Each issue is dedicated to an in-depth review of a single topic, updated to within three months of publication. These topics are not exclusively medical but may also cover such things as child abuse and public policies toward children. Competent book reviews. Indexed in *Adolescent Mental Health Abstracts, Current Contents in Clinical Practice,* and *Index Medicus.*

H126 **PEDIATRIC MENTAL HEALTH** Santa Monica, Calif.,
Pediatric Projects, 1982- . Bimonthly. Individuals, $24/year;
libraries, $30/year; $28/year foreign. From: P.O. Box 1880,
Santa Monica, CA 90406.
A bimonthly for people who work for children and families in health
care, with news of play, preparation, and parenting services and announcements of relevant publications (often as bibliographies) in each
issue. Altogether it contains some 180 references per year. For example, in 1982, issues included bibliographies on families of hospitalized
children, publications on pediatric psychosocial care, resource citations
on family cultural beliefs about pediatric illness, and "ways to facilitate
communication with migrant families from any culture." Provides its
own index.

H127 **PEDIATRICS** Edited by Jerold F. Lucey. Evanston, Ill.,
American Academy of Pediatrics, 1948- . Monthly. $42/year.
From: P.O. Box 1034, Evanston, IL 60204.
Wider in scope than the *Journal of Pediatrics,* includes commentary,
reviews, and clinical concerns. A typical issue might include material
on the concerns of mothers seeking care in pediatricians' offices, reducing the toll of infant injuries, teenage pregnancy, and acute medical intervention with gypsies. Indexed in *Biological Abstracts, Chemical
Abstracts, Excerpta Medica,* and *Index Medicus.*

H128 **PERINATOLOGY-NEONATOLOGY: THE   JOURNAL   OF
MATERNAL-FETAL AND NEONATAL HEALTH CARE**
Edited by Hal Spector. Los Angeles, Barrington Publications,
1977- . Bimonthly. $40/year. From: 825 S. Barrington Ave.,
Los Angeles, CA 90049.
Deals largely with sound practices surrounding delivery and neonatal
care; reports on research in understandable language.

H129 **PHYSICAL & OCCUPATIONAL THERAPY IN PEDI-
ATRICS: The Quaterly Journal of Developmental Therapy**
Edited by Suzann K. Campbell. New York, Haworth, 1980-
Quarterly. Individuals, $32/year; institutions, $60/year; libraries, $75/year. From: 28 E. 22nd St., New York, NY 10010.
Provides both theme and general issues on topics related to developmental therapy for a transdisciplinary audience. Generally, attempts to
combine clinical and research applications within a developmental context with substantial sections of book reviews (some 75 per year) and
annotated bibliographies. The Winter 1982 issue, for example, had

lengthy signed reviews of nine books and contained an annotated bibliography of 40 items on motor development in children with Down's
syndrome. The Spring 1983 special theme issue on aquatics contained
an extensively annotated bibliography that cited around 25 books and
journal articles and three films. Indexed in *Biological Abstracts, Cumulative Index to Nursing and Allied Health Literature, Excerpta Medica*, and
Psychological Abstracts.

H130 **PRACTICE DIGEST: A Quarterly Publication of the Nation-
      al Association of Social Workers** Edited by Betty Sancier.
      Albany, N.Y., The National Association of Social Workers,
      1978- . Quarterly. Members, $15/year; nonmembers, $25/year;
      student members, $10/year; student nonmembers, $15/year.
      From: 49 Sheridan Ave., Albany, NY 12210.
A professional periodical intended to improve social work practice and
provide a forum for the exchange of practice information by publishing
descriptive reports of social work experience in both new and established fields. Includes case studies and articles on topics such as agencies working together and building on the strengths of minority groups.
Can be helpful to other professionals collaborating with social workers.

H131 **PRINCIPAL** Edited by Sally Banks Sakariya. Reston, Va., Na-
      tional Association of Elementary School Principals, 1920- .
      Quarterly. Free with membership; individuals, $85/year; institu-
      tions, $50/year. From: 1920 Association Dr., Reston, VA
      22091.
An award-winning journal that collects and disseminates information
for elementary and middle school principals and provides a good overview of elementary school administrative concerns. Includes thoughtful
series on topics such as the ways children learn, as well as detailed
reporting on such research as the Study of School Needs of One-Parent
Children. Indexed in *Education Index.*

H132 **PSYCHOLOGY IN THE SCHOOLS** Edited by Gerald B.
      Fuller. Brandon, Vt., Clinical Psychology Publishing Co.,
      1964- . Quarterly. Individuals, $25/year, $27/year foreign; insti-
      tutions, $60/year, $62/year foreign. From: 4 Conant Sq., Bran-
      don, VT 05733.
Intended to bridge the gap between the problems of the schools and
findings in psychology, this quarterly is directed toward an audience of
school psychologists, counselors, teachers, and personnel workers.
Articles range from theory and research to opinion and practice. Most
issues have sections on evaluation and assessment, educational prac-

tices and problems, strategies in behavioral change, general articles, and literature reviews. Typically, this review section includes fairly lengthy signed reviews of six or seven books, with a supplementary listing of books received. Reviews around 24 books each year and lists an additional 60. Indexed in *Child Development Abstracts, Current Contents, Current Index to Journals in Education, Education Index, Exceptional Child Education Resources, Language and Language Behavior, Psychological Abstracts,* and others.

H133 **PUBLIC WELFARE** Edited by Bill Detweiler. Washington, D.C., American Public Welfare Assn., 1943- . Quarterly. $20/year. From: 1125 15th St., NW, Washington DC 20005.

Includes feature articles on topics like foster family care, aid to families with dependent children, and surviving hard times. Reviews perhaps 8 books per year on public policy issues and provides brief synopses of approximately 70 additional books. Abstracted in *Social Work Research and Abstracts.*

H134 **RESIDENTIAL GROUP CARE & TREATMENT** Edited by Ord Matek. New York, Haworth, 1982- . Quarterly. Individuals, $32/year; institutions, $48/year; libraries, $83/year. From: 28 E. 22nd St., New York, NY 10010.

Aims at providing a forum on philosophies and practices in residential treatment and/or residential group care, wherein differences can be discussed and evaluated. Each issue includes an editor's page and thoughtful reviews of approximately four or five books. Articles deal with such topics as residential care as preparation for adoption or the therapeutic aspects of a residential recreation experience. Indexed in *Biological Abstracts, Bulletin Signalétique, Child Development Abstracts and Bibliography, Criminal Justice Abstracts, Current Index to Journals in Education, Exceptional Child Education Resources, National Criminal Justice Reference System, Psychological Abstracts, Rehabilitation Literature, Sage Family Studies Abstracts, SOPODA, Social Work Research and Abstracts,* and *Sociological Abstracts.*

H135 **ROEPER REVIEW: A JOURNAL ON GIFTED EDUCATION** Edited by Ruthan Brodsky. Bloomfield Hills, Mich., Roeper City and Country School, 1978- . Quarterly. Individuals, $20.00/year; institutions, $27.50/year. From: P.O. Box 329, Bloomfield Hills, MI 48103.

An excellent refereed journal that focuses on the philosophical, moral, and academic issues that relate to the lives and experiences of the gifted and talented and translates them into practice—in homes, schools, and the community. Open to many approaches and positions, it includes 15–20 articles per issue and always contains articles on programs, teachers, research, and parenting. Most issues cluster additional articles in a few large themes, such as perceptions of giftedness, the preschool gifted child, the application of developmental theories, and community resources. The individual articles generally include substantial bibliographic references. The journal itself has two review sections—one for classroom materials and the other for professional books (usually around seven of the latter in each issue). Indexed in *Current Index to Journals in Education, Education Index,* and *Psychological Abstracts.*

H136 **SCHIZOPHRENIA BULLETIN**   Edited by Samuel J. Keith and Loren R. Mosher. Washington, D.C., National Institute of Mental Health, Center for Studies of Schizophrenia, 1969– . Quarterly. $21/year. From: U.S. Government Printing Office, Washington, DC 20402.

The bulletin's purpose is to facilitate the dissemination and exchange of information on schizophrenia. Articles are in the public domain. Indexed in *Current Contents, Excerpta Medica, Index Medicus, Index to Government Periodicals,* and *Psychological Abstracts.*

H137 **SEX ROLES: A JOURNAL OF RESEARCH**   Edited by Phyllis A. Katz. New York, Plenum, 1974– . Monthly. $115/year. From: 233 Spring St., New York, NY 10013.

A cross-disciplinary journal of research and theory, including social, political, and economic aspects. Typically includes articles on topics like gender role socialization, measures of play behavior, and male responses to female competence. Includes reviews of research and book reviews. Indexed in *Current Contents, Excerpta Medica, Psychological Abstracts, Sage Family Studies Abstracts,* and *Sociological Abstracts.*

H138 **SOCIAL CASEWORK: The Journal of Contemporary Social Work**   Edited by Robert A. Elfers. New York, Family Service Association of America, 1920– . Monthly, except August and September. Individuals, $25.00/year; institutions, $37.50/year. From: 44 E. 23rd St., New York, NY 10010.

Directed primarily to the interests of social work practitioners and family life educators. Contains articles that illuminate a facet of social work theory or practice, that report professional experimentation or research, or that are relevant to the social problems of the day and to the concerns of social workers. Includes articles on adolescents, children, child abuse and neglect and similar topics, reader comment, and anywhere from 40 to 50 book reviews yearly. Indexed in *Current Contents, Exceptional Child Education Resources, Hospital Literature Index, Language and Language Behavior Abstracts, Psychological Abstracts, Social Sciences Citation Index, Social Sciences Index, Social Work Research and Abstracts,* and *Sociological Abstracts.*

A 50-year cumulative index to issues from 1920 to 1979 is available from JAI Press (individuals, $50; institutions, $95) at Box 1678, 36 Sherwood Pl., Greenwich, CT 06830. It includes an overview of the journal and separate author, title, subject, and book review indexes.

H139 **SOCIAL WORK** Edited by Carol H. Meyer. New York, National Association of Social Workers (NASW), 1956- . Bimonthly. Free to members; nonmembers, $35/year; institutions, $45/year. From: 7981 Eastern Ave., Silver Spring, MD 20910.

A professional journal that covers social work practices, techniques, research, and contemporary social problems; includes many articles on topics like adolescents, adoption assistance, child support, childhood illnesses and problems, family life-styles, funding, family violence, and other topics related to children. Each article is preceded by a short abstract. Reviews more than 100 books per year. Indexed in *Excerpta Medica, Hospital Literature Index, P.A.I.S. Bulletin, Psychological Abstracts, Social Sciences Index,* and *Social Work Research and Abstracts.*

Two other NASW periodicals that often contain relevant articles are *Health and Social Work* (1976- , quarterly, individuals, $40/year; institutions, $45/year) and *Social Work in Education* (1978- , quarterly, individuals, $35/year; institutions, $70/year).

H140 **STUDIES IN ART EDUCATION: A Journal of Issues and Research in Art Education** Edited by Jean C. Rush. Reston, Va., National Art Education Assn., 1959- . 4 issues/year. $25/year. Add $5 in Canada and elsewhere. From: 1916 Association Dr., Reston, VA 22091.

A good source of articles and research on creativity, aesthetic structure, spatial organization, and affective aspects of cognition. Reviews approximately eight relevant books yearly. Indexed in *Education Index.*

H141 **STUDIES IN FAMILY PLANNING** Edited by Valeda Slade. New York, Population Council, 1963- . Bimonthly. Free. From: One Dag Hammarskjöld Plaza, New York, NY 10017.

Good for reports on family structure and conditions in developing countries like India and Africa, with articles on topics that include infant and child mortality. Contains perhaps four abstracts of journal articles and four book abstracts per issue. Indexed in *Biological Abstracts, Current Contents, Excerpta Medica, Index Medicus,* and *Social Sciences Citation Index.*

H142 **TELEVISION & CHILDREN**   Edited by Nicholas B. Van Dyck. Princeton, N.J., National Council for Children and Television, 1978– . Quarterly. $25/year. From: 20 Nassau St., Suite 200, Princeton, NJ 08542.

An ongoing source of information, research, and opinion on the interactions between children and television, with a concentration on primetime television. Reports research by the council and others on the effects and consequences of television watching, which absorbs so much of the time of American children.

H143 **TOPICS IN LEARNING AND LEARNING DISABILITIES** Edited by D. Kim Reid and Wayne P. Hresko. Rockville, Md., Aspen Systems Corp., 1981– . Quarterly. $38/year. From: 1600 Research Blvd., Rockville, MD 20850.

Each topical issue includes literature reviews and useful summaries of current thought and research on one particular theme (e.g., language intervention or reading comprehension). Each article contains a substantial bibliography; some issues have final articles that summarize or interpret the whole issue.

H144 **UNICEF NEWS**   Edited by Brian Miller. New York, UNICEF Information Division, 1968– . Quarterly. $6/year. From: 443 Mt. Pleasant Rd., Toronto, Ontario M4S 2L8, Canada.

Covers broad issues on children and their families around the world, focusing on development projects.

H145 **THE URBAN REVIEW: Issues and Ideas in Public Education** Edited by David E. Kapel and William T. Pink. New York, Agathon, 1966– . Quarterly. Individuals, $16.50/year; libraries and institutions, $33.00/year. From: 49 Sheridan Ave., Albany, NY 12210.

Deals with issues and ideas such as student disruptions, student fears, the repercussions of academic failure, suggested policies for bilingual education, and recommendations for improving individualized education programs. Includes empirical studies, theoretical papers, and practical solutions and a special department prepared by the staff of the ERIC Clearinghouse on Urban Education that summarizes recent research. Indexed in *Education Index* and *Psychological Abstracts.*

H146 **WHO CHRONICLE** Geneva, World Health Organization (WHO), 1966- . Bimonthly. $11/year. From: Organisation Mondiale de la Sante, 20 Avenue Appia, CH-1211 Geneva 27, Switzerland.
Records the principal health activities undertaken in various countries with WHO assistance. Topics include those health problems of children that can be satisfactorily solved only through the cooperation of many countries. Published in Arabic, English, French, Russian, and Spanish. Indexed in *Chemical Abstracts* and *Index Medicus.*

H147 **WORKING MOTHER: The Magazine for Working Mothers** Edited by Vivian Cadden. New York, McCall, 1978- . Monthly. $9.95/year. From: 230 Park Ave., New York, NY 10169.
A service magazine directed toward the 6 million working women who are mothers of infants and young children, with articles aimed at helping these women simultaneously manage homes, jobs, and their children's needs. Each issue has sections on home, job, children, and food and usually contains sound, sensible advice on topics like day care, child support, dealing with picky eaters, how and when to fire the babysitter, and making the most of maternity leave.

H148 **WORLD HEALTH** Edited by John Bland. Geneva, World Health Organization (WHO), 1958- . 10 issues/year. $13.75/year. From: Organisation Mondiale de la Sante, 20 Avenue Appia, CH-1211 Geneva 27, Switzerland.
Has an attractive format and includes many illustrations, with interesting reports on WHO activities. Basically concerned with broad international public health issues such as diabetes, infant mortality, clean water, and air pollution that require cooperation and interdisciplinary efforts for solution. Versions are published in Arabic, English, French, Persian, Portuguese, Russian, and Spanish. Indexed in the *P.A.I.S. Bulletin.*

H149 **YOUNG CHILDREN** Edited by Jan Brown. Washington, D.C., National Association for the Education of Young Children (NAEYC), 1946- . Bimonthly. $20/year. From: 1834 Connecticut Ave., NW, Washington, DC 20009.
A refereed journal for adults concerned with young children; includes intelligent, readable, well-illustrated articles on theory, practice, and research, as well as two excellent review sections on books for children and professionals and selected lists of new books. In the May 1983 issue, feature articles dealt with the art of storytelling, child care prac-

tices in Japan and the United States, and preschool work habits. Additional departments and features included a Washington update; a calendar of events; a research review on television and young children; a public policy report on building coalitions for young children; cogent editorials; news of NAEYC's business, elections, and officers; a thoughtful editorial on four-year-old children attending school; and details of an accreditation project concerned with quality care for early childhood programs. Indexed in *Current Contents, Current Index to Journals in Education, Education Index,* and *Psychological Abstracts.*

H150 **ZERO TO THREE: Bulletin of the National Center for Clinical Infant Programs** Edited by Sally Provence. Washington, D.C., National Center for Clinical Infant Programs, 1980– . Five issues/year. $12/year. Add $5 for Canada and foreign. Quantity discount. From: 733 15th St., NW, Washington, DC 20005.

An interesting, informative, well-written, interdisciplinary newsletter reaching more than 11,000 practitioners, policymakers, teachers, researchers, care givers, and librarians who are concerned about the quality of life for infants and their families. Topical articles on subjects like infant depression may be extended with case notes, bibliographies, and treatment suggestions. *Zero to Three* also includes book reviews (perhaps six or more per issue) and reviews of audiovisuals, calls for papers, notes on conferences, and information on the center.

10 / Directories

Bibliographies, abstract journals, and reviews lead to books and print materials; mediaographies lead to audiovisuals; and directories, as the word indicates, point to a place. Directories in this chapter lead not to printed materials but, rather, directly to persons, organizations, or funding sources. Although these sources should be tapped early in a search for information, I have placed this chapter at the end of the section on printed materials as a bridge to the chapters in the next section, which arrange selected organizations by broad interest categories. Bibliographies and index services often provide addresses of their sources or include these in a directory appendix.

A wide range of directories is included here since so many organizations and agencies deal in some way with children. Nevertheless, I have left out some well-known directories (such as *The National Directory of State Agencies, Research Centers Directory,* and the *Encyclopedia of Information Systems and Services*) to keep the length of this chapter and book within reason. In general, I prefer to include lesser known and underused directories. As the annotations indicate, some directories list other directories concerned with the same general areas; others cull their information from existing directories. These and other directories can be located through the *Directory of Directories* (I28) and the *Directory Information Service,* a comprehensive guide to directories in all fields. The *American Reference Books Annual* (D28), a comprehensive guide to new reference materials, attempts to review all reference books of national significance and is worth scanning for new directories. Similarly, the *P.A.I.S. Bulletin* (G39) can be scanned semimonthly or yearly under "Directories" to locate new directories on children. The descriptor "Directories" in ERIC's *Resources in Education* (G46) uncovers directories processed through ERIC clearinghouses into the ERIC system.

Many organizations compile directories of officers, divisions, or members as an ongoing process, whereas periodicals often include directory information or provide directory issues. Because of funding problems, some directories compiled by organizations are occasional or sporadic. Commercial publishers who have compiled commercially viable directories tend to publish these every year or every other year. I have tried to indicate the frequency of ongoing directories and the latest available edition of less-regular directories. Information on the latest edition of ongoing directories can be checked through *Books in Print* (D31) or the *Directory of Directories* (I28). Data bases, as described in Chapter 11, often contain directory-type information. Statistical directories are noted in Chapter 15, and some directories prepared for parents are included in Chapter 17.

During the last few years, several directories have been developed that exclusively cover children and youth. These include the *National Directory of Children & Youth Services,* now issued every two years; *The National Children's Directory,* issued only once; and the *Youth Serving Organizations Directory,* which provides information on many organizations serving children under the age of 12. *Children's Media Market Place* also is considered in this chapter rather than in the chapter on children's books because it covers media other than print. There have always been directories for the parents of handicapped children; some are included here and others in Chapter 17. Three very useful directories are *The Help Book* (P5), *Help for the Handicapped Child* (P6), and *How to Get Help for Kids* (P7). I have included very few directories of schools or educational resources in general, since they are thoroughly covered in *A Guide to Sources of Educational Information* (B7).

In addition to these formal publications, government agencies and organizations concerned with the well-being of children have compiled many brief and extremely helpful directories of or for relevant agencies and advocates. Although they can be ephemeral, many are listed here, since they are so well targeted. The House Select Committee on Children, Youth, and Families is currently working on such a guide, *Federal Programs Affecting Children* (I42). Publications by agencies of the U.S. government can be located in many depository libraries; libraries or organizations concerned with children often acquire some of the fugitive directories issued by concerned organizations.

This chapter is divided into three sections: guides to people, guides to funding sources, and guides to organizations.

GUIDES TO PEOPLE

Only a few of the guides to professionals concerned in some way with children are included in this section. Other sources to check are membership rosters and directories of professional organizations that list members and their interests. Biographical directories in the *Directory of Directories* can lead to these sources, as can Loretta Walker's *Membership Directories of American Professional Societies: A Checklist* (Schenectady, N.Y., Union College, Schaffer Library, 1979). Generally, membership directories, like the *American Dental Directory,* the *Directory of Medical Specialists,* or the *NASW Register of Clinical Social Workers,* combine information on the backgrounds, geographic locations, and specializations of the persons listed. They often provide background information on the profession, indicate the qualifications for inclusion, and, in this way, guarantee that individuals included have at least "paper" qualifications. In the section on organizations, some of these directories are subsumed under the names of their parent organizations.

General biographical directories, like *Current Biography* and *Who's Who,* as well as geographic directories, such as *Who's Who in the West,* are worth searching for biographical data. Some announcement services, abstract journals, and indexes provide addresses of authors for convenience in obtaining reprints. Since women tend to be underrepresented in standard "who's who" directories, biographical guides that concentrate on women,

such as the *World's Who's Who of Women,* are helpful supplementary tools. Computer searches of biographical data bases are
now possible. (For example see I1 and the discussion on pp. 265
of Chapter 11.)

Several dictionaries and encyclopedias annotated in Chapter 2
contain extensive biographical information, especially the *Dictionary of Behavioral Science* (A4), *The Language of Mental
Health* (A15), *Basic Handbook of Child Psychiatry* (A26), *Encyclopedia of Social Work* (A30), and the *International Encyclopedia
of the Social Sciences* (A32). Some multifaceted data bases, such
as FAMILY RESOURCES DATABASE (J24), provide directory-like
access to experts and/or researchers.

I1   **AMERICAN MEN AND WOMEN OF SCIENCE: Social
        and Behavioral Sciences**   13th Edition. Edited by the Jaques
        Cattell Press. New York, R. R. Bowker, 1978. 1,645 pp. $69.95.
Contains listings of 24,000 Americans and Canadians important in the
social and behavioral sciences, including political science, psychology,
sociology, business, and administration, with geographic and discipline
indexes. Names were taken from the seven-volume *American Men and
Women of Science* (1976). *American Men and Women of Science: Physical and Biological Sciences* is now in its 15th edition (1982, 7 vols.,
$495/set) and lists 130,000 scientists. Both use formats that provide
names, birthplace and date, personal data on marriage and children,
education, career honors and rewards, memberships, research interests
and activities, occupations, and addresses. These data bases are now
available as MWSC through BRS and as FILE 236 in DIALOG.

A similar directory set, *Directory of American Scholars* (8th Edition,
1982, 4 vols., $295/set or $90 each), covers scholars in history; English, speech, and drama; foreign languages, linguistics, and philology;
and philosophy, religion, and law.

I2   **BIOGRAPHICAL DIRECTORY OF THE AMERICAN
        ACADEMY OF PEDIATRICS**   1st Edition. Edited by the
        Jaques Cattell Press. New York, R. R. Bowker, 1980. 940 pp.
        $95.
One of a new directory series by Bowker, this includes lists of officers,
board members, staff, committees, and past presidents of the American
Academy of Pediatrics, as well as biographies of 18,300 members arranged geographically. Includes name, birthplace and date, personal

data, education, career honors, research, occupations, information on membership status, internships and residencies, postgraduate training, licensure and certifications, academic experiences, professional interests, mailing address, and telephone number.

Bowker has compiled a similar directory for the American Public Health Association (1979, 1,207 pp., $54.50), covering 26,000 members, and one for the American Psychiatric Association (1977, 1,573 pp., $49.50), covering 23,000 members. (Sometimes these agencies simultaneously issue briefer, less-expensive directories on their own.)

I3   **BIOGRAPHY INDEX** Bronx, N.Y., H. W. Wilson, 1946– . Quarterly, with bound annual and three-year cumulations. $55/year in the United States and Canada; $65/year foreign. Cumulative volumes, $100 each; $130 foreign.

A general index to biographical materials appearing in approximately 2,400 periodicals, as well as individual and collective biographies, obituaries, and biographical materials from books that are not primarily biographies. Includes a name alphabet and an index by profession and occupation.

I4   **THE COMPENDIUM: Persons of Eminence in Exceptional Education** Novato, Calif., Academic Therapy, 1974. 271 pp. (Out of print)

An interesting biographical index of leaders, innovators, thinkers, pioneers, and controversial personalities in exceptional education. Individuals included here were nominated by their colleagues for recognized contributions in teaching, writing, research, or community endeavors that advanced the status or education of exceptional children.

I5   **DIRECTORY OF PROFESSIONALS AND RESEARCHERS IN THE AREA OF BLACK FAMILIES, INCLUDING CHILD SOCIALIZATION & CHILDREARING** Compiled for the National Council of Family Relations by Marie Ferguson Peters. Storrs, Conn., University of Connecticut, School of Home Economics and Family Studies, 1980. 22 pp. Single copy free (paper). From: Marie Ferguson Peters, University of Connecticut, Storrs, CT 06268.

A project completed with financial support of the National Council of Family Relations and the School of Home Economics and Family Studies at Storrs. Arranged alphabetically by surnames, it provides name, position, work location, phone, and research interests for approximately 100 researchers concerned with black families and/or children. As such, it serves as a guide to some current research and the institutions where this research is taking place.

I6 **NASW REGISTER OF CLINICAL SOCIAL WORKERS, 1982** 3rd Edition. Silver Spring, Md., National Association of Social Workers, 1982. 671 pp. $50. From: 7981 Eastern Ave., Silver Spring, MD 20910.

This register was compiled as a "direct response to the voiced needs of consumers, legislators, agencies, insurance companies, and that segment of the social work profession which engages in direct clinical practice," since clinical social workers provide more direct treatment services than psychologists or psychiatrists. Most of the book is an alphabetic listing of 9,000 qualified individuals within city and state, but the directory also contains definitions of social work, the education and experience criteria for inclusion in the directory, a code of ethics, and similar information.

I7 **WHO'S WHO BIOGRAPHICAL RECORD: CHILD DEVELOPMENT PROFESSIONALS** Compiled by the editors of *Who's Who in America.* Chicago, Ill., Marquis Who's Who, 1976. 515 pp. $55.

Covers (although not completely) 9,000 child-development specialists previously scattered through many directories. Includes child psychologists, counselors, researchers, special education teachers, preschool directors, and college professors of child development and educational psychology, among others. Contains standard biographical data and books authored, with information verified by biographees.

DIRECTORIES OF SOURCES OF FUNDS OR ASSISTANCE

Since the *Resource Directory for Funding and Managing Nonprofit Organizations,* discussed in item B13 in Chapter 3, is such an outstanding guide for locating materials on funding sources, I am including only a few basic funding directories here. More are discussed in *A Guide to Sources of Educational Information* (B7) and in Carol Kurzig's *Foundation Fundamentals: A Guide for Grantseekers* (New York, The Foundation Center, 1981, 148 pp.,

$6.50 [paperback]). This last guide includes comprehensive bibliographies and detailed research examples. Newsletters and periodicals (discussed in Chapter 9) are useful for keeping current with new programs and the real (as opposed to paper) requirements for government and foundation funding. *Children Today* (H32) is a good official window on Washington, whereas newsletters like *Child Protection Report* (H27) take readers behind the scenes. *The Federal Register* officially supplements the *Catalog of Federal Domestic Assistance* (I8), and the commercial *Federal Grants and Contracts Weekly* contains the latest information on upcoming grants and requests for proposals (RFPs). Publications like the *Grantsmanship Center News* also provide timely information and suggestions. Most entries on federal programs include information on funding, especially *Federal Programs Affecting Children* (I42).

I8   **CATALOG OF FEDERAL DOMESTIC ASSISTANCE** Executive Office of the President and Office of Management and Budget. Washington, D.C., U.S. Government Printing Office, 1965- . Annual loose-leaf with updates; subscription basis preferred. $32/year.

The basic U.S. government compendium of federal programs, projects, services, and activities that provide assistance or benefits to the American public, both on individual and organizational bases. It describes authorizing statutes, the nature of program activities, eligibility and restrictions, and deadlines; also provides names of Washington and local contacts. The *Catalog* indexes agency programs, functions, popular names, subjects, applicant eligibility, deadlines, and deleted and new programs. Available on-line as FAPRS (J4).

I9   **GRANTS FOR CHILDREN AND YOUTH** New York, The Foundation Center, 1983. $30 (computer printout). (Comsearch Broad Topics)

Includes information on 3,800 grants issued in 1982 that support services and activities for infants, children, and youths to age 18, as well as research and advocacy programs related to the health and welfare of youth. This is one of a series of broad subject searches prepared by The Foundation Center in 1983 that provide indexes of foundations with addresses and notes on limitations, a keyword index to the field, and an index of recipient organizations. Another Comsearch Broad Topic covers *Grants for Women and Girls* ($28). Contact The Foundation

Center ((800) 424-9836) for a list of other broad searches or geographic area searches.

I10　**HANDBOOK OF FEDERAL RESOURCES ON DOMESTIC VIOLENCE**　By Interdepartmental Committee on Domestic Violence. Rockville, Md., National Clearinghouse on Domestic Violence, 1980. 261 pp. Single copy free while supply lasts (paper). From: National Institute of Mental Health, 5600 Fishers Lane, Rockville, MD 20857.

Although the clearinghouse has been discontinued, this directory can be used to identify pertinent government funding for domestic violence programs. The book is arranged alphabetically by government agency, then by Office of Management and Budget numbers. It includes a detailed subject index and table of contents. Programs listed may still be useful to combat violence in families.

I11　**INTERNATIONAL FOUNDATION DIRECTORY**　2nd Edition. London, Europa Publications, 1980. 378 pp. $65. From: Gale Research Co., Book Tower, Detroit, MI 48226.

Lists foundations, trusts, and other nonprofit institutions that operate internationally and provides information on a wide range of more than 1,000 foundations in 45 nations worldwide. Information includes purpose, activities, background, financial data (when available), addresses, and phone numbers. The *Guide to European Foundations* (Torino, Italy, Ecizii Della Fordazione Sri, 1979) is another useful guide to foundations in 16 European countries.

DIRECTORIES OF ORGANIZATIONS, ASSOCIATIONS, PROGRAMS, DATA BASES, AND GOVERNMENT AGENCIES

This subsection lists broad directories covering many organizations, as well as other brief directories compiled to meet immediate needs. Some of these may be out of print or hard to obtain but are included because they are valuable and available in some libraries. The growth of commercial directories on children is a good sign. Chapter 17 contains some valuable directories oriented mainly toward parents and nonprofessionals, including *The Help Book* (P5), *Help for the Handicapped Child* (P6), and *How to Get Help for Kids* (P7).

I12   **ADOPTION AGENCIES, ORPHANAGES AND MATER-
NITY HOMES: AN HISTORICAL DIRECTORY** Com-
piled by Reg Niles. Garden City, N.Y., Phileas Deigh Corp.,
1981. 2 Vols. (in one book). 478 pp. $32.
A directory compiled by a search consultant in the adoptee's rights
movement. Arranged first by state, then by city or town, it covers adoption agencies, orphanages or children's homes with at least 15 beds,
and maternity homes for unmarried mothers in the United States and
Canada. It also includes maternity hospitals and hospitals deemed to be
significant for adoptees and excludes agencies that closed before 1900.
Niles provided as much information as he could find on 9,262 agencies
that may be concerned with prior adoptions. For each, he tried to include name, address, source of name, date established or incorporated,
affiliated agencies, auspices, function, umbrella organization (such as
order of nuns or name of diocese), restrictions, and so on. The directory includes an interesting bibliography arranged by state, province,
and country, and also by topic, with such subjects as black market children. The category termed "General" is an interesting source of historical data on human service agencies.

I13   **CATALOG OF FEDERAL YOUTH PROGRAMS** Prepared
for the Office of Youth Development, Division of Youth Activities by Lawrence Johnson & Associates. Washington, D.C.,
U.S. Government Printing Office, 1977. 392 pp. $7.50 (paper).
Intended as a single source of information on federally supported youth
programs, this guide describes youth programs in all departments,
under the name of the department, with indexes by subject, popular
name, and agency. Includes definitions. Easy to read, but less detailed
and up-to-date than the current *Catalog of Federal Domestic Assistance.*

I14   **CATALOG OF HUMAN SERVICES INFORMATION
RESOURCE ORGANIZATIONS: An Exploratory Study of
Human Services Information Clearinghouses** Prepared by
Applied Management Sciences, Inc. and Cuadra Associates.
Rockville, Md., Project SHARE, 1980. 320 pp. (Human Services
Monograph Series, No. 15.) Out of print, but available for $28
from: National Technical Information Service, 5825 Port Royal
Rd., Springfield, VA 22161. (NTIS No. SHR-0101701; confirm
price when ordering)
A formatted directory to some 150 human services information clear-
inghouses. For each, it includes address and telephone number, operat-
ing organization and sponsoring agency, purpose, target clientele, ser-

vices and availability of services, publications, fees, materials collected, number and forms of holdings, and year founded. Although some of the organizations included have gone out of business or changed addresses, this catalog is informative and clear on the organizations it lists.

I15   **A CHILD ADVOCATE'S DIRECTORY OF CONGRES-
      SIONAL AND FEDERAL OFFICES AND AGENCIES**
      Washington, D.C., Coalition for Children and Youth, 1979. 97
      pp. Paper. (Out of print)
Accurate up to October 1979, this directory includes congressional committees and federal agencies and offices with responsibilities for major programs affecting children and youth. Historically valuable, with names and phone numbers and an annotated list of the members of the now defunct Coalition for Children and Youth.

I16   **A CHILD ADVOCATE'S GUIDE TO CAPITOL HILL:
      97TH CONGRESS** Washington, D.C., Children's Defense
      Fund, 1981. 45 pp. Paper. (Out of print) (Printed as a public ser-
      vice by Aetna Life and Casualty)
Provides a very thorough exposition of congressional committees concerned with children through 1981.

I17   **CHILDREN'S MEDIA MARKET PLACE** 2nd Edition.
      Edited by Carol A. Emmens. New York, Neal-Schuman, 1982.
      353 pp. $24.95 (paperback).
The second edition, revised and expanded, is a directory of sources of children's media, including such things as television shows, video, animated films, radio programs, and juvenile magazines—essentially, media intended for children preschool through grade 8 and, to a degree, for the adults who work with children.

It is a two-part directory. The first (major) part is a series of 21 annotated lists and bibliographies that include publishers (by format, subject, or special interest); audiovisual producers and distributors, similarly classified; periodicals (for children, professionals and parents, review sources, and reviewers); wholesalers; juvenile book stores; juvenile book clubs; agents for children's properties; children's radio program sources; children's television program sources; media organizations; public library coordinators of children's and young adult services; state school media offices; examination centers; calendar of events and conferences; awards for children's media; and a bibliography of tools for selecting children's media. The second part is an alphabetic index with addresses and telephone numbers of the sources in the guide. Extensive though it is, I found gaps and inaccuracies in its bookstore and library sections for my local geographic area of California. Nevertheless, it is an impressive tool.

I18   **CONSUMER'S GUIDE TO MENTAL HEALTH AND RELATED FEDERAL PROGRAMS** Edited by John J. Cohrssen and Louis E. Kopolow. Washington, D.C., National Institute of Mental Health, 1979. 204 pp. Single copy free (paperback). From: NIMH, 5600 Fishers Lane, Rockville, MD 20857.

Like the *Catalog of Federal Youth Programs* (I13), this guide seems to be excerpted from the *Catalog of Federal Domestic Assistance*. It includes services for health entitlements, social services, including welfare services, and child support services; financial assistance; education programs; and general programs for children. Every section includes some programs for children—for example, the child care food program, the food stamp program, the national school lunch program, the WIC program (a food program for women, infants, and children), and the summer food service program are all under the heading "Food." For each, it describes the program, the intended beneficiaries, and how to apply. A detailed classified table of contents indexes these agencies. Appendixes provide regional addresses of various agencies.

I19   **DATABASES AND CLEARINGHOUSES: Information Resources for Education** 5th Edition. Compiled by Ruth Gordon and Jay Smink. Columbus, Ohio, National Center for Research in Vocational Education, Resource and Referral Center, 1982. 119 pp. $8.75 (paperback). (ED 225 602)

Offers formatted, descriptive summaries of 64 clearinghouses and 56 data bases considered useful in education. The data base summaries in Section I provide full descriptions of 12 education data bases and 3 multidisciplinary data bases pertinent to education, with briefer descriptions of 41 other data bases having some relevance to education. All are national, commercially available, computer-accessible data bases. Information for the first 15 data bases includes major areas, size, date established, types of source materials, the frequency with which new information is added, and whether thesauri or search aids are available.

Profiles for clearinghouses include the full name and acronym of the clearinghouse; a description of its functions, services, and major publications; its date of establishment and the sponsoring organization; the kinds of documents or materials on which it bases its information; the forms or formats in which the information is retrievable; and the contact person. The book includes an introduction, lists of references, a subject index, and a resource index.

240

I20   DESCRIPTIVE STUDY OF SELECTED NATIONAL
       YOUTH SERVING ORGANIZATIONS By Dan James.
       Washington, D.C., U.S. Department of Agriculture, Science
       and Education Administration, 1979. 131 pp. Price not available
       (paper).
Detailed descriptions of 14 well-known voluntary organizations work-
ing with children and youth, based on interviews and questionnaires.
Organizations include the Boy Scouts, the Girl Scouts, Future Farmers
and Future Homemakers, Camp Fire, 4-H, Junior Achievement, Red
Cross Youth Service, United States Youth Soccer Association, United
Neighborhood Center of America, Young Men's Christian Association
(YMCA), and Young Women's Christian Association (YWCA). Summary tables cover histories, programs, membership by decades, current
youth membership, youth served by age, membership by sex, residence, race and/or ethnic group, sources of funds, program budgets,
and organizational staffing.

I21   DIRECTORY FOR EXCEPTIONAL CHILDREN: A List-
       ing of Educational Facilities, 1984–85   10th Edition. Edited
       by Porter Sargent Staff. Boston, Mass., Porter Sargent, 1984.
       Annual. $40.
A basic directory of public and private facilities for exceptional children,
issued since 1965 and completely revised and updated with each edition
by a competent, dedicated staff. The main section describes more than
3,000 institutions for the entire range of developmental, organic, and
emotional handicaps, including boarding schools, residential and day
facilities, outpatient clinics, and summer sessions. Separate sections
cover such things as academic programs for the learning disabled; facilities for the emotionally disturbed, the orthopedically or neurologically
handicapped, and the mentally retarded; psychiatric and guidance
clinics; and schools for the blind/partially sighted and the deaf/hard-
of-hearing.
    These categories are subdivided by state and town, so it is easy to
locate or compare programs in the same geographic regions. They are
formatted to describe facilities, staff, fees, enrollment, and requirements for acceptance, as well as therapeutic, remedial, academic, and
vocational services provided. Opportunities for scholarship and financial assistance also are reported. Because this book is intended for all exceptional children, it is not limited to sources available only to the
wealthy but, rather, lists state and federal agencies and personnel,
associations, societies, and foundations that may offer additional assis-

tance and information. There is a general alphabetic index to the whole volume.

I22   **DIRECTORY OF ACCREDITED AGENCIES**   By the Council on Accreditation of Services for Families and Children. New York, 1979. 47 pp. Free to members; nonmembers, $6 (paper). From: 67 Irving Pl., New York, NY 10003.
The council, incorporated in 1977, offers accreditation through a lengthy process, laid out in its *Provisions for Accreditation,* including a self-study, an on-site review, and an evaluation of the team report. The directory is updated by a newsletter.

I23   **DIRECTORY OF AGENCIES: U.S. VOLUNTARY, INTERNATIONAL VOLUNTARY, INTERGOVERNMENTAL** By the National Association of Social Workers. Washington, D.C., 1980. 104 pp. $6 (paperback).
A directory of more than 300 social work agencies arranged in alphabetic order with geographic and subject indexes. Provides full information for agencies, including names, addresses, phone numbers, directors, number and type of members, purposes and activities, and publications. More than 50 of the organizations listed are concerned with children and youth.

I24   **DIRECTORY OF CANADIAN HUMAN SERVICES/REPERTOIRE DES SERVICES SOCIAUX AU CANADA** Ottawa, Canadian Council on Social Development, 1982. 770 pp. $35.00, plus $2.50 postage and handling. From: 55 Parkdale Ave., Box 3505, Station C, Ottawa, Ontario K1Y 4G1, Canada.
Uses a bilingual format to provide a complete list of human services available in Canada; it contains 22,000 listings on more than 14,000 organizations. Public agencies are asterisked for easy reference; names and addresses are included, geographically divided.

I25   **DIRECTORY OF CANADIAN PROFESSIONALS PROMOTING HEALTH EDUCATION FOR CHILDREN AND YOUTH, 1983-84** Compiled by Gordon Mutter. Ottawa, Health Promotion Directorate, 1983. Pagination and price not available. From: Health Promotion Directorate, Health and Welfare Canada, 450 Jeanne Mance Bldg., Ottawa, Ontario K1A 1B4, Canada.
Identifies officials responsible for child and youth health education at the local, provincial, and national levels; intended to help professionals in private and public agencies share and exchange information.

I26   **DIRECTORY OF CHILD ADVOCACY PROGRAMS**
       Compiled by U.S. Children's Bureau. Washington, D.C., Ad-
       ministration for Children, Youth, and Families, 1978. 101 pp.
       Paper. (Out of print)
Arranges programs by state and indexes them by areas of interest. For
each organization, it includes name, address, telephone number, contact person, purpose, and advocacy activities.

I27   **DIRECTORY OF DIOCESAN AGENCIES OF CATHOLIC
       CHARITIES AND NCCC MEMBER INSTITUTIONS IN
       THE UNITED STATES, PUERTO RICO, AND CANADA**
       Washington, D.C., National Conference of Catholic Charities,
       1922– . Annual. $7.50. From: NCCC, Publications Dept., 1346
       Connecticut Ave., NW, Suite 307, Washington, DC 20036.
Annual publication that lists members by diocese under states. Listings
include around 550 branch offices and diocesan agencies and 200 additional member institutions, including those for dependent, neglected,
or delinquent children and youth; maternity homes; settlements; day
care centers; and community service and social development programs.

I28   **DIRECTORY OF DIRECTORIES (DOD)** An Annotated
       Guide to Business and Industrial Directories, Professional and
       Scientific Rosters, and Other Lists and Guides of All Kinds. 3rd
       Edition. Edited by James M. Ethridge. Detroit, Mich., Gale
       Research, 1985. 1,322 pp. $125.
The second edition of this impressive directory lists and describes
7,820 directories in 16 subject areas. In essence, these are separate subject directories with entries arranged alphabetically by title in a directory
format. The index section consists of a good, detailed subject index and
a comprehensive title index. It includes around 60 directories on children, with many others that are peripherally relevant, especially in the
directory sections for social sciences and humanities, health and
medicine, education, public affairs and social concerns, and law and
government. Other sections deal with business; banking and finance;
agriculture; science and engineering; biographical directories; religious, ethnic, and fraternal affairs; genealogical, veterans, and patriotic
affairs; travel, hobbies, and leisure; and sports and outdoor recreation.
All include organizations that deal in some way with children. The
Directory of Directories is also helpful in locating membership directories of relevant organizations.
     Between the biennial editions, *DOD* is updated by the *Directory In-
formation Service* ($75/two issues), which lists and describes approxi-
mately 1,000 additional organizations.

I29   **DIRECTORY OF HOMEMAKER–HOME HEALTH AID SERVICES: In the United States, Puerto Rico and the Virgin Islands**   New York, National Homecaring Council, 1982. Not paged. $10 (paperback). From: 67 Irving Pl., New York, NY 10003.
This geographically arranged annual, prepared with the assistance of a computer, lists around 5,000 agencies and service units that provide homemaker or health aid services. It also offers a separate listing of approximately 145 local agencies accredited or approved by the council.

I30   **DIRECTORY OF MEMBER AGENCIES**   (Family Service Association of America) Compiled by Joan Fenton. New York, Family Service Association of America, Annual. 1984 edition, 91 pp., $16.25. From: 44 E. 23rd St., New York, NY 10010.
A two-part directory (the first section is on the United States; the second is on Canada) intended mainly for internal use in interagency correspondence and referral of clients. Each entry includes a description of the area served by the agency and a list of its branch or district offices. Includes a page of supplemental resources.

I31   **DIRECTORY OF MEMBER AGENCIES AND ASSOCIATES OF THE CHILD WELFARE LEAGUE OF AMERICA**   Compiled by the Child Welfare League of America. New York, 1977– . Annual. $10 (paper). From: 67 Irving Pl., New York, NY 10003.
Lists accredited public and private agencies by state, with telephone numbers, services, and names of the directors. The introduction describes the league's services and provides the names of its officers and board members; also states the provisions for accreditation.

I32   **A DIRECTORY OF NATIONAL HEALTH, EDUCATION, AND SOCIAL SERVICE ORGANIZATIONS CONCERNED WITH YOUTH**   Prepared by the National Family Planning and Reproductive Health Association Staff. Rockville, Md., Department of Health, Education, and Welfare, U.S. Public Health Service, Bureau of Community Health Services, 1979. 55 pp. Price not available (paper).
A useful directory that describes organizations and their membership and publications, and lists directors, regional or state officers, addresses, and phone numbers.

I33   **DIRECTORY OF NATIONAL INFORMATION SOURCES ON HANDICAPPING CONDITIONS AND RELATED SER-**

VICES 2nd Edition. Clearinghouse on the Handicapped, Office of Human Development Services, Office for Handicapped Individuals. Washington, D.C., U.S. Government Printing Office, 1980. 263 pp. $8 (paperback). (DHEW Publication No. OHDS 80-22007)

An inventory of information resources for handicapped persons and those working in their behalf—mostly national organizations that respond to inquiries from the public and professionals. It provides, in excellent format, clear descriptions of various organizations—advocacy, consumer, voluntary health; information data banks and vendors; Federal Government; trade and professional; and facilities, schools, and clinics. It also details the information services of these organizations. Appendixes include information on sports and religious organizations serving the handicapped and an annotated list of 30 directories of services and resources for the handicapped. Many of the organizations are related in some way to the needs of handicapped or exceptional children. Gale Research's *Handicapping Conditions and Services Directory* (1981, $28) was derived from the 1976 edition of this directory.

I34   **DIRECTORY OF ONLINE DATABASES** Santa Monica, Calif., Cuadra Associates, 1981– . Quarterly. $75/year.

A competent, ongoing quarterly that provides two comprehensive data base directories each year, in the spring and fall. Each of these has a pocket to hold the smaller updates issued in winter and summer. The Spring 1983 issue provided concise descriptions of 1,596 on-line data bases arranged alphabetically by name. These cover the types and services of each data base; its producer and on-line services; and its content, coverage, updating features, and limiting conditions. Recent issues include address lists for data base producers and on-line services and a master index with all known names, acronyms, and cross-references to data bases, systems, and services. The *Directory* has a subject index and is useful for users who want further details on possible computer search services other than those included in Chapter 11.

Cuadra Associates notes that (as of August 1984) more than 2,400 data bases are available through 345 on-line services worldwide and that the number of on-line data bases is growing at approximately 35 percent annually and the number of on-line services at around 40 percent.

I35   **DIRECTORY OF RESIDENTIAL TREATMENT CENTERS, 1982–83** 9th Edition. Reston, Va., International Halfway House Assn., 1983. Biennial. $12. From: P.O. Box 2337, Reston, VA 22090.

A geographic arrangement (state, then city) of halfway houses (community-based residential treatment centers) designed to help the socially handicapped reenter society. It includes transitional residencies and therapeutic communities but excludes those for the medically ill and long-term residential care programs. For each, this directory includes ages and sexes served, capacity, and function. Some of these centers house children as young as five years of age.

I36   **DIRECTORY OF SOCIAL WELFARE RESEARCH CAPABILITIES: A Working Guide to Organizations Engaged in Social Work and Social Work Research**   Compiled by Richard J. Estes. Ardmore, Pa., Dorrance, 1981. 129 pp. (Out of print) (Research Report No. 80-12)
Estes surveyed 200 social work organizations and agencies to identify 75 social welfare–related research units in the United States and Puerto Rico. The result is an intricately coded directory that can be searched for research priorities, special populations, fields of practice, and practice modes. It provides information on size and composition of research staff, affiliations, relations to sponsoring institutions, funding patterns, and research publications. A good tool for locating research organizations and their work.

I37   **DIRECTORY OF SPECIAL LIBRARIES AND INFORMATION CENTERS**   8th Edition. Edited by Brigitte T. Darnay. Detroit, Mich., Gale Research, 1983. 2 Vols. Vol. I: 1,640 pp., $280. Vol. II: 836 pp., $235.
Volume I provides descriptions of some 15,000 special libraries and information centers, networks, consortia, and computerized services, with updated entries arranged alphabetically. It includes a subject index with numerous entries under the headings of child abuse, child development, child welfare, children, the gifted child, the exceptional child, children's literature, and children's play. Volume II contains geographic and personnel indexes.

I38   **EDUCATION DIRECTORY**   Separate parts published by the Department of Education and the National Center for Education Statistics. Washington, D.C., U.S. Government Printing Office, 1912- . Prices vary.
A series issued by the Federal Government since 1912, now largely discontinued but still available in depository libraries. Three of the four parts are relevant and relatively current. These three are

1. *Educational Associations 80-81.* 1980. 127 pp. Lists national, state, regional, and college associations, foundations, and the like. Subject index.
2. *Local Education Agencies.* 1980. 175 pp. Covers all elementary and secondary school systems in the United States; for each state, it includes school systems, superintendents, number, grades, and enrollments.
3. *State Education Agency Officials.* 1981. 81 pp. Lists principal officers of state education agencies.

The *Standard Education Almanac* (N21) covers much of the same data.

I39   **ENCYCLOPEDIA OF ASSOCIATIONS '85**   19th Edition. Edited by Denise S. Akey. Detroit, Mich., Gale Research, 1984. 4 Vols. Vol. 1: *National Organizations of the U.S.,* $185. Vol. 2: *Geographic and Executive Index,* $165. Vol. 3: *New Associations and Projects,* $180 (paper) (a periodical supplement to Volume 1, cumulatively indexed). Vol. 4: *International Organizations 1984,* $145 (paperback) (with cumulative alphabetic and keyword index).
The standard directory—found in most large libraries—that arranges 18,140 organizations into 17 categories, including relevant categories of education, business, social welfare, and cultural and public affairs. The new *Social Service Organizations and Agencies* and the *Youth-Serving Organizations Directory,* also by Gale, are both more convenient for locating agencies concerned with children, but the *Encyclopedia of Associations* includes some relevant sources not covered in either.

I40   **FAMILY RESOURCE COALITION PROGRAM DIREC-TORY, AUGUST, 1982**   Chicago, Ill., Family Resource Coalition, 1982. Unpaged, 29 charts. $5 (paper). From: 230 N. Michigan Ave., Suite 1625, Chicago, IL 60601.
An interim directory arranged by state in chart form, covering the names, addresses, and services of identified family resource and parent support programs. The coalition intends to compile a more comprehensive directory that will include population served, staff size, volunteer component, fees charged, funding sources, and more.

I41   **FEDERAL INFORMATION RESOURCES AND SYS-TEMS: A Directory Issued by the Comptroller General**

Washington, D.C., U.S. Government Printing Office, 1980.
1,196 pp. $20. (Congressional Sourcebook Series)
One of a series of three volumes issued by the General Accounting
Office to fulfill its responsibilities for monitoring and maintaining a
data base of current inventories of requirements for recurring reports,
evaluation studies, and other information sources and systems. This
one describes federal source systems maintained by executive agencies
that contain fiscal, budgetary, or program-related information. It can be
used to locate data-gathering systems or data banks related to children.
Another volume in this series, *Federal Evaluations,* is an inventory of
program and management evaluation reports produced by or for departments, agencies, and commissions of the Federal Government. Its
index, too, can be searched to locate evaluations of programs. The first
volume in the set, *Requirements for Recurring Reports to the Congress,*
describes requirements for various reports to Congress from the executive, legislative, and judicial branches of government.

I42   **FEDERAL PROGRAMS AFFECTING CHILDREN**   Com-
      mittee Print prepared for the House Select Committee on Chil-
      dren, Youth, and Families by the Congressional Research Ser-
      vice of the Library of Congress; coordinated by Jan Fowler.
      Washington, D.C., U.S. Government Printing Office, 1984. 232
      pp. $5.50 (paper).
This directory summarizes federal programs involving the expenditure
of federal dollars that provide assistance or services to children and
their families. The programs included directly affect children in the
areas of income maintenance, nutrition, social services, education,
health, housing, and taxation. This compilation omits addresses of information sources, but it does provide formatted information on each
program's legislative authority; the federal, state, and/or local agencies
that administer the program; a brief program description; information
on numbers or extent of children's participation in the program; and
program funding levels in fiscal years 1981, 1982, and 1983. An appendix by the Congressional Research Service includes some comparable
data on funding in 1970 and 1975; another appendix includes titles of
General Accounting Office reports on these programs.

I43   **A GUIDE TO ORGANIZATIONS, AGENCIES, AND FED-
      ERAL PROGRAMS FOR CHILDREN**   Edited by Joyce
      Lynn. Washington, D.C., Day Care and Child Development Re-
      ports, 1980. 36 pp. Paper. (Out of print)

An intelligently assembled directory, still available in some libraries. Includes foundations.

I44 **HANDBOOK OF PRIVATE SCHOOLS** An Annual Descriptive Survey of Independent Education. Edited by Porter Sargent Staff. Boston, Mass., Porter Sargent, 1915– . Annual. 1983 Edition, 1,472 pp., $31.

A leading directory of independent schools, carefully revised each year, arranged by regions and states. Provides complete statistical and descriptive data on enrollments, tuitions, administrators, faculty, special programs, athletic and recreational programs, school histories, and other details. Covers around 1,800 elementary and secondary boarding and day schools. The frequently revised Porter Sargent *Guide to Summer Camps and Summer Schools* is a comparative source for around 1,100 summer programs in the United States, Canada, Mexico, and abroad.

I45 **HANDICAPPED CHILDREN'S EARLY EDUCATION PROGRAM, 1982–83 OVERVIEW AND DIRECTORY** Prepared by the U.S. Department of Education, Technical Assistance Development System for Special Education Programs. Washington, D.C., U.S. Government Printing Office, 1983. 181 pp. $6 (paperback). (ED 1.32/4:982–83)

A directory of projects supported by Special Education Programs grants and contracts in the Handicapped Children's Early Education Program (HCEEP). An overview of HCEEP's activities is presented.

I46 **HEALTH ORGANIZATIONS OF THE UNITED STATES, CANADA AND THE WORLD** A Directory of Voluntary Associations, Professional Societies and Other Groups Concerned with Health and Related Fields. 5th Edition. Edited by Paul Wasserman. Detroit, Mich., Gale Research, 1981. 500 pp. $74.

A comprehensive listing of health organizations arranged alphabetically by organization title, with a selected keyword index of organizations, a list of subjects and cross-references, and a subject index to organizations. Some 80 organizations are listed under "child health," with additional entries under specific diseases, "pediatrics," "parenthood," and "obstetrics and gynecology."

I47 **INTERNATIONAL DIRECTORY OF MARKETING RESEARCH HOUSES AND SERVICES (The Green Book)**

New York, American Marketing Assn., 1963– . Annual. 22nd
Edition, 1984, 359 pp., $50. From: 420 Lexington Ave., Suite
1733, New York, NY 10170.
Provides a means for locating private companies that conduct and
report research to meet the information needs of those who advertise
to children. Some of these companies issue statistical or other data on
children, babies, or adolescents for their clients. The directory is organized by firm name and includes products, services, and names of principal executives.

I48   **INTERNATIONAL DIRECTORY OF MENTAL RETAR-
       DATION SOURCES** Revised Edition. Edited by Rosemary
       F. Dybwad. Washington, D.C., President's Committee on Men-
       tal Retardation, 1977. 360 pp. (Out of print) (Simultaneously
       published by the International League of Societies for the Men-
       tally Handicapped, Brussels, Belgium)
Published as part of an effort to develop and maintain an "international
exchange of knowledge and information on all aspects of mental retardation." Includes contributions from more than 60 countries, made
possible through the collaboration of professionals, volunteers, state
officials, and international public servants. The first part deals with international organizations; the second part with individual countries.
Each entry provides background information on the country and indicates the names, addresses, and scopes of government agencies and
voluntary organizations.

I49   **INVENTORY OF INFORMATION RESOURCES IN THE
       SOCIAL SCIENCES** Prepared by the University of Bath for
       the Organisation for Economic Co-operation and Development.
       Edited by J. M. Brittain and S. A. Roberts. Lexington, Mass.,
       Saxon House/Lexington Books, 1975. 237 pp. Price not avail-
       able.
Identifies 442 organizations that offer information sources for social
scientists. Sources come from 12 European countries, Canada, and
Japan; 24 are multi- or international. Sources are arranged alphabetically by country, and then by organization. For each source listed, the
entry covers address, title, type of service, fields covered, size,
language, availability of files, current system, and charges. This is an interesting guide to international data systems but needs to be browsed,
because the index does not indicate the range of services that cover
children in some way.

I50   **MENTAL AND DEVELOPMENTAL DISABILITIES DI-
RECTORY OF LEGAL ADVOCATES** Washington, D.C.,
Commission on the Mentally Disabled, American Bar Assn.,
1981. 18 pp. $3 (paper); quantity discount. From: 1800 M St.,
NW, Washington, DC 20036.
A compact guide to a variety of legal advocates, arranged by type and
including national organizations, institutional advocacy projects, developmental disabilities protection and advocacy agencies, state advocacy
agencies, private attorneys, law clinics and public interest programs,
legal services, state bar association projects, and selected local bar
association projects. A scope note for each type of service is followed by
listings of the names, addresses, and telephone numbers of relevant
organizations. In some cases, these are subdivided by state. The commission has a Resource Center and publishes the *Mental Disability Law
Reporter.*

I51   **THE NATIONAL CHILDREN'S DIRECTORY** An Organizational Directory and Reference Guide for Changing Conditions for Children and Youth. Edited by Mary Lee Bundy and
Rebecca Glenn Whaley. College Park, Md., Urban Information
Interpreters, 1977. 303 pp. (Out of print) (UISP Publication No.
16)
A competent directory by an alternative publisher that provides information on 204 national organizations dealing with children, 464 local
organizations arranged by state, and listings of alternative programs
and federal agencies. The editors perceive children—especially poor
and minority children—as a powerless and victimized group. The
organizations included are those engaged in institutional reform, legislative lobbying, litigation, research, publishing, or information dissemination (other than publishing). Hence, while the organizations contained in this directory overlap with those in other directories, the descriptions may differ in perspective and emphasis.
   Descriptive categories cover reform activities, objectives, publications, funding sources, and typical directory data. The book includes
essays on issues related to children and youth, such as child hunger,
health care, and day care for profit, and a useful 300-item annotated
bibliography entitled "Reference Sources for Citizen Action" by Erika
Teal (mostly materials from the early 1970s). It also offers a separate
listing of around 225 periodicals dealing with children and youth affairs, mostly published by groups listed in this directory.

I52   **NATIONAL DIRECTORY OF CHILDREN & YOUTH
SERVICES '83–'84: The Reference Handbook for Professionals** 3rd Edition. Compiled by the Editors of *Child Protection*

Report. Washington, D.C., CPR Directory Services Co., 1983. 600 pp. $49 (paperback).

A comprehensive guidebook to agencies delivering services to children and youth, updated every two years by the editors of *Child Protection Report* and intended for professional care providers, program managers, administrators, and policymakers. The main section, arranged by state, includes the names, addresses, phone numbers, and managers of every social services agency, health department, and juvenile court/ youth agency in major cities, counties, and states in the United States. This section also includes listings of some 2,500 licensed private providers of services—such as residential care, treatment, or assistance—for victims of abuse or neglect, sexual assault or rape, and alcohol and drug abuse. The second section includes several unannotated directories of federal children's program managers in Washington; congressional committees responsible for social services, health, and juvenile justice legislation; runaway youth shelters throughout the country; federally funded clearinghouses and resource centers; and national professional and advocacy organizations that serve children.

I53   **NATIONAL DIRECTORY OF INTERCOUNTRY ADOP-TION SERVICE RESOURCES** By Betsey R. Rosenbaum and Arlene Lishinsky of the American Public Welfare Association (APWA) for the Department of Health and Human Services, Office of Human Development Services. Washington, D.C., U.S. Government Printing Office, 1980. 212 pp. $6.50 (paperback). (DHEW Publication No. OHDS 80-30252)

This directory is a listing of service resources within the United States for families seeking to adopt internationally. It was developed as a companion document to the APWA's *Intercountry Adoption Guidelines.* Organized by state, it includes descriptions of state public welfare services (if available), local offices of international child-placement agencies, domestic child-placement agencies, and adoptive parent groups involved with international adoption. The directory information for the state public agencies includes the names of contact persons for official correspondence on state adoption laws and procedures, licensing information, listings of resources, and public agency services, as well as the administrator of the Interstate Compact on the Placement of Children. For international child-placement agencies located in the United States, the directory includes addresses; telephone numbers; directors; contact persons; and the agency's foreign contacts, services, and requirements. For domestic child-placement agencies, the directory indicates the services provided, to whom they are available, and applicable restrictions.

I54   **NATIONAL DIRECTORY OF PRIVATE SOCIAL AGEN-
       CIES, 1983** Queens Village, N.Y., Croner, 1983. $45 (loose-
       leaf).
A loose-leaf directory with monthly supplements covering 10,000 private social agencies in the United States. These are classified by services
offered and then listed by states and cities. Includes homes, agencies,
and welfare organizations that either give direct help to applicants or
refer them to the proper location. The first part lists services under categories, with reference numbers; the second part is arranged geographically and provides names and addresses of organizations. Relevant
areas include casework, family service/financial assistance, foster
home placement for children, group work (psychiatric) in institutional
settings, protective services for children, and residential homes for children. There is no evaluation of the agencies listed.

I55   **NATIONAL DIRECTORY OF PROGRAMS PROVIDING
       COURT REPRESENTATION TO ABUSED AND NE-
       GLECTED CHILDREN** By the National Legal Resource
       Center for Child Advocacy and Protection. Washington, D.C.,
       1979. 12 pp. $2 (paper). From: 1800 M St., NW, Washington,
       DC 20036.
A compilation of special programs providing court representation to
maltreated children. These projects include those affiliated with courts,
legal service agencies, bar associations, law schools, and public defend-
ers. The directory also suggests national legal programs that provide
technical support for these projects. The directory is kept current with a
bimonthly newsletter, *Legal Response Child Advocacy and Protection.*

I56   **PUBLIC WELFARE DIRECTORY 1984/85** Edited by Amy
       Weinstein. Washington, D.C., American Public Welfare Assn.,
       1984. 448 pp. $50 prepaid.
A knowledgeable four-part annual guide to welfare services at the
federal and state levels in the United States and at the federal and provincial levels in Canada. Includes very intelligent, structured discussions of the responsibilities, services, and functions of individual
government agencies and their backgrounds and is updated frequently
enough to be current. Entries include agency name, address, phone
number, key personnel, types of service, and clientele. The directory
contains citations of other sources of information; a discussion of international social service, with the names of voluntary agencies with international programs or functions; and the texts of some documents to

facilitate and standardize procedures, including a time zone map, the Interstate Compact on the Placement of Children, and the Uniform Child Custody Jurisdiction Act.

157　**REPORT ON FEDERAL GOVERNMENT PROGRAMS THAT RELATE TO CHILDREN** Compiled by the Federal Interagency Committee for the International Year of the Child. Washington, D.C., U.S. Government Printing Office, 1979. 125 pp. $6 (paperback).

A compilation of the child-related activities and programs of 28 executive branch agencies, intended to assess existing programs for children and to determine the gaps and barriers in the delivery of services to children. Includes descriptions of agency programs, authorizing legislation, and appropriations. Some agencies that did not have specific legislated mandates for children described the ways their general programs affected children.

158　**SELECTED TITLE V CRIPPLED CHILDREN SERVICES, 1981** McLean, Va., Association of State and Territorial Health Officials Foundation, 1983. 17 pp. $2.50 prepaid (paper). (ASTHO Publication No. 64)

Describes the services and expenditures of the nation's state crippled children's agencies, using tables, illustrations, and text.

159　**SELECTED TITLE V MATERNAL AND CHILD HEALTH SERVICES, 1981** McLean, Va., Association of State and Territorial Health Officials Foundation, 1983. 78 pp. $3.50 prepaid (paper). (ASTHO Publication No. 65)

Describes services and examines funding patterns of state maternal and child health programs. Includes tables and illustrations.

160　**SERVICE DIRECTORY OF NATIONAL VOLUNTARY HEALTH AND SOCIAL WELFARE ORGANIZATIONS, 1980** 14th Edition. Edited by Elma P. Cole. Washington, D.C., National Assembly, 1980. 110 pp. $8, including postage (paper). From: 1346 Connecticut Ave., NW, Suite 424A, Washington, DC 20036.

A directory of some 100 voluntary organizations intended to help national, state, and local organizations identify sources for potential help in dealing with health and welfare matters. Descriptions contain purpose, programs, national services, and publications. Includes a title index and a guide to other directories.

161 **SERVICES FOR FAMILIES OF OFFENDERS: AN OVER-
VIEW** Washington, D.C., U.S. Government Printing Office,
1981. 54 pp. $3.25 (paper).
Examines the emotional and practical needs of families when family
members are incarcerated. The second section lists programs throughout the United States that help meet family needs.

162 **SOCIAL SERVICE ORGANIZATIONS** Edited by Peter
Romanofsky and Clarke A. Chambers. Westport, Conn.,
Greenwood, 1978. 2 Vols., continuously paged. 823 pp. $65.
(The Greenwood Encyclopedia of American Institutions)
A historical directory or encyclopedia that provides concise histories of
some 200 national and local social welfare agencies, selected for inclusion because of their historical significance, longevity, size, influence,
or presence of prominent national figures. Many agencies are represented here, including advocacy agencies, volunteer agencies, direct service
agencies, and agencies that attempted to influence public policies.
Many of the organizations labored, one way or another, to improve the
circumstances of children and childhood. The histories (mostly by
Romanofsky, but 30 signed by other specialists) indicate the origin,
leaders, and significant accomplishments of each agency and its relationship to other agencies and the events of its times. Each contains a
bibliography of additional sources. Aided by a detailed table of contents
and subject index, the histories provide a rich resource for locating information on child welfare in the United States. The book is part of the
multivolume *Greenwood Encyclopedia of American Institutions Series.*
Appendix 3 classifies 22 of the agencies as being concerned with child
welfare. A companion volume is entitled *Fraternal Organizations;* these
organizations also were often active in child health and welfare projects.

163 **SOCIAL SERVICE ORGANIZATIONS AND AGENCIES
DIRECTORY** A Reference Guide to National and Regional
Social Service Organizations, Including Advocacy Groups,
Voluntary Associations, Federal and State Agencies, Clearing
Houses and Information Centers. Edited by Anthony T. Kruzas
et al. Detroit, Mich., Gale Research, 1982. 525 pp. $60.
The first edition of this convenient new directory identifies and de-
scribes the scope of 6,700 national and regional social service
organizations. These are classified in 47 subject chapters and then sub-
divided by type—as national organizations, state government agencies,
Federal Government agencies, and clearinghouses and information

centers. Chapters most relevant for children deal with adoption, family services, child welfare, child abuse and neglect, deaf/hearing impaired, education, blind/visually impaired, exceptional children, family services, gifted children, recreation, juvenile justice, and youth. In general, the divisions are very good for those concerned with social issues and conditions (although additional chapters on mental health and social action would be useful). The chapters are well arranged and easy to browse. Additional relevant organizations in other sections can be located through the detailed table of contents or the name and keyword index, although this is not as thorough as it could be.

164 **U.S. FACILITIES AND PROGRAMS FOR CHILDREN WITH SEVERE MENTAL ILLNESSES: A** Directory, **1977** By the National Institute of Mental Health. Washington, D.C., U.S. Government Printing Office, 1977. 515 pp. Single copy free while supply lasts (paperback). From: National Institute of Mental Health, 5600 Fishers Lane, Rockville, MD 20857.
A joint effort of the National Institute of Mental Health and the National Society for Autistic Children, this publication describes the programs and facilities for children diagnosed as autistic, schizophrenic, psychotic, or otherwise severely disturbed. Descriptions, up-to-date as of 1976, are based on institution responses to a 59-item questionnaire that covered capacity (including waiting list and average stay), fees, admissions criteria, program, staff, physical description, and parental participation.

165 **WASHINGTON INFORMATION DIRECTORY** Washington, D.C., Congressional Quarterly, 1975– . Annual. 1984 Edition, 900 pp., $36.
An excellent annual guide (published each May) to approximately 5,000 official and unofficial agencies in the Washington, D.C. area; handy for quick reference. Organized mainly by 16 subject chapters (none, unfortunately, on children) it groups agencies into three categories—executive agencies, Congress, and private nongovernment organizations—and provides names, addresses, and brief descriptions for each. For most subject chapters, it provides annotated bibliographies of sources of information. The congressional appendix includes each member's office address, telephone number, key staff members, committee assignments, and district offices. Other appendixes deal with executive departments, federal agencies, foreign embassies, national labor unions, regional federal information sources, religious

organizations, and state and local officials. There is an excellent subject index with many references to children and an agency and organization index.

I66   **WHERE TO WRITE FOR VITAL RECORDS: BIRTHS, DEATHS, MARRIAGES, AND DIVORCES** Compiled by the National Center for Health Statistics. Washington, D.C., U.S. Government Printing Office, 1982. 18 pp. $3.25 (paper).

A helpful reference tool (replacing four earlier publications) for all those who need copies of vital registration records. *Where to Write* lists addresses, fees, and instructions for vital records offices for each state and the District of Columbia, New York City, American Samoa, the Canal Zone, Guam, Puerto Rico, the Trust Territory of the Pacific Islands, and the Virgin Islands.

I67   **WHO KNOWS? WHO CARES? FORGOTTEN CHILDREN IN FOSTER CARE** Compiled by Joseph E. Persico. New York, National Commission on Children in Need of Parents, 1979. 96 pp. $6.50 (paper). From: Child Welfare League of America, 67 Irving Pl., New York, NY 10003.

A trenchant analysis of our foster care situation that contains many directory appendixes, including a chart directory of federal programs affecting children, resource persons, significant reports and studies, state policy planners, and administrators of children's services.

I68   **YOUTH-SERVING ORGANIZATIONS DIRECTORY** 2nd Edition. Edited by Annie M. Brewer. Detroit, Mich., Gale Research, 1980. 1,179 pp. $52.

A convenient directory composed of 1,191 entries concerning young people aged 12–20, taken from three other Gale reference directories (*The Research Centers Directory,* 6th Edition; *Directory of Special Libraries,* 5th Edition; and *Encyclopedia of Associations,* 13th Edition). Within this age group, it covers organizations with youths as members; organizations that teach, heal, or administer to the young directly or through organizations; and organizations with a large scope that includes young persons. This directory does not include all the child-centered organizations listed in its three Gale sources, but many are relevant for children under 12. Entries are numbered and are accessible through a keyword index based on organization title. The words *child* and *children* turn up often in the index. Entries include founding date, number of members, staff activities, departments, publications, and information on annual meetings.

PART III

Nonprint Sources
on the Child

11 / Computerized Retrieval Sources

This chapter discusses some computerized retrieval sources useful for child workers. Although at first glance the tools in this chapter might seem to offer a new approach to accessing information on children, most are computerized counterparts of the works discussed in Chapters 2–10.

Computerized sources that compile and dispense information on people and organizations are comparable to the directories in Chapter 10. Ongoing bibliographies of particular types of documents are counterparts of *Books in Print* (D31), *Monthly Catalog of United States Government Publications* (D36), and *Book Review Index* (D43). These use authors and titles as access points to verify citations and to locate additional information. Most data bases in this chapter, however, have evolved from the printed abstracting and indexing sources cited and discussed in Chapter 8.

Although data bases offer rapid access and Boolean searches that can combine several factors in one search, they still generally use factors and indexing approaches developed over time and can be understood best as developments of particular prototypes. One major advantage they offer, other than rapidity, is the ability to search for several aspects simultaneously (e.g., age groups and topics; geographic areas and target groups; or topic, agency, and year). Well-designed print tools may offer some of these advantages through clever indexing, cross-references, hierarchical subject terms, or divisions over time. In fact, in many

259

data bases, multifocus (Boolean) searches may result in false drops if the indexing is not good or the searcher is not skilled. Since on-line time equals money, it is important for searchers to clarify their questions. It is also a good idea to be familiar — or at least acquainted with — the print prototype, if one exists. In general, it is a good idea to run initial searches on a data base through the parent agency (if such services are offered) using their vocabularies (thesauri), questionnaires, and search aids.

Another theoretical advantage to data bases is currency. Even though some print indexes, like the *P.A.I.S. Bulletin* and the *Readers' Guide,* are updated and cumulated frequently, no print index can add items daily, as NEWSSEARCH does; thus, printed indexes to grants and funds inevitably contain some whose deadline has passed. Despite the lure of potential currency, some bibliographic data bases are rather sluggish in entering materials. ERIC's entries in *Current Index to Journals in Education* are essentially no more current in computer-accessible format. The *International Bibliography* of the Modern Language Association is two years out-of-date in print or on-line. In fact, some data bases (such as BRS's PRE-MED/PRE-PSYCH data base) were established because other data bases were slow in entering data.

I have tried to include the data bases that are most significant for information on children, but nearly all of them contain some information on children. Several described here do not contain a high proportion of child-related information, but their rapid access and targeted approaches make them far more valuable than their print counterparts. Some are very general, or seem almost beside the point, yet contain so much data that even the small proportion on children becomes significant. For these, multiple points of access and rapid searches open up their files.

On the other hand, because of the browsing capability of print formats, it can be worthwhile to stay with print versions of indexes that contain a great deal of information on children, if they are well indexed and/or well organized, brief, inexpensive, or frequently updated. Whatever their advantages and new qualities, computer searches are not panaceas and are still best used by those who understand the structures and uses of their print counterparts.

Except for the full-text data bases offered in legal fields, searches usually still result in bibliographic citations rather than the documents cited. Some vendors offer an order service for add-on fee plus costs. Their main advantage is speed in placing the order. Still, full-text searching of data bases will likely increase in the near future.

Until very recently, data base searches were largely limited to academics and researchers whose parent organizations—engineering, research, and business firms and universities—could afford to purchase tapes or pay for services. Today, such searches are available for a fee at many libraries and, perhaps more important, outside libraries to that section of the public with access to microcomputers or terminals and modems. This powerful searching mechanism is now available—not too expensively—to individuals who subscribe directly to bargain offers of "after hours" searches at lower rates. I have discussed a few such sources under "Vendors" (pp. 262–264).

I have divided the data bases into several groups that correspond to the type of information provided: directory information, current news, and bibliographic data. The bibliographic section is further divided into two sections. Data bases in the first section are comparable to the ongoing bibliographies in Chapter 5 and deal solely with periodical titles, books, or documents. Those in the second section are comparable to the indexes in Chapter 8, although some listed here are not available in print versions, and some off-target titles that are cumbersome in print are included only here.

Two major statistical data bases are incorporated into Chapter 15. Chapter 7 cites data bases that can be searched to locate audiovisuals. The computerized data bases of the following organizations are discussed in Chapter 12: the Juvenile Justice Clearinghouse (K29), National Child Welfare Training Center (K38), Business and Professional Women's Foundation (K53), Catalyst (available on BRS) (K54), Group Child Care Consultant Services (K27), National Referral Center (K56), Project SHARE (K58), Resource and Referral Service (K60), International Children's Centre (K70), International Labour Office (K71), and International Refugee Integration Resource Center (K72).

Infotecture Europe (1981– , Toronto, Espial Productions, 18 issues/year) is an English-language source for European data bases. The computerized data files of the Institute for Child Behavior Research (L42) are mentioned in Chapter 13. The National Maternal and Child Health Clearinghouse (see L25) and National Health Information Clearinghouse (L27) have data bases of relevant topics, agencies, and organizations. The Test Collection of ETS (M1) file is now available on-line through BRS and is covered in Chapter 14. Other organizations covered in Chapters 12 and 13 and periodical indexes in Chapter 8 will be on-line in the near future.

Since there are nearly 2,000 data bases, I have inevitably omitted many that may be useful occasionally. These can be located through vendor catalogs and some of the directories listed in Chapter 10, particularly *Databases and Clearinghouses* (I19) and *Directory of Online Databases* (I34). Another recommended information source is Vivian Sessions's frequently updated *Directory of Data Bases in the Social and Behavioral Sciences* (New York, Science Associates/International). The American Society for Information Science (ASIS), under the editorship of Martha Williams, publishes *Computer Readable Bibliographic Data Bases: A Directory and Data Sourcebook,* which is updated with a looseleaf service.

Since the field is proliferating rapidly, the aforementioned titles, like the vendors that follow and this chapter as a whole, may be subject to rapid obsolescence. Nevertheless, even though the chapter might be incomplete, it should provide useful broad outlines and details of tools that will continue to be useful.

VENDORS

The vendors that follow can serve as points of access for most searches and most data bases involving children. Mead Data Central (J3) offers access to full-text searches, rather than to abstracts or bibliographic citations. Both BRS (J1) and DIALOG (J2) offer cross-indexing or cross-referencing of their own data bases to help subscribers or users choose appropriately.

J1   BIBLIOGRAPHIC RETRIEVAL SERVICES, INC. (BRS)
1200 Route 7, Latham, NY 12110. (518) 783-1161, (800)
833-4707

Bibliographic Retrieval Services was established in 1976 to provide innovative, cost-effective on-line retrieval services to such large users as universities, libraries, businesses, and professional offices. It included 88 data bases as of December 1984, with a subscription access plan that charges by the number of connect hours (from $750/year for 25 hours to $3,800/year for 240 hours, plus royalty fees for some data bases). A nonsubscription use plan also is available. It provides its subscribers with an on-line directory index to choose among files and a MERGE program that allows users to combine in one file information from data bases like ERIC and PsycINFO. Other distinctive features of BRS are its on-line searching of reference tools and catalogs, specialized retrieval software, and a comprehensive system for setting up and searching private data bases (some of which have gone public). The system is on-line 22 hours per day (it is closed from 4 A.M. to 6 A.M. Eastern Standard Time) Monday through Saturday; it is closed on Sunday from 4 A.M. to 6 A.M. and from 2 P.M. to 7 P.M.

BRS/AFTER DARK, available from 6 P.M. local to 4 A.M. (Eastern Standard Time) Monday through Friday, all day Saturday, and Sunday from 6 A.M. to 2 P.M. Eastern Standard Time, then from 7 P.M. to 4 A.M. Eastern Standard Time, offers 39 BRS data bases to subscribers with personal computers and modems for charges as low as $6–$25 per hour, with a monthly minimum of $12 and a one-time start-up fee of $75. These offer simplified, less-sophisticated searching of BRS data bases in a menu-driven program that offers suggestions or options at each step. This service includes electronic mail, a newsletter, and instant software delivery.

J2   DIALOG INFORMATION RETRIEVAL SERVICE 3460
Hillview Ave., Palo Alto, CA 94304. (415) 858-3810, (800)
227-1927; (800) 982-5838 in California

An offshoot of Lockheed Corporation, DIALOG is an enormous bibliographic retrieval service that has 75 million records in more than 175 data bases in 17 major categories, including science, technology, business, economics, social sciences, medicine, current events, and directories, all described in a convenient catalog. On-line service fees, based entirely on use, range from $25/hour to $300/hour (although most are less than $100). Typically, a ten-minute search is $5–$17. DIALOG offers its users access to service that will supply copies of documents located through searches at $4.50 plus cost. Other options include a selective dissemination of information (SDI) service that automatically keeps users updated in the areas they specify. DIALOG is available 22 hours a day (it is closed from 10 P.M. to midnight Eastern Standard Time) Monday through Thursday. DIALOG closes at 8 P.M. on Friday, is open from 8 A.M.–8 P.M. on Saturday, and is closed Sunday.

KNOWLEDGE INDEX is DIALOG's after-hours service for the desk-top-computer set. It covers 23 of the more popular data bases for a flat fee of $24/hour from 6 P.M. to 5 A.M. Monday through Thursday, 6 P.M. to midnight Friday, 8 A.M. to midnight Saturday, and 3 P.M. to midnight Sunday and holidays. It has an initial subscription fee of $35, which includes an instruction manual and two free hours of search time. To inquire about KNOWLEDGE INDEX, call (800) 227-1927.

J3   **MEAD DATA CENTRAL**   P.O. Box 933, Dayton, OH 45401.
       (513) 865-6800, (800) 543-6862
Mead Data Central, which acquired THE NEW YORK TIMES INFORMATION BANK in 1983, offers full-text searching of more than 60 newspapers, magazines, wire services, newsletters, and government documents, as well as the *Encyclopedia Britannica,* in a service called NEXIS. Until it acquired the INFORMATION BANK, it required its users to use Mead terminals; but (as of late 1983) it now allows access through certain customer-provided equipment.

Mead's other service, LEXIS, is a data base for law offices and libraries, with full-text searching of 13 legal information files.

DIRECTORY DATA BASES

Two types of directory data bases are discussed in this section: directories of people and directories of funds. There are also directories of associations, however; in particular, *The Encyclopedia of Associations* (I39) is on-line through DIALOG. Other directory data bases cover such things as research in progress—for example, SMITHSONIAN SCIENCE INFORMATION EXCHANGE (SSIE), which is now available through the National Technical Information Service (J34). The FAMILY RESOURCES DATABASE, BILINGUAL EDUCATION BIBLIOGRAPHIC ABSTRACTS (BEBA), and ERIC also offer directory information.

People

American Men and Women of Science and *Marquis Who's Who in America* are both available on-line through DIALOG. The former holds some 130,000 biographies of scientists, broadly construed, and is updated yearly. The latter includes around 75,000 records and is updated quarterly. The contents of the biographies are the same as the print versions, but they are searchable through more aspects than name, geography, and specialty in this format.

The ELECTRONIC YELLOW PAGES—PROFESSIONALS is available only on-line. Based on data taken from the yellow pages of telephone books (and cross-checked with other sources), it indexes professionals in medicine, engineering, and accounting, as well as hospitals, medical laboratories, and clinics. Records include county name, telephone number, a Standard Industrial Classification Code, and the size of the office. The ELECTRONIC YELLOW PAGES provides more than 1.5 million names and is updated semiannually.

Another interesting guide to biographical data is Gale Research's BIOGRAPHY MASTER INDEX, which indexes almost 2 million names from 600 biographical dictionaries and directories, author's handbooks, and similar guides. Output includes the name, birth and death dates of the person, and citations to the sources that include information on that person. This is very handy for finding information on persons not listed in major directories. These tools are all available through DIALOG.

The FAMILY RESOURCES DATABASE, BILINGUAL EDUCATION BIBLIOGRAPHIC ABSTRACTS, SCHOOL PRACTICES INFORMATION FILE, and other bibliographic data bases provide information on people.

Funding Sources

The data bases here are similar to the directories of funding sources noted in Chapter 9. It is particularly valuable for occasional users to search such directories on-line, especially if time is short or grant parameters are complex, although Comsearch's *Grants for Children and Youth* cited in Chapter 10, item I9, is worth looking at first.

J4　　**FEDERAL ASSISTANCE PROGRAMS RETRIEVAL SYS-TEM (FAPRS)**　Office of Management and Budget, Budget Review Division, Federal Program Information Branch. Washington, DC 20503. (202) 395-3112

A computerized means of identifying federal programs and research projects appropriate for a community's developmental needs in such areas as social services, health, employment, education, and housing. Based on the *Catalog of Federal Domestic Assistance* (18), a compendium of federal programs, projects, and services, FAPRS matches the characteristics of a community with the requirements of these programs. Input requires the name and population of the area for which the search is being made, the county in which it is located, and the specific needs. The output is a list of the names and identifying numbers of applicable federal programs from the *Catalog*.

Every state has a designated access point for FAPRS, many with free searches or searches costing as little as $5. The entire data base can also be obtained from the National Technical Information Service and is available through private timesharing companies. Contact the source or your local federal information clearinghouse for more information.

J5　　**FOUNDATIONS GRANTS INDEX**　The Foundation Center, 888 Seventh Ave., New York, NY 10106. (212) 975-1120

One of three data bases from The Foundation Center; all correspond to printed indexes with the same name but are updated every two months rather than yearly. This includes information on grants of $5,000 or more awarded by 400 major philanthropical institutions (excluding grants to individuals). Grants can be searched through descriptors of field, categories of aid, keywords used in the abstract, or the recipient's name (using synonyms like *child* and *children*). Retrieval can be narrowed to state or city of recipients, year authorized, grant amount, type of recipient, or state of foundations. This is useful for locating or verifying foundations in appropriate interest or geographic areas.

Other data bases include NATIONAL FOUNDATIONS, which identifies 21,000 private U.S. foundations. This can be used to generate lists of foundations by geographic location (such as state, city, and zip code). Information, which is derived from Internal Revenue Service returns, includes financial data. The FOUNDATION DIRECTORY includes more detailed information on approximately 3,400 foundations. These can all be searched directly or through DIALOG.

J6   GRANTS   Oryx Press, 2214 N. Central at Encanto, Suite 103, Phoenix, AZ 85004. (602) 254-6156

Provides information on more than 1,500 currently available grants offered by federal, state, and local governments, private foundations, associations, and commercial organizations—updated monthly. Its print equivalent is the *Grant Information Index.* It is available from DIALOG and System Development Corporation at approximately $60.00/hour on-line, plus $0.30 per off-line record.

BIBLIOGRAPHIC DATA BASES

Current News and Happenings

Although these services are considerably more expensive than the many newsletters that also keep readers current regarding events that affect children, there are times when "up-to-the-minute" coverage is worth any cost. The data bases that follow provide rapid access to stories covered by general newspapers and magazines; one abstracts the *Congressional Record.* I have treated them as bibliographic data bases, but they are more concerned with facts than sources.

J7   CONGRESSIONAL RECORD ABSTRACTS   Capitol Services, Inc., 415 Second St., NE, Washington, DC 20002. (301) 951-1389

An ongoing index of the *Congressional Record,* the official daily journal of the proceedings of Congress, prepared by a data base publisher. Covers all public laws, bills and resolutions, reports and schedules of committees and subcommittees, floor actions and activities, executive communications, debates and speeches, and materials inserted by members of Congress. Useful for locating legislation relating to children and families. A sample record is shown in Figure 6.

   Materials can be searched by subject or bill title. The specific subject descriptor "Social Services—Children and Families" retrieves abstracts that are primarily and specifically related to children. Educational and day care issues should be searched by specific topic. An "Editors Code

```
File135*:Congressional Record 1981 - Jun 26 1984
        Set Items Description
        ---  -----  -----------

 ss hr(w)5600 and co=98
          1    10 HR(W)5600
          2 76437 CO=98
          3     5 1 AND 2

  t 3/5/2-5
3/5/2
   176054
   House suspended rules &  passed HR 5600,  revise &  extend programs under
PHS Act titles X & XX; 290-102 vote (Roll Call No.  223)  H5526,  following
7-1 division H5512; text H5506. Stmts by WAXMAN H5507,  5509 discusses 3-yr
authorizations for preventive health & health services block grant,  family
planning, & adolescent family life demonstration projects; MOLINARI  H5507;
DANNEMEYER  H5508,  5510 opposes failure to include family planning program
into state &  local block grants,  earmarking rape crisis  &   hypertension
services,  &  23% authorization increase over President's budget;  PORTER,
MADIGAN H5509; BEILENSON, FAUNTROY H5510; LELAND, S.MORRISON, WEISS H5511.
   Source: 98-078    Page: H5506
   JUNE 11, 1984
   Subfile: HOUSE PROCEEDINGS
   Descriptors: HEALTH-PUBLIC HEALTH PROGRAMS .(3011); PROCUREMENT-GRANT-IN-
-AID PROVISIONS .(1905); SOCIAL SERVICES-CHILDREN & FAMILIES .(4306);  ROLL
CALL VOTES .(6400); FLOOR DEBATE .(6500)

3/5/3
   173785
   C/Energy & Commerce reported HR 5600,  extend &  revise titles X &  XX of
PHS Act; H.Rpt. 98-804.
   Source: 98-069    Page: H4579
   MAY 23, 1984
   Subfile: HOUSE PROCEEDINGS
   Descriptors:     HEALTH-PUBLIC    HEALTH    PROGRAMS    .(3011);    SOCIAL
SERVICES-CHILDREN & FAMILIES .(4306)

3/5/4
   172651
   House C/Energy & Commerce approved HR 5600, revise & extend titles X & XX
of Public Health Service Act.
   Source: 98-063    Page: D650
   MAY 15, 1984
   Subfile: DIGEST
   Descriptors:    HEALTH-PUBLIC    HEALTH    PROGRAMS    .(3011);    SOCIAL
SERVICES-CHILDREN & FAMILIES .(4306)

3/5/5
   170705
   * HR 5600 WAXMAN, revise &  extend programs under PHS Act titles X &  XX;
C/Energy & Commerce.
   Source: 98-055    Page: H3391
   MAY 3, 1984
   Subfile: HOUSE PROCEEDINGS
   Descriptors:    HEALTH-PUBLIC    HEALTH    PROGRAMS    .(3011);    SOCIAL
SERVICES-CHILDREN & FAMILIES .(4306)
   NEW BILL
```

Figure 6   The descriptor "Social Services—Children & Families" is useful for searching CONGRESSIONAL RECORD ABSTRACTS. This search was conducted through DIALOG and is reproduced with permission.

Sheet," available from Capitol Services, is helpful in locating appropriate terms.

Capitol Services also produces *Federal Register Abstracts,* which covers federal regulations.

Custom searches are available through the producer and usually cost from $25 to $100, with free estimates. *Congressional Record Abstracts* is on-line with DIALOG, where it covers the 47th and subsequent Congresses for about $75.00/hour on-line and $0.15 per full record off-line.

J8 **THE INFORMATION BANK (INFOBANK)** (Registered trademark of The New York Times.) Mead Data Central, P.O. Box 933, Dayton, OH 45401. (513) 865-6800

A computerized information service based on *The New York Times,* providing on-line or on-demand access to materials published originally in the *Times* and/or three other data bases of information abstracts. Starting with June 1, 1980, every type of story appearing in the *Times* is entered in complete full-text form. Materials can be located through controlled vocabularies or free-text searches. INFOBANK adds approximately 1,800 items per month.

The INFORMATION BANK contains 2 million items in abstract form from *The New York Times* and 60 other newspapers; wire services; the Gallup Poll; topical magazines; and various weeklies, monthlies, and quarterlies published since 1969. Information is derived from current news stories, editorials, articles, essays, and surveys. Major areas are current affairs; business; and economic, social, and political information, with some 15,000 items added each month.

The DEADLINE DATA ON WORLD AFFAIRS, also from Mead, provides geopolitical information on countries, states, and world organizations, including age distribution, health care, life expectancy, and infant mortality statistics.

ADVERTISING AND MARKETING INTELLIGENCE (AMI) has more than 125,000 abstracts on advertising and marketing from more than 60 trade and professional publications, including information on products for children. It, too, is available from Mead Data Central.

J9 **NATIONAL NEWSPAPER INDEX** Information Access Company, 404 Sixth Ave., Menlo Park, CA 94025. (414) 367-7171, (800) 227-8431

Provides citations for five national newspapers; *Christian Science Monitor, The New York Times, Wall Street Journal, Los Angeles Times,* and *The Washington Post* for 1979 to date. All are indexed from cover to cover except for weather charts, stock market tables, crossword puzzles, and horoscopes. The subject headings are modifications of Library of Congress subject headings, so that terms starting with *child* and *children* are good access points.

NEWSSEARCH, also from Information Access Company, is the index to the current month's magazine, journal, and newspaper literature—from *Magazine Index, National Newspaper Index,* and *Legal Resource Index.* These are updated daily and kept in the NEWSSEARCH data base approximately 45 days before being transferred.

Both the *National Newspaper Index* and NEWSSEARCH are available on DIALOG.

Books, Documents, or Periodicals Only

Librarians who are concerned with verifying information on publications for purchase, reference, or cataloging purposes are responsible for the creation of numerous data bases that can also be used to locate books or other formats by subject, author, title, or date. In general, these are similar or identical to the print tools cited in Chapter 5. This section notes a few on-line data bases that are useful for verifying information on books, government publications, and periodicals. These items, of course, can also be verified through those subject indexes or abstract services—in print or on-line—that index or abstract books or public documents (e.g., the *P.A.I.S. Bulletin*). Similarly, the indexing and abstracting services in Chapter 8 usually provide information on the titles, addresses, prices, and frequencies of the periodicals they abstract or index.

Basically, sources that were originally designed for purchase information cover items in print or for sale and provide price and other helpful information. Those designed for cataloging or historical record cover various categories (such as national bibliographies) and may include slightly different data. *Books in Print* (J10) is the most comprehensive source; BOOKSINFO, issued by Brodart (Williamsport, Pa.) and available through BRS, includes English-language books from 10,000 U.S. publishers and 200 foreign publishers. It contains fewer titles than *Books in Print,* but subject searching is considered easier.

Other book record on-line files used by librarians include LC MARC, which contains complete bibliographic data on English-language books cataloged by the Library of Congress since 1968, with foreign books added from 1970 through 1979. REMARC covers the older publications of the Library of Congress from 1897 to 1980 over various time spans. Both are available through DIALOG and can be searched through Library of Congress subject headings, as well as through author, title, series, and publication date.

Book Review Index (D43) is also available on-line through DIALOG. Its citations to reviews in some 400 journals can be searched by author, title, periodical title, year of publication, and type of document (e.g., children's books and children's periodicals). Titles can be located through synonyms for *child, childhood,* and *children* in the index.

J10 **BOOKS IN PRINT (BIP)** R. R. Bowker, 205 E. 42nd St., New York, NY 10017. (212) 916-1600

The most comprehensive file on books, covering titles about to be published and titles recently out of print, as well as those in print. Uses author and title access as well as Library of Congress subject headings for books published or distributed in the United States. Other points of access are publisher, price, international standard book number (ISBN), and type of binding. The BIP file covers the books cited in the print version of *Books in Print, Subject Guide to Books in Print, Scientific and Technical Books in Print, Medical Books in Print, Business and Economic Books in Print, Paperbound Books in Print, Forthcoming Books, Subject Guide to Forthcoming Books, Children's Books in Print, Subject Guide to Children's Books in Print, Religious Books in Print, Large Type Books in Print,* and *Books in Print Supplement.* This data base is available through DIALOG and BRS.

J11 **GPO MONTHLY CATALOG** U.S. Government Printing Office, 5236 Eisenhower Ave., Alexandria, VA 22304. (703) 446-2135

An on-line equivalent of the *Monthly Catalog of United States Government Publications,* with materials from 1976 to date. Materials on children can be searched by agency, title, note, abstract, and descriptor. The file is available on BRS and DIALOG for approximately $35.00/hour on-line, plus $0.10 per record off-line.

A GPO PUBLICATIONS REFERENCE FILE, available only from DIALOG, provides access to public documents in print or forthcoming from the Superintendent of Documents. It includes materials from 1971 to date; materials on children can be searched by title, descriptor, and note.

J12   **ULRICH'S INTERNATIONAL PERIODICALS DIREC-TORY**   R. R. Bowker, 205 E. 42nd St., New York, NY 10017. (212) 916-1600
Covers the periodicals in *Ulrich's International Periodicals Directory,* as well as those in *Irregular Series and Annuals, Sources of Serials,* and *Ulrich's Quarterly*—a total of more than 100,000 serials (regular, irregular, and annual) from 65 publishers in 181 countries. These can be searched through any word in their titles (or former or alternative titles). Entries include information on status (e.g., discontinued), name and address, frequency of publication, circulation, subject areas, and the names of abstracting or indexing services that cover the publication. Also includes Dewey decimal classification and international standard serial numbers. ULRICH's is available on DIALOG for $65.00/hour on-line and $0.20 per record off-line.

INDEXING AND ABSTRACTING DATA BASES

Many of the indexing and abstracting data bases listed here are counterparts of the print tools listed in Chapter 8 and are more fully described there. Some of the sources in Chapter 8 are planning to go on-line in the near future, including *Chicago Psychoanalytic Literature Index* (G8), *Cumulative Index to Nursing and Allied Health Literature* (G13), *Kindex* (G29), and *Refugee Abstracts* (G43). Similarly, some of the organizations in Chapter 12 are likely to computerize their files soon.

Bibliography of Bioethics (G5) and *Population Index* (G35) are subsumed under the discussion of MEDLARS. Other data bases, such as HISTORICAL ABSTRACTS, are available both in print and on-line, but are described in this chapter only, since the computer form seems more valuable for locating materials on childhood.

A few very important data bases listed in this chapter have no exact current print counterparts (although they may have generated some subject bibliographies or bibliographic surveys). These include BILINGUAL EDUCATION BIBLIOGRAPHIC ABSTRACTS, BIRTH DEFECTS INFORMATION SERVICE, CHILD ABUSE AND NEGLECT, FAMILY RESOURCES DATABASE, and MENTAL HEALTH ABSTRACTS.

J13   **AGRICOLA**   National Library of Agriculture, 10301 Baltimore Blvd., Beltsville, MD 20705. (301) 344-3778

The cataloging and indexing base of the National Library of Agriculture, with comprehensive worldwide coverage of journals and monographs in agriculture and related areas, totaling 1.7 million volumes. Contains a substantial amount of material on nutrition, housing, rural development, and family economics relevant to child welfare. AGRICOLA is available through BRS and DIALOG for approximately $35.00/hour on-line and $0.10/record off-line.

J14   **AMERICAN HISTORY AND LIFE**   ABC-Clio, Inc., P.O. Box 4397, Santa Barbara, CA 93103. (805) 963-4221

This valuable interdisciplinary data base corresponds to *America: History and Life,* a three-part print base comprising *Part A: Article Abstracts and Citations, Part B: Index to Book Reviews,* and *Part C: American History Bibliography,* from 1964 on. It contains abstracts of articles and citations of reviewed books and dissertation abstracts from *Dissertation Abstracts International* on U.S. and Canadian history from prehistoric times to the present, as well as area studies, current affairs, and studies of historical interest taken from some 2,000 American and foreign journals and dissertations. Book review and dissertation citations have been included since 1974. Materials can be searched by author, title, type of document, historical period, journal name, year of publication, journal announcement, country of publication, and subject descriptor. Subject terms such as "youth," "child," and "children" can be used to narrow retrieval of book reviews, articles, and dissertations.

At the end of 1983, AMERICAN HISTORY AND LIFE contained more than 5,000 citations related to children and childhood (out of 160,000 records); it is updated six times a year. In addition to its value in locating historical and humanistic materials not easily found elsewhere, this file can be used to locate materials on groups of Americans (e.g., Mexican Americans) or the peoples and cultures of particular geographic locations. Its annual subject index is useful as a vocabulary list.

It is available through DIALOG at approximately $65.00/hour on-line and $0.15/record off-line.

J15   **BASE D'INFORMATION ROBERT DEBRÉ (BIRD)** In-
      ternational Children's Centre (ICC) Documentation Service,
      Chateau de Longchamp, Bois de Boulogne, 75016 Paris, France.
      (506) 79 92

This data base is an extension of the 500,000-item reference library of
the International Children's Center (K70). It incorporates some
15,000 items per year (1,200 per month), carefully chosen from the
870 periodical titles, 600 documents, and 700 books accessed each year
by the center and entered in the data base within a month of receipt.
BIRD covers information on all aspects of child life, from conception
through adolescence. Although it encompasses materials in French,
English, and Spanish and can be accessed in all three languages, it gives
maximum coverage to documents in French, especially those originat-
ing in developing countries (these comprise 30 percent of the data
base). The data base uses BRS software and can be searched through
keywords in French, English, and Spanish, as well as through authors,
titles, and such general descriptors as "premature," "legislation," and
"statistics." Purchasable tools include a list of descriptors (200 French
francs), a user's manual (70 francs), and a catalog of periodicals (60
francs). The data base can be searched through the Documentation Service of ICC or the French supplier, G. CAM-Serveur, Tour Maine Montparnasse, 33, avenue du Maine, 75755 Paris, Cedex 15, France. All
references given are for documents available from ICC; photocopies are
available to all interested users.

J16   **BILINGUAL   EDUCATION   BIBLIOGRAPHIC   AB-
      STRACTS (BEBA)** National Clearinghouse for Bilingual
      Education (NCBE), 1555 Wilson Blvd., Suite B2-605, Rosslyn,
      VA 22209. (703) 522-0710, (800) 336-4560

The National Clearinghouse for Bilingual Education has constructed a
bibliographic data base that contains citations to print and nonprint
materials on all aspects of bilingual and bicultural education, including
journal articles, research reports, conference papers, bibliographies,
reference materials, reviews, program descriptions, and curricular
materials. This data base goes beyond the details of education and contains all sorts of information on approximately 5 million children
nationwide, including minority children, refugee children, and other
children who—for one reason or another—do not speak English fluent-
ly. These entries are similar to those in ERIC and include abstract and

Journal Article Citation

BEBA Accession Number......	AN	BE001649 8005.
Title.....................	TI	HELP FOR DANA FAST HORSE AND FRIENDS.
Publication Date...........	YR	79.
Author....................	AU	GIPP, GERALD E.
Source Journal Citation....	SO	AMERICAN EDUCATION, V15 N7 P18–21 AUG-SEP 1979.
Issue Code (J=Journal).....	IS	J.
Publication Type Codes.....	PT	080. 141.
Descriptive Notes..........	NT	4 P.
Major Descriptors..........	MJ	AMERICAN-INDIANS. EDUCATIONAL-LEGISLATION. TEACHER-EDUCATION. BILINGUAL-EDUCATION. AMERICAN-INDIAN-EDUCATION.
Minor Descriptors..........	MN	OUTREACH-PROGRAMS. FINANCIAL-SUPPORT. EDUCATIONAL-FINANCE. TEACHER-PROGRAMS. SCHOOL-PERSONNEL. LITERACY-EDUCATION. HIGH-SCHOOL-EQUIVALENCY-PROGRAMS. FELLOWSHIPS. ALASKA-NATIVES. EXTERNAL-DEGREE-PROGRAMS. TEACHER-INTERNS. COMMUNITY-COLLEGES. UNIVERSITIES. COLLEGE-PROGRAMS. FEDERAL-PROGRAMS. FEDERAL-LEGISLATION. AMERICAN-INDIAN-CULTURE. RESERVATIONS-INDIAN.
Identifiers................	ID	*INDIAN EDUCATION ACT 1972.
Language Codes.............	LC	L-0. M-0. N-0. P-0. Q-0. R-0. S-0. T-0. U-0.
Abstract...................	AB	IN RESPONSE TO FINDINGS OF HIGH DROPOUT RATES, LOW ACHIEVEMENT LEVELS, AND LOW SELF-ESTEEM AMONG INDIAN CHILDREN, AS WELL AS A SHORTAGE OF INDIAN TEACHERS AND PRINCIPALS, CONGRESS PASSED THE INDIAN EDUCATION ACT IN 1972. AMONG THE PROGRAMS AUTHORIZED BY THE LEGISLATION ARE: (1) BILINGUAL EDUCATION PROGRAMS IN MORE THAN 1,000 SCHOOL DISTRICTS IN 42 STATES; (2) BASIC LITERACY, HIGH SCHOOL EQUIVALENCY, AND JOB TRAINING PROGRAMS FOR 10,000 ADULTS; (3) 260 FELLOWSHIPS FOR UNDERGRADUATE AND GRADUATE STUDY IN PROFESSIONS IN WHICH INDIANS HAVE BEEN UNDERREPRESENTED; AND (4) EDUCATION STAFF TRAINING PROGRAMS FOR 800 INDIANS AND ALASKA NATIVES. TO SOLVE GEOGRAPHIC PROBLEMS AND RESPOND TO TRIBAL PREFERENCES, THREE APPROACHES TO TRAINING INDIAN TEACHERS WERE DEVELOPED: (1) COMMUNITY COLLEGE-UNIVERSITY AFFILIATION, IN WHICH TRIBAL COUNCIL-FOUNDED COMMUNITY COLLEGES OFFER TEACHER PREPARATION COURSES IN CONJUNCTION WITH A DEGREE-GRANTING UNIVERSITY; (2) UNIVERSITY OUTREACH, IN WHICH TEACHER INTERNS ARE TAUGHT IN THEIR HOME PUEBLOS BY UNIVERSITY STAFF MEMBERS; AND (3) CAMPUS-BASED PREPARATION, IN WHICH RESIDENT OR COMMUTING INTERNS TAKE ALL COURSEWORK ON CAMPUS. (DS).

Figure 7 Sample BEBA citation with key to fields.

language notes. Information on availability of documents is included as part of the data element of the BEBA citation. Subject descriptors stem from the ERIC *Thesaurus* (A37). See Figure 7 for a sample BEBA citation.

The clearinghouse performs custom searches of its data bases through the mail for a fee of $10.00 for up to 100 citations from BEBA and/or ERIC. (Other data bases can be searched for $10.00/base, plus $0.15/citation.) Searches on file are available at $2.50 for up to 50 pages; $5.00 for 51–75 pages. Turnaround time is three weeks. For custom searches, NCBE requests a full description of the topic, with information on language, ethnic group, age, educational level, and subject. Searches also are available through BRS.

J17 **BIRTH DEFECTS INFORMATION SYSTEM (BDIS)** Center for Birth Defects Information Services, 171 Harrison Ave., Box 403, Boston, MA 02111. (617) 956-7400
An on-line human genetics information service for health professionals, researchers, and medical media, developed at Tufts–New England Medical Center in 1978 under a grant from the March of Dimes Birth Defects Foundation, with computer capability assisted by the Massachusetts Institute of Technology. This service notes that as many as 16 percent of all deliveries involve birth defects (thus, as many as half a million of the 3.5 million children born in the United States each year have some form of birth anomaly, and 250,000 are born with major birth defects).

BIRTH DEFECTS INFORMATION SYSTEM's Information Retrieval Facility contains articles, prepared by specialists, on more than 1,000 birth defects. These articles, which are updated regularly, summarize the clinical features, natural history, complications, treatment, prognosis, and inheritance of each birth defect. BDIS's Diagnostic Assist Facility accepts case descriptions, asks pertinent questions, and provides a list of the best matches from a knowledge base of 600 conditions. Its Unknowns Registry Facility stores clinical, demographic, and epidemiologic information on cases for which there is no clear diagnosis. The center is currently compiling the *Genetic Services Directory.*

Access to BDIS is via computer terminals over standard telephone lines, directly or through a communications network, and through personal computers. Subscribers are billed $15.00/month for services, plus $10.75/hour on-line connect changes and $3.50/article retrieved. There is a $50.00 charge for each clinical case processed for diagnosis. There is no charge for the Unknowns Registry.

A BDIS training program is available. The quarterly newsletter, *Tielines,* provides news of this data base.

J18 **CHILD ABUSE AND NEGLECT (CAN)** National Center on Child Abuse and Neglect Children's Bureau, P.O. Box 1182, Washington, DC 20013. (202) 245-2856; clearinghouse, (301) 251-5157

The Child Abuse and Neglect file contains three types of materials: bibliographic references to books and periodical articles, descriptions of ongoing research projects, and listings of service programs (with only two years coverage of research and service projects). This data base — with some 12,000 citations — covers all the areas of child abuse, including definition, identification, prevention, and treatment. Print publications of CAN — *Child Abuse and Neglect Research: Projects and Publications* (1978, free), *Child Abuse and Neglect Programs* (1976, $7), and *Child Abuse and Neglect Audiovisuals* (1983, $20) — are extensive but not kept current.

The bibliographic file goes back to 1965 and contains a wide range of data; it is valuable for literature searches on topics like infanticide, adolescent parents and child maltreatment, adolescent abuse, laws that mention emotional or psychological mistreatment, laws on sexual exploitation of children or child pornography, cultural values and child abuse, cross-cultural aspects of child abuse and neglect, infant mortality, religion and religious affiliation related to child abuse, and prenatal influences. The file is available directly through the center via mail and from DIALOG for $35.00/hour on-line and $0.10/record off-line.

J19   **COMPREHENSIVE DISSERTATION INDEX** University Microfilms International, 300 N. Zeeb Rd., Ann Arbor, MI 48106. (313) 761-4700, (800) 521-0600

This system contains all doctoral dissertations and master's theses accepted by accredited educational institutions in the United States and many from Canadian and European institutions — more than 800,000 altogether, updated monthly. Doctoral dissertations are covered from 1861, master's theses from 1962 to the present. Corresponding print data bases are *Dissertation Abstracts International* (G17), *American Doctoral Dissertations,* and *Masters Abstracts.* COMPREHENSIVE DISSERTATION INDEX covers searches in all subject disciplines, including education, psychology, sociology, and library and information science. Since other data bases also contain theses and dissertations, the best use of this data base is for searches limited exclusively to dissertations and/or theses. *Datrix Keyword Frequency List* is an aid for users. Service is available directly as DATRIX II (Direct Access to Reference Information — A Xerox Service) or through BRS and DIALOG as COMPREHENSIVE DISSERTATION INDEX for approximately $70.00/hour on-line and $0.20/record off-line. DATRIX II custom mail searches cost $15.00.

J20   **CONGRESSIONAL INFORMATION SERVICE (CIS)**
4520 East-West Highway, Suite 800, Bethesda, MD 20814.
(301) 654-1550, (800) 638-8380
Corresponds to *CIS/Index* (G10), where it is more fully described. It
contains abstracts and citations to the publications of all U.S. Senate,
House, and joint committees and subcommittees, including reports,
hearings, documents, prints, and legislative histories or public laws,
and can be searched by title, descriptor, committee code, congressional
session, document type, witness name or affiliation, journal announcement, report number, or GPO number. CIS is available on DIALOG and
System Development Corporation's ORBIT and covers materials from
1970 to date. Charges are approximately $90.00/hour on-line and
$0.25/record off-line.

J21   **CRIMINAL JUSTICE PERIODICAL INDEX (CJPI)**   Uni-
      versity Microfilms International, 300 N. Zeeb Rd., Ann Arbor,
      MI 48106. (313) 761-4700, (800) 521-0600
Offers citations to journal literature in the criminal justice field from
some 120 journals on justice and law enforcement, from 1975 to date.
It contains approximately 90,000 records, is updated monthly, and is
relevant for such topics as family courts, juvenile delinquency, and
child abuse. CJPI corresponds to the printed *Criminal Justice Periodical
Index* and can be searched by author, title, subject descriptor, journal
name, or year of publication. This file is particularly valuable for recent
materials and for reviews of criminal justice textbooks. It is available
through DIALOG for approximately $55.00/hour on-line and $0.15/rec-
ord off-line.

J22   **EDUCATIONAL RESOURCES INFORMATION CENTER
      (ERIC)**   National Institute of Education, ERIC Processing and
      Reference Facility, 4833 Rugby Ave., Suite 301, Bethesda, MD
      20814. (301) 656-9753
The major data base for materials on education, and the data base that
will yield the greatest number of references on children. It covers the
journal literature of *Current Index to Journals in Education* (G15) and
the report information of *Resources in Education* (G46) and includes
almost 500,000 citations on all aspects of education from rural and
urban education to early childhood education; management, counseling, and personnel services; tests, measurement, and evaluation; education of the handicapped, disadvantaged, and gifted; vocational and
career education; higher education; and particular curriculum areas.
ERIC also includes general and therapeutic aspects such as bibliotherapy, play therapy, values clarification, and art and dance therapy.

Search vocabulary is from the *Thesaurus of ERIC Descriptors* (A37) and can narrow searches by age or grade level. Searchers also can look for particular kinds of documents, such as bibliographies or reference books. Other user aids are the *ERIC Identifier Authority List, Descriptor Usage Report,* and *ERIC Processing Manual.*

The microfiche entries uncovered through *Resources in Education* can be perused in approximately 650 locations throughout the country. They are listed in the *Directory of ERIC Microfiche Collections,* which is available from the address above. ERIC also issues the *Directory of ERIC Search Services,* which describes some 450 organizations that provide searches of the ERIC data base, many free or for a modest fee. *A Guide to Sources of Educational Information* (B7) describes state education agencies that offer inexpensive ERIC searches. Beyond these sources, ERIC can be searched through BRS, DIALOG, and SDC.

J23 **EXCEPTIONAL CHILD EDUCATION RESOURCES (ECER)** Council for Exceptional Children (CEC), 1920 Association Dr., Reston, VA 22091. (800) 336-3728, (703) 620-3660 in Virginia

A comprehensive data base of published and unpublished literature on the education of handicapped and gifted children that corresponds to the printed *Exceptional Child Education Resources* (G20), where it is more fully described. It is particularly useful for searches on topics such as developmental disabilities, although searching broader topics, like child abuse, will locate entries not found in other data bases. ECER uses the *Thesaurus of ERIC Descriptors* (A37) and, like it, can be searched by age or grade level. Approximately 30 percent of the items in ECER are in the ERIC data base, but ECER's annotations of journal articles are fuller. ECER also includes commercial books relevant to special education, doctoral dissertations on exceptional children, and nonprint materials—mostly those used for parent or teacher education.

Custom searches of ECER and ERIC are performed for nonmembers of CEC for around $35 for up to 50 citations from one data base and $50 for up to 100 citations from both data bases. Reprints of previously performed searches are available for $10 each. ECER can also be searched through DIALOG and BRS and through many of the same sources that search ERIC.

J24 **FAMILY RESOURCES DATABASE** National Council on Family Relations (NCFR), Family Resource and Referral Center, 1219 University Ave., SE, Minneapolis, MN 55414. (612) 331-2774

FAMILY RESOURCES DATABASE is an interdisciplinary data base concentrating on information on the family, the only comprehensive collection that bridges the gaps among data bases in medicine, sociology, psychology, and education. It combines the abstract files of the *Inventory of Marriage and Family Literature* (D35) with the extensive collections of the Family Resource and Referral Center, which contain citations to and some abstracts of a great variety of materials, including journal articles, monographs, government publications, reports, audiovisual materials, programs, research, organizations, individuals, tests and assessments, and instructional materials on marriage and the family, broadly construed. General subject areas include trends and change in marriage and the family, organizations and services to families, family relationships and dynamics, issues related to reproduction, sexual attitudes and behavior, marriage and divorce (including custody and child support), and families with special problems. The last category includes child abuse, family stress, families and disasters, children of divorce, families with handicapped or learning disabilities, and other relevant topics.

FAMILY RESOURCES DATABASE covers bibliographic and biographical data from 1970 on, with some historical references—around 53,000 items total. These include popular, juvenile, and instructional materials; books and monographs, government publications, newsletters and periodicals, journal articles, audiovisuals, dissertations, proceedings, scholarly materials, and information on works in progress; and entries for organizations, research centers, and individuals with expertise in various marriage and family topics. Perhaps 14,000 citations relate to children and youth. Many are abstracted. Topics can be searched by classification code or by keywords and their synonyms; searches can be narrowed to particular types of publications, time spans, or geographic areas. This data base covers journal literature from 1973 to the present and nonjournal references back to 1970, with some historical information included. FAMILY RESOURCES can be searched through BRS, with a royalty fee of $25.00/hour on-line, plus $0.20/citation on-line and $0.15/record off-line, and through DIALOG for $57.00/hour on-line and $0.25/record off-line.

J25   **HISTORICAL ABSTRACTS** ABC-Clio, Inc., P.O. Box 4397, Santa Barbara, CA 93103. (805) 963-4221
HISTORICAL ABSTRACTS, the companion to AMERICAN HISTORY AND LIFE (J14), contains abstracts and citations to international literature in history, culture, economics, and politics, excluding the United States and Canada. It corresponds to the printed *Historical Abstracts: Part A,*

Modern History Abstracts (1450–1914) and *Part B, Twentieth Century Abstracts* (1914 to present). It indexes journals published since 1973 and books and dissertations published since 1980, with a total of 191,000 citations through 1984, updated six times a year. HISTORICAL ABSTRACTS can be searched through terms like "child," "childhood," "children," and their synonyms in the title abstract or descriptor. Since *American History and Life* covers the United States and Canada, this file is reserved for international topics. It contains more than 2,000 items on children and is available through DIALOG for $65.00/hour on-line and $0.15/record off-line.

J26 **LANGUAGE AND LANGUAGE BEHAVIOR ABSTRACTS (LLBA)** Sociological Abstracts, P.O. Box 22206, San Diego, CA 92122. (619) 565-6603

The computer equivalent of *Language and Language Behavior Abstracts* (G30) from 1973 on, LLBA allows searches to be narrowed by age and educational levels and searches through terms such as "child," "childhood," and their equivalents in titles, abstracts, and descriptors. Includes materials on language acquisitions, bilingualism, sociolinguistics and language planning, speech and hearing problems, and interpersonal behavior and communications. LLBA issues a *User's Reference Manual.*

The Linguafranca division of Sociological Abstracts will perform computer searches for a minimum of $20.00, plus $0.15/record off-line, with free cost estimates. Only Linguafranca can retrieve citations prior to 1973.

The standard data base includes some 63,000 records and is searchable through DIALOG at approximately $55.00/hour on-line and $0.15/record off-line.

J27 **LEGAL RESOURCE INDEX** Information Access Company, 404 Sixth Ave., Menlo Park, CA 94205. (415) 367-7171, (800) 227-8431

The LEGAL RESOURCE INDEX data base, which merges *Legal Resource Index* and *Current Law Index,* contains citations to legal and law-related journal literature from 1980 to date, including 660 law journals and 5 law newspapers, as well as legal monographs and government publications. Topics related to children can be located by searching the title, identifier, and descriptor paragraphs with terms like "infant," "juvenile," "children," "childhood," and "youngsters." Because of inconsistencies in legal terminology, these synonyms will retrieve some articles dealing with adolescents. LEGAL RESOURCE INDEX can be searched through DIALOG at $90.00/hour on-line and $0.20/record off-line.

J28   **LIBRARY AND INFORMATION SCIENCE ABSTRACTS
       (LISA)** The Library Assn., 7 Ridgemont St., London WC1E
       7AE, England. (01) 636-7543
This is the only on-line file devoted to library and information science
and corresponds to the print file *Library and Information Science Abstracts.* It covers books, journal articles (from 300 periodicals), bulletins, conference proceedings, and technical reports on publishing,
technical processes, and users and user behavior, from 1969 on. As an
international data base, it contains materials in languages other than
English, so searches must be narrowed by language. Topics on children
can be located by searching titles, abstracts, subject headings, and descriptor paragraphs. LISA has issued the *LISA List of Classification Codes*
and a list of periodicals. LISA is available through DIALOG and SDC for
approximately $74.00/hour on-line and $0.25/record off-line.

J29   **MAGAZINE INDEX** Information Access Company, 404
       Sixth Ave., Menlo Park, CA 94025. (415) 367-7171, (800)
       227-8431
Comparable in scope to the *Readers' Guide to Periodical Literature,* it
provides citations to 435 popular magazines published in the United
States and Canada, covering magazines indexed from 1959 to 1969 and
from 1972 to date. It offers access to a wide range of child-related topics
in business, current affairs and public policy, education, health, medicine, social sciences, life-style, and travel. These topics may be searched by titles, abstracts, or descriptors, with an additional entry point
through "named people." MAGAZINE INDEX is available through
DIALOG for around $75.00/hour on-line and $0.20/record off-line.

J30   **MEDICAL LITERATURE ANALYSIS AND RETRIEVAL
       SYSTEM (MEDLARS)** National Library of Medicine
       (NLM), MEDLARS Management Section, 8600 Rockville Pike,
       Bethesda, MD 20209. (301) 496-6193
MEDLARS is the National Library of Medicine's computer-based system
that provides rapid access to the journal literature of the health sciences—some 4 million references dating back to 1964. The articles, indexed at the rate of more than 200,000 per year, are taken from 3,000
journals in many languages and medical specialties; they appear in print
each month in *Index Medicus* (G24) and the *International Nursing
Index* (G27) and are also published in a variety of recurring bibliographies.
    MEDLINE (MEDLARS On-line) is a nationwide system for searching
the MEDLARS data base through computer terminals in 1,100 medical

institutions throughout the country. It provides citations and abstracts to virtually every area in the field of biomedicine, including behavioral disorders, hospital literature, population, psychiatry, medical specialties, and clinical practice. Since 1975, approximately 40 percent of the records contain author abstracts taken from the printed articles.

Since the file size is approximately 4 million records, it is important to limit a search to the desired language and to be as specific as possible. Topics on children can be searched using *Medical Subject Headings* (A34), terms from its indexes, or synonyms in the title or abstract paragraphs.

Other computerized search services from NLM are CATLINE, which provides access to books cataloged by the National Library of Medicine; TOXLINE, which provides access to literature on toxicology and pharmacology; and AVLINE, which provides information on audiovisuals used for health science education. BIOETHICSLINE is the computerized counterpart of *Bibliography of Bioethics* (G5), and POPLINE corresponds to *Population Index* (G35). The data bases are available from NLM from 3 A.M. to 9 P.M. Eastern Standard Time. The National Library of Medicine and medical library networks also can provide photocopies, purchase information, and interlibrary loan for cited items. MEDLINE can also be searched through BRS, DIALOG, the AUSTRALIAN MEDICINE NETWORK, BLAISE (British Library Automated Information Service)-LINK, and DIMDI (Deutsches Institut für Medizinische Dokumentation und Information).

J31   **MENTAL HEALTH ABSTRACTS**   IFI/Plenum Data Company, 3202 Kirkwood Highway, Suite 203, Wilmington, DE 19808. (302) 998-0478, (800) 368-3093

MENTAL HEALTH ABSTRACTS is the continuation of the file established by the National Clearinghouse for Mental Health Information (NCMHI) in 1969. It covers the world literature on mental health and mental illness, including such areas as child development, child psychiatry, crime and delinquency, child mental illness, and social issues involving children. Its orientation is perhaps less theoretical than PsycINFO (J37), and it tends to include more on the legal and administrative aspects of mental health and on psychopharmacology.

It can be searched by age levels in the identifier field and by terms relating to children in the title and/or abstract. The *Mental Health Abstracts User Guide* is available from IFI/Plenum for $10.

The NCMHI data base included selected articles from 1,200 high-yield journals from 41 countries in 21 languages, as well as books, monographs, technical reports, workshop and conference proceedings, and symposia. Documents were abstracted in English in 200–300 words; these abstracts were the main source of index terms selected by an automatic indexing operation. In 1982, when NCMHI was discontinued, its file incorporated 450,000 abstracts. It was taken over by IFI/Plenum, who now update the data base monthly with around 1,500 items. It contains 495,000 items and is growing rapidly.

The ongoing file is available through DIALOG as MENTAL HEALTH ABSTRACTS for $30.00/hour on-line and $0.10/record off-line. See Figure 8 for a sample record from MENTAL HEALTH ABSTRACTS.

J32 **MODERN LANGUAGE ASSOCIATION BIBLIOGRAPHY (MLA Bibliography)** Modern Language Association of America, 62 Fifth Ave., New York, NY 10011. (212) 741-7863
This data base, which corresponds to the *MLA International Bibliography of Books and Articles on the Modern Languages and Literature,* provides citations on literature, linguistics, languages, and folklore—some 469,000 records altogether, including journal articles, books, and essays. It is a source for children's literature and communicative behavior. The title and descriptor approaches must be narrowed to limit retrieval to items related to children. The MLA BIBLIOGRAPHY is available through DIALOG and BRS for $55.00/hour on-line and $0.15/record off-line.

J33 **NATIONAL CRIMINAL JUSTICE REFERENCE SERVICE (NCJRS)** U.S. Department of Justice, National Criminal Justice Reference Service, National Institute of Justice, Box 6000, Rockville, MD 20850. (301) 251-5500
Includes citations and abstracts of materials collected by the National Criminal Justice Reference Service, an international clearinghouse of practical and theoretical information on criminal justice and law enforcement. Includes published and unpublished research reports; program descriptions and evaluations; books; dissertations; handbooks and standards; journal articles; and audiovisual materials. Although NCJRS covers fewer items than the CRIMINAL JUSTICE PERIODICAL INDEX (J21) (200 versus 650 journals), its abstracts provide detailed information on article contents and it covers a variety of materials, such as books. Children are not apt to be criminals, but NCJRS is worth searching for materials on such topics as juvenile dependency and neglect, runaways, and status offenders. Most entries in NCJRS are from 1972 to date. It is searchable through DIALOG.

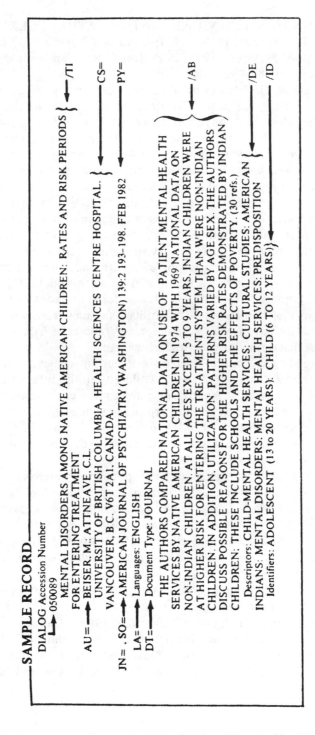

SAMPLE RECORD

DIALOG Accession Number
→ 050089

MENTAL DISORDERS AMONG NATIVE AMERICAN CHILDREN: RATES AND RISK PERIODS } → /TI
FOR ENTERING TREATMENT

AU= → BEISER, M.; ATTNEAVE, C.L.
UNIVERSITY OF BRITISH COLUMBIA. HEALTH SCIENCES CENTRE HOSPITAL. } CS=
VANCOUVER, B.C. V6T 2A1. CANADA.

JN = . SO= → AMERICAN JOURNAL OF PSYCHIATRY (WASHINGTON) 139:2 193-198. FEB 1982 PY=

LA= → Languages: ENGLISH
DT= → Document Type: JOURNAL

THE AUTHORS COMPARED NATIONAL DATA ON USE OF PATIENT MENTAL HEALTH
SERVICES BY NATIVE AMERICAN CHILDREN IN 1974 WITH 1969 NATIONAL DATA ON
NON-INDIAN CHILDREN. AT ALL AGES EXCEPT 5 TO 9 YEARS. INDIAN CHILDREN WERE
AT HIGHER RISK FOR ENTERING THE TREATMENT SYSTEM THAN WERE NON-INDIAN
CHILDREN. IN ADDITION, UTILIZATION PATTERNS VARIED BY AGE SEX. THE AUTHORS
DISCUSS POSSIBLE REASONS FOR THE HIGHER RISK RATES DEMONSTRATED BY INDIAN
CHILDREN: THESE INCLUDE SCHOOLS AND THE EFFECTS OF POVERTY. (30 refs.)
} → /AB

Descriptors: CHILD-MENTAL HEALTH SERVICES: CULTURAL STUDIES: AMERICAN
INDIANS: MENTAL DISORDERS: MENTAL HEALTH SERVICES: PREDISPOSITION
} → /DE
Identifiers: ADOLESCENT (13 to 20 YEARS): CHILD (6 TO 12 YEARS) } → /ID

Figure 8 Sample record from MENTAL HEALTH ABSTRACTS, File 86, produced by IFI/Plenum.

J34   **NATIONAL TECHNICAL INFORMATION SERVICE
(NTIS)** National Technical Information Service, Office of
Data Base Services, 5285 Port Royal Rd., Springfield, VA
22161. (703) 487-4807, 487-4808

Created by Congress in 1950 to provide technical reports and other information products to business, educators, government, and the public, NTIS is the sales agent for research sponsored by U.S. and foreign governments, as well as development reports prepared by technical groups, grantees, and government contractors. It corresponds to *Government Reports Announcement and Index* and, in part, to *Abstract Newsletters.* NTIS contains almost 900,000 records, many from the Department of Energy, the National Aeronautics and Space Administration, and the Department of Defense. It does not contain a large proportion of information on children but is a very large file that includes more than 2,000 citations from the U.S. Environmental Protection Agency and 6,000 from the U.S. Department of Health and Human Services each year. Some 6,775 records dealt with children and 12,490 with families as of January 1985. NTIS is valuable for such federal research areas as delivery of human services, military families, runaways, and aggression and for out-of-print or superseded reports of U.S. government agencies that cannot be procured elsewhere.

Research relating to children can be searched by agency or by synonyms for "child," "childhood," and "children" in the titles or in the paragraphs of the abstracts. Appropriate descriptors can also be found in the thesauri developed by the government agencies that contribute to NTIS, including the *Health Care Microthesaurus. A Reference Guide to the NTIS Bibliographic Data Base* provides helpful details on contents, organization, and services.

NTIS performs custom searches for $125; published searches cost $35 for the first copy and $10 for each additional copy. Three bibliographic searches are *Day Care Centers: Children and Youth, 1964–August 1981* (129 citations; PB 81-808966); *Developing Countries: Rearing of Children, January 1973–May 1981* (60 citations; PB 81-863953); and *Sourcebook of Extant Data Bases on Developmentally Disabled Children* (directory; PB 81-154155).

NTIS is also available through BRS, DIALOG, and SDC and through four non-U.S. vendors: European Space Agency–Information Retrieval Service (ESA-IRS); Informationsystem Karlsruhe (INKA); Canadian Institute for Scientific and Technical Information (CISTI); and Radio Swiss Limited, Berne, Switzerland (DATA-STAR). Most of these vendors offer citations from 1964 to date for approximately $45.00/hour on-line and $0.15/record off-line.

J35   **P.A.I.S. (PUBLIC AFFAIRS INFORMATION SERVICE) INTERNATIONAL** Public Affairs Information Service, 11 W. 40th St., New York, NY 10018. (212) 736-6734, 736-6629

The P.A.I.S. data base contains the files of the *P.A.I.S. Bulletin* (G39) from 1976 to date and the *P.A.I.S. Foreign Language Index* (G40) from 1972—some 206,000 citations, updated quarterly. This public policy data base (described more fully in Chapter 8) is valuable for social, economic, and political issues involving children, with an emphasis on facts and statistics rather than theory. It is also a good source for information on prominent persons. Microfilms of original documents are available from the Photographic Services of the New York Public Library. P.A.I.S. INTERNATIONAL is available through DIALOG for $60.00/ hour on-line and $0.15/record off-line.

J36   **PRE-MED (PREM)** Bibliographic Retrieval Services, Inc., 1200 Route 7, Latham, NY 12110. (518) 783-1161, (800) 833-4707

——   **PRE-PSYC (PREP)** Bibliographic Retrieval Services, Inc., 1200 Route 7, Latham, NY 12110. (518) 783-1161, (800) 833-4707

These two files are discussed together, since they are similar and may soon be merged by their producer. PRE-MED provides current on-line access to recent (preceding three or four months) citations in 125 medical journals covered by the *Abridged Index Medicus*. Records appear in this file within two weeks of the time they appear in medical libraries; subsequently, within two to three months, they appear in MEDLINE.

PRE-PSYC contains early references to articles in 98 major psychology journals that are subsequently indexed in PsycINFO and SOCIAL SCISEARCH. References (approximately 1,000 per month) are entered as early as possible; the file dates from fall 1981.

These files were created to lessen the time lag in the fields of medicine and clinical psychology and should be used to supplement the major tools. Both are available through BRS.

J37   **PsycINFO** American Psychological Assn., 1400 N. Uhle St., Arlington, VA 22201. (202) 833-5908, (800) 336-4980

Covers the world's literature on psychology and related social and behavioral sciences, with citations and abstracts for books, journals, technical reports, dissertations, research reviews, conference reports, and monograph and book reviews—around 420,000 citations altogether, updated monthly. Originally identical to the print *Psychological Ab-*

Childhood Play Development — (cont'd)
B Psychogenesis
  Psychosocial Development
R Childhood Play Behavior
  Childrens Recreational Games
  Emotional Development

Childhood Psychosis [67]
UF Infantile Psychosis
B Psychosis
N Childhood Schizophrenia
  Early Infantile Autism
  Symbiotic Infantile Psychosis
R Autistic Children
  Emotionally Disturbed

Childhood Schizophrenia [67]
B Childhood Psychosis
  Psychosis
  Schizophrenia
R Early Infantile Autism
  Symbiotic Infantile Psychosis

Childlessness [82]
SN State of having no children.
B Family Structure
R Family Planning Attitudes

Childrearing Attitudes [73]
R Attitudes/
  Family Relations
  Parental Attitudes

Childrearing Practices [67]
SN Limited to human populations.
B Family Relations
N Child Rearing

Childrens Apperception Test [73]
B Personality Measures
  Projective Personality Measures
  Projective Techniques

Childrens Manifest Anxiety Scale [73]
UF CMA Scale
B Nonprojective Personality Measures
  Personality Measures

Childrens Personality Questionnaire [73]
B Nonprojective Personality Measures
  Personality Measures

Childrens Recreational Games [73]
B Games
  Recreation
R Childhood Play Behavior
  Childhood Play Development
  Toys

Chile [82]
B South America

Chimpanzees [73]
B Mammals
  Primates (Nonhuman)
  Vertebrates

Chinchillas [73]
B Mammals
  Rodents
  Vertebrates

Chinese Americans

Chlorpromazine [67]
UF Thorazine
B Adrenolytic Drugs
  Amines
  Antiemetic Drugs
  Antihypertensive Drugs
  CNS Affecting Drugs
  CNS Depressant Drugs
  Neuroleptic Drugs
  Phenothiazine Derivatives
  Sedatives
  Tranquilizing Drugs

Chlorprothixene [73]
B Adrenolytic Drugs
  Amines
  Antiemetic Drugs
  Antihistaminic Drugs
  Antispasmodic Drugs
  Minor Tranquilizers
  Neuroleptic Drugs
  Phenothiazine Derivatives
  Tranquilizing Drugs

Choice Behavior [67]
SN Motivational or judgmental processes involved in the decision or tendency to select one alternative over another or others. Used for human or animal populations.
B Cognitive Processes
  Decision Making
R Classification (Cognitive Process)
  Freedom
  Psychological Reactance

Cholecystokinin [82]
SN Hormone secreted by upper intestinal mucosa on contact with gastric contents, it stimulates contraction of the gallbladder. Also, a neurotransmitter.
UF Pancreozymin

Toilet Training
Weaning
R Father Child Relations
   Feeding Practices
   Mother Child Relations
   Parent Child Relations
   Parent Training
   Parental Attitudes
   Parental Role
   Sociocultural Factors

Children 67
SN Ages 0–12 years. Used in noneducational contexts. Application of terms designating age is mandatory for ages 0–19.
UF Childhood
    Youth (Children)
B   Developmental Age Groups
N   Infants
    Neonates
    Only Children
    Preschool Age Children
    School Age Children
R   Adopted Children
    Autistic Children
    Childhood Development
    Elementary School Students
    Foster Children
    Illegitimate Children
    Intermediate School Students
    Junior High School Students
    Kindergarten Students
    Nursery School Students
    Predelinquent Youth
    Primary School Students
    Stepchildren

Chloral Hydrate 73
B   Anticonvulsive Drugs
    Hypnotic Drugs
    Sedatives

Chloralose 73
B   Hypnotic Drugs

Chlordiazepoxide 73
UF Librium
B   Amines
    Benzodiazepines
    Minor Tranquilizers
    Tranquilizing Drugs

Chloride Ions 73
B   Chemical Elements
    Electrolytes
    Nonmetallic Elements

Chlorimipramine 73
B   Amines

Chlorisondamine 73
B   Amines
    Antihypertensive Drugs
    Ganglion Blocking Drugs

Chloroform 73
B   Anesthetic Drugs
    General Anesthetics

B   Hormones
    Peptides

Cholesterol 73
B   Steroids

Choline 73
UF Choline Chloride
B   Vitamins
R   Acetylcholine
    Cholinesterase
    Succinylcholine

Choline Chloride
Use Choline

Cholinergic Blocking Drugs 73
UF Anticholinergic Drugs
    Cholinolytic Drugs
    Parasympatholytic Drugs
N   Atropine
    Benactyzine
    Homatropine
    Nicotine
    Orphenadrine
    Scopolamine
    Trihexyphenidyl
R   Antiemetic Drugs
    Antispasmodic Drugs
    Cholinergic Nerves
    Cholinesterase
    Cholinomimetic Drugs
    Drugs/
    Hallucinogenic Drugs
    Parasympathetic Nervous System

Figure 9 Terms from the *Thesaurus of Psychological Index Terms* (A39) are used to search the PsycINFO data base. This page is reproduced with permission of the American Psychological Association, publisher of *Psychological Abstracts* and the PsycINFO Database (Copyright © by the American Psychological Association), and may not be reproduced without its prior permission.

stracts (G36), it is now 25 percent more extensive, since *PA* dropped dissertations and certain other categories in 1980. Its search terms are provided in the *Thesaurus of Psychological Index Terms* (A39) (see Figure 9), which can be used to access information on particular child populations such as "Adopted children" or "Autistic children." Other representative terms for child-related topics are "Battered child syndrome," "Child discipline," "Childhood play behavior," "Childhood schizophrenia," "Father-child relations," "Feeding practices," "Parent training," "Play therapy," and "Toy selection." It is also possible to search for synonyms of "child," "children," and "childhood" in the title and abstract files. Because this is an international index, users should limit searches to desired languages and publication types.

For the occasional user, PASAR (PSYCHOLOGICAL ABSTRACTS SEARCH AND RETRIEVAL SERVICE) can provide mail access, with guidelines that help construct useful search statements. Typically, searches cost between $50 and $70. *PsycINFO Users Reference Manual* is another helpful tool. The data base can be leased by information agencies or accessed through BRS, DIALOG, SDC, and two non-U.S. vendors: DATA-STAR and DIMDI (Deutsches Institut für Medizinische Dokumentation und Information).

J38   **SCHOOL PRACTICES INFORMATION FILE (SPIF)**
       Bibliographic Retrieval Services, Inc., Education Service Group, 1200 Route 7, Latham, NY 12110. (518) 783-1161, (800) 833-4707

This file, designed specifically for educators and administrators, contains descriptions of current educational resource programs, practices, materials, and other products from school systems and school districts, publishers, and public organizations. It includes curriculum materials in most subject fields and grade levels, school business practices, special education programs, in-service programs for educators, and national and state validated programs. It can be searched by subject (ERIC descriptors), author, publisher/producer, type of resource, grade level, target audience, funding source, source of data, and geographic source. Age and grade levels should be used to narrow searches. Descriptions include contact persons and availability. SPIF is available exclusively through BRS and the TIMESHARE system of the Minnesota Educational Computing Consortium.

J39   **SOCIAL SCISEARCH** Institute for Scientific Information, 3501 Market St., University City Science Center, Philadelphia, PA 19104. (215) 386-0100, (800) 523-4092

A multidisciplinary data base derived from 1,500 of the world's most important social science journals, with the addition of relevant articles selected from 2,500 additional journals in the natural, physical, and biomedical sciences from 1973 to date. An on-line equivalent of *Social Sciences Citation Index* (G48), with more than one million citations, it allows searching through the author's cited references and forward to articles that cite a particular work, as well as through the traditional approaches—title words and phrases, authors, names, corporate source, and so on. Citation searching allows users to locate and retrieve articles that include a specific author's work in its bibliography or references. Since there is no thesaurus, title searches should include synonyms of "child," "children," and "childhood." SOCIAL SCISEARCH is available through BRS, DIALOG, and DIMDI, with different prices for subscribers and nonsubscribers.

J40 **SOCIOLOGICAL ABSTRACTS (SA)** P.O. Box 22206, San Diego, CA 92122. (714) 565-6603

On-line equivalent of *Sociological Abstracts* (G53) for sociology and related disciplines in the social and behavioral sciences. Covers original research, reviews, discussions, monographs, conference reports, panel discussions, and case studies in 1,400 journals. Includes 130,000 citations from 1963 to date.

The Sociosearches of Sociological Abstracts, Inc., offer searches of SA and optional cross-data base searches in the humanities and social sciences (including ERIC, NTIS, SOCIAL SCISEARCH, LLBA, HISTORICAL ABSTRACTS, and FOUNDATION GRANTS). Prices for single-term searches in SA range from $20.00 up, plus $0.15 for each abstract. SA is also searchable through DIALOG for $55.00/hour on-line and $0.15/record off-line.

12 / Child-Related Organizations

This chapter and Chapter 13 describe the publications and information services of some American and Canadian organizations and clearinghouses that supply information on the well-being of children in the United States and Canada. These are but a handful of the groups that serve children; I am including mainly those national organizations, professional associations, and government agencies that emphasize public information and education and that have the time, funds, and ability to provide direct information through clearinghouses, publications, networks, or responses to questions. I have omitted many fine organizations devoted largely to research or direct service. Many other organizations can be located through the directories annotated in Chapter 10 and the source guides listed in Chapter 3. Organizations that supply information in the special areas of tests and assessments, statistics, and children's books are annotated in Chapters 14–16. I have placed organizations that deal with health, safety, nutrition, handicaps, specific diseases, and family values in Chapter 13.

The information in this chapter and Chapter 13 is based on responses to questionnaires mailed in 1982 and 1983; the descriptions were then reverified with the organizations around spring 1984. In keeping with my interdisciplinary approach, organizations are arranged in a few broad, general classes. For convenience in browsing, however, this chapter covers general agencies, social service agencies, media groups, and others that do

293

not fit into Chapter 13. International organizations or groups that supply information primarily on children outside the United States and Canada appear at the end of this chapter.

Many of the organizations herein address their material or information toward parents, professionals, and the general public; I have listed some representative publications. Publications of groups not included in this book can be found in *Associations' Publications in Print* (D29). Clearinghouses and data bases accessed primarily via computer are annotated in Chapter 11. The organizations listed here are willing to forward brochures and lists of publications; however, sending a stamped, self-addressed envelope would be helpful.

GENERAL AND CHILD ADVOCACY ORGANIZATIONS

On October 1, 1982, 10 new resource centers—the Consolidated Regional Resource Centers for Children, Youth, and Families—under the Department of Health and Human Services, Office of Human Development Services (Administration for Children, Youth, and Families) began offering services in the areas of adoption, child abuse and neglect, and child welfare. A list of these regional centers and two national resource centers is given in Figure 10.

K1   **ADAM WALSH CHILD RESOURCE CENTER, INC.**
     1876 N. University Dr., Suite 306, Ft. Lauderdale, FL 33322.
     (305) 475-4847
A nonprofit organization dedicated to making America safer for children. Its programs are aimed at preventing the abduction and molestation of children and bringing about positive changes in systems that serve children. It is a prime source of information for parents who want to know how to protect their children and effect positive changes for all children.

The center is working in the areas of legislation, Federal Bureau of Investigation policy, and public awareness. It urges that all children be fingerprinted and offers a free pamphlet entitled *Safety Tips,* which instructs parents on how to teach their children to protect themselves and suggests things parents can do to further ensure their child's safety. Materials from the center include the Safety With Strangers Program, designed for use with elementary school children (20 slides, audiocassette, and instructional manual; $50/set); *Fingerprinting Children: A How-To Manual* ($5); and *Private Zone* ($3), a booklet on sexual assault prevention skills for parents to read and discuss with their children. A publications list is available from the center on request.

K2   **AMERICAN CAMPING ASSOCIATION (ACA)** Bradford Woods, Martinsville, IN 46151-7902. (317) 342-8456
A consultant and accreditation agency on organized camping and a nonprofit educational organization for owners, operators, and staffs of camps for children, youth, and adults. Its library includes 5,000 books, and it is a prolific publisher of books on camping, outdoor education, day care camp programs, parent guidance, nature appreciation, and working with children and youth in the outdoors. It publishes the *Parents' Guide to Accredited Camps* each January (1983, $5.95), which provides descriptions of 2,400 camps, with cross-references to activities, and lists of camps that serve special populations (e.g., asthmatic, blind, limited mobility, wheelchair restricted).

K3   **AMERICAN CHILD CARE SERVICES** 532 Settlers Landing Rd., P.O. Box 548, Hampton, VA 23669. (804) 722-4495
A small, privately endowed nonprofit foundation engaged primarily in children's welfare and educational activities that relate to "serving those who serve children." For this purpose, it operates two interesting and helpful information agencies: the Child Care Personnel Clearinghouse and the Child Care Information Center.

The Child Care Information Center has been recording, duplicating, and distributing audiotape cassettes in the fields of child care, child development, and early childhood education on a low-cost, nonprofit basis since 1971. Its excellent *Cassette Tape Catalogs* are described in F7. It now owns and distributes more than 3,000 cassettes based on conferences, seminars, workshops, and symposia that are useful for in-service programs, self-study, or professional development for child care workers, social workers, day care providers, and natural and adoptive parents.

The Child Care Personnel Clearinghouse is a service that coordinates employment information at all levels in the child care field, serving students and recent graduates as well as experienced personnel. Its purpose is to facilitate contact between children's institutions and qualified employees. The semiannual *Help Kids* ($1/issue) lists jobs in the child-

Consolidated Regional Resource Centers for Children, Youth, and Families

REGION I

New England Resource Center for Children and Families
Judge Baker Guidance Center
295 Longwood Avenue
Boston MA 02115
Project Director: Christina Crowe
617/232-8390

REGION II

Region II Resource Center on Children and Youth
Cornell University Family Life Development Center
College of Human Ecology
Ithaca NY 14853
Project Director: Frank Barry
607/256-7794

REGION III

Region III Resource Center for Children, Youth and Families
Virginia Commonwealth University
School of Social Work
1001 West Franklin Street
Richmond VA 23284

Project Director: Henry Gunn
804/257-6231

REGION VI

Region VI Regional Resource Center for Children, Youth and Families
University of Texas at Austin, School of Social Work
Austin TX 78712
Project Director: Rosalie Anderson
512/471-4067

REGION VII

Region VII Children, Youth and Family Center
University of Iowa Institute of Child Behavior and Development
Oakdale Campus
Iowa City IA 52319
Project Director: Charles Abel
319/353-4791

REGION VIII

Region VIII Family Resource Center
University of Denver
Graduate School of Social Work
Denver CO 80208
Project Director: Burt Annin
303/753-2886

REGION IV

Southeastern Regional Resource Center for Children and Youth Services
University of Tennessee
School of Social Work
1838 Terrace Avenue
Knoxville TN 37996-3920
Project Director: Jean Blankenship
615/974-6015

REGION V

Region V Resource Center on Children and Youth Services
University of Wisconsin - Milwaukee
P.O. Box 786; School of Social Welfare
Milwaukee WI 53201
Project Director: Adrienne Haeuser
414/963-4184

REGION IX

Region IX Consolidated Resource Center for Children and Youth Services
California State University - Los Angeles
5151 State University Drive
Los Angeles CA 90032
Project Director: Shelley Brazier
213/224-3283

REGION X

Northwest Resource Center for Children, Youth, and Families
University of Washington
School of Social Work
4101 - 15th Avenue N.E.
Seattle WA 98195
Project Director: Diane Brannon
206/545-1669

Figure 10 Consolidated Regional Resource Centers for Children, Youth, and Families.

welfare field by state, with a list of job information sources on the back. Twice a year, the clearinghouse conducts a nationwide survey of more than 3,000 institutions and agencies to locate jobs that can be filled by students or recent graduates. This information is published in the *Summer* and *Fulltime Job Lists,* which are circulated in placement offices and other college locations. Copies of these lists are also available for $1.

K4   **AMERICAN HUMANE ASSOCIATION (AHA)** P.O. Box 1266, Denver, CO 80201. (303) 695-0811
The AHA, a nonprofit membership organization, has been concerned with preventing cruelty to children since 1877. Its current areas of emphasis include education in the field of child abuse and neglect for the general public, for professionals in social service and child-protection agencies, and for policy analysis and information dissemination/advocacy. The Child Protection Division conducts the National Study on Child Neglect and Abuse Reporting, a systematic collection of data from official reports on the nature, incidence, and characteristics of child abuse. This is available as an annual report.

A long-time leader in this field, AHA has compiled *Child Protective Services Standards* ($0.50) and *Guidelines for Schools* ($5.00 per 100 copies). Its books include *The Fundamentals of Child Protection* ($2.50) and the important *Child Protective Services Entering the 1980's—A Nationwide Survey* (628 pp., $15.00), which uses tables and descriptions to compare methods and policies in states and counties. *Sexual Abuse of Children: Implications for Treatment,* edited by Wayne Holder ($7.50), deals specifically and realistically with the growing problem of sexual abuse.

K5   **AMERICAN PSYCHOLOGICAL ASSOCIATION (APA)** 1200 17th St., NW, Washington, DC 20036. (202) 955-7742
Founded in 1892, the world's largest association of psychologists aims to advance psychology as a science and profession and as a means of promoting human welfare through research and dissemination of knowledge in the biological, behavioral, cognitive, and social foundations of behavior. Some of the information activities, such as PsycINFO, *Psychological Abstracts,* and *PsycSCAN: Developmental Psychology,* are discussed in Chapters 8 and 11, and certain publications are discussed in Chapters 2 and 14. Many of their abstract compilations, such as *PsycINFO Retrospective: Learning and Communication Disorders, 1971–1980* (508 pp., $31.50) and *PsycINFO Retrospective: Mental Retardation, 1971–1980* (468 pp., $31.50), are most valuable for research on children.

Beyond these activities, APA has 40 interest-area divisions; many of these—including the Division of Child, Youth, and Family Services—address research and clinical issues relating to the status and well-being of children and youth and their families. Other divisions with a special interest in children and family issues are the Division on Developmental Psychology, the Society for the Psychological Study of Social Issues, the Division of Clinical Psychology, the Division of School Psychology, the Division on Mental Retardation, the Division of the Psychology of Women, and the Division of Psychology and the Law.

The *APA Guide to Research Support* (1981, 376 pp., $23.00) is a comprehensive handbook on federal funding of behavioral science research that identifies areas in 250 programs, with suggestions for writing proposals. During the last year, APA studies have dealt with many issues involving children, such as the Family Protection Act and the impact of media violence on children. The January 1983 issue of *American Psychologist* focuses on children, youth, and family policy. The October 1979 issue of *American Psychologist* deals with "Psychology and Children: Current Research and Practice." APA also offers specialty guidelines (e.g., for school psychologists), and *Standards for Providers of Psychological Services* (single copy free). Its monthly newspaper, the *APA Monitor,* typically includes a number of articles on children's issues, such as unmet needs, child advocacy, and runaways, and reports on current APA activities affecting the well-being of children.

An APA Task Force on Children, Youth, and Families was established at the central office in 1982. It recommended that a permanent Committee on Children, Youth, and Families be established.

K6   **AMERICAN   PUBLIC   WELFARE   ORGANIZATION (APWA)** 1125 15th St., NW, Suite 300, Washington, DC 20005. (202) 293-7550

Founded in 1930, APWA is a nonprofit organization of individuals and agencies concerned with the effective administration and delivery of human services. Members include virtually all state and territorial public welfare agencies, more than 900 local governments and nonprofit agencies, and 6,000 individuals. Its goals are to promote the development of sound and progressive policies in human services and to strengthen the skills of professionals employed in human services. Its staff can provide information on public policy and administration in such areas as adoption; child abuse; day care; family services; foster care; interstate placement of children; child health; youth services; Aid to Families with Dependent Children (AFDC); funding; and protective services for children, youth, and families.

Its publications include the *Public Welfare Directory* and various standards developed by APWA staff in conjunction with federal agencies, such as the *Intercountry Adoption Guidelines, National Directory of Intercountry Adoption Services Resources,* and *Standards for Foster Family Services Systems.*

A Guide to Delivery of Child Protective Services (1981, 240 pp., $15) is a manual with a framework to help agencies analyze their child-protection service functions and develop appropriate skills and standards. APWA's *Reference Guide to Child Abuse and Neglect Materials Available from States and Counties* (1981, 31 pp., $4) contains abstracts of materials prepared by state and county agencies with directions on how to obtain them. Its *Survey of the Use and Functioning of Multidisciplinary Teams in Child Protective Services* (1981, 30 pp., $4) is intended to improve the knowledge base and functioning of such teams. APWA has published several brief documents dealing with confidentiality, cultural responsiveness, worker burnout, and the like, in child-protection services.

Other comprehensive surveys include *The Law of Adoption Records: A Survey of State Statutes* (1980, 66 pp., $6), which covers adoption registries, "contact-consent" systems, and laws regarding the sealing of and access to birth certificates. *The Rights of Putative Fathers in Adoption Proceedings: A Review of State Statutes,* by Laurie Davis et al. (1980, 49 pp., $5) is another overview and summary of state statutes, as is the *Withdrawal of Parental Consent to Adoption: A Survey of State Statutes,* by Ruth Lovald (1981, 29 pp., $4).

Other publications include the *Congressional Record Index,* a weekly digest of bills and regulations on human services ($100/year). *Public Welfare* is a quarterly ($20/year) that offers many articles on human services and legal problems of children and families. Reprints are available for a low cost.

A source of information on domestic refugees, APWA formerly issued a biweekly *Refugee Reports* and a quarterly *Journal of Refugee Resettlement* under a short-lived grant from the Office of Refugee Resettlement. Contact *Refugee Reports* at (202) 667-0782 for back issues.

K7   ASSOCIATION FOR CHILDHOOD EDUCATION INTERNATIONAL (ACEI) 11141 Georgia Ave., Suite 200, Wheaton, MD 20902. (301) 942-2443

An international nonprofit organization, founded in 1892, concerned with the education and well-being of children from infancy through early adolescence. Members include teachers, librarians, parents, administrators, day care personnel, and other care givers in more than 70 countries. Major focuses include child development, early and later childhood education, early adolescent education, day care, and effective reading and writing activities. ACEI activities include regional, national, and international conferences and publications. Typically, these reflect careful research, broad-based views, and fresh thinking on a wide range of issues affecting children. Included are an excellent periodical— *Childhood Education* (H26) —and a newsletter—*ACEI Exchange* (10 issues/year; $20/year; free, with associate membership), which provides practical ideas and association news. Around 65 low-cost bulletins, booklets, and leaflets are in print; several excellent publications deal with evaluating children's books or play equipment. Well-known classics include *Play: Children's Business* ($4) and *Selecting Educational Equipment for School and Home* ($4). Every three years, ACEI issues the *Bibliography of Books for Children.*

K8   **ASSOCIATION OF JUNIOR LEAGUES, INC. (AJL)** 825
      Third Ave., New York, NY 10022. (212) 355-4380
AJL is the international advisory and consulting organization for 253 Junior Leagues throughout the United States, Canada, and Mexico, with a combined membership of 155,000 women. The Junior Leagues are educational and charitable associations, established to promote voluntarism, to develop the potential of members for voluntary participation in community affairs, and to demonstrate the effectiveness of trained volunteers in meeting community needs.

Junior Leagues have many programs for children throughout the United States, including programs on adoption, child abuse and neglect, parental support, child placement, child advocacy, child care/day care, child health, child safety, foster care/children in placement, hospital services, juvenile justice, mental health/counseling, physical rehabilitation/services for the disabled, runaway youth, screening and testing, special education, substance abuse, teenage pregnancy/sexuality/parenting, and youth groups/recreation. Some of these programs are information sources through publications, libraries, video documentations, or thoroughly researched position papers.

One current program for children is Child Watch, developed by the Children's Defense Fund in collaboration with AJL. In more than 70 communities, Child Watch volunteers have interviewed social welfare administrators, advocates, and lay persons in an effort to monitor the impact of 1981 and subsequent federal budget cuts on children's services. Four areas—child welfare, Aid to Families with Dependent Children, child care, and child health—are the focus of the interviews. The findings are handled by individual projects and have included public hearings, citizen education forums, and the development of projects designed to address some of the gaps in services uncovered by the AJL volunteers.

The headquarters office is most helpful in documenting league activities. It issues a series of fact sheets on the league and compiles an annual report on children and youth projects. The semiannual *Junior League Review* includes well-written reports and a valuable "Networking" section that is a classified directory of projects; it is updated by the bimonthly *AJL Newsline*. *Child Care: Options for the Eighties* identifies a number of major issues and strategies.

K9   CANADIAN COUNCIL ON CHILDREN AND YOUTH (CCCY)   (Le Conseil Canadien de l'Enfance et de la Jeunesse) 323 Chapel St., Ottawa K1N 7Z2, Canada. (613) 238-6520

This national voluntary organization founded in 1958 has three major purposes: to identify and act on issues affecting children in Canada; to publish research, books, and articles for and about children; and to serve as an umbrella for all other child-related voluntary organizations. For its users, it maintains a resources/information/documentation segment that serves as the Referral and Information Centre. The center covers agencies, culture, education, health, law, native populations, recreation, urban environment, and other topics with books, periodicals, reference books, newspaper clippings, and a cross-reference system with more than 5,500 cards. It is open to the general public and to specialists in all fields concerned with children.

Since its clients include government agencies, elected representatives at all levels, the Young Men's Christian Association, and all child-related organizations, CCCY is active in many fields, including learning disabilities, child abuse, children's broadcasting, children's play, cultural opportunities for children, and a Canadian bill of rights for children. Current areas of concern are child pornography, violence in sports, day care standards and services, and follow-through on the Charter of Rights and Freedoms. CCCY was instrumental in helping to establish the Canadian Ministry of Youth. Other recent concerns include the Native People's Publishing Project, which is producing a textbook for high school students and an activity book for the primary grades, and an updating of recommendations on emotional and learning disorders through analysis and comparison of provincial actions in legislation, health care, education, and social services.

Publications (in French and English) include copies of CCCY presentations to Parliamentary Committees; an occasional newsletter, *Action;* the *Child Abuse Bibliography;* fair play codes; position papers; posters;

and a handbook on children in sports. Other publishing areas are friendship, play, and children and culture. The play series, in particular, has worldwide sales and is especially popular in Australia, Sweden, Switzerland, and the United States. A complete list of CCCY publications is available on request.

K10 **CENTER FOR ARCHITECTURE AND URBAN PLANNING** University of Wisconsin, School of Architecture and Urban Planning, P.O. Box 413, Milwaukee, WI 53201. (414) 963-4014

The center develops, coordinates, and disseminates research on all aspects of architecture and urban planning and publishes an extensive series of reports and working papers. The Children's Environments Project, part of the center, has developed planning and design guides for nearly every aspect of children's environments. One relevant title is *Case Studies of Child Play Areas and Child Support Facilities,* by Uriel Cohen et al. (1979, 405 pp., $15.00) — a substantial study of 50 child care centers and play environments. The research forms for this study are in a separate appendix that is sold for $2.00. The research resulted in two reports: *Recommendations for Child Play Areas* (1979, 380 pp., $15.00), a highly regarded report with 75 patterns for planning and designing children's play areas, and *Recommendations for Child Care Centers* (1979, 450 pp., $17.50), which provides criteria and 115 patterns.

Other guides and guidelines are *Planning and Design Guidelines: Child Care Centers and Outdoor Play Environments—Synopsis* (1979, $1.00), *Mainstreaming the Handicapped: A Design Guide* (1979, 64 pp., $5.00), *The Application of Research to the Design of Therapeutic Play Environments for Exceptional Children* (1980, 12 pp., $1.00), and *Design Patterns for Children's Environments* (1980, 15 pp., $1.00). The center's *Bibliography on Children and the Physical Environment* costs $7.50.

K11 **CENTER FOR EARLY ADOLESCENCE** Carr Mill Mall, Suite 223, Carrboro, NC 27510. (919) 966-1148

Associated with the Department of Maternal and Child Health in the School of Public Health, University of North Carolina at Chapel Hill, this center focuses on early adolescence — that is, the years between the ages of 10–15, a time of great physical, social, and emotional growth. It works to increase the effectiveness of agencies, professionals, and volunteers who work with young adolescents in and out of school and in the areas of adolescent development, related issues, and after-school programs. Through information dissemination, constituency building, and networking, the center encourages policy setters and practitioners to expand the opportunities open to adolescents for positive growth and responsible social involvement. It houses an extensive collection of books, periodicals, program materials, curricula, and bibliographies. Requests for information are answered personally. Its training division develops curriculum materials and provides continuing education programs for professionals and agencies that work with young adolescents.

Publications include training curricula for parents and middle grade school personnel; books and monographs on topics like adolescent development, family interaction, after-school programming, parenting, and education; and bibliographies and resource lists on these topics. The center's occasional newsletter, *Common Focus,* covers programs, research, books, films, and continuing education opportunities for professionals who work with young adolescents and is distributed free. Publications include *Early Adolescence: What Parents Need to Know* (1982, 37 pp., $3.75 including postage), a handbook that provides readable, accurate information on the physical, intellectual, and social development of adolescents and how their development affects family structures; it contains checklists and an annotated list of resources for parents. Other titles are *Understanding Early Adolescence: A Framework,* (1980, 52 pp., $4.00 plus $2.00 postage and handling) and *Schools for Young Adolescents: Adapting the Early Childhood Model* (1980, 39 pp., $2.75, plus $1.00 postage and handling). Call or write for a current publications brochure.

K12   **CHILD CARE EMPLOYEE PROJECT (CCEP)**   P.O. Box 5603, Berkeley, CA 94705. (415) 653-9889
A national support and resource center in the area of child care working conditions, with publications of interest to child care personnel. Its goals are to improve the salaries, working conditions, and status of child care workers and to increase public awareness about the importance of child care work and the training and skills it demands. Its informative publications include a competent quarterly newsletter, *Child Care Employee News,* for $5.00/year, that contains national news of interest to child care workers. *CCEP Handouts* are short papers ($2.50 each) that cover such topics as "Staff Evaluation" and "Special Stresses of Infant Caregiving." Its *Salary Surveys: How? Why? Who? When? Where?* (31 pp., $3.50) is a clear and comprehensive guide to conducting surveys. Brochures and a complete list of publications are available on request.

K13   **CHILD CARE LAW CENTER**   625 Market St., Suite 815, San Francisco, CA 94105. (415) 495-5498

The purpose of the Child Care Law Center is to foster the development of high-quality, affordable child care programs through education, publication, advocacy, policy development, legal representation, and referral and consultation. Its services are available to parents, attorneys, child care providers, policymakers, government and community agencies, unions, and employers. It has a Legal Resource Bank that collects cases, court decisions, legislation, law review articles, and other materials relevant to the key legal issues in child care. It has more than 25 publications dealing with child care centers, employer-supported child care, family day care, and parent information. These include bibliographies, tips on retaining a lawyer, information on child abuse, employee taxes, child care contracts, and other legal aspects of child care.

K14 **CHILD FIND, INC.** 7 Innis Ave., P.O. Box 277, New Paltz, NY 12561. (914) 255-1848

A national nonprofit agency for locating missing children in the United States, supported completely by private donations, Child Find maintains a toll-free number (1-800-431-5005) only for child victims and for spotters. It notes that 150,000 children are reported missing each year, of whom 100,000 are the victims of illegal, noncustodial parental kidnappings, and that most of these children are never seen again. Child Find maintains a register of missing children (with photographs) to aid searching parents and produces the annual *Child Find Directory of Missing Children,* which it hopes to distribute widely in schools and day care centers. It works with law enforcement officials, school authorities, and local and state agencies to maximize the exchange of information. Its quarterly *Child Find Newsletter* reports on legislation, safety-awareness programs, and returned children. A prevention measure, *Childfinder Kit,* costs $10 and includes abduction precautions for parents and children, an identification package, step-by-step instructions, and a bibliography of related films and books.

K15 **CHILDREN'S DEFENSE FUND (CDF)** 122 C St., NW, Washington, DC 20001. (202) 628-8787

A national public charity supported by foundations, corporate grants, and individual donations; its goal is to encourage this nation to meet the survival needs of all children by ensuring that the needs of children and families are placed higher on our national public policy agenda. It carries out long-range, consistent advocacy by monitoring federal and state legislative and administrative policies and engages in research, public education, community organization, network building, technical assistance, and formation of coalitions on specific issues.

The staff of CDF includes health, education, child welfare, mental health, and child care specialists; researchers; public policy and data analysts; lawyers; networkers; and community organizers. Its four program areas are education, child health and mental health, child welfare, and child care and family-support services.

Since 1982, the two major goals of the Children's Defense Fund have been to protect the federal framework of children's programs, especially those meeting the survival needs of homeless, poor, handicapped, and minority children, and to counter the massive budget assault on entitlement programs, such as Medicaid, food stamps, and Aid to Families with Dependent Children, that help the young and the poor.

CDF is cooperating with the Junior Leagues in a Child Watch program that monitors the effects of relevant budgets cuts in communities across the country. The *Child Watch Manual* ($0.50) provides step-by-step monitoring methods. CDF's Children's Public Policy Network consists of organizations working on behalf of children, with a toll-free number ((800) 424-9602) that provides information and support.

A monthly newsletter, *CDF Reports,* keeps members abreast of national and local developments affecting children. At the beginning of each new Congress, CDF issues its *National Legislative Agenda for Children,* setting down priorities. Its statistical works and data books include *Children and the Federal Budget* (1981, 40 pp., $2.50 [paperback]), which explains the federal budget process for child advocates. *Children and Federal Child Care Cuts* (1983, 96 pp., $7.50 [paperback]) reports on the findings of a survey of individual states, which revealed lower child care budgets in 32 states and lower child care standards in 33. *Children and Federal Health Care Cuts* (1983, 67 pp., $3.50 [paperback]) reports a similar survey on the impact of health budget reductions on state maternal and child health services. Each year for the last four years, CDF has published the *Children's Defense Budget* (N39). The most recent issue (1984) is a comprehensive analysis of the effects of the current budget on child care, education, Medicaid and maternal and child health, child welfare, food stamps, AFDC, and other programs that affect children and youth.

Other publications that present careful research effectively and briefly include *Employed Parents and Their Children: A Data Book* (1982, 78 pp., $8.00), *Children Without Health Care* (1981, $2.20), *Unclaimed Children: The Failure of Public Responsibility to Children in Need of Mental Health Services* (1982, $10.50), and *Time to Stand Up for Your Children: A Parent's Guide to Child Advocacy* (1982, $2.50). Some are cited in this book; a complete list is available from CDF on request.

K16 **CHILDREN'S FOUNDATION** 1420 New York Ave., NW, Suite 800, Washington, DC 20005. (202) 347-3300
A national advocacy organization for children and those who care for them, established in 1969. Initially, it concentrated on the implementation of federal food assistance for children. Currently, its major concerns are child care—especially family day care—and the problems created by the growing feminization of poverty. The Children's Foundation concentrates on the job development and support aspects of child care and on empowerment through leadership development and is also a forum for grassroots concerns. Its ultimate aim is a national full-employment policy, with jobs and income support for women and families in need. Its National Family Day Advisory Panel works with 100 day care associations comprised of women who care for children in their homes; it helped to establish the National Association for Family Day Care (NAFDC).

Publications include a newsletter—the *National Family Day Care Bulletin*—and the *Factsheet on Child Care Food Program in Family Day Care Homes*. The Children's Foundation still works with food through training, technical assistance, and establishing sponsorships for the U.S. Department of Agriculture's child care food program. In 1979, it issued the *WIC* [Women, Infants, and Children] *Directory of Special Supplemental Food Programs for Women, Infants, & Children.*

The Southern Regional Office is at 88 Walton St., NW, Atlanta, GA 30303, (404) 522-2232. The Western Regional Office is at 227 E. Palace Ave., Santa Fe, NM 87501, (505) 988-9686.

K17 **CHILDREN'S LEGAL RIGHTS INFORMATION AND TRAINING PROGRAM (CLR)** 2008 Hillyer Pl., NW, Washington, DC 20009. (202) 332-6575
A nonprofit organization established in 1975 to provide legal information and training to nonlegal professionals engaged in the delivery of services to children and youth and their families. Its clientele includes social workers, educators, health-care providers, juvenile justice personnel, law enforcement officers, and individuals in related fields. Activities include workshops and conferences, often for specific agency needs and involving the preparation of written materials. The director, Roberta Gottesman, wrote *The Child and the Law* (Q119), a university text on the legal rights of children. CLR's *Children's Legal Rights Journal* (H31) is annotated in Chapter 9. Another project is a legal tapes program that concentrates on state laws on children's rights in areas like foster care and juvenile justice programs.

K18   **CHILDREN'S RIGHTS, INC.** P.O. Box 11458, Washington, DC 20008.
This group works with parents, legislators, legal professionals, psychiatrists, psychologists, educators, social workers, and law enforcement professionals to increase public awareness and legislative reform on child snatching and child restraint issues. It provides testimony for state, federal, and international legislation. Its quarterly newsletter *Our Greatest RESOURCE. . .Our Children* is available for $5.00/year, and the *Handbook for Parents Victimized by Child-Snatching or Child-Restraint* costs $7.50.

K19   **CHILD WELFARE LEAGUE OF AMERICA (CWLA)** 67 Irving Pl., New York, NY 10003. (212) 254-7410
A federation of leading child welfare agencies in the United States and Canada, founded in 1920 to increase knowledge and promote better understanding of child welfare problems and to improve care and services for deprived, neglected, and dependent children and their families. It includes nearly 400 agencies—public and private, religious and non-sectarian—and works to improve services to children through consultation, advocacy, regional conferences, research, training, surveys, publications, and special projects. Membership is open to indirect service organizations such as planning councils and educational and advocacy groups and to individuals such as professionals, volunteers, students, parents, legislators, and others who support the CWLA's purposes and programs.
   CWLA conducts research and agency and community surveys; develops standards for services; produces public information materials; and maintains a library and information service. Its publications range broadly, covering developmental disabilities, administration and finance, board membership, adoption, foster family care and foster family education, and standards. Two new works in CWLA's *Standards Series* are *CWLA Standards for Organization and Administration of All Child Welfare Services* (1984, $10.50) and *CWLA Standards for Service to Children in Their Own Homes* (1984, $7.50). Other standards publications deal with adoption services, residential centers for children, child protective services, day care, foster family care, and group home services. CWLA's adoption project, Permanent Families for Children, issues its own publications.
   Other recent publications are Thomas Troyer's *The New Tax Law: A Guide for Child Welfare Organizations* (1981, $3.00); *Getting Started as a Residential Child Care Worker? A Guide for Beginners,* by J. E. Crone (1983, $5.50); and *Child Welfare Services for Children with Developmen-*

tal Disabilities, by Ronald Hughes and Judith S. Rycus (1983, $6.95). CWLA's bimonthly *Child Welfare* (H34) has a multidisciplinary approach to the problems of children. Its library and information service houses approximately 4,000 books and documents and 147 periodical titles.

K20 **CLEARINGHOUSE ON CHILD ABUSE AND NEGLECT INFORMATION** Department of Health and Human Services, Children's Bureau, National Center on Child Abuse and Neglect, P.O. Box 1182, Washington, DC 20013. (301) 251-5157

A major function of this clearinghouse is to provide concerned professionals and members of the general public with up-to-date information on various aspects of child maltreatment. The primary source of information is a data base of documents, research projects, programs, audiovisuals, and state laws on child abuse and neglect, drawn from many of the sources in Chapter 11. Its computerized data base also is discussed in that chapter. The clearinghouse surveys research projects annually and ongoing programs for victims and parents twice a year. As part of its effort to meet information needs, it prepares a series of annotated bibliographies on major topics, which are updated frequently. It distributes its own documents only. Titles include *Costs and Cost Effectiveness of Programs to Eliminate Child Abuse and Neglect.* A current list of documents is available on request.

K21 **EDUCATIONAL INFORMATION RESOURCES CENTER (ERIC)** ERIC Processing and Reference Facility, 4833 Rugby Ave., Suite 301, Bethesda, MD 20814. (301) 656-9723

ERIC is a national bibliographic network for nonbook literature of education, originally founded in 1965 to organize and disseminate the results of exemplary programs, research and development efforts, professional papers, committee reports, and other educational information. It publishes and distributes these materials in an uncopyrighted microfiche format and indexes them in *RIE* and other tools (paper, computerized, and microfiche). More than 240,000 documents were in the ERIC data base in February 1985. ERIC also offers an index to 700 educational periodicals in *RIE* and *CIJE* (both are discussed in Chapter 8). Computerized access is discussed in Chapter 11.

Now a part of the U.S. Department of Education, ERIC's components include 16 clearinghouses (see Figure 11), the ERIC Processing and Reference Facility (a clearinghouse for clearinghouses), and assorted public and commercial distribution channels. The most important clear-

List of ERIC Network Components

CLEARINGHOUSES

ERIC Clearinghouse on
Adult, Career, and Vocational Education
Ohio State University
1960 Kenny Road
Columbus, Ohio 43210
Telephone: (614) 486-3655

ERIC Clearinghouse on
Counseling and Personnel Services
University of Michigan
2108 School of Education Building
Ann Arbor, Michigan 48109
Telephone: (313) 764-9492

ERIC Clearinghouse on
Educational Management
University of Oregon
Eugene, Oregon 97403
Telephone: (503) 686-5043

ERIC Clearinghouse on
Elementary and Early Childhood Education
University of Illinois
College of Education
Urbana, Illinois 61801
Telephone: (217) 333-1386

ERIC Clearinghouse on
Handicapped and Gifted Children
Council for Exceptional Children
1920 Association Drive
Reston, Virginia 22091
Telephone: (703) 620-3660

ERIC Clearinghouse on
Higher Education
George Washington University
One Dupont Circle, Suite 630
Washington, D.C. 20036
Telephone: (202) 296-2597

ERIC Clearinghouse on
Information Resources
Syracuse University
School of Education
130 Huntington Hall
Syracuse, New York 13210
Telephone: (315) 423-3640

ERIC Clearinghouse for
Junior Colleges
University of California
96 Powell Library Building
Los Angeles, California 90024
Telephone: (213) 825-3931

ERIC Clearinghouse on
Languages and Linguistics
Center for Applied Linguistics
1611 North Kent Street
Arlington, Virginia 22209
Telephone: (703) 528-4312

ERIC Clearinghouse on
Reading and Communication Skills
National Council of Teachers
of English
1111 Kenyon Road
Urbana, Illinois 61801
Telephone: (217) 328-3870

ERIC Clearinghouse on
Rural Education and Small Schools
New Mexico State University
Box 3AP
Las Cruces, New Mexico 88003
Telephone: (505) 646-2623

ERIC Clearinghouse on
Science, Mathematics, and Environmental Education
Ohio State University
1200 Chambers Road, Third Floor
Columbus, Ohio 43212
Telephone: (614) 422-6717

ERIC Clearinghouse on
Social Studies/Social Science Education
855 Broadway
Boulder, Colorado 80302
Telephone: (303) 492-8434

ERIC Clearinghouse on
Teacher Education
American Association of Colleges
for Teacher Education
One Dupont Circle, N.W., Suite 616
Washington, D.C. 20036
Telephone: (202) 293-7280

ERIC Clearinghouse on
Tests, Measurement, and Evaluation
Educational Testing Service
Rosedale Road
Princeton, New Jersey 08540
Telephone: (609) 921-9000 ext. 2176

ERIC Clearinghouse on
Urban Education
Teachers College, Columbia University
Box 40
525 West 120th Street
New York, New York 10027
Telephone: (212) 678-3437

National Institute of Education
(Central ERIC)
Office of Dissemination and
Resources
Washington, D.C. 20208
Telephone: (202) 254-5555

ERIC Document Reproduction Service *(EDRS)*

Computer Microfilm International,
Corporation (CMIC)
3030 N. Fairfax Drive, Suite 200
Arlington, Virginia 22201
Telephone: (703) 841-1212

ERIC Processing and Reference Facility
4833 Rugby Avenue—Suite 303
Bethesda, Maryland 20014
Telephone: (301) 656-9723

Oryx Press
3930 E. Camelback Road, Suite 206
Phoenix, Arizona 85018
Telephone: (602) 956-6233

Figure 11   ERIC clearinghouse and distribution facilities comprise an educational information network that contains significant information on children.

inghouses for children are those on Elementary and Early Childhood Education, Handicapped and Gifted Children, Rural Education and Small Schools, and Urban Education. Usually established at ongoing professional organizations, universities, or other institutions, the ERIC clearinghouses acquire, assess, review, and abstract the documents and periodical articles covered each month in *RIE* and *CIJE*. All answer requests for information in their fields; all perform custom computer searches of the ERIC data base for varying fees.

A recent study indicates that some form of ERIC information is available at more than 3,000 different locations in the United States, including institutes of higher education, libraries, and information services for educators. ERIC itself produces two ongoing directories, usually updated every two years: the *Directory of ERIC Microfiche Collections* (latest edition, 1983) and the *Directory of ERIC Search Services*. ERIC is a heavily used system with a great deal of information on children and is now involved in a two-year project designed to make its materials more accessible to educational practitioners.

There are many "ready reference" guides to ERIC, available free while the supply lasts from the ERIC facility. *All About ERIC* is available from U.S. government bookstores and from the U.S. Government Printing Office, Washington, DC 20402. A slide/tape kit, *ERIC: What It Is, How to Use It* (Revised Edition) is now available from the National Audiovisual Center, Washington, DC 20409 (Attn.: Order Section) for $94. The ERIC Document Reproduction Service (EDRS), c/o Computer Microfilm International Corporation, 3030 N. Fairfax Dr., Suite 200, Arlington, VA 22201, is the source for subscriptions to microfiche sets or individual copies in paper or microfiche.

K22 **ERIC CLEARINGHOUSE ON ELEMENTARY AND EARLY CHILDHOOD EDUCATION (ERIC/EECE)** University of Illinois, 805 W. Pennsylvania Ave., Urbana, IL 61801. (217) 333-1386

The scope of this clearinghouse is the physical, social, cultural, and educational development of children from birth through age 12, including prenatal factors, parent behavior, educational theory and practices, community services, other groups and institutions, physical settings, and theoretical and philosophical issues.

ERIC/EECE produces two bimonthly newsletters. The first is *ERIC/EECE Newsletter* ($5.00/year), which provides brief reports of current research and new programs and practices; announcements of books, activity kits, films, and the like; and summaries and bibliographies of ERIC documents—altogether a handy, compact guide to ERIC and other sources on children up to age 12. The second is *MicroNotes on Children and Computers* ($8.00/year), a newsletter for people who work with children and computers that includes reports of current research, programs, and practices, as well as announcements of relevant resource materials. ERIC/EECE also issues papers covering a wide range of topics for researchers, students, teachers, program directors, and policymakers, including topic papers, literature reviews, research papers, bibliographies, and conference proceedings.

Its free *Resource Lists* provide up to two pages of current ERIC citations on many topics; titles include *Child Development, Child Health and Nutrition, Computers and Children, Day Care, Early Childhood Education, Infants, Kindergarten, Multicultural Education, Elementary Education, Parents, Stress in Schools,* and *Television and Children.*

Other annotated bibliographies deal with aspects of child development, child rearing and parent/school cooperation, day care, and educational concerns. *An International Bibliography of ERIC Resources: Elementary and Early Education* (1981, 90 pp.) is available for $5.00. *Talks with Parents* (1983, 80 pp.) costs $6.95. A complete publications list is available on request.

ERIC/EECE performs custom computers searches in its scope areas (on all BRS and DIALOG data bases) and will estimate costs if requested. It prefers to run searches through personal appointment or telephone order but will also handle mail requests.

ReadySearches—duplicate printouts of at least 35 citations from the ERIC data base—are updated every six months and are available for $10.00 each. Some topics are *Effects of Divorce on Children, Elementary Education and Computers, Infants and Their Caregivers,* and *Bilingual Education.* A full list is available on request.

K23   ERIC   CLEARINGHOUSE   ON   URBAN   EDUCATION (ERIC/CUE) Columbia University, Teachers College, Box O, 525 W. 120th St., New York, NY 10027. (212) 678-3437
Primary areas of interest are the education of urban and minority children and youth, especially blacks, Puerto Ricans, and Asian-Americans. Considers urban education from grade 3 through college, urban and minority social institutions and services, and the relationship between urban and minority life and school performance. Its *Urban Diversity Series* includes documents like *Home, School and Community in Adolescent Education* and *More Effective Schooling: From Research to Practice.* Prices of these monographs vary. The *IRCD Bulletin* is a backlist series of review articles that synthesize concepts and current practices and cost $0.50 or $1.00 per issue, with topics like *Parent Participa-*

tion in Urban Schools. The ERIC/CUE *Digest Series* provides important urban education information in a brief format; numbers in this series are free. Titles include *Improving the Mathematical Skills of Low Achievers* and *Microcomputers: Equity and Quality in Education for Urban Disadvantaged Students.* Complete publications lists are available on request.

K24   **GESELL INSTITUTE OF HUMAN DEVELOPMENT**   310
       Prospect St., New Haven, CT 06511. Administration, Vision, and Clinical Services, (203) 777-3481; Developmental Department, (203) 776-8125; Medical Department, (203) 789-1911

A private nonprofit institute whose pioneer work, founded on the studies begun by Dr. Arnold Gesell in 1911, deals with child growth and development in a multidisciplinary fashion. Its books, tests, approaches, and findings have proved valuable for educators, pediatricians, psychologists, and parents. Its basic interests are child development, child behavior, child psychology, and developmental assessment. The Gesell Developmental Examination, promoted by the Developmental Department, assesses physical (motor), adaptive, language, and personal/social development. A major task of this department is training educators and psychologists in the concepts of developmental assessment. The Medical Department carries out a practice of family medicine and does medical detective work for children and adults with chronic illness. Its research studies include environmental, nutritional, and biochemical aspects of child and family health. The Vision Department is interested in the relationship between vision and other behavior.

The institute staff has written many books. Among these are the well-known Gesell, Ilg, and Ames series on child development: *Infant and Child in the Culture of Today, The Child from Five to Ten,* and *Youth: The Years from Ten to Sixteen,* as well as books on individuals aged one to six. Other publications deal with school readiness, testing, and home behavior; these include testing aids and computers, tapes, and articles. The institute's newly published *Directory of Developmental Placement Programs* (1983, $5.50) includes an annotated bibliography and research data. Complete lists are available on request. Its newsletter, *Update* ($20/year), reports research and institute news, as well as forthcoming workshops and seminars.

K25   **GIRLS CLUBS OF AMERICA**   National Resource Center,
       441 W. Michigan St., Indianapolis, IN 46202. (317) 634-7546

A national resource center serving as both an informational clearinghouse and a repository for accumulating data on girls and their special needs in order to bring together research, theory, and practice to improve girls' lives. Its collection includes more than 3,000 books and monographs, 500 pamphlets, 150 periodicals, and 550 microfiche. Publications deal with programs, sports, policies, girls at risk, career awareness, employment skills, decision-making skills, and the like. Titles include *What Do We Know About Girls?* (1982, $4.95) and *Facts and Reflections on Female Adolescent Sexuality* ($3.75). Other publications are available from the headquarters office at 205 Lexington Ave., New York, NY 10016.

K26 **GRAHAM (FRANK PORTER) CHILD DEVELOPMENT CENTER** Highway 54, Bypass West 071A, Chapel Hill, NC 27514. (919) 966-4121

This group's current major interest areas are pediatrics, day care, mental retardation, learning disabilities, the socially disadvantaged, and public policy. Its programs in these areas include research, demonstration and curriculum development, public policy analysis, and outreach and training under contract. Projects and publications can be followed in the center's newsletter, *Developments.* Many of its reports are available through ERIC; some have been commercially published by Walker Educational Book Corporation (720 Fifth Ave., New York, NY 10019). Two well-known projects are the Carolina Abecedarian Project, a longitudinal comparison of high-risk infants, and Project CARE (Carolina Approach to Responsive Education), which compares two preschool preventive educational programs. Reports and reprints of papers on these projects are available. *Learningames for the First Three Years,* by Joseph Sparling and Isabelle Lewis ($2.95 [paper]), organizes 100 growth games. Catalogs and status reports are available on request.

K27 **GROUP CHILD CARE CONSULTANT SERVICES (GCCCS)** University of North Carolina, School of Social Work, Chapel Hill, NC 27514. (919) 966-5466

GCCCS, founded in 1956, is the child welfare services arm of the School of Social Work at the University of North Carolina; it focuses on the improvement of public and private agency services to children, youth, and families. These include preventive and protective services, foster family care, permanency planning programs, adoption services, community-based group home agencies, juvenile justice programs, and the residential care and treatment of children and youth. In these areas, it offers technical assistance, curriculum development, and various forms of training programs to improve agency services. GCCCS's library includes thousands of books, pamphlets, and 85 periodical titles; it performs computer searches for members and provides low-cost loans or photocopies for nonmembers. Publications include the excellent *Starting Points* (B16); around 45 publications are in print, including practice monographs, reports of proceedings, profiles of group homes, and guides for practitioners. Prices range from $1 for *Standards of Job Performance for Child Care Administrators* to $465 for their *Basic Course for Residential Child Care Workers,* with guides, seven student and seven instructor manuals, and five tapes (sections can be purchased separately). The *Training Course for Licensors of Residential Group Child Care and Child Placement Agencies* costs $55. Brochures and a publications catalog are available on request.

K28 **INSTITUTE FOR CHILDHOOD RESOURCES (ICR)**
1169 Howard St., San Francisco, CA 94103. (415) 864-1169
Founded in 1977 to create a library/resource center on children's services and to house Parent and Child Care Resources, the publishing branch of the institute. The resource center, open by appointment, includes books, research documents, toys, and other educational equipment, with an emphasis on infant care, early childhood, and child care. Services include consultation, instruction, workshops, and research and development. Publications include *The Whole Child: A Sourcebook, Confronting the Child Care Crisis* (Q99), *Choosing Childcare: A Guide for Parents* (Q97), *Child Care: A Comprehensive Guide* (Human Sciences Press, 4 vols.), and *The Toy Chest: A Sourcebook.*

K29 **JUVENILE JUSTICE CLEARINGHOUSE** National Criminal Justice Reference Service (NCJRS), 1600 Research Blvd., Box 6000, Rockville, MD 20850. (800) 638-8736
A clearinghouse on programs and practices for juvenile justice professionals, active since 1972 and sponsored since 1979 by the National Institute for Juvenile Justice and Delinquency Prevention. It collects program descriptions, project reports, research studies, and evaluations and maintains information on these in a computerized data base with on-line search and retrieval capabilities. It is accessible to anyone involved with juvenile justice, including planners, researchers, concerned citizens, and school authorities. It covers all subjects on prevention and treatment. Current hot topics include school violence, status offenders, child abuse and neglect, due process, jailing of children, delinquency prevention, and serious or violent juvenile offenders. Other important areas include child pornography and prostitution,

learning disabilities, runaways, alternative education, and substance abuse.

NCJRS, with a data base of 75,000 documents, offers topical bibliographies, directories, and brochures; prompt response to queries; free documents in paper and microfiche; descriptions of operating programs; and referrals to other information sources. All items in the collection may be borrowed by interlibrary loan. The National Institute of Justice, principal sponsor of NCJRS, publishes the bimonthly *NIJ Reports,* a journal of news about criminal and juvenile justice research that includes abstracts of recent publications and products. Subscription is free within the United States. *Topical Searches* (bound bibliographies with catalog data and complete abstracts of 30 documents) are available for $5.00 each. Custom searches are $48.00; *Topical Bibliographies* (up to 200 citations) are $17.50. A products and services list is available on request.

K30   **KEMPE (C. HENRY) NATIONAL CENTER FOR THE PREVENTION AND TREATMENT OF CHILD ABUSE AND NEGLECT**   1205 Oneida St., Denver, CO 80220. (303) 321-3963

The Kempe Center, founded in 1958, is an advocacy, research, and treatment organization that works with families and professionals to prevent and treat child abuse through education, evaluation, consultation, and treatment programs, as well as national and international symposia. Since its founding, it has been an important leader in this area. Its outstanding publications and audiovisuals on child abuse and neglect are prepared for audiences that range from the general public to junior high, high school, and college students writing term papers; professional child workers; grant writers; parents; and lay persons working with parents. A publications catalog is available for $1.00; the audiovisual catalog is annotated in item F5. Activities and programs are reported in *Kempe Center News,* free on request.

Its library, which includes approximately 1,000 books, 100 audiovisuals, and 1,800 articles on all aspects of child abuse and neglect (legal, social, therapeutic, developmental, nutritional, and so on), offers individual memberships for $5.00 plus mailing costs. These extend search and checkout privileges for circulating items and in-house use of reference items. Agency memberships are $25.00 per year plus mailing costs. Topic Searches for articles in the files are $5.00 plus $0.20/page photocopy charge; Topic Searches for articles and books in the library are $15.00 (which includes checkout of three books) plus a photocopy charge of $0.20/page.

K31   **NATIONAL ART EDUCATION ASSOCIATION (NAEA)**
1916 Association Dr., Reston, VA 22091. (703) 860-8000
An organization for art educators, supervisors, and administrators that
is one of the few groups concerned with the aspects of children related
to aesthetics, creativity, and the visual arts. Journals include *Art Education* and *Studies in Art Education.* Books, pamphlets, and films deal with
art for the preprimary child, art education advocacy and practices from
elementary school through college, art careers and skills, art and cognition, art in special education, art history, and safety.

K32   **NATIONAL ASSOCIATION FOR CREATIVE CHILDREN
AND ADULTS (NACCA)**   8080 Springvalley Dr., Cincinnati,
OH 45236. (513) 631-1777
A nonprofit membership organization founded in 1974 to provide assistance and direction to individuals and groups seeking to enlarge the
scope of their creative talents. Publishes *The Creative Child and Adult
Quarterly,* which contains insights into theories and applications of creativity research. Other publications include compilations of creative
writing, vignettes, musical compositions, and the *Three-Way Developmental Growth Check List for Giftedness-Talent-Creativity* ($25).

K33   **NATIONAL ASSOCIATION FOR GIFTED CHILDREN**
5100 N. Edgewood Dr., St. Paul, MN 55112. (612) 784-3475
A membership organization of educators, parents, and community
people interested in the development of gifted children. Its goals are to
serve as a public advocate for the needs of the gifted; to promote research and development into the nature and education of the gifted; to
encourage and assist local and state organizations in supporting gifted
education; and to disseminate information on gifted children to parents, school personnel, and public officials. Membership includes the
Gifted Child Quarterly and *Communique* newsletter. Publications available from the organization include guides to programs and lobbying,
such as *Chapter Development Booklet* ($5); *Successful Programs* ($12),
which covers 100 programs; and *Guiding the Gifted Child* ($12); as well
as materials for parents, teachers, and teenagers. A complete list of publications and tapes is available on request.

K34   **NATIONAL ASSOCIATION FOR THE EDUCATION OF
YOUNG CHILDREN (NAEYC)**   1834 Connecticut Ave.,
NW, Washington, DC 20009. (202) 232-8777, (800) 424-2460
Founded in 1926 to serve and act on the needs and rights of young chil-
dren, with primary emphasis on providing services and resources for

adults who work with or on behalf of young children from birth to age eight. Members are engaged in a wide range of early childhood services, including research, teaching, directing programs, child advocacy, teacher education, parenting, and licensing. NAEYC's information services include pamphlets, books, conferences, bibliographies, and information referrals on a wide range of topics related to early childhood education and child development. It has published many helpful pamphlets and brochures, including *How to Choose a Good Early Childhood Program.* Comprehensive membership includes an excellent journal entitled *Young Children* (H149) and around half a dozen books a year that reflect current research and practice. These outstanding publications are available to nonmembers at low cost and cover nearly every area of child development and early childhood education from motor development to cognitive development, language development, outdoor play, family relationships, and research reviews. Some recent significant titles are *Fundraising for Early Childhood Programs: Getting Started and Getting Results* (1982, 88 pp., $3.85) and *How to Generate Values in Children* (1984, 112 pp., $12.00). NAEYC plans to open the Child Care Information Service in 1985.

K35   **NATIONAL ASSOCIATION OF COUNSEL FOR CHIL-DREN (NACC)**   1205 Oneida St., Denver, CO 80220. (303) 321-3963
A membership organization comprising primarily attorneys and lay persons directly engaged in children's law, but open to other advocates of the legal interests of children. It provides self-training and education for these legal representatives; supports the regulation of legal professionals and others who represent children to ensure that the representation is of adequate quality; and supports the position of children through amici curiae briefs, advice, and consultation. It publishes and distributes materials on children's law at its annual seminars and distributes free its *Guidelines for the Guardian Ad Litem of a Maltreated Child.* NACC's periodic newsletter, *The Guardian,* provides cases, advocacy articles, and information on conferences for members. Members and affiliates share recent cases, model forms and briefs, and innovative approaches to legal and administrative representation of children.

K36   **NATIONAL BLACK CHILD DEVELOPMENT INSTI-TUTE (NBCDI)**   1463 Rhode Island Ave., NW, Washington, DC 20005. (202) 387-1281
A nonprofit national membership advocacy and service organization founded in 1970 and dedicated to improving the quality of life for black children through public policy advocacy and service. Although its na-

tional efforts have focused on child development, child care, child welfare, and education issues, it has a dual advocacy structure that allows local affiliates to work on issues that are significant in their geographic areas, such as community development, adoption, foster care, or financial issues. Membership is open to all persons and agencies concerned about black children—parents, educators, child care providers, ministers, physicians, lawyers, social workers, child welfare administrators, and community workers.

NBCDI publishes a quarterly newsletter, *The Black Child Advocate,* and a periodic legislative alert, *The Black Flash.* Both deal with child development, education and child welfare issues, and suggested action for child advocates. NBCDI publications include *Guidelines for Adoption Services to Black Families* ($2.20, including postage and handling), *The Status of Black Children in 1980* ($3.20), and *Who Bears the Burden? Black Children in America: Impact of the President's FY'85 Budget Proposals* ($5.75). A complete list of publications is available on request.

K37   **NATIONAL CHILD SUPPORT ENFORCEMENT REFERENCE CENTER**   6110 Executive Blvd., Room 820, Rockville, MD 20852. (301) 443-5106

This active center maintains a clearinghouse of child support materials; conducts searches; serves as an information exchange service; and publishes materials, including its *Annual Report.* It collects and disseminates information on child support legislation and on techniques and procedures used by child support enforcement agencies across the country. These and other materials relevant to child support are pulled together in a free annual *Information Sharing Index,* which is updated at midyear. The 1983 edition is a substantial volume with 14 sections covering history and general items, fiscal/statistical aspects, legislative/regulation, location, establishment of paternity, enforcement of support, management and operation, public affairs, systems, state plans and procedures, training, audiovisuals, techniques for effective management of program operations (TEMPOs), and information memoranda. Audiovisuals can be borrowed for a two-week period.

Other free materials are the monthly *Child Support Report,* periodic *Abstracts of Child Support Techniques,* quarterly *Child Support Enforcement Statistics,* the *History and Fundamentals of Child Support Enforcement, A Legislator's Guide to Child Support Enforcement,* and the *Guide to State Child Support and Paternity Laws.*

The parent body, the National Institute of Child Support, has developed courses relating to child support that cover history, management, supervisory skills, enforcement techniques, interviewing, and establishment of paternity.

K38   **NATIONAL CHILD WELFARE TRAINING CENTER (NCWTC)** University of Michigan, School of Social Work, 1015 E. Huron St., Ann Arbor, MI 48104. (313) 763-4260

The mission of the National Child Welfare Training Center is to develop state and local capacities to provide child welfare services through education and training, with emphasis on work with racial and ethnic minorities. The center performs research, technical assistance, network building, information sharing, and the dissemination of unpublished documents to Regional Resource Centers, schools, state agencies, and others. They issue a quarterly catalog entitled *Sources* that includes descriptions of noncommercial materials useful in the education and training of child welfare staffs. The materials include syllabi, teaching guides, manuals and handbooks, and, occasionally, monographs, position papers, evaluation studies, bibliographies, and descriptions of audiovisual materials. Subject areas range from adolescents to case reviews, child abuse, values, and volunteers. The NCWTC Information System covers more than 5,000 such resources; it includes an index of 125 descriptors, a user's guide, and 5,000 catalog cards with availability information.

The center has other publications; *A Sourcebook in Child Welfare: Serving Black Families and Children* and *A Sourcebook in Child Welfare: Serving Chicano Families and Children,* for example, are comprehensive collections of nondeficit resource materials. The center also issues free research reports from national surveys on the current state of training and education in social work education programs and state agencies, such as *Master's and Bachelor's Programs, Doctoral Programs,* and *Faculty and Field Instructor Report.* A project *Craft* notebook includes training materials for child welfare staffs who place children with special needs. NCWTC has a library of 1,000 book and 15 periodical titles. Its new computerized information system is available as of April 1984.

K39   **NATIONAL CLEARINGHOUSE FOR BILINGUAL EDUCATION (NCBE)** 1555 Wilson Blvd., Suite 605, Rosslyn, VA 22209. (703) 522-0710, (800) 336-4560

NCBE, which began operation in 1977, is set up to help the U.S. educational system meet the needs of 5 million school-age children who have minority-language backgrounds. Its functions are to provide information on bilingual education and related background areas (such as legislation and policies); to coordinate information gathering, processing, and sharing among educators working with minority-language students; to conduct public information activities; and to operate a computerized data base on bilingual education. This data base, BILINGUAL

EDUCATION BIBLIOGRAPHIC ABSTRACTS (BEBA), is discussed in Chapter 11 (J16).

NCBE's interest areas include culture, parent and community involvement, and tests and measurements. Its other dissemination/information activities include a competent bimonthly newsletter, *Forum,* which includes articles, reports, announcements of publications, legislation, reviews, and a calendar of bilingual events. Other publications include bibliographies, directories, surveys and statistics, and information packets on topics like parent and community involvement in bilingual education. Certain publications are available as sets of microfiche. A current products list and brochure are available on request.

K40 **NATIONAL COMMITTEE FOR PREVENTION OF CHILD ABUSE (NCPCA)** 332 S. Michigan Ave., Suite 1250, Chicago, IL 60604-4357. (312) 663-3520

Established in 1972 in response to the increasing incidence of infant deaths due to purposely inflicted injury, the NCPCA was formed to help prevent child abuse, which it defines to include nonaccidental physical injury, emotional abuse, neglect, sexual abuse, and exploitation of children. It is dedicated to involving concerned citizens in actions to prevent these abuses, focusing principally on primary prevention. Its goals are to stimulate greater public awareness, to promote the development of programs, to advocate for needed change, and to establish cooperation among organizations that relate the problems of child abuse. To that end, it attempts to expand knowledge on prevention, to disseminate that knowledge, and to put that knowledge into action through community programs nationwide. Methods include media campaigns, publications, conferences and workshops, a national evaluation project, advocacy efforts, and technical and consultative services. Its excellent low-cost publications are described in a catalog, free on request. These include an excellent 12-page directory entitled *Selected Child Abuse Information and Resources* ($0.25, quantity discount), which lists state NCPCA branches, as well as classified, annotated lists of other organizations, including programs for children and teenagers, statistical sources, and directories. Other titles are *Annotated Bibliography of Legal Articles on Child Abuse* (1979, $4.00), which annotates 175 items published from 1961 to 1975; *Foster Parenting Abused Children* (1982, $4.00); *Physical Child Neglect* (1981, $3.00); and *Understanding Sexual Child Abuse* (1978, $3.50).

K41 **NATIONAL CONFERENCE OF STATE LEGISLATURES (NCSL)** 1125 17th St., Suite 1500, Denver, CO 80202. (303) 292-6600 (State-Federal Relations Office: 222 N. Capitol St., NW, Washington, DC 20001)

This organization, funded by the states, is the official representative for 7,500 state legislators and their staffs. Its goals are to improve the quality and effectiveness of state legislatures and to foster interstate communication and cooperation, as well as a strong, cohesive voice in the federal system. Although its services are for a limited clientele, it will exchange information with other organizations.

The conference offers technical assistance through research, testimony preparation, bill drafting, and state workshops; it established an information clearinghouse for its Children and Youth Program in June 1979. This clearinghouse collects and distributes state statutes, law journal articles, statistical data, court decisions, research reports, and the like. It also provides guidance to experts in the children and youth field.

Its Children and Youth Program consolidates formerly separated children and youth projects and, in September 1983, produced the *Children and Youth Program Information Clearinghouse Reference List* (27 pp., $5.00), which lists available materials for legislators and legislative staffs on child abuse and neglect, background and demographics, budget and fiscal concerns, child support standards and legislation, child custody, parent locator services, paternity, child welfare, child mental health, courts, child care, child health, foster care, grandparent visitation rights, and interstate and international enforcement.

NCSL's own publications include the introductory *Legislator's Guide to Child Support Enforcement* (1980, 58 pp., $5.00) and the substantial *In the Best Interest of the Child: A Guide to State Child Support and Paternity Laws* (1981, 148 pp., $18.50), which brings together exemplary statutes from all 50 states and categorizes laws. Another relevant work from its series on current legislative interest is the *Legislator's Guide to Youth Services* (1982, 106 pp., $13.50). Copies of NCSL's works are free to legislators and state libraries and can be purchased by others.

K42   **THE NATIONAL CONSORTIUM FOR CHILD MENTAL
      HEALTH SERVICES**   1424 16th St., NW, Washington, DC
      20036. (202) 462-3754
The consortium is a coalition of 17 national, professional, provider, and consumer organizations concerned with promoting and protecting mental health services for children. Members meet quarterly to exchange information about ideas on public policy and programs serving mentally ill children and adolescents. It is open to "anyone connected with child mental health services."

K43 **NATIONAL LEGAL RESOURCE CENTER FOR CHILD ADVOCACY AND PROTECTION** American Bar Assn., (ABA), 1800 M St., NW, Suite 200, Washington, DC 20036. (202) 331-2250

This program of the Young Lawyers Division of the American Bar Association was set up to help improve the quality of legal representation in child welfare judicial proceedings. It serves the legal profession and those who work in the legal system as the national source of technical assistance on the legal aspects of child welfare and has published more than 20 books and monographs and supported around 40 child advocacy projects. Publications are excellent and to the point. Areas of interest include child abuse and neglect, child sexual abuse and exploitation, foster care and adoption, child custody, termination of parental rights, and the representation of children in domestic relations cases. Its newsletter, *Legal Response: Child Advocacy and Protection,* includes book reviews, bibliographies, news and articles on legislation and court actions, and relevant awards. The *National Directory of Programs Providing Court Representation to Abused and Neglected Children* is $1.00. Other titles are *Alternative Means of Family Dispute Resolution,* a massive textbook costing $25.00, and *Recommendations for Improving Legal Intervention in Intrafamily Child Sexual Abuse Cases* ($5.00). *Child Sexual Abuse and the Law* ($8.50) is a detailed state survey and analysis of laws and legal issues relating to intrafamily sexual abuse.

K44 **NATIONAL ORGANIZATIONS ADVISORY COUNCIL FOR CHILDREN (NOAC)** 331 E. 38th St., New York, NY 10016. (212) 686-5522

An umbrella organization that works actively with more than 500 private voluntary groups to expand programming for children. NOAC serves as a catalyst to promote activities for children and families; conducts periodic workshops, conferences, and training programs for the general public; and publishes an annual journal and a periodic newsletter. As an umbrella organization, it offers a good overview of the needs of children.

K45 **NATIONAL SOCIAL SCIENCE AND LAW CENTER, INC. (NSS&LC)** 1825 Connecticut Ave., NW, Suite 401-S, Washington, DC 20009. (202) 797-1100

A nonprofit organization, funded by the Legal Services Corporation, dedicated to applying social science methods to the legal problems of the poor. It answers research requests from its clientele—legal services attorneys, local community groups, public interest law firms, civil rights groups, and neighborhood legal services programs. Its sources include its own reference library of more than 6,000 indexed publications, as well as its own computer data processing capabilities and access to major data bases and library facilities in the nation's capital. NSS&LC manuals for client groups include an annotated bibliography, *Sources on Statistical Information on the Low-Income Population* (1981, 41 pp., $4). Other recent publications include *Functions of Welfare: A Review of the Longitudinal Research on AFDC Households* (1983, 32 pp. plus 10 appendixes, $5) and other well-done guides and analytical surveys of poor families and children. A brochure and current publications list are available on request.

K46 **NATIONAL/STATE LEADERSHIP TRAINING INSTITUTE ON THE GIFTED AND THE TALENTED (N/S-LTI-G/T)** Civic Center Tower Bldg., 316 W. 2nd St., Suite PH-C, Los Angeles, CA 90012. (213) 489-7470
An organization whose purpose is to train adults who work with gifted and talented children. During the past 10 years, it has assisted regional, state, intermediate, and local educational agencies and parent groups in planning, improving, and implementing educational programs for gifted and talented children. It publishes extensively in the areas of program, curriculum, and staff development; parenting; advocacy; and the disadvantaged gifted.

K47 **TOY MANUFACTURERS OF AMERICA** 200 Fifth Ave., New York, NY 10010. (212) 675-1141
A trade organization for manufacturers of toys, games, and holiday decorations. Its major purpose is to provide services to member manufacturers, but it also will answer consumer queries on toy selection and safety through its booklet, *ABC's of Toys & Play* (single copies free; slight charge for multiple copies). This organization also publishes the free *Toy Industry Fact Book* every two years.

K48 **USA TOY LIBRARY ASSOCIATION** 5940 W. Touhy Ave., Chicago IL 60648. (312) 763-7350
An association formed in the fall of 1983 by a diverse group of practitioners—directors of toy libraries, medical doctors, psychologists, educators, and librarians—who share a belief that play and toys are vital in the early development and education of all children. Membership is open to individuals, organizations, professionals, and lay persons. The monthly newsletter, *Child's Play,* is planned as an update on new toys, funding opportunities, new books, articles and films on play and child

development, toy library administrative techniques, and other relevant materials. Current emphases include the development and extension of toy libraries, therapeutic use of toys, and toys in early childhood education. The group hopes to issue an annual directory, a guide to good toys, and an operating manual for toy libraries and to conduct workshops on therapeutic play intervention programs and toy library operations. Discounts on toy purchases are available to members.

MEDIA ORGANIZATIONS

This section covers four organizations concerned in different ways with children and the media. Many others are contained in the *Children's Media Market Place* (I17). Since these are a self-sufficient unit, I have gathered them together. Some of the organizations in Chapter 16 also are concerned with media other than books. The National PTA (L68), too, has worked extensively in this area.

K49 **ACTION FOR CHILDREN'S TELEVISION (ACT)** 46
       Austin St., Newtonville, MA 02160. (617) 527-7870
Action for Children's Television is a 16-year-old nonprofit children's advocacy group with 20,000 members nationwide concerned with promoting diversity in children's television programming and in stemming excessive commercialization of television for young audiences. It publishes a biannual news magazine, *RE:ACT* ($15/year, free with membership) that reflects its concern about media issues relating to children, including traditional broadcast television, cable television, low-power television, radio, and other technologies. ACT has published numerous booklets; kits; time charts; guides to programming; bibliographies; reference lists; a 16mm film; and *Fighting TV Stereotypes: An ACT Handbook,* which deals with images of women and minorities in programs for children and adults.

K50 **CHILDREN'S ADVERTISING REVIEW UNIT** Council
       of Better Business Bureaus, 845 Third Ave., 17th Floor, New
       York, NY 10022. (212) 754-1353
An investigative arm of the National Advertising Division of the Council of Better Business Bureaus, the Children's Advertising Review Unit was established in 1974 "to assure the truth, accuracy, and sensitivity

of advertising directed to children" under age 12. Although supported by business, it is part of a nonprofit organization directed to the public interest and maintains a clearinghouse on research in children's advertising. Its annotated bibliography, *Children and Advertising,* is reviewed in Chapter 6 (E37). Free publications include two pamphlets: the detailed *Children's Advertising Guidelines* and *An Eye on Children's Advertising,* which describes the review and evaluation of child-directed advertising in all media. When advertising is found to be inaccurate or unfair to children's perceptions, the Children's Unit seeks modification or discontinuance through voluntary cooperation. Cases and their resolution are reported in a free monthly press release, *NAD Case Report.*

K51 **MEDIA ACTION RESEARCH CENTER (MARC)** 475 Riverside Dr., Suite 1370, New York, NY 10115. (212) 865-6690

An independent nonprofit organization, established in 1974 with a grant from the Lilly Foundation and the United Methodist Church to study the impact of television; disseminate its findings in understandable language; bring about positive change; and help viewers improve their strategies for intentional, selective viewing. It offers training events in television awareness and has produced the comprehensive *Television Awareness Training: The Viewer's Guide* (280 pp., $12.95) for all viewers and *Growing with Television: A Study of Biblical Values and the Television Experience* ($36.45 for a starter kit) primarily for church educators.

K52 **NATIONAL COUNCIL FOR CHILDREN AND TELEVISION (NCCT)** 20 Nassau St., Suite 215, Princeton, NJ 08540. (609) 921-3639

A group established in 1977 to attempt cooperative rather than adversarial approaches in considering the needs of children and the legitimate needs of the television industry, with members from advertising, broadcasting, communication research, child development, child advocacy, and education. Educational services include an NCCT speaker's bureau that offers presentations to parent groups, regional workshops for teachers, a listener's bureau that brings producers and writers into classrooms, annual research conferences, annual writers' workshops, and annual workshops and quarterly seminars in New York and Los Angeles. The NCCT Clearinghouse provides information on child development, education, policies, communications, and audience research to members, professional associates, and students on request. The *NCCT Clearinghouse Index* is published annually; the *NCCT Informa-*

tion Service, an annotated packet of reprints of current articles, news clippings, and research abstracts, is distributed monthly (for $100/ year) in combination with subscription to their quarterly, *Television & Children* (H142).

LIBRARIES, CLEARINGHOUSES, AND GENERAL RESEARCH ORGANIZATIONS

This section includes libraries, clearinghouses, and similar information sources that contain hard-to-find information on children, even though their focus is broader than or different from the area of childhood. Some cover extensively the problems of women in the work force. To keep the length of this book manageable, I have had to omit many organizations, particularly libraries and library organizations such as the Council of Planning Librarians and the National Library of Medicine, which contribute significantly in organizing information and compiling bibliographies. These can be located through directories of libraries.

K53   **BUSINESS AND PROFESSIONAL WOMEN'S FOUNDA-TION**   Marguerite Rawalt Resource Center, 2012 Massachusetts Ave., NW, Washington, DC 20036. (202) 293-1200
The small, nonprofit parent organization focuses mainly on women's employment and economic issues. It aims to promote economic and social sufficiency through sponsored research, publications, educational grants, and library services. The Rawalt Resource Center is a national center on women's employment issues, with a valuable, focused library of 20,000 books, pamphlets, speeches, news clippings, and periodicals. This service provides public reference and referral by mail, telephone, and personal visits; interlibrary loan services; and photocopying at $0.10/page; as well as information packets or research summaries on topics that are requested frequently. The center is now putting its catalog on-line and will shortly offer computerized information retrieval through a public data base that will provide nationwide access to materials on women and economic issues. Relevant publications are *Model of Quality Day Care* (supply limited, but loan copies available); *Women and Poverty: A Research Summary* (1982, $1.00); and *Determinants and Consequences of Maternal Employment: An Annotated Bibliography, 1968–80* (E59).

K54   CATALYST 14 E. 60th St., New York, NY 10022. (212)
759-9700
A nonprofit organization founded in 1962 to promote the full participation of women in business and the professions through working with employers, educators, counselors, women, and the media. Its Library and Audiovisual Center contains more than 5,000 cataloged items— 4,000 books, 125 periodicals, 2,000 vertical files, and 500 career files—on women in the labor force; career options for women; and related economic, legislative, and social trends. The Catalyst Audiovisual Center reviews materials in the *Catalyst Media Review* ($12.00/ year). The CATALYST RESOURCES FOR WOMEN (CRFW) data base on women and employment is available through BRS. It includes more than 3,000 documents on two-career family issues such as child care, alternative work patterns, parenting, and relocation. Journal articles, studies, books, reports, bibliographies, audiovisual resources, and magazine and newsletter articles are cited with publisher and source information and a descriptive abstract. Royalty fees for CRFW are $15.00/ hour, $0.25/off-line citation and $0.15/on-line citation, plus a *Thesaurus* for $10.00. For persons without terminals, Catalyst staff will conduct searches of BRS data bases.

Catalyst has compiled relevant bibliographies and directories, including *Resources on Parenting and Child Care* ($4.00, updated quarterly); *Corporations and Two-Career Families: Directions for the Future* ($5.00); and *Two-Career Families: An Annotated Bibliography of Relevant Readings,* ongoing bibliographies from the library.

K55   HUMAN RELATIONS AREA FILES (HRAF) 755 Prospect St., P.O. Box 2054, Yale Sta., New Haven, CT 06520. (203) 777-2334
This substantial data bank and research tool is a unique cross-referenced social science information retrieval system designed for cross-cultural research in anthropology and related behavioral disciplines such as sociology, psychology, and political science (see Figure 12). The files contain materials in the life sciences and the humanities, as well as geographic data, and are based on a line-by-line analysis of 3.3 million page references from more than 5,300 selected sources covering 320 nations and cultures.

The HRAF files, which have been in existence more than a quarter century, are a continually expanding collection of (mostly) primary source materials—including books, articles, and unpublished manuscripts—on a large sample of cultures and societies representing all major areas of the world. These files are arranged first by culture and

Cleanliness training 863
Cradle songs and lullabies . . 533
Disparagement. 784

Medical care 758
Preventive medicine. 751

855 CHILD CARE--supervision, care, and support of children from earliest independence (e.g., walking, talking) to puberty; distribution of responsibility among parents and other relatives; institutionalized care (e.g., day nurseries); beliefs and standards concerning proper clothing, feeding, and housing of children; provisions for physical and mental health; protection from physical and social dangers (e.g., confinement, removal of dangerous objects); attitude of adults toward children (e.g., indulgent, indifferent, censorious); spoiling and coddling; mistreatment and neglect of children; etc. See also:

Care of orphans. 736
Discipline and training. . . . 86*
Family relationships 593

Medical care 758
Preventive medicine. 751

856 DEVELOPMENT AND MATURATION--concepts and standards of physical, mental, and emotional behavior and development during infancy and childhood; data on infant behavior; methods of promoting and influencing growth (e.g., molding of head, magical rituals); adjustments to growth; data on maturation (e.g., age at creeping, standing, walking, talking, cooperation); attitudes toward and special treatment of development events (e.g., teething, growth of hair and nails, increases in weight and stature); reactions and adjustments to retardation and precocity; etc. See also:

Ceremonies during infancy
  and childhood 852
Cranial deformation. 304

Data on physical growth and
  mental development. 145
Education. 87*
Socialization. 86*

857 CHILDHOOD ACTIVITIES--extent to which a special culture of childhood exists; children's play; imitative activities (e.g., make-believe); habits of rest and sleep; children's playgroups, cliques, and gangs; quarreling and fighting; children's explorations and haunts; tasks performed by children and age at which each is undertaken (e.g., errands, chores, care of younger children); etc. See also:

Age-grades 561
Baby talk. 195
Child betrothal. 584
Children's games, toys, and
  playthings. 524
Daily routine. 512
Education. 87*

Ingroup antagonisms. 578
Mutual aid 476
Primary groups 571
Quest for guardian spirits . . 787
Residence changes by children. 591
Socialization. 86*

Figure 12 The Human Relations Area Files contain much ethnographic and anthropological data related to children and youth. These categories are reproduced from the *Outline of Cultural Materials,* by George P. Murdock et al. 5th Revised Edition. New Haven, Conn., Human Relations Area Files, Inc., 1982.

then by 716 numerical subject categories (79 broad subjects) based on George P. Murdock's *Outline of Cultural Materials* (5th Revised Edition, New Haven, Conn., 1982). HRAF does not focus on children and youth, but a great deal of relevant information can be found in its files. Major areas include 85–Infancy and Childhood, 86–Socialization, 88–Adolescence, 15–Behavior Process and Personality, 16–Demography, and 87–Formal Education. These classification numbers can be used to locate relevant materials originally placed in the Cultural Files, thus greatly reducing the time spent searching for such materials.

The complete files, in 5″ × 8″ paper format, are distributed to sponsoring member institutions. The HRAF-Microfiles, 4″ × 6″ microfiche copies of 80,000–100,000 file pages per year, are distributed to 250 associate member institutions worldwide. Although hours and accessibility vary, these collections are generally open to researchers and educators. A list of available file sources can be obtained from HRAF on written request.

One especially useful HRAF publication, produced to assist the field worker in research, is the *Field Guide to the Ethnological Study of Child Life,* 2nd Edition, 1966, 79 pp. (out of print).

K56 **NATIONAL REFERRAL CENTER** Library of Congress, 2nd St. and Independence Ave., SE, 5th Floor, Washington, DC 20540. (202) 287-5670 for referral services; (202) 287-5680 for information

A free referral service established in 1962 that directs persons with questions to the organizations that might be able to answer these questions. It works from a subject-indexed computerized data base that lists information on 13,000 organizations of various types. File descriptions indicate the organization's special fields of interest and the information services it provides. The file is accessible at the Library of Congress through computer terminals and also is available at certain federal agencies that use the Department of Energy's RECON Computer Network. The center also handles requests made in person, by mail, or telephone. Although it originally focused on science and technology, it now systematically covers all areas in the United States, with a few international and foreign resources.

From time to time, the National Referral Center compiles directories of information resources covering a broad area. These are published by the Library of Congress under the general title *A Directory of Information Resources in the United States* and varying subtitles and are sold by the U.S. Government Printing Office, Washington, DC 20402. One relevant title is *Directory of Federally Supported Information Analysis Centers* (4th Edition, 1979, 87 pp., $4). Under the title *Who Knows?* the center issues informal lists of resources on particular topics, free while the supply lasts. They must be requested individually by topic. A list on children was issued in 1980; a complete set of titles is available on request.

K57 **NATIONAL SELF-HELP CLEARINGHOUSE** City University of New York, Graduate School and University Center, 33 W. 42nd St., New York, NY 10036. (212) 840-1258

An organization for lay people and professionals interested and/or involved in any facet of self-help—health, mental health, or community or common problems. In addition to its clearinghouse function, its major activities are encouraging, supporting, and conducting training activities and research. It has compiled the *Directory of Self-Help Groups* ($6.50); a guide entitled *Developing a Directory of Self-Help Groups* ($2.00); and a newsletter, *Self-Help Reporter* (5 issues/year, $10.00), whose reports on groups and regional clearinghouses usually include parent or health groups involving children. There are 24 regional clearinghouses on self-help. *Help: A Working Guide to Self-Help Groups* is available from the publisher, New Viewpoints, Inc., Dept. EJ, 730 Fifth Ave., New York, NY 10019 ($10.65, including postage and handling).

K58 **PROJECT SHARE** P.O. Box 2309, Rockville, MD 20852. (301) 251-7150

A unique information clearinghouse developed by the Department of Health and Human Services (DHHS) to improve the planning, management, and delivery of human services. This data base includes information on innovative projects funded by DHHS, state reorganizations, local projects, and current research. Publications include the quarterly *Journal of Human Services Abstracts* (G28); topical annotated bibliographies; monographs; occasional papers; *SHARING,* the bimonthly newsletter ($15/year); and reference and referral services.

K59 **REFUGEE POLICY GROUP (RPG)** Resource Center, 1424 16th St., NW, Suite 401, Washington, DC 20036. (202) 387-3015

A repository for major documents and other information on refugees and refugee assistance, primarily designed to serve organizations, policymakers, and researchers. Includes materials on international and domestic refugee issues.

K60 **RESOURCE AND REFERRAL SERVICE (RRS)** Ohio State University, 1960 Kenny Rd., Columbus, OH 43210. (800) 848-4815, ext. 234; (614) 486-3655 in Ohio, Alaska, and Hawaii
RRS, operating out of the National Center for Research in Vocational Education at Ohio State University, collects and disseminates information on a wide variety of educational organizations, with some emphasis on groups concerned with educational research. It maintains an on-line data base—RESOURCE ORGANIZATIONS AND MEETINGS FOR EDUCATORS (ROME)—through BRS that covers more than 1,000 professional and nonprofit organizations and advocacy groups in education and related disciplines. ROME includes information on regional, national, and international meetings; workshops; seminars; and conferences and symposia. It includes title, dates, location, contact information, sponsors, and costs. ROME also is used to prepare short directories—*Mini-Lists* —of topics of current interest; titles include *Preventing Child Abuse and Neglect* and *Microcomputers in Education*. Each *Mini-List* describes the scope, purpose, and relevant publications of perhaps 8–12 organizations and is distributed free. Telephone consultation also is available.

K61 **THE URBAN INSTITUTE** 2100 M St., NW, Washington, DC 20037. (202) 833-7200
A nonprofit, multidisciplinary, policy research organization dedicated to objective information; it investigates the full range of domestic social and economic problems and policies, as well as specifically urban problems. Most work is supported through grants and projects. The institute has eight research centers, including health policy, housing, and social services research. Relevant publications include *Monitoring the Outcomes of Social Services* (2 vols., 1977, $7.00); *Day Care in the Next Decade* (1980, 14 pp., $1.75); *Prevention in Child Welfare* (1979, 11 pp., $1.00); and *A Public Assistance Data Book* (1977, 344 pp., $10.00), which compiles information on public assistance programs in 50 states. *Public Policies Towards Adoption* (1979, 84 pp., $5.00) addresses the criteria that agencies use to select adoptive parents.

INTERGOVERNMENTAL, FOREIGN, AND INTERNATIONAL ORGANIZATIONS

Although this book is primarily concerned with children in the United States, this section annotates a few major international or foreign agencies that compile, tabulate, or dispense information on children in other countries. Information stems from questionnaires distributed in 1982 and 1983, supplemented by research. These organizations, which were typically formed in response to the sufferings of children in war, tend to view children more globally and holistically than official agencies and child-centered professions in the United States. Organizations concerned with maternal health, infant nutrition, and breast-feeding also seem to have an international or multinational scope.

Many other international organizations, particularly divisions of Unesco or organizations concerned with development—for example, the Organisation for Economic Co-operation and Development (OECD)—have publications or information centers that deal with children in some way. Demographic data will deal with infant mortality, as will studies of drought in the Sahel or studies of food, agriculture, and rural development. Documents libraries and the *Yearbook of International Organizations* are sources to search for additional information. The 1981 *Yearbook,* published by the International Chamber of Commerce and the Union des Associations Internationales in Belgium, is available from Unipub (Box 433, Murray Hill Sta., New York, NY 10157) for $150; it covers nearly 15,000 organizations. Publications of the United Nations and some other international organizations are listed and annotated in the publications catalog of Unipub, available from the headquarters office at 1180 Avenue of the Americas, New York, NY 10036, with prices in U.S. dollars. Catalogs and lists of new publications for particular agencies are available on request.

Other organizations (such as Direct Relief International, P.O. Box 30820, Santa Barbara, CA 93105) that have international responsibilities toward child victims but do not disseminate information are not included here; these can be located through international directories of voluntary organizations.

The International Board on Books for Young People (IBBY) is discussed in Chapter 16.

K62 AGENCY FOR INTERNATIONAL DEVELOPMENT (AID) International Development Cooperation Agency

(IDCA), Office of Health, Bureau of Science and Technology, Room 709, SA-18, Washington, DC 20523, (703) 235-8950; Office of Nutrition, Room 320, (703) 235-9062. AID, whose purpose is to provide assistance to developing countries, is active in many areas that affect third-world children. Areas of interest include alleviation of malnutrition; nutrition education; child and infant nutrition; nutrition surveys; and prevention of childhood diseases via immunization and oral rehydration therapy for diarrheal disease. Services are for persons and organizations active in the field of nutrition and health in developing countries. Some services are free. Publications include agency policy statements; annotated bibliographies; and reports of projects, such as *Maternal and Infant Nutrition* (1982), which reports on three years of activity in improving maternal and infant feeding practices.

AID has contractually sponsored two information clearinghouses; one is directed by the American Public Health Association and is discussed in item K64, and the other is directed by Management Sciences for Health, located in Washington, D.C.

Another AID agency concerned indirectly with children is the Office of Women in Development, IDCA, New State, Room 3534, 320 21st St., NW, Washington, DC 20523 (202) 632-3992. Its areas of interest are economic, agricultural, and rural development issues related to the concerns, needs, and roles of women in less-developed countries. It has a library collection of around 6,000 reports, documents, books, and periodicals on women in development issues, arranged by country and covering areas like health, economics, and nutrition that strongly affect children. On-site use can be arranged. Publications include bibliographies, research reports, specific projects, and newsletters. A publications list is available. The staff provides services and publications at no cost, but priority is given to women in less-developed countries and people in government who work directly with these countries.

K63   CENTRO INTERNAZIONALI STUDI FAMIGLIA (CISF)
Via Monte Rosa, 21 Milano 20149, Italy. Telephone: 46 97 251
CISF, established in 1973, is associated with the *Gruppo Periodici* (Publishing Group) of the Societa San Paolo (publisher of the *Famiglia Cristiana*). It is a specialized center for the study, documentation, and promotion of the family, often collaborating with international governmental and nongovernmental organizations. It has a documentation center that collects, selects, and publishes information on the family. Materials from various countries are classified and published in *DOC-CISF*. The library and documentation center are open to the public.

CISF publishes an Italian-language review (six issues/year)—*La Famiglia Oggi*—with summaries in English and French, which typically includes three or four articles on a specific family theme and sections on counseling, CISF activities, international documents on family life, bibliographies, and book reviews. Issues have dealt with topics like sex education, family and work, family and drugs, marriage preparation, and family politics. CISF also publishes Italian-language bibliographies on specific themes, including a substantial 205-page bibliography on juvenile delinquency and deviant behavior of minors. A scientific committee composed of sociologists, psychologists, doctors, theologians, and others is responsible for formulating policy, study, and research.

K64 **CLEARINGHOUSE ON INFANT FEEDING AND MA-TERNAL NUTRITION** (Also known as Centre de Documentation sur la Nourriture du Nouveau-Ne et la Nutrition de la Mere and Centro de Documentacion sobre Alimentacion Infantil y Nutricion Materna.) American Public Health Assn., 1015 Fifteenth St., NW, Washington, DC 20005. (202) 789-5600

The clearinghouse, an international center for information and materials, includes research on breast-feeding, infant feeding, and maternal nutrition, as well as materials on programs, training, and legislation. Documents are classified by subject, country, and author.

It is funded by the Agency for International Development and was established to assist governments and institutions developing workshops of educational programs on infant feeding and maternal nutrition. For these groups, it prepares bibliographies, reading lists, information packets, and briefing materials. It also responds to specific requests for information from individuals by providing lists of references from the collection or the names of persons or institutions that may be able to answer these requests.

Its newsletter, *Mothers and Children: Bulletin on Infant Feeding and Maternal Nutrition,* is issued free three times a year to health practitioners and governments in developing countries. The final page includes a list of resources: publications, materials, training, conferences, and legislation. Other sections include questions and answers, news, articles, summaries of journal articles, program descriptions, and book reviews, all well illustrated.

K65 **DEFENSE FOR CHILDREN INTERNATIONAL** (Also known as Defense des Enfants International and Defensa de los Niños Internacional.) P.O. Box 359, CH-1211 Geneva 4, Switzerland. (022) 20 83 45

The purpose of this international membership organization, founded in July 1979 (the International Year of the Child), is child advocacy at the international level—that is, the promotion of awareness and respect for the fundamental rights of children throughout the world. It accomplishes its purpose through information, studies, reports on cases, situations, issues, and initiatives in the area of child advocacy and through handling individual cases of violation that require international mediation or intervention. This organization attempts to identify, study, and offer solutions in situations where children's rights are not adequately protected. It fosters and assists initiatives at all levels to improve respect for children's rights, and it disseminates information on all aspects of children's rights issues from an international perspective. All individuals (professional and nonprofessional) and organizations (governmental and nongovernmental) are welcome to join or use the facilities of the organization.

Defense for Children International participates in human rights and child welfare information networks to identify organizations that can locate information on child welfare and child rights, acting as the focal point and central address for the referral of cases of child maltreatment that have not found national solutions, such as violations of children's rights in Iran, the disappearance of children in Argentina, or children imprisoned with adults. A documentation service is in the process of being set up. It is the secretariat for international nongovernmental efforts to ensure optimal formulation of the Convention on the Rights of the Child currently being drafted in the United Nations.

Publications include a quarterly information sheet for members; ad hoc publications as needed; and an excellent and informative quarterly, *International Children's Rights Monitor,* which is described more fully in item H79. So far, their *Iketsetseng Series on the Health and Welfare of Children,* published for the World Health Organization, includes an informative publication entitled *Child Labour: A Threat to Health and Development* (1981, 85 pp.).

K66   INFORMATION CENTER ON CHILDREN'S CULTURES
United States Committee for UNICEF, 331 E. 38th St., New York, NY 10016. (212) 686-5522, ext. 402/403

A UNICEF-sponsored group established to introduce American children to children around the world, especially in developing countries, the center is used by teachers, writers, librarians, UNICEF personnel, and media people, but is also open to the public, including children. Its multicultural, multimedia, multilanguage (mostly English) library contains 17,000 books, 15,000 photographs, 50 periodical titles, records, slides, filmstrips, and other media, as well as a realia collection of some 510 games, toys, musical instruments, and children's clothing. The center answers questions and is a major information source on children's cultures. It provides excellent information sheets and bibliographies of well-chosen children's literature for almost all countries and areas of the world. Bibliographies are free with a stamped, self-addressed, legal-size envelope.

Other center materials cover topics such as *Masks Around the World, Making Music Around the World,* and *Food Supply—A Global Perspective.* The center will mail on request its brochure and book lists/information sheets, as well as a catalog of publications and educational material produced by the U.S. Committee for UNICEF. These include excellent color slide sets for children on cultures and global issues; posters; kits; albums; and cassettes of music, games, and books. The committee also distributes films on UNICEF's work, suitable for all age groups. These deal with topics like childhood disability, health and nutrition, and profiles of children's needs in Asia, Africa, Latin America, and the Middle East. A list is available free from UNICEF Films, at the same address.

K67   **INTER-AMERICAN CHILDREN'S INSTITUTE** (Instituto Interamerican del Niño.) 8 de Octubre 2904, Montevideo, Uruguay. (80) 23 13; (80) 12 19

A specialized agency of the Organization of American States (OAS) concerned with all areas related to children; originally founded in 1927 to deal with "problems related to motherhood, childhood, adolescence, and the family in the Americas, and to adopt measures conducive to their solution." Its five technical units include special and preschool education, sociolegal studies, health and drug dependence, data processing, and civil registration and statistics. It is governed through a Directing Council, which includes representatives of all member countries and oversees the implementation of policies set at the Pan-American Child Congress held every four years. Activities include technical assistance, research, training of adults who work with children, improving the collection and comparability of statistics, and promoting the improvement of legislation for child and family protection. Clients include governments in American countries and child and family protection experts and institutions. Publications include the Spanish-language *Boletin,* which does an admirable job of combining research articles and current reporting, as well as technical reports that deal with subjects like early intervention with multihandicapped children, responsibilities of child-development experts working with high-risk children; and English-language reports on *New Trends in Family*

Law and *Outline of the Law of Minors in Latin America.* It has a library of around 10,000 books, as well as pamphlets, periodicals, films, and filmstrips.

K68   **INTERNATIONAL BUREAU OF EDUCATION (IBE)**   15, Route des Morillons, 1218 Grand-Saconnex, Geneva, Switzerland. (022) 98 14 53; Telex 22644
Founded in 1925 as a private organization, IBE became the first intergovernmental education agency in 1929. Since becoming an integral part of Unesco in 1969, it serves all member states as a source of information on comparative education. To this end, it coordinates and publishes its studies on comparative education with other institutions pursuing similar objectives. It maintains an international library and a permanent international exhibition on education. The Documentation and Information Center (IBEDOC) contains 80,000 books, 2,500 periodical titles, 250,000 microfiche, and numerous audiovisual items and is a major documentation and dissemination source that can be accessed by computer. Publications, in English, French, and Spanish (and sometimes other languages), include an acquisitions list; a newsletter on innovations; a quarterly newsletter, *IBEDOC Information;* and an ongoing bibliographic source, *Educational Documentation and Information* (D33). IBE is now producing the *List of Current Bibliographic Sources in Education.* Documents are distributed through Unipub in the United States (Box 433, Murray Hill Sta., New York, NY 10157). A complete list, including national distribution agents, is available on request.

IBE convenes an International Conference on Education at least every two years. Reports from this conference often are listed in the annual *International Yearbook of Education.* For example, the 1982 *Yearbook* contains national conference reports from 1981 on the structures of national education systems.

K69   **INTERNATIONAL CATHOLIC CHILD BUREAU (ICCB)** (Also known as Bureau Catholique de l'Enfance, Oficiana Internacional Catolica de la Infancia, and Internationales Katholisches Buro für das Kind), 65 rue de Lausanne, CH-1202 Geneva, Switzerland. (022) 31 32 48
An international organization founded in Paris in 1948, ICCB groups organizations and individuals committed to serving the interests of children and to respecting the Catholic identity of the organization. It has permanent representatives at the United Nations in New York and Geneva and at Unesco in Paris. It identifies and defends the needs of the child as seen from a Christian perspective, provides a forum for the

exchange of information among those working with children, and serves as child advocate in national and international debates on all issues, including spiritual and moral. It collaborates with other international organizations concerned with children and conducts international conferences and seminars. Topics have included street children, children and publicity, and comparative studies on re-education. The current three-year program (1984–1987) is centered on the theme, the Child and the Spiritual Void. It has a documentation center that collects information on its areas of interest and compiles bibliographies. Some recent topics are *Children of Divorced or Single Parents* (June 1982), *The Child and Death* (August 1982), and *Refugee Children* (August 1982). ICCB has used specialized commissions to work in such areas as handicapped children and religious education of children; some legislation has resulted from its work. Its Charter for Children's Books has provided guidelines in many countries, and it was the initiator and a major force in the International Year of the Child.

Publications include a French quarterly, *Enfants de partout,* and *L'Enfance dans le monde,* which is published three times a year in French and English as an information service for those concerned with child welfare. Approximately half the publication is devoted to internal news from ICCB (including reports from representatives and the United Nations), the other half goes beyond ICCB to report or announce world events, relevant meetings, services, books, periodicals, and films.

K70 **INTERNATIONAL CHILDREN'S CENTER (ICC)** (Also known as Centre International de l'Enfance and Centro Internacional de la Infancia.) Chateau de Longchamp, Bois de Boulogne 75016, Paris, France. (506) 79 92

The International Children's Center was founded in Paris in 1949, following negotiations between Unesco and the French government, as a new type of agency devoted entirely to improving the well-being and health of the child and the family, especially in developing countries. It is concerned with all aspects of the child (medical and nonmedical) from conception to age 20. As a consequence, ICC resources are "at the disposal" of specialized agencies and sections of the United Nations (such as the World Health Organization), as well as national institutions for maternal and child care. Its clientele are all who share an interest in children's problems, including doctors, health workers, social workers, and educators.

ICC's basic working concepts involve the continuity of human development (with an emphasis on the delicate periods of childhood and adolescence), the necessity of a global approach to the problems of childhood and adolescence, and the accordance of priorities to activities for family promotion and community development in national plans for economic and social development. Its departments include one for education and training (its major activity); an epidemiological pilot station; and a department of information, documentation, and publications. The documentation center includes a multinational, multilanguage library of 9,000 books and 870 periodicals covering all aspects of childhood, adolescence, motherhood, and the family—all indexed and abstracted. Its bibliographic card file, with 500,000 references, answers worldwide requests and is now being converted to an on-line data base, BASE D'INFORMATION ROBERT DEBRÉ (J15). New references (around 1,200 per month) are now processed on magnetic tape; the data base is available through the supplier G. CAM-Serveur Tour Maine Montparnasse, 33, avenue des Maine, F-75755 Paris, Cedex 15, France (53 87 072), as well as through the documentation service. The Department of Information also collaborates with technical services to publish *Bibliographic Bulletins;* three are published regularly on the following topics: prevention of famine and malnutrition, immunizations, and family health and family planning. Another, on childhood accidents, is published in collaboration with the World Health Organization's Regional Office for Europe.

Other activities of ICC are multinational teaching programs, courses, seminars, surveys, and publishing. Its technical reports in English, French, and Spanish (often on topics like breast-feeding, screening and integration of handicapped children, and family planning) are frequently distributed to national agencies or to offices of UNICEF and the World Health Organization or prepared collaboratively with organizations such as the U.S. Department of Health and Human Services. Some of these reports are issued at several levels (for mass media, policy-makers, health workers, and academics); ICC is particularly concerned with developing information on early childhood. Since 1950, ICC has published from one to five books or monographs each year. It also publishes two periodicals, *Children in the Tropics* and *Courrier,* that are discussed in items H30 and H39, respectively.

K71   **INTERNATIONAL   LABOUR   OFFICE   (ILO)** (Also known as Bureau International du Travail [BIT] and Oficina Internacional del Trabajo [OIT].) Central Library and Documentation Branch, CH-1211 Geneva 22, Switzerland. (022) 99 86 75
Founded in 1919 "to advance the cause of social justice" as a contribution to ensuring universal and lasting peace, ILO has long been concerned with child labor as part of promoting human rights in the labor

field, as well as assisting in creating employment, providing training, and improving the conditions of work and life. The ILO has a tripartite structure that involves workers, employers, and governments in all its constituent bodies. In 1946, it became the first specialized agency associated with the United Nations.

The ILO library includes 1 million books, reports, and bound volumes and 8,000 periodicals; in 1965, it acquired a computerized catalog, the LABORDOC data base, which grows at the rate of 600 items per month. LABORDOC is used to produce a monthly publication, *International Labour Documentation.* (In the United States, LABORDOC is available through SDC's ORBIT; in Canada, it is accessible through the International Development Research Centre.) The library will perform searches for qualified users. With a mandate to conserve and disseminate information, it tries to reach all policymakers, planners, researchers, teachers, and practitioners whose concerns are related to the world of work. It maintains special collections (reference, statistics, periodicals, and files on particular nations) and microfiche services (library catalog, ILO publications and documents, and a register of periodicals).

The monthly library publication, *International Labour Documentation,* contains bibliographic references with English-language abstracts and descriptors to recent acquisitions in the ILO library and separate subject indexes in English, French, and Spanish. It provides worldwide coverage of labor laws, industrial relations, vocational training, working conditions, and labor-related aspects of other fields.

ILO publishes many monographs, pamphlets, and journals, including the *Year Book of Labour Statistics* (trilingual), *Legislative Services, Social and Labour Bulletin, Bulletin of Labour Statistics,* and the *International Labour Review* (bimonthly, $28.50/year). The last publication is worth consulting for articles on child labor. A recent news bulletin, *Women at Work* (two issues/year, $11.50), is issued by the Office of Women Workers; it includes reports on subjects like maternity leave and working mothers. A catalog of publications is available free from ILO publications, ILO, CH-1211 Geneva 22, Switzerland.

K72 **INTERNATIONAL REFUGEE INTEGRATION RESOURCE CENTRE (IRIRC)** (Also known as Centre International d'Echanges d'Informations sur l'Integration des Refugies.) 5–7 avenue de la Pais, CH-1202 Geneva, Switzerland. (022) 31 02 61

IRIRC is a computer-based documentation and information center charged with the responsibility of gathering, storing, and disseminating information on all aspects of refugee reception, resettlement, and integration, including child refugees. Its primary responsibilities are to intergovernmental, governmental, and nongovernmental refugee-assisting organizations, but it anticipates that its data bank will be available for computer searching by researchers and the staffs of academic institutions in the near future. In the meantime, IRIRC issues the well-done *Refugee Abstracts* (G43) and is compiling a directory of organizations that assist refugees, as well as a directory of experts and a thesaurus. IRIRC is a project of the United Nations High Commissioner for Refugees.

K73 **INTERNATIONAL UNION FOR CHILD WELFARE (IUCW)** (Also known as l'Union Internationale de Protection de l'Enfance.) 1 rue de Varembe, CH-1211 Geneva 20, Switzerland. (022) 34 12 20

IUCW, founded in 1920, is an international nongovernmental organization dedicated to the service of children and adolescents throughout the world; in fact, the original five-point Declaration of the Rights of the Child was promulgated by IUCW in 1923. It is a federation of national public and private institutions working in the fields of family and child welfare, with 191 member organizations from 90 countries. It helps these organizations pool experience and exchange information through regional and international meetings, advisory groups, and cooperative or comparative international studies in areas like adoption, children of migrant workers, and early childhood education. It offers assistance in child advocacy, training of child workers, conference planning, and the publication and dissemination of information. Its library, the International Documentation Centre, has around 15,000 books and 250 periodical titles and issues a *Library Supplement* to IUCW's excellent quarterly, *International Child Welfare Review* (available in English, French, and Spanish—see item H80). Occasional papers include *The Protection of Children in Armed Conflicts.*

The priorities of IUCW's recently formed International Standing Committee on Child Abuse (Commission Internationale Permanente de l'Enfance Maltraitee) are to coordinate international activities in child abuse; to identify agencies dealing with child abuse at the national and international levels; to gather, disseminate, and publish information; and to motivate and assist nations in developing child abuse treatment and prevention services.

K74 **INTERNATIONAL UNION OF FAMILY ORGANISATIONS (IUFO)** (Also known as Union International des Organismes Familiaux.) 28 Place Saint-Georges, 75441 Paris, Cedex 09, France. (878) 07 59, (281) 19 46

An umbrella organization that contains more than 300 government and nongovernment organizations from some 60 countries. Members range from family associations and movements to research centers and social security offices, all of which share the common aim of improving the living conditions of families. IUFO participates in projects in more than 100 countries, working largely through technical commissions and study groups in such areas as education, family policy, family movements, family action among the working class, and rural families. It holds regional meetings for representatives from continents or groups of countries; since 1948, it has held one or more annual meetings on significant topics ranging from juvenile delinquency (Geneva, 1948) to child nutrition (Dakar, 1980). Publications include reports of these conferences and reports of study groups. IUFO is now planning to establish an affiliated International Family Institute in Madrid, which will include research and publications on family matters, as well as an International Documentation Center of publications relating to social work for the benefit of the family.

K75 **NATIONAL CHILDREN'S BUREAU (NCB)** 8 Wakley St., Islington, London EC1V 7QE, England. (01) 278-9441

An independent voluntary organization consisting primarily of groups concerned with children but also open to individuals, NCB has an interdisciplinary perspective on the well-being of children in the family, school, and society. Although it is British, it has a global perspective in practice. Its activities include improving communication and cooperation among education, medicine, and social work professionals and between voluntary and official services; evaluating existing services; encouraging new developments and new knowledge; and making available existing knowledge on children's developments and needs. Its quarterly publication, *Concern,* reports on bureau activities and includes articles arising from research and development work of NCB and other groups.

NCB's Information Service and Library—open to visitors—includes 6,000 books and pamphlets and 100 periodical titles; photocopies are available at cost. Exemplary telephone reference services are provided to members. NCB undertakes an immense amount of direct and bibliographic research in child health, welfare, and education on topics like foster care, child abuse, and stepchildren. Abstracts and summaries of research and reports are issued as two-page *Highlights.*

Other information packets—available at a modest cost—include *Film-lists* of films about children, arranged by topic (currently 29 lists are available on topics including adolescence, education, ethnic minorities and race relations, mental handicaps, physical handicaps, and preschooling). *Booklists* (usually around four pages long) contain up-to-date references of articles and books on 120 separate topics ranging from accidents to youth work. A new *Briefing Papers* series includes ideas, information sources, and a bibliography of books and media. Titles include *Leaving Residential Care, Latchkey Schemes,* and *Respite Care. Organisations Lists* include addresses, telephone numbers, and brief annotations of organizations in 13 areas, such as care and development of children, children's rights, and so on. The Voluntary Council for Handicapped Children also issues its own set of *Factsheets.*

In recent years, NCB has continued and published on the National Child Development Study, a unique longitudinal study of 16,000 children in England, Scotland, and Wales born between March 3 and 9, 1958. Other major studies have dealt with children growing up in one-parent families, adoptive children, and gifted children. NCB has completed a major evaluation of preschool centers and sponsored an inquiry into the problem of handicapped children and their families that resulted in the formation of the Voluntary Council for Handicapped Children.

The bureau has published more than 70 books and 320 articles. Recent titles include *A Fairer Future for Children* (Macmillan, 1980) and *The Needs of Children* (2nd Edition, Hutchinson, 1980). One helpful booklet, *Children in the UK: Signposts to Statistics* (1982), lists key sources under 24 topics. Reference books include the out-of-print *Index of Documentary Films about Children* (3rd Edition, 1977) and *Sources of Information about Children* (1974). It also has designed and produced developmental record charts to map a child's individual progress from birth.

K76   **NATIONAL FOUNDATION FOR EDUCATIONAL RE-SEARCH IN ENGLAND AND WALES (NFER)** The Mere, Upton Park, Slough, Berkshire SL1 2DQ, England. Slough 74123

Areas of concern for NFER are education, psychology, psychometrics, and sociology in support of applied research in public-sector education in England and Wales. It conducts and disseminates information on such research and cooperates with national and international organizations. NFER maintains a source file of other educational research projects in the United Kingdom that from time to time has been compiled into various registers. NFER research and other British research is reported in the foundation's newsletter, *Educational Research News,* and its journal, *Educational Research.* A register of United Kingdom research on special education is in preparation.

NFER's library contains 12,500 books and 400 periodical titles, with computer access to BLAISE-LINE for the *British Education Index*. What NFER offers is detailed in a series of around 20 *Research Information* brochures that cover areas like research and testing, statistics, computer services, information services, and educational policy information. Two particularly relevant brochures are *Teaching Styles and Pupil Performance at the Primary Level* (RI/31) and *Information for Parental Choice* (RI/38).

The primary concern of NFER's research is education; recent publications deal with nursery education, early school experiences, the transition to school, and the needs of handicapped and disabled children. Its publishing house is NFER-Nelson (Darville House, 2 Oxford Road E., Windsor, Berkshire SL4 1DF, England), which also publishes some works of the National Children's Bureau (K75). Recent titles include *Children with Disabilities and Their Families: A Review of Research* (1982), *The Coordination of Services for Children Under Five* (1982), and *The Education of Three-to-Eight Year Olds in Europe in the Eighties* (1982). Such reports often include American and European practices, experiences, and research. NFER-Nelson also publishes, distributes, and assists in developing educational/psychological tests and other assessment procedures.

K77 **TEACHING AIDS AT LOW COST (TALC)** Institute of Child Health, 30 Guildford St., London WC1N 1EH, England. Mail order address: P.O. Box 49, St. Albans, Hertfordshire AL1 4AX, England. (0727) 53869

A charity affiliated with the Institute of Child Health to provide low-cost aids for teaching child health to child health workers in developing countries. Its scope includes nutrition, health planning and primary health care, and development, and it provides highly illustrated manuals for rural medicine. Medical items, sold at very low costs, include printed materials; slides and slide sets on topics like diarrhea, malnutrition, and child development; and excellent weight and growth charts. A catalog is available on request.

K78 **UNITED NATIONS CHILDREN'S FUND (UNICEF)** (Also known as Fonds des Nationas Unies pour l'Enfance and Fondo de las Naciones Unidas para la Infancia.) 866 U.N. Plaza, New York, NY 10017. (212) 754-1234

Created in 1946 by the United Nations General Assembly as the United Nations International Children's Emergency Fund, UNICEF was established on a short-term basis to meet the emergency needs of suffering children in post-war Europe after the phasing-out of activities of the U.N. Relief and Rehabilitation Agency (UNRRA). In 1953, UNICEF was given an indefinite mandate to carry on long-range programs for children of the developing countries of Africa, Asia, and Latin America. The organization's name was changed to The United Nations Children's Fund, but the acronym UNICEF was maintained. In 1959, the General Assembly adopted the Declaration of the Rights of the Child, which provided a framework for the broadening of UNICEF activities to include support for education, social services, and training. In 1979, UNICEF was the lead agency for the International Year of the Child and subsequently was given responsibility by the General Assembly for drawing attention to needs and problems common to children in both developing and industrialized countries. Its primary focus and all of its program activities, however, remain concentrated on the situation of children in developing countries.

UNICEF's major effort is directed toward improving the survival, health, and development prospects of children through a focus on effective actions that can be undertaken at a cost manageable by any community and society. Crucial to the spreading of these actions and improvement is the involvement of communities and families in planning and support. This community-based services approach relies on workers selected from and chosen by the community—linked by paraprofessional or other intermediate supervisory staff to the technical and financial resources of the national services.

The fund is financed entirely by voluntary contributions from governments and private sources. Typically, the major contributions to UNICEF projects come from the country being assisted. UNICEF collaborates with other organizations in advocacy, fund-raising, and program implementation.

UNICEF staff numbers approximately 2,400, with some 1,900 stationed in the field. There are 87 field offices, with headquarters in New York and Geneva. UNICEF currently works with the governments of more than 110 developing countries. Ongoing publications, most of which are available in English, French, and Spanish, include the annual *State of the World's Children Report* and a biennial review, *Les Carnets de l'Enfance/Assignment Children*. Other recent publications include *Reaching Children and Women of the Urban Poor, Current Views on Nutrition Strategies, UNICEF and the Household Fuels Crisis,* and *The Impact of the World Recession on Children*.

The United States Committee for UNICEF, at 331 E. 38th St., New York, NY 10016, produces a free quarterly, *News of the World's Children,* that reports UNICEF activities.

K79 **WORLD HEALTH ORGANIZATION (WHO)** CH-1211
Geneva 27, Switzerland. (022) 91 22 27; Telex 27821
A specialized agency of the United Nations with primary responsibility
for international health matters and public health, WHO serves as an information exchange for the health professions in 164 member states. It
promotes the development of comprehensive health services; the prevention and control of disease; and the improvement of health personnel, planning, and research. Areas most relevant to the well-being of
children include maternal and child health projects and research, provision of safe water supplies, and prevention of malnutrition. The Division of Family Health issues publications such as *The Incidence of Low
Birth Weight: A Critical View of Available Information* (1980), and a
WHO Working Group in Faro, Portugal wrote *Early Detection of Handicap in Children* (1979). *The World Health Statistics Quarterly* and
World Health Statistics Annual contain health and vital statistics on children and infants. WHO's research activities can be followed in the *Bulletin of the World Health Organization,* and the *WHO Chronicle* provides a
monthly record. *World Health* magazine is published by WHO for the
lay reader (10 issues/year). Publications or catalogs of publications of
the Pan American Health Organization (regional office of WHO for the
Americas) and WHO can be obtained from the WHO Publications Center, 49 Sheridan Ave., Albany, NY 12210.

13 / Health, Handicapping Conditions, and Family Concerns

This chapter covers a few organizations whose major or exclusive concerns are health, nutrition, handicapping conditions, and family well-being. Although there is considerable overlap among these areas, and the concerns of the organizations frequently coincide, I have used these divisions to facilitate browsing. Please read all sections or use the index to locate all organizations. The groups in this chapter, like those in Chapter 12, generally appreciate stamped, self-addressed envelopes and/or a modest contribution in return for their hard-pressed services.

HEALTH AND NUTRITION ORGANIZATIONS AND CLEARINGHOUSES

This section deals with the physical aspects of child well-being; it includes lay and professional organizations and government agencies that function as information sources or are willing to provide information relating to child health, nutrition, or medicine for children from conception through age 12. Since birth defects are considered *the* major child medical problem in this country according to such knowledgeable sources as the March of Dimes, I have included organizations concerned with child life from conception. Similarly, nutrition is considered by some to be the major environmental factor in child health. Regretfully, many competent organizations that concentrate on one single childhood disease or work only in one locality or region have been omitted because of space considerations; however, these can be located through the National Health Information Clearinghouse (L27) and the National Referral Center (K56), as well as through the directories of handicapping conditions and health discussed here and in Chapter 10. Some international health organizations are included in the international section of Chapter 12.

L1   **ALLIANCE FOR PERINATAL RESEARCH SERVICES (APRS)**   Box 6358, Alexandria, VA 22306. (703) 765-6300
An interdisciplinary group interested in consultation, research, literature, and services relating to pregnancy, childbearing, and child rearing. APRS has books, pamphlets, periodicals, audiotapes, a speaker's bureau, workshops, and in-service training programs.

L2   **AMERICAN ACADEMY OF PEDIATRICS (AAP)** P.O. Box 927, Elk Grove Village, IL 60007. (312) 228-5005, (800) 433-9016. (Office of Government Liaison: 1331 Pennsylvania Ave. NW, Suite 721 N, Washington, DC 20004-1703. (202) 662-7460, (800) 336-5475.)
A membership association of physicians certified in the care of infants, children, and adolescents, founded in 1930 to serve as an advocate for children and to ensure a high caliber of pediatric practice. AAP now has more than 27,000 fellows in 66 countries. Its purpose is "the attainment by all children of their full potential for physical, emotional, and social health," carried out through the establishment of standards and liaison with other groups concerned with children. Significant contributions include the creation of a separate administrative unit for child health programs, the development of guidelines for immunization, the creation of public and legislative awareness of lead paint hazards, and participation in Project Head Start. Their public education campaigns and their excellent inexpensive publications for health professionals and the general public are of continuing value. Research projects pursued by AAP have studied many issues on how child health care is financed, organized, and delivered—particularly to high-risk or low-income children.
    Some valuable titles for professionals are *Handbook of Common Poisonings in Children* (2nd Edition, 1983, 180 pp., $15); *Sports Medicine Health Care for Young Athletes* (1983, 326 pp., $15), *Adoption of*

Children (3rd Edition, 1976, 124 pp., $10); *Pediatric Nutrition Handbook* (1984, price not set), *Guidelines for Perinatal Care* (1983, price not set); *Hospital Care of Children and Youth* (3rd Edition, 1978, 120 pp., $15); *Recommendations of Day Care Centers for Infants and Children* (1980, 66 pp., $10); and *Demographic and Socioeconomic Fact Book on Child Health Care* (1980, 88 pp., $10). AAP's *Report of the Committee on Infectious Diseases* (19th Edition, 1982, 450 pp., $15), known as the *Red Book* since it was first published in 1938, is a quick reference guide to the control of more than 100 communicable diseases that provides summaries of diseases, recommended immunization schedules, and drug dosages. These manuals are written by committees of pediatric experts and are published as quality paperbacks to ensure widespread distribution. Reprints of articles in *Pediatrics* (H127) also are distributed at low cost. Topics include accident prevention, adolescence, drugs, environmental hazards, government and children, illness and handicapping conditions, immunization, learning disabilities, medical ethics, neonatal care, nutrition, pediatric practice, physical fitness and sports, radiology, and screening.

Patient education materials (mostly pamphlets, newsletters, brochures, and posters) are sold in lots of 100 to physicians for distribution to patients. These include the excellent *Child Health Record;* first aid charts; and materials on accidents, safety, and community health. Lists of publications and a brochure are available on request.

L3   **AMERICAN ALLIANCE FOR HEALTH, PHYSICAL EDUCATION, RECREATION, AND DANCE (AAHPERD)** 1900 Association Dr., Reston, VA 22091. (703) 476-3460, 476-3481

The concerns of this membership organization include health, leisure, therapeutic recreation, safety, physical movement, motor activities, and dance and the application of all these to the handicapped. It is an exemplary research organization, which diligently collects, organizes, and publishes in its areas of interest. (Typically, materials on childhood movement and development of motor skills are less thoroughly treated elsewhere.) AAHPERD's 1984–1985 publications catalog (available on request) provides annotations, subject organization, and cross-references for more than 200 print and audiovisual items, including bibliographies and compilations of research. A few of its excellent titles are *Testing for Impaired, Disabled, or Handicapped Individuals* (1975, $5.50); *Children Learn Physical Skills* (1974, 2 vols.: *Birth to Three* and *Four to Six,* $8.35 each); *Movement Activities for Places and Spaces* (1982, $5.20); and *Movement Education for Preschool Children* (1980,

$7.90). Their six-volume *Basic Stuff Series I* (1981, $34.10) includes *Exercise Physiology, Kinesiology, Motor Learning, Psychosocial Aspects of Physical Education, Humanities in Physical Education,* and *Motor Development.* The three-volume *Basic Stuff Series II* (1981, $17.80) deals with *Early Childhood (Ages 3–8), Childhood (Ages 9–12),* and *Adolescence (Ages 13–18).* Periodicals include *Health Education; Journal of Physical Education, Recreation, and Dance;* and *Research Quarterly for Exercise and Sport.*

L4   **AMERICAN ASSOCIATION OF PSYCHIATRIC SER-VICES FOR CHILDREN (AAPSC)**   1522 K St., NW, Suite 1112, Washington, DC 20005. (202) 833-9775
A multidisciplinary group of child mental health agencies and professionals founded to ensure high-quality standards for child clinical services, to provide a national focus for interdisciplinary cooperation, to support research projects, and to provide a clearinghouse for information relevant to child mental health. AAPSC serves as the Washington advocate for its membership and services to children and monitors and reviews proposed legislation in its quarterly newsletter. It answers inquiries and provides consulting services for professionals.

L5   **AMERICAN COLLEGE OF NURSE-MIDWIVES**   1522 K St., NW, Suite 1120, Washington, DC 20005. (202) 347-5445
A professional organization of certified nurse-midwives whose goal is the "improvement of services for mothers and babies" through ensuring the quality of education and practice of nurse-midwives by such mechanisms as accreditation of its educational programs, examination and certification of its graduates, definitions of functions, standards and qualifications for the practice of nurse-midwifery, written guidelines for quality, provisions for continuing education, and research. Its books, pamphlets, and periodicals are available at reasonable prices.

L6   **AMERICAN FOUNDATION FOR MATERNAL AND CHILD HEALTH**   30 Beekman Pl., New York, NY 10022. (212) 759-5510
Collects information on the effects of prenatal drugs and obstetric management on mothers and infants, testifies in this area, and sponsors interdisciplinary conferences. Has a substantial library of clippings and articles available on-site.

L7   **AMERICAN PUBLIC HEALTH ASSOCIATION (APHA)**   1015 15th St., NW, Washington, DC 20005. (202) 789-5600

A membership organization that covers all disciplines and specialties in the public health spectrum. Its *Washington News Letter* provides a summary of health-related legislative activities from Washington and federal agencies. The monthly *American Journal of Public Health* includes commentary and articles, as well as an excellent structured book section. The monthly newspaper, *The Nation's Health,* also reports on legislation and policy issues. APHA has 24 special sections, including Maternal and Child Health and School Health Education and Services.

L8   **AMERICAN SCHOOL HEALTH ASSOCIATION (ASHA)**
P.O. Box 708, Kent, OH 44240. (216) 678-1601
A national membership organization for all professionals concerned with the health of school-age children, it seeks to promote comprehensive and constructive school health programs, incorporating health services, health education, and a healthful school environment. It works with school systems, individuals, corporations, and other agencies to gather, coordinate, and distribute health information. It develops teaching guidelines, sets standards for health education, and participates in health education studies. Publications include *School Health in America* (3rd Edition, 1981, $5.00); *Health Instruction: Guidelines for Planning Health Education Programs, K–12* (1983, $8.95); and *A Multidisciplinary Approach to Learning Disability* (1978, $5.95).

L9   **ASSOCIATION FOR THE CARE OF CHILDREN'S HEALTH (ACCH)**   3615 Wisconsin Ave., NW, Washington, DC 20016. (202) 244-1801
A multidisciplinary membership organization founded in 1965 with the intent of fostering and promoting the well-being of children and families in health care settings through education, planning, research, and interaction. Its membership now includes parents and concerned consumers, administrators, architects, various child care specialists, and all types of health professionals. It is an international organization, but most of its 3,700 members reside in the United States and Canada. There are more than 45 affiliates working locally. Special study sections deal with areas like infancy, adolescent care, ambulatory and critical care, chronic conditions, design and environment, research, and parent and family issues.

Its publications include an excellent informative newsletter, *ACCH Network; Children's Health Care* is the official journal. It also prepares and distributes inexpensive posters; pamphlets for parents, teachers, and teens (available individually or at bulk rates); and books, directories, and bibliographies on various aspects of child health care. Some useful titles include *Directory of Child Life Activity Programs in North America* (1981, 69 pp., $5), which provides information on more than 325 programs. *Directory of Hospital Psychosocial Policies and Programs* (1982, 110 pp., $8) lists policies and programs in 286 children's hospitals and hospitals with pediatric residencies in the United States and Canada. *Research Booklet: A Directory of Projects and People Involved in Psychosocially-oriented Children's Health Research* (1984, 59 pp., $5) summarizes current research of ACCH members.

Some bibliographies are *The Adolescent and Health Care: An Annotated Bibliography* (1982, 36 pp., $6) and *The Child and Health Care: A Bibliography* (1982, 75 pp., $7). Other publications provide suggestions and guidelines for activity programs, references on health care, ethical perspectives for professionals, and information for parents. ACCH is the founder of Children and Hospitals Week, a public education campaign that was started in 1981 to increase public, parental, and professional knowledge of the needs of children in the health care system. Other ACCH activities include parent-network training and technical assistance to staffs of hospitals, school systems, and libraries to sensitize them to the needs of sick or handicapped children and to help them work with parents to develop local programs.

L10   **CHILD AMPUTEE PROSTHETICS PROJECT**   University of California, 100 Veteran Ave., Los Angeles, CA 90024. (213) 825-5201

A multidisciplinary treatment center for congenital limb deficiency and acquired amputation for children under age 21 that includes the services of physicians, occupational and physical therapists, prosthetists, and social workers. Regardless of geographic location or financial condition, it accepts anyone with a skeletal deficiency of the extremities as a continuing patient. Its textbook, *The Limb Deficient Child* (1982), is available from C. C Thomas for $32.50. Single copies of a pamphlet, *The Child With a Limb Deficiency: A Guide for Parents* (1979), are available at a nominal cost.

L11   **CHILDREN IN HOSPITALS**   31 Wilshire Park, Needham, MA 02192.

A nonprofit membership organization of parents and health care professionals that attempts to educate all those concerned with the need for continued and ample contact between parents and children when either is hospitalized. It encourages hospitals to adopt flexible visiting policies and to provide live-in accommodations when possible. The $5.00 membership fee includes an informative newsletter on issues relating to children's hospitalization and injuries. Its brochures, available for $0.20 each, list references for books and articles and suggestions for handling hospitalizations. Children in Hospitals offers discounts on books and brochures dealing with hospitalization and has a survey of hospital policies.

L12   **CHILDREN'S NUTRITION RESEARCH CENTER**   Baylor College of Medicine, Texas Children's Hospital, 6621 Fanin, Houston, TX 77030. (713) 791-3200, 790-4796

A national facility of the U.S. Department of Agriculture Agricultural Research Service, whose research mission is to develop precise methods for investigating nutrient requirements for infants and for investigating relationships between nutrition, growth, and development. Beyond that, it seeks to quantify nutritional standards for dietary intake and for measuring nutritional status in pregnant and lactating women and of children from conception through adolescence. It has attracted scientists from around the world.

L13   **CONSUMER PRODUCT SAFETY COMMISSION (CPSC)**   Washington DC 20007. (Street address: 5401 Westbard Ave., Bethesda, MD 20016.) (800) 638-CPSC; (800) 492-8363 in Maryland; (800) 638-8333 in Hawaii, Alaska, Virgin Islands, and Puerto Rico

Evaluates the safety of products sold to the public, with jurisdiction over more than 15,000 consumer products; develops safety standards; and provides a hot line for obtaining safety information or reporting hazardous products. It will provide printed materials on different aspects of consumer safety on request. Areas relating to children include crib design; a CPSC toy manufacturer holiday safety program designed to help consumers select appropriate toys; a smoke detector campaign; and investigation of ways to cooperate with industry to reduce children's carcinogen exposure from rubber and plastic children's products. Works with industry groups, such as the Juvenile Products Manufacturers Association, to set voluntary standards and seeks mandatory regulations when this cannot be done satisfactorily.

A most valuable product commissioned by CPSC and prepared by the Highway Safety Research Institute of the University of Michigan at Ann Arbor is *Anthropometry of Infants, Children, and Youths to Age 18 for Product Safety Design* (1977), a massive 638-page study of 87 standard traditional and functional body measurements taken by anthropometrists on a representative sampling of infants, children, and youths aged 2 weeks to 18 years. This document reports summary statistics for

16 age groups, with photographs and illustrations and data on deviations for males, females, and combined groups. This depository publication is available in libraries that collect government documents and from the Society of Automatic Engineers, 400 Commonwealth Dr., Warrendale, PA 15096 for $27.50 (paperback).

L14   FOOD AND NUTRITION INFORMATION CENTER (FNIC) U.S. Department of Agriculture, Human Nutrition Information Service, National Agricultural Library Bldg., Beltsville, MD 20705. (301) 344-3719

This center acquires books, journals, and audiovisuals on human nutrition, food technology, and food science management at all levels, from children's materials to industry reports and sophisticated professional information. Audiovisuals include motion pictures, filmstrips, slides, videocassettes, transparencies, posters, charts, and games. All these are indexed in AGRICOLA, the bibliographic data base discussed in item J13. The Food and Nutrition microfiche program consists of the Base Collection (1,057 105mm × 148mm microfiche, $375) and the 1983 update (1,176 microfiche, $2,825).

They also are cited in the quarterly *Food and Nutrition Resource Guide* (1983– , $95/year), which similarly covers print and nonprint materials at all levels. Relevant areas are nutrition education, children's books, curricula, anthropometry, world health, and dietary goals. In addition, these items have been compiled into *Audiovisual Resources in Food and Nutrition* (F6) and the *Food and Nutrition Bibliography* (distributed by Oryx Press, 2214 N. Central Ave. at Encanto, Phoenix, AZ 85018).

Because of budget restrictions, FNIC has had to limit its lending services to federal and state government agencies (state-level personnel only); faculty of colleges and universities; libraries and information centers; research institutions; school districts and individual schools; nutrition education and training-program staffs; head start and day care staffs; personnel with the Supplemental Food Program for Women, Infants, and Children (WIC); Commodity Supplemental Food (CSF); and cooperative extension at the federal, state, and county levels.

L15   FOOD AND NUTRITION SERVICE U.S. Department of Agriculture, 3101 Park Center Dr., Alexandria, VA 22302. (703) 756-3281

This agency provides food assistance to eligible participants to enable them to purchase a greater variety of foods to improve their diets. It also helps provide food service to children in schools, day care homes, child care institutions, recreational centers, and residential summer camps. It provides specified nutritious food supplements to pregnant and nursing women and children up to five years old and donates foods to various food program outlets.

Publications of the Food and Nutrition Service of the U.S. Department of Agriculture are available while the supply lasts from the U.S. Government Printing Office and free from regional offices of the Food and Nutrition Service. Some titles (with Food and Nutrition Service ordering numbers) are *Child Care Food Program* (PA-1299), *Food Chart—Child Care Food Program* (PA-1165), and *How WIC Helps—Eating for You and Your Baby* (PA-1198).

L16   **FOOD RESEARCH AND ACTION CENTER (FRAC)** 1319 F St., NW, Suite 500, Washington, DC 20004. (202) 393-5060
Organized in 1970 as a nonprofit law firm and advocacy center to work with the poor and near-poor to alleviate hunger and malnutrition in the United States. With a staff of nutritionists, attorneys, and community workers, FRAC works primarily with federal food programs, including food stamps, child care food, school lunch and breakfast, and WIC programs, although it increasingly works at the state and local levels. As an advocacy agency, it monitors programs and supplies information to Congress, community groups, and the general public. Its monthly newspaper, *Foodlines* ($20/year), provides a broad focus on hunger and economic issues, with current information on food programs and budget issues. Its *Guides* and *Profiles* of food programs are practical, clear, and informative. Titles include *FRAC's Guide to Quality School Lunch and Breakfast Programs* (1982, $2.00); *The Supplemental Food Program for Women, Infants, and Children (WIC: A Success Story)* (1981, $0.50); and *FRAC's Guide to State Legislation* (1983, $10.00).

L17   **HUMAN GROWTH FOUNDATION**   4930 W. 77th St., P.O. Box 20253, Minneapolis, MN 55420. (612) 831-2780
A voluntary, nonprofit organization composed of physicians, concerned parents, and friends of children with growth problems, dedicated to helping medical science understand the process of growth, particularly dwarfism. It supports research, training, and treatment programs and is a clearinghouse for families who face growth problems and who need medical or financial aid or moral support. The Human Growth Foundation publishes a bimonthly newsletter, *Human Growth Ink,* that includes reports on research and activities. Its pamphlets cover topics like *Patterns of Growth, Growth Hormone Deficiency,* and *Achondroplasia* ($0.20 each) and *Short Stature and Dwarfism* ($0.05).

L18   **THE HUMAN LACTATION CENTER LTD.**   666 Sturges Highway, Westport, CT 06880. (203) 259-5995
The Human Lactation Center, incorporated as a nonprofit membership organization in 1975, is funded largely through publication sales, contributions, and grants. Its major areas of concern are the social patterns of breast-feeding and weaning and the relationship of lactation to ovulation. Its major activities are field work with mothers and children ' and research, teaching, and publishing on maternal and infant feeding practices, childbirth, lactation, and natural methods of family planning. It maintains an extensive library on these subjects.

The center publishes occasional papers and a newsletter, *The Lactation Review* (single issues, $3.75), that includes scholarly, interesting, clearly written articles on such topics as contaminants of breast milk, charts on drugs for nursing mothers, weaning practices, the politics of breast-feeding, conference reports, book and film reviews, and bibliographies. Other publications include *The Tender Gift: Breastfeeding* (now published by Schocken Books) and *Breastfeeding and Food Policy in a Hungry World* (Academic Press).

Current pursuits include national and international consultation with governments, industry, and medical institutions; conferences on breast-feeding for hospitals; and study of the relationship between lactation and reproduction for researchers in anthropology, nutrition, and public health.

L19   **INTERNATIONAL ASSOCIATION OF PARENTS & PROFESSIONALS FOR SAFE ALTERNATIVES IN CHILDBIRTH (NAPSAC)**   P.O. Box 428, Marble Hill, MO 63764. (314) 238-2010
A membership forum to promote education on the principles of natural childbirth by facilitating communication and cooperation among parents, medical professionals, and childbirth educators. It is particularly concerned with assisting parents-to-be in assuming more personal responsibility for pregnancy, childbirth, infant care, and child rearing. It works for the establishment of family-centered maternity care in hospitals and for the establishment of maternity and childbearing centers and safe home birth programs. NAPSAC has a certification program for maternity services and compiles the annual *Directory of Alternative Birth Services and Consumer Guide* (1982, $5.95), which includes 4,500 names and addresses of alternative health care professionals, birth centers, and childbirth educators. NAPSAC serves as a source of information to hospitals, home birth services, government agencies, professional organizations, and news media. Members receive a quarterly

newsletter, *NAPSAC News,* and discounts on other well-researched publications that include materials on childbirth, nutrition, breast-feeding, children's books on new babies, and miscellaneous titles (on fathering, circumcision, and the like).

L20   JUVENILE DIABETES FOUNDATION (JDF) 23 E. 26th St., New York, NY 10010. (212) 689-2860
Established in 1970, JDF raises funds for the support of research on diabetes and provides educational programs and information on juvenile diabetes. Local volunteers offer group counseling and educational lectures. Publications include pamphlets and fact sheets on symptoms, problems encountered in treatment, insulin reactions, and the like. A quarterly newsletter, *Dimensions in Diabetes,* reports on activities and research.

L21   LA LECHE LEAGUE INTERNATIONAL (LLL) 9616 Minneapolis Ave., Franklin Park, IL 60131. (612) 455-7730
An international organization founded 25 years ago by seven mothers to provide information, encouragement, and support to mothers who wanted to nurse their babies; this has developed into the theme of fostering "good mothering through breast-feeding." Its main emphasis is mother-to-mother support through almost 10,000 experienced, trained volunteers, but La Leche is open to everyone and shares its expertise with others. Its information on breast-feeding practices includes a library of 600 books, 150 pamphlets, and 12 periodical titles. The library can provide bibliographies and articles on breast-feeding research and management. Its quarterly high-quality *Breastfeeding Abstracts* ($7/year) reviews books and abstracts articles for health professionals. The member newsletter is *La Leche League News.*

La Leche publications include books, packets, and other materials on pregnancy, childbirth, nutrition, and parenting for both professionals and parents. It publishes a free directory of La Leche representatives and provides phone counseling or referral to a counselor. Materials are available from headquarters or through local groups. Typical titles are *The Womanly Art of Breastfeeding* (1981, 368 pp., $12.50; paperback, $7.50), *Nursing Baby Packet* (13 pamphlets, $3.75), *Breastfeeding and Drugs in Human Milk* (1984, $5.95), and the *Selected Bibliography of Published Articles on Breastfeeding, 1980–83* (1984, $2.00). La Leche publications are available in Afrikaans, Arabic, Chinese, Danish, Dutch, English, French, German, Hebrew, Indonesian, Italian, Japanese, Korean, Laotian, Polish, Portuguese, Spanish, Vietnamese, and Yupik. La Leche also loans its materials—in the United States only—in braille, large type, cassette tape, and reel-to-reel tape.

L22   **MARCH OF DIMES BIRTH DEFECTS FOUNDATION (MOD)**   1275 Mamaroneck Ave., White Plains, NY 10605. (914) 428-7100

This group, originally the National Foundation for Infantile Paralysis, turned its attention to birth defects in 1958, after its research had lead to the elimination of polio. It notes that birth defects are the nation's largest child health problem. Its purpose is to prevent birth defects or—if this is not yet possible—to improve treatments to ameliorate their effects on newborns and infants. The March of Dimes supports birth defects research, funds service programs at hospitals, and sponsors health education programs for professionals and the general public through its headquarters office and 700 chapters across the country.

Its professional publications include a series of nursing modules on perinatal and postpartum care; an original articles series on birth defects; and the *Birth Defects Compendium,* which describes and illustrates more than 1,000 defects. It reprints pertinent journal articles in its *Perinatal Reprint Series.*

Publications for the general public deal with nutrition, adolescent pregnancy, and other materials for schools, youth agencies, and health care institutions. Media include packets, printed matter, exhibits, and audiovisuals for purchase and loan, dealing largely with prenatal care and education for parenthood. *Starting a Healthy Family* is an interdisciplinary program of materials for classes in junior and senior high schools.

Its Center for Birth Defects Information Services (operated through Tufts New England Medical Center) offers access to the computerized BIRTH DEFECTS INFORMATION SYSTEM (J17) to certain professionals at major medical centers.

It provides a referral service to genetic counseling centers around the world. Catalogs of professional publications and of public health education materials are available free.

L23   **NATIONAL CANCER INSTITUTE (NCI)**   Office of Cancer Communications (OCC), Public Inquiries Section, 9000 Rockville Pike, Bldg. 31, Room 10A18, Bethesda, MD 20205. (301) 496-5583

Founded in 1937 under President Franklin Roosevelt, NCI is the Federal Government's principal agency for research on cancer prevention, diagnosis, treatment, and rehabilitation and for the dissemination of information on the control of cancer. It is one of 11 research institutes of the National Institutes of Health and has developed an international cancer research data bank to collect, catalog, store, and disseminate the

results of cancer research worldwide. The Office of Cancer Communications prepares and distributes a wide variety of materials for patients, the general public, and health professionals. Publications are free, although orders for professional publications are limited to three titles.
Relevant materials include *Young People with Cancer: A Handbook for Parents* (No. 82-2378), which covers treatments, side effects, and issues for most forms of childhood cancer, with a glossary, bibliography, list of reading materials, and a fold-out drug chart. *Diet and Nutrition: A Resource for Parents of Children with Cancer* (No. 82-2038) contains information on nutrition, side effects of cancer and treatments, diets for children, and ways to encourage children to eat. *The Leukemic Child* (No. 82-863) is a parent-to-parent account by a mother who provides advice to other parents of leukemic children. *Students with Cancer: A Resource for the Educator* (No. 80-2086) is designed for teachers who have students with cancer. Other patient and professional materials, including annotated bibliographies and cancer-education materials, also are available. Write for a current publications list.

L24 **NATIONAL CENTER FOR CLINICAL INFANT PROGRAMS** 733 15th St., NW, Suite 912, Washington, DC 20005. (202) 347-0308
The focus of the center, which works with professionals from many disciplines concerned with infant health, mental health, and development, is to increase the general public's awareness of the importance of the first three years of life and to support professional initiative in the field of infant mental health and development. It supports its work through national and regional training institutes, fellowship programs, and consultation with policymakers. Its excellent bulletin, *Zero to Three,* is described in item H150. The center also issues a *Clinical Infant Report* series. Report No. 1, *Psychopathology and Adaptation in Infancy and Early Childhood: Principles of Clinical Diagnosis and Preventive Intervention* (1981, $25.00), presents experiences and accomplishments in both normal and disturbed infants (birth to age four years) and their caretakers. Report No. 2, *Infants and Parents: Clinical Case Reports* (1983, $32.50), provides detailed case studies illustrating diagnostic and therapeutic issues and methods. Its free booklet, *Infancy in the Eighties: Social Policy and the Earliest Years of Life* (1983), provides a summary of the needs of children in the first years of life and the implications of such knowledge for public policy. A brochure of publications is available on request.

L25　NATIONAL CENTER FOR EDUCATION IN MATERNAL AND CHILD HEALTH (NCEMCH)　3520 Prospect St., NW, Washington, DC 20057. (202) 625-8400
The purpose of this organization (previously the National Clearinghouse for Human Genetic Diseases) is to serve the full range of programs and constituencies of the Maternal and Child Health Block Grant and the Division of Maternal and Child Health. These areas include human genetics, nutrition, sudden infant death syndrome, nursing, child health, maternal health, and prevention of disease and illness. Clients are health professionals, educators, state government programs, and the general public. NCEMCH services, now free, include the identification, listing, and dissemination of single copies of a wide variety of government publications in its areas of interest, including professional and public education materials. The *Publications List,* available on request, is a valuable annotated list of government documents on child and maternal health. Other publications include the *Directory of Clinical Genetic Service Centers,* the *Federal Maternal and Child Health Resources Guide,* and the *National List of Voluntary Support Organizations.* The NCEMCH library includes 500 books, 3,500 pamphlets, and 1,500 periodicals. This group has been most prompt in providing services.

The National Maternal and Child Health Clearinghouse (NMCHC) ((202) 625-8410) operates out of this center, as does the National Sudden Infant Death Syndrome Clearinghouse (L30). NMCHC undertakes the distribution of approximately 500 publications in the field of human genetics and broad areas of maternal and child health and has an automated data base of topics, agencies, and organizations related to these areas. It also provides current fact sheets, subject lists, and referral lists in this field and maintains mailing lists of agencies, organizations, and individuals for the timely dissemination of new publications.

L26　NATIONAL CENTER FOR HEALTH EDUCATION (NCHE)　30 E. 29th St., New York, NY 10016. (212) 689-1886
NCHE, an outgrowth of the President's Committee on Health Education in 1971 and the Health Education Resource Center, is a private sector agency that considers itself the linchpin in a communications and service network linking front-line practitioners, professionals, educators, managers, communicators, and decision makers concerned with all aspects of education for health. With the Mental Health Materials Center, it has just produced a massive compilation of evaluated print and audiovisual materials in mental health and health education.

L27 **NATIONAL HEALTH INFORMATION CLEARING-HOUSE (NHIC)** P.O. Box 1133, Washington, DC 20013-1133. (703) 522-2590 in Virginia and metropolitan Washington; (800) 336-4797 elsewhere in the United States

This clearinghouse was established to help consumers and health professionals locate health information through identification of health information resources and channeling of requests for information to appropriate resources. Its subject areas are health education, health promotion, and other topics related to health in general. The data base contains descriptions of more than 2,000 health organizations. NHIC maintains a library collection of health and medical directories and reference books, books on health promotion, health periodicals, and files on 800 health topics. It generally answers questions by channeling inquiries to the appropriate organization or by providing names of organizations, but it will provide sources of particular publications or information on topics for which no organizations have been identified. It has produced excellent resource lists on current health concerns. NHIC is a project of the DHHS Office of Disease Prevention and Health Promotion.

L28 **NATIONAL PERINATAL ASSOCIATION (NPA)** 1311A Dolley Madison Blvd., Suite 3A, McLean, VA 22101. (703) 556-9222

Membership in NPA comprises those involved in the many disciplines related to the care of mothers and infants, including obstetricians, gynecologists, neonatologists, nurses, nurse-midwives, social workers, hospital administrators, nutritionists, dietitians, outreach educators, and consumers—basically all professions involved in any way with prenatal and neonatal care. Its objectives are to promote optimal perinatal care, facilitate the education of health care professionals, serve as an education/legislation resource center, and foster multidisciplinary and interdisciplinary cooperation. NPA is currently involved in the general growth of state perinatal organizations and legislative surveillance, reported in its quarterly newsletter, the *NPA Bulletin*. It sponsors annual education conferences on many topics that provide continuing education credits to all health care professionals. Membership is available at large or through existing regional/state perinatal organizations.

L29 **NATIONAL REYE'S SYNDROME FOUNDATION** P.O. Box RS, Benzonia, MI 49616. (616) 882-5521

This organization was founded in 1976 to educate the lay public, medical professionals, and politicians about the existence and devastation of this national health problem affecting previously healthy children under age 18. The foundation's coordination and information activities include promoting and initiating research in the areas of etiology, treatment, basic sciences, and neuropsychological follow-up; encouraging coordination of efforts of various centers in treatment and prevention of Reye's Syndrome (RS); establishing RS as a reportable disease in every state; sponsoring a multicenter study group of recognized authorities; and encouraging involvement of the Federal Government in supporting RS research. The organization publishes a semiannual newsletter, *The R.S. Reporter,* and brochures on Reye's Syndrome; compiles bibliographies; refers inquirers to appropriate agencies or information sources; distributes low-cost print materials; and rents or sells its film, *Portrait of a Killer.* Its awareness programs include films and speakers. Brochures are available on request; donations are appreciated.

L30   **NATIONAL SUDDEN INFANT DEATH SYNDROME CLEARINGHOUSE** 3520 Prospect St., NW, Washington, DC 20057. (202) 625-8410
Founded in 1980 by the Bureau of Community Health Services to provide information and educational materials on sudden infant death syndrome (SIDS), the major cause of death of infants between the ages of one month and one year. Its clientele includes health care professionals, community-service personnel (including counselors, funeral directors, clergy, death investigators), parents, and the general public; it is the central source for the exchange of program and educational materials for affiliated organizations and for information and counseling programs. Its data base of literature supports reference and general inquiries. The clearinghouse produces its own two-page fact sheets, a catalog of audiovisuals, and a selected bibliography on grief counseling and Sudden Infant Death Syndrome research. It also produces a newsletter, *Information Exchange.* Fact sheets cover SIDS and grief counseling for professionals, parents, and the general public. Titles include *What Is SIDS?* (1983), *What Parents Should Know About SIDS* (1983), *Facts About Apnea* (1983), *Parents and the Grieving Process* (1982), *The Grief of Children* (1982), and *The Grief Process* (1983). All fact sheets are free up to five copies.

L31   **NUTRITION INFORMATION SERVICE (NIS)** Ryerson Polytechnic Institute, 350 Victoria St., Toronto, Ontario M5B 2K3, Canada. (416) 979-5000, ext. 6903
An active library and information service with materials and survey publications on child nutrition. Its *Infant Feeding: An Annotated Bibliog-*

raphy is reviewed in item E91. NIS also has issued *A Directory of Canadian Organizations Involved in Food and Nutrition* ($10 prepaid) and the *Index of Free and Inexpensive Food and Nutrition Information Materials* ($11 prepaid), which covers materials on infant feeding, school lunches, WIC programs, and other child-nutrition topics. Additional publications are bibliographies and manuals on food and nutrition for the disabled, athletes, and the aged, as well as on school materials.

L32   **PEDIATRIC PROJECTS, INC.** P.O. Box 1880, Santa Monica, CA 90406. (213) 459-7710
A nonprofit corporation providing services for and distributing publications and therapeutic play materials to people who work with children in health care and their families. Includes a consultant service; a bimonthly newsletter, *Pediatric Mental Health;* a toy store that includes medically oriented toys and games, such as the Sugar Babe diabetic teaching doll, nurse and doctor hand puppets, and medical figures; an at-cost reprint service dealing with play, preparation, and parenting; bibliographies of children's books on specific disabilities and on coping with illness; lists of professional publications on research and practice in psychosocial care; and a bookstore that carries books for professionals and children. Professional books deal with such topics as preparation for stress, play therapy, parents and families, and teaching school children about the hospital. Books for children cover attitudes toward disability, health, illness, and death; bilingual books; and books on going to the doctor, dentist, emergency room, and so on. Pediatric Projects' own publications include *Preparing Well Young Children for Possible Hospitalization: The Issues* (1983, $12).

L33   **POISON CONTROL DIVISION**   Food and Drug Administration, Bureau of Drugs, 5401 Westbard Ave., Bethesda, MD 20016. (301) 496-7691
This division, formerly the National Clearinghouse for Poison Control Centers, evaluates the toxic hazards of medicine and household chemicals and supplies information on antidotes, symptoms, and treatment. The division obtains its information from industrial formulas, technical reports, and scientific journals. It then provides analyses of products to poison control centers in the states. These, in turn, provide round-the-clock information services to the medical profession.

L34   **SPINA BIFIDA ASSOCIATION OF AMERICA (SBAA)** 343 S. Dearborn St., Chicago, IL 60604. (800) 621-3141, (312) 663-1562 in Illinois

An action-oriented national association founded in 1973 by parents of children with spina bifida and adults with spina bifida, SBAA now has an information resource center with free handouts and pamphlets—a public-awareness program that reached 42 million Americans in 1983. It works mostly through chapters that publish newsletters and testify on spina bifida. The headquarters office distributes publications for children, teachers, parents, and the general public at a small charge. It funds five research projects and an annual conference on current medical techniques, as well as a leadership training seminar. Its newsletter, *Insights,* reports on products, medical treatments and therapies, federal activities, new books, and major issues. Titles include *Straight Talk— Parent to Parent* ($1.50) and *Learning Disabilities and the Person with Spina Bifida* ($1.50).

ORGANIZATIONS CONCERNED WITH HANDICAPPING CONDITIONS

This section contains a few of the many agencies that provide information relative to the concerns of handicapped children. Many of the directories in Chapter 10 can provide additional information, especially the *Directory of National Information Sources on Handicapping Conditions and Related Services* (I33), issued by the Clearinghouse on the Handicapped (L37). The Coordinating Council for Handicapped Children (L39) is an umbrella organization for all organizations dealing with handicaps, and the Clearinghouse on the Handicapped keeps tabs on organizations concerned with handicaps.

L35   **AMERICAN ASSOCIATION OF CHILDREN'S RESIDEN-TIAL CENTERS (AACRC)**   1346 Connecticut Ave., NW, Suite 318, Washington, DC 20036. (202) 463-7065
A national organization representing interdisciplinary mental health facilities that provide a therapeutic living experience, individual and group therapy, and parent or family therapy. AACRC was founded in 1957 to provide effective advocacy to maintain and enhance sound clinical practice in children's residential treatments. It publishes *Residential Treatment News,* which contains information on legislation, programs, grants, upcoming conferences, and appropriate publications, and compiles an informative *Directory of Organizational Members.*

Other information activities include an annual conference, which incorporates most of its papers in *Contributions to Residential Treatment.*

L36 ASSOCIATION FOR CHILDREN AND ADULTS WITH LEARNING DISABILITIES (ACLD) 4156 Library Rd., Pittsburgh, PA 15234. (412) 341-1515, 341-8077
A membership organization founded by concerned parents in 1964 to define and find solutions to the entire spectrum of learning problems and to educate the public about learning disabilities. It is open to professionals, adults with learning disabilities, and parents of learning-disabled children and advocates an interdisciplinary approach. ACLD has 50 state affiliates, 800 local chapters, and more than 60,000 members. The headquarters office provides general information, and the local chapters provide referrals to treatment centers and physicians. The resource center at national headquarters has 500 publications for sale and rents films. Lists of materials are available on request. Its Governmental Affairs Committee provides information and recommends action on legislation that might affect children with learning disabilities or their families. A bimonthly newsletter, *Newsbriefs* ($5.00), covers current developments, legislative activities, national news, new programs, and projects and materials in the area of learning handicaps. ACLD conducts research on such issues as the link between learning disabilities and delinquency. Its annual conferences cover all aspects of learning disabilities, including new technology. *Selected Conference Proceedings* is available for $13.95. ACLD has a library of books, pamphlets, periodicals, and films. Its services are open to everyone.

L37 CLEARINGHOUSE ON THE HANDICAPPED U.S. Department of Education, Office of Special Education and Rehabilitative Services, Switzer Bldg., Room 3132, 330 C St., SW, Washington, DC 20202. (202) 732-1245, 732-1248
Created by the Rehabilitation Act of 1973 to enhance the flow of disability-related information to handicapped individuals, parents, and their service providers. Areas of interest are handicapping conditions and related services, federal legislation, programs, and funding. Publications include the *Directory of National Information Sources on Handicapping Conditions and Related Services,* summaries of legislation and federal regulations affecting the handicapped, and the *Pocket Guide to Federal Help for the Handicapped Person.* The clearinghouse's bimonthly newsletter, *Programs for the Handicapped,* focuses on federal activities affecting the handicapped. It also announces new publications and services. This newsletter and single copies of most clearinghouse publications are free.

L38   **CLOSER LOOK**   P.O. Box 1492, Washington, DC 20013.
Established primarily for the parents of handicapped children, with a
focus on the educational rights of the handicapped, especially as guaranteed under P.L. 94-142, the Education of All Handicapped Children
Act. Closer Look answers requests for information and makes referrals
by mail. It publishes *Closer Look,* primarily for parents, twice a year.

L39   **COORDINATING COUNCIL FOR HANDICAPPED CHILDREN (CCHC)**   220 S. State St., Room 412, Chicago, IL
      60605. (312) 939-3513
CCHC, first organized in 1969, is a coalition of 85 parent and professional organizations working together to actualize civil, social, and economic rights, as well as rights to employment, transportation, and safety for
handicapped children. An umbrella agency that covers all handicaps, it
provides information and referral services, advocacy, and workshops
for parents and professionals. It provides help to handicapped people of
all ages by answering specific requests; through public information
campaigns; through conferences and radio and television interviews;
and by sending spokespersons to federal and state legislative hearings.
CCHC assists parent groups working for better services for disabled children. Its weekly Parents' Rights Training Sessions and monthly workshops are free.
   Publications include fact sheets covering topics like *Income Tax
Deductions, Supplemental Security Income Benefits, How to Prepare for a
Successful Due Process Hearing,* and *How to Participate Effectively in Your
Child's IEP Meeting* and substantial books and directories with titles
such as *How to Organize an Effective Parent/Advocacy Group and Move
Bureaucracies* ($6) and *How to Get Services by Being Assertive* ($6).

L40   **COUNCIL FOR EXCEPTIONAL CHILDREN (CEC)**   1920
      Association Dr., Reston, VA 22091. (703) 620-3660
A national membership organization founded in 1922 that covers the
entire scope of special education and exceptional children—mental retardation; physical and learning disabilities; communication disorders;
homebound, hospitalized, and gifted children; and children with emotional, cognitive, visual, motor, and auditory handicaps. Its aim is to
promote the education of handicapped and gifted children through
publications, conventions and conferences, advocacy activities, and
maintenance of an information center and data base. It is open to special
education teachers and administrators, school psychologists, social
workers, students, parents, and other individuals concerned with
improving the quality of life for exceptional children. CEC houses the
ERIC Clearinghouse on Handicapped and Gifted Children, which pre-

pares abstracts for EXCEPTIONAL CHILD EDUCATION RESOURCES (J23) and the ERIC system, and runs custom searches on this data base and ERIC for interested individuals. The ECER data base contains some 50,000 citations to books, government documents, research reports, teaching guides, films, filmstrips, tapes, and doctoral dissertations. Around 200 periodicals are scanned regularly. Reprints of computer searches are available. Its library collection contains 10,000 books and 25,000 periodical issues, as well as the ERIC microfiche, and can be used on-site.

CEC periodicals include *Exceptional Children* and *Teaching Exceptional Children.* Division periodicals include *Behavioral Disorders, Diagnostique, Journal of Childhood Communication Disorders, Journal of the Division of Early Childhood, Career Development for Exceptional Individuals, Education and Training of the Mentally Retarded, Teacher Education & Special Education,* and *Journal for the Education of the Gifted.* Other publications deal with early childhood education, creative teaching, professional support, behavioral disorders, delivery of services, prevention of child abuse and neglect, attitudes, and affective education. *Microcomputers in Special Education: Selection and Decision Making Process* ($7.95) is a recent publication. An organization brochure and a list of publications are available on request.

L41 **DEVEREUX FOUNDATION** Devon, PA 19333. (215) 964-3000
A nonprofit organization, the Devereux Foundation is a nationwide network of day and residential treatment centers for children and young adults who are emotionally disturbed or mentally handicapped. It serves approximately 1,800 children at treatment facilities at or near Devon, Pennsylvania and through therapeutic programs in California, Texas, Massachusetts, Connecticut, Georgia, and Arizona. Its publications include the IMAGE (Individual Motor Achievement through Guided Education) program kit, with exercise activities and various Devereux Behavior Rating Scales (for children, adolescents, and elementary school behavior) as well as films. The foundation answers queries, conducts seminars, and provides advisory services at cost to professionals, agencies, and concerned parents.

L42 **INSTITUTE FOR CHILD BEHAVIOR RESEARCH** 4157 Adams Ave., San Diego, CA 92216. (619) 281-7165
A nonprofit corporation charted by the state of California in 1967 to perform research on the causes and treatments for autism and other behavioral disturbances, to foster such research, and to serve as an infor-

mation and referral service for parents and professionals dealing with autistic children and adults. One purpose is to serve as a link between parents of autistic children, who are scattered geographically, and researchers throughout the world who need carefully diagnosed samples of children for research purposes. Referrals are made with parental consent. A high priority of the institute is the development of improved methods for diagnosing children with severe behavioral disorders; it has developed the *Diagnostic Check List, Form E-2* for this purpose and provides diagnoses (by questionnaire) for autistic and similarly labeled cases. *Form E-2* is available in English, French, Spanish, German, Italian, and Japanese. *Form E-3* is designed to obtain detailed information on biological factors and evaluations of treatment. Information from these forms constitutes the institute's data files, available at cost on computer tapes, on some 8,000 autistic children. (It is comparable to the BIRTH DEFECTS INFORMATION SYSTEM [J17]). These research data are available at certain universities and medical centers. The institute can make searches for a charge.

Other services of the institute include the maintenance of a directory of physicians who use nutritional approaches to the treatment of behavioral and mental problems. It offers 60 publications, both popular and scientific, all available for a modest price. Representative titles are *The Differentiation of Childhood Psychoses* ($0.40), a *Book List* on autism and related problems ($0.25), and *Junk Food, Megavitamins, and Child Behavior* ($0.75). The award-winning film *Infantile Autism: The Invisible Wall* can be rented for $15.00/week. The library has a collection of approximately 200 books, 100 pamphlets, 400 periodicals, and 2 films. It loans only films, but other materials can be used on-site.

L43   INTERNATIONAL PARENTS' ORGANIZATION (IPO)
3417 Volta Pl., NW, Washington, DC 20007. (202) 337-5220
IPO is an association of affiliated parents, founded in 1957, within the Alexander Graham Bell Association for the Deaf. Its goal is to give the parents of hearing-impaired children the chance to work together for better conditions for their children—educationally, socially, and vocationally—through auditory/oral education. It provides parents and the public with information on hearing impairment and hearing conservation and is a clearinghouse for the exchange of ideas among parents and between parents and professionals. It publishes a semiannual magazine for parents, *Our Kids Magazine.* Membership in IPO is automatic with membership in the Bell Association and includes access to the Volta Bureau Lending Library, a valuable source of information on parent-

ing, psychosocial aspects of hearing impairment, communication, hearing, and audiology. Bell activities include an educational journal, *The Volta Review;* a newsletter, *Newsounds;* publications; audiovisual aids; and a children's rights program.

L44   LEKOTEK 613 Dempster St., Evanston, IL 60201. (312) 328-0001

A parent resource center and toy library for families of handicapped children, Lekotek trains parents in the use of remediation materials and lends materials to members for home use. Its concerns are children with special needs (from birth to age 19) and their families. Its publications include training materials for Lekotek leaders and an award-winning film, *Hidden in Play.* Lekotek's most recent work is *The Lekotek Guide to Good Toys* (1983, $12.95, plus $1.50 shipping and handling), which groups toys into developmental categories (e.g., gross, motor, fine motor, infant stimulation, and adaptive toys) and arranges toys within these categories by order of complexity, along with price information, illustrations, and sources. Its library includes 200 books, 50 newsletters and pamphlets, and 3,000 toys. This organization is the United States's link to the International Conference of Toy Libraries. Lekotek also holds a training course three times a year for Lekotek leaders. Successful completion can earn participants two graduate credit hours.

L45   MENTAL HEALTH LAW PROJECT (MHLP) 2021 L St., NW, Suite 800, Washington, DC 20036. (202) 467-5730

A nonprofit public-interest organization that is a national leader in law-reform advocacy for people labeled mentally or developmentally disabled. Its goal is to establish access to suitable mental health, education, and social services in humane surroundings, rather than in mental institutions or retardation centers. MHLP has spearheaded the development of a nationwide network of advocates representing mentally disabled children and adults in their efforts to secure public services. Its *Washington UPDATE* newsletter, which provides a concise overview of federal legislative and policy changes affecting mentally disabled people, is sent to individuals donating $20 or more and is free to nonprofit advocacy organizations actively representing disabled people. Periodic action-oriented *Alerts* are sent to everyone who has requested inclusion on the mailing list. MHLP has produced a mental health legislative guide published by the American Bar Association. Its publications list is available on request.

L46   **NATIONAL ASSOCIATION FOR DOWN'S SYNDROME
(NADS)**   P.O. Box 63, Oak Park, IL 60303. (312) 543-6060
A nonprofit organization of parents and professionals involved with
Down's syndrome individuals that attempts to keep its members informed in areas such as education, recreation, rehabilitation, research,
and legislation. Information activities include a newsletter, *NADS
NEWS,* four general meetings per year, a parent support program, the
collection and distribution of pamphlets, and the production of an excellent bibliography.

L47   **NATIONAL DOWN SYNDROME SOCIETY (NDSS)**   70
      W. 40th St., New York, NY 10018. (212) 764-3070, (800)
      221-4602
A very active national organization founded in 1979 that disseminates
information to genetic counselors, teaching hospitals, new parents,
nursing associations, health maintenance organizations, special education centers, and the general public. It compiles information on early
education and parent support groups nationwide and raises funds and
awards research scholarships for research into Down's syndrome. It has
a hot-line service available with general information on Down's syndrome, as well as local educational services in cities and towns across
the country. NDSS publishes an annual report, a suggested reading list,
a fact sheet on Down's syndrome, and an information booklet (also
available in Spanish) entitled *This Baby Needs You Even More,* which
contains a background statement on NDSS. New activities in 1984 include awards for science writers, the production of films for professional
groups, and a neuroscience symposium.

L48   **NATIONAL EASTER SEAL SOCIETY**   2023 W. Ogden
      Ave., Chicago, IL 60612. (312) 243-8400, 243-8880
Founded in 1919, Easter Seal is the oldest and largest voluntary organization providing direct rehabilitation services to disabled persons in the
United States. Its nationwide program of research, education, and treatment includes publication of its professional journal, *Rehabilitation Literature* (G44), which provides compact reviews and abstracts of rehabilitation. Easter Seal also publishes a variety of excellent, inexpensive
booklets, bibliographies, and brochures on rehabilitation and disabilities for professionals, parents, and persons with disabilities. Topics include accessibility for wheelchairs to public places; attitudes toward
handicapped persons; awareness of their needs; dental care; learning
disabilities; speech, language, and hearing; employment; and psychological aspects of being handicapped. There are 10 bibliographies on
the areas of rehabilitation and disabilities for $0.30 each. Some other

relevant titles are *For Parents, For Teachers, Brain Injury and Learning Disorders in Children,* and *Periodicals that Publish Articles Concerning Persons Who Have Disabilities.* Other low-cost, high-quality publications include *Understanding Stuttering: Information for Parents* (1979, 39 pp., $0.80), *Children on Medication: A Guide for Teachers* (1980, 3 pp., $0.30), *Self-Help Clothing for Children Who Have Physical Disabilities* (1979, 64 pp., $1.25), *Camps for Children with Disabilities* (1982, 6 pp., single copy free with self-addressed, stamped envelope), *Feeding the Cerebral Palsied Child* (chart, single copy free with self-addressed, stamped envelope), and a *Learning Disabilities* packet for $3.75. Their publications catalog can be obtained by sending a stamped, self-addressed envelope to the above address.

**L49 NATIONAL INFORMATION CENTER FOR HANDI-
CAPPED CHILDREN AND YOUTH (NICHCY)** P.O. Box 1492, Washington, DC 20013. (703) 522-3322
Supported by the Special Education Programs of the U.S. Department of Education, this information and referral center has recently inaugurated the National Exchange Network that provides a two-way nationwide flow of information on projects and progress that involve services to the handicapped. NICHCY offers free periodic newsletters and other print materials of interest to parents, professionals, advocates, and anyone else concerned with handicapped children and youth. It convened an invitational Parent Group Round Table Meeting in August 1983 and from this derived an interesting table of the training and information needs of various groups, such as parents and families, parent organizations and leaders, children and youth with handicaps, and service providers. Inclusion on the NICHCY mailing list is free.

**L50 NATIONAL SOCIETY FOR CHILDREN AND ADULTS
WITH AUTISM (NSAC)** 1234 Massachusetts Ave., NW, Suite 1017, Washington, DC 20005. (202) 783-0125
A nationwide agency (formerly the National Society for Autistic Children) with more than 100 chapters, dedicated to the education and welfare of people with autism. Its priorities are research and education, and it is concerned not only with autism but also with childhood schizophrenia and other profound behavioral and/or communicative disorders. NSAC publications include a bimonthly newsletter, *The Advocate* (individuals, $15.00/year; students, $7.50/year); conference proceedings; *Critical Issues in Educating Autistic Children and Youth* ($15.00); *Children Apart* ($1.00); and *How They Grow: A Handbook for Parents of Young Children with Autism* ($2.00).

NSAC's Information and Referral Service can provide reading lists and film lists and will answer questions. Its holdings include 300 books, 25 pamphlets, and 15 periodicals. The NSAC bookstore makes available more than 130 popular and professional items on autism.

L51 **ORTON DYSLEXIA SOCIETY** 724 York Rd., Baltimore, MD 21204. (301) 296-0232

An international, nonprofit scientific and educational association concerned with the study, treatment, and prevention of developmental dyslexia. Members include parents, neurologists, speech and reading therapists, educators, and social workers. The organization disseminates information on dyslexia and provides guidance to resources for testing, teaching, and teacher training. Branches offer workshops, group meetings, parent support groups, and meetings for dyslectics. The headquarters office distributes its newsletter, *Perspectives on Dyslexia,* free to members. Its annual, the *Annals of Dyslexia,* is a professional journal on specific language ability (members, free; nonmembers, $9.50). Some publications are *Sex Differences in Dyslexia* ($15.00); *Reading, Writing, and Speech Problems in Children* ($5.00); *Dyslexia* ($2.00); packets of reprints for parents, educators, and physicians; and many other items, including assessment guidelines, checklists, and reprints. Brochures and publications lists are available on request.

L52 **PARENT EDUCATIONAL ADVOCACY TRAINING CENTER** 228 S. Pitt St., Room 300, Alexandria, VA 22314. (703) 836-2953

A private, nonprofit, professionally staffed organization concerned with the parent's role in the special education planning process. Its purposes are to train parents of handicapped children to become effective advocates for their children and to train teams of parents and educators to provide training for parents in their communities. Activities include parent training courses, parent/professional training courses, information and referral to local community agencies, and consultation to individual families and to local and state agencies. *Negotiating the Special Education Maze* (Prentice-Hall, 1982, $7.95) was prepared under the center's auspices.

FAMILY CONCERNS AND VALUES

This section covers organizations whose major focus is centered on particular values connected with or implicit in family life. Many of the organizations in the previous chapters and in the two preceding sections are oriented toward or founded by parents or deal with such family issues as adoption, but I have classified them in other categories if they were concerned with broader or particular social, welfare, health, or advocacy issues. For example, La Leche (L21) is strongly concerned with values and parenting, but I have included it in the health and nutrition section of this chapter because of its focus on breast-feeding. In this section, I have included groups that are concerned with home learning or other interactions among family, children, and education.

L53   **CENTER FOR PARENT EDUCATION** 55 Chapel St., Newton, MA 02160. (617) 964-2442
A nonprofit, public service organization established in 1978 by Burton L. White, who formerly headed the Harvard Preschool Project. In addition to adding to the knowledge base on child development, the two major thrusts of the center are public education through the use of such mass communication media as radio, television, books, and magazines and the provision of support services for professionals in the field of education for parenthood. The center is most competent at assessing children, training practitioners, and evaluating training materials. Activities include workshops for professionals and provision of speakers and consultants for conferences and projects. Its active publishing and provisioning program includes an informative bimonthly *Newsletter* ($20.00/year), which contains feature articles on important topics and current events; listings of useful resources; and reviews of books, toys, audiovisuals, and other professional or educational materials. Additional publications include policy papers, research reports, and assessment manuals. Three interesting miscellaneous items are *Film Critiques: Critical Evaluations and Information on Audiovisual Materials Pertaining to Education for Parenthood* ($10.00), *Standard Equipment Useful to Those Raising a Baby* (1980, $3.00), and *A Guide to Reading a Popular Book on Early Development and Parenting* ($7.50).

L54   **CENTER FOR THE IMPROVEMENT OF CHILD CAR-
      ING (CICC)**   11331 Ventura Blvd., Suite 103, Studio City, CA
      91604. (213) 980-0903
A nonprofit research, training, and community service organization
concerned with parent training programs; training of parenting instructors; and research on parenting programs to make them more sensitive
to the characteristics of different parent populations, with some special-
ization into black parenting. Publications include *Effective Black Parenting: A Review and Synthesis of Black Perspectives* ($9); *Critiques of
Parent Training Manuals* ($6); and *Training Parenting Instructors: A Na-
tional Model for Training Mental Health, Social Service and Education Personnel to Deliver Group Parent Training Services in Their Agencies* ($20).
A complete list of publications is available on request.

L55   **COMMITTEE FOR SINGLE ADOPTIVE PARENTS**   P.O.
      Box 15084, Chevy Chase, MD 20815.
An information and support service for present and prospective single
adoptive parents of both sexes; open only to unmarried individuals or
to agencies. Membership and services are chiefly for residents of the
United States and Canada. This group, which has been active since
1973, also informs public and private agencies of legislation and research applying to adoption by a single person. Its publications include
Source List, which provides current newsletter information and updated
lists of sources of adoptable children that will accept unmarried applicants. Its *Handbook for Single Adoptive Parents* (1982, $6) covers the
mechanics of adopting a child born in the United States or another
country, a guide to the tasks of single parenthood, case histories, and
surveys by social workers.

L56   **THE COMPASSIONATE FRIENDS, INC.**   P.O. Box 1347,
      Oak Brook, IL 60521. (312) 323-5010
A self-help organization with 400 chapters as of January 1984 offering
friendship and understanding to bereaved parents. Its purposes are to
help parents resolve the grief they experience on the death of a child
and to foster the physical and emotional health of bereaved parents and
siblings. Each chapter develops its own resources, newsletters, libraries, and community of caring people and is encouraged to establish
professional liaison advisory committees with local doctors, nurses,
clergy, social workers, psychologists, funeral directors, and others. The
headquarters office assists in the development of chapters, libraries,
telephone groups, and programs and serves as a referral agency to local
chapters. Publications include the quarterly *Compassionate Friends*

Newsletter, which contains organization news; book reviews; poems; and sensitive, well-handled articles on topics like sibling grief. Publications include two fine booklets— *When a Baby Dies* ($2.25, quantity reduction) and *The Grief of Parents. . .When a Child Dies* ($1.75, quantity reductions) —as well as helpful brochures such as *Stillbirth, Miscarriage and Infant Death: Understanding Grief; Caring for Surviving Children; Suggestions for Clergy;* and *Suggestions for Doctors and Nurses.* These brochures are available in quantities of 50 for $5.00. A general brochure is available on request.

L57 FAMILY RESOURCE COALITION 2100 N. Michigan Ave., Suite 1625, Chicago, IL 60601. (312) 726-4750
A new grassroots coalition of family resource programs extending throughout the United States and Canada committed to encouraging the growth of family resource programs and to sharing information and mutual assistance among programs. Major concerns include community parent education and parent support groups. It publishes the quarterly *Family Resource Coalition Report* (free to members; nonmembers, $9), which frequently focuses on specific themes like rural support or teenage parenting), and an annual directory based on its computerized clearinghouse; this contains information on family resource programs, other programs working with families, and related materials. The coalition offers a national referral service for parents, as well as technical assistance for groups who wish to develop family resource programs or networks or to educate the public on the effectiveness and importance of preventive community-based support for families. It prepares, produces, and distributes materials on training, resources, and advocacy activities in these areas. *Programs to Strengthen Families: A Resource Guide* ($8) is a recent publication that describes the background of the family support movement and provides detailed profiles of 70 diverse programs.

L58 FATHERHOOD PROJECT Bank Street College, 610 W. 112th St., New York, NY 10025. (212) 663-7200, ext. 235
The Fatherhood Project collects and shares information on all kinds of programs and policies that support male participation in child rearing, including issues regarding employment (e.g., paternity leave and alternative work schedules), law (e.g., custody mediation, child support enforcement policies), health (e.g., pre- and postnatal classes for new fathers), education (for boys and men through the life span), and social and supportive services for all kinds of fathers (e.g., single fathers, teenage fathers, and gay fathers). It encourages the nurturing capacity

of males of all ages and ethnic and racial backgrounds, from all types of families. Publications include a national catalog of innovative programs and policies, *Fatherhood U.S.A.* (Garland, 1984, 348 pp., $14.95 [paperback]), and a state-of-the-art analysis of fatherhood and social change entitled *The Future of Fatherhood.*

L59 **GROWING WITHOUT SCHOOLING** 729 Boylston St., Suite 308-CRS, Boston, MA 02116. (617) 437-1550
An advocacy agency founded for home schooling as an alternative to compulsory education, it is concerned with offering help to parents who have taken or wish to take their children out of school to learn at home. Assistance includes a bimonthly newsletter/magazine, *Growing Without Schooling* ($15/year), that connects parents interested in the same concept. The publication includes directory information, information on court cases and pending legislation, personal tips, and accounts. A mail-order bookstore of supportive materials operates from the same address. Information is available on receipt of a stamped, self-addressed envelope.

L60 **HOME AND SCHOOL INSTITUTE (HSI)** Special Projects Office, 1201 16th St., NW, Washington, DC 20036. (202) 466-3633
HSI is founded on the belief that all families have strengths and abilities to help their children and that all schools and agencies have capacities to work effectively with families. It seeks to aid families to help their children fulfill their potential and to help school and community agencies reach out to families. The scope is family education—generally for families with children from preschool to junior high—including training for family involvement and materials for educating children at home without duplicating the work of the schools. It provides workshops for parents, schools, and social and health agencies; curricula and parent programs for schools; child-abuse prevention curriculum and staff/parent workshops for health and social service agencies; and public service television and radio presentations. Its books for parents cover home-learning activities for children of varying ages and disabilities and the *Survival Guide for Busy Parents* ($12), intended to help working parents, single parents, and young parents.

L61 **INTERNATIONAL CONCERNS COMMITTEE FOR CHILDREN (ICCC)** 911 Cypress Dr., Boulder, CO 80303. (303) 494-8333

A charitable and educational organization whose experienced volunteers work to educate professionals, the public, and prospective parents on ways to provide assistance to homeless children through sponsorship, fostering, and adoption. It provides information both on procedures and the availability of adoptable domestic and foreign children and maintains a *Listing Service* ($10 donation requested), updated at least six times annually, that covers foreign-born children in the United States whose adoptions have disrupted, as well as children badly in need of adoptive homes and parents looking for that "special child" who will fit into their family. ICCC's *Newsletter* ($8 donation requested), published at least quarterly, contains legislative news and information on refugee and sponsorship advocacy. Its annual *Report on Foreign Adoption,* with nine current updates ($10 donation requested), includes approximate costs, waiting periods, and types of children available from a number of individual agencies and other organizations perceived as working morally, ethically, and legally in adoptive placement. ICCC actively gathers and distributes information by recognized experts in adoption.

L62   INTERPERSONAL   COMMUNICATIONS   SERVICES, INC. (ICS)   7052 W. Lane, Eden, NY 14057. (716) 649-3493

ICS is a private, nonprofit corporation providing resources and services to facilitate more effective communication between family members and other groups, such as students, teachers, and co-workers. Program and training activities include an eight-week course called "Toward Effective Parenting"; a "Family Cluster" project for mutual support among families; a variety of intergenerational programs; a Television Awareness Training series of modules; and a program to help parents and leaders deal with children and grief. ICS publishes a newsletter, *For Parents. . .to Increase the Joys of Effective Parenting* (5 issues/year, $10.00, bulk rate available) that offers a Christian/human relations perspective on effective parenting. Each issue includes resources, television tips, "together time," communications skills, and articles that cover such topics as how to be a supportive parent, ways to prepare children for peace, and Biblical understanding of the parent/child relationship. Other tools from ICS include a *Parent Education Resource List* ($1.00), *School Resources for Improving Relationships* ($2.00), *Christian Family Celebration Pac* ($7.95), and materials on feelings, communication, family relationships, and children's books. *Children's Books Which Focus on Death* ($5.00) covers the ways books deal with religious, emotional, and intellectual issues.

L63   **METRO-HELP, INC.**   2210 N. Halsted St., Chicago, IL
60614. (312) 929-5854
A telephone information and referral service, a crisis information center, and a message center where parents and runaways can leave messages for each other. Since its founding in 1971, more than 1.2 million troubled young people have called Metro-Help for assistance. It runs the National Runaway Switchboard ((800) 621-4000; (800) 972-6004 in Illinois) in addition to local lines such as Metro-Help Regional Service and Sex Info-Line and handles Rideboard and Agency Information Service Calls. National Runaway Switchboard callers include children as young as age 5, with more than 40 percent of the calls coming from or concerning children between the ages of 11 and 15; the young callers include runaways, prerunaways, and "throwaways"—children thrown out of their homes by their parents. Family problems are expressed by 32.2 percent of the group.

L64   **NATIONAL CENTER FOR FAMILY STUDIES**   The Catholic University of America, St. John's Hall, Washington, DC 20064. (202) 635-5453
Established in 1979 at The Catholic University of America, this is now an all-university center with the mission of supporting contemporary family life through research, education, and service activities in the areas of family policy, family health, and human services, including family ministries. Its projects are undertaken in the context of values that include the partnership of families and institutions in fulfilling family functions; emphasis on the prevention of family breakdown through family support and self-help; promotion of family-centered services; and sensitivity to the traditions, values, and practices of families with differing racial, ethnic, structural, and religious backgrounds. Two monthly newsletters are *American Family* (H7), published by the Clearinghouse on Family Policy and Programs, and *American Catholic Family,* published by the Clearinghouse on Families and Religion. The Family Impact Seminar, founded in 1976, is the policy research and analysis unit associated with the center since 1982. It aims to encourage a family perspective in developing, monitoring, and implementing policies and has used its family impact analysis approach in major studies on foster care and teenage pregnancy. Publications include *Toward an Inventory of Federal Programs with Direct Impact on Families* (1978, 35 pp., $3). A list of publications is available on request.

L65   **NATIONAL COMMITTEE FOR ADOPTION (NCFA)**
1346 Connecticut Ave., NW, Suite 326, Washington, DC 20036. (202) 463-7563

This organization provides an information and referral service on adoption and related services (such as adolescent pregnancy services and counseling) to young women and girls experiencing unplanned pregnancies, and their families. Other clients include couples and families interested in adopting children; infants; children with special needs; children from other countries; and families needing postlegal counseling and services. NCFA operates a National Adoption Hotline. Publications include the *National Adoption Hotline Resource Directory* ($17.49), a comprehensive list of 600 agencies and groups in 50 states that provide services to young, single, or troubled parents; adoption services; and counseling for infertile couples. Its *National Adoption Hotline Training Manual* costs $6.20, and the *Complete Hotline Volunteers Resource Binder,* which includes the preceding two items, is $75.00. The committee's newsletter, *National Adoption Reports,* includes legal news and book reviews, media information, and organization news and is free to members. NCFA also issues a *Model Legislation Series* that includes a *Model Act for the Adoption of Children with Special Needs* ($6.00) and *An Act to Establish a Mutual Consent Voluntary Registry and to Provide for the Transmission of Nonidentifying Information on the Health History and the Genetic and Social History of Adoptees* ($2.00). Other productions include a miniposter for the National Adoption Hotline and a brochure on *The Adoption Option,* both available in quantity only.

L66   NATIONAL COMMITTEE FOR CITIZENS IN EDUCATION (NCCE)   410 Wilde Lake Village Green, Columbia, MD 21044. (301) 997-9300, (800) NETWORK

NCCE, a membership organization supported by individuals, corporations, foundations, and sale of publications, runs the Parents' Network and is concerned with the issues of parent and citizen participation in public education in the belief that schools improve and children do better in school when parents are involved. It gathers, creates, and disseminates information to members through publications, legislative activities, and working with groups that share its concerns. It monitors federal and state legislative and executive activities relating to public schools and advises members on the implications of these activities. For example, it brought the issue of school records to a national audience and supplied information that was incorporated into the Family Educational Rights and Privacy Act of 1975. Its publications include filmstrips and books on such topics as organizing parent groups and parents' rights. Its monthly newsletter, *NETWORK* (8 issues/year during school term, $8.00), does a good job of reporting public school issues and problems at all levels. Other publications include *Parent Right Cards* (a card-listing of the rights of parents), handbooks, and books.

Some representative titles and prices are *Parent Participation—Student Achievement: The Evidence Grows, An Annotated Bibliography* (1981, $4.25); *Single Parents and the Public Schools: Results of a National Survey* (1981, $4.25, plus $1.00 postage); *You Can Improve Your Child's School* (1980, $6.95); and *The Rights of Parents in the Education of Their Children* (1977, $4.95). Other publications deal with special education, testing, federal legislation, funding, budgeting, school politics, and leadership. The Parents' Network includes 300 local groups of parents.

L67 **NATIONAL COUNCIL ON FAMILY RELATIONS (NCFR)** 1910 W. County Rd. B, Suite 147, St. Paul, MN 55113. (612) 633-6933
An interdisciplinary membership organization for professionals in the family field open to practitioners, academicians, and interested lay persons. Publications include a newsletter and three journals: the *Journal of Family History* (H97), *Family Relations* (H67), and the *Journal of Marriage and the Family*. Other publications include titles such as the *Guide to Graduate Family Programs, Standards and Criteria for the Certification of Family Life Educators,* and *An Overview of Content in Family Life Education*. It cooperates with Sage to produce the NCFR–Sage Book Series. Its Family Resource and Referral Center is a national family information referral service of more than 4,000 books and other items that draws its resources on the family from the fields of medicine, psychology, sociology, and education. On-line service of the FAMILY RESOURCES DATABASE is discussed extensively in item J24.

L68 **NATIONAL PTA** 700 N. Rush St., Chicago, IL 60611. (321) 787-0977
A voluntary membership organization founded in 1897 as the National Congress of Parents and Teachers and traditionally concerned with child welfare and parent involvement in education. Its basic purposes are to promote the welfare of children and youth at home, school, community, and place of worship; to raise the standards of home life; to secure adequate laws for the care and protection of children and youth; and to encourage close relations between the home and school and between educators and the general public to meet these goals. Today the PTA has 5.2 million members in 26,000 local associations and serves as an interface between schools and parents by interpreting school objectives to parents and parents' needs to schools. In recent years, it has initiated active programs and position statements on such areas as alcohol and drug education, sex education, environmental education, and television programming.

Its publications program includes around 50 inexpensive booklets and monographs, 10 films, filmstrips, recordings, and posters on many aspects of education. Its prize-winning periodical, *PTA Today* (7 issues/year, $4), is supplemented by a newsletter, *What's Happening in Washington* (8 issues/year, $3), which competently reports federal legislation in areas of PTA concern, taking in a broad range of issues affecting children and education, from asbestos hazards to block grants and immunization. Sometimes, as with television-viewing-skills development, the PTA compiles well-documented reports or overviews. Its recent booklet, *Looking in on Your School: A Workbook for Improving Public Education* (1983, $3), is designed to help parents, community leaders, and school board members evaluate their public schools.

The National PTA has substantial collections of materials in areas like standardized testing, television viewing, adolescent sexuality, parental education, and health education—altogether some 3,500 books, 30 file drawers of pamphlets, 50 boxes of documents, 5 file drawers of photographs, 575 periodicals, and more. Other information activities include an annual convention; programs; exhibits; leadership and legislative workshops; and special projects, such as its safety belt campaign school discipline.

L69   NATIONAL RESOURCE CENTER ON FAMILY BASED SERVICES   University of Iowa, School of Social Work, N118 OH, Iowa City, IA 52242. (319) 353-5076

Established to assist state child and family welfare agencies develop family-based alternatives to foster care, the center provides technical assistance and consultation for the planning and implementation of family-based social service programs. Its free quarterly newsletter, *Prevention Report,* highlights the progress of public and voluntary agencies in this area, with profiles of particular states and programs, a legislative update, topical articles, and notification of new resources for prevention. Center publications include the *Annotated Bibliography of Family Based Services* (1982, $3), the *Annotated Directory of Exemplary Family Based Programs* (1984, $5), *Family-Centered Social Services: A Model for Child Welfare Agencies* (1983, $7), a variety of family-based training materials, and an audiovisual presentation. The center also has a library of more than 2,000 items, including books, pamphlets, leaflets, articles, brochures, clippings, newsletters, journals, videotapes, and a film. A complete list of materials and prices is available on request.

L70   PARENTS WITHOUT PARTNERS, INC. (PWP)   7910 Woodmont Ave., Bethesda, MD 20814. (301) 654-8850, (800) 638-8078

A national and international mutual help organization of single parents—the widowed, divorced, separated, or never married—who are bringing up children alone or, although not having custody, are concerned with the upbringing of their children. Its tasks and purposes are to support single parents and their children in all aspects of single parenting through such activities as rap sessions, family outings, and provision of information on topics like child support and divorce law. Publications include *Single Parent Magazine* (10 issues/year, $9) and many brochures, reading lists, and booklets on relevant topics. Titles of some bibliographies are *Remarriage/Stepparenting Bibliography* and *Separation and Divorce: Annotated Bibliography*. These all are included in a *Single Parent Survival Packet*. PWP's information center—open to parents and researchers—has substantial uncataloged vertical files and more than 800 books.

L71   **SCHOOL AGE CHILD CARE PROJECT (SACC)** Wellesley College Center for Research on Women, Wellesley, MA 02181. (617) 431-1453

A national information and technical assistance resource committed to promoting and enhancing the development of formal and informal programs and services for children ages 5 through 12 before and after school and at those times when there is a need for care and supervision. SACC provides information, technical assistance, and consultation to parents, schools, child care and youth-serving agencies, and policymakers on ways to organize, design, and implement services for children. It issues a very informative *SACC Newsletter* that reports on programs nationwide, announces resources and conferences, and reviews books. Other well-done publications include a *School-Age Child Care: Bibliography and Resource List* ($5.00 postpaid, with reprints). *School-Age Child Care: An Action Manual* (Boston, Auburn House, 1982, 486 pp., $14.95 postpaid) is a guide to organizing, designing, and managing child care programs for school-age children and is addressed to parents, school administrators, community organizers, and anyone else interested in starting child care programs. *School-Age Child Care: A Policy Report* (1983, $10.00 postpaid) is addressed primarily to policymakers and advocacy groups. SACC has numerous articles, research papers, and program materials (including videotapes and slides) on the topic and offers loans and photocopies to nonmembers.

L72   **SOUTHWEST EDUCATIONAL DEVELOPMENT LABORATORY (SEDL)** 211 E. Seventh St., Austin, TX 78701. (512) 476-6861

An educational development laboratory with some expertise in parent involvement and parent education; it developed a Parenting Materials Information Center—apparently not currently funded—which included around 4,000 items on all aspects of parenting. Some of these tools are described in *Parenting in 1977,* a bibliography available in many libraries. At one time, the center offered a free literature search on parenting materials. This has been replaced by the Positive Parent program, which offers 12 booklets at $4.50/set or $0.35 each (less with quantity orders) and 26 video spots on effective parenting skills. Some reference publications are *Paraprofessionals in Early Education of the Handicapped: Literature Review and Annotated Bibliography* (1977, $6.00) and *Media and Materials for Early Childhood in the 1980's: A Survey of Preschool Personnel* (1981, $2.00). Reference and survey works on toys and games include *Toy Preference and Safety Knowledge* (1981, $3.50), which surveys teachers' knowledge of toy selection and safety, and *Toys: More than Trifles for Play* (1981, $6.00), which reviews the toy industry, educational claims for toys, safety standards and precautions, toy selection, and toy libraries. Other works deal with basic skills and with cognitive aspects of games and informal learning. A publications list is available on request.

L73 **TRIADOPTION LIBRARY** P.O. Box 638, Westminster, CA 92684. (714) 892-4098
A nonprofit special library that gathers, preserves, and disseminates information related to extended families, with a focus on separation and reconciliation of families separated by divorce, surrender, adoption, geography, or the inability to communicate. Its services include a computerized referral service to search and support organizations; individual guidance for those seeking information on relatives; classes, seminars, and conferences; a speakers' bureau: and publications. Some titles are *The Adoption Searchbook, The Adoption Encounter Group,* and *Searching for Minors.* The Triadoption Library contains city, telephone, and microfiche directories; related titles in genealogy, fiction, law, sociology, and autobiography; audio- and videocassettes; volumes compiled from articles in law, psychological, and medical journals; and newspaper and magazine clippings. Its genealogical archives contains surname card files and family histories submitted by family members. Modest fees are charged to cover costs.

L74 **UNION COLLEGE CHARACTER RESEARCH PROJECT** 266 State St., Schenectady, NY 11203. (518) 370-6012

This research project, associated with Union College, is concerned with the moral and character development of children and youths. Activities include group training for parents of preschool children and publications for parents and professionals. Titles include *Let Me Introduce Myself* (1976, 128 pp., $7.95), *Your Baby's First 30 Months* (1981, 160 pp., $5.95), *Religious Education of Preschool Children* (1981, 196 pp., $5.95), *When a Story Would Help* (1981, 84 pp., $2.45), and *Celebrating the Second Year of Life* (1979, 148 pp., $5.95)—all on infancy and preschool children. Professional publications include *Evaluating Moral Development* (1980, 230 pp., $6.95), *Character Development in College Students* (1982, 329 pp., $10.95), and *Athena's Mirror: Moral Reasoning in Poetry, Short Story and Drama* (1982, 376 pp., $12.95). A library of books, pamphlets, and periodicals can be used on-site.

L75   **THE VANIER INSTITUTE OF THE FAMILY/L'INSTI-TUT VANIER DE LA FAMILLE**   151 Slater St., Suite 207, Ottawa K1P 5H3, Canada. (613) 232-7115
The Vanier Institute, established in 1965, is a national membership association (open to individuals and groups) to promote the well-being of families and the quality of life in a familial society. Program areas include communications; media and technology; learning and the family; research and knowledge development; and work, economy, and the family. Its Resource and Information Centre includes more than 5,500 books, 330 vertical files, and 176 periodicals. The institute has issued a substantial number of publications in French and English (although some are in one language only). Most of these are concerned with policy issues on the family. Two interesting bibliographies are *Varieties of Family Lifestyles: A Selected, Annotated Bibliography* (300 references, 1977, $1.50) and *Perspectives on Learning: A Selected Annotated Bibliography* (1976, $2.50), with many references on the family and learning. Its quarterly newsletter, *Transition* (free, although a contribution of $10.00 is appreciated), reports on its own work and that of other groups and individuals concerned with the family; it includes reviews, summaries from current journals, guest opinions, and reference materials.

L76   **WORK AND FAMILY INFORMATION CENTER**   The Conference Board, 845 Third Ave., New York, NY 10022. (212) 759-0900
A new service, established in 1983, designed to meet the needs of the business community and other organizations concerned with work and family relations. It collects, analyzes, and disseminates information on trends in family characteristics of the work force, personnel policies

and practices that are beneficial to the families of workers, major actions on relevant legislative and regulatory issues, and innovative employer partnerships with government agencies or community groups. Its services are available to Conference Board Associates, government and social service agencies, foundations, educational and research institutions, the media, and other groups involved with work and family issues.

PART IV

Special Subjects

14 / Measurements, Tests, and Assessments

This chapter, in an effort to be holistic, combines measurements, tests, and assessments from the fields of growth, development, health, intelligence, suitability for schooling, and anthropometry. Tests and assessments are first concerned with ascertaining some normal level and then measuring and differentiating among departures from this norm. The majority of tests and assessments, however, seem to be concerned with locating or screening for children at risk, children with special needs, or children lacking a knowledge of the predominant culture or testing language. This chapter is far from a complete guide to tests and assessments involving children, but I hope it will provide users with some background on the range of childhood tests and assessments and guides to other sources of tests. It provides tests for individual children and for groups of children, tests that can be administered by parents or volunteers, and measurements that require clinical judgment. It includes not only reference books and bibliographies but also handbooks, texts, manuals, and anthologies that cover issues and provide points of view, including parental and professional perspectives. Items were selected for clarity, comprehensiveness, practicality, recency, and interdisciplinary value. Since *A Guide to Sources of Educational Information* (B7) has a substantial chapter on educational tests and assessments, I have included here only a few titles from this field. *Selecting Materials for Instruction: Issues and Policies* (O66) similarly covers organizations such as the SOI (Structure of

Intellect) Institute (214 Main St., El Segundo, CA 90245) and the Learned Society of Intelligence Education in Tokyo that focus on Guilford's intellectual abilities rather than subject matter or standard intelligence. Although most of the materials here are based largely on the American experience, I have included several with an international perspective.

There are many types of tests for children, but I am including only one major organization—the Educational Testing Service (ETS), which now operates the National Assessment of Educational Progress; the ERIC Clearinghouse on Tests, Measurement, and Evaluation; and the Test Collection. Other organizations concerned with educational and psychological testing are covered in Chapter 18 of *A Guide to Sources of Educational Information*. The Test Collection and the ERIC Clearinghouse on Tests, Measurement, and Evaluation both keep up with organizations concerned with tests and measurements. The National Center for Health Statistics, which is treated in Chapter 15, appraises child health; indicators, a form of appraisal, are also treated in Chapter 15. Some organizations in Chapter 13 are similarly concerned with evaluating disabilities or health.

The appraisal of specialized areas, such as mathematical thinking, artistic ability, or musical competence, are usually followed by organizations like the National Council of Teachers of Mathematics and The National Art Educator's Association. Usually their compilations and research are entered into the ERIC data base. PsycINFO follows psychological tests, whereas various medical indexes and data bases cover health appraisals and medical screening. The FAMILY RESOURCES DATABASE is a good source for family measurement instruments. The National Auxiliary Publications Service (NAPS) of the American Society for Information Science (ASIS) is a microfiche depository for some unpublished tests (ASIS/NAPS, P.O. Box 3513, Grand Central Sta., New York, NY 10017).

The *Glossary of Measurement Terms* (A12) and *Manual on Terminology and Classification in Mental Retardation* (A19) are relevant dictionaries. The *Encyclopedia of Pediatric Psychology* (A29) discusses pediatric tests, and the *Basic Handbook of Child Psychiatry* (A26) covers psychiatric testing. Various annuals in Chapter 5, especially *Advances in the Behavioral Measurement of Children*

(D10) update the field. Pertinent bibliographies in Chapter 6 include *Annotated Bibliography on Perceptual-Motor Development* (E8), *Bibliography on Human Intelligence* (E21), *Child Health Assessment* (E34), *The Education of Poor and Minority Children* (E66), and *The Gifted Student* (E84). The Film Archives on Child Development, described in item F13, is an important pictorial resource.

ORGANIZATIONS

M1 **EDUCATIONAL TESTING SERVICE (ETS)** Rosedale Rd., Princeton, NJ 08541. ERIC/TM, (609) 734-5181; Test Collection, (609) 734-5686

The Test Collection of ETS is an extensive library of tests and assessment instruments. It is a reference resource for those engaged in education, research, advisory services, and related activities. The collection includes around 12,000 tests cataloged by author, title, and subject and backed by reference books on tests. The director, Marilyn Halpern, estimates that several thousand of these tests are suitable for use with children between birth and 12 years of age. Probably 1,300–2,000 tests cover personality, attitudes, interests, and vocational skills. Supplementary files include addresses of foreign and American test publishers, references to test reviews, and a large collection of test-publisher catalogs.

The hardworking, competent staff of four continually prepares and updates approximately 200 bibliographies of tests covering various subjects and/or different populations. Publications include *Major U.S. Publishers of Standardized Tests* (free, updated as necessary) and an excellent newsletter, *News on Tests* ($25/year, $27/year foreign), that includes announcements and descriptions of new tests, reference materials in the area of testing, and information on conferences and organizations. It is an outstanding current-awareness source with a yearly index that serves as a convenient checklist for new tests and references.

The Test Collection also produces bibliographies ($3 each) that cover relevant areas such as *Achievement Batteries, Preschool–Gr. 3; Behavior Rating Scales, Gr. 4–6; Manual Dexterity; Infant Development; Piagetian Measures; Moral Development; Culture-Fair and Culture Relevant Tests; Social Skills, Birth–9; Children's Attitudes Toward Parents; Spanish*

Speakers, Preschool–Gr. 3; Auditory Skills; and *Attitudes Toward School and School Adjustment, Gr. 4–6.*

Its series, *Tests in Microfiche,* backed by annotated indexes, have been issued since 1975 in sets of 40–100 titles for around $100/set. These make available in microfiche format a variety of educational, psychological, and related research instruments that have not been published by commercial test publishers; many are related to children. ETS microfiche test sets are now available at more than 500 locations. Lists of these collections and the titles in each set and lists of bibliographies are available on request.

The Test Collection answers specific mail and telephone requests free of charge and distributes free minibibliographies of several citations in response to reference questions. In addition, the Test Collection file is now available on-line as a publicly searchable, computer-retrievable data base through BRS (J1) so researchers and others can run their own computer searches on the Test Collection data base. The Test Collection staff will continue to respond to reference requests.

The ERIC Clearinghouse on Tests, Measurement, and Evaluation (ERIC/TM), a separate unit in ETS, collects, evaluates, processes, and disseminates information in five areas of interest: tests and information on tests, all types of measurement instruments, program evaluation, cognitive development after infancy and early childhood, and general learning theory applied to humans. It publishes three series of interpretive summaries: *TM Reports,* monographs on such topics as assessment of learning disabilities and intelligence testing; *Highlight,* annotated bibliographies on topics like competency testing of teachers and minimum-competency testing; and *Updates,* minibibliographies or brief fact sheets on the evaluation of gifted programs and student evaluation of teacher performance. ERIC/TM also offers customized searches of ERIC and social science data bases. Its 1977 *Directory of Information on Tests* costs $3.

**M2   NATIONAL ASSESSMENT OF EDUCATIONAL PROG-
RESS (NAEP)** Rosedale Rd., Box 2923, Princeton, NJ 08541. (800) 223-0267

NAEP is a government-mandated, continuing national survey of the knowledge, skills, understanding, and attitudes of 75,000–85,000 children and youths at the ages of 9, 13, and 17, and young adults from 25 to 35. These ages, which correspond to the end of primary, intermediate, secondary, and formal postsecondary education, are considered key points in the education system. (In recent assessments, however, out-of-school 17-year-olds and 25- to 35-year-olds have not been included.) NAEP gathers information on the degree to which educational goals are being met and makes this information available so that problem areas can be identified and priorities established. Only reading and mathematics *must* be assessed, but 10 areas have been examined in a revolving plan: art, careers and occupational development, citizenship, literature, mathematics, music, reading, science, social studies, and writing. Periodic small-scale probes provide specific information on limited areas like life skills or consumer skills for particular age groups. Reports group achievement by geographic region, community size and type, sex, race, and level of parents' education. More than 125 reports have been issued and are available through the ERIC system and ETS offices. Many have been printed as government documents. ETS, which now administers the project, hopes to make this data base more accessible through improved communication methods, perhaps by linking it to other national data bases.

ETS, which succeeds the Education Commission of the States as the overseer agency for NAEP, has issued a detailed framework of its approach in *National Assessment of Educational Progress Reconsidered: A New Design for a New Era* (NAEP Report 83-1), free on request. NAEP believes that the new collection design will help in using data for policy decisions. A free quarterly *NAEP Newsletter* covers current assessment activities and findings. The last issue of the year usually includes a good summary. Leaflets summarizing assessment findings in particular areas are usually available free. Full reports are available from NAEP, ERIC, and GPO. A complete list of publications is available from NAEP, whose distribution center also makes available data tapes of NAEP assessments.

PUBLICATIONS

M3   **AAHPERD HEALTH RELATED PHYSICAL FITNESS TEST MANUAL**   By the American Alliance for Health, Physical Education, Recreation, and Dance. Reston, Va., 1980. 80 pp. $3.95 (paperback). From: P.O. Box 704, Waldorf, MD 20610.

This test is designed to screen children and youths from ages 6 to 17 on items related to health status in childhood and adult years. The manual evaluates aspects of physiological and psychological functioning that are believed to offer significant protection against degenerative diseases such as musculoskeletal disorders, obesity, and coronary disease. It concentrates on cardiovascular function, body composition, strength, and flexibility—components basic to fitness. AAHPERD also sells Cumulative Fitness Records, Personal Fitness Records, and Class Composite Records at low prices. A Health Related Physical Fitness Sample Kit ($4.25) contains the manual and sample forms.

M4   APPRAISAL OF INDIVIDUAL DEVELOPMENT (AID) SCALES By Appalachia Educational Laboratory (AEL). Charleston, W.Va., not dated. *AID Scales User's Manual,* with scales, $8; *AID Scales,* $6. From: Educational Communications, Inc., 9240 S.W. 124th St., Miami, FL 33176.

An experimental set of scales that assesses the preschooler's development in 59 developmental competency areas in 49 competency clusters. Areas correspond to the competency base that Appalachia uses in its *Day Care and Home Learning Activities Plans* and its *Classroom Learning Activity Plans.*

M5   ASSESSING CHILDREN WITH SPECIAL NEEDS: A PRACTICAL GUIDE FOR THE USE OF PSYCHOLOGICAL, BEHAVIORAL, AND EDUCATIONAL MEASURES By Thomas and Aline Mahan. New York, Holt, Rinehart & Winston, 1981. 229 pp. $10.95 (paperback).

Geared toward teachers, school psychologists, and graduate students in education, this book uses an active involvement method and case studies to demonstrate how to use assessment measures effectively to improve teaching/learning interactions. The first part provides overviews of the basic characteristics of standard educational and psychological assessment instruments and the use of assessment data in making decisions. Includes detailed discussions of the evaluation of behavioral characteristics, perceptual abilities, motor skills, creativity, and critical thinking.

M6   ASSESSING THE HANDICAPS AND NEEDS OF MENTALLY RETARDED CHILDREN Edited by Brian Cooper. New York, Academic Health, 1981. 268 pp. $24.50.

Eighteen essays based on papers read at a small multidisciplinary colloquium at the Central Institute of Mental Health in Mannheim, West Germany involving European pediatricians, psychiatrists, neurologists, clinical workers, educational psychologists, and biostatisticians. Papers deal with topics like estimating needs, the neurological and neurophysiological bases of handicaps, means of assessing mental handicaps, patterns and profiles in mental handicaps, assessing family situations, assessing and evaluating special care, early diagnosis, and prevention.

Valuable for its interdisciplinary, international perspective. Includes an index.

M7 ASSESSING THE LEARNING DISABLED: Selected Instruments, The Diagnostician's Handbook 3rd Edition. Edited by August J. Mauser. Novato, Calif., Academic Therapy, 1981. 288 pp. $12.50 (paperback).

A well-organized book that provides concise annotations for more than 300 evaluation instruments for children and adults with learning disabilities. These are categorized into broad areas such as preschool readiness, reading readiness, diagnostic reading, survey tests, oral reading, mathematics abilities, creativity tests, social adjustment, and miscellaneous items. Information on tests includes source, age range suitability, administration time for each test, and particular distinguishing characteristics of each test. The book has an alphabetic index, publishers' names and addresses, and comprehensive selected reading lists.

M8 ASSESSMENT INSTRUMENTS IN BILINGUAL EDUCATION: A Descriptive Catalog of 342 Oral and Written Tests By the Northwest Regional Educational Laboratory, Center for Bilingual Education. Los Angeles, California State University, National Dissemination and Assessment Center, 1978. 485 pp. $5.95. From: 5151 State University Dr., Los Angeles, CA 90032. (Also in ERIC as ED 173 373)

Provides thorough descriptions of 342 different tests in 38 languages (although most are English or Spanish) from preschool through adult level. Separate chapters cover language proficiency, language dominance, self-concept and personality measures, sociocultural measures, reading and reading readiness, general achievement, aptitudes and interests, and miscellaneous. Most chapters are further divided into tests in English, Spanish, and other languages. Descriptions include name, test developer, source, copyright or development date, language, description, age or grade level, administration time, scoring methods and availability of scores, cost per student, and a sample item. Descriptions also note whether the test is for groups or individuals and whether it is commercial or locally developed. Indexes list instruments, publishers, and local projects.

M9 THE ASSESSMENT OF PSYCHOPATHOLOGY AND BEHAVIORAL PROBLEMS IN CHILDREN: A Review of Scales Suitable for Epidemiological and Clinical Research (1967-1979) By Helen Orvaschel, Diane Sholomskas, and

Myrna M. Weissmen. Rockville, Md., National Institute of
Mental Health, Division of Biometry and Epidemiology, 1980.
85 pp. $4.50 (paper). (Mental Health Services Systems Reports,
Series AN, Epidemiology No. 1) (Also in ERIC as ED 213 749)
A monograph issued by the Division of Biometry and Epidemiology to
keep the scientific community abreast of current research; it summarizes and supplies bibliographic references for 44 current (post-1967)
scales suitable for epidemiologic studies of children and adolescents
under age 18. These include tests of intelligence, intellectual functioning, brain dysfunction, organicity (dysfunction due to structural change
in the central nervous system), learning disabilities, personality, infant
development, perception, cognitive development, and projective tests.
The apparent purpose is to assess the prevalence of psychopathology in
children. Tests are divided into psychiatric interviews, general psychopathology scales, specific syndrome (e.g., anxiety, depression) scales,
and miscellaneous scales. Areas covered for each are purpose and properties of the scale, methods of obtaining information, informant, content, and psychometric properties. All 44 scales are summarized in
tables designed to help investigators choose those appropriate for their
study groups. The addresses and phone numbers of scale developers
are included.

M10   ASSESSMENT OF RISK IN THE NEWBORN: Evaluation
      During the Transitional Period   By C. J. Lepley. White Plains,
      N.Y., March of Dimes Birth Defects Foundation, 1980. 24 pp.
      Free to professionals, from local chapter of March of Dimes
      (paper). (Module 4, Part A)
One of a series of Nursing Staff Development Programs issued by the
March of Dimes Birth Defects Foundation. This one emphasizes the
knowledge and techniques necessary to assess the newborn during the
first six hours of life, with particular attention given to the uses and interpretation of neonatal assessments most commonly used in the delivery room and nursery. Includes brief discussions of appropriate nursing
interventions and assessments necessary during the first 24 hours. Although it does not address specific interventions for high-risk newborns, it does provide assessments to assist nurses in identifying newborns at risk.

M11   THE BABY CHECKUP BOOK: A PARENT'S GUIDE TO
      WELL BABY CARE   By Sheilah Hillman et al. New York,
      Bantam Books, 1982. 334 pp. $6.95 (paperback).

A very clear, well-organized explanation of checkups (physical examinations) during the first 15 months of life, arranged chronologically in 11 chapters that progress from the first few minutes of life to the 15-month checkup. Includes checklists, photographs, and score tables that indicate what physicians are looking for and why they perform these tests. Defines and explains hard-to-find terms like *Apgar.* Written in consultation with three physicians.

M12 **BASIC DEVELOPMENTAL SCREENING: 0–4 YEARS** 3rd Edition. By Roland S. Illingworth. Boston, Mass., Blackwell Scientific Publications, 1982. 64 pp. Price not available.
Intended as a simple, practical guide to developmental screening to enable the busy doctor to rapidly eliminate developmental and/or neurological abnormalities and to know when to seek a specialist's advice. Includes only those screening tests that do not require any apparatus more complicated than firm cardboard. Logically arranged, with chapters on developmental history and interpretations; includes an index.

M13 **BEHAVIORAL ASSESSMENT: A PRACTICAL HANDBOOK** 2nd Edition. Edited by Michel Hersen and Alan S. Bellack. New York, Pergamon, 1981. 603 pp. $45.00; paperback, $19.50.
Includes 15 chapters in three sections—fundamental issues, assessment strategies, and evaluation for treatment planning. The emphasis is on methodology, with case descriptions for specific disorders. Includes chapters on assessing children in inpatient and outpatient settings.

M14 **CHILD HEALTH ASSESSMENT PART 2: THE FIRST YEAR OF LIFE** Hyattsville, Md., Bureau of Health Manpower, Division of Nursing, 1979. 222 pp. $7.50 (paper). (DHEW Publication No. HRA 79-25)
A report of methods developed and validated by the Nursing Child Assessment Project to study and observe children and their environment during the first year of life, including physical, mental, and social growth and development.

M15 **CHILDREN AT RISK: A HANDBOOK OF THE SIGNS AND SYMPTOMS OF EARLY CHILDHOOD DIFFICULTIES** By Gary A Crow. New York, Schocken Books, 1978. 280 pp. $12.95.
A guide to help teachers, parents, and others working with children from ages five to eight identify some 100 significant early signs and

symptoms that may indicate that these children need special attention and help. Particular symptoms were selected from a total of 450 that Crow uncovered in a substantial literature search. For convenience, they are categorized as physical/organic, emotional/social, academic/ classroom, and environmental/family. Chapters on each of the subgroups include case histories and a detailed "symptom profile," or individual record-keeping form.

M16 **THE CLINICAL INTERVIEW OF THE CHILD** By Stanley I. Greenspan, with Nancy Thorndike Greenspan. New York, McGraw-Hill, 1981. 224 pp. $17.95.

A clinician's guide that provides a how-to, systematic framework for interviewing all kinds of children at all ages. Includes ways to observe the child's physical and neurological status, overall mood, capacity for human relationships, emotional or affect proclivities, means of coping with anxiety, and capacity for thematic organization. The book explains how to set up and conduct interviews, suggests special strategies for different ages or developmental capacities, and helps clinicians understand their own subjective responses to the children they observe.

M17 **CLINICAL METHODS IN PEDIATRIC DIAGNOSIS** By Balu H. Athreya. New York, Van Nostrand Reinhold, 1980. 289 pp. $24.50.

The basic aim of this clearly written guide is to elicit history and physical findings and to use a logical approach in describing physical findings. It suggests methods of history taking (including a basic outline for pediatric history), observation, and physical examination oriented toward child patients and approaches for delineating specific complaints. Covers the general physical examination, as well as detailed but generally simple methods for examining body regions and systems. It has separate chapters on assessing child development and behavior and examining the newborn. Includes an index.

M18 **COMPETENCY BASED EDUCATION SOURCEBOOK** 1st Edition. By Oregon Competency Based Education Program. Portland, Oreg., Northwest Regional Educational Laboratory, 1977. 752 pp. $28.50. From: Northwest Regional Educational Laboratory, Office of Marketing, 300 S.W. Sixth Ave., Portland, OR 97204. (2nd Edition [1978] available from ERIC as ED 163 660)

A comprehensive reference guide of successful programs based on student competencies, compiled for planners, teachers, and administrators, with indexes by component, title, and originator. Materials are grouped into four areas: identification of instructional outcomes, measurement of outcome attainment, promotion of instructional outcomes, and management of programs.

M19   DEVELOPMENTAL   PSYCHOMETRICS: A   Resource Book for Mental Health Workers and Educators   By Jack L. Fadely and Virginia N. Hosler. Springfield, Ill., C. C Thomas, 1980. 158 pp. $13.75; paperback, $9.75.

A handbook for social workers, mental health workers, allied health personnel, and general and special education teachers that presents a holistic method for assessing the developmental levels of children and adolescents in language, intelligence, personality, perceptual motor skills, and social concepts. The authors begin with a general introduction to the current status of developmental evaluation, stressing the multidimensional nature of behavior and assessment. Chapters review broad areas like intelligence, development, and learning; the school/community interface; the preschool child; perceptual motor development; learning skills assessment; personality factors; and social behavioral assessments. For each area, the authors consider the developmental aspects, the assessment procedures, and the implications for learning and remediation and sometimes review specific tests. Overall, the work is practical, concise, and reasonably clear. Includes an index.

M20   DIRECT OBSERVATION AND MEASUREMENT OF BE-HAVIOR   By S. J. Hutt and Corinne Hutt. Springfield, Ill., C. C Thomas, 1978. 224 pp. $18.50.

Two researchers at the Human Development Research Unit of the Park Hospital for Children in Oxford, England set down their experiences in recording and measuring behavior and discuss studies that illustrate their methodologies and techniques. Methodologies are drawn mainly from studies of children and animals; techniques include sequential analysis, tape recording, checklists, event recorders, motion pictures, and videotaping. Behavior elements, social behavior, and the effects of drugs on behavior were observed. The book has a subject index, an author index, and substantial references, as well as a glossary of "motor patterns of four-year-old nursery school children."

M21   DIRECTORY   OF   UNPUBLISHED   EXPERIMENTAL MENTAL MEASURES   By Bert A. Goldman and John Christian Busch. New York, Human Sciences Press, 1974– . Vol. 1: 1974, 223 pp., $26.95; Vol. 2: 1978, 518 pp., $34.95; Vol. 3: 1982, 448 pp., $39.95.

A directory (primarily for researchers) of experimental test instruments not produced commercially at the time of publication; based on an exhaustive review and careful search of tests in some 40 education and psychology journals. Volume 1 covers 1970; Volume 2, 1971 and 1972; and Volume 3, 1973. Volumes for 1974–1979 are now in preparation. Items covered are thoroughly annotated and arranged by categories such as achievement, aptitude, and problem solving. Volume 3 has an author/title index.

M22 **DISCOVERY AND NURTURANCE OF GIFTEDNESS IN THE CULTURALLY DIFFERENT** By E. Paul Torrance. Reston, Va., Council for Exceptional Children, 1977. 101 pp. (Out of print) (Available from ERIC as ED 145 621)
Identifies some important issues and trends on the use of standardized tests for giftedness in the culturally different (i.e., not "mainstream" or middle class) and suggests 18 nonpsychometric measures for identifying giftedness among such children.

M23 **EARLY ADOLESCENT COMPETENCIES** Edited by Clifford H. Sweat. Danville, Ill., Interstate Printers & Publishers, 1979. 69 pp. $4.75.
A compilation of articles examining the competencies that are supposedly basic to the development of early adolescents (largely in the middle school/junior high years), ranging from academic to cultural (music and art), physical, social, and vocational (career development) aspects. Since these competencies are basically related to education and because the purposes of education are poorly defined for this age group, there is a fuzzy feel to this book as a whole, although some sections (mathematics, for example) are relatively precise. The concepts and criteria expressed, however, are not readily available elsewhere.

M24 **EARLY CHILDHOOD ENVIRONMENTAL RATING SCALE** By Thelma Harms and Richard M. Clifford. New York, Columbia University, Teachers College, 1980. 38 pp. $5.95 (paper).
A 37-item research instrument designed to enable teachers, directors, trainers, and state licensing staff to assess objectively the adequacy of environments for children between the ages of two and six. Areas covered are space, daily schedule, types of supervision, and experiences. The scale includes clear directions, information on reliability and validity, and a guide for training observers.

M25 **EARLY IDENTIFICATION OF EMOTIONALLY HANDI-
CAPPED CHILDREN IN SCHOOL** 3rd Edition. By Eli M.
Bower. Springfield, Ill., C. C Thomas, 1982. 320 pp. $26.75.
A classic—now in its third edition—that provides an in-depth study of
the early identification and treatment of emotionally handicapped children in school. The new edition covers the implications of P.L. 94-142
and the Early Periodic Screening, Diagnosis and Treatment (EPSDT)
program. It deals with history and research, as well as the use and interpretation of screening tests.

M26 **AN EDUCATOR'S GUIDE TO PSYCHOLOGICAL TESTS:
DESCRIPTIONS AND CLASSROOM IMPLICATIONS**
By Constance Tarczan. Springfield, Ill. C. C Thomas, 1972. 128
pp. $8.75 (spiral-bound).
A concise introductory guide to standardized psychological tests geared
toward teachers of special education, with descriptions of the most commonly used and cited tests, a chapter on basic statistical terminology,
descriptions of statistical techniques, and discussions of concepts such
as intelligence quotient and mental age.

M27 **EXAMINATION OF THE CHILD WITH MINOR NEU-
ROLOGICAL DYSFUNCTION** 2nd Edition. By Bert C. L.
Touwen. London, Spastics International Medical Publications,
and Philadelphia, Pa., J. B. Lippincott, 1979. 139 pp. $25
(paper). (Clinics in Developmental Medicine No. 71) From:
J. B. Lippincott, E. Washington Sq., Philadelphia, PA 19105.
Concerned mainly with the neurological examination of children without apparent neurological problems, referred to specialists because of
behavioral and/or learning difficulties. This edition, which is thoroughly revised, discusses the relationships between neurological dysfunction
and behavior in children and provides techniques for examination (sit-
ting, standing, reflexes, and so forth) and for detection of minor neurological dysfunctions. Illustrated with photographs and black-and-
white drawings.

M28 **FAMILY MEASUREMENT TECHNIQUES: ABSTRACTS
OF PUBLISHED INSTRUMENTS, 1935–1975** Revised
Edition. By Murray A. Strauss and Bruce W. Brown. Minneapo-
lis, University of Minnesota Press, 1978. 668 pp. $32.50.
Contains abstracts of 813 tests used in family measurement, based on a
thorough literature search. One section covers parent/child and sibling/

sibling measures for conflict and integration, role differentiation and
performance, interpersonal competence, and multivariable measures
of parent/child relations—131 pages altogether, subdivided into many
smaller topics. Another section (164 pages) deals with similar measures
that cover husband/wife and parent/child variables. Sex and premarital
relations are dealt with in a 39-page section. Entries provide full bibliographic information, an abstract, a sample question from the test, indication of test length, ordering information, and further references
when available. Reliability/validity evaluations are not included, since
less than half the instruments have them. The book has author, test
title, and subject indexes.

M29 **GESELL AND AMATRUDA'S DEVELOPMENTAL DIAG-
NOSIS: The Evaluation and Management of Normal and Abnormal Neuropsychologic Development in Infancy and Early
Childhood** 3rd Edition. Edited by Hilda Knobloch and Benjamin Pasamanick. Hagerstown, Md., Harper & Row, 1974. 537
pp. $26.75.
The most recent edition of the classic work of Arnold Gesell and Catherine Amatruda on diagnosing developmental problems. Broad areas,
covered in 20 chapters and 5 appendixes, include development; defects
and deviations in development; ways to protect early childhood development through screening, guidance, and management; training for developmental diagnosis; and the clinical aspects of child adoption. Appendixes supply information on techniques and equipment, audiovisual
aids, and a bibliography.

M30 **A GUIDE TO ASSESSMENT INSTRUMENTS FOR LIM-
ITED ENGLISH SPEAKING STUDENTS** By Barbara P.
Pletcher et al. New York, Santillana, 1978. 55 pp. $9.50 (paper-
back).
Covers available assessment instruments for elementary school children whose first language is Chinese, French, Navajo, Portuguese,
Spanish, or Tagalog, arranged by language. Instruments, normed on
children residing in the United States, are designed to yield widely applicable scores. Descriptions include source, purpose, target ethnic
group, score interpretation, grade range, administration time and requirements, author, and costs. Includes language dominance tests,
tests of language proficiency, attitude and self-concept inventories,
measures of cognitive style, and achievement tests in mathematics or
multisubject areas.

M31 **HANDBOOK FOR MEASUREMENT AND EVALUATION IN EARLY CHILDHOOD EDUCATION** By William Lawrence Goodwin and Laura A. Driscoll. San Francisco, Calif., Jossey-Bass, 1980. 632 pp. $27.95. (Social and Behavioral Science Series)

A handbook that combines three topics usually treated separately. Intended to provide guidelines to improve early childhood education through measurement and evaluation. Includes an examination of the status of early childhood education, followed by seven chapters on measurement in early childhood education and four on evaluation.

M32 **HANDICAPPED CHILDREN: EARLY DETECTION, INTERVENTION AND EDUCATION: Selected Case Studies from Argentina, Canada, Denmark, Jamaica, Jordan, Nigeria, Sri Lanka, Thailand and the United Kingdom** Paris, Unesco, 1981. 142 pp. $17.50. From: Unipub, Box 433, Murray Hill Sta., New York, NY 10157.

Supplies current information on identification of and intervention in early handicap problems in numerous countries, along with a discussion of current plans and experimental programs. Includes charts and references.

M33 **IDENTIFYING HANDICAPPED CHILDREN: A Guide to Case Finding, Screening, Diagnosis, Assessment and Evaluation** Edited by Lee Cross and Kenneth Goin. New York, Walker, 1977. 127 pp. $7.95 (paperback).

A textbook that includes a 62-page annotated bibliography of screening, diagnosis, and assessment instruments, with information on prices and availability.

M34 **IQ TESTS FOR SCHOOL CHILDREN (How to Test Your Child's Intelligence)** By Martin Lutterjohann. Translated from the German by Hanna Gunther. New York, Stein and Day, 1980 (originally published in Munich in 1977). 232 pp. $5.95 (paperback).

Tests for children between the ages of 6 and 14, arranged by age, with explanations for parents on how to determine school readiness and the like. Discusses ways to train for perception, concentration, language, memory, math aptitude, logical thinking, and creative thinking. The author also has issued *IQ Tests for Children* (1978, 179 pp., $4.95 [paperback]), which covers tests for children from infancy to age six.

M35 MANUAL OF PHYSICAL STATUS AND PERFOR-
MANCE IN CHILDHOOD, Vol. 1: Physical Status; Vol. 2:
Physical Performance   By Robert M. Malina and Alex F.
Roche. New York, Plenum, 1983. 2,270 pp. $310.
A three-part set in two volumes that summarizes most extant research
on anthropometric measurements of children and provides an extensive listing of annotated references. Volumes 1A and 1B cover measurements of the body as a whole and of specific body parts. Volume 2
presents complementary data on functional measurements, including
body composition, physiological data, and physical performance.
Tables include data on representative samples of U.S. and Canadian
children, as well as samples from other geographic areas. They cover
standards and measurements of obvious utility, such as stature, weight,
and physical fitness peformance. Other measurements are more unusual (e.g., fingernail growth and skin pH) but undoubtedly are valuable
for research in child health and for designing appropriate environments. The work includes measurements for all health workers: den-
tists, radiologists, biologists, nutritionists, physical educators, and
kinesiologists.

M36   MENTAL MEASUREMENTS YEARBOOK (MMY)   8th
Edition. Edited by Oscar K. Buros. Lincoln, University of Nebraska Press, 1978. 2 Vols. $140.
This irregular yearbook, issued since 1941, is the standard source of information on published tests in education, psychology, and industry,
especially commercial tests sold in the United States. Covers tests and
test reviews and books and book reviews, all cross-indexed by authors,
test titles, and topics. Each edition supplements rather than supplants
the previous editions. Indexes include directories of periodicals and
publishers, indexes of books and test titles, an index of names, and
classified indexes of tests and reviews. Each edition has a section on
how to use the yearbook.
   For each test, detailed information is given on subject populations,
normative data, alternative forms, scoring services, administration
time, costs, references (in books, journal articles, and dissertations),
and, when possible, reviews by qualified professionals and ordering
information.

M37   MIRRORS FOR BEHAVIOR III: An Anthology of Observation Instruments   3rd Edition. Edited by Anita Simons and E.
Gil Boyer. Wyncote, Pa., Communications Materials Center,
1974. $22.95.

A supplement to the 17-volume out-of-print *Mirrors for Behavior,* this edition contains charts, abstracts, and descriptions of 99 observation instruments from a wide variety of systems (although most are in learning environments). Instruments deal with observation of families, infants, early education, small groups, animals, content analysis, and so on. For each test, information is provided on the subject of observation, the number of subjects observed, the collection methods reported, category dimensions, settings, coding units, needed personnel, and uses of the test as reported by the author.

M38 **THE NEUROLOGICAL ASSESSMENT OF THE PRE-TERM AND FULLTERM NEWBORN INFANT** By Victor and Libby Dubowitz. London, Spastics International Medical Books, and Philadelphia, Pa., J. B. Lippincott, 1981. 112 pp. $25. (Clinics in Developmental Medicine, No. 79) From: J. B. Lippincott, E. Washington Sq., Philadelphia, PA 19105.

One of a series of handbooks issued by Spastics International. Another is *The Neurological Examination of the Full Term Newborn Infant* (2nd Edition, 1977, 68 pp., $21, Clinics in Developmental Medicine, No. 63). These are simple, yet detailed, manuals based on clinical experience and current neurological concepts and practices. The *Neonatal Behavioral Assessment Scale* (2nd Edition, 1984, not yet paged or priced, Clinics in Developmental Medicine, No. 88) provides tools to study the behavior of the newborn.

M39 **OBSERVING AND RECORDING THE BEHAVIOR OF YOUNG CHILDREN** 2nd Edition. By Dorothy H. Cohen and Virginia Stern. New York, Teachers College Press, 1978. 176 pp. $7.50 (paperback).

An effective introduction to the skills of perceptive child observation in 11 chapters that cover ways to record behavior, use of materials, interactions with other children, dramatic play, relationships with adults and behavior in adult-directed activities, clues to cognitive functioning, language development, and others. Includes references for further reading.

M40 **PEDIATRIC SCREENING TESTS** Edited by William Frankenburg and Bonnie W. Camp. Springfield, Ill., C. C Thomas, 1975. 549 pp. $31.25.

A 16-chapter guide divided into four parts. The first part covers the principles of screening and the criteria to be considered in selecting diseases and screening tests. The other three parts cover procedures and pathology in screening for physical problems, screening sensory processes, and screening for psychopathology. Chapters in parts 2–4 start with general definitions and overviews of particular diseases, list the pros and cons of screening, and then follow up with reviews of tests that include where to obtain the test, the approximate cost of the test, the age range it is suitable for, administration requirements, and a critical review of the test (usually by two experts). Includes an index of all tests.

M41 **PRESCHOOL SCREENING: THE MEASUREMENT AND PREDICTION OF CHILDREN AT-RISK** By Keith E. Barnes. Springfield, Ill., C. C Thomas, 1982. 266 pp. $2.50.
An introductory text on the essential components of preschool screening, covering the testing process and measurements that can be performed by volunteers, health technicians, and paraprofessionals. These include measurements in education, mental health, and public health; measures of hearing and vision, speech and language, general development, and academic readiness; and experimental-research measures. Measures are described clearly in narrative form, giving an overview of the history and background of the test and what is known of its validity, reliability, and applications, with intelligent suggestions for applications obviously based on a great deal of experience. The book includes a bibliography, author and title indexes, and a directory of publishers.

M42 **PRESCHOOL TEST DESCRIPTIONS: Test Matrix and Correlated Test Descriptors** By H. Wayne Johnson. Springfield, Ill., C. C Thomas, 1979. 304 pp. $24.75 (spiral-bound).
A guide to 130 preschool tests to help in the appraisal and educational programming of young handicapped children. Two-page descriptions are arranged alphabetically by title with formatted information on source, date, cost, administration, appropriateness, interpretation, and technical aspects. Matrixes provide quick reference guides for selecting tests and for choosing among selection criteria. The book includes a clear description of the author's procedures and rationales and is useful for all preschool assessments.

M43 **PSYCHIATRIC EVALUATION OF CHILDREN** 3rd Edition. By James E. Simmons. Philadelphia, Pa., Lea & Febiger, 1981. 311 pp. $13.50.
A valuable exposition of the fundamentals of psychiatric evaluation, intended as a practical guide for physicians in training for child psychia-

try. Simmons uses a medical model for diagnosis and emphasizes the importance of carefully classifying child patients before jumping to conclusions or into therapy. He suggests that clinicians examine their own attitudes toward children and the predicaments these children are in. Whatever the theoretical meaning of fantasies and behavior, he believes that prognosis depends on whether the child can distinguish fantasy from reality and has the capacity to move toward maturity. *Psychiatric Evaluation of Children* also covers family evaluation, individual interviews, and the importance of using family members as allies in helping the child.

M44　**THE PSYCHOEDUCATIONAL ASSESSMENT OF PRE-SCHOOL CHILDREN** Edited by Kathleen D. Paget and Bruce A. Bracken. New York, Grune & Stratton, 1983. 551 pp. $32.50.

Contains comprehensive discussions of the issues, techniques, instruments, and procedures for formal and informal assessment of preschool children between the ages of two and six, organized into specific skill areas for an audience of school, child, and clinical psychologists, counselors, early-childhood educators, special educators, physicians, social workers, and audiologists. Twenty chapters cover cognitive, personality, and behavioral assessment, as well as language assessment, gross and fine motor development, speech assessment, creativity, neuropsychology, legal issues, auditory and visual functioning, giftedness, and cultural difference. All chapters have extensive current bibliographies; some use tables and charts. Includes a glossary and an index.

M45　**THE PSYCHOLOGICAL ASSESSMENT OF CHILDREN** 2nd Edition. By James O. Palmer. New York, Wiley, 1983. 634 pp. $37.50.

A broad, developmentally oriented review of the problems, issues, techniques, and procedures involved in the psychological assessment of children. Arranged in six sections (22 chapters) covering the hypothesis of assessment, methods of data collection, procedures in assessment, analysis of assessments, special problems (e.g., assessing infants and preschool children, physically handicapped children, children with developmental and learning disabilities and traumatic brain damage, children from different cultures, and children in the courts), and recommendations. Essentially a practitioner's handbook for psychologists, counselors, and psychiatrists that views children's disturbances primarily as developmental deviations due to stress.

M46 **PSYCHOLOGICAL ASSESSMENT OF HANDICAPPED INFANTS AND YOUNG CHILDREN** By Gordon Ulrey and Sally J. Rogers. New York, Thieme-Stratton, 1982. 241 pp. $19.95.

Although this book is directed primarily at psychologists, it seems useful to anyone involved in assessing, treating, or teaching very young handicapped children. In the first few chapters, the authors deal with such complex issues as children's milieus, handicapping conditions, and behavior. Subsequent chapters deal with assessing children with motor handicaps, visual handicaps, hearing impairments, and language disorders—emphasizing throughout the importance of systematic observation as part of the total assessment, the strengths and weaknesses of specific tests, and the need to translate assessment into a relevant treatment program.

M47 **PSYCHOLOGICAL TESTING OF CHILDREN: A CONSUMER'S GUIDE** By Stanley D. Klein. Boston, Mass., Exceptional Parent Press, 1977. 117 pp. $4.95, plus $1.75 postage and handling, prepaid. From: 605 Commonwealth Ave., Boston, MA 02215.

A clear exposition of psychological testing, directed toward parents, that emphasizes psychological assessment of children with disabilities. Covers test logic and construction; psychological assessment; administration, scoring, and interpretation; intelligence testing; personality testing; tests for brain injury; and achievement, aptitude, and interest tests.

M48 **SCREENING AND EVALUATING THE YOUNG CHILD: Handbook of Instruments to Use from Infancy to Six Years** By Lois E. Southworth, Rosemary L. Burr, and Andrea Ewell Cox. Springfield, Ill., C. C Thomas, 1981. 216 pp. $16.75; paperback, $13.50.

Provides detailed descriptions of approximately 200 instruments, most administered individually, but some to groups.

M49 **SCREENING GROWTH AND DEVELOPMENT OF PRESCHOOL CHILDREN: A GUIDE FOR TEST SELECTION** By Sharon R. Stangler, Cathee J. Huber, and Donald K. Routh. New York, McGraw-Hill, 1980. 326 pp. $12.95.

A systematic approach to assessment during the first five years of life—based on normal growth and development—to provide guidance in selecting and using appropriate developmental screening tests. The first three chapters, essentially literature surveys with references, deal with normal growth and development, concepts of screening, and assessment of screening tests. The chapter on normal growth and development includes many tables and milestones of growth and illustrations of newborn reflexes. Chapters 4–8 (also with references) cover five categories of screening tests: physical growth, general development (which includes neuromotor, psychosocial, and self-help), hearing, speech and language, and vision. In each of these, a general discussion is followed by formatted reports on specific tests that indicate test author, source, purpose, age, manual and forms, type, time, screener, environment, equipment, appropriateness, reliability, validity, acceptability, simplicity, and cost, as well as criteria for referring a child to a specialist.

Suggested criteria for selecting tests are acceptability, simplicity (ease of teaching, learning, administration), cost (equipment, personnel, cost/benefit), appropriateness (prevalence/applicability), reliability (precision), and validity (accuracy). The appendixes include a worksheet for calculating the validity of screening tests and growth charts.

M50 SEE HOW THEY GROW—MONITORING CHILD
GROWTH FOR APPROPRIATE HEALTH CARE IN DE-
VELOPING COUNTRIES By David Morley and Margaret
Woodland. New York, Oxford University Press, 1980. 265 pp.
$15.95.
Prepared by the Tropical Child Health Unit of the Institute of Child Health in London for doctors, nurses, and other health workers in developing countries to aid their understanding of the entire process of a child's physical, mental, and social development and growth. The book demonstrates how to improve child health and overcome malnutrition by monitoring growth through a simple chart that Professor Morley developed and modified in many countries. Provides a background and layout for the charts, suggests ways of keeping these charts, and discusses the weight curves of malnourished children and the growth curves for specific diseases (e.g., measles, tuberculosis, diarrhea, and malaria). Some chapters deal with breast-feeding and the birth interval, children at risk, the growth chart as a measure of child nutrition in the community, community involvement, and the role of part-time health workers. Includes references and appendixes.

M51 SOCIOEMOTIONAL MEASURES FOR PRESCHOOL
AND KINDERGARTEN CHILDREN By Deborah Klein
Walker. San Francisco, Calif., Jossey-Bass, 1973. 256 pp.
$23.95. (Social and Behavioral Science Series)

A comprehensive guide to 143 socioemotional measures for use with children aged three to six, compiled from a thorough search and intended for a variety of users, including child psychologists, child-development specialists, counselors, social workers, kindergarten teachers, and administrators. The first part of the book has a most helpful discussion of rationales and background for organizing the measurement field in terms of educational objectives and the values and disadvantages of each type of test. The second part groups tests in six categories: attitudes, general personality and emotional adjustment, interests or preferences, personality or behavior traits, self-concept, and social skills or competency. Each measure is fully described, including title and date, author, appropriate age range, measurement technique, background sources, administration time and method, content examples, scoring procedure, examiner requirements, norms, validity, reliability, and historical notes. Includes name, author, and general indexes, as well as references and an appendix of journals surveyed.

M52 **SPECIAL EDUCATION INDEX TO ASSESSMENT MATERIALS** Albuquerque, N. Mex., National Information Center for Educational Media, 1980. 127 pp. $21 (paperback).
Includes annotated citations of nearly 1,500 items in the NICSEM (National Information Center for Special Education Materials) data base published between 1940 and 1980. Covers aptitude and achievement tests; motor, sensory, and communication skills; speech pathology; development and interpretation of tests; and professional materials on testing procedures.
The arrangement is intricate, thorough, and cumbersome (the key to the arrangement is inside the back cover). Citations are arranged alphabetically by title. A classified index ("hierarchy") follows alphabetic, permuted, and outline guides to the hierarchy. This complex arrangement, however, enables users to locate items by cost, source, subject, disability, grade level, and media.

M53 **STANDARDS FOR EDUCATIONAL AND PSYCHOLOGICAL TESTS AND MANUALS** Revised Edition. By a Joint Committee of the American Psychological Assn., American Educational Research Assn., and National Council on Measurement in Education. Washington, D.C., American Psychological Assn., 1974. 76 pp. $5 (paperback).
A well-organized set of guidelines and criteria for publishers and users of tests that discusses interpretation, dissemination of information,

standards for reliability and validity, and uses of tests, among other topics. Good index.

M54 **STUDENT LEARNING STYLES: DIAGNOSING AND PRESCRIBING PROGRAMS** Edited by Thomas F. Koerner. Reston, Va., National Association of Secondary School Principals, 1979. 137 pp. $7 (paperback).
An overview of learning styles that includes instruments and means of identifying learning styles, with suggestions for using that knowledge to help students and for matching teaching to learning styles. Appendixes include references to representative learning-style instruments.

M55 **TEMPERAMENTAL DIFFERENCES IN INFANTS AND YOUNG CHILDREN** Newark, N.J., Ciba Pharmaceutical Co., 1982. 320 pp. $35. (Ciba Foundation Symposium, No. 89) From: P.O. Box 12832, Newark, NJ 07101.
A symposium on measurable individual differences in temperament in infants and young children that examines research and explores the relationship between personality and temperament. It suggests ways that identification of temperamental characteristics can promote better care and education of babies and young children and help institute preventive measures for children at risk.

M56 **TESTING AND ETHNIC MINORITY STUDENTS: AN ANNOTATED BIBLIOGRAPHY** By James A. Vasquez, Sandra E. Gonzales, and Mary E. Pearson. Rosslyn, Va., National Clearinghouse for Bilingual Education, 1980. 28 pp. $3 (paper).
A useful sampling of around 110 items of research literature on educational and psychological testing of ethnic minority students that deal with theory, practice, and experiments. Includes a wide range of tests and measurement instruments, as well as discussions that relate testing to different theories of intelligence, racial differences on test scores, and the appropriate/inappropriate use of educational and psychological measurements. Intelligence quotient tests, scholastic achievement and aptitude tests, readiness tests, and tests used for selection purposes are covered. Other articles explore factors that may influence test performance and the consequences of testing policy.

M57 **TESTING IN FOREIGN LANGUAGES, ESL, AND BILINGUAL EDUCATION, 1966–1979: A SELECT ANNOTATED ERIC BIBLIOGRAPHY** Edited by Sophia Behrens et al. Washington, D.C., ERIC Clearinghouse on Language and Linguistics, Center for Applied Linguistics, 1980. 340 pp. $8.75 (paper). (Language in Education: Theory and Practice, Vol. 3, No. 24)

A computer-produced annotated bibliography on foreign-language testing that combines in one book all locatable references from the ERIC data base from 1966 through 1979 on foreign-language testing, testing in bilingual education, and testing in English as a second or foreign language. Similar to *RIE* in format, it is divided into four main sections: document resumes, journal article resumes, subject index, and author index.

M58 **TESTING IN PRACTICE: A GUIDE TO THE PREPARATION AND MARKING OF TESTS, FORMAL EXAMINATIONS AND INFORMAL ASSESSMENTS** By Bill Peddie and Graham White. Auckland, New Zealand, Heinemann Educational Books, 1979. 67 pp. $3.25 (paper). From: Heinemann Educational Books, 4 Front St., Exeter, NH 03833.

A simple, practical, pamphlet presentation of educational testing theory for teachers and administrators, intended to clarify the nature of the testing process and to deploy classroom testing as an aid to teaching rather than a process that dominates the teaching/learning situation. Offers many useful suggestions on such topics as improving reliability, preparing objective tests, question banking, and diagnostic feedback.

M59 **TESTS: A COMPREHENSIVE REFERENCE FOR ASSESSMENTS IN PSYCHOLOGY, EDUCATION, AND BUSINESS** Edited by Richard C. Sweetland and Daniel J. Keyser. Kansas City, Mo., Test Corporation of America, 1983. 976 pp. $49.95.

A new, valuable ready reference that classifies and briefly describes more than 3,000 tests for all age groups. The main sections—psychology, education, and business—are subdivided into smaller topics, such as children and child development, child personality, intelligence and related topics, educational development, and preschool readiness. Achievement tests in many subjects are provided for all age groups. The section on special education includes tests for giftedness, learning disabilities, physical and mental handicaps, and special education. The student evaluation section includes tests that deal with behavior problems, student attitudes, and personality factors. The formatted test descriptions include coded visual keys, a statement of the test's purpose, a description of the test, and relevant cost and availability information. There are good cross-references between sections for tests that are relevant to more than one area, as well as author and test title indexes. *Tests* also includes lists of publishers and test-scoring services and special indexes for the visually impaired.

M60   **TESTS AND MEASUREMENTS IN CHILD DEVELOP-MENT: Handbook I** By Orval G. Johnson and James W. Bommarito. San Francisco, Calif., Jossey-Bass, 1971. 518 pp. $29.95.

This volume and *Tests and Measurements in Child Development: Handbook II* (M61) constitute a central resource of information on published and unpublished measures suitable for children. *Handbook I* describes 300 unpublished psychological measures of child behavior, suitable for children between birth and age 12, gathered from the literature from 1956 through 1965. The tests included in this volume are not included in the *Mental Measurements Yearbook* (M36). Descriptions include author and title of the test, age level, source, variable(s) studied, and reliability and validity.

M61   **TESTS AND MEASUREMENTS IN CHILD DEVELOP-MENT: Handbook II** By Orval G. Johnson. San Francisco, Calif., Jossey-Bass, 1976. 2 Vols. $59.95/set. (Jossey-Bass Behavioral Science Series)

This two-volume handbook continues the work of *Handbook I* with 900 psychological tests suitable for children up to age 18, located through a survey of 148 journals in psychology, psychiatry, education, exceptionality, and sociology from 1966 through 1974. The materials in *Handbook II* are arranged in 11 broad categories: cognition, personality and emotional characteristics, perceptions of environment, self-concept, qualities of care-giving and home environment, motor skills and sensory perception, physical attributes, attitudes and interests, social behavior, vocational tests, and "unclassified tests." Within these categories, tests are arranged alphabetically by title.

For each test, information is given on author, title, variable(s) studied, type of measure, description of measure, reliability and validity, source, and bibliography. The book also includes an index of authors and measures, a subject index, and a list of journals searched.

M62   **TESTS AND TESTING OF BILINGUAL CHILDREN: A BIBLIOGRAPHY OF LITERATURE** Compiled by Judith Kirsch. Rosslyn, Va., National Clearinghouse for Bilingual Education, 1981. 71 pp. $7.90 (paper).

Another topical selected bibliography from the BEBA data base. Includes 85 entries—journal articles, research reports, government documents,

and other documents—indexed with descriptors from the *ERIC Thesaurus* on such things as test selection, validity, reviews, bias, and
interpretation. Each entry contains bibliographic and source information and a comprehensive abstract.

M63 **TESTS APPROPRIATE FOR USE WITH AMERICAN IN-
DIANS** Princeton, N.J., Educational Testing Service, Test
Collection, 1982. 9 pp. $3. Microfiche. (ED 213 546) From:
ERIC Document Reproduction Service, P.O. Box 190, Arling-
ton, VA 22210.
Describes 13 standardized tests appropriate for use with American
Indian students from preschool through high school. Provides authors,
copyright date, appropriate age level, test format, and publishers.

M64 **TESTS IN PRINT III: AN INDEX TO TESTS, TEST
REVIEWS AND THE LITERATURE OF SPECIFIC
TESTS** 3rd Edition. Edited by James V. Mitchell, Jr. Lincoln,
University of Nebraska Press, 1983. 1,150 pp. $85.
An index and update of tests and documents in the *Mental Measurements Yearbook* (M36). Includes test titles, parts and subtests, copyright dates, groups for whom the tests are intended, publication dates,
authors, and publishers. Contents are arranged by types of tests and
cross-referenced to test reviews and citations in *MMY.* Personal name
and test title indexes, as well as a directory of publishers.

15 / Statistics

Statistics in general is an area that is well served by compilations, indexes, and data bases. The major sources of statistical information discussed in this chapter include the *American Statistics Index* and the *Statistical Reference Index,* both from Congressional Information Service (J20) and available in print or on-line. Since many statistics originate in government, they can be followed or verified through the *Monthly Catalog* (D36) in print or on-line; Johns Hopkins's POPLINE provides access, through MEDLARS (J30), to population statistics. Other tools in this chapter are compendiums or catalogs of statistics by different agencies. If the documents are produced by the Federal Government, they should be available in depository libraries and purchasable from the U.S. Government Printing Office (GPO), with a limited number of copies available free (in some cases) from the issuing agencies. Federal statistical publications are reported in three *Subject Bibliographies* available free from GPO: *Educational Statistics* (SB-083), *Statistical Publications* (SB-273), and *Vital and Health Statistics* (SB-121). Public affairs periodical indexes, such as the *P.A.I.S. Bulletin* and *Refugee Abstracts,* are good ongoing sources of information on statistics, as are newsletters of child advocacy organizations.

Although indexing tools and documents are helpful, national statistics on children are not well integrated despite the fact that many federal, state, and local agencies collect information on children's health, education, welfare, behavior, nutrition, development, incarceration, and maltreatment as part of their ongoing responsibilities. Unfortunately, the agencies that collect these data do not necessarily have common definitions, common standards for age-group division, comparable measurements, similar tabulation techniques, and so on. (These, in fact, may differ even within the same agency.) In the last few years, data on children have been collected but not published, whereas existing data sets (such as national surveys and large-scale longitudinal studies) are not analyzed, according to H. W. Watts and F. P. Santos, of Columbia University's Center for the Social Sciences, in *The Allocation of Human and Material Resources to Childrearing in the United States: A Theoretical Framework and Analysis of Major Data Sources* (New York, Columbia University, Center for Social Sciences, 1978). Under the Reagan administration, at least 50 major statistical programs have been eliminated or reduced. Many of these canceled programs—such as surveys of family budgets, housing, health, and nutrition—are of vital concern to children. Useful summaries, like the *National Immunization Survey* and the *Status of Children, Youth, and Families,* were discontinued. Since indexing systems like *American Statistics Index* pick up only published reports, data are no longer directly available to the public, even though they may still be collected. In other cases, information that is collected is not used when appropriate. For example, the U.S. Department of Education in 1982 used 1970 census data rather than 1980 census data in allocating $2.9 billion in grants to states for educating poor children during the 1982–1983 school year.

Other revelant data appear not to be collected at all. For example, several million children are served by public social service agencies in 3,100 counties and $1 billion is expended annually in services for children under Title IV (including Aid to Families with Dependent Children, Child Welfare Services, and the Work Incentive Program) and Title XX (Grants to States for Services) of the Social Security Act. Yet, it is not known how many children receive services, who they are, why they come to the agencies, or what services they receive. Some states and counties can answer some of these questions, but answers are not easily available at the national level. The Office of Human Development Services (OHDS) is attempting to fill this gap with its Voluntary Cooperative Information System, designed to gather statistical data on OHDS-funded programs from the state agencies administering them. The American Public Welfare Association staff, with a State Advisory Committee, consultants, and a subcontractor, have put together a plan and collected some child welfare information on this basis. See item N35 for an example.

The Children's Bureau — an overview agency for children — collected information on the number of children served by public and voluntary agencies in each state and whether children were living with their parents, in foster homes, or in institutions. This function was transferred to the National Center for Social Statistics, whose latest report (1975) covers only 31 states, and these incompletely; the latest complete report, 1971, is, of course, badly out-of-date.

There has been no comprehensive survey of child welfare programs since the Jeter Study (1961), when child welfare services were usually administered through specialized child welfare units at state and local levels, with strong leadership supplied by the Children's Bureau. At that time, federal funds supported a range of state services (and training for these services), such as family counseling, homemaker service, day care, and protective services. Some 400,000 children received public child welfare services, and another 125,000 received "casework services."

Sporadic compilations of statistics, such as chart books or profiles assembled for the International Year of the Child (1979) or the White House Conference on Children are available. *American Families and Living Arrangements* was produced by the 1980 White House Conference on Families. The Bicentennial brought forth *America's Children, 1976;* the Year of the Child resulted in the *Status of the World's Children.*

Another complicating fact in assembling and compiling statistical data on children is that the data can be collected in an amazing variety of ways — through surveys (partial or complete); geographic sampling; interviews and questionnaires in schools and neighborhoods; assessment of school progress; physical and psychological examinations; school, medical, and arrest records; and birth and death certificates. Some of these data are exact, some are approximate, and some are not quite applicable. Needs-assessment approaches measure conditions for which some program or service is available or possible and are almost inevitably based on the ideals and existence of the program or service. The social-indicators approach seeks to measure significant child or family characteristics in the context of social change. Some of the tests and assessments in Chapter 14 occasionally overlap with the statistical sources in this chapter.

In general, statistical information on children is compiled by many agencies within our federal establishment—as well as by states, cities, regions, and other areas—and not always coordinated. The Office of Human Development has, at least for now, discontinued the *Status of Children, Youth, and Families,* which covered health, education, and socioeconomic factors. The new House Select Committee on Children, Youth, and Families, however, has compiled a modest statistical assessment in *U.S. Children and Their Families: Current Conditions and Recent Trends* (May 1983). Since the committee plans to develop an up-to-date profile and information base on children and youth, it may become possible, through congressional pressure, to more effectively rationalize and coordinate national statistics on children. In the meantime, advocacy groups, such as the Children's Defense Fund, are actively engaged in extracting relevant information from unwieldy compilations.

Rather than preparing a substantial profile of present federal agencies and their collections, I provide a hasty overview of some of what has been and is currently collected. Finding the right agency, like finding the right index or data base, requires an analysis of aspects: legal, health, economic, educational. Finding the appropriate bureau for past statistics requires reading the fine print in the *Statistical Abstract of the United States* (N23) or knowing who used to do what. Terms related to children, however, will uncover statistics in most indexes. The Clearinghouse on Child Abuse and Neglect, the National Child Support Reference Center, and the National Bilingual Education Clearinghouse, among others, also collect statistics in their areas of interest. The Immigration and Naturalization Service of the U.S. Department of Justice publishes an *Annual Report* on alien children, and the U.S. Department of Education issues numerous publications on children in school. State statistics can be followed through the *Statistical Reference Index* (N24), as well as annual reports or journals of state agencies for health, welfare, rehabilitation, social services, and human resources.

AN OVERVIEW OF SOME FEDERAL AGENCIES COLLECTING INFORMATION ON CHILDREN

1. Administration for Children, Youth, and Families, U.S. Department of Health and Human Services, Hubert H. Humphrey Bldg., 200 Independence Ave., SW, Washington, DC 20201, (202) 755-7762. Although the abolishment of the agency's Research and Evaluation Division and the discontinuation of certain reports may give pause, this agency is still compiling the *Status of Handicapped Children in Head Start Programs.* It is a source of poverty status, child health needs, and the demographics of Pacific and Asian-American families.

2. Bureau of Labor Statistics (BLS), U.S. Department of Labor, Washington, DC 20212, (202) 523-1327. Covers marital and family characteristics of workers, labor force activities of married women, and children of working mothers. These are discussed in its helpful *Major Programs, Bureau of Labor Statistics,* which is available free. BLS's *Monthly Labor Review* is covered in item H119. The bureau also issues *Databooks* on groups like working women.

The Women's Bureau of the U.S. Department of Labor, 200 Constitution Ave., NW, Washington, DC 20210, (202) 563-6611. A helpful source of information on topics like employers and child care and other programs related to working mothers.

The Employment Standards Administration, Washington, DC 20210. Produces and distributes factsheets and brochures on child labor standards and laws, as well as the numbers of minors employed legally or in violation of child labor provisions.

3. Bureau of the Census, U.S. Department of Commerce, Washington, DC 20233, (301) 763-4100. The *Census of Population* covers the number and distribution of U.S. inhabitants by age, sex, marital status, race, and employment status, among

other factors. The Census Bureau also issues subject reports and social indicators; its *Current Population Reports Series* P20, P23, P25, and P60 are among the more relevant. These deal with household and family composition, marital status and living arrangements, income, and ethnic variations in income. The bureau has produced a *Factfinder for the Nation Series* that describes the scopes and applications of its principal censuses and surveys. Titles include *Reference Sources,* which describes publications; *History and Organization;* and *Population Statistics. Telephone Contacts for Data Users* includes telephone numbers for regional offices.

    4. Family Economics Research Group, Agricultural Research Service, U.S. Department of Agriculture, Federal Bldg., Room 442A, Hyattsville, MD 20782, (301) 436-8461. The department has always been a source of information on food and nutrition. Currently, it is researching family economics and the cost of raising a child. *Family Economics Review* (H61) reports this research.

    5. Office of Policy Development and Research, U.S. Department of Housing and Urban Development (HUD), 451 7th St., NW, Washington, DC 20410, (202) 755-5600. Its statistics and reports on housing incorporate information on housing type and density, market and rental practices affecting families, special needs of family housing, environments of families with children, and the like.

    6. U.S. Department of Justice, 633 Indiana Ave., NW, Washington, DC 20531, (202) 724-7782. The Bureau of Justice Statistics collects information on incarcerated and delinquent children. Its *Report to the Nation on Crime and Justice* incorporates statistics from the Office of Juvenile Justice and Delinquency Prevention, among other sources. Legal periodicals and data bases are also good sources.

    7. National Center for Education Statistics (NCES), 400 Maryland Ave., SW, Room 1001, Washington, DC 20202, (301) 436-7900. Typically covers such facets as pupil enrollment, characteristics of students, educational outcome, and measures of academic achievement. NCES prepares an annual report, the *Condition of Education,* and a *Digest of Education Statistics.*

    8. National Center for Health Statistics (NCHS), 3700 East-West Highway, Hyattsville, MD 20782, (301) 436-8500. Issues

Vital Statistics Reports on the rates of marriage, divorce, birth, and death; children involved in divorces; duration of marriages; health expenditures; children's behavioral patterns; and hospital coverage of families. Its yearly report, *Health: United States,* includes information on child health and overviews of topics related to infant mortality and the use of health services. A complete cumulative listing of the *Vital and Health Statistics* series from 1962 through 1979 is contained in the center's *Catalog of Publications* (DHHS Publication No. [PHS] 80-1301). For the latest listing of NCHS reports, check the *Catalog* and the quarterly *Publication Note.*

9. U.S. Social Security Administration, Office of Research and Statistics, Altmeyer Bldg., 6401 Security Blvd., Room 138, Baltimore, MD 21235, (301) 597-2927. Collects data on family assistance and on social security recipients, including young widows and their children. Some titles are *AFDC Standards for Basic Needs* (N30), the new *Quarterly Public Assistance Statistics,* (1982–), and *A Chartbook: Aid to Families with Dependent Children.*

INTERNATIONAL SOURCES

International statistics are gathered by international agencies, especially the World Health Organization, UNICEF, Unesco, and other agencies noted in the international section of Chapter 12. They are cited in some of the periodicals discussed in Chapter 9, as well as in compilations such as *State of the World's Children, 1984* (N22). Recent *Draper Fund Reports,* especially the December 1982 report, *Children: The Right to Be Wanted,* include statistics on children. These reports are issued by the Population Crisis Committee of the Draper Fund, 1120 19th St., NW, Suite 550, Washington, DC 20036. One of the *Population Briefings* (No. 10, July 1982) of this agency is a helpful directory of major private organizations in the population field. The Population Reference Bureau (N1) is another major source. *The World Health Statistics Quarterly* (1947–) and the *World Health Statistics Annual* (N68) are good sources for health statistics. The National Children's Bureau (F1) has produced the exemplary *Children in the U.K.: Signposts to Statistics,* which arranges sources by topics and includes addresses and citations.

ORGANIZATIONAL SOURCES

Since statistics are accessible through the *American Statistics Index* (N2) and *Statistical Reference Index* (N24), I am including only one organization here, although I have brief descriptions of some federal agencies in the previous section and descriptions of some survey organizations in the section on surveys on pp. 446–447. In the future, if federal statistics collections continue to decline, we may have to depend more on organizations like the American Hospital Association and the American Academy of Pediatrics to collect data for the public sector as well as for their own professions.

N1 **POPULATION REFERENCE BUREAU (PRB)** 1337 Connecticut Ave., NW, Washington, DC, 20036-1897. (202) 785-4664

The Population Reference Bureau is a private nonprofit organization that has been "telling the world about population" since 1929 through publications and information services. It is considered a prime information source on national and international population dynamics. Members (students, $5/year; primary/secondary teachers, $10/year; university instructors, $15/year; other individuals, $25/year; libraries, $30/year; institutions, $100/year) receive bimonthly issues of *Intercom,* a lively international news magazine; four quarterly issues of *Population Bulletin*—perceptive, concise studies of population topics; an annually updated *World Population Data Sheet* wall chart; and a quarterly population education newsletter, *Interchange.*

In collaboration with UNICEF, PRB has prepared an excellent *1982 World's Children Data Sheet.* This chart, which is available for $1.00 in French, Spanish, or English, contains 15 columns of data on children in 165 countries, including demographics, economic status, health, education, and nutrition. An accompanying teacher's guide, *Children: A Constant Concern,* is also available for $1.00. Bulk rates are available for both.

The bureau's demographic data—taken from publications of the United Nations Population Division—use infant mortality estimates for less-developed countries that take into account data from all available censuses, surveys, and registration systems.

Relevant *Population Bulletins* ($3.00 each) include *The Value and Cost of Children* (1977, out of print); *America's Baby Boom Generation: The Fateful Bulge* (1980; 9 slides available for $4.50); *The World Fertility Survey: Charting Global Childbearing* (21 slides, including map, $10.50).

PRB's *Reports on the World Fertility Survey* are clear, nontechnical PRB staff analyses of national surveys conducted between 1974 and 1981, which allow the first standardized comparison of worldwide fertility trends.

The *Population Handbook* (1982, $4.00, bulk rates available) is a lively guide to demographic basics that contains sources of population information. It comes in two English-language editions ("Original" — largely United States—and "International") and has been adapted in Spanish (for Latin America), French (for Francophone Africa), Arabic (for the Middle East), and Thai.

PRB has a Population Film Library with a collection of more than 40 films, filmstrips, and slide/tape programs on population dynamics and related topics. (Send a stamped, self-addressed envelope for a free catalog.)

The Library and Information Service responds to mail, telephone, or walk-in queries and also offers on-line bibliographic research of two major population data bases, POPLINE (created and maintained by Johns Hopkins University's Population Information Program and Columbia University's Center for Population and Family Health and also available through MEDLARS [J30]) and POPULATION BIBLIOGRAPHY (created and maintained by the Carolina Population Center of the University of North Carolina).

The Demographic Information Services Center (DISC), staffed with demographers, statisticians, and systems analysts, offers personalized, in-depth data and analyses for individual clients seeking professional interpretation of population trends and demographic variables for future planning.

PRINT SOURCES

This section is divided into three parts: The first includes significant reference works (indexes, bibliographies, compendiums, and directories) leading to statistical information sources on children. The second part is an alphabetic listing of other statistical publications on children. The third section annotates a few relevant surveys.

The Latin root for the word *statistics* is *status,* meaning *state.* The Greek word *statistik* means the study of political facts and figures. As these imply, most statistics are gathered by government organizations as a bureaucratic responsibility. They may not be disseminated quickly (or at all) by these bureaus or correlated with related statistics. They are usually available at some headquarters offices, however, and can be obtained by determined searchers. I hope that the guides in this section will increase their accessibility.

The source guides in the first part of this section can be supplemented by an excellent publication of the Children's Defense Fund that was cited in Chapter 3, *Where Do You Look? Whom Do You Ask? How Do You Know?* (B19). The *Guide to Population/ Family Planning Information Sources* (B5) is a good source of statistical information, and the *Population Index* (G35) is valuable for locating statistics and demographic information on families. A *Review of Head Start Research Since 1969* (E128) has extensive statistical analyses of research. Two periodicals discussed in Chapter 9 are most helpful—the *Family Economics Review* (H61) and the *Monthly Labor Review* (H119).

Encyclopedias, too, can be a good source (as of date of publication). For example, the *Encyclopedia of Social Work* (A30) contains statistics on child health and welfare from the 1940s to date and issues updated statistics between editions.

INDEXES, GUIDES, AND COMPENDIUMS

N2   **AMERICAN STATISTICS INDEX (ASI)** Washington,
     D.C., Congressional Information Service, 1973– . Monthly,
     with quarterly cumulated *Index* and *Abstracts.* Sold on a service
     basis, depending on type of institution and total library budget.
An outstanding indexing journal by the publishers of *CIS/Index* (G10)
that provides detailed abstracts and excellent indexing of 7,500 statisti-

cal publications from some 500 sources in the Federal Government. The ongoing publications are backed by a supplement that provides statistics from the early 1960s to 1974. Each abstract includes the name of the issuing agency, the type of publication, complete bibliographic information (including numbers assigned by different federal agencies), a detailed description of the subject matter, and an outline of specific content. The *Index* is in several parts. The first covers subjects and names of places, agencies, corporations, and individuals; the second is an index of economic, geographic, and demographic categories (for comparative data); the third section consists of supplementary indexes that provide access by title or agency report number.

Congressional Information Service, which publishes the *Statistical Reference Index* (N24), also can provide partial or complete microfiche files of publications cited and indexed in *ASI,* as well as individual on-demand copies. The data base can be searched on-line.

N3   **AMERICA'S CHILDREN AND THEIR FAMILIES: KEY FACTS** Washington, D.C., Children's Defense Fund, 1982. 81 pp. $5.50 (paper).
One of a series of publications issued by this leading child advocacy organization, *America's Children and Their Families* is an inclusive, easy-to-understand compendium of statistics on family structure, income and poverty, employment, child care, health, education, social services, and other topics, garnered from the Bureau of the Census and other government sources. These statistics indicate that the situation of American children has deteriorated considerably compared to 10 years ago.

N4   **AMERICA'S CHILDREN 1976: A Bicentennial Assessment** Washington, D.C., National Council of Organizations for Children and Youth, 1976. 87 pp. Paperback. (Out of print)
A significant and realistic fact book on American children that uses charts, maps, and illustrations. Separate sections treat children in poverty, child health, family changes, and other child care needs. Somewhat comparable to *Children in the World* (N9) but at a national level.

N5   **CATALOG OF PUBLICATIONS OF THE NATIONAL CENTER FOR HEALTH STATISTICS 1979-83** Hyattsville, Md., National Center for Health Statistics, 1981- . Free. From: 3700 East-West Highway, Hyattsville, MD 20782.
Contains a listing of NCHS reports published during the last five years, with a complete cumulative listing of the *Vital Statistics Reports,* which includes more than 500 individual publications. Other NCHS data are

published in *Advance Data from Vital Statistics,* which releases early findings from NCHS surveys. In general, NCHS reports are of two types: those related to the health status of people and those related to health facilities and occupations. The catalog includes order blanks for in-print reports and information on how to obtain out-of-print reports from the National Technical Information Service. It is updated between editions by a periodic *Publication Note.*

N6 **CHARACTERISTICS OF AMERICAN CHILDREN AND YOUTH** By Jerry T. Jennings. Washington, D.C., U.S. Bureau of the Census, 1982. 64 pp. $4.50 (paper). (Current Population Reports, Special Studies, Series P-23, No. 114)

An ongoing statistical report on the demographic, educational, and economic characteristics of persons under age 25 compiled from government surveys, decennial censuses, and related statistics. It is intended to provide a readily accessible and comprehensive set of data on children under age 14 and youth aged 14–25. Areas covered are population growth and distribution, migration, education, family and marital status, living arrangements, fertility, mortality and health, labor force participation, occupation, income and poverty status, voting, and crime and victimization. Also provides historic perspectives on some topics. Includes 9 charts, 53 tables, definitions, explanations, information on data sources, and estimates of reliability.

N7 **CHILD AND FAMILY INDICATORS: A REPORT WITH RECOMMENDATIONS** Edited by Harold W. Watts and Donald J. Hernandez. Washington, D.C., Social Science Research Council, Center for Coordination of Research on Social Indicators, 1982. 66 pp. Free while supply lasts (paper). From: 1755 Massachusetts Ave., NW, Washington, DC 20036.

A report, partly funded by the Foundation for Child Development, that examines available statistics on children and families in the United States, assesses their adequacy for describing and analyzing the conditions of children, and suggests new measures and ways to improve existing measures. Provides an overview of data collected on children and families. Since the Advisory Group on Child and Family Indicators (of the center's Advisory and Planning Committee of Social Indicators) undertook its work, many data-collection sources have been jeopardized by proposed cuts in budget and personnel, so that the admittedly inadequate extant sources may not even be maintained. The major recommendations made in this publication are (1) to maintain and improve basic data-collection programs; (2) to publish a biennial report on children; (3) to establish a data archive for child indicators; (4) to develop new indicators and new questions; and (5) to replicate and institute new surveys—in particular, the National Health Examination Surveys should be replicated.

N8   **CHILD CARE: DATA AND MATERIALS** 3rd Edition. U.S. Senate, Committee on Finance, December 31, 1977. Washington, D.C., U.S. Government Printing Office, 1978. 316 pp., 60 tables, 6 appendixes. $7.

An impressive compilation of data on areas related to child care: children of working mothers, current child care arrangements, costs of child care, federal involvement in child care, standards and licensing, and the like.

N9   **CHILDREN IN THE WORLD** By Magda Cordell McHale and John McHale, with Guy F. Streatfeild. Washington, D.C., Population Reference Bureau, 1979. 72 pp. $3 (paperback). From: 1337 Connecticut Ave., NW, Washington, DC 20036.

A chart book of statistics prepared for the International Year of the Child (1979). Covers stages of the life cycle; the number and location of children in the world; languages and religion; indicators for health, nutrition, social, and economic conditions; handicapped children; education; employment; and outlook for the future. Charts are logically arranged and indexed.

N10   **THE CONDITION OF EDUCATION, 1984 EDITION** Washington, D.C., U.S. Department of Education, National Center for Education Statistics, 1975- . Annual. $7. From: U.S. Government Printing Office, Washington, DC 20402. (Document No. 065-000-00200-1)

An excellent annual statistical survey that provides up-to-date overviews of conditions in society that affect all levels of education, as well as educationally disadvantaged adults. Each chapter includes a text, followed by tables and charts. The report is especially important for bilingual educators because it contains information on the preliminary results of the U.S. Department of Education's efforts to estimate the number and distribution of 5- to 17-year-olds who speak a language other than English at home (approximately 10 percent of this age group counted in the 1980 census were in this category). The *Condition of Education for Hispanic Americans* (1980, $6.50 [paperback]) gives a statistical overview of Hispanics in the United States and their participation in education and employment. A related annual, the *Digest of Education*

Statistics (1982, $7.50) provides tabular data on nearly every facet of American education from preschool through graduate school.

N11 **CURRENT LISTING AND TOPICAL INDEX TO THE VITAL AND HEALTH STATISTICS SERIES, 1962–1978** Hyattsville, Md., National Center for Health Statistics, 1979. 27 pp. Free while supply lasts. (DHEW Publication No. [PHS] 79-1301) From: 3700 East-West Highway, Hyattsville, MD 20782.

A helpful index to surveys and series; includes the names of individual reports from the National Health Examination Surveys and the Nutrition Examination Survey (Series 11) under "Children and youths." Other relevant sections are Series 20, which contains the titles of mortality reports, including mortality by age and infant mortality; Series 21, which contains more data on natality, marriage, and divorce, including information on children of divorced couples and natality statistics analyses; and Series 23, *Data for the National Survey of Family Growth,* which has additional titles on children. Supplemented by the *Catalog of Publications of the National Center for Health Statistics 1979–83* (N5).

N12 **DEVELOPMENT OF CHILDHOOD SOCIAL INDICATORS** By Nicholas Zill II, Heidi Sigal, and Orville G. Brim, Jr. In: *America's Unfinished Business: Child and Family Policy,* by E. Zigler et al., New York, Cambridge University Press, 1982, Chap. 13. Also issued separately by Child Trends, New York, not dated.

Contains good narrative overviews of the social indicator movement and the sources and availability of data on children's living conditions, physical health, educational achievement, statistical compendiums, local studies, needs assessments, sample surveys, and major surveys and their sources. Includes substantial references and a statistical "exhibit" that covers the structure and economics of family life, children's health, children in school, and children no longer in school.

N13 **EMPLOYED PARENTS AND THEIR CHILDREN: A DATA BOOK** Washington, D.C., Children's Defense Fund (CDF), 1982. 78 pp. $8 (paper).

This data book on work force trends is an outgrowth of an Aspen Institute/CDF seminar of linkages between work and family, intended to provide information and help design public policies to meet the needs of children with working parents.

N14 **ETHNIC STATISTICS: A COMPENDIUM OF REFER-ENCE SOURCES** By Deborah Pomerance and Diane Ellis. Arlington, Va., Data Use and Access Laboratories, 1978. 148 pp. (Out of print, but available through NTIS as PB 283 378; paper, $14.50; microfiche, $4.50)
Includes detailed abstracts of 92 federal data sources from 11 U.S. agencies and departments from which ethnic and racial information can be derived. It also offers narrative descriptions of six major agencies, with indexes by subject, ethnic or racial group, and title. Many of these sources contain information on children in general and on minority children. The detailed descriptions include the purpose of the census or survey responsible for the data, the time frame, geographic coverage, frequency, subject parameters and limitations, and specific racial or ethnic groups for which data are provided.

N15 **FACTS AT YOUR FINGERTIPS: A Guide to Sources of Statistical Information on Major Health Topics** Hyattsville, Md., National Center for Health Statistics (NCHS), 1977– . Irregular. Free while supply lasts. (DHEW Publication No. [PHS] 79-1246) From: 3700 East-West Highway, Hyattsville, MD 20782.
Bibliographic information on reports and directory information on their sources comprise this publication of NCHS. Some relevant areas are adolescent health, adoptions, birth defects, births, child health, and child abuse, as well as general topics relating to vital statistics and chronic disease. Under each topic, NCHS sources are listed first, followed by other government sources, and then by private sources.

N16 **FAMILY PLANNING: IMPACT ON THE HEALTH OF WOMEN AND CHILDREN** By Deborah Maine. New York, Center for Population and Family Health, 1981. 56 pp. Free while supply lasts (paperback). From: 60 Haven Ave., B-3, New York, NY 10032.
A well-documented chart book with an outstanding bibliography. Covers the health of women and children in developing countries, as affected by family planning, using mortality data. The first chapter deals with child health and family planning.

N17 **FEDERAL STATISTICAL DIRECTORY** Washington, D.C., Office of Federal Statistical Policy and Standards, 1935– . Annual. $5.
Provides names and agencies of key persons engaged in statistical programs and related activities.

N18   **HEALTH STATUS OF CHILDREN: A REVIEW OF SUR-
VEYS 1963-1972**   Washington, D.C., Bureau of Community
Health Service, 1978. 259 pp. Price not available (paper).
(DHEW Publication No. [HSA] 78-5744)
Pulls together information from NCHS surveys involving children's
health and nutrition. It is an overview of the health status of children
and youth between 1963 and 1972 and a follow-up to a 1963 Children's
Bureau publication entitled *Illness Among Children,* which was based on
the National Health Surveys from 1957 to 1961. This report, prepared
by the University of California School of Public Health at Berkeley,
summarizes the findings of four health surveys and three nutritional
surveys, covering acute and chronic illness, dental care, and disparities
in health care for low-income and minority children. These reports
were not exclusively surveys and interviews but did involve (collectively) clinical examinations, laboratory tests, measures of growth,
hospital and medical records, and biochemical and developmental
evaluations. The whole report includes 108 tables.

Health surveys reviewed include *The Health Interview Survey,
1969-1972; The Health Examination Survey: Physical Findings for Children and Youths, 1963-1965* and *1966-1970; The Hospital Discharge
Survey, 1968-1971;* and *Adolescent Health in Harlem, 1968-1970.*

Nutrition surveys reviewed include *Preliminary Findings of the First
Health and Nutrition Examination Survey, 1971-1972; The U.S. Ten-State
Nutrition Survey, 1968-1970;* and *A Study of the Nutritional Status of Pre-
School Children in the United States, 1968-1970.*

N19   **HEALTH, UNITED STATES: A Comprehensive Summary
of U.S. Health Statistics**   Washington, D.C., U.S. Government Printing Office, 1976-. Annual. $7.
Includes analytical articles on selected topics of interest, as well as detailed statistical tables on health status and determinants, utilization of
health resources, health care resources, and health care expenditures.

N20   **THE NATION'S FAMILIES: 1960-1990**   By George Mas-
nick and Mary Jo Bane. Boston, Mass., Auburn House, 1980.
175 pp. $19.95; paperback, $10.95.
An important volume of assessments and forecasts of social changes involving families. Includes data and tables on current population, household, and life-style trends. Chapters deal with life-course variables,
trends in household and family structures, labor force participation and

attachment by women, women's contributions to family income, and families and government.

N21 STANDARD EDUCATION ALMANAC, 1982-83 15th Edition. Chicago, Ill., Marquis Academic Media, 1968- . Annual. $55.
Intelligently combines data on education in the United States and Canada from more than 60 information sources. Includes the *Annual Gallup Poll on the Public's Attitudes Toward the Public Schools,* as well as statistics on education and directories of organizations.

N22 STATE OF THE WORLD'S CHILDREN, 1984 Edited by James P. Grant. Oxford, England, Oxford University Press, 1980- . Annual. 1984 Edition, 126 pp., $6.95 (paperback).
The 1984 edition includes three parts: a moving essay on the state of the world's children; a "Lifelines" section with essays on the children's revolution; and a statistical section that contains economic and social statistics relating to children, including indicators for nutrition, health, education, demography, and economics.

An expanded version in hardcover is available for $19.95. This version also contains "The Impact of World Recession on Children and Ideas in Action."

N23 STATISTICAL ABSTRACT OF THE UNITED STATES
By the Bureau of the Census. Washington, D.C., U.S. Government Printing Office, 1879- . Annual. $15; paperback, $11.
The standard summary of statistics on the social, political, and economic organization of the United States.

N24 STATISTICAL REFERENCE INDEX (SRI) Edited by Darlene J. Montgomery. Bethesda, Md., Congressional Information Service, 1980- . Monthly, with annual cumulation. Price varies, depending on type of library and publications received.
Similar to the *American Statistics Index* (N2), except that *SRI* abstracts and indexes statistics outside Federal Government sources. It covers periodicals, annuals, monographs, and recurring serials from business organizations, commercial publishers, universities, associations, state agencies, and the like. It is a good source for business, welfare, and economic information, as well as for reports of independent research. Abstracts are arranged by code number under the issuing source; each issue includes a subject and name index, a categories index, a titles

index, and an issuing-sources index. *SRI* offers microfiche copies for approximately 90 percent of the publications identified through the index.

N25 **THE STATUS OF CHILDREN, YOUTH, AND FAMILIES, 1979–** Washington, D.C., Administration for Children, Youth, and Families, 1980–. Biennial. Discontinued.

A continuation and expansion of *The Status of Children* (1975 and 1977). Includes a chapter on demographic trends and one on life-cycle development that attempt to capture the factor of time over the life cycle. Other chapters deal with the status of children (in numbers, mobility, family setting, economic environment, health and nutrition, and education, with a supportive bibliography); the status of youth; families; and the status of research on children, youth, and families. All have substantial references. The *American Statistics Index* reported in late 1983 that the publication was discontinued, although the data is still compiled by the agency.

N26 **SUBJECT INDEX TO CURRENT POPULATION RE- PORTS: December 1980** Washington, D.C., U.S. Depart- ment of Commerce, 1981. 49 pp. $4.75 (paper). (Current Popu- lation Reports, Special Studies, Series P-23, No. 109)

A convenient single index to the extensive *Current Population Reports,* helpful in locating the titles and dates of appropriate reports. The most relevant reports are indexed under "Children and youth." Others can be found under "Blacks," "Geographic areas," "Households and families," "Income," "Poverty," "School enrollment," and "Spanish and ethnic."

N27 **WHERE TO FIND BLS DATA ON CHILDREN AND YOUTH** Washington, D.C., Bureau of Labor Statistics, 1979. 13 pp. Free (paper). From: Bureau of Labor Statistics, Inquiries and Correspondence, Washington, DC 20212.

Annotates BLS sources on children and youth and indicates how to obtain these publications. Areas include Special Labor Force Reports that provide in-depth studies of certain categories of workers (as women who head families or working mothers), *Monthly Labor Review* articles, current employment information, news releases, occupational materials, data on price and living conditions, and other sources of information.

N28   **WHERE TO FIND BLS STATISTICS ON WOMEN**   By
      Beverly L. Johnson. Washington, D.C., Bureau of Labor
      Statistics, 1980. 10 pp. Free (paper). (Report 612) From:
      Bureau of Labor Statistics, Inquiries and Correspondence,
      Washington, DC 20212.
Similar in intent to N27, but uses a tabular format to indicate ongoing
sources of information on women. Covers labor force status, earnings
and hours of work, education, membership in labor organizations, occupational injuries and illnesses, and sources of unpublished data.

N29   **WORLD ATLAS ON THE CHILD**   Washington, D.C., The
      World Bank, 1979. 40 pp. Paper. (Out of print) From: 1818 H
      St., NW, Washington, DC 20433.
Prepared in observation of the International Year of the Child (1979);
brings together basic statistical information on income, population,
child health, education, and other child-related data from 185 nations.
Uses maps (mostly based on 1975 data) for a visual presentation of the
status of children around the world, based on indicators that include
gross national product, population, number of children, life expectancy
at birth, infant mortality, death rates of children between 1 and 4, rates
and numbers of children in the labor force, and education data. Statistical annexes present data for each country arranged by region, with comparisons for different years.

ADDITIONAL SOURCES

N30   **AFDC STANDARDS FOR BASIC NEEDS**   Washington,
      D.C., U.S. Social Security Administration, 1955- . Annual
      (formerly irregular). Free. From: Office of Research and
      Statistics, 1875 Connecticut Ave., NW, Washington, DC 20009.
Discusses standards and maximums used by the states to determine
eligibility of citizens for Aid to Families with Dependent Children.

N31   **AMERICAN FAMILIES AND LIVING ARRANGEMENTS**
      Washington, D.C., Bureau of the Census, 1980. (Current Popu-
      lation Reports, Series P-23, No. 104)
Chart book prepared for the 1980 White House Conference on
Families.

N32   ANNUAL STATISTICS REVIEW, FINAL REPORT, FOOD AND NUTRITION PROGRAMS Washington, D.C., U.S. Department of Agriculture, Food and Nutrition Service, 1969–70– . Annual. Free while supply lasts.
Includes detailed statistics on child nutrition programs and family food assistance programs.

N33   AVAILABILITY OF CHILD CARE FOR LOW INCOME FAMILIES: Strategies to Address the Impact of the Economic Recovery Tax Act of 1981 and the Omnibus Budget Reconciliation Act of 1981 By June H. Zeitlin and Nancy Duff Campbell. In: *Clearinghouse Review, 16*(4):285–313, August–September 1982. Washington, D.C., National Clearinghouse for Legal Services, 1982.
Supplies statistics, legal background, and strategies vis-à-vis child care for low-income families. Footnotes indicate other sources of data.

N34   BLOOD LEAD LEVELS FOR PERSONS 6 MONTHS–74 YEARS OF AGE: UNITED STATES, 1976–80 By Joseph L. Annest et al. Hyattsville, Md., National Center for Health Statistics, 1982. 24 pp. Free (paper). (Advance Data from Vital and Health Statistics, No. 79; DHHS Publication No. [PHS] 82-1250)
The statistics in this report are the first national estimates of lead levels in whole blood obtained on a representative sample of the U.S. population. NCHS plans additional detailed descriptive statistics on blood levels in particular populations. This report presents statistics for three age categories: children aged 6 months–5 years; youths aged 6–17 years; and adults aged 18–74 years. The study indicates that lead levels decrease with age and that some groups are particularly high-risk. Four percent of the youngest group in general had elevated blood lead levels, but 12 percent of young black children and 18.5 percent of low-income black children had elevated blood lead levels.

N35   CHARACTERISTICS OF CHILDREN IN SUBSTITUTE AND ADOPTIVE CARE: A Statistical Summary of the VCIS National Child Welfare Data Base Compiled by Toshia Tatara for the Voluntary Cooperative Information System (VCIS). Washington, D.C., 1983. 120 pp. $12 (paper). From: 1125 15th St., NW, Washington, DC 20005.

Statistical summaries of national child-welfare data gathered from public child-welfare agencies for 1981-1982; includes aggregate state statistics for substitute care and adoption services.

N36 **CHILDREN IN CUSTODY: Advance Report on the 1979 Census of Public and Private Juvenile Facilities** Washington, D.C., Office of Justice, Assistance, Research, and Statistics, 1980-81. Biennial. Part I: *Public Facilities,* 1980; Part II: *Private Facilities,* 1981. (Out of print)
A two-part report covering public and private facilities, with selected comparisons to earlier years. Covers capital and operating expenses, with some additional information on the facilities, staffs, and residents.

N37 **CHILDREN OF WORKING MOTHERS, 1983** Washington, D.C., Bureau of Labor Statistics, 1983. 19 pp. $3. (BLS Bulletin No. 2158)
Findings from the annual survey of marital and family characteristics of workers. Covers family size, type of family, employment status of parents, and family income in the preceding year. Data are collected in March. Children included are under the age of 18.

N38 **CHILDREN, PROBLEMS, AND SERVICES IN CHILD WELFARE PROGRAMS** By Helen R. Jeter. Washington, D.C., Children's Bureau, 1963. 291 pp. (Out of print)
Other than the less-complete *National Study of Social Services to Children and Their Families* (N53), this report on a 1961 survey is the last extensive study of services to children by social welfare agencies.

N39 **CHILDREN'S DEFENSE BUDGET: An Analysis of the President's Fiscal 1985 Budget and Children** Washington, D.C., Children's Defense Fund, 1984. 280 pp. $12.95 (paperback). From: 122 C St., NW, Washington, DC 20001.
A comprehensive analysis of the effect of the president's budget on child care, education, Medicaid, maternal and child health, child welfare, food stamps, Aid to Families with Dependent Children, youth employment, and other programs involving children. This is the fourth consecutive year that CDF has published this analysis. A 1981 pamphlet, *Children and the Federal Budget,* explains the federal budget process and suggests when and how child advocates can influence budget decisions.

N40   **CHILDREN'S ENGLISH AND SERVICES STUDY: LAN-
GUAGE MINORITY CHILDREN WITH LIMITED ENG-
LISH PROFICIENCY IN THE UNITED STATES** By
Michael O'Malley. Rosslyn, Va., National Clearinghouse for
Bilingual Education, 1981. 87 pp. $3 (paperback).

A collaborative study by the National Institute of Education, the National Center for Education Statistics, and the Office of Bilingual Education to determine the number of children in the United States with
limited proficiency in English and the types of services they receive in
school.

N41   **CHILD SUPPORT ENFORCEMENT: ANNUAL REPORT
TO CONGRESS**   Washington, D.C., U.S. Office of Child Sup-
port Enforcement, 1976– . Annual. Free. From: National Child
Support Enforcement Reference Center, 6110 Executive Blvd.,
Room 820, Rockville, MD 20852.

Includes a chapter detailing financial, statistical, and program data obtained from federal reports completed by the states. Covers collections,
expenditures, case loads, and requests processed and provides background on support enforcement and related research studies.

N42   **CONCEPTUALIZATION AND MEASUREMENT OF
HEALTH FOR CHILDREN IN THE HEALTH INSUR-
ANCE STUDY**   By Marvin Eisen et al. Santa Monica, Calif.,
Rand, 1980. 314 pp. $10 (paper).

Part of a Rand study to investigate the effects of different forms of
health-care financial arrangements in the United States. Includes tables
and bibliographic references.

N43   **DEMOGRAPHIC AND SOCIOECONOMIC FACT BOOK
ON CHILD HEALTH CARE: A Survey of Trends in the
United States** By the American Academy of Pediatrics.
Evanston, Ill., 1980. 88 pp. $10.

Presents data for pediatricians and child-health advocates in comparative chart, graph, and map forms. Five sections deal with pediatric
population and demographic data, a medical manpower profile, utilization of medical services and facilities, a pediatric practice profile, and a
national health care profile. In addition to birth, infant mortality, and
fertility rates, the first section includes information on 10 leading
causes of death; the second section includes statistics on pediatricians
and family practitioners; and the third section gives children's hospital
statistics.

N44   **DIGEST OF DATA ON PERSONS WITH DISABILITIES**
Prepared by the Rehab Group, Inc. under contract to the Congressional Research Service, Library of Congress. Washington, D.C., U.S. Government Printing Office, 1979. 141 pp. $6.50 (paper).
A readable compendium with a glossary of terms that provides detailed information on data sources for persons with disabilities. Areas include work, education, health, income, limitations, mental health, and federal programs.

N45   **DIMENSIONS OF POVERTY IN LATIN AMERICA AND THE CARIBBEAN**   Edited by Francisco Galdames. Santiago, Chile, Americas Regional Office of UNICEF, 1982. 167 pp. Price not available (paper).
A two-column book in Spanish (*Dimensiones de las Pobreza en America Latina y el Caribe*) and English, prepared to make known the magnitude and diverse facets of extreme poverty, especially as they relate to children. Includes chapters on general and demographic background, nutrition, health, housing, education, income distribution and employment, and synthetic indicators. Contains 135 detailed bilingual charts based on quantitative data on such things as infant mortality (by country), proportion of poor families, and proportion of families without piped water. Has an excellent bibliography. According to this book, more than 50 million children are without resources to satisfy their primary or essential needs, and the risk of death in early childhood remains excessively high. The UNICEF office in Chile has compiled many helpful Spanish-language statistical and narrative reports on children in Latin America, including *El Niño en America Latina y el Caribe* (1979); *El Niño en el Peru* (1978); and *Pobreza, Necesidades Basicas y Desarrollo* (1982).

N46   **EDUCATION: THE CRITICAL FILTER**   A Statistical Report on the Status of Girls and Women in Elementary and Secondary Education. By Matilda Butler. San Francisco, Calif., Women's Educational Equity Network, 1979. $4.25 (paperback).
An easy-to-read statistical summary of the status of girls and women vis-à-vis student enrollment; role portrayal in instructional materials, courses, athletics, and extracurricular activities; and such educational outcomes as grades, aptitudes, graduation, future study intentions, and attitudes. Also covers professional training and salaries. Indicates sources throughout.

N47 **FAMILY BACKGROUND, EARLY DEVELOPMENT, AND INTELLIGENCE OF CHILDREN 6-11 YEARS, UNITED STATES** Hyattsville, Md., National Center for Health Statistics, 1977. 42 pp. Paper. (Data from the National Health Survey, Series 11, No. 142)
Analyzes the relationship of estimated intelligence to factors in children's backgrounds, including prenatal care, condition at birth, early developmental history, preschool educational experiences, and present medical problems.

N48 **FAMILY DAY CARE IN THE UNITED STATES; FINAL REPORT** Washington, D.C., Administration for Children, Youth, and Families, 1981. 7 Vols. (National Day Care Home Study) (Out of print, but available from: ERIC Document Reproduction Service, P.O. Box 190, Arlington, VA 22210, as ED 211 218. Check for price.)
The *Final Report Series* of the National Day Care Home Study project covers data on family day care providers, the children in their care, and the children's parents. Volume I is a summary of findings; Volume V, *Family Day Care Systems Report,* presents an extensive descriptive and statistical analysis of the day care institutions that administer family day care systems.

N49 **INDICATORS OF CHILD HEALTH AND WELFARE: Development of the DIPOV Index** By Leonard S. Kogan, Shirley Jenkins et al. New York, City University of New York, Center for Social Research, 1974. Paged in sections. $17.50. Distributed by Columbia University Press.
Uses indicators based on discrimination and poverty—including health and welfare attributes and characteristics and resource and service statistics on children—in contexts that include children, broken down by geographic area.

N50 **INDICATORS OF SOCIAL WELL-BEING FOR U.S. COUNTIES** By Peggy J. Ross, Herman Bluestone, and Fred K. Hines. Washington, D.C., U.S. Department of Agriculture, Economic Development Division, 1979. 18 pp. $1.50 (paper). From: Washington, DC 20250. (Rural Development Research Report, No. 10)
Applies four composite indexes of social well-being to 3,097 U.S. counties and depicts these by U.S. county maps and mean index scores of counties, grouped by rural/urban orientation and metropolitan/nonmetropolitan status. Thus, the map is an overview of the geography of

well-being in the United States. Indexes, constructed from the 1970 population census, are socioeconomic, health, family status, and alienation. The report has a statistical supplement, entitled *Indexes and Rankings for Indicators of Social Well-Being for U.S. Counties.*

N51 **INEQUALITY OF SACRIFICE: THE IMPACT OF THE REAGAN BUDGET ON WOMEN** By the Coalition on Women and the Budget. Washington, D.C., 1983. 82 pp. $2 (paper). From: National Women's Law Center, 1751 N St., NW, Washington, DC 20036.

An overview of the effects of the fiscal year 1984 budget on the total spectrum of women, including women in families, Aid to Families with Dependent Children, child-nutrition programs, child care, and food stamps. Includes an 11-page directory of resource organizations.

N52 **NATIONAL ANALYSIS OF OFFICIAL CHILD NEGLECT AND ABUSE REPORTING; ANNUAL REPORT** Denver, Colo., American Humane Assn., Child Protection Division, Annual. $3 (paper). From: 9725 E. Hampden Ave., Denver, CO 80231.

Statistical report by state and selected detail by case type. Also covers distribution of case by case type, type of maltreatment, service provided, sex of adult or adults responsible, child's race or ethnicity, family stress factors, and the relationship between the child and the perpetrator. With many cross-tabulations.

N53 **NATIONAL STUDY OF SOCIAL SERVICES TO CHILDREN AND THEIR FAMILIES** By Ann W. Shyne and Anita G. Schroeder. Rockville, Md., Westat, Inc. for National Center for Child Advocacy, 1978. 160 pp., plus six appendixes. Inquire about price ((301) 251-1500). *Overview,* 26 pp., $1.40 (single copy free while supply lasts; paper). From: Westat, Inc., 11600 Nebel St., Rockville, MD 20852.

An attempt to gather information on children and families who receive child public welfare, why they have been referred, and the nature of the services they receive. Describes the paucity of knowledge in this area. This survey was based on a representative sample of children being served by 315 public social service departments in the United States in March 1977—a total of 9,579 children of the 1.8 million receiving public social services. Areas covered are demographic and social characteristics of the children, living arrangements and family circumstances, introduction to the agency, agency service plans and activities, and agency staff.

N54   NATIONAL STUDY OF THE INCIDENCE AND SEVERITY
      OF CHILD ABUSE AND NEGLECT Washington, D.C.,
      Office of Human Development Services, 1981–1982. 3 Parts.
      Part I: *Executive Summary,* 1982, 17 pp., price not available
      (paper); Part II: *Study Findings,* 1981, 56 pp., $3.20 (paper);
      Part III: *Study Methodology,* 1982, 191 pp., single copy free
      (paper). From: LSDS, Dept. 76-A2, Washington, DC 20402.
Another contract report by Westat, Inc. (see N53), under the sponsorship of the National Center on Child Abuse and Neglect, on the
number and characteristics of children who were the victims of physical
assault; sexual exploitation; emotional abuse; and physical, emotional,
and educational neglect from May 1979 to April 1980, using nationwide
estimates based on a survey of 550 community agencies serving 26
counties in 10 states. Data on each county were collected over a
12-month period from child-protection agencies and from selected
schools, hospitals, courts, and police departments. It was found that
adolescents from ages 15 to 17 were the primary victims of maltreatment and that only around one-half of these case had been reported to
child-protection agencies.

N55   NUTRITION, GROWTH AND DEVELOPMENT OF
      NORTH AMERICAN INDIAN CHILDREN Edited by
      William M. Moore, Marjorie M. Silverberg, and Merrill S. Read.
      Washington, D.C., U.S. Government Printing Office, 1972. 246
      pp. Paperback. (Out of print) (DHEW Publication No. [NIH]
      72-76)
These papers, based on a conference for researchers, clinicians, and
Indian representatives, cover perspectives, diets, growth, nutritional
status, child-rearing practices, and cultural change, with statistics on
health, growth, and nutritional status. Subject and author indexes.

N56   PERSPECTIVES ON WORKING WOMEN: A DATA-
      BOOK Washington, D.C., Bureau of Labor Statistics, 1980. 8
      Parts. 105 pp. $5.50 (paper). (Bulletin 2080)
Provides detailed information on women's labor force participation, in
eight sections, with most information based on the Current Population
Survey. Part III focuses on working women's marital, family, and child
status; Part V examines earnings; and Part VI looks at data by race and
Hispanic origin.

N57 **PORTRAIT OF INEQUALITY: BLACK AND WHITE CHILDREN IN AMERICA** By Mary Wright Edelman. Washington, D.C., Children's Defense Fund, 1980. 116 pp. $5.50 (paper).
Reports on social and economic conditions of black children in the United States from 1969 to 1979, with data on family structure, child care, unemployment, education, health, housing, and crime. Includes 44 pages of descriptions and solutions and 59 pages of tables.

N58 **PRELIMINARY NATIONAL ASSESSMENT OF THE NUMBERS AND CHARACTERISTICS OF JUVENILES PROCESSED IN THE JUVENILE JUSTICE SYSTEM** By T. Edwin Black and Charles P. Smith. Washington, D.C., National Institute for Juvenile Justice and Delinquency Prevention, 1981. 194 pp. Not priced (paper). (Reports of the National Juvenile Justice Assessment Centers)
Reports on the number of persons under age 18 processed nationally in the official juvenile justice system. Primarily concerns the processing of juvenile delinquent and status offenses, not the cases of victimized or dependent children.

N59 **PROFILES OF CHILDREN: 1970 WHITE HOUSE CONFERENCE ON CHILDREN** Washington, D.C., U.S. Government Printing Office, 1970. 187 pp. Paper. (Out of print)
A substantial chart book with tables and references and a great deal of useful information. The first section deals with children entering the 1970s; others cover the prenatal period, infancy, the preschool years of 1–6, and the school years of 6–13. A companion volume, *Profiles of Youth,* was prepared for the 1971 White House Conference on Youth.

N60 **PROFILES OF FAMILIES IN POVERTY: EFFECTS OF THE FY 1983 BUDGET PROPOSALS ON THE POOR: A Working Paper** By Tom Joe. Washington, D.C., Center for the Study of Social Policy, 1982. Paged in sections. $10 (paper). From: 236 Massachusetts Ave., NE, Washington, DC 20002.
Analyzes the effects on the poor of the Reagan administration's 1982 program changes and 1983 proposals. Includes a detailed appendix on "total monthly disposable income for working and non-working AFDC mothers with two children." Chapters include "Hurting the Truly Needy," "Penalizing the Working Poor," and "Long Range Effects of the Budget Proposals."

N61   **PROJECTIONS OF NON-ENGLISH LANGUAGE BACK-
GROUND AND LIMITED ENGLISH PROFICIENT PER-
SONS IN THE UNITED STATES TO THE YEAR 2000:
Executive Summary**   By Rebecca Oxford et al. Rosslyn, Va.,
National Clearinghouse for Bilingual Education, 1980. 34 pp.
$3.40 (paper).
Presents statistical projections up to the year 2000—broken down by
language, age, and state—of persons not speaking English or limited in
the English language. Both groups are expected to increase, based on
the Current Population Survey, census projections, and the Children's
English and Services Survey. The full paper of 148 pages is available
from the clearinghouse for $0.10/page.

N62   **A PUBLIC ASSISTANCE DATA BOOK**   By Tondy H.
Campbell and Marc Bendick, Jr. Washington, D.C., The Urban
Institute, 1977. 344 pp. $10. From: 2100 M St., NW, Washing-
ton, DC 20037.
Presents 104 variables describing public assistance benefits and their
administration in state and metropolitan areas of the United States,
mostly collected for use in a study of error rate in eligibility determination and benefit computation in Aid to Families with Dependent Children. Variables are categorized as characteristics of public assistance
clients, public assistance eligibility and benefit policies, characteristics
of public assistance staff, public assistance program operations, and
public assistance program performance. The authors published another
paper, *The Anatomy of AFDC Errors,* with The Urban Institute in 1977.

N63   **SEXUAL EXPLOITATION OF CHILDREN—A PROBLEM
OF UNKNOWN MAGNITUDE**   Washington, D.C., U.S.
General Accounting Office (GAO), 1982. 63 pp. Up to five
copies free; additional copies, $3.25 each (paper). From: Docu-
ment Handling and Information Services Facility, P.O. Box
6015, Gaithersburg, MD 20760.
Compiled by GAO in response to a request by the Subcommittee on
Select Education; covers teenage prostitution and child pornography
and governmental (federal, state, and local) efforts to curb these activities. Based on a literature search, a survey sent to all states and police
departments and mayors of large cities, and an intensive investigation
in New York and Los Angeles. The report includes an estimate of the
number of children involved, the reasons for their involvement, the effects on children of sexual exploitation, social services and proposed
solutions, and a lengthy bibliography.

N64 SOCIAL INDICATORS III: SELECTED DATA ON SO-
CIAL CONDITIONS AND TRENDS IN THE UNITED
STATES: A Publication of the Federal Statistical System
Washington, D.C., Bureau of the Census, 1980. 585 pp. $19
(paper).
An impressive compilation with a glossary of terms and attractive color
charts. Uses 11 categories to determine social indicators: population
and the family; health and nutrition; housing and the environment;
transportation; public safety; education and training; work; social security and welfare; income and productivity; social participation; and
culture, leisure, and use of time. Each section begins with public perceptions and is divided further. Includes retrospective information to
show trends. An appendix provides sources of data. Many tables
throughout relate to children: for example, death rates for children and
teenagers; selected causes and years, 1950–1977; and infant mortality
by race, 1960–1977.

N65 STATE REPORTS ON WOMEN AND CHILD WAGE
EARNERS, 1870–1906 By M. Aldrich. In: *Library History
(U.S.)*, Vol. 21, pp. 86–90, 1980.
Lists state labor bureau reports dealing with women and child workers
from 1897 to 1906 from the National Archives.

N66 THE TOY INDUSTRY FACTBOOK New York, Toy Manufacturers of America, 1979– . Annual. Free while supply lasts.
From: 200 Fifth Ave., New York, NY 10010.
Developed to meet the needs of analysts and marketers with statistical,
marketing, and economic information on the toy industry; provides a
profile of the industry in a question-and-answer format. Includes data
on types, quantities, distribution, and prices of toys sold over the last
five years and nonstatistical information on advertising and advertising
guidelines.

N67 USDA ESTIMATES OF THE COST OF RAISING A
CHILD: A GUIDE TO THEIR USE AND INTERPRETA-
TION By Carolyn S. Edwards. Washington, D.C., U.S. Department of Agriculture, Agricultural Research Service, 1981. 57
pp. Paper. (Out of print) (Miscellaneous Publication No. 1411)
"This guide describes the USDA estimates of the cost of raising a child,
provides the estimates updated to June 1980 price levels, and answers
the most frequently asked questions about their use and interpretation." Indicates the costs of raising a child for urban, rural nonfarm,

and farm children by region, age, and cost levels; figures include clothing, housing, medical care, education, and transportation (see Figure 5 in Chapter 9). This monograph also provides information on the related costs of having a baby, child care costs, and higher education costs. It is updated in *Family Economics Review* (H61).

N68 **WORLD HEALTH STATISTICS ANNUAL, 1939/1946–** Geneva, Switzerland, World Health Organization, 1951– . 36 Swiss francs.
Contains life tables (life expectancies, births, deaths), information on vital statistics, and causes of death for all ages in all countries.

N69 **WORLD REFUGEE SURVEY 1982** By the U.S. Committee for Refugees. New York, American Council for Nationalities, 1982. 62 pp. $4 (paperback).
An annual comprehensive survey of major refugee situations, mainly by country of asylum. Comprises a number of articles on refugee problems and U.S. policies.

N70 **WORLD SCHOOL-AGE POPULATION UNTIL YEAR 2000: Some Implications for the Education Sector** Paris, Unesco, Office of Statistics, 1981. 159 pp. Free while supply lasts. From: 7, place de Fontenoy, 75700 Paris, France.
Includes two related studies: The first is an overall quantitative analysis of trends and projects of the world school-age population from 1960 to 2000. The second explores the implications for educational planning. This office produces many interesting statistical analyses involving children and young people, including *Comparative Analysis of Male and Female Enrollment and Illiteracy* (1980, 165 pp.) and *The Allocation of Resources to Education Throughout the World* (1980, 101 pp.), both free while the supply lasts.

SURVEYS

Major public-opinion-poll organizations include the Gallup Organization, 53 Bank St., Princeton, NJ 08540, (609) 924-9600, which issues the *Gallup Opinion Index—Political, Social, and Economic Trends,* as well as a Gallup poll on education, which is

reprinted in *Phi Delta Kappan.* The polls of the National Opinion
Research Center (NORC), 6030 S. Ellis Ave., Chicago, IL 60637,
(312) 753-1300 tend to focus on single topics and are reported in
a newsletter and a publications bibliography. The Roper Center,
at Yale University Center, Box 1732, Yale Sta., New Haven, CT
06520, serves as an international depository, in machine-
readable form, for survey data from academic and commercial
publications. It discusses its own and other survey results in its
monthly *Public Opinion.* The Institute for Social Research of the
University of Michigan, Box 1248, Ann Arbor, MI 48106, (313)
764-8382, covers all social science fields, including such child-
related areas as child rearing, impact of television on children,
and delinquency. The *Bibliography of Research in Children, Youth,
and Family Life at the Institute of Social Research* is available on
request. The files and research of the institute were used to
compile the *American Social Attitudes Data Sourcebook* (N72)
and *Five Thousand American Families: Patterns of Economic Progress* (N76).

PUBLICATIONS

N71   **AMERICAN FAMILIES: 1980** By James Schriver et al.
      Princeton, N.J., Gallup Organization, 1980. 223 pp. $49. From:
      American Research Corp., P.O. Box 7849, Newport Beach, CA
      92660.
A comprehensive survey of American families—part of a public refer-
endum relating to the White House Conference on Families—based on
interviews with 1,592 adults in March 1980. Includes tables and
surveys.

N72   **AMERICAN SOCIAL ATTITUDES DATA SOURCE-
      BOOK, 1947-1978** By Philip E. Converse et al. Cambridge,
      Mass., Harvard University Press, 1980. 441 pp. $25.
A unique record of trends in social and economic attitudes of adult
Americans, culled from the archives of the Survey Research Center at
the University of Michigan. Includes questions that have been asked
over time on topics that vary from views on women's roles to life
quality, family financial situations, the state of the national economy,

and war and peace. Uses text, tables, and graphs to demonstrate continuity and change in perspectives and supplements these opinions with
government data.

N73 **CHILDREN'S SEXUAL THINKING: A Comparative Study
of Children Aged 5 to 15 Years in Australia, North America,
Britain and Sweden** By Ronald and Juliette Goldman.
Boston, Mass., Routledge & Kegan Paul, 1982. 485 pp. $24.95.
One of the few surveys actually involving children, this book is based
on interviews and discussions with hundreds of children in four areas.
Topics examined were how children perceive aging, parental roles, sex
identity, sex roles of children and adults, conception, gestation and
childbirth, and related subjects. Results were scored on criteria based
on realism and discussed in the light of developmental theories of
childhood.

N74 **FAMILIES AT WORK: STRENGTHS AND STRAINS**
Study conducted for General Mills, Inc. by Louis Harris and
Associates. Minneapolis, Minn., General Mills, 1981. 87 pp.
Free while supply lasts (paper). (The General Mills American
Family Report, 1980–81) From: General Mills, Inc., Public Affairs Dept., P.O. Box 1113, Minneapolis, MN 55440.
A survey based on interviews in November and December 1980 with
six groups: a national cross-section, teenagers, human resource executives, labor leaders, family traditionalists, and feminists. Areas covered
include the benefits and strains of work on family life, the effects of
working on child care, priorities and demands, and benefits and work
policies perceived to be helpful to families.
   This report and that annotated in item N75 are part of General Mills'
American Family Program, designed to identify genuine social concerns, to provide data that illuminate these concerns, and to share findings with public- and private-sector leaders. It consists of biennial
reports, alternated by forums or specific initiatives. Other reports in the
series include *The American Family and Money (1974–75)* and *Raising
Children in a Changing Society (1976–77)*. All present information very
well.

N75 **FAMILY HEALTH IN AN ERA OF STRESS** Study con-
ducted by Yankelovich, Skelly and White. Minneapolis, Minn.,
General Mills, 1979. 192 pp. Free while supply lasts (paper).
(The General Mills American Family Report, 1978–79) From:

General Mills, Inc., Public Affairs Dept., P.O. Box 1113,
Minneapolis, MN 55440.
Deals with the attitudes and practices of adults and teenagers that affect
other family members. It notes that almost half of all American families
are cutting back in some essential health area in order to cope with
inflation. The proportions are higher for low-income families, minorities, and single parents.

N76 **FIVE THOUSAND AMERICAN FAMILIES: PATTERNS
OF ECONOMIC PROGRESS** Compiled by the Institute for
Social Research of the University of Michigan. Vol. 1: *An Analysis of the First Five Years of the Panel Study of Income Dynamics*
(Report PB 236 457/8GA); Vol. 2: *Special Study of the First Five
Years of the Panel Study of Income Dynamics* (Report PB 236
458/6GA). Springfield, Va., National Technical Information Service, 1974. Vol. 1: 439 pp.; Vol. 2: 377 pp. Inquire about price.
Although outdated, this is a most impressive survey source on family
economic data, covering income as related to educational level, family
dynamics, and parent/child relations.

N77 **HOW IS WORK AFFECTING AMERICAN FAMILIES? A
REPORT FROM THE EDITORS OF BETTER HOMES
AND GARDENS** Des Moines, Iowa, Meredith Corp., 1981.
88 pp. Free while supply lasts (paper). From: Locust at 17th,
Des Moines, IA 50336.
A report based on the attitudes and opinions of 32,588 respondents to
an "American Family" questionnaire in the June 1981 issue of *Better
Homes and Gardens.* Pages 47–54 deal with children.

N78 **IS GOVERNMENT HELPING OR HURTING AMERICAN
FAMILIES? A REPORT FROM THE EDITORS OF
BETTER HOMES AND GARDENS TO THE WHITE
HOUSE CONFERENCE ON FAMILIES** Des Moines,
Iowa, Meredith Corp., 1980. 80 pp. Free while supply lasts
(paper). From: Locust at 17th, Des Moines, IA 50336.
Summarizes attitudes and opinions of 46,817 respondents to an
"American Family" questionnaire in the March 1980 issue of *Better
Homes and Gardens.* Covers policies affecting children, child care and
family solidarity, education, health and safety, housing, taxes, and
economic policies.

N79   STATISTICAL HIGHLIGHTS FROM THE NATIONAL
      CHILD CARE CONSUMER STUDY   By Administration for
      Children, Youth, and Families. Washington, D.C., 1978. 28 pp.
      Single copy free (paper). (DHEW Publication No. [OHDS]
      78-31096)
Summary of parent practices and attitudes toward child care taken from
the National Child Care Consumer Study, involving the extent and use
of day care, with information on preferences and the public role.

N80   WHAT'S HAPPENING TO THE AMERICAN FAMILY?
      A REPORT FROM THE EDITORS OF BETTER HOMES
      AND GARDENS   Des Moines, Iowa, Meredith Corp., 1978.
      214 pp. Free while supply lasts (paper). From: Locust at 17th,
      Des Moines, IA 50336.
This report summarizes the attitudes and opinions of some 302,602 respondents to a questionnaire appearing in the September and October
1977 issues of *Better Homes and Gardens*. Section V deals with relationships with children. Section VI deals with teenagers. Other relevant sections are on health, education, and housing.

16 / Children and
Books

Several perspectives on the interrelations between children and books are combined here. Children's literature is a well-developed field with an extensive collection of reference books, including bibliographies and abstract journals. Children's librarians and school librarians are also expert organizers of children's books, with their own perspectives and reference works; these books could and should be used far more extensively by professionals in other fields. Typically, librarians are concerned not only with the value and the aesthetic components of children's literature, but also are experts in using books for information, with a pragmatic knowledge of what appeals to children. English teachers and language-arts teachers have another perspective on children's books and expertise in the area of reading, an area that involves a detailed study of children's ways of learning. Since educators use textbooks and other print materials in teaching children, included in this chapter are tools that list or provide means of evaluating the books that are used in schools. *Selecting Materials for Instruction* (O66) provides many more criteria and references.

Bibliotherapy, a therapeutic application of books, is a professional tool that uses the knowledge and skills of both librarianship and psychology. Its premises and practices are thoroughly discussed in *The Bookfinder* (O26 and O27) and *Books to Help Children Cope with Separation and Loss* (O29). This ties in particularly well with the resources of previous chapters. For example,

Chapter 6 contains several bibliographies of psychological references on hospitalized or bereaved children, whereas this chapter
contains bibliographies or guides to books to help bereaved or
hospitalized children deal with their stress.

Print resources for the fields of children's librarianship and
children's literature are certainly far more extensive than the
works annotated in this chapter. For example, I have omitted
reference works dealing with children's authors and illustrators,
indexes to plays and poetry, and guides to information books. I
have included only a salient sample of reference tools—those
that were most widely useful—as well as guides to further
sources for those who wish to pursue this area. Three valuable
guides are *Information Sources in Children's Literature* (O58),
Children's Literature: A Guide to Reference Sources (O11), and
Choosing Books for Young People (O40). The American Library
Association (O2) has published the convenient *Selecting Materials for Children and Young People: A Bibliography of Bibliographies and Review Sources.* Another excellent starting point is *Children and Books* (O30), with bibliographic appendixes that
provide a very-well-rounded perspective on children's literature
that encompasses the viewpoints of librarians, educators, literary
types, and developmental specialists. *Children's Media Market
Place* (I17), a directory discussed in Chapter 10, is a guide to
children's books, among other media; it includes lists of publishers, selection tools, periodicals for children, bookstores, and
book clubs. Some of the periodicals in Chapter 9 review children's books; these are noted in their annotations. Two helpful
dictionaries are *A Dictionary of Reading and Related Terms* (A7)
and *The Living Word Vocabulary* (A18).

Although children's literature has its own abstract journal—
Children's Literature Abstracts (O37)—many other periodical indexes and data bases provide relevant materials. *Library and Information Science Abstracts* (J28) and *Library Literature* (New
York, H. W. Wilson, 1921- , sold on a service basis) are sources
for the library perspective; *Education Index* (G19) and the ERIC
(J22) sources cover educational applications; *Psychological Abstracts* (G36), *Child Development* (H24), and other psychologi-
cal/behavioral sources might cover the developmental and psychological abstracts; social issues in children's books may be

discussed in social science indexes and data bases; and language, literature, and reading data bases and indexes are also worth consulting for language and literary concerns. Folklore is covered to a certain extent in anthropological tools; *Folk Literature and Children* (E81) is one relevant bibliography. Fairy tales and mythology have their own reference works. Some health care organizations provide bibliographies for or about ill or hospitalized children.

Following are some major organizations and printed guides. Other organizations listed in Chapters 12 and 13 also provide information on books for children. Among these are the Information Center on Children's Cultures (K66), the Association for Childhood Education International (K7), Pediatric Projects, Inc. (L32), and the National Black Child Development Institute (K36). The Sex Information and Education Council of the United States (80 Fifth Ave., Suite 801, New York, NY 10011) is a major source of information on printed materials dealing with sexuality and sex education.

Typically, schools of education and schools of library science at the university level contain substantial library collections dealing with books and children and/or children's literature, and public libraries have professional collections on children's literature adjacent to the books for children in their children's or young adults' rooms. The Library of Congress has a Children's Literature Center (Room 140H) that maintains an extensive collection of reference books and provides reference and bibliographic services on children's literature (see item O11).

Although bibliographic control of book reviews is important to experts in children's literature, it seems less significant for most child workers. Most review publications are subsumed under the names of the organizations that follow.

ORGANIZATIONS

O1 **AMERICAN ASSOCIATION OF SCHOOL LIBRARIANS (AASL)** 50 E. Huron St., Chicago, IL 60611. (312) 944-6780
An affiliate of the American Library Association, concerned with the role of librarians in schools, AASL has much experience in dealing with

controversy related to children's materials. Its *School Library Media Quarterly* ($15/year) reviews all kinds of children's books and media and contains frequent articles on issues like censorship and selection.

O2　**AMERICAN LIBRARY ASSOCIATION (ALA)** 50 E. Huron St., Chicago, IL 60611. (312) 944-6780
A national professional group that publishes numerous helpful periodicals, guides, reviews, and bibliographies. Its periodical, *Booklist* (22 issues/year, $40.00), is an excellent review source. It has commissioned and published an excellent regional *Reading for Young People* series and the *History of Children's Literature: A Syllabus with Selected Bibliographies* (1980, 312 pp., $70.00).

ALA's divisions include the Office for Intellectual Freedom, which issues a newsletter and publishes on topics like censorship and access to materials. Some items available from ALA's order department are *Challenged Materials* (1981, $0.10) and *Pressure Groups and Censorship* (1981, $2.00).

The Association for Library Service to Children (ALSC) is the ALA division concerned with children from preschool through the eighth grade. It is interested in improving and extending library services to children and in evaluating and selecting library materials for this group. It publishes many relevant discussions and reading lists, including an annual list of *Notable Children's Books*. Some relevant titles and prices are *Building a Children's Literature Collection* (1978, $4.75); *Directory: Coordinators of Children's Services and Young Adult Services* (1981, $5.50); *Information: A Necessity for Survival; Strategies for the Promotion of Children's Books in a Developing Country* (1981, $1.00); *Selected List of Children's Books of Information about Exceptional Children* (1980, $0.35); *Selecting Materials for Children and Young Adults: A Bibliography of Bibliographies and Review Sources* (1980, $7.00); and *Standards of Criticism for Children's Literature* (1971, $0.50).

O3　**AMERICAN PRINTING HOUSE FOR THE BLIND (APH)** 1839 Frankfort Ave., P.O. Box 6085, Louisville, KY 40206. (502) 895-2405
The world's largest publishing house for visually impaired persons, founded in 1858. It produces print materials and tangible aids that are distributed through other groups, like the Division for the Blind and Physically Handicapped of the Library of Congress. APH has been the official publisher of school materials for blind children since 1879, producing braille, large-type books, cassettes, and talking books, as well as teaching devices based on sound, touch, and memory. These in-

clude sensory and textured aids for early childhood education, globes, maps, and music materials. Catalogs are available on request. A *Central Catalog* provides a title index for locating materials for the blind and visually handicapped in depository libraries throughout the United States.

O4   CENTER FOR CHILDREN'S BOOKS (CCB)   1100 E. 57th St., Chicago, IL 60637. (312) 753-3450

An examination center for children's books, with a collection of 20,000 volumes of children's trade books published during the last five years— including both classics and outstanding books and a professional collection of reference books, pamphlets, periodicals, and catalogs on children's literature and reading. The purpose of the center is to help adults learn to evaluate children's books with strong critical standards that include appeal, literary quality, readability, and developmental values. It competently reviews virtually all children's trade books in a review journal, *Bulletin of the Center for Children's Books*. Selections from this journal are published approximately every 10 years as *The Best in Children's Books.*

Although the center is not generally open to the public, qualified visitors can get passes to use the collection on-site.

O5   CHILDREN'S BOOK COUNCIL (CBC)   67 Irving Pl., New York, NY 10005. (212) 254-2666

A nonprofit organization of children's book publishers founded in 1945 to encourage the reading and enjoyment of children's literature. It cooperates with many educational and interest groups to provide lists of award-winning books and other recommended titles. Lists include *Classroom Choices for 1982, Children's Book Showcase, Children's Books: Awards and Prizes, Notable Children's Trade Books in the Field of Social Studies,* and *Outstanding Science Trade Books for Children.*

CBC is the official headquarters of Children's Book Week (now Book Week) and promotes this event with attractive display materials and publications. It also promotes a Summer Reading Program and a Year-Round Reading Program, with specific themes, displays, and instructional materials. *Calendar,* which appears three times every two years, covers holidays and events concerning children and books, with interviews of authors and listings of free and inexpensive items. A one-time handling fee of $10 places you on the mailing list permanently.

CBC's library, which serves as an examination center for children's trade books, retains for three years sample copies of all juvenile books produced by cooperating publishers. Award-winning books and a professional collection on children's literature are in a permanent collection. Altogether, CBC holds some 8,000 books, 35 periodical titles, a complete file of Book Week posters from 1919 to date, and relevant vertical-file materials on children's books. Visitors may use the collection on-site.

O6   **COUNCIL ON INTERRACIAL BOOKS FOR CHILDREN (CIBC)**   1841 Broadway, New York, NY 10023. (212) 757-5339
Founded in 1966 to effect basic changes in books and other media and to promote learning materials that embody the concepts of cultural pluralism, CIBC has extended its scope from combating racist and sexist stereotypes to encompass stereotypes relating to age and handicapping conditions. Its *Interracial Books for Children Bulletin* features critical analyses of racist and sexist stereotypes in children's books and instructional materials. A recent issue dealt with homophobia, a fear of homosexuals or homosexuality. CIBC's Racism and Sexism Resource Center is a national referral center and publisher of books, pamphlets, audiovisuals, lesson plans, and teaching strategies, with particular emphasis on analyzing racism and sexism in teaching materials. Publications include *Ten Quick Ways to Analyze Children's Books for Racism and Sexism* ($0.10) and *Stereotypes, Distortions, and Omissions in U.S. History Textbooks* ($7.95). A detailed catalog will be sent on request.

CIBC has a children's book collection of around 1,000 titles related to third-world and feminist themes and reference materials on its areas of interest.

O7   **CURRICULUM ADVISORY CENTER (CAS)**   500 S. Clinton St., Chicago, IL 60607. (312) 939-1333
Founded in 1961, CAS is one of the very few agencies that attempts to review textbooks and other traditional curriculum materials. Its *Curriculum Review* is a well-indexed and well-organized periodical ($35/year, 5 issues/year) that combines reviews of materials in basic subject areas like language arts, mathematics, science, and social studies, with cluster reviews of trade books that are useful for learning. It has a national staff of reviewers who are simultaneously subject specialists and active classroom teachers or professors.

O8   **EDUCATIONAL PRODUCTS INFORMATION EXCHANGE (EPIE) INSTITUTE**   P.O. Box 620, Stony Brook, NY 11790.

A nonprofit membership group for educational consumers that also reviews textbooks and curriculum materials and trains teachers in evaluation. Its publications include quarterly *EPIE Reports,* which cover new developments in curriculum materials, and a monthly newsletter, *EPIEgram,* that offers advice, warnings, consumer alerts, and news.

O9 **INTERNATIONAL BOARD ON BOOKS FOR YOUNG PEOPLE (IBBY)** Leonhardsgraben 38 a, CH-4051 Basel, Switzerland. (06) 25 34 04

Founded in Zurich in 1953, this international organization promotes worldwide understanding through children's books and reading and encourages high literary and artistic standards and the wide distribution of literature for children. Goals include the establishment of national and international libraries and the publication of imaginative and challenging books for young people. It encourages commercial exchange among publishers so that the best children's literature of each country will be translated into as many languages as possible. IBBY also encourages the development of books for children in countries that do not possess a large body of children's literature and the publication of books that keep children in touch with their own heritage, language, and customs.

Composed of national sections (e.g., Irish, Austrian) from many countries, IBBY has been commissioned by Unesco to compile an international directory of specialists in children's literature. It issues a compact international directory of cooperating organizations entitled *IBBY's International Guide to Sources of Information about Children's Literature.* Its quarterly, *Bookbird,* provides criticism, news, reviews of children's books, and news of international publishing, with articles by authors, artists, librarians, and educators.

O10 **INTERNATIONAL READING ASSOCIATION (IRA)** 800 Barksdale Rd., P.O. Box 8139, Newark, DE 19711. (302) 731-1600

A nonprofit professional organization of classroom teachers, reading specialists and researchers, college teachers, administrators, parents, librarians, psychologists, and others interested in improving reading instruction, with councils and affiliates in 30 countries. IRA encourages research on and study of the reading process and issues journals for reading teachers at various levels. *The Reading Teacher* (8 issues/year) is for elementary teachers. *The Reading Research Quarterly* publishes in the area of reading research. An annual membership fee of $30 includes either one of these publications; a $45 annual fee includes both.

Other publications include the annual *Summary of Investigations Relating to Reading;* numerous publications on literacy, motivation, attitudes, and creativity; thorough analyses and suggestions on reading in the areas of science, mathematics, social studies, poetry, and career education; diagnostic tools in reading—from informal to criterion referenced; books and brochures for parents; cross-cultural information; and approximately 20 annotated bibliographies that cover everything from *Migrant Education* (1982, $2.50) to *Vision/Visual Perception* (1982, $4.50) and *Sex Differences and Reading* (1976, $2.00). A catalog is available on request. IRA has a library of 10,000 books and 200 periodical titles.

O11 **LIBRARY OF CONGRESS, CHILDREN'S LITERATURE CENTER** Washington, DC 20540. (202) 287-5535
The Library of Congress, our national depository for copyrights, contains nearly 200,000 volumes of juvenile literature acquired since 1870, including juvenile books in other languages and rare books in the Rare Book Division. The Children's Book Section has custody of a small reference collection on the history and criticism of children's books. This includes basic catalogs, indexes, bibliographies, subject lists, review media, professional journals, and books on folklore, storytelling, and the writing and illustration of children's books. In 1966, it began a dictionary (author/title/subject) catalog and an illustrator catalog of annotated cards for new children's books that will eventually cover all children's books in print. It first issued Virginia Haviland's *Children's Literature: A Guide to Reference Sources* in 1966 and updates it periodically with supplements. It also issues *Children's Books: A List of Books for Preschool through Junior High School Age,* an annual, annotated, selected list of new juvenile books. From time to time, it issues catalogs of exhibits, background on children's authors, bibliographies of folklore, and so forth. One particularly useful bibliography is *Children & Poetry* (1979). All publications are available from the U.S. Government Printing Office, Washington, DC 20402.

The library's Children's Book Section answers reference and research inquiries and provides bibliographic information on children's books, but does not serve children.

O12 **LIBRARY OF CONGRESS, DIVISION FOR THE BLIND AND PHYSICALLY HANDICAPPED (DBPH)** 1291 Taylor St., NW, Washington, DC 20542. (202) 287-5100
A major source of free-loan materials for blind and physically impaired persons. Services were extended for blind children in 1952 and, in 1956, to those whose physical impairments (reading disabilities as well

as muscular weaknesses) prevented them from reading standard print. For such persons, DBPH produces books and magazines in recorded disks and cassettes, braille, and larger type. These are listed in a series of catalogs available on request, mailed postage-free to users, and distributed through a network of regional and local libraries.

The reference section of DBPH will answer, at no charge, queries on blindness and physical impairments. Inquiries may be submitted directly or through cooperating libraries. This section also publishes and distributes free pamphlets, periodicals, and more substantial publications on disabling conditions and on its services. It *Sources of Large-Type Books* lists publishers, sellers, and lenders, and its *National Organizations Concerned with the Visually and Physically Handicapped* is an annotated guide to 65 organizations.

O13 **MODERN LANGUAGE ASSOCIATION (MLA)** 62 Fifth Ave., New York, NY 10011. (212) 741-5588

Founded in 1883 to promote study, criticism, and research on the literature and language of English and foreign languages, MLA is a leading source of information on modern languages and literatures. Its Division on Children's Literature produces a yearly guide entitled *Children's Literature* in cooperation with the Children's Literature Association. MLA's *International Bibliographies,* available in print and on-line through DIALOG and BRS, provides international coverage of literature, language, folklore, and linguistics. A catalog of publications is available on request.

O14 **NATIONAL COUNCIL OF TEACHERS OF ENGLISH (NCTE)** 1111 Kenyon Rd., Urbana, IL 61801. (217) 328-3870

A nonprofit membership organization—the world's largest subject matter association—with 100,000 members, mostly English and language teachers at all levels. Its Children's Literature Assembly publishes a quarterly *Bulletin* ($5/year or $13/three years) that covers topics like historical fiction or violence in children's literature. NCTE is also the headquarters office of the ERIC Clearinghouse on Reading and Communication Skills and a substantial publisher in its own right, with some 400 publications in print. Many of its publications deal in some way with introducing books to or sharing books with children. One of the best is *Raising Readers: A Guide to Sharing Literature with Young Children* (1980, 192 pp., $10.95), which combines creative activities and motivations with specific titles. Other publications are concerned with standards and with censorship, such as the well-known *Student's Right to Read.*

O15 **WILLIAM S. GRAY RESEARCH COLLECTION IN READING** Alvina Treut Burrows Institute, Inc., Box 49, Manhasset, NY 11030. (516) 869-8457
An indexed microfiche collection of some 10,000 titles on reading research from 1884 on, with citations from more than 450 research journals and 250 publishers, probably the most comprehensive collection extant. The Burrows Institute, which houses and distributes this collection, is a nonprofit association established in 1976 to encourage research in reading and the language arts. It houses other related collections on methodology, early textbooks, and the like, and plans to expand services to include publication and on-line computer searches.

BOOKS

O16 **THE AGING ADULT IN CHILDREN'S BOOKS & NON-PRINT MEDIA: AN ANNOTATED BIBLIOGRAPHY** By Catherine Townsend Horner. Metuchen, N.J., Scarecrow, 1982. 242 pp. $15.
This comprehensive, although unevaluative, survey of 50 years of children's fiction (and other media directed toward children) has aging human adults playing significant roles. The first part contains an annotated bibliography with lengthy plot summaries but no evaluations, followed by title and author/subject indexes. Includes around 300 fiction titles arranged by grade level—preschool and primary, intermediate, and middle and high school. The second section, arranged by media, covers filmstrips, movies, videotapes, records, cassettes, games, magazine articles, textbooks, and nonfiction books and has its own subject index. Since the author attempts to be comprehensive, some materials are out of print, and others are not recommended.

O17 **AMERICAN INDIAN STEREOTYPES IN THE WORLD OF CHILDREN: A READER AND BIBLIOGRAPHY** By Arlene B. Hirschfelder. Metuchen, N.J., Scarecrow, 1982. 296 pp. $17.50.
A two-part anthology/bibliography resulting from concern about the images of American Indians presented to children—"put together to try and shock adults into realizing that the world of contemporary American infants and young children is saturated with inappropriate images of Indians. . .in children's story and text books. . ." The first (anthology) section includes seven articles that describe and analyze

the imagery of American Indians in children's fiction, adolescent novels, school textbooks, paintings and sculptures, toys, and YWCA and YWCA programs. The second (bibliography) section is divided into two parts: stereotypes and corrective materials—123 items altogether, with excellent annotations. There are separate indexes for the reader and bibliography sections.

O18 **A TO ZOO: SUBJECT ACCESS TO CHILDREN'S BOOKS** By Carolyn W. Lima. New York, R. R. Bowker, 1982. 464 pp. $29.95.
A competent, if complex, subject guide to children's picture books, based on the collection of the San Diego Public Library and fairly comprehensive up to 1979. Contains a subject heading section of 445 terms, followed by a subject guide that provides author/title access to 4,400 picture books and a bibliographic guide that gives full information. Title and illustrator indexes.

O19 **BEHAVIOR PATTERNS IN CHILDREN'S BOOKS: A BIBLIOGRAPHY** Compiled by Clara J. Kircher. Washington, D.C., The Catholic University of America Press, 1966. 132 pp. (Out of print)
This interesting older effort organizes 507 books for children from preschool to ninth grade in separate chapters devoted to 24 categories of desirable behaviors (e.g., "the value of honesty," "a spirit of generosity," "spiritual values," and "acceptance of a stepparent"). These chapters are followed by selected readings and behavior, author, and title indexes. *Behavior Patterns in Children's Books* is a replacement for the earlier *Character Formation Through Books: An Application of Bibliotherapy to the Behavior Problems of Childhood,* which annotated 386 books for a wider age range.

O20 **BEST BOOKS FOR CHILDREN: PRESCHOOL THROUGH THE MIDDLE GRADES** 2nd Edition. Edited by John T. Gillespie and Cristine B. Gilbert. New York, R. R. Bowker, 1981. 629 pp. $29.95.
Arranged by curricular or interest areas, this is an annotated, classified listing of 13,000 available, up-to-date, accurate, relevant titles recommended in (usually three) book review sources.

O21 **THE BEST IN CHILDREN'S BOOKS: The University of Chicago Guide to Children's Books/The University of Chicago Guide to Children's Literature, 1973–1978** Edited by Zena

Sutherland. Chicago, Ill., University of Chicago Press, 1981.
547 pp. $25.

The Best in Children's Books is a bibliography of selected titles from the
Bulletin of the Center for Children's Books that demonstrates the center's exemplary approach to evaluation. Annotations indicate potential
uses, child appeal, and literary quality. Books are arranged by author
and indexed by title, developmental values, curricular applications,
reading levels, and subjects.

O22   **BEST OF THE BEST**   2nd Edition. Edited by Walter Scherf.
      Munich, Germany, Verlag Dokumentation, 1976. 344 pp.
      $21.50. Distributed by R. R. Bowker, 1180 Avenue of the
      Americas, New York, NY 10036.

A listing of books for children between the ages of 3–15, selected for excellence from 110 countries, in the language of the country of origin.

O23   **BIBLIOGRAPHY OF BOOKS FOR CHILDREN**   Edited by
      Sylvia Sunderlin. Washington, D.C., Association for Childhood
      Education International, 1937– . Triennial. 1983 Edition,
      members, $8.50; nonmembers, $10.00 (paperback).

This triennial guide to some 1,500 quality English-language books suitable for elementary and preschool children between the ages of 3 and
13 is compiled by a committee of children's librarians and teachers.
Typically, issues cover picture books, easy reading fiction, story collections, and nonfiction and reference books arranged by Dewey decimal
classification. Citations provide author, price, date, pages, publisher,
grade levels, and symbols for awards. Each new edition adds and
deletes books, and each includes author and title indexes and a directory of publishers. The current issue includes a guide to children's
magazines, newspapers, and reference books.

O24   **BIBLIOGRAPHY ON DISABLED CHILDREN: A Guide to
      Materials for Young People Aged 3 to 17 Years**   Compiled by
      the Canadian Association of Children's Librarians, Committee
      on Library Service to Disabled Children. Ottawa, Canada,
      Canadian Library Assn., 1981. 50 pp. $5.50 (paperback).

An annotated guide to books, films, and filmstrips arranged by major
disabilities (e.g., general, emotional disorders, hearing impairment,
learning disabilities, mental retardation, physical disabilities, and visual
impairments) and intended to help individuals who work with disabled
children locate materials that explain these handicapping conditions
and portray them candidly and realistically, yet with understanding.

Within the chapters on disabilities, materials are divided by format and then by reading age levels (3–7, 8–12, and 13–17 years). Citations are annotated and include publisher and date of publication.

O25   **A BICULTURAL HERITAGE: Themes for the Exploration of Mexican and Mexican-American Culture in Books for Children and Adolescents**   By Isabel Schon. Metuchen, N.J., Scarecrow, 1978. 164 pp. $11.

A resource guide to children's literature on the customs, life-styles, heroes, folklore, and history of Mexican and Mexican-American cultures for teachers and libraries dealing with school-age children.

O26   **THE BOOKFINDER: A Guide to Children's Literature about the Needs and Problems of Youth Aged 2–15**   Edited by Sharon S. Dreyer. Circle Pines, Minn., American Guidance Service, 1977. 649 pp. $37.50

O27   **THE BOOKFINDER II: A Guide to Children's Literature about the Needs and Problems of Youth Aged 2–15**   Edited by Sharon S. Dreyer. Circle Pines, Minn., American Guidance Service, 1981. 2 volumes in one book. $37.50.

Bookfinder and *Bookfinder II* form a unique set of reference works that identify, categorize, and describe juvenile books that can help children cope with ordinary or severe life challenges. The first title (O26) covers 1,031 children's books published up to 1975; the second (O27) covers 723 books published since 1975. Most of these books deal with contemporary children; approximately 90 percent are fiction (although the criteria merely specified that these books should deal constructively and helpfully with real-life situations faced by children). Both have a unique split-page format; the upper part (essentially a separate volume) consists of author, topical, and title indexes, with a recapitulation of the uses and history of bibliotherapy. The topical index is extremely helpful and comprises 450 psychological, behavioral, and developmental themes ranging alphabetically from abandonment to work attitude and including such areas as adoption, courage, death, divorce, and parental control. For each theme, there are one to several dozen books. The lower part of the split page arranges books alphabetically by author and then by title, with annotations that provide clear summaries of plots, characters, themes, and subthemes. The split-page format enables users to keep the index open to a particular area while browsing titles in the annotation section.

O28 **BOOKS IN SPANISH FOR CHILDREN AND YOUNG ADULTS: An Annotated Guide/Libros Infantile y Juveniles en Español: Una Guia Anotada** By Isabel Schon. Metuchen, N.J., Scarecrow, 1978. 165 pp. $11.
This is a guide to Spanish-language books, by Hispanic authors, for children from preschool through high school. Most books in this guide were published after 1973 and originated in Argentina, Chile, Colombia, Cost Rica, Cuba, Ecuador, Guatemala, Mexico, Peru, Puerto Rico, Spain, Uruguay, and Venezuela. Includes materials on life-style, folklore, heroes, history, fiction, poetry, theatre, and classical literature.

O29 **BOOKS TO HELP CHILDREN COPE WITH SEPARATION AND LOSS** 2nd Edition. By Joanne E. Bernstein. New York, R. R. Bowker, 1983. 439 pp. $29.95.
An annotated guide to 633 books that can help children between the ages of 3 and 16 deal with various areas of separation and loss. The first part contains a discussion of separation and divorce and their effects on children, as well as a discussion of bibliotherapy, with explicit suggestions for adult guides and a discussion of selection criteria. The second part, the bibliography, is topically arranged and covers separation from schools and neighborhoods; hospitalization; and coping with divorce, death or loss, adoptions, stepparents, and the like. Annotations indicate plots and themes, strengths and limitations, reading and interest levels, and price. The third section suggests readings on separation and loss and on bibliotherapy for adults. Suitable for counselors, therapists, and lay adults, with a directory of service organizations. Indexed by author, title, subject, interest level, and reading level (the last three are most detailed and helpful).

O30 **CHILDREN AND BOOKS** 6th Edition. By Zena Sutherland and May Hill Arbuthnot. Glenview, Ill., Scott, Foresman, 1981. 678 pp. $21.95.
This deservedly classic work is continually reorganized and updated to provide a well-rounded and current perspective on the interrelations of children and books. The first section is an overview of children's needs and interests; the second deals with books for young children. The third, the heart of the book, deals with types of children's literature. Areas covered are folk tales, fables, myths and epics, modern fantasy, poetry, modern fiction, historical fiction, biography, and information books (encompassing science, social science, religion, the arts, activi-

ties and experiments, and references). For each genre, the authors discuss major authors and representative titles for younger, middle, and older children. The chapters in the fourth section provide valuable guidance in bringing children and books together. The fifth part covers issues such as censorship, sexism, access to materials, internationalism, and the impact of television. Appendixes provide book-selection aids, substantial lists of background references for adults, addresses of children's book publishers, and lists of award-winning books. Indexed by subject, title, and author/illustrator. A most helpful and attractive work, illustrated with reprints from children's books.

O31 **CHILDREN'S BOOK REVIEW INDEX (CBRI)** (Annual clothbound volumes.) Edited by Gary C. Tarbert. Detroit, Mich., Gale Research, 1975- . Annual. *Children's Book Review Index: 1983,* 1984, 450 pp., $65.
Annual index to reviews of children's books derived from the *Book Review Index* (D43), arranged alphabetically by author in the main section and indexed by title. Entries include book author and title, journal source code, and citation. The *Children's Book Review Index: A Master Cumulation, 1969–1981* (1982, 4 vols., $240) provides citations to some 150,000 reviews of 35,500 books. CBRI information from 1975 on is searchable on-line through DIALOG's BOOK REVIEW INDEX data base.

O32 **CHILDREN'S BOOKS AND MAGAZINES: A MARKET STUDY** By Judith S. Duke. White Plains, N.Y., Knowledge Industry Publications, 1979. 236 pp. $24.95.
This relatively current analysis of the marketing aspects of children's literature covers such economic aspects as market trends, book clubs, magazines, audiovisual markets, and sales predictions, as well as the demographic, economic, and social trends that affect the market. It also includes profiles of 25 leading publishers.

O33 **CHILDREN'S BOOKS FOR TIMES OF STRESS: An Annotated Bibliography** By Ruth J. Gillis. Bloomington, Indiana University Press, 1978. 322 pp. (Out of print)
A computer offprint that combines good selections and adequate annotations of 261 books for young children from preschool age to third grade faced with new or stressful situations such as moving, eyeglasses, death, divorce, hospitalization, jealousy, and sibling rivalry. Unfortunately, the format (all uppercase letters) is difficult to read, and citations omit number of pages, price, and place of publication. Reviews are noted but not cited. Annotations are repeated in full (rather than being

indexed) under as many as nine redundant headings. Points of access include emotions, behavior, situations, family members, and self-concept. Despite these flaws, the books (which include many picture books) are well chosen for young children and are not duplicated in other guides.

O34   **CHILDREN'S BOOKS IN PRINT**   New York, R. R. Bowker, 1962– . Annual. $42.50.

Similar to *Books in Print* (D31), this comprehensive bibliography provides author, title, and illustrator access to all in-print books for children from preschool through grade 12 (using levels assigned by the publishers) —around 45,000 books each year. Entries provide author, title, price, publisher, appropriate grade level, binding, illustrator, series information, and catalog card number. Includes a directory of publishers. A companion volume, the *Subject Guide to Children's Books in Print,* indexes these books by Library of Congress subject headings and also gives complete ordering information. Searchable on-line through the BOOKS IN PRINT data base.

O35   **CHILDREN'S BOOKS OF INTERNATIONAL INTEREST: A Selection from Four Decades of American Publishing** 2nd Edition. Edited by Virginia Haviland. Chicago, Ill., American Library Assn., 1978. 77 pp. $5 (paperback).

An annotated selection of approximately 350 "intrinsically excellent, enriching, and enduring" children's books, representing the best of American book publishing and considered worthy of exporting and reproducing. Includes picture books and reading books for younger children and fiction, folklore, poetry, biography, history, the arts, science, and nature books for older children, carefully selected and evaluated for value and appeal by successive committees of librarians.

O36   **CHILDREN'S CATALOG**   14th Edition. Edited by Richard H. Isaacson and Gary L. Bogart. New York, H. W. Wilson, 1981. 1,277 pp., plus annual supplements, 1982–1985. $54.

First issued in 1909, this basic, comprehensive guide for selecting library collections for children up through the sixth grade is considered an essential reference source for children's librarians. The 14th edition, prepared by an advisory committee of children's library specialists and reviewed by a panel of children's librarians and teachers of children's literature, comprises almost 6,000 recommended in-print titles. These are arranged like a library: nonfiction by Dewey decimal classification, followed by fiction, story collections, and easy books. Entries include standard bibliographic data with approximate grade levels, price, and recommended Sears subject headings and critical and descriptive notes. The second section is an author, title, subject, and analytic index that provides excellent access—even to individual stories or fairy tales. The third part is a directory of publishers and distributors.

H. W. Wilson also prepares the *Junior High School Library Catalog* (4th Edition, 1980, with four annual supplements, 1981–1984, $62) and the *Senior High School Library Catalog.*

O37   **CHILDREN'S LITERATURE ABSTRACTS** Edited by Colin Ray. Powys, Wales, Children's Libraries Section of the International Federation of Library Associations, 1973- . Quarterly. $15/year. From: Bont Dolgadfan, Llanbrynmair, Powys SY19 7BB, Wales.

This international abstract journal to periodical articles on children's literature and reading and allied topics is arranged in 14 sections, with author and title indexes. Covers around 100 entries in each issue, with an annual index.

O38   **CHILDREN'S LITERATURE: AN ISSUES APPROACH** By Masha K. Rudman. Lexington, Mass., D. C. Heath, 1976. 433 pp. $14.95 (paperback).

An issues-oriented guide (from a theme-centered course in children's literature) with eight chapters on issues important to young children under age 12: siblings, divorce, death and old age, war, sex, blacks, native Americans, and females. Each chapter includes a discussion of the issue, with criteria for selecting books on this topic; a section on the ways these books relate to the topic; suggestions for teachers or other adults to personalize or extend a discussion; suggestions to children for critical reading; annotated lists of other sources for adults; and an annotated list of books for children. Altogether, approximately 1,350 books are annotated, with some indication of grade or interest level. The book contains an excellent final chapter on using children's books in reading programs. Appendix C is a well-annotated guide to some 40 other guides to children's literature. Includes publisher's addresses, lists of award-winning books, an author/illustrator index, a title index, and a fine subject index that also covers themes and skills.

O39   **CHILDREN'S WRITINGS: A BIBLIOGRAPHY OF WORKS IN ENGLISH** Compiled by Jane B. Wilson. Jefferson, N.C., McFarland, 1982. 169 pp. $24.95.

A 737-item, partially annotated, eclectic bibliography of English-language works by and about young authors (under age 21) from the sixteenth through the twentieth centuries, with author, title, and subject indexes. The work, which is based on four earlier bibliographies of works by young authors, provides a rich assortment of books, periodicals, and newspapers—not all easy to locate. Unfortunately, it tends to have extensive annotations for well-known authors and brief or no annotations for those who are lesser known. Contains two particularly interesting essays on seven-year-old writers and teenage-girl diarists.

O40   CHOOSING BOOKS FOR YOUNG PEOPLE: A Guide to Criticism and Bibliography, 1945–1975   By John R. T. Ettlinger and Diana Spirt. Chicago, Ill., American Library Assn., 1982. 238 pp. $25.
A comprehensive 600-item bibliography of works that select, criticize, or list books for young people. The annotations are clear, and the subject index is adequate, but the book is too long to browse and is probably more valuable for research in trends and attitudes toward reading or children's literature than practical help for those working directly with children. Arranged by author, with a subject index.

O41   CONCEPTIONS AND MISCONCEPTIONS: Sexuality in Children's Books   Oakland, Calif., Association of Children's Librarians of Northern California, 1978. 34 pp. $2 (paperback).
Competently selects, annotates, and evaluates 120 trade books on sex for preschool through eighth grade children. Topics cover birth, reproduction, puberty, sexual identity, sexuality, sexual tensions, and relationships; most titles are nonfiction. Criteria for inclusion are readability; accuracy; positive viewpoint; biologically informative language; and precise, labeled illustrations. The annotations are helpful in delineating content and approaches, assets, and limitations. Books are arranged by level, then by broad topic, with an author/title index.

O42   CREATIVE USE OF CHILDREN'S LITERATURE   By Mary Ann Paulin. Hamden, Conn., Library Professional Publications (Shoe String), 1982. 730 pp. $49.50.
An attractive composite of suggestions and bibliographies of books that covers some 5,000 books and 785 media entries. Most of the book is arranged by topic, theme, and curriculum area, under which books, games, and other related resources are described and discussed. Suggests ways to expand school literature experiences with puppetry, music, games, dramatics, and art. Title and subject indexes.

O43 **THE DISABLED CHILD IN THE LIBRARY: MOVING INTO THE MAINSTREAM** By Linda Lucas and Marilyn Karrenbrock. Littleton, Colo., Libraries Unlimited, 1983. 220 pp. $19.50.
An introduction to both public and school library services for disabled children that provides information on various disabilities and details about the kinds of materials, equipment, services, and facilities these children need.

O44 **EARLY READING DEVELOPMENT: A BIBLIOGRAPHY** (Classifications and Introductions to the Literature) By Elizabeth Hunter-Grunden and Hans Grunden. New York, Harper & Row, 1981. 384 pp. $77.95.
Comprehensively surveys the literature on reading development up to age seven.

O45 **EDUCATIONAL PRODUCTS FOR THE EXCEPTIONAL CHILD: A Catalog of Products Funded by the Bureau of Education for the Handicapped** Edited by Shellie Roth for Biospherics, Inc. Phoenix, Ariz., Oryx, 1981. 971 pp. $65.
This illustrated catalog brings together in one place products developed for handicapped and "special" children under the auspices of the Bureau of Education for the Handicapped. Materials are organized into categories, with an introductory overview for each. Categories include activities of daily living, affective education, assessment, evaluation, measurement, basic skills, early childhood education, education of the gifted and talented, finance, productivity, management, and personnel preparation. Each item is described and illustrated, with information on its goals, intended users, subject areas, patterns of use, claims and assurances, materials and personnel requirements, and contact addresses. Descriptions are clearly written and usually free of educational jargon.

O46 **THE ELEMENTARY SCHOOL LIBRARY COLLECTION: A Guide to Books and Other Media, Phases 1-2-3** 13th Edition. Edited by Lois Winkel, assisted by Margaret Edsall et al. Newark, N.J., Bro-Dart Foundation, 1982. 1,104 pp. $69.95.
Recommended as a basic collection of books and media for elementary school libraries serving children from preschool through sixth grade. It includes 8,586 book titles and 4,554 nonprint items such as filmstrips, kits, recordings, pictures, games, slides, transparencies, and charts. It is similar in organization to the *Children's Catalog* (036), but is more

related to school curriculum, although the high-quality materials are similarly selected, with phases 1, 2, and 3 suggested for priority in purchasing. The first section is a catalog using the Dewey decimal classification and integrating audiovisuals with books. This is subdivided into six sections: reference, nonfiction, fiction, easy, periodicals, and professional. Entries for each item include all information from a typical catalog card, with subject headings, descriptive annotations, interest and reading-level estimates, price, order information, and suggested phase. The second section includes well-done author, title, and subject indexes. One appendix lists books and media particularly suitable for preschool children; another lists books for independent beginning readers by reading levels; a third is a directory of publishers, producers, and distributors.

O47 **EL-HI TEXTBOOKS IN PRINT**   New York, R. R. Bowker, 1969– . Annual. $42.50.
One of the Bowker series, revised each spring, that lists and indexes some 35,000 elementary, junior, and senior high textbooks and supplementary materials. These are arranged into broad categories (largely corresponding to curriculum areas) and then subdivided. *El-Hi* provides access to guidance materials, maps, tests, reference books, and professional books. Each entry provides information on title, edition, author, editor, publisher, binding, price, series affiliation, grade level, illustrator, publication date, and related teaching materials. The book includes indexes to authors (editors, translators, and so on), titles, and publishers' series, as well as the usual list of publishers.

O48 **FIFTEEN CENTURIES OF CHILDREN'S LITERATURE: An Annotated Chronology of British and American Works in Historical Context**   By Jane Bingham and Grayce Scholt. Westport, Conn., Greenwood, 1980. 540 pp. $35.
A scholarly work, arranged by time period, that covers the historical background, development of books, and treatment of children from the sixth to the twentieth centuries, with an annotated chronology of each period.

O49 **GIRLS ARE PEOPLE TOO! A Bibliography of Nontraditional Female Roles in Children's Books**   By Joan E. Newman. Metuchen, N.J., Scarecrow, 1982. 195 pp. $12.50.
Annotates 540 mostly recent children's books selected on the basis of the "nontraditionality" (or initiative, individuality, dignity, intelligence, and/or creativity) of the main female characters. Books are ar-

ranged by age (primary and intermediate) and then by fiction and nonfiction, with subcategories for such groups as the handicapped, blacks, native Americans, and other minorities. Includes an interesting chronology of events dealing with women.

O50 **A GUIDE TO FAMILY READING IN TWO LAN-GUAGES: THE PRESCHOOL YEARS** By Theodore Andersson. Rosslyn, Va., National Clearinghouse for Bilingual Education, and Los Angeles, California State University, 1981. 81 pp. $1.25 (paper).
Provides research background on early learning and preschool reading of the bilingual child and suggests practical ways to encourage young children to read in two languages.

O51 **A GUIDE TO REFERENCE BOOKS FOR SCHOOL MEDIA CENTERS** 2nd Edition. By Christine Gerhart Wynar. Littleton, Colo., Libraries Unlimited, 1981. 377 pp. $28.50.
Some 2,000 reference books carefully chosen for school media centers (from kindergarten to 12th grade) are evaluated and annotated in this guide. Arranged by broad subjects, with an author/title/subject analytical index. Items are easy to find and thoroughly annotated. Sources of reviews are indicated.

A briefer guide, *Reference Books for Children* (Metuchen, N.J., Scarecrow, 1981, 273 pp., $14.50 [paperback]) is similar in scope but annotates only 900 books, most published within the last five years. It includes a good introduction to reference services for children, as well as criteria on reference works.

O52 **A GUIDE TO SUBJECTS & CONCEPTS IN PICTURE BOOK FORMAT** 2nd Edition. By Yonkers Public Library Children's Services. Dobbs Ferry, N.Y., Oceana Publications, 1979. 163 pp. $15.
Not a buying guide but a guide for locating subjects, ideas, or themes in children's picture books at the preschool and early primary levels, based on the picture-book collection of the Yonkers Public Library. Topics and titles are easily located, since books are listed under specific, logically arranged subjects like "Weather—Wind."

O53 **A GUIDE TO THE SELECTION AND USE OF READING INSTRUCTIONAL MATERIALS** By Freda Browns and Diane Arnell. Washington, D.C., Alexander Graham Bell Association for the Deaf, 1981. 102 pp. $11.95 (paperback).

A helpful guide to reading materials by two teachers of the deaf who
subscribe to the language-experience approach to teaching reading to
hearing-impaired students. Includes a wide range of materials, such as
basal reading series, supplementary readers, workbooks, library books,
skill builders, newspapers and periodicals, reference materials, and
filmstrips and tapes. Suggests criteria for evaluation and provides descriptive comments. The fifth chapter is an annotated compilation of
books and resources on the theory and practice of teaching reading. Appendixes include lists of American and Canadian publishers and professional organizations. Title index.

O54 **HANDBOOK FOR STORYTELLERS** By Caroline Feller
     Bauer. Chicago, Ill., American Library Assn., 1977. 381 pp. $20;
     paperback, $12.
Contains many practical ideas for storytellers that emphasize program
planning, oral interpretation, and the art of narrative. Includes bibliographies and suggested equipment.

O55 **HEALTH, ILLNESS, AND DISABILITY: A Guide to
     Books for Children and Young Adults** By Pat Azarnoff. New
     York, R. R. Bowker, 1983. 259 pp. $29.95.
An annotated guide to some 1,000 fiction and nonfiction titles dealing
with health issues, such as health habits, medical treatments, serious
illness, hospitalization, and disability—considered suitable for children
with illness or disabilities, as well as for other young family members,
classmates, and friends. These books—published from 1960 through
1983—were all in print as of mid-1983. Books are arranged by author
and indexed by title and health subject (e.g., brain injury, radiation
therapy, skeletal system). The detailed subject index is supported by a
helpful subject-groupings section that contains descriptions and comments, making subjects very easy to find. Entries include a full bibliographic description with prices, categorization as fiction or nonfiction,
appropriate grade level, and an annotation (usually one or two sen-
tences) that describes the book's content, particularly as it concerns the
physical or emotional well-being of children. The author is a child-
development teacher concerned with health and mental health. The
book can be used as a working tool by social workers, health-care
professionals, child psychologists, child-development specialists,
parents, teachers (especially teachers of mainstreamed, disabled, or
chronically ill students), and other adults who deal with sick children.
Includes a directory of publishers with addresses.

O56 **HELPING CHILDREN COPE** By Joan Fassler. New York, Free Press, 1978. 162 pp. $12.95.

A bibliographic essay that cites 203 items to help young children between the ages of four and eight deal with stress-producing situations like death, separation, illness, hospitalization, and changes in life-style. Items were chosen for use by and with children, based on professional literature and feedback from teachers.

O57 **HELPING CHILDREN COPE WITH DEATH: GUIDELINES AND RESOURCES** Edited by Hannelore Wass and Charles A. Corr. New York, Hemisphere, 1982. 194 pp. $24.95. (Series in Death Education, Aging, and Health Care)

One of a series intended for parents, clergy, medical professionals, and counselors involved with children. The guidelines cover children's views of death, the role of pastoral counselors, and death education. Resources include an extensive listing of books for children of various age groups, books for adults, and an annotated list of media items. The annotations are quite helpful; the book contains a topical index and information on distributors. Wass and Corr have also written *Childhood and Death* and the well-recognized *Death Education: An Annotated Resource Guide.*

O58 **INFORMATION SOURCES IN CHILDREN'S LITERATURE: A Practical Reference Guide for Children's Librarians, Elementary School Teachers and Students of Children's Literature** By Mary Meacham. Westport, Conn., Greenwood, 1978. 256 pp. $29.95. (Contributions in Librarianship and Information Science, No. 24)

Provides useful evaluative descriptions of some 200 information sources on literature for children up to the sixth grade, including review media, selection aids, science books, book awards, authors, and illustrators. The book is helpful to the novice in that it reprints sample pages of the works discussed. Appendixes include criteria for evaluation, an annotated guide to further reading, and suggested titles on organizing and operating a library/media center.

O59 **INTRODUCING MORE BOOKS: A Guide for the Middle Grades** By Diana Spirt. New York, R. R. Bowker, 1978. 240 pp. $13.95.

Books recommended for children between the ages of 9 and 14 are arranged under developmental goals such as "understanding physical and emotional problems" and "getting along in the family." Titles are annotated and analyzed by theme, with teaching ideas and suggestions of additional (similar) titles.

O60 **MULTICULTURAL RESOURCES FOR CHILDREN** By Margaret S. Nichols and Peggy O'Neill. Stanford, Calif., Multi-cultural Resources, 1977. 205 pp. $5 (paperback). From: P.O. Box 2945, Stanford, CA 94305.
A guide to a multicultural collection of nearly 10,000 items arranged by major culture areas: black, Spanish speaking, Asian American, Pacific Island, and native American. For each area, the collection includes folk tales and legends, materials for young children, art and music, popular readings, high-interest/low-vocabulary materials, social studies materials and series, bilingual materials, pictures, posters, maps, study prints, periodicals, games, simulations, and examples of creative productions by children. Includes a directory of foreign publishers and more than 200 items on evaluating multicultural materials.

O61 **NOW UPON A TIME: A CONTEMPORARY VIEW OF CHILDREN'S LITERATURE** By Myra Pollack Sadker and David Miller Sadker. New York, Harper & Row, 1977. 475 pp. $22.50.
This work on children's books (mostly contemporary) deals with topics such as family, sex, aging, death, women and minorities, ecology, humor, war and peace, and censorship. Discusses ways to use literature creatively in teaching.
    Appendix A is an annotated bibliography of fiction and nonfiction books that depict the handicapped. It is intended to sensitize children to the problems and aspirations of handicapped individuals.

O62 **OPENING DOORS FOR PRESCHOOL CHILDREN AND THEIR PARENTS** 2nd Edition. By the Association for Library Service to Children, Preschool and Parent Education Committee. Chicago, Ill., American Library Assn., 1981. 90 pp. $6 (paperback).
A three-section guide to quality literature for preschool children and their parents. The first section is an extensive (141-item) bibliography of books and media for parents of preschool children, emphasizing such preschool activities and play as puppetry and storytelling. The second section—selected with the aid of children's librarians nation-wide—annotates 320 titles for children, including picture books, folk-tales, alphabet books, songbooks, and nursery rhymes—both classics

and contemporaries. The third section covers nonprint materials: films, filmstrips, recordings, toys, and realia, with information on developmental skills and appropriate age levels. Entries provide complete bibliographic citations but no prices. The author/title index includes the toys and realia.

O63 **READING AND THE BLACK ENGLISH SPEAKING CHILD: AN ANNOTATED BIBLIOGRAPHY** Compiled by Jean R. Harber and Jane N. Beatty. Newark, Del., International Reading Assn., 1978. 47 pp. $2.50 (paperback). (IRA Annotated Bibliography Series)
This well-done bibliography of 145 items offers practical annotations slanted toward teachers. Covers factors that influence reading performance, testing, and suggested strategies, among other topics.

O64 **RELIGIOUS BOOKS FOR CHILDREN** Compiled by Pat Pearl. Bryn Mawr, Pa., Church and Synagogue Library Assn., 1983. 36 pp. $5 (paper). From: P.O. Box 1130, Bryn Mawr, PA 19010. (A CSLA Bibliography)
An extensive, critical, current annotated guide for selecting religious books for children from preschool through sixth grade, compiled under the auspices of the Church and Synagogue Library Association and limited to books with religious subjects or strong overt religious themes. Intended for parents, teachers, and librarians, it has high professional standards and fills a gap in bibliographies of children's literature. It is arranged in eight chapters that cover bible reference works and stories, the Old Testament, the New Testament/Jesus Christ, Christian theology, church and churches, Judaism, (other) religions, and religious holidays. Chapters are subdivided into smaller areas such as creation, Moses, church buildings, and Buddhism, with books for preschool through elementary children listed before those for middle school and up. Citations include prices, age levels, subject headings, and Dewey decimal numbers, as well as style, strengths, and limitations. Asterisks indicate books that are exceptional or exceptionally important. Subject and author indexes.

   The author reviews and is a frequent author of religious books for children. The CSLA, a nonprofit membership group concerned with congregational library service, has published other relevant works, including the similar, well-done *Helping Children Through Books: A Selected Booklist* (1979, 31 pp., $3.75) and supplementary booklists for young children and youth.

O65   **RESEARCH IN CHILDREN'S LITERATURE: AN ANNO-**
       TATED BIBLIOGRAPHY Compiled by Dianne L. Monson
       and Bette J. Peltola. Newark, Del., International Reading Assn.,
       1976. 96 pp. $3 (paperback). (IRA Annotated Bibliography
       Series)
A report on 322 studies completed between 1960 and 1974, divided
into three chapters: dissertations and ERIC documents (177 annotated
items); journal articles (from 1965 to 1974); and related studies,
including books, monographs, and unpublished library school master's
theses. The indexes, intended to identify relationships among the
studies, are by general subject, sample characteristics, evaluation
instruments, and types of study. Most of the studies are content analyses or experimental in nature, but there are also surveys, comparative
studies, and literary analyses. Approximately half the items are published research.

O66   **SELECTING   MATERIALS   FOR   INSTRUCTION** By
       Marda Woodbury. Littleton, Colo., Libraries Unlimited. Vol. 1:
       Issues and Policies, 1979, 382 pp., $23.50; $28.00 foreign, Vol 2:
       Media and Curriculum, 1980, 245 pp., $23.50; $28.00 foreign.
       Vol 3: *Subject Areas and Implementation,* 1980, 335 pp., $23.50;
       $28.00 foreign. All three titles for $56.40.
Three comprehensive, clearly written handbooks that use the perspectives of teachers, parents, librarians, curriculum developers, and education theorists to help educators choose materials appropriate for a wide
array of learning situations. Includes discussions, usually followed by
annotated lists of key organizations and publications. Uses sample
policies, checklists, criteria, diagrams, charts, and evaluation forms to
clarify and amplify the discussions. All volumes are well indexed.
    Issues and Policies covers the basics and policies of materials selection
in schools, with overviews of budgeting, instructional materials, and
the selection process. Separate chapters deal with fairness and bias;
parent and community involvement; basic learning materials; indivi-
dualization; and the problems and issues involved in choosing materials
for special education, gifted education, and young children.
    Media and Curriculum provides guidance in selecting materials in
particular media and explores some problems and solutions to selecting
and locating free materials, federally funded materials, and materials
from government agencies. Media covered include pictures, toys,
games, recyclables, and standard print and audiovisual formats.
    Subject Areas and Implementation covers criteria and sources for par-
ticular subject areas, including science materials, mathematics, the

environment, affective education, health education, narcotics education, nutrition, sex and family life, social studies and social sciences, legal education, multicultural education, foreign-language and bilingual education, language arts, consumer education, and career education. It also deals with handling controversies and teaching educators how to select instructional materials.

O67 THE SINGLE-PARENT FAMILY IN CHILDREN'S BOOKS: An Analysis and Annotated Bibliography, with an Appendix on Audiovisual Material By Catherine Townsend Horner. Metuchen, N.J., Scarecrow, 1978. 172 pp. $11.
Similar to Horner's *The Aging Adult in Children's Books & Nonprint Media* (O16), this is a selection of 215 children's books for readers in the intermediate grades. Since 41 percent of the items covered were published before 1965, the value of this publication is partly research rather than simply book selection or bibliotherapy. Titles are well-annotated and arranged by cause of the single-parent status (e.g., widowhood, divorced, orphan with single parent). The book has an intricate coding chart and provides access by relative (grandmother, mother, father, aunt, and so forth).

O68 THE STORYTELLER'S SOURCEBOOK: A Subject, Title, and Motif Index to Folklore Collections for Children By Margaret Read MacDonald. Detroit, Mich., Gale Research, with Neal-Schuman, 1982. 818 pp. $49.95.
A reference tool to folktales in children's books (all folktales contained in the *Children's Catalog, 1961–1981*, as well as a few 1981 titles, older titles still in use, and collections reviewed in *Booklist* from 1960 through 1980). Covers 556 folktale collections and 389 picture books, with materials arranged by motif and indexed by motif, title, subject, and ethnic/geographic factors. An additional 72 collections are listed only in the ethnic/geographic index. Intended primarily as a finding aid for storytellers and secondarily as a reference tool for folklore scholars. The motif section, arranged according to Stith Thompson's motif index, includes plot summaries; the subject index (from Apple to Zeus) is most thorough.

O69 THE USES OF ENCHANTMENT: THE MEANING AND IMPORTANCE OF FAIRY TALES By Bruno Bettelheim. New York, Knopf, 1976. 328 pp. $15.00. Available in paperback from Random House, $3.95.

An impassioned, scholarly presentation of the values of fairy tales as growth experiences for children. Bettelheim, an educator and therapist, sees fairy tales as mirrors reflecting inner human development. This book examines a few popular fairy tales in terms of the developmental stages and tasks they represent and shows their meanings and applications for children.

O70   **YOUNG PEOPLE WITH PROBLEMS: A Guide to Biblio-therapy**   By Jean A. Pardeck and John T. Pardeck. Westport, Conn., Greenwood, 1984. 176 pp. $29.95.

Young People with Problems is a bibliotherapeutic handbook for adults working with children and adolescents that provides background information on bibliotherapy with examples of practical limitations. It contains 10 chapters on 10 issues that are identified as major problem areas for young people: alcohol and drug abuse, divorce and separation of parents, emotional and behavioral problems, moving to a new home, physical handicaps, serious illness and death of family members, sexual awareness, sibling relationships, stepparents, and teenage pregnancy and abortion. The authors, both social workers, seem well aware of the potential uses of bibliotherapy for troubled youngsters, but less aware of the range of books for children and young adults that deal with these problem areas. Titles are not always well chosen or current; some are substandard or out-of-date.

17 / Parenting and Parent Education Materials

This chapter includes resource guides directed primarily to parents and compilations of parent-education materials intended for parents, teenagers, and professionals. It is divided into three sections: reference guides and encyclopedias, special handbooks, and bibliographies of parent-education materials. Other materials suitable for parents can be found in the audiovisual bibliographies listed in Chapter 7, the directories annotated in Chapter 10, and the periodicals and periodical indexes in Chapters 8 and 9. The appendix contains other works that might interest parents. Many of the bibliographies in Chapter 6 are relevant to parent education, especially *Family Support Counseling for Parents of Exceptional Children* (E77), *Foster Family Services Selected Reading List* (E82), and *Resources for Early Childhood* (E127). Of the periodical indexes in Chapter 8 and the data bases in Chapter 9, the most useful sources are probably those produced by ERIC, the Council on Exceptional Children, and the FAMILY RESOURCES DATABASE.

Many organizations—from local adult schools to national and international organizations—offer curricula on various aspects of parenting. Home economists deal with family budget and food management; health experts with child health; consumer educators with food, budget, health, and the like; and social workers, psychologists, and educators with family dynamics.

I have not included any organizations in this chapter; however, many of the organizations in Chapter 13 were founded by

or involve parents, and child advocacy organizations in general
are also advocates for parents in some sense or another. Organizations concerned with health or with handicapped children inevitably work with or for parents. Nutrition groups, such as the
Human Nutrition Information Service at the National Agricultural Library, produce parent-oriented publications. Some of the
original education laboratories, such as the Education Development Center, Appalachia Educational Center, and Southwest
Educational Development Laboratory, have worked extensively
in this area; their publications can generally be followed through
ERIC. Overall, the section on family values in Chapter 13 is
probably the most relevant to parents. The term "parent education" in the index will lead to additional entries.

Many helpful publications on parenting have been produced
by the Federal Government. Single copies of some are available
free from the issuing agencies and/or from the National Center
for Education in Maternal and Child Health, 3520 Prospect St.,
NW, Suite 1, Washington, DC 20057. Publications go out of
print very quickly, but they can be found in libraries and can be
copied.

ENCYCLOPEDIAS AND SOURCE BOOKS

P1   **CARING FOR YOUR CHILD: A Complete Medical Guide**
      By William E. Homan and the editors of *Consumer Guide*. New
      York, Harmony Books, 1979. 192 pp. $10.95.
Written by a pediatrician with years of experience in children's
diseases, this encyclopedia provides alphabetically arranged profiles of
163 common health problems, diseases, and conditions that afflict children from infancy through adolescence. For each item, it provides a description to help parents identify the probable cause, information on diagnosis (i.e., are laboratory tests needed, can it be diagnosed at home),
home treatments, doctors' treatments, precautions, and related topics.
Articles are clear and easy to understand without being simplistic. The
volume includes an index and cross-references, a helpful chart of symptoms, and line drawings.

P2 **CHILD CARE ISSUES FOR PARENTS AND SOCIETY: A Guide to Information Sources** By Andrew and Rhoda Garoogian. Detroit, Mich., Gale Research, 1977. 367 pp. $40. (Social Issues and Social Problems Information Guide Series, Vol. 2)

A guide to recent nontechnical information sources on child care, arranged alphabetically by broad subjects and then subdivided by types of materials. The materials were especially selected for their value to parents and include books, pamphlets, government publications, audiovisuals, and organizations. Many deal with specific areas in child development, health, and exceptional children. The book is somewhat similar in level to *Resources for Early Childhood* (E127), with briefer annotations. Appendixes include a brief survey of indexes, a list of children's magazines, a list of poison-control centers arranged by state, and a directory of book publishers. Includes author, title, subject, and organization indexes.

P3 **CHILD HEALTH ENCYCLOPEDIA: The Complete Guide for Parents** By the Boston Children's Medical Center and Richard I. Feinbloom. New York, Delacorte Press, 1975. 561 pp. $15.

Compiled for parents by medical specialists, this is a readable, well-researched compendium. Its general articles on child health care, safety and accident prevention, and emergency treatment are followed by a 400-page section of alphabetic entries on childhood diseases and conditions.

P4 **THE ENCYCLOPEDIA OF CHRISTIAN PARENTING** Compiled by Leslie R. Keylock. Old Tappan, N.J., Fleming H. Revell, 1982. $16.95.

A one-volume encyclopedia with a rather fundamentalist perspective on the practical and spiritual aspects of family life and parenting, intended to meet the everyday concerns of Christian parents. It combines in alphabetic order some 170 articles ranging from abortion to working mothers. Although a few of the articles are original, most are excerpts from larger works (many from the 1968 *New Encyclopedia of Child Care and Guidance*). The range and selection of topics is quite broad and commendably includes spiritual, religious, and ethical aspects of child rearing that are missing from many parental compilations. It contains much valuable information, well arranged, indexed, and updated by bibliographies that include works published as recently as 1979 and 1981. The compiler has selected wisely in many instances: Articles on creativity, nightmares, or the gifted child could benefit all parents and

professionals. Others on topics like death, delinquency, and depression
have an interesting and helpful religious perspective. In some cases,
however, the approach is definitely limited. The article on music, for
example, deals almost exclusively with the Satanic aspects of rock
music and suggestive lyrics, and the article on working mothers covers
only the financial and social pressures of work.

P5   **THE HELP BOOK** By J. L. Barkas, New York, Scribner's,
      1979. 667 pp. $3.50 (paper).
An annotated directory of more than 5,000 programs and services offering assistance for all kinds of medical, financial, psychological, legal,
and educational problems—arranged alphabetically into 50 broad areas
such as adoption, aging, and alcoholism. The section on children is further subdivided into advocacy and multipurpose groups, state agencies,
child rearing, child/youth participation groups, education, employment, food and nutrition, handicaps, health, legal rights, and mental
health and retardation. There is a separate section on parenting (including day care), as well as relevant sections on juvenile delinquency,
kidnapping, runaways, legal services, suicide prevention, safety, sex
education, and therapy. The book is intended for individuals and
professionals. It is not indexed, but each section has an introduction
and cross-references.

P6   **HELP FOR THE HANDICAPPED CHILD** By Florence
      Weiner. New York, McGraw-Hill, 1973. 221 pp. (Out of print)
A well-organized, thoroughly researched, ready-reference guide to the
labyrinth of services—voluntary, private, and governmental—for handicapped children, intended for physicians, agency personnel, and
parents. The first part, arranged by handicap (e.g., allergies/asthma,
arthritis, birth defects), provides definitions, descriptions, treatments,
prognoses, medical progress and medical goals, drug therapy, tests,
services, relevant associations, and educational implications. The work
includes an excellent section on government services and a good subject index.

P7   **HOW TO GET HELP FOR KIDS: A Reference Guide to Ser-
      vices for Handicapped Children** Edited by Barbara Zang.
      Syracuse, N.Y., Gaylord, with Neal-Schuman, 1980. 245 pp.
      $29.95 (paperback).
A helpful national guide to services, agencies, and sources of information for the parents of handicapped children, compiled by the network
organizer of the Children's Defense Fund (K15) and useful for profes-

sionals and parents. Its 1,800 entries are arranged geographically under topic. Six major sections deal with community services, state services for handicapped children, government services, health plans and insurance information, recreation for the handicapped, and emergency services. These are subdivided as appropriate (for example, recreation includes scouts, summer camps, and recreational programs). Essays by professionals provide overviews of the status of services in the area of education, diagnosis, finances, legal services, respite care, and parent support groups. Entries for agencies include addresses and telephone numbers. *How To Get Help for Kids* contains an annotated bibliography of 108 items (government documents, pamphlets, books, and brochures). The appendix includes sources of recreation information and assistance and a general index to the agencies in the different sections.

P8 **THE MOTHERS' AND FATHERS' MEDICAL ENCYCLOPEDIA** Revised Edition. Virginia E. Pomeranz and Dodi Schultz. Boston, Mass., Little, Brown, 1977. 562 pp. $17.50.

A well-cross-referenced, current, readable work with 2,200 alphabetically arranged entries. As a home reference, it combines the functions of a parents' dictionary of medical terms; a first aid manual; and an information source on child development, child health, and preventive care for children from infancy through college. The entry on poisoning, for example, assembles potentially toxic household substances in one list, with emergency procedures opposite each page of the list. Helpful appendixes include a list of poison-control centers, information on selecting a doctor, root clues to medical terms, a vital statistics appendix for entering children's medical histories, and space for emergency telephone numbers.

P9 **PARENT'S ENCYCLOPEDIA OF INFANCY, CHILDHOOD, & ADOLESCENCE** By Milton I. Levine and Jean H. Seligman. New York, Crowell, 1974. 554 pp. $12.50; paperback, $3.95.

The major emphases of this competent encyclopedia are child health and development. Alphabetically arranged, it contains lengthy and helpful articles on topics like adoption and accidents and shorter articles on topics like wryneck. It is particularly successful in explaining health issues and medical problems in a thorough, jargon-free manner. The appendixes include directories of poison-control centers, genetic-counseling centers, community mental health centers, and parent agencies, as well as an annotated classified bibliography. No index, but good cross-references.

P10   **A PARENT'S GUIDE TO DAY CARE**   Washington, D.C.,
Administration for Children, Youth, and Families, 1980. 74 pp.
Paper. (Out of print)
The fourth section of this pamphlet includes lists of child care agencies
and organizations, ethnic and other special organizations, federal agencies supporting day care, state day care agencies, federal agencies for
children with handicapping conditions, national organizations for children with handicapping conditions, single parents and parent groups,
and agencies for child abuses or neglect and crisis situations.

P11   **PARENT'S YELLOW PAGES**   Edited by Frank Caplan for
the Princeton Center for Infancy and Early Childhood. Garden
City, N.Y., Anchor/Doubleday, 1978. 512 pp. $9.95 (paperback).
Each article in this A to Z manual provides overviews of some 130
topics in child rearing, with recommended ways to handle problems
and undertakings, supplemented with suggested readings, information
on specific equipment, and lists of service organizations that might be
helpful. General areas include health, education, nutrition, safety, law,
and consumer awareness. No index, but cross-references and a detailed
table of contents.

P12   **WHERE TO GET HELP FOR YOUR FAMILY**   Revised
Edition. By Anne M. Tansey. St. Meinrad, Ind., Abbey, 1977.
204 pp. $3.95 (paperback).
A guide to 157 social service agencies directed toward a lay audience.
Agencies are arranged by name under category; entries include a brief
history of each agency, together with current activities, publications,
and special projects.

P13   **THE WHOLE BIRTH CATALOG: A Sourcebook for
Choices in Childbirth**   Edited by Janet Isaacs Ashford et al.
Trumansburg, N.Y., Crossing Press, 1983. 313 pp. $14.95
(paperback).
A comprehensive guide to pregnancy, childbirth, and early parenting
that reviews more than 1,000 completely cited books, pamphlets,
magazines, and newspapers and describes products, resources, and
organizations. It is arranged by broad topics such as being pregnant,
giving birth, family living, and working for change. Although it focuses
on pregnancy and birth, *The Whole Birth Catalog* includes many titles
and sections on infancy and early childhood. Relevant topics under
"being pregnant" include fetal development, nutrition in pregnancy,

and drugs and hazards. Relevant sections under "giving birth" are infants at risk, stillbirth, and infant death. There are individual titles on areas like early jaundice, circumcision, breast and bottle feeding, immunization, neonatal diseases, and birth marks. The "Living in Family" section has many pertinent topics, with excellent evaluative reviews of books and pamphlets on baby-care basics, baby products, child health and safety, and being parents. Additionally, the book provides information on networks, organizations, and audiovisuals, a helpful foreword, a medical glossary, and a good index.

P14   **THE WHOLE CHILD: A SOURCEBOOK** By Stevanne Auerbach. New York, Putnam, 1981. 320 pp. $17.95 (paperback).

Reviews, analyzes, and condenses information on phases of childhood from conception to school age in a lively, easy-to-use format. The first section, "Getting Ready," covers the decision to have a child; the second section is an alphabetically arranged guide to the whole experience of childhood. Appendixes include a directory of organizations.

SPECIAL HANDBOOKS

This section includes a few handbooks devoted to particular populations useful for parents.

P15   **THE BLACK PARENTS HANDBOOK: A Guide to Healthy Pregnancy, Birth, and Child Care** By Clara J. McLaughlin. New York, Harcourt, Brace, Jovanovich, 1976. 220 pp. $5.95 (paperback).

A clear presentation of basic information on pregnancy, birth, and child rearing, with good coverage of environmental, genetic, and medical problems of black parents. Emphasis is on child rearing, with a discussion of developmental tasks for children to age six and practical advice in such areas as first aid, accident prevention, immunization, sex education, and discipline.

P16   **THE FATHER'S ALMANAC** By S. Adams Sullivan. Garden City, N.Y., Doubleday, 1980. 165 pp. $9.95 (paperback).

Arranged somewhat chronologically in 12 chapters that go from baby's arrival to record keeping and cover aspects of job, family, everyday life, special events, teaching, learning with kids, playing with kids, working with kids, and further readings in between. Easy to read and straightforward, the *Father's Almanac* should be indispensable to an inexperienced father and valuable to any father. Indexed.

P17 **PRIME-TIME PARENTING** By Kay Kuzma. New York, Rawson, Wade, 1980. 305 pp. $13.95.

A handbook for busy parents written by a working mother with a doctorate in child development. Deals forthrightly with the problems that working parents, single parents, and overextended homemakers face in providing quality care for their children, despite the constraints of time. Covers preventive discipline, short cuts, ways to solve family and job conflicts, family identity, and the specific problems of working parents. Includes a detailed section on child care that covers every possible alternative. Throughout, it has many creative, positive approaches to problem solving. Indexed.

BIBLIOGRAPHIES AND PROGRAMS

P18 **AN ANNOTATED BIBLIOGRAPHY FOR CHILD AND FAMILY DEVELOPMENT PROGRAMS** By Dingle Associates for the Administration for Children, Youth, and Families. Washington, D.C., 1977. 126 pp. Paper. (Out of print)

Part of a project to develop a framework for providing comprehensive services to families and encouraging parents' involvement with their children's development. This bibliography lists four kinds of materials: audiovisuals, organizations and projects, newsletters and journals, and written materials (arranged by subject). The last category occupies most of the book. Subjects include child abuse, child care services, child development, early childhood education, exceptional children, health and nutrition, home-based materials, interracial and nonsexist materials, parent education, program information, and teenage parents/ education for parenthood. Contains author/organization and subject indexes.

P19 **AN ANNOTATED BIBLIOGRAPHY ON CHILDREN** Prepared by the U.S. Department of Health, Education, and Welfare Library for the White House Conference on Children, December 13–18, 1970. Washington, D.C., 1970. 75 pp. Paper. (Out of print). (AOA Publication No. 216-A)

Includes around 500 references published from 1965 to 1970, arranged alphabetically by author.

P20   **A CATALOG OF PARENT INVOLVEMENT PROJ-ECTS—A COLLECTION OF QUALITY PARENT PROJ-ECTS FOR ASSISTING CHILDREN IN THE ACHIEVE-MENT OF BASIC SKILLS** By Norberto Cruz, Nancy J. Holland, and Monica Garlington. Arlington, Va., InterAmerica Research Associates, 1981. 60 pp. Paper. (Apparently out of print but available from ERIC, ED 226 842.)

A catalog of projects (rather than materials) that pursue the involvement of parents in assisting their children develop basic skills, based on a nationwide search of projects using parents as tutors. Describes selected projects and indicates the features that would be most relevant for replication. The projects selected support parents as primary educators of their children, provide activities and/or training for parents, and promote learning activities for children that foster positive self-images for children and effective parenting skills. The first section covers comprehensive parenting projects; the second, educational materials and information service projects; and the third, home-based service delivery projects. The fourth section contains ordering information on specialized materials available from projects. Includes indexes by alphabet, implementation method, state, and subject area.

P21   **EXPLORING CHILDHOOD: Program Overview and Catalog of Parenting/Child Development Materials, 1980–82** By the Education Development Center (EDC). Newton, Mass., EDC School and Society Programs, 1980. 32 pp. Free (paper). From: 55 Chapel St., Newton, MA 02160.

A catalog of materials of an outstanding parenting/child development program originally developed and tested for high school students but now widely used in Head Start programs, social service agencies, parenting centers, church groups, adult education centers, and other community groups. Materials—available at cost—come in all media as integrated programs covering healthy development, infancy, family and society, child-abuse prevention and treatment, preschool, children, single-parent families, children with special needs, and materials for program leaders and teachers. EDC's network of regional coordinators and field associates is available to provide training and technical assistance to groups using these materials.

P22   **FAMILY LIFE AND CHILD DEVELOPMENT: A Selective, Annotated Bibliography, Cumulative Through 1975**   By the Book Review Committee of the Child Study Association of America/Wel-Met, Inc. New York, Child Study Press, 1976. 45 pp. $2.50 (paper).
An annotated list of 320 publications deemed especially valuable by the Child Study Association's Book Review Committee. Materials, largely selected for parents, range from simple to more technical and are arranged in broad topics with intelligent subdivisions. Areas covered include marriage and the family, human development, sex education, disabilities, schools and learning, mental health education, and social problems and the family. Subdivisions in the family section include special situations (such as stepchildren, twins, and moving) and everyday situations. Annotations are succinct but helpful.

P23   **FAMILY LIFE AND CHILD DEVELOPMENT: A Selective, Annotated Bibliography, Cumulative Through June 1979**   By the Jewish Board of Family and Children's Services. New York, 1979. 43 pp. $3 (paper). From: 120 W. 57th St., New York, NY 10019.
An excellent annotated list of 362 publications by the Book Review Committee of the Jewish Board of Family and Children's Services, slanted toward parents and libraries and continuing the work of the Child Study Association (see P22). It is intended as a selective guide of current knowledge, but it does include some technical (asterisked) publications that seem appropriate. The topics are similar to those listed in P22—nicely updated, with books arranged alphabetically by title under subject. Citations include price and date (not pages) and very-well-written annotations. The book includes a detailed table of contents and an author and title index.

P24   **GETTING INVOLVED: Basic Educational Skills Project**   An Annotated Bibliography in the Areas of Curriculum, Parent Involvement, Teacher Attitudes and Behaviors, and Continuity. Washington, D.C., Head Start Bureau, 1981. 144 pp. $5 (paper). (DHHS Publication No. [OHDS] 81-31168)
Intended as a resource guide for administrators, staff, and parents working with children in school and at home to implement a Basic Educational Skills Program. Most of the entries focus on younger children and include books, articles, pamphlets, posters, films, records, and multimedia packages. Other items in the *Getting Involved* series include such booklets as *Your Child and Reading*.

P25 **HEALTHY MOTHERS COALITION DIRECTORY OF EDUCATIONAL MATERIALS** Compiled by the Healthy Mothers, Healthy Babies Coalition. Washington, D.C., U.S. Department of Health and Human Services, Public Health Service, 1983. 202 pp. Single copy free (paper). From: 721 Hubert H. Humphrey Bldg., 200 Independence Ave., SW, Washington, DC 20029.

A work-in-progress compendium of print and audiovisual materials on prenatal and infant care intended for use by the public, with how-to materials for health professionals who work with pregnant women and with babies up to one year old. The nontechnical materials are aimed at pregnant women, teenagers, expectant fathers, women planning pregnancy, parents of newborns, and siblings. Materials are arranged in alphabetic order under the names of participating coalition organizations (e.g., American College of Nurse-Midwives, American Red Cross). The catalog includes a brief description of each organization and general instructions for ordering materials. Item listings include format, physical description, publication date, price, and availability in languages other than English. In many cases, annotations are provided. The book includes a brief directory of other sources of information and subject and title indexes to listed items.

P26 **NUTRITION EDUCATION RESOURCE GUIDE: An Annotated Bibliography of Educational Materials for the WIC and CSF Programs** 2nd Edition. By the Food and Nutrition Information Center. Beltsville, Md., Human Nutrition Information Service, 1983. 202 pp. Single copy free (paperback). From: National Health Information Clearinghouse, P.O. Box 1133, Washington, DC 20013-1133. (Bibliographies and Literature of Agriculture Series, No. 24)

A resource guide to 346 evaluated print and audiovisual nutrition education materials developed to assist state and local staffs of the Special Supplemental Program for Women, Infants and Children (WIC) and the Commodity Supplemental Foods Program (CSF) in educating participants in these programs (i.e., pregnant and lactating women and infants and young children). Each entry includes title, author, abstract, appraisal, source, format, availability, cost, reading level (when applicable), and subjects assigned.

P27 **OFF TO A GOOD START: A Resource for Parents, Professionals and Volunteers** Washington, D.C., Administration for Children, Youth, and Families, 1981. 279 pp. (Out of print)

A desk reference of information relevant to the family, with some 250 citations to journal articles, audiovisuals, and books. Each entry provides author, title, source, funding, abstract, and address when available. Includes an index.

P28　**PARENTING: AN ANNOTATED BIBLIOGRAPHY** By the Committee on Infant and Preschool Child, American Academy of Pediatrics. Washington, D.C., Administration for Children, Youth, and Families, 1978. 34 pp. Paper (Out of print)
A resource for parents, services, and health professionals, issued jointly by the Children's Bureau, the American Academy of Pediatrics, and the National Center on Child Abuse and Neglect to help prevent child maltreatment by building more effective child-rearing skills and more satisfying parenthood. Books were chosen on the basis of content excellence, readability, availability, and popularity, with an effort to include representative and diverse views. *Parenting* provides guidelines, as well as books that offer support and alternatives. It includes books on parenting for parents, teenagers, and pediatricians, as well as books on particular aspects such as discipline, divorce, single parents, and working mothers. It also contains bibliographies, other sources of information, and an author index.

P29　**PARENTING IN 1977: A LISTING OF PARENTING MATERIALS** By the Parenting Materials Information Center. Austin, Tex., Southwest Educational Development Laboratory, 1977. 182 pp. Paper. (Out of print)
A comprehensive listing of some 3,700 items (print and nonprint) dealing with various aspects of parenting, parent involvement, and/or parent education, divided into 15 subject areas including child abuse, discipline, education, exceptional children, health and safety, language and intellectual development, and social and emotional development. Many of the items deal with the application of research findings, not the research itself. Entries provide title, author, copyright date, pagination or length, price, and publisher. The Parenting Materials Information Center (no longer active) used to offer literature searches in this area. This guide can be found in many libraries.

P30　**PUBLICATIONS FOR PARENTS AND EDUCATORS OF HANDICAPPED CHILDREN** Compiled by Phyllis M. Quinn. Washington, D.C., American Physical Therapy Assn. (APTA), not dated. 5 pp. Free with self-addressed, stamped envelope (paper). From: 1156 15th St., NW, Washington, DC 20005.

One of a series of helpful bibliographies issued by APTA that provides sources, authors, titles, prices, and, sometimes, annotations of 51 well-selected books and pamphlets. Other similar, free, topical bibliographies available from APTA are *Communication* (10 items, 2 pp.), *Directories* (13 items, 2 pp.), *Equipment for the Handicapped* (12 items, 2 pp.), *Physical Activities and Recreation* (36 items, 3 pp.), *Psychology* (9 items, 1 p.), *Rights of the Handicapped* (7 items, 1 p.), and *Teaching and Testing Material* (39 items, 4 pp.).

P31 **A READER'S GUIDE FOR PARENTS OF CHILDREN WITH MENTAL, PHYSICAL, OR EMOTIONAL DISABILITIES** By Coralie B. Moore and Kathryn Gorham Morton. Rockville, Md., Bureau of Community Health Services, 1976. 144 pp. $3.50 (single copy free while supply lasts; paper). From: National Center for Maternal and Child Health, 3520 Prospect St., NW, Suite 1, Washington, DC 20057.

A two-part guide compiled with the help of 100 parents and professionals. The first part covers basic reading; how to teach, train, and play at home; firsthand accounts; background readings on issues like advocacy, behavior modification, and prevention; and sources of further information. The second part is arranged by disability and includes learning disabilities, mental retardation, autism, physical handicaps, epilepsy, hearing impairments, cleft palate, and multiple handicaps. Many of these sections are subdivided into similar sections.

P32 **STEPPARENTING: With Annotated Bibliography** By Renata Espinoza and Yvonne Newman. Rockville, Md., National Institute of Mental Health, Center for Studies of Child and Family Mental Health, 1979. 63 pp. Single copy free (paper). (DHEW Publication No. [ADM] 78-579)

Combines a review of recent research and a bibliography of popular literature on stepparenting. Nicely covers special problems of stepfamilies such as discipline, money, relatives, guilt, myths, names, adoption, incest, and visitation.

P33 **UNDERSTANDING ADOPTION: Resources and Activities for Teaching Adults About Adoption** By the Social Science Education Consortium (SSEC) and Children's Home Society of Minnesota. $14.95 (kit). From: SSEC, 855 Broadway, Boulder, CO 80302.

Includes a four-part sourcebook with guidelines, reproducible handouts, transparency masters, and a pamphlet entitled *Understanding Adoption as a Family-Building Option.* Activities can be used with social workers and mental health specialists, as well as adoptive parents, biological parents, and adopted adults.

APPENDIX

Multidisciplinary Handbooks and Compendiums

This appendix consists of multidisciplinary handbooks and compendiums that I encountered in libraries, bookstores, and reviews while researching this book and that I thought were too good to omit. There are undoubtedly many more of equal value, but these are intended as a starting point for a multidisciplinary library. Additional titles can be located through reference tools in the main chapters, especially *Books in Print, Associations' Publications in Print,* and targeted bibliographies. The organizations in Chapters 12 and 13 are knowledgeable about handbooks or guides in particular areas of interest. Some produce their own handbooks. Although the subjects overlap, there are so many that I have divided them into broad subject areas for convenience in browsing.

CHILD ADVOCACY, CHILDREN'S RIGHTS, AND CHILD PROTECTION

Some legal handbooks also deal with these areas, as do handbooks on children with special needs.

Q1   **CHILDREN'S RIGHTS AND THE MENTAL HEALTH PROFESSIONS** Edited by Gerald P. Koocher. New York, Wiley-Interscience, 1976. 259 pp. $35. (Wiley Series on Personality Processes)

Twenty-four contributors provide multiple perspectives on children's rights. Broad areas include the responsibility of service delivery to children (such as children's rights in custody disputes, as research participants, children's rights to know the results of clinical evaluations, and their rights in family dysfunctions). Other areas explored are children's rights vis-à-vis teaching, research, and treatment institutions; due process in commitment, punishment, juvenile court, and abuse; and policy issues like testing, drug administration by professionals, and abuse of drugs by children.

Q2   **THE CHILDREN'S RIGHTS MOVEMENT: Overcoming the Oppression of Young People** By Beatrice Gross and Ronald Gross. Garden City, N.Y., Doubleday, 1977. 390 pp. (Out of print)
A collection of articles that include many of the concerns and approaches in examining institutions that deal with children.

Q3   **A COMMUNITY APPROACH: THE CHILD PROTECTION COORDINATING COMMITTEE** Washington, D.C., National Clearinghouse on Child Abuse and Neglect Information, 1979. 63 pp. plus appendixes. $6.30. (The User Manual Series)
Covers the development, organization, and external and internal functions of such a committee. Includes standards and a bibliography.

Q4   **EQUAL RIGHTS FOR CHILDREN** By Howard Cohen. Totowa, N.J., Littlefield, Adams, 1980. 172 pp. $4.95 (paperback).
A legal handbook that covers social policy, child protection, historical background, borrowed capacities, child agents, children's rights to political participation, rights in court, and rights of privacy. The author believes that all adult rights should be extended to children. Includes notes and a bibliography.

Q5   **HELPING IN CHILD PROTECTIVE SERVICES: A CASEWORK HANDBOOK** Englewood, Colo., American Humane Assn., 1981. 252 pp. $10.
A step-by-step approach to child protective services, with a glossary, selected references, and an index.

Q6   **HOW TO ORGANIZE AN EFFECTIVE PARENT/ADVOCACY GROUP AND MOVE BUREAUCRACIES** Chicago,

Ill., Coordinating Council for Handicapped Children, 1982. 130 pp. $6. From: 220 S. State St., Room 412, Chicago, IL 60604. An effective parent advocacy handbook by an organization that has succeeded in moving bureaucracies. Covers every conceivable angle from gaining tax exempt status to uncovering buried talents, training parents, lobbying, recruiting volunteers, and raising money.

CHILD DEVELOPMENT AND PSYCHOLOGY

Included in this section are a few handbooks and compendiums on all aspects of child development—physical, psychological, cognitive, emotional, social, moral, and religious—from professional and parental perspectives; it overlaps somewhat with the entries on child health, special needs, and child psychiatry. The books here are accessible and understandable, but not necessarily classics. The tests and assessment methods in Chapter 14 deal with child-development norms. Some of the parent education materials in Chapter 17 also relate to this topic.

Q7   A BASIS FOR SENSORIMOTOR DEVELOPMENT— NORMAL AND ABNORMAL: The Influence of Primitive, Postural Reflexes on the Development and Distribution of Tone By Mary R. Fiorentino. Springfield, Ill., C. C Thomas, 1981. 174 pp. $19.75.
A practical, well-illustrated work by an occupational therapist, directed toward therapists and educators. Uses photographs and text to outline the nature of sensorimotor development from birth to age 15 months. Compares normal and abnormal development with examples of such things as extension against gravity, righting reactions, and the development and distribution of muscle tone. The final chapters deal with recording methods, case reviews, and early diagnostic signs.

Q8   DEVELOPMENT JOURNEY: A Guide to the Development of Logical and Moral Reasoning and Social Perspective By Mary M. Wilcox. Nashville, Tenn., Abingdon, 1979. 286 pp. $10.95.
Wilcox's belief is that the process of developing a values system builds on logical reasoning (after Piaget), moral reasoning (after Kohlberg),

and faith development. Several chapters incorporate practical applications.

Q9   ENCOURAGING LANGUAGE DEVELOPMENT By Phyllis Hastings and Bessie Hayes. London, Croom Helm, 1981. 68 pp. $11 (paperback). (Special Education Series)
A very practical, easily understood guide to language problems and their remediation, with background on language and language development from basic to higher level skills. Includes sections on teaching language through physical activities and the importance of oral muscular competence as a prerequisite for speech.

Q10   THE ESSENTIAL PIAGET Edited by Howard E. Gruber and J. Jacques Voneche. New York, Basic Books, 1977. 881 pp. $35.00; paperback, $18.50.
An interpretive reference to the work of Piaget that clarifies his ideas and underlying themes.

Q11   FIRST CHILD, SECOND CHILD. . .Your Birth Order Profile By Bradford Wilson and George Edington. New York, McGraw-Hill, 1981. 286 pp. $11.95. Available in paperback from Zebra (475 Park Ave. S., New York, NY 10016), $1.95.
Covers the effect of birth order on personality. The first part deals with the major birth orders—oldest, middle, youngest—divided by sex.

Q12   GROWING UP FORGOTTEN: A Review of Research and Programs Concerning Early Adolescence By Joan Lipsitz. Lexington, Mass., D. C. Heath, 1977. 267 pp. $5.95 (paperback).
A comprehensive guide that covers research, schools, service institutions, handicapped young adolescents, families, voluntary organizations, and the juvenile justice system. Has an impressive bibliography and index.

Q13   THE HAND AS A GUIDE TO LEARNING By Ester Cotton. London, Spastics Society, 1981. 47 pp. £1.
A two-part illustrated booklet that reviews the movements and functions of the normal hand and discusses abnormal movement patterns (as in cerebral palsy). It also suggests equipment and exercises for teaching grasp, hold, and release and covers group activities in schools and nurseries for working out functional goals for children.

Q14 **HANDBOOK OF CROSS-CULTURAL HUMAN DEVEL-OPMENT** Edited by Ruth H. Munroe, Robert L. Munroe, and Beatrice B. Whiting. New York, Garland STPM, 1981. 888 pp. $80.

A prospectus and review of the field of cross-cultural studies, with 6 chapters on perspectives, 4 on early experiences and growth, 5 on cognitive and moral development, and 11 on socialization and outcomes. Author and subject indexes.

Q15 **HANDBOOK OF DEVELOPMENTAL PSYCHOLOGY** Edited by Benjamin B. Wolman et al. Englewood Cliffs, N.J., Prentice-Hall, 1982. 960 pp. $79.95.

A 50-chapter encyclopedic guide to developmental psychology that covers research methods in 10 chapters, followed by 8 chapters on infancy, 7 on childhood, and 7 on adolescence, with the remainder on adulthood, including an interesting chapter on the child's effect on the parent. Developmental theories are very well covered. Author and subject indexes.

Q16 **HANDBOOK OF INFANT DEVELOPMENT** Edited by Joy D. Osofsky. New York, Wiley-Interscience, 1979. 954 pp. $58.95. (Wiley Series on Personality Processes)

Presents a comprehensive review of ideas, data, and issues in the research on infancy from birth to two years, including prenatal and perinatal influences such as medication. Also covers parent/infant and infant/infant relationships. Intended for teachers, researchers, and scholars, this handbook contains a good subject index.

Q17 **HUMAN GROWTH, Volume 3: Neurobiology and Nutrition** Edited by Frank Falkner and J. M. Tanner. New York, Plenum, 1979. 624 pp. $39.50.

A scholarly compendium of the embryology and development of the special senses, including maturation and organization of the brain; sexual differentiation of the brain; and the effects of nutrition, the environment, and genetics. Chapters include illustrations and summaries. Although technical, it is well organized for reference use. Volumes 1 and 2, at the same price, deal with prenatal and postnatal growth, respectively.

Q18 **INFANT PERCEPTION: FROM SENSATION TO COGNITION, Volume I: Basic Visual Processes** Edited by Leslie B.

Cohen and Philip Salapatek. New York, Academic, 1975. 496 pp. $54.
Devoted entirely to visual perception, this book deals with a two-dimensional pattern perception continuum from basic sensing and neurophysiological functions to information processing and memory. Volume 2, by the same editors, is entitled *Perception of Space, Speech, and Sound* (1975, $43). The set sells for $83.

Q19 LANGUAGE ACQUISITION By Jill G. DeVilliers and Peter A. DeVilliers. Cambridge, Mass., Harvard University Press, 1978. 312 pp. $14.
A clear summary of language acquisition. Covers critical periods and kinds of experiences needed to learn language, as well as genetic aspects and language acquisition in developmentally disabled children.

Q20 THE MAGIC YEARS By Selma Fraiberg. New York, Scribner's, 1968. 305 pp. $5.95 (paperback).
An engaging, easy-to-read, authoritative, and comprehensive guide that traces child development from birth to age six, with examples and anecdotes. Each period is treated in separate sections, with one or two chapters on personality development followed by one or more chapters on the problems of child rearing at that particular stage.

Q21 THE ORIGINS OF INTELLIGENCE IN CHILDREN By Jean Piaget. New York, International Universities Press, 1966 (originally published in 1952). $6.95 (paperback).
A classic presentation of six stages in sensorimotor development, in which Piaget used his own children as illustrations.

Q22 THE PHILOSOPHY OF MORAL DEVELOPMENT: Moral Stages and the Idea of Justice By Lawrence Kohlberg. New York, Harper & Row, 1981. 256 pp. $22.95.
Like Piaget, Kohlberg uses six developmental stages; in this instance, the stages concern moral development, from avoiding punishment to distinguishing between legality and justice. The book is based in part on classroom experiences.

Q23 PIAGET'S THEORY: A PRIMER By John L. Phillips. San Francisco, Calif., Freeman, 1981. 192 pp. $14.25; paperback, $6.50. (Psychology Series)

An easy-to-read summary and introduction to Piaget's theory of cognitive development; suitable for parents and professionals.

Q24 **THE PSYCHOLOGY OF SEX DIFFERENCES** By Eleanor E. Maccoby and Carol N. Jacklin. Stanford, Calif., Stanford University Press, 1974. 2 Vols. in one. $37.50 (hardcover); paperback: Volume 1, $8.95; Volume 2, $6.95.
A comprehensive survey of research that covers the origins of physical and psychological sex differences; Volume 2 includes an extensive annotated bibliography.

Q25 **RELIGIOUS THINKING FROM CHILDHOOD TO ADOLESCENCE** By Ronald Goldman. New York, Seabury, 1968. 276 pp. $6.95 (paperback).
Describes the abilities of students aged 6–17 years to understand religious concepts and examines the development of religious thinking within the context of maturation of cognitive processes.

Q26 **RESEARCH ON RELIGIOUS DEVELOPMENT: A Project of the Religious Education Association** New York, Hawthorn, 1971. 904 pp. (Out of print)
A comprehensive review of research literature that summarizes 25 years of research by Catholic, Jewish, and Protestant scholars. Covers cognitive change in areas like prayer and children's perceptions of God.

CHILD LIFE AND CHILDHOOD

This section includes a few aspects of children's lives that, although important, are not usually considered in texts or handbooks of child development. Most of these titles refer to children in the United States.

Q27 **THE CHILD AND TELEVISION DRAMA** By the Group for the Advancement of Psychiatry, Committee on Social Issues. New York, Mental Health Materials Center, 1982. 123 pp. $14.
An overview of contemporary children's television programming in America (live actors, violence, cartoons, and educational) that exam-

ines the audience and television's effects on children's judgment and behavior. Provides a bibliography for further reading.

Q28 CHILDHOOD: A SOCIAL CONSTRUCT By Ann H. Reuf and Dorothy Kurz. Lexington, Mass., Xerox Individual Publishing, 1977. 245 pp. (Out of print)

A selection of readings that focuses on the social framework surrounding childhood; discusses differing current and past concepts of childhood, vis-à-vis western and nonwestern values and American institutions.

Q29 CHILDREN OF WAR By Roger Rosenblatt. Garden City, N.Y., Doubleday, 1983. 201 pp. $13.95.

A moving journalistic account of the feelings and lives of children in trouble sites around the world, whose daily reality includes death, assassination, war, and chaos.

Q30 CHILDREN'S EXPERIENCE OF PLACE: A Developmental Study By Roger Hart. New York, Irvington, 1979. 518 pp. $27.50. Distributed by Wiley-Halsted, 605 Third Ave., New York, NY 10158.

A difficult-to-describe book that uses text, photographs, and graphics to convey the ways children act, sense, think, feel, and get to know their place in the world. The author's eclectic participant observance of the "phenomenal landscape" includes his own observations, interviews with parents and children, model building, photo-recognition tasks, and active play and exploration. Areas covered are children's spatial activities, place knowledge, place values and feelings, and place use.

Q31 CHILDREN'S FRIENDSHIPS By Zick Rubin. Cambridge, Mass., Harvard University Press, 1980. 165 pp. $8.95; paperback, $3.95. (Developing Child Series)

A low-key anecdotal discussion of children's friendships that considers the developmental nature of these friendships and suggests ways that adults can structure the environment or provide support when friendship problems occur.

Q32 CHILDREN'S GAMES IN STREET AND PLAYGROUND: Chasing, Catching, Seeking, Hunting, Racing, Dueling, Exerting, Daring, Guessing, Acting, Pretending By Iona Opie and Peter Opie. London, Oxford University Press, 1969. 371 pp. $40.

Concerned solely with the games that children from age 6 to 12 play of their own accord when out-of-doors and out of sight, based on interviews with more than 10,000 children. Around 2,500 games and game-rhymes are described and indexed. Histories of some games are included.

Q33   **THE CHILDREN WE TEACH**   By Nina Ridenour. New York, Mental Health Materials Center, 1967. 32 pp. $1.

A very concise, sensitive guide to help teachers understand the emotional needs and individuality of the various types of students they encounter in their classes and the interpersonal problems that may evolve. Also useful for parents, counselors, group leaders, recreation supervisors, and other adults who work with children.

Q34   **A CHILD'S JOURNEY: FORCES THAT SHAPE THE LIVES OF OUR YOUNG**   By Julius Segal and Herbert Yahraes. New York, McGraw-Hill, 1979. 354 pp. $5.95 (paperback).

An easy-to-read, always interesting review of the research on the various forces that shape a child's life and personality, including genetics, parental role, child-rearing practices, school, peer pressures, social problems, and government policies.

Q35   **THE SERIOUS BUSINESS OF GROWING UP: A Study of Children's Lives Outside School**   By Elliot A. Medrich and Judith A. Raizen. Berkeley, University of California Press, 1982. 420 pp. $24.50.

A study of the use of out-of-school time by 764 children ages 11 and 12 in Oakland, California. The study was divided into five areas: things children do on their own or with friends, family activities, household chores and outside jobs, organized activities, and television-viewing time. Some issues explored were the interactions of race, gender, and economic status; the impact of a working mother; and the effect of television on the ways children spend their time.

HEALTH AND NUTRITION

Books for both parents and professionals are covered in this section, which overlaps somewhat the sections on special needs and child development. Additionally, some significant books on child health from a parental perspective are included in Chapter 17. The *Encyclopedia of Pediatric Psychology* (A29) is treated in Chapter 2. Health screening and assessment tools are annotated in Chapter 14.

Q36   **AMERICA'S POISONED PLAYGROUNDS: CHILDREN AND TOXIC CHEMICALS**   By Louis Freedberg. Oakland, Calif., Youth News, 1983. 54 pp. $5.95, plus $1.00 postage (paper). From: Conference on Alternative State and Local Policies, 2000 Florida Ave., NW, Washington, DC 20009.

A factual briefing and exposé, based on a six-month survey of urban parks and playgrounds by Youth News and the Conference on Alternative State and Local Policies. This book documents a variety of toxic hazards found in children's playgrounds and reveals that play areas are often built without adequate testing for toxic chemicals, constructed in potentially dangerous areas such as landfills or garbage dumps, erected near freeways or in mixed residential/industrial areas, and built with equipment that uses wood preservatives at higher-than-safe levels. It also indicates that there is inadequate collaboration between health departments and public works. Includes recommendations for action at city, county, and state levels, as well as annotated lists of publications and organizations.

Q37   **BETTER HEALTH FOR OUR CHILDREN: A NATIONAL STRATEGY**   The Report of the Select Panel for the Promotion of Child Health to States, Congress and the Secretary of Health and Human Services. By the U.S. Public Health Service. Rockville, Md., 1981. 4 Vols. Volume 1: *Major Findings and Recommendations*, $9.50; Volume 2: *Analysis and Recommendations for Selected Federal Programs,* $4.75; Volume 3: *A Statistical Profile,* $8.50; Volume 4: *Background Papers,* $10.00. From: U.S. Government Printing Office, Washington, DC 20402.

Recommendations from a select panel deal with every aspect of children's health, including serious unmet needs in child and maternal health and the weaknesses and strengths of federal policies. The panel's analyses are based on Volume 3, *A Statistical Profile;* Volume 4, *Background Papers,* was commissioned by the panel for use in its deliberations.

Q38 **CHILD ABUSE AND NEGLECT: A Medical Reference** Edited by Norman S. Ellerstein. New York, Wiley, 1981. 355 pp. $40.

An exhaustive presentation of the medical issues involved in cases of abused and neglected children. Most of the chapters deal with specific organ system manifestations; some cover medical testimony, photography, and legal issues; and a few offer scholarly discussions of broad issues in the areas of etiology and prevention. Although it is intended as a medical reference, most of the text can be comprehended by lay persons.

Q39 **CHILDREN WITH CHRONIC ARTHRITIS: A Primer for Patients and Parents** By Gordon F. Williams. Littleton, Mass., PSG Publishing, 1981. 365 pp. $25.

Includes illustrations and clear, thorough discussions of such disease processes as inflammation, autoimmunity, and joint contracture, as well as family reactions to disease.

Q40 **THE CHRONICALLY ILL CHILD: A Guide for Parents and Professionals** By Audrey T. McCollum. New Haven, Conn., Yale University Press, 1981. 273 pp. $7.95 (paperback).

Practical advice and support for parents and other caretakers of chronically ill children. Covers the physical and emotional difficulties experienced by the children and the pressures experienced by their families and suggests ways to meet these challenges while showing concern for the quality of the ill child's life. Includes a subject index and an appendix of service organizations.

Q41 **CHRONIC OBSTRUCTIVE PULMONARY DISEASE— CARE OF THE CHILD AND ADULT** By Dorothy L. Sexton. St. Louis, Mo., C. V. Mosby, 1981. 292 pp. Price not available.

Uses clear diagrams to explain the respiratory system and covers lung diseases prevalent in infants, children, and adults, including neonatal respiratory distress, cystic fibrosis, asthma, and chronic bronchitis. For each, it includes preventive measures, pathological development, treatment, and course. The final chapters deal with associated psychological problems.

Q42 **COMMON ORTHOPEDIC PROBLEMS IN CHILDREN** By Jacob F. Katz. New York, Raven, 1981. 202 pp. $27.

Encompasses common conditions found in the musculoskeletal systems of children from infancy to adolescence, including congenital anomalies, genetic diseases, developmental deformities, tumors, injuries, and infections, with material largely arranged by anatomy. Discussion covers diagnosis, clinical course, natural history, and an overview of therapy. The book has a good index, a comprehensive glossary, and a generous supply of photographs. It is intended for medical students but is relatively understandable by a lay person.

Q43   **CURRENT PEDIATRIC DIAGNOSIS & TREATMENT**
       7th Edition. By C. Henry Kempe, Henry K. Silver, and
       Donough O'Brien. Los Altos, Calif., Lange Medical, 1982.
       1,066 pp. $26.
An up-to-date reference and source for all child-health professionals, translated into Spanish, French, Italian, Polish, Turkish, and Serbo-Croatian and revised every two years. This publication covers just about everything—from removing embedded fishhooks to counseling parents of a dying child. Well organized in 38 chapters, with a substantial, accessible index, it covers all body systems, accidents and emergencies, poisoning, developmental problems of childhood, and diagnosis and therapies and includes tables of normal and therapeutic values.

Q44   **DIARRHEA AND MALNUTRITION: Interactions, Mechanisms, and Interventions** Edited by Lincoln C. Chen and
       Nevin S. Scrimshaw. New York, Plenum, 1983. 318 pp. $39.50.
Summarizes the current state of knowledge of diarrhea—a major source of morbidity and mortality among children in poor countries, yet a disease that can be easily and effectively treated with simple, low-cost techniques. Relates feeding practices to diarrhea and covers the protective effects of breast-feeding and other effective interventions.

Q45   **DISEASES OF CHILDREN** 4th Edition. By Hugh Jolly.
       Oxford, Blackwell Scientific, 1981. 760 pp. $32.50. Distributed
       by C. V. Mosby, 11830 Westline Industrial Dr., St. Louis, MO
       63141.
A frequently updated, comprehensive book by a London physician, notable for its global perspective. Emphasizes the taking of family history and social history and suggests ways for improving communication with patients. Provides excellent coverage of pediatric problems likely to be encountered in children from tropical areas or developing nations.

Q46 FOOD ADDITIVES AND HYPERACTIVE CHILDREN
By C. Keith Connors. New York, Plenum, 1980. 184 pp. $21.50.
This book, designed to be read by both nonprofessionals and professionals, presents carefully documented studies on the relationships between food additives and child behavioral and learning problems. It includes an exploration of the effects of artificial coloring on learning, visual-motor function, and impulse control and a discussion of the possible role of food allergies in hyperactive behavior. Includes an exhaustive bibliography and descriptions of special diets.

Q47 GROWING UP HEALTHY: A Parent's Guide to Good Nutrition By Myron Winick. New York, Morrow, 1982. 240 pp. $10.50.
Timely, scientifically sound, and well indexed. Covers nutrition developmentally from breast-feeding and infancy through adolescence, with separate treatment of topics like illness and anorexia. Includes an excellent review of changes involved in adaptation to pregnancy and what is known about maternal nutrition and fetal development.

Q48 HANDBOOK OF PEDIATRICS 14th Edition. Edited by Henry K. Siler, C. Henry Kempe, and Henry B. Bruyn. Los Altos, Calif., Lange Medical, 1983. 883 pp. $13.
A helpful synopsis of the symptoms and treatments of childhood diseases, with valuable sections on topics like growth and development and nutrition.

Q49 HUMAN MILK IN THE MODERN WORLD: Psychosocial, Nutritional, and Economic Significance By Derrick B. Jelliffe and E. F. Patrice Jelliffe. Oxford, Oxford University Press, 1978. 500 pp. $34.50.
A comprehensive account that reviews and evaluates modern scientific information on aspects of human milk and breast-feeding that have not been brought together before. It views the problems stemming from the transfer from breast- to bottle-feeding from many nutritional, psychological, social, medical, and economic angles. Some consequences—the weakening of the mother-infant bond for instance—are obvious; others—such as economic costs and the reduction in resistance to disease—are less apparent. This book draws together a great deal of information on the consequences and implications of changing patterns in infant feeding for children, mothers, families, communities, and the world. It includes a 75-page bibliography, a list of audiovisuals, addresses of concerned groups, and an industry code of ethics.

Q50   INFANT MORTALITY AND THE HEALTH OF SOCIE-
TIES   By Kathleen Newland. Washington, D.C., Worldwatch
Institute, 1981. 56 pp. $2 (paper). (Worldwatch Paper No. 47)
Covers the levels and trends of infant mortality and, behind that, the
physical and social environments that effect these trends. Suggests
ways to attack the "roots of infant mortality."

Q51   MALNUTRITION AND BRAIN DEVELOPMENT   By
Myron Winick. New York, Oxford University Press, 1976. 169
pp. $18.95.
Presents an overview of malnutrition during the growing period; documents the clinical and epidemiological evidence of its effects on cellular
growth, myelination, and metabolic processes; and describes the effect
of malnutrition on these processes at critical periods of development.

Q52   NUTRITION CASEBOOK ON DEVELOPMENTAL DIS-
ABILITIES   By Ninfa Saturnino Springer. Syracuse, N.Y., Syracuse University Press, 1982. 208 pp. $20.00; paperback,
$12.95.
Intended primarily for parents and professionals (such as teachers,
nurses, and physical therapists) who deal with developmentally disabled persons. It helps provide an understanding of nutrition-related
problems and the nutrition interventions that can be used to manage
them. The *Nutrition Casebook* covers nutrition screening and assessment, the nutritional status of selected children, growth retardation,
various feeding and eating problems, drug-nutrient interactions, and
resources for nutrition. It contains a glossary, a substantial list of
readings, seven appendixes for different kinds of diet therapy, and an
index.

Q53   PARENTS' GUIDE TO ALLERGY IN CHILDREN   By
Claude A. Frazier. New York, Grosset & Dunlap, 1978. 338 pp.
$3.95 (paperback).
A very helpful guide to all types of allergies, with a detailed index and
many charts and tables.

Q54   PEDIATRIC NUTRITION HANDBOOK   2nd Edition.
Evanston, Ill., American Academy of Pediatrics, 1984. Not yet
paged or priced.
Extraordinarily inclusive and clear, with chapters on basic nutrients, assessment of nutritional status, normal eating patterns, and clinical
applications, among other topics. Well referenced, organized, and
indexed.

Q55 **PEDIATRIC NUTRITION IN DEVELOPMENTAL DIS-ORDERS** Edited by Shusma Palmer and Shirley Ekvall. Springfield, Ill., C. C Thomas, 1978. 613 pp. $54.50.
A monumental work in four sections and 74 chapters. The first section, consisting of 20 chapters, concerns nutrition and developmental disorders arranged by disease. The second section, with 52 chapters, deals with nutrition and hereditary metabolic disorders. The 26 chapters of the third section deal with nutrient deficiency disorders, and the final section covers preventive nutrition and supplementation. Four appendixes include food requirements and assessment forms. There are helpful chapters on nutrition education, vitamin and mineral deficiencies, and toxicities. The whole is a most impressive work.

Q56 **PEDIATRIC PATHOLOGY** Edited by Colin L. Berry. Berlin, Springer-Verlag, 1981. 697 pp. $82.50.
A surprisingly readable guide to materials on pediatric pathology that tend to get buried in books on general pathology. Covers the organ systems (health, liver, lungs, and so on), as well as such areas as congenital malformations and metabolic disorders. Well indexed for reference use, with current journal references.

Q57 **SCHOOL HEALTH IN AMERICA: A Survey of State School Health Programs** 3rd Edition. By Anne S. Castile and Stephen J. Jerrick. Kent, Ohio, American School Health Assn., 1982. 220 pp. $5.
The bulk of this book is a state-by-state summary of the status of school health programs in the various states, compiled to provide a starting point for improving and expanding health programs. The first part introduces the studies, summarizes their findings, and indicates some standards for personnel and programs.

Q58 **A SIGH OF RELIEF: THE FIRST-AID HANDBOOK FOR CHILDHOOD EMERGENCIES** Produced by Martin I. Green. New York, Bantam, 1977. 199 pp. $8.95 (paperback).
The first part of this handbook deals with preventive measures for home, toy, school, water, and playground safety; first aid supplies; drug identification; immunization schedules; and the like. The second, after a general discussion on assessing the emergency, arranges emergencies alphabetically from "Back and neck injuries" through "Bites," "Bleeding," and "Transportation." Suggestions are clear and appropriate. A quick reference and an emergency index guide are included.

Q59 SOURCEBOOK ON FOOD AND NUTRITION 3rd Edition. By Joannis S. Scarpa et al. Chicago, Ill., Marquis Academic Media, 1982. 549 pp. $49.50.
The "spanning the ages" section of this compilation includes eight chapters on nutrition and food in infancy, adolescence, and childhood.

Q60 TAKING CARE OF YOUR CHILD: A PARENTS' GUIDE TO MEDICAL CARE By Robert H. Pantell, James F. Fires, and Donald M. Vickery. Reading, Mass., Addison-Wesley, 1977. 409 pp. $10.95; paperback, $9.95.
Another intelligently arranged, well-done guide to common medical problems of children. This one makes information accessible through a diagram of a child keyed to problems and pages; a classified list of complaints (e.g., injuries, abdomen, skin); and a topical subject index.

SPECIAL NEEDS

Titles here overlap those under health, development, and psychiatry. Ideally, these are books with multiple perspectives, including parental, educational, social, psychological, and medical concerns of children with special needs. Two handbooks on dying children are included. Many organizations in Chapter 13 are concerned with children with special needs. Assessments and measurements are treated in Chapter 14.

Q61 ADJUSTMENT TO SEVERE PHYSICAL DISABILITY: A METAMORPHOSIS By C. DeLoach and B. Green. New York, McGraw-Hill, 1981. 310 pp. $17.95. (Special Education Series)
A text for parents, families, and professionals that deals with the ways societal conceptions affect or impede physical, psychological, or social adjustment and the laws, services, environmental changes, and technological advances for disabled persons.

Q62 AUTISM: A PRACTICAL GUIDE FOR PARENTS AND PROFESSIONALS Edited by Maria J. Paluszny. Syracuse, N.Y., Syracuse University Press, 1980. 200 pp. $9.95 (paperback).
An interdisciplinary, jargon-free discussion by five specialists of autism and its treatment.

Q63 **BILINGUAL SPECIAL EDUCATION RESOURCE GUIDE**
Edited by Carol H. Thomas and James L. Thomas. Phoenix,
Ariz., Oryx, 1982. 204 pp. $25.
A comprehensive tool to help educators meet the needs of students
who are both handicapped and bilingual and/or bicultural. Covers the
needs of children, ways to communicate with their parents, means of
assessing these children, appropriate curricula, and career opportunities. The second section covers agencies, programs, materials, and data
bases that offer information and assistance.

Q64 **CARE OF THE CHILD FACING DEATH** Edited by Lindy
Burton. Boston, Mass., Routledge & Kegan, 1974. 225 pp.
$18.50.
Written to help parents and professionals deal with their fears and anxieties and the fears and anxieties of children. Covers problem areas
such as pain, heavy treatment regimes, and the siblings of a dying child.

Q65 **CARE OF THE NEUROLOGICALLY HANDICAPPED
CHILD; A BOOK FOR PARENTS AND PROFESSIONALS**
By Arthur L. Prensky and Helen S. Palkes. New York, Oxford
University Press, 1982. 330 pp. $24.95.
Provides good delineations of the roles and training of professionals
who work with or appraise neurologically handicapped children. Chapters deal with common neurological disorders such as epilepsy, cerebral
palsy, birth defects, mental retardation, learning and language disabilities, neuromuscular disease, and hyperactivity. Includes a chapter
on legal services that covers legal aspects of education, employment,
community service, and parental support.

Q66 **CHILDREN WITH HANDICAPS: A MEDICAL PRIM-
ER** By Mark L. Batshaw and Yvonne M. Perret. Baltimore,
Md., Brookes, 1981. 464 pp. $18.95.
A comprehensive developmental guide, starting with genetics, birth
defects, and prenatal diagnosis, followed by chapters on birth, the first
few weeks of life, and prematurity. Additional chapters deal with nutrition; normal and abnormal development of the central nervous and
locomotor systems; and specific disabilities such as cerebral palsy,
epilepsy, hyperactivity, and sensory defects.

Q67 **CHILD WELFARE SERVICES FOR CHILDREN WITH
DEVELOPMENTAL DISABILITIES** By Ronald C. Hughes
and Judith S. Rycus. New York, Child Welfare League of
America, 1983. 64 pp. $6.95.

The basic concept of this short, well-written book is that the disabled child is not the problem but rather has a problem needing help. Uses case studies backed by excellent research to cover the nature, myths, and needs of developmentally disabled children; the family/child-welfare services available to them; and the interactions between these. Intended to help child-welfare agencies examine their own roles and responsibilities.

Q68   **COORDINATING SERVICES FOR HANDICAPPED CHILDREN: A HANDBOOK FOR INTERAGENCY COLLABORATION**   Edited by Jerry Elder and Phyllis Magrab. Baltimore, Md., Brookes, 1980. 264 pp. $13.95 (paperback).

An interdisciplinary text for educators, administrators, and health professionals to facilitate the delivery of adequate and coordinated services to disabled children from birth to age 21.

Q69   **DISABLED CHILD**   By A. Wisbeach. Brighton, England, Oxford Regional Health Authority, 1980. 53 pp. Inquire about price. From: 2 Foredown Dr., Postslade, Brighton BN4 2BB, England.

Helpful information on equipment and adaptations—such as wheelchairs, special devices, clothing, and equipment—to help children toward independence.

Q70   **THE DYING CHILD: The Management of the Child or Adolescent Who Is Dying**   2nd Edition. By William M. Easson. Springfield, Ill., C. C Thomas, 1981. 126 pp. $11.95 (paperback).

A psychiatrist's psychosocial approach to the care and management of terminally ill children and adolescents.

Q71   **EARLY MOVEMENT EXPERIENCES AND DEVELOPMENT: Habilitation and Remediation**   By Joseph P. Winnick. Philadelphia, Pa., Saunders, 1979. 525 pp. (Out of print)

Covers the roles of movement and play experiences in human development; suggests ways for professionals to remediate or habilitate physical, motor, perceptual, academic, and cognitive development through play, physical recreation, and physical education activities; describes handicapping conditions related to movement; suggests teaching and assessment methods for these areas; and reviews research. Logically arranged by types of handicaps, with bibliography and author and subject indexes. Intended primarily for teachers.

Q72   EDUCATING THE CHRONICALLY ILL CHILD   By Susan B. Kleinberg. Baltimore, Md., Aspen, 1982. 349 pp. $29.95.

A useful reference book that covers history, current legal status, medical issues, and educational strategies for groupings of specific chronic illnesses, with helpful guidelines for teaching children in the classroom, hospital, and home. Includes illustrations and a medical glossary. Should be useful for parents, nurses, teachers, social workers, and other health workers and educators.

Q73   AN EDUCATION HANDBOOK FOR PARENTS OF HANDICAPPED CHILDREN   Edited by Stanley I. Mopsik and Judith A. Agard. Cambridge, Mass., Ware Press, 1980. 287 pp. $15.95 (paperback).

A good guide to finding the right school, fair treatment, and needed funds.

Q74   EDUCATOR'S RESOURCE GUIDE TO SPECIAL EDUCATION: Terms-Laws-Tests-Organizations   By William E. Davis. Boston, Mass., Allyn and Bacon, 1980. 270 pp. $26.95.

Includes terms, acronyms, tests, legislation, and a directory of agencies and organizations. Valuable for parents, professionals, and students, with terms for medicine, psychology, law, statistics, and other disciplines, as well as practical examples.

Q75   EMOTIONALLY TROUBLED CHILD: A Guide for Parents and Teachers in the Early Recognition of Mental and Nervous Disorders in Children   By Robert L. Mason, Jr. et al. Springfield, Ill., C. C Thomas, 1976. 196 pp. $18.50.

Covers children from preschool through adolescence with a checklist of symptoms and directory information.

Q76   GROWING UP HANDICAPPED: A Guide to Helping the Exceptional Child   By Evelyn W. Ayrault. New York, Continuum, 1977. 216 pp. $9.95.

Appendixes include 13 directories.

Q77   A HANDBOOK OF MEDICAL, EDUCATIONAL, AND PSYCHOLOGICAL INFORMATION FOR TEACHERS OF PHYSICALLY HANDICAPPED CHILDREN   By Harold D. Love and Joe E. Walthall. Springfield, Ill., C. C Thomas, 1977. 219 pp. $16.75.

This simple handbook of medical, educational, and psychological information for teachers of physically handicapped children presents the essentials of diagnosis, treatment, and prognosis in concise lay language. Covers history, anatomy, diseases and physical disabilities, sensory disabilities, and school problems (including problems of architecture, psychological testing, and placement). Includes a glossary and an index.

Q78 **HANDBOOK OF SPECIAL EDUCATION** Edited by James M. Kauffman and Daniel P. Hallahan. Englewood Cliffs, N.J., Prentice-Hall, 1981. 992 pp. $69.95.
Intended as a basic reference work for students and professionals in special education and for school personnel concerned with their education. Covers theory and research, as well as practical problems of service delivery, teaching techniques, and child management, with chapters on community, architectural planning, psychoactive drugs, and emergency medical procedures. Introduction includes historical trends and a comparative study of special education in Europe. Author and subject indexes.

Q79 **HOLISTIC HEALTH CARE FOR CHILDREN WITH DE-VELOPMENTAL DISABILITIES** By Una Haynes. Baltimore, Md., University Park Press, 1981. 178 pp. $17.95.
A transdisciplinary guide intended for professionals planning programs for infants or young children with developmental disabilities. Covers methods of handling, self-care, and positioning, as well as general health and safety, with well-selected abstracts from fields like physical therapy that deal in some way with developmental disabilities.

Q80 **HOW TO BUILD SPECIAL FURNITURE AND EQUIP-MENT FOR HANDICAPPED CHILDREN** By Ruth B. Hoffman. Springfield, Ill., C. C Thomas, 1974. 100 pp. $10.50 (spiral binding).
Simple, straightforward plans requiring only rudimentary skills, tools, and materials.

Q81 **THE MULTIPLY HANDICAPPED CHILD** Compiled and edited by James M. Wolf and Robert M. Anderson. Springfield, Ill., C. C Thomas, 1974. 488 pp. $48.75 (photocopy edition, spiral binding).
An older, but comprehensive, collection of readings developed to meet the needs of those who serve exceptional children in almost any capaci-

ty. Covers frameworks, specific disabilities, treatments, and studies. There are extensive indexes and a bibliography with nearly 1,200 items.

Q82 **THE NON-COPING CHILD: A Handbook for the Teacher of the Failing Child** By Sister Mary Consilia. Novato, Calif., Academic Therapy, 1978. $31.50 (loose-leaf).
A very thoughtful approach to the syndrome of not coping, educational approaches and types of schooling, the effects of labeling children, and management and diagnostic procedures for teachers. Includes bibliographic references.

Q83 **RAISING A HYPERACTIVE CHILD** By Mark A. Stewart and Sally W. Olds. New York, Harper & Row, 1973. 312 pp. $14.37.
Covers the problems a hyperactive child faces at school and at home at different ages and suggests practical methods for establishing a healthy climate and appropriate rules, helping the child help himself, and so on. Also deals with the hazards and values of drugs and special education.

Q84 **RAISING THE YOUNG BLIND CHILD: A Guide for Parents and Educators** By Shulamith Kastein. New York, Human Sciences, 1980. 208 pp. $19.95.
The author, associated with the New York Foundation for the Blind, emphasizes parenting techniques and stresses the uniqueness of each blind child.

Q85 **A RESOURCE GUIDE FOR PARENTS AND EDUCATORS OF BLIND CHILDREN** By D. Willoughby. Baltimore, Md., National Federation of the Blind, 1979. 142 pp. $5.95.
Written in a family perspective, with suggestions on how to overcome obstacles and help children grow toward independent, responsible adulthood.

Q86 **THE SILENT GARDEN: UNDERSTANDING THE HEARING-IMPAIRED CHILD** By Paul Orden and Suzanne Lipsett. New York, St. Martin's, 1982. 227 pp. $12.95; paperback, $7.95.
A helpful guide for all those who work with deaf children, by an author who himself is deaf. Stresses verbal and nonverbal communication and explores parents' options in schooling. Includes an index and an appendix on services and equipment.

Q87 TEACHING CHILDREN WITH SEVERE COMMUNICA-
TION DISORDERS By Betty Van Witsen. New York, Teachers College Press, 1977. 147 pp. $10.50 (paperback).
A valuable how-to book that provides detailed principles and techniques for teaching children with severe communication and behavioral
disorders. The first section covers the symptoms and behaviors that dif-
ferentiate these children from learning disabled or mentally retarded
children. Includes activities that can be used at home and has a separate
chapter on medications.

CHILD SOCIAL WORK, PSYCHIATRY, AND PSYCHOTHERAPY

Joseph Noshpitz's *Basic Handbook of Child Psychiatry* (A26) is
an excellent reference for all aspects of child psychosis and neu-
rosis. This section includes a few supplementary titles. It overlaps
to an extent with the sections on special needs, child health, and
child development. Some assessment tools and techniques are
discussed in Chapter 14.

Q88 CHILDREN AT RISK: A HANDBOOK OF THE SIGNS
AND SYMPTOMS OF EARLY CHILDHOOD DIFFICUL-
TIES By Gary A. Crow. New York, Schocken, 1978. 288 pp.
$12.95; paperback, $6.95.
Includes symptoms, profiles, and therapies, as well as a bibliography
and index.

Q89 DISORDERED THINKING AND COMMUNICATION IN
CHILDREN By Mahin Hassibi and Harry Breuer, Jr. New
York, Plenum, 1980. 207 pp. $25.
A synthesis of the literature since the 1920s, with conceptual frame-
work, case studies, clinical descriptions, guidelines for differential diag-
nosis, and therapies. Includes a substantial bibliography.

Q90 HANDBOOK OF TREATMENT OF MENTAL DISOR-
DERS IN CHILDHOOD AND ADOLESCENCE Edited by
Benjamin B. Wolman et al. Englewood Cliffs, N.J., Prentice-
Hall, 1978. 475 pp. $59.95.

Thirty-two experts cover the entire field of child psychopathology in 24 chapters dealing with basic approaches to treatments for specific syndromes and disorders. Subject and author indexes.

Q91 **A PRIMER OF CHILD PSYCHOTHERAPY** 2nd Edition. By Paul L. Adams. Boston, Mass., Little, Brown, 1982. 213 pp. $14.95.

An informal, lucid book intended primarily for residents in psychiatry. Discusses psychological development and the external influences—family, school, health care, and the like—that affect the outcomes of treatment. Extensive discussion of aspects of referrals and a good chapter on the initial interview.

Q92 **PSYCHOPHARMACOLOGY IN CHILDHOOD AND ADOLESCENCE** Edited by Jerry M. Weiner. New York, Basic Books, 1977. 226 pp. $15.

Provides a well-organized, authoritative source of information on the expanding range of psychopharmacology for childhood and adolescent disorders. Covers basic issues and clinical applications in a holistic perspective. Index.

Q93 **SEXUAL ABUSE: INCEST VICTIMS AND THEIR FAMILIES** By Jean Goodwin. Littleton, Mass., John Wright/PSG, 1982. 209 pp. $22.

Integrates clinical experiences in evaluating and treating incest victims, with a thorough review of the literature; contains examples, diagnostic techniques, and interventions.

Q94 **SOCIAL WORK WITH ABUSED AND NEGLECTED CHILDREN** Edited by Kathleen C. Faller. New York, Free Press, 1981. 268 pp. $19.95.

An interdisciplinary text by authors in the fields of social work, pediatrics, psychology, psychiatry, and law. The book emphasizes teamwork across disciplines in identifying, assessing, and treating child abuse and neglect. It reviews the factors that should guide social workers in intervention and offers good coverage of sexual abuse, adolescent issues, nonaccidental child injuries, and the child-welfare system.

Q95 **WINDOWS TO OUR CHILDREN: A Gestalt Therapy Approach to Children and Adolescents** By Violet Oaklander. Moab, Utah, Real People Press, 1978. 335 pp. $9 (paperback).

A handbook of alternative therapies for helping children grow that includes fantasy, play therapy, role enactment, meditation, and body movement, among others. Includes a bibliography.

CHILD CARE

This section includes a few handbooks and guides for parents and for providers, as well as others that deal with policy issues. Other materials on child care can be found in legal handbooks; statistical sources are in Chapter 15. Organizations concerned with child care and day care can be located through the index of this book.

Q96   **ADMINISTERING DAY CARE AND PRESCHOOL PRO-GRAMS**   Edited by Donald T. Streets. Boston, Mass., Allyn & Bacon, 1982. 400 pp. $24.95.
A coherent, comprehensive guide to administering early childhood learning centers, written by knowledgeable contributors. Includes such areas as recruiting and selecting personnel and daily and fiscal management.

Q97   **CHOOSING CHILDCARE: A GUIDE FOR PARENTS**   By Stevanne Auerbach. New York, Dutton, 1981. 192 pp. $5.75.
A well-organized guide for working parents that uses checklists to explore the pros and cons of having a sitter come to the home, using family day care, or choosing a day care center.

Q98   **CONDITIONS FOR LEARNING**   By Lois Murphy and Ethel Leeper. Washington, D.C., U.S. Department of Health, Education, and Welfare, 1976. 40 pp. $4.50. (Caring for Children Series; S/N 017-090-00015-1) From: U.S. Government Printing Office, Washington, DC 20402.
Sets out the activities, the environment, and the parental follow-through necessary for a child care center to provide healthy and proper conditions for learning. Considers ways to use time, space, size, and the like, to encourage observation, discovery, comparison, organization, problem solving, supposition making, planning, and adaptation. Useful for parents and staff.

Q99 **CONFRONTING THE CHILD CARE CRISIS** By Stevanne Auerbach. Boston, Mass., Beacon, 1979. 127 pp. $10.50.

Uses extensive statistics and quotes from research to examine the child care crisis at federal, state, and local levels, pointing out red tape, overlapping services, mismanagement, and wasted resources at the federal level. Includes an in-depth examination of the child care situation in San Francisco. Appendixes lead to additional sources of information.

Q100 **THE DAY CARE BOOK** By Grace Mitchell. New York, Stein and Day, 1979. 239 pp. $10.

Helpful guidelines for parents on how to look for and evaluate day care facilities and how to cope if these facilities are less than ideal.

Q101 **DAY CARE: SCIENTIFIC AND SOCIAL POLICY ISSUES** Edited by Edward F. Zigler and Edmund W. Gordon. Boston, Mass., Auburn House, 1982. 515 pp. $24.95; paperback, $12.95.

A collection of articles that combine recent research on the effects of day care with policy analyses on the delivery of day care. Authors include Senators Orrin Hatch and Edward Kennedy and professionals from the fields of psychology, psychoanalysis, early childhood education, economics, pediatrics, and public health.

Q102 **DEVELOPING AND ADMINISTERING A CHILD CARE CENTER** By Dorothy June Sciarra and Anne G. Dorsey. Boston, Mass., Houghton Mifflin, 1979. 393 pp. $21.95.

Outlines the major components of developing and running a child care center, including safety, health, equipment, and staff. Includes many sample forms.

Q103 **DEVELOPING PROGRAMS FOR INFANTS AND TODDLERS** Washington, D.C., Association for Childhood Education International, 1977. 76 pp. $3.25 (paper).

A practical written publication by 11 child care educators that offers guidelines for developing child care programs, with examples of varied programs for normal and handicapped children. Useful for practitioners, policymakers, and parents.

Q104 **FUNDAMENTALS OF GROUP CHILD CARE: A Textbook and Instructional Guide for Child Care Workers** By Jack Adler. New York, Harper & Row, 1981. 357 pp. $26.

A comprehensive guide that covers history, criteria, child development, tasks, methodology, and relationships, with instructions and reviews for some areas.

Q105 **GUIDELINES FOR DAY CARE SERVICE** New York, Child Welfare League of America (CWLA), 1972. 32 pp. $3.25 (paper).
A condensed, nontechnical version of CWLA's *Standards for Day Care Service* that provides an overview of the details of organizing an agency and the services, programs, and facilities it should provide. Includes a glossary and selected references.

Q106 **THE INFANT CENTER: A Complete Guide to Organizing and Managing Infant Day Care** By Emily Herbert-Jackson et al. Baltimore, Md., University Park Press, 1977. 224 pp. $19.95 (paperback).
A detailed description of ways to establish, organize, and operate an infant day care center, with information on quality-control systems. Appendixes provide references and information on equipment and supplies.

Q107 **LEGAL HANDBOOK FOR DAY CARE CENTERS** By Lawrence Kotin for the Administration for Children, Youth, and Families. Washington, D.C., 1983. 143 pp. $4.50. (HE 23.1008:D 33/4)
Provides a comprehensive basis from which day care centers can identify legal issues and review pertinent laws.

Q108 **NURSERY SCHOOL & DAY CARE CENTER MANAGEMENT GUIDE** Revised Edition. By Clare Cherry, Barbara Harkness, and Kay Kuzma. Belmont, Calif., Fearon-Pitman, 1978. $19.95 (loose-leaf).
Covers administration, finance, space and equipment, staff, enrollment, parents, health, safety, children's programs, community relationships, and food management and nutrition for a hypothetical community nursery school for children aged two and older.

FAMILY PERSPECTIVES AND SOCIAL POLICIES

The family-concerns organizations annotated in Chapter 13, the parenting materials of Chapter 17, and the historical perspectives discussed in Chapter 4 are supplemented by this section. Some child care issues are discussed in items Q96–Q108 of this appendix. Surveys and statistics are covered in Chapter 15.

Q109 CHANGING AMERICAN FAMILY By Hoyt Gimlin. Washington, D.C., Congressional Quarterly, 1979. 207 pp. $7.50. (Editorial Research Reports)
Originally published as 10 separate *Editorial Research Reports* between 1976 and 1978, *Changing American Family* examines many social and economic factors affecting family life today, including single-parent families, family violence, teenage pregnancy, housing outlook, and youth unemployment.

Q110 CHANGING IMAGES OF THE FAMILY Edited by Virginia Tuftie and Barbara Myerhoff. New Haven, Conn., Yale University Press, 1979. 416 pp. $30.
Goes to the sources of family images in the arts, history, law, and contemporary society. Four chapters deal with the family in Europe and early America; five with the family in literature, art, and the mass media; four with the contemporary American family; and three with law, politics, and ethics.

Q111 FAMILIES AND WORK: TRADITIONS AND TRANSITIONS Washington, D.C., American Association of University Women, 1982. 78 pp. Members, $6.50; nonmembers, $10.00; plus $2.25 for postage and handling. From: 2401 Virginia Ave., NW, Washington, DC 20037.
A very-well-done survey of multiple aspects of families and work. The first part provides perspectives in nine chapters that include discussions of conflicts in values, loyalties, and life-styles; strengths and strains; two-earner families; single-parent families; choosing nonpaid work; and caring for families. Seven chapters on cultural diversity survey mixed, black, Hispanic, native American, Asian–Pacific American, rural, and urban white ethnic families. Nine chapters deal with public and private policies (government, corporations, labor, and the like), and two provide projections. Includes references and suggested resources.

Q112 FAMILIES TODAY: A RESEARCH SAMPLER ON FAMILIES AND CHILDREN Edited by Eunice Corfman. Rockville, Md., National Institute of Mental Health, 1979–1980. 2 Vols., 1,013 pp. Vol. 1: $9.50; Vol. 2: $10.00. (NIMH Science Monograph No. 1)

A highly interesting "sampler" of research papers on the family, with a section of abstracts as the last chapter. Articles in Volume 1 are grouped into areas on the family as an enduring unit, marriage and divorce, parents and children, and families and the outside world. Volume 2 covers families in distress, mental illness and the family, and strengthening the family. Intended as a resource document for the White House Conference on the Family and the International Year of the Child, it provides invaluable background information for therapists, counselors, students, social workers, researchers, and parents.

Q113 **THE FUTILITY OF FAMILY POLICY** By Gilbert Y. Steiner. Washington, D.C., The Brookings Institution, 1981. 221 pp. $18.95.
A senior fellow of the Brookings Governmental Studies program traces the evolution of family policy as a political issue and details how politicians and policies have dealt with intractable problems like abortion, adolescent pregnancy, child care, child support, aid to dependent children, foster care, and domestic violence. Because these issues are too complicated to fit them into a package with universal appeal, Steiner believes a national family policy is highly unlikely.

Q114 **AN OUNCE OF PREVENTION: CHILD HEALTH POLITICS UNDER MEDICAID** By Anne-Marie Foltz. Cambridge, Mass., MIT Press, 1982. 254 pp. $32.50.
A study of the implementation of the Early and Periodic Screening, Diagnosis and Treatment Program (EPSDT) of Medicaid, with a chronology of events and very interesting commentary. Covers problems among the states, Federal Government, and private health care delivery systems as they affect children's health care. Appendixes include health care standards.

Q115 **STEPFAMILIES: A COOPERATIVE RESPONSIBILITY** By Frederick Capaldi and Barbara McRae. New York, New Viewpoints/Vision Books, 1979. 192 pp. $10.95; paperback, $6.95.
Includes an overview of past and current concepts of the family in society and insight into the anatomy of the many roles of the members of a stepfamily, with practical advice on problems and confusions.

Q116 **YOUNG CHILDREN AND SOCIAL POLICY** Edited by William M. Bridgeland and Edward A. Duane. In: *Annals of the American Academy of Political and Social Science, 461*:9–144, May 1982.

Covers family, health, education, and public policy areas for young children in 13 indexed articles.

LAW

This multidisciplinary section attempts to locate handbooks on all aspects of law involving children.

Q117 **A BILL OF RIGHTS FOR CHILDREN** By Henry H. Foster, Jr. Springfield, Ill., C. C Thomas, 1974. 96 pp. $7.75 (paperback).
Describes the various rights children should be accorded, such as the right to be regarded as a person; to be supported, maintained, and educated; and to receive fair treatment.

Q118 **CHILD ABUSE AND THE LAW: A LEGAL PRIMER FOR SOCIAL WORKERS** By Barbara A. Caulfield. Chicago, Ill., National Committee for Prevention of Child Abuse, 1979. 64 pp. $4.50 (paperback).
Introduces child abuse laws and indicates their applications for social workers.

Q119 **THE CHILD AND THE LAW** By Roberta Gottesman. St. Paul, Minn., West Publishing, 1981. 223 pp. $8.95 (paperback).
A course book for professionals who work with children as social workers, doctors, educators, and juvenile justice personnel, intended to provide answers to the questions of practitioners. Chapters deal with the juvenile justice system, child abuse and neglect, medical care, evidence, moot court script, foster care and placement, adoption, custody, education, and student rights. It includes a table of cases, with summaries of leading cases; an appendix of constitutional amendments; a bibliography keyed to chapters; and an index.

Q120 **THE CHILD AND THE LAW** (Papers and Proceedings of the First World Conference of the International Society on Family Law, April 1975.) Edited by Frank Bates for the International Society of Family Law. Dobbs Ferry, N.Y., Oceana, 1976. 2 Vols. $80.
Papers from this first world conference cover international aspects of child/parent relationships, as well as various national legal practices

relating to child welfare, foster homes, custody, adoption, treatment of illegitimate children and children of divorced families, family courts, and medical and psychiatric practices.

Q121 CHILD PROTECTION: THE ROLE OF THE COURTS By Hortense R. Landau et al. Washington, D.C., National Center on Child Abuse and Neglect, 1980. 75 pp. plus appendix. Single copy free (paperback). From: U.S. Government Printing Office, Dept. 76, Washington, DC 20402. (Include [OHDS] 80-30256 on the order.)

A manual designed to help users of the juvenile courts understand the process and procedures in child abuse and neglect cases (one of a series of manuals based on the *Draft Federal Standards for Child Abuse and Neglect Prevention and Treatment Programs and Projects.* Provides an overview and definitions of child abuse and neglect, overviews of the juvenile court process, the use of witnesses, case preparation, and the proving of child maltreatment. Other chapters deal with court-ordered treatment and the proceedings involving American Indian children. It includes a bibliography and an appendix of standards related to the judicial system.

Q122 CHILD PSYCHIATRY AND THE LAW Edited by Diane H. Schetky and Elissa P. Benedek. New York, Brunner-Mazel, 1980. 297 pp. $25.

A four section, 18-chapter compilation of pertinent issues by experienced psychologists, psychiatrists, social workers, and lawyers. The first section, an introduction to forensic child psychiatry, covers the juvenile justice process, court evaluations, and the expert witness. The second section deals with child custody, dependency, and neglect. The third covers the juvenile offender. The fourth deals with such special issues as the child as witness, competency and criminal responsibility, commitment proceedings for mentally ill or mentally retarded children, personal injury to children, and legal issues in the practice of child psychiatry. There is a good subject index that ties the work together.

Q123 CHILD SUPPORT IN AMERICA: THE LEGAL PERSPECTIVE By Harry D. Krause. Charlottesville, Va., The Michie Company, 1981. 700 pp. $30.

This volume, intended for state attorneys, private attorneys, and judges, describes, analyzes, and evaluates child-support enforcement laws and regulations at the state and federal levels and examines the ways these laws interact. Includes recent decisions and a thorough treatment of the establishment of paternity for children born to unmarried parents. Includes a subject index.

Q124 **COMPARATIVE LICENSING STUDY: Profiles of State Day Care Licensing Requirements** Compiled by Dr. Raymond Collins. Washington, D.C., Administration for Children, Youth, and Families, 1982. 6 Vols. (Out of print)
A comparative licensing study of child care licensing laws and regulations in all 50 states, the District of Columbia, Guam, Puerto Rico, and the Virgin Islands.

Q125 **DIVORCE, CHILD CUSTODY, AND THE FAMILY** By the Group for the Advancement of Psychiatry. New York, Mental Health Materials Center, 1980. 192 pp. $12.95.
Provides a mental health perspective on the ways that divorce and child-custody decisions affect family members. Covers the historical and legal aspects of custody determinations and makes a case for the family approach to decision making. Also considers the role of litigation for the mental health professional. The appendix includes reprints of existing statutes and has an extensive bibliography as well as source references for each chapter. Valuable for parents and all concerned professionals.

Q126 **THE DIVORCE HANDBOOK: Your Basic Guide to Divorce** By James T. Friedman. New York, Random House, 1982. 170 pp. $12.50.
Written for a lay audience in question-and-answer format, this book proceeds chronologically through the divorce process. Relevant areas include dealing with children and custody decisions and determining child support and visitation rights. Clearly written, with a glossary, checklists, guides, and sample schedules for such things as child support. A bibliography lists some other popular treatments for both adults and children.

Q127 **THE EDUCATOR AND CHILD ABUSE** By Brian G. Fraser. Chicago, Ill., National Committee for Prevention of Child Abuse (NCPCA), 1977. 38 pp. $2.50 (paperback).
This booklet by the executive director of NCPCA is intended to help educators meet their legal responsibilities. Includes a discussion of the legal status of the educator regarding child abuse, as well as suggestions for a model school policy on reporting child abuse and what to look for.

Q128 **A GUIDE TO STATE CHILD SUPPORT AND PATERNI-
TY LAWS: In the Best Interest of the Child**   By Carolyn K.
Royce and Lawrence R. Young. Washington, D.C., National
Conference of State Legislators, Child Enforcement Beneficial
Laws Project, 1982. 148 pp. $18.50.
A comprehensive compilation that includes classified exemplary stat-
utes from all 50 states, plus references.

Q129 **JOINT CUSTODY: AN ALTERNATIVE FOR DIVORC-
ING FAMILIES**   By Mel Morgenbesser and Nadine Nehis.
Chicago, Ill., Nelson-Hall, 1981. 176 pp. $15.95.
A clearly written reference work for the concept of joint custody, suitable for social workers and family counselors as well as lawyers. Examines the social, legal, and economic aspects of joint custody from the
parents' and children's perspectives. In addition to interviews with parents, children, and therapists, the book includes sample legal agree-
ments, references, suggested readings, and an index.

Q130 **JOINT CUSTODY AND CO-PARENTING—SHARING
YOUR CHILD EQUALLY**   By Miriam Galper. Philadelphia,
Pa., Running Press, 1980. 207 pp. $6.95 (paperback). From:
125 S. 22nd St., Philadelphia, PA 19103.
The author, a divorced mother and social worker, covers the legal,
financial, scheduling, and living arrangements implicit in shared custody, with quotes from children and parents that address the concerns of
parents and legal and mental health professionals. Includes a list of
selected readings on separation and divorce.

Q131 **JUVENILE JUSTICE STANDARDS: Standards Relating
to. . .**   Compiled by the Institute of Judicial Administration
and the American Bar Assn. Cambridge, Mass., Ballinger,
1979–. 23 Vols. $250; paperback, $125.
The Institute of Judicial Administration and the American Bar Association have completed 23 volumes in their ongoing set of standards to
serve as guidelines for legislators, judges, and nonprofit organizations
concerned with child and family welfare. Significant volumes cover the
rights of minors, abuse and neglect, schools and education, police handling of juvenile problems, noncriminal behavior, juvenile delinquency
and sanctions, and youth service agencies. Write Ballinger (54 Church
St., Harvard Sq., Cambridge, MA 02138) for current catalog.

Q132 **LAW OF ADOPTION**   4th Edition. By Morton L. Leavy and Roy D. Weinberg. Dobbs Ferry, N.Y., Oceana, 1979. 117 pp. $5.95. (Legal Almanac Series, No. 3)

A brief but thorough legal handbook that covers the history, process, and legal aspects of adoption in 10 chapters, with charts that list such things as the appropriate court and residence requirements for particular states. Appendixes cover recent court cases and procedures for foreign adoption and provide the text of the Uniform Adoption Act as well as New York State's Standards of Practice for Adoption Services. The book contains a brief glossary and an index. The same publisher has issued a similar publication, *Law of Support.*

Q133 **LAW OF JUVENILE JUSTICE WITH A NEW MODEL JUVENILE COURT ACT**   By Sol Rubin. Dobbs Ferry, N.Y., Oceana, 1976. 119 pp. $5.95. (Legal Almanac Series, No. 22)

A critical handbook by a long-time creator and observer of juvenile and family court law. The first part provides background information on the juvenile justice system, including the courts, those in court (juveniles and the adults contributing to their neglect or delinquency), children in detention homes, disposition of children's cases, and children's rights. The second part is a proposed Model Juvenile Court Statute in 33 sections; its introductory chapters consider many issues involving children and justice.

Q134 **THE LEGAL ASPECTS OF PROTECTIVE SERVICES FOR ABUSED AND NEGLECTED CHILDREN: A Manual**   By Barbara A. Caulfield. Washington, D.C., U.S. Government Printing Office, 1978. 121 pp. Paperback. (Out of print)

A manual designed to assist social workers in state and local protective service agencies but valuable for a wider audience. Includes working definitions of child abuse and neglect, a glossary of legal terms, advice on reading legal citations, and a good overview of legal procedures. Sections deal with investigation and diagnosis, when to go to court, the trial, rights of parents and children, interstate questions (on such things as custody and placement), and advanced legal concepts. Good index.

Q135 **LEGAL ISSUES IN PEDIATRICS AND ADOLESCENT MEDICINE**   By Angela Roddey Holder. New York, Wiley, 1977. 350 pp. $55.

A clearly written, thorough coverage of the interactions between pediatrics and the law by the executive director of Yale's program in law, science, and medicine. It discusses conflicts and controversies in elucidating the laws that pertain to children from before birth to adolescence, with unusually detailed treatment of issues involved during the prenatal period. Other chapters deal with the child and death; the minor's consent to treatment; the minor as research subject; pediatricians and the schools; pediatricians and the courts; the minor and the psychiatrist; and minors, contraception, and abortion. Includes tables of cases and an index.

Q136 **LEGAL RIGHTS OF CHILDREN** By Robert M. Horowitz and Howard A. Davidson. Colorado Springs, Colo., Shepard's/ McGraw-Hill, 1984. 674 pp. $70.

Well organized, current, and thorough, this book provides overviews and specifics on federal and state laws that deal with almost every conceivable issue that involves children and the law: primary rights to physical, intellectual, and emotional nurture; rights in schools, mental institutions, and juvenile courts; family living, including adoption, divorce, custody, foster care, and grandparents' visitation rights; taxation and property rights; public benefit programs such as Aid to Families with Dependent Children and Social Security; maltreatment and exploitation; economic rights; decedents' estates; and more. Well arranged for reference, with indexes by subject, statutes, cases, and regulations. An appendix lists relevant publications by the American Bar Association.

Q137 **A LEGISLATOR'S GUIDE TO CHILD SUPPORT ENFORCEMENT** By Carolyn K. Royce and Deborah E. S. Bennington. Denver, Colo., National Conference of State Legislators, 1980. 58 pp. $5 (paper). From: 1125 Seventeenth St., Suite 1500, Denver, CO 80208.

A clearly written guide to help state lawmakers shape public policy for child-support enforcement, with a glossary and an appendix of resources that can provide more information on particular issues. Includes an overview of demographics (i.e., statistics on the extent of the problem) and state, legislative, and national perspectives. The final chapter offers a checklist for reviewing a child-support enforcement program.

Q138 **LITTLE SISTERS AND THE LAW** Compiled by Catherine Milton et al. for the American Bar Assn., Female Offender Resource Center. Chicago, 1977. 81 pp. (Out of print)

An impressive collection of information on the double standard implicit in the treatment of girls under age 18 in our juvenile justice system. For example, although almost 75 percent are charged only with status offenses, they are often held in detention for greater periods of time than boys and are less frequently placed in community programs. This report, based on an extensive survey, includes statistics, case histories, state profiles, and information on support services and programs. The book includes extensive references and an excellent resource section.

Q139 **MODEL CHILDREN'S CODE AND CHILDREN'S COURT RULES** 2nd Edition. Albuquerque, N. Mex., American Indian Law Center, 1982. 94 pp. $12.50. From: P.O. Box 4456—Station A, 1117 Stanford, NE, Albuquerque, NM 87196.
This manual, prepared with the assistance of the U.S. Department of Labor, was intended as a model meeting the legal, cultural, and economic needs of American Indian tribes. It contains an ordinance section with commentary on the rights of minors, court jurisdiction, shelter care and detention facilities, warrants and custody orders, adjudicatory and adoption hearings, abuse and neglect, and the relinquishing of parental rights. This edition incorporates changes in the law and includes sections of the Indian Child Welfare Act of 1978 and a new section on adoption.

Q140 **NEW TAX LAW: A GUIDE FOR CHILD WELFARE ORGANIZATIONS** By Thomas A. Troyer, Walter B. Slocombe, and Robert A. Boisture. New York, Child Welfare League of America, 1982. 17 pp. $3.00, plus $1.50 postage and handling.
Valuable for any nonprofit organization working with children.

Q141 **P.L. 94-142: RELATED FEDERAL LEGISLATION FOR HANDICAPPED CHILDREN AND IMPLICATIONS FOR COORDINATION** By Susan Learner. Washington, D.C., National Education Assn., 1978. 28 pp. (Out of print)
Covers all types of federal legislation related to handicapped children: education programs, health programs, programs for child development, and social services. It includes the texts of assorted legislation, an overview of existing coordination among federal programs, a chart of rehabilitation services provided by each program, and a bibliography.

Q142 **PROTECTION OF ABUSED VICTIMS: STATE LAWS AND DECISIONS** Compiled by Irving J. Sloan. Dobbs

Ferry, N.Y., Oceana, 1982– . $35 for binder and subscription service (loose-leaf).
A loose-leaf service addressed to social workers, law enforcement officers, and lawyers concerned with the field of family violence, arranged by topic and state. The first binder, on child abuse, includes a broad narrative survey; significant judicial decisions; state reporting laws arranged by topic; tables, charts, and relevant case studies; and materials on court roles, evidence, and reporting procedures. Provides definitions of abuse and neglect in the courts, in welfare programs, in criminal codes, and in reporting laws. This service plans future binders on sexual abuse, guardianship, spouse abuse, and abuse of the elderly, among other topics.

Q143 **RIGHTS OF JUVENILES: THE JUVENILE JUSTICE SYSTEM** 2nd Edition. By Samuel M. Davis. New York, Clark Boardman, 1980. Paged in sections. $50 (loose-leaf).
A treatise on juvenile justice legislation and case decisions. Covers philosophy and jurisdiction of the juvenile court, waiver of jurisdiction, the prejudicial process, the adjudicatory process, and the dispositional process, as well as future directions of the juvenile court. The treatment is legalistic, thorough, and coherent. The book includes the Uniform Juvenile Court Act, a chart of selected state statutes, a bibliography, a table of cases, and an index that enables users to easily locate relevant law.

Q144 **SCHOOLS AND THE LAW** 5th Edition. By E. Edmund Reutter, Jr. Dobbs Ferry, N.Y., Oceana, 1981. 118 pp. $5.95. (Legal Almanac Series, No. 17)
A remarkably concise overview of the legal framework for education, focusing on the public schools. Chapters cover laws determining what is taught (state guides, requirements, and prohibitions); how it is taught; to whom it is taught (compulsory attendance laws, admission requirements, and so on); and laws concerning those who teach, administer schools, or learn. Additional chapters deal with church/state relations and education and race relations and education.

Q145 **SOME EMERGING ISSUES IN LEGAL LIABILITY OF CHILDREN'S AGENCIES** By Carol M. Rose. New York, Child Welfare League of America, 1978. 68 pp. $6.90 (paper).
Provides an overview of children's constitutional rights (as distinct from parental rights) in the light of recent judicial decisions and the agency/child relationship. Covers treatment issues (e.g., protection,

privacy, and the right to refuse); placement issues (e.g., procedural rights, consent, home stability, and discrimination); and disclosure and record keeping. Some leading cases and statutes are treated in an appendix.

Q146 **STATE LAWS AND REGULATIONS ON GENETIC DIS-ORDERS** By the National Clearinghouse for Genetic Diseases. Rockville, Md., 1980. 80 pp. Price not available. (DHHS Publication No. [HSA] 81-5243)
Includes summaries of state and territorial laws concerning human genetic disorders such as cystic fibrosis, hemophilia, and phenylketonuria.

Q147 **UNIFORM CHILD SUPPORT GUIDELINES** Compiled by the Washington State Association of Superior Court Judges, Family Law Committee, and Office of the Administrator for the Courts. Available through the National Conference of State Legislatures.
A compilation of research intended to suggest guidelines for judges, attorneys, and litigants in establishing appropriate levels of child support.

Q148 **YOUTH AND THE LAW** 4th Edition. By Irving J. Sloan. Dobbs Ferry, N.Y., Oceana, 1981. 120 pp. $5.95. (Legal Almanac Series, No. 46)
A comprehensive overview of the law concerning persons under age 18; designed for young persons and for social workers and law enforcement workers who deal with children and youth. Starts out with an overview of state laws and jurisdictions. Relevant areas include child abuse; support, guardianship, and adoption; and child labor. The book also provides forms for pleading in juvenile court and adoption and guardianship forms, as well as selected statutes on child abuse and juvenile courts. Includes an index.

Index

544

Issues and Policies, O66
Italian, A24

Jacklin, Carol N., Q24
James, Dan, I20
James, William, E76
Jansen, Julie M., H114
Jarvis, Peggy, H17
Jelliffe, Derrick B., D6, H110, Q49
Jelliffe, E. F. Patrice, D6, Q49
Jennings, Jerry T., N6
Jensen, Lydia M., p. 176
Jerrick, Stephen J., Q57
Jeter, Helen R., N38
Jeter Study, p. 419
Jewish Board of Family and Children's
    Services, E5, P23
*Jewish Family: A Survey and Annotated
    Bibliography,* E93
Jews, E93
Joe, Tom, N60
Johns Hopkins, p. 417
Johns Hopkins University, N1
Johnson, Beverly L., N28
Johnson, H. Wayne, M42
Johnson, Orval G., M60, M61
Joint custody, Q129, Q130
*Joint Custody: An Alternative for Divorcing
    Families,* Q129
*Joint Custody and Co-Parenting—Sharing
    Your Child Equally,* Q130
Jolly, Hugh, Q45
Jones, Dorothy M., E44
Jones, R. B., H21
Jordan, June B., G20
Journal for the Education of the Gifted, L40
Journal of Abnormal Psychology, H84
Journal of Adolescent Health Care, H85
Journal of Aesthetic Education, H86
*Journal of Autism and Development
    Disorders,* H87
Journal of Child Care, H88
*Journal of Childhood Communication
    Disorders: Bulletin of the Division for
    Children with Communication
    Disorders,* H89, L40
Journal of Child Language, H90
*Journal of Child Psychology and Psychiatry
    and Allied Disciplines,* H91
Journal of Child Psychotherapy, H92

Journal of Children in Contemporary Society,
    H93
Journal of Clinical Child Psychology, H94
Journal of Drug Education, H95
Journal of Experimental Child Psychology,
    H96
Journal of Family History, H97, L67, p. 47
Journal of Family Issues, H98
Journal of Family Law, H99
Journal of Genetic Psychology, H100
Journal of Human Services Abstracts, G28,
    K58, p. 144
Journal of Juvenile Law, H101
Journal of Learning Disabilities, H102
Journal of Marriage and the Family, L67
Journal of Nurse-Midwifery, H103
Journal of Pediatric Psychology, H104
Journal of Pediatrics, H105
*Journal of Physical Education, Recreation,
    and Dance,* L3
Journal of Psychohistory, C10, H106, p. 47
Journal of Refugee Resettlement, K6
*Journal of School Health: Official Journal of
    the American School Health
    Association,* H107
Journal of Social Issues, H108
*Journal of the American Academy of Child
    Psychiatry,* H109
Journal of the Division of Early Childhood,
    L40
Journal of Tropical Pediatrics, H110
*Journal of Youth and Adolescence: A
    Multidisciplinary Research Publication,*
    H111
Junior High School Library Catalog, O36
Junior League Review, K8
*Junk Food, Megavitamins, and Child Behav-
    ior,* L42
Juvenile & Family Court Journal, H112
Juvenile & Family Law Digest, H113
Juvenile court, Q133, Q143, Q147
Juvenile delinquency, B18, C3, G2, Q122
    see also Criminal justice
Juvenile Diabetes Foundation (JDF), L20
Juvenile justice, A13, B19, H112, N58,
    Q12, Q119
Juvenile Justice Clearinghouse, K29
*Juvenile Justice Standards: Standards
    Relating to. . .,* Q131
Juvenile justice systems, Q121, Q122,